LOVE'S LABOUR'S LOST

for Marion and Bill, with fond memories of your wonderful hospitality on my Oxfordian visit to Chicago, 2 Feb. 2002,

Felicia Londre

SHAKESPEARE CRITICISM

PHILIP C. KOLIN, *General Editor*

LOVE'S LABOUR'S LOST
CRITICAL ESSAYS

EDITED BY

FELICIA HARDISON LONDRÉ

ROUTLEDGE
NEW YORK AND LONDON

First paperback edition published in 2001 by
Routledge
29 West 35th Street
New York, NY 10001

Published in Great Britain by
Routledge
11 New Fetter Lane
London EC4P 4EE

Routledge is an imprint of the Taylor & Francis Group.

10 9 8 7 6 5 4 3 2 1

Library of Congress Cataloging-in-Publication Data

Love's labour's lost : critical essays / edited by Felicia Hardison Londré.
     p. cm.
    Includes bibliographic references.
    ISBN 0-8153-0984-8 (alk. paper)
    ISBN 0-8153-3888-0 (pbk.)
    1. Shakespeare, William, 1564-1616. Love's labour's lost.
    I. Londré, Felicia Hardison, 1941- . II. Series:Garland
reference library of the humanities ; vol. 1643. III. Series:
Garland reference library of the humanities. Shakespeare
criticism ; v. 13.
  PR2822.L68 1997
  822.3'3–dc21
                                              97-526
                                              CIP

Printed on acid-free, 250-year-life paper
Manufactured in the United States of America

To the memory of
Stephen J. Hemming
(1959–1996)
and his many Shakespearean roles
at American Players Theatre

CONTENTS

Part III. *Love's Labour's Lost* on Stage

General Editor's Introduction

The continuing goal of the Garland Shakespeare Criticism series is to provide the most influential historical criticism, the most significant contemporary interpretations, and reviews of the most influential productions. Each volume in the series, devoted to a Shakespearean play or poem (e.g., the sonnets, *Venus and Adonis, The Rape of Lucrece*), includes the most essential criticism and reviews of Shakespeare's work from the seventeenth century to the present. The series thus provides, through individual volumes, a representative gathering of critical opinion of how a play or poem has been interpreted over the centuries.

A major feature of each volume in the series is the editor's introduction. Each volume editor provides a substantial essay identifying the main critical issues and problems the play (or poem) has raised, charting the critical trends in looking at the work over the centuries, and assessing the critical discourses that have linked the play or poem to various ideological concerns. In addition to examining the critical commentary in light of important historical and theatrical events, each introduction functions as a discursive bibliographic essay that cites and evaluates significant critical works—essays, journal articles, dissertations, books, theatre documents—and gives readers a guide to the research on a particular play or poem.

After the introduction, each volume is organized chronologically, by date of publication of selections, into two sections: critical essays and theatre reviews/documents. The first section includes previously published journal articles and book chapters as well as original essays written for the collection. In selecting essays, editors have chosen works that are representative of a given age and critical approach. Striving for accurate historical representation, editors include earlier as well as contemporary criticism. Their goal is to include the widest possible range of critical approaches to the play or poem, demonstrating the multiplicity and complexity of critical response.

In most instances, essays have been reprinted in their entirety, not butchered into snippets. The editors have also commissioned original essays (sometimes as many as five to ten) by leading Shakespearean scholars, thus offering the most contemporary, theoretically attentive analyses. Reflecting some recent critical approaches in Shakespearean studies, these new essays approach the play or poem from many perspectives, including feminist, Marxist, new historical, semiotic, mythic, performance/staging, cultural, and/or a combination of these and other methodologies. Some volumes in the series even include bibliographic analyses that have significant implications for criticism.

The second section of each volume in the series is devoted to the play in performance and, again, is organized chronologically, beginning with some of the earliest and most significant productions and proceeding to the most recent. This section, which ultimately provides a theatre history of the play, should not be regarded as different from or rigidly isolated from the critical essays in the first section. Shakespearean criticism has often been informed by or has significantly influenced productions. Shakespearean criticism over the last twenty years or so has usefully been labeled the "Age of Performance." Readers will find information in this section on major foreign productions of Shakespeare's plays as well as landmark productions in English. Consisting of more than reviews of specific productions, this section also contains a variety of theatre documents, including interpretations written for the particular volume by notable directors whose comments might be titled "The Director's Choice," histories of seminal productions (e.g., Peter Brook's *Titus Andronicus* in 1955), and even interviews with directors and/or actors. Editors have also included photographs from productions around the world to help readers see and further appreciate the way a Shakespearean play has taken shape in the theatre.

Each volume in the Garland Shakespeare Criticism series strives to give readers a balanced, representative collection of the best that has been thought and said about a Shakespearean text. In essence, each volume supplies a careful survey of essential materials in the history of criticism for a Shakespearean text. In offering readers complete, fulfilling, and in some instances very hard to locate materials, volume editors have made conveniently accessible the literary and theatrical criticism of Shakespeare's greatest legacy, his work.

Philip C. Kolin
University of Southern Mississippi

Acknowledgments

My joy in working on a play I love so dearly was much enhanced by the generous support of so many scholars, archivists, and theatre artists.

In the final months of what turned out to be a much longer than anticipated undertaking, Carol Banks helped me complete the transfers to disk and pointed out my editorial inconsistencies; her assistance was invaluable. Ron Engle also came to the rescue by tracking down a missing line in a review from a now-defunct newspaper.

Peter Evans at Hosei University in Tokyo made numerous inquiries to insure that this collection would include *the* outstanding piece of Japanese scholarship on the play. Professor Toshio Murakami introduced me to the right translator for the late Professor Nakanori's article: Toru Iwasaki, son-in-law of Koshi Nakanori and a prominent scholar in his own right. All of my work in Japan was made possible by Yoshiteru Kurokawa, Dean of the Faculty of Letters at Hosei University.

I am also grateful for the genuine interest and support of David Bevington and C.J. Gianakaris, both of whom represent the best in Shakespeare scholarship as well as open-mindedness and tolerance for all points of view. Others who have taken a lively interest in my Shakespeare-related work include Edward Amor, Suzanne Burgoyne, Kevin Doyle, Julia Gábor, Franklin J. Hildy, David and Debra Krajec, Gyorgy Lengyel, Andrew McLean, Doina Zaharia (University of Sibiu, Romania), and the late Kenneth Kloth.

Members of the Shakespeare Oxford Society have been very generous in their support of my work. I especially want to thank Gerald Downs for giving me a first edition of Eva Turner Clark's 1933 book; Richard Whalen for many stimulating long-distance conversations; Gary Goldstein, editor of *The Elizabethan Review*; the Honorable Paul H. Nitze; and Charles Vere, Lord Burford.

Twenty-five years ago I directed a college production of *Love's Labour's Lost*. Perhaps this volume has its origin in that happy experience. Some of those who worked with me then have remained constant in their friendship, and I should like to remember them here: Gary J. Lenox, Steven Roy Fish, John Leon Miller, and Pat Thom. It was then too that I first worked with twelve-year-old Stephen J. Hemming, who grew up to be one of Wisconsin's "most popular and gifted actors." As Damien Jaques observed (*Milwaukee Journal Sentinel*, 21 April 1996): "On stage, his work was notable for its intelligence, versatility and precise focus. Off stage, the actor was witty, charming and personable." To Steve this book is dedicated.

I appreciate the patience of all the contributors of original essays, who sent in their work quite promptly and then had to wait a year or two for me to finish my part. They are Toru Iwasaki, Mari Pappas, John Ezell, Gerald Freedman, Péter Huszti, Daniel J. Watermeier, Theodore Swetz, and Melia Bensussen. Philip C. Kolin, general editor of the Garland Shakespeare Criticism series, and Phyllis Korper at Garland Publishing have been unfailingly generous in their assistance.

After reading *Love's Labour's Lost* over and over again during the last three years, I find increasing delight in it. In these days when "the western canon" is frequently under siege by those who would turn literary studies into sociology, it is important to renew regularly our acquaintance with the classics, which are classics only because of their timeless power to touch our emotions, provoke our thinking, shed light on our humanity, and amaze us by what can be done with language. Thus I would like to take this opportunity to express my love for just a few of the great writers who continue to inspire me: Mikhail Bulgakov, Anton Pavlovich Chekhov, Emily Dickinson, Federico García Lorca, Johann Wolfgang von Goethe, Li Po (a.k.a. Li Bai), Abraham Lincoln, Alfred de Musset, Evgeny Shvarts, Natsume Soseki, Mark Twain, Edith Wharton, Tennessee Williams, and, above all, the one who wrote under the name William Shakespeare.

Felicia Hardison Londré
University of Missouri
Kansas City

Illustrations

PART I
INTRODUCTION

LOVE'S LABOUR'S LOST
AND THE CRITICAL LEGACY

Felicia Hardison Londré

In an essay signaling key developments in modern Shakespeare production, Roger Warren asserts that "two achievements of the twentieth-century stage stand out above all others in their contribution to the interpretation of Shakespeare." The first is discovery of the enhanced relevance of the history plays when they are performed as a cycle, and "the other main achievement of the modern stage has been to establish *Love's Labour's Lost* as one of Shakespeare's major plays." Of the latter milestone, he notes further that "this has been done on stage rather than in the study" (268–70).

The essays in the present volume, representing both the stage and the study, clearly illustrate our century's accelerating appreciation of this long-unsung masterpiece of language and style. Having chosen *Love's Labour's Lost* as my own first directorial venture into Shakespeare (1970) and having seen five utterly captivating productions of it between 1974 and 1994, I am repeatedly astonished at the derogatory remarks the play has accumulated from the pens of eminent literary critics, especially in the nineteenth century. From the pens of performance critics we have nothing at all for a couple of centuries, as the play had no recorded performance between 1604 and 1839—a 235–year hiatus! Indeed, it is Shakespeare's only play that failed to reach the stage in the eighteenth century. To see *Love's Labour's Lost* "established" as "one of Shakespeare's major plays" alongside *Hamlet*, *Romeo and Juliet*, and others of the standard repertoire is as gratifying as witnessing the triumph of any deserving underdog.

And what an underdog! *Love's Labour's Lost* gives us entrée into a Renaissance-era lifestyles-of-the-rich-and-famous, golden world of beautiful people—young, attractive, clever, sophisticated people—who ultimately sense that beauty really resides in the soul and must be cultivated there. Even the low-life characters of this comedy do not simply mark time (as we might accuse Elbow in *Measure for Measure* or the Gardeners in *Richard II* of doing), but instead they actively strive for grace by exercising their mental faculties, by emulating their betters (a time-honored means of self-improvement), and by drawing upon their creative resources to make a gift of entertainment for no other motive than to please and honor some foreign guests. In sum, we are looking at a world where people across the social spectrum are attempting, albeit sometimes misguidedly, to better themselves, not materially or politically, but in terms of their innate potential as human beings. It's an idea whose time is about due to come again.

Adding to the appeal of *Love's Labour's Lost* is the fascinatingly complex Don Adriano de Armado, who belongs to the Spanish gentry but loves a country wench, who perorates as fancifully as the French lords but does it in prose, who embodies both the "man of great spirit" and the melancholic. Also among the play's beauties (pun intended) are the Princess and her three ladies. They and Jaquenetta together endow *Love's Labour's Lost* with more female speaking roles than almost any other play of Shakespeare. Whether or not this circumstance has been a particular stimulus, the play has generated a high incidence of excellent critical studies by women, including groundbreaking book-length studies by Eva Turner Clark (1933) and Frances A. Yates (1936), as well as numerous perceptive analyses from the decades of feminist criticism.

The characters' (and the author's) sheer delight in bandying words is infectious. Ironically, the very whimsicality with which words are handled in this comedy indicates a genuine respect for them. In language and spirit, the modern equivalent of *Love's Labour's Lost* might be a cross between Enid Bagnold's *The Chalk Garden* (1955) and the 1994 movie *Ed Wood*. About the former, Noël Coward was heard to say at the opening performance: "For those who love *words*, darling! For those who love *words*. . . ." And the latter charmingly depicts the title character's Holofernes-like, unbounded enthusiasm for an expressive medium that he cannot fully grasp.

In our image-oriented era, *Love's Labour's Lost* refreshingly challenges our verbal skills. The fact that the modern theatregoer will not understand every word or all the puns in this play does not exclude him or her from the fun; it merely places the theatregoer in the position of the child, and children are remarkably receptive to Shakespeare in performance. Unlike most adults, the child doesn't erect a mental block at the sound of every unfamiliar word; the child rather intuits meaning from context without worrying about possible inexactitudes. Thus, when I directed *Love's Labour's Lost*, I attempted to tease out the child within the adult theatregoer by emphasizing the play's playfulness. Taking my cue from the abundance of word play and word games, I sought physical reification of the language in actual play and games. My setting, on a grass-carpeted arena stage, was a little golden playground: a metallic gold merry-go-round at center, a gold jungle gym, gold-painted see-saw, and two side-by-side swings with pink roses twined about their golden ropes. For the concluding song, the Owl and the Cuckoo were pulled into the playing area in little gilded coaster wagons.

Those who prefer literal meaning to metaphor must resign themselves to the fact that there are elements of this play that will probably never be satisfactorily explained, like Moth's "Concolinel" (presumably a lost song, but there can be no certainty of this). And there are points that may be explained in footnotes but will never be satisfactorily communicated to a modern theatre audience. For example, Costard's line "O! marry me to one Frances—I smell some l'envoy, some goose in this" (III.1.118–119) probably refers teasingly to the coming of the French envoy Simier in 1579 to seek Queen Elizabeth's consent to marry François, duc d'Alençon. Because such "complexities and suggestions of topicality have given carte blanche to a bizarre range of speculation," William C. Carroll noted (bemusedly rather than superciliously, one presumes) in his 1976 book, "the play has always been the darling of the Shakespearean lunatic fringe." (5).

THE FAQs ABOUT *LOVE'S LABOUR'S LOST*

While it is not possible to clear every textual hurdle in the play, there are some frequently-asked questions about *Love's Labour's Lost* that can be answered briefly and perhaps with some plausibility:

Why does the play's title have two apostrophes in most modern editions whereas both the Quarto and First Folio editions use none? The title page of the Quarto edition (1598) proclaims it "A PLEASANT Conceited Comedie CALLED Loves labors lost." The First Folio (1623) lists it as *Loves Labour lost* on the table of contents page, and as *Loves Labour's lost* at the top of the first page of text. The title used on this book is the one that appears on the Third Folio, the one which, as the choice of most editors, has gained familiarity. The simplest way to make sense of those apostrophes is to read the title as signifying that "love's labour is lost."

How should Berowne's name be pronounced? Although the Second Folio and some early editors used the French spelling Biron (based upon Marshal Biron who served Henri IV of France), its pronunciation was undoubtedly anglicized to "beroon" with the accent on the latter syllable, as indicated by scansion of the lines in which it occurs and by its rhyming with "moon" in IV.3.228.

Why should the low-life characters be bound by vows taken by the lords? The restrictions apply "within a mile of [Navarre's] court"; that is, inside the palace and within the walled confines of the surrounding gardens and out-buildings.

What is the nature of the business concerning Aquitaine that brings the Princess of France to the court of Navarre? Because the text offers so few references to the business aspect of the Princess's visit, and because there is no historical basis for a transaction between France and Navarre involving Aquitaine, it is difficult to see what this is about. Kristian Smidt found it strange that "the ostensible reason for the French embassy which leads to so much conflict and complication, the redemption of the mortgage on Aquitaine, should be quickly and consistently forgotten, with only one brief reminder (IV.1.5), until the Princess at parting almost casually mentions 'my great suit so easily obtain'd.'" That "great suit" was, according to Smidt, the undignified task of "pressing Navarre to buy Aquitaine for money which was originally loaned to the Princess's father" (108). Smidt's further analysis of this matter (108–110) is quite helpful. John Turner succinctly summarizes the business: "The ladies from the French court . . . have come to Navarre as a negotiating team to conduct a particularly delicate piece of diplomatic business—to take back again the half that has already been once repaid of a debt owed by France to Navarre and to forfeit instead the possibly overvalued territories in Aquitaine that had been laid in surety against that debt" (32).

What is this thing called Euphuism that is always mentioned in connection with Love's Labour's Lost? Arising from a self-consciousness about linguistics and literature that characterized Renaissance Italy, France, Spain, and England, Euphuism was an effort to explore and expand the possibilities of the English language through rhyming, antithesis, alliteration, "taffeta phrases, silken terms precise, three-piled hyperboles, spruce affectation," and lexical borrowings from classical Greek, Latin, and contemporary foreign languages. This courtly fad peaked in 1578. With its numerous examples of the movement's characteristic verbal conceits (including the most rhymed lines in any Shakespeare play), Love's Labour's Lost is a textbook example of Euphuism. The other major Euphuist works were John Lyly's *Euphues, the Anatomy of Wit* (1578) and *Euphues and His England* (1579) as well as Anthony Munday's *The Mirror of Mutability* (1579). Both Lyly and Munday were at times employed as secretaries to the Earl of Oxford, who was the movement's acknowledged ringleader at court.

At this point, it is necessary to touch upon the Shakespeare authorship question as it relates to this play. While many leading Shakespearean scholars still adhere to the traditional claim that the plays and sonnets of Shakespeare were written by William Shakspere of Stratford-upon-Avon (whose principal documented activities were business dealings in malts and grains), increasing numbers of scholars are open to looking more closely at the extensive historical and textual evidence that supports Edward De Vere, seventeenth Earl of Oxford, as the Bard behind the pseudonym William Shake-speare. The authorship question is complex and cannot be adequately presented here. Suffice it to say that responsible scholars now acknowledge at least that there are grounds for continuing investigation of the issue from both the so-called Stratfordian and Oxfordian points of view and that keeping the issue open to objective scholarly debate can illuminate many facets of the Shakespeare canon. Indeed, significant contributions to our understanding of the Elizabethan era have come out of research undertaken from both perspectives. An essay exemplifying such advancements of knowledge as a product of Oxfordian research—drawing upon hitherto neglected materials at the Huntington Library—was prepared especially for this collection, but was unfortunately withdrawn by the author at the last minute for personal reasons. However, Eva Turner Clark's book *The Satirical Comedy Love's Labour's Lost* (1933) is unsurpassed as the seminal work on the play by an Oxfordian. Those interested in the arguments for Oxford's authorship of the entire Shakespeare canon may consult Eva Turner Clark's *Hidden Allusions in Shakespeare's Plays* (1931), as well as the cited books by Charlton Ogburn, Dorothy and Charlton Ogburn, and Richard Whalen.

Numerous in-jokes, personal references, and depictions of manners betray the virtual certainty that *Love's Labour's Lost* was written by an intimate of the court. The characters into which the author is most likely to have projected himself are the quick-witted Berowne and Don Armado (which is interesting in the light of De Vere's having cast himself as an "allowed fool" at Elizabeth's court). When Armado brags that the king would "with his royal finger, thus, dally with my excrement, with my mustachio" (V.1.95–96), court insiders surely recalled how Queen Elizabeth sometimes touched Oxford's chin to tease him about the sparseness of his beard. Armado goes on to talk of staging some show or firework for the king (V.1.102–4); Oxford had staged fireworks for the queen in Warwickshire in 1572. Oxford loved to pun upon his names, often using the word "ever" to refer to "E. Vere," as in "verse . . . variation . . . ever . . . every word doth almost tell my name" (Sonnet 76). At the end, Spring—called Ver—sings of cuckoldry, which was very much on Oxford's mind after 1576. Whether or not one accepts the Oxfordian view, some kind of courtly connection is indicated, as noted in several essays in this collection: Hazlitt, Campbell, Barber, Miller.

The affinities of *Love's Labour's Lost* with Euphuism—in addition to many of the play's topical references—make 1578 a likely date for the first draft; and indeed, as indicated in my own study of foreign elements in *Love's Labour's Lost* (included in this collection), there was a play performed at court in January 1579 that might well have been an early version of the play we know. Conversely, the orthodox dating of the play to the 1590s (to make it fit the dates of Shakspere of Stratford-upon-Avon) posits that the author based his in-jokes upon topics that had been fashionable at court twelve to fifteen years earlier. How would a young man fresh from a small rural town have dared to write one of his first plays for and about court society? In fact, how could one who spoke Warwickshire dialect have acquired the verbal facility and sophistication to lampoon a linguistic fad that had flared briefly among courtiers when he was only fourteen?

Besides Euphuism, another clear influence on the play is the Italian *commedia dell'arte*, as shown by many scholars, including Richard David in his Introduction to the Arden edition (xxxi–xxxii) and Oscar J. Campbell (whose study appears in this collection). The multivalent Don Armado, for whom scholars have detected several possible prototypes among prominent figures in Elizabethan England, derives primarily from the *miles gloriosus* (braggart soldier) of Roman comedy, who evolved into the Capitano of *commedia dell'arte*. Similarly, the stock characters of the pedant or *dottore* and the clownish servants or *zanni* may be seen as progenitors of Holofernes and Costard. Documentation of visits by Italian *commedia* companies to England in the late sixteenth century is sparse (see Campbell's essay). Oxford, however, is known to have attended at least one *commedia dell'arte* performance during his travels in Italy in 1575–76.

EARLY LITERARY CRITICISM

Whatever the identity of the poet-dramatist William Shakespeare, *Love's Labour's Lost* has generated considerable wonderment on the part of the critics that the author of *Hamlet* and *Twelfth Night* could also have written what they perceived as an inferior play. Thus, much criticism—from Robert Tofte's flippant remarks of 1598 (a selection included in this book) until well into the nineteenth century—is devoted to attacking the play's deficiencies or to defending it as legitimately belonging to the Shakespeare canon by pointing out the occasional flash of familiar genius. Charles Gildon's passage on *Love's Labour's Lost* in his "Remarks on the Plays of Shakespear" (1710, included in this collection) is a case in point. Gildon calls this "one of the worst of Shakespear's Plays, nay I think I may say the very worst," but ends his commentary by citing a "well contriv'd" plot device and a selection of lines that offer "some pretty Reflections." Examining the play more closely, Samuel Johnson (1765, selections included in this collection) found it "often entangled and obscure" with much of it so "vulgar" that it ought not have been performed before "a maiden queen"; yet he also concedes "many sparks of genius." Edward Capell, in his introduction to his edition of Shakespeare's plays (1768) attributed the play's "blemishes" to a different standard of literary beauty: "the measure we call dogrel, and are so much offended with, had no such effect upon the ears of that time." However, Capell did appreciate the "ease and sprightliness of dialogue" and "quick turns of wit" in *Love's Labour's Lost*.

Although nineteenth-century critics continued to judge the play largely in the same vein as their predecessors, the century did bring greater variety in critical perspectives. In Samuel Taylor Coleridge's 1811 lecture on *Love's Labour's Lost*, as reported by Tomalin (included in this collection), the play triggered a stream of associations from the fad for child actors to precepts on child-rearing. By 1818, however, when he wrote out his lecture on the play (also included), Coleridge was focusing more directly on the text itself. William Hazlitt's infamous remark that "if we were to part with any of the author's comedies, it should be this" opens his 1817 essay (included in this collection), but he—like the eighteenth-century critics—begrudgingly finds some aspect to commend; in his view, it is certain characterizations that redeem the play. Taking a populist view, Charles Knight noted in 1849 that no character seems to have any actual work to do: "the schoolmaster appears to be without scholars, . . . the constable without watch and ward," Jaquenetta without duties in the dairy, Costard never called to the plow. Knight traced the play's movement from affectation and "false refinement" to the homely and familiar, "as the more natural characters, one by one, trip up the heels of the more affected." W.W. Lloyd in 1856 saw the play as a reflection of its time, especially as it exhibited "detailed manners of the follies . . . which were rife under Elizabeth." J.A. Heraud (1865) found the Elizabethan period best reflected "in the academical aspects." Because the pulpit was an important educational medium, "the schoolmaster and the curate are accordingly intruded into the play, and exhibited in contrast with the uninstructed constable." Heraud further saw *Love's Labour's Lost* as having "no incident, no situation, no interest of any kind; the whole play is, literally and exclusively, 'a play on words.'"

A number of foreign commentaries on Shakespeare also appeared in the nineteenth century, especially in Germany, led by August Wilhelm von Schlegel. His treatment of *Love's Labour's Lost* (1808, included in this collection), though plot centered, betrays a romantic sensibility by its emphasis on the play's variety of tone. It has been said that literary criticism consists fundamentally in recounting the matter of the original work; the critic's vocabulary and points of emphasis intrinsically constitute a point of view. In this instance, the point of view is of particular interest in that it is largely to Schlegel's credit that German-speaking peoples have maintained a longstanding allegiance to *unser Shakespeare* ("our" Shakespeare). Schlegel's translations of Shakespeare's plays are yet today more often used for German-language productions than are those of any other individual translator. Another German scholar, Hermann Ulrici, while analyzing the dialectical interaction of forces in *Love's Labour's Lost*, tended to see the play from a moral standpoint. In his 1839 essay, he read a lesson in "the thorough worthlessness of wit and talent when exclusively directed to festive and social amusement. . . . The highest splendour and pleasures of life, wit and talents, without the earnestness and profundity which a thoughtful mind lends to them, are a mere false tinsel, while learning and science, abstracted from, and undirected to the realities of life, are equally worthless and unsubstantial." He further expressed concern that the play "lightly and wickedly trifles with broken oaths," but excused this largely on the grounds that "the violation is made to incur a grave penalty." Georg G. Gervinus, writing in 1849, combined moral and aesthetic approaches: "it is a comedy that ends in tears. Certainly this conclusion is in opposition to all aesthetic antecedence, but the catastrophe is genuinely Shakespearian; for moral rectitude was ever the poet's aim rather than a strict adherence to the rules of art." To those who had criticized the severity of the comedy's ending, Gervinus replied that "a kind of moral stupidity is requisite to believe that after this agitating conclusion, sophistry, playfulness, and jesting can begin afresh, and comedy resume its place." According to Gervinus, Shakespeare knew exactly what he was doing with his artistically unorthodox tactics.

French appreciation of Shakespeare came only in the 1830s with Romanticism's overthrow of the long-established neoclassical strictures. Still, as late as 1865, A. Mézières focused on the English bard's lack of logic and his recourse to forced and improbable situations, as when all four of the young nobles in *Love's Labour's Lost* swear to avoid women, then fall in love in the same instant, and later seek solitude in the same spot where each, thinking himself alone, reads aloud a sonnet he has written. In 1867 Emile Montégut observed how extensively the play seems to have been reworked, leaving it with a patched and asymmetrical quality. He did, however, acknowledge the accuracy of Shakespeare's depiction of French manners and attitudes ("Even their bad taste is French"!). François-Victor Hugo, the leading nineteenth-century translator of Shakespeare into French, interpreted *Love's Labour's Lost* as Shakespeare's critique of Queen Elizabeth's affectation and her despotic efforts to prevent her court favorites from marrying. The play is thus, in his 1868 analysis, a plea for love as a force of nature in opposition to the virgin queen's "monkish fanaticism."

THE GROWTH OF CRITICAL APPRECIATION FOR THE PLAY

The later nineteenth century brought more positive assessments of the play's worth. According to the English scholar J.O. Halliwell-Phillips (1879), "a complete appreciation of *Love's Labour's Lost* was reserved for the present century, several modern psychological critics of eminence having successfully vindicated its title to a position amongst the very best productions of the great dramatist." The Irish critic Edward Dowden promoted a biographical approach to Shakespeare criticism with his 1875 book *Shakspere: A Critical Study of His Mind and Art.* "The play is chiefly interesting as containing Shakspere's confession of faith with respect to the true principles of self-culture," he asserted. Then, based upon his conception of the author's views, combined with a nineteenth-century paternalism, Dowden found that "Berowne, the exponent of Shakspere's own thought, . . . is yet a larger nature than the Princess or Rosaline. *His* good-sense is the good-sense of a thinker and of a man of action. When he is most flouted and bemocked, we yet acknowledge him victorious and the master; and Rosaline will confess the fact by-and-by." F.J. Furnivall's 1877 comments on *Love's Labour's Lost* also mined the spurious biographical vein: "He brings his Stratford out-door life and greenery, his Stratford countrymen's rough sub-play, on to the London boards. . . ."

The aesthetic approach yielded greater riches. Swinburne, for example, emphasized the poetry in the play he called "a lyrical farce." He rhapsodized in 1880 that "in *Love's Labour's Lost* the fancy for the most part runs wild as the wind, and the structure of the story is as that of a house of clouds which the wind builds and unbuilds at pleasure. Here we find a very riot of rhymes, wild and wanton in their half-grown grace as a troop of 'young satyrs, tender-hoofed and ruddy-horned'; during certain scenes we seem almost to stand again by the cradle of new-born comedy, and hear the first lisping and laughing accents run over from her baby lips in bubbling rhyme; but when the note changes we recognise the speech of gods. For the first time in our literature the higher key of poetic or romantic comedy is finely touched to a fine issue." Walter Pater, the leading English exponent of literary aestheticism, wrote only three essays on Shakespeare, and one of them was on *Love's Labour's Lost* (1878, published in 1885, included in this collection). An American scholar, Thomas R. Price, published two essays on *Love's Labour's Lost*, both in the journal *Shakespeariana*. The longer piece (1890) analyzes the play first in terms of Shakespeare's poetic interpretation of nature, and then for his understanding of human character. Price's shorter piece (1889, included in this collection) zeroes in on some of the wordplay in the text. Another American, Denton J. Snider (ca. 1890), examined the text as a dialectic between Learning (as an end in itself) and Love (in both its "ethical" and sensual forms). While his division of the play into "three movements" implies an aesthetic evaluation of its structure, an underlying moral approach is evident.

The Danish critic George Brandes discussed the play's treatment of love and language in an essay written in 1895–96 and published in 1898. He elucidated the continental antecedents of Euphuism and observed that "strictly speaking, it is not against Euphuism itself that Shakespeare's youthful satire is directed in *Love's Labour's Lost*. It is certain collateral forms of artificiality in style and utterance that are aimed at." But he found Shakespeare unable to rise above the excesses he was mocking, and this mired the work in "tediousness." E.K. Chambers also grumbled that "little in Shakespeare is more tedious than certain parts of *Love's Labour's Lost*" (1905), but he attributed the problem to the topical nature of much of the wit.

In 1880 Sidney Lee drew upon a variety of sources to write what was probably the first systematic study of the historical context for many aspects of *Love's Labour's Lost*, with references ranging from the court of Henri IV in France to the sojourn of the Russian envoy Pisemsky in England. This approach has appealed to a number of twentieth-century scholars, including Campbell, Harbage, and Londré in this volume. Other historiographical source studies include those of Abel Lefranc (1936), Eva Turner Clark (1933), Fred Sorenson (1935), Frances A. Yates (1936), Dorothy and Charlton Ogburn (1952), Evert Straat (1959–60), Dinesh Biswas (1971), Hugh M. Richmond (1979), Mary Ellen Lamb (1985), and Maurice Hunt (1992). Austen K. Gray (1924) conjectured compellingly about the circumstances of the original production, speculating that it was performed on 2 September 1591 in the park of Titchfield House, the Earl of Southampton's estate. However, G.P.V. Akrigg (1968) noted that there is "no evidence of a play or actors at Titchfield" (193). Much of Akrigg's discussion of *Love's Labour's Lost*'s historical context is also conjectural, though solidly based upon careful research and intelligently framed parameters.

The knotty problem of dating the play's original composition is often treated in conjunction with studies of its historical context, beginning with investigations by J.O. Halliwell-Phillips (1879) and H.B. Charlton (1918). A clear and succinct survey of the related topics of dating, sources, texts, and evidence of revision is Richard David's introduction to the Arden edition. Rupert Taylor, in his 1932 book on the date of *Love's Labour's Lost*, drew heavily upon historical evidence surrounding the quarrel between Thomas Nashe and Gabriel Harvey to support his arguments for 1596 as the date of composition. Alfred Harbage's 1962 essay (included in this collection) marshalls textual and historical arguments not only supporting the generally accepted early placement of the play within the Shakespeare canon, but also for dating it as early as 1589–90. My own essay, much indebted to Eva Turner Clark and Dorothy and Charlton Ogburn, accepts an even earlier date of original composition, 1578, with revisions made in approximately 1592 and again before its 1598 quarto publication. Internal evidence of revision includes "the Katharine-Rosaline tangle" in II.1, a sequence in which lines attributed to Katharine in the Quarto are given to Rosaline in the Folio. This is the subject of articles by Georges Lambin (1959) and John Kerrigan (1982), and it figures in Stanley Wells's analysis of folio variants (1982, included in this collection). Several different textual problems are given close scrutiny in G. Lambrechts's 1964 article published in French.

One aspect of historical analysis of *Love's Labour's Lost* has held particular fascination for scholars from the time of William Warburton (1747): tying its characters to actual historical figures. Warburton's proposal of John Florio as the prototype for Holofernes set off a 150–year scholarly debate over that particular contention, and started the ball rolling for other such "identifications." Frances Yates accepted Florio as the original of Holofernes, but other scholars have seen elements of Holofernes' character in Gabriel Harvey (Looney, Clark), in George Chapman (Acheson), in Richard Lloyd (Lefranc) and in various Elizabethan schoolmasters whose names have come down to us. Taking her cue from Yates's linkage of the play with Sir Walter Ralegh's putative School of Night, Muriel C. Bradbrook (1936) argued strongly for Ralegh as the one being parodied in the character of Don Armado. Armado, however, has also been tied to Gabriel Harvey (Taylor), the Duke of Parma (Lamb), Monarco, and Antonio Pérez, as noted in my essay in this collection. In two articles (1935, 1940), Daniel C. Boughner placed his analyses of Don Armado's character and provenance in a general historical context. Some aspects of Moth can be explained in terms of the Flemish governor La Motte (Lamb), while Richard David pointed out similarities between Moth and Thomas Nashe. Navarre, Berowne, Longaville, and Dumain have clear parallels in Henri IV and the well-known French noblemen Biron, Longueville, and the Duc de Mayenne (despite the fact that the historical Duc de Mayenne had little in common with the other three). Berowne and Rosaline adumbrate Benedick and Beatrice of *Much Ado About Nothing*, and both couples exhibit the sort of quick-witted banter that reportedly went on between Edward De Vere and the bewitching, black-haired lady-in-waiting Anne Vavasor (Ogburn). Katharine and Maria had counterparts among the ladies attending Marguerite de Valois (Richmond). Maurice Hunt found the model for the Princess of France not in Marguerite, but in Queen Elizabeth. Sir Philip Sidney may well have lent some facets to Boyet's character (Looney), and/or Boyet may be founded upon the French minister Pibrac (Lefranc). These are but a few examples of the many topical character references that have been proposed by scholars. Of course, rarely does a dramatist transfer a personality whole-cloth from a living person to a character for the stage; it is not unusual to take inspiration from several living sources and fuse them into a multifaceted character.

Those who focus on the characters' ties to actual historical figures tend to see the play as a satire. Kenneth Muir warned (1979), however, that "the guying of Shakespeare's contemporaries is much less important than the satire of various kinds of literary affectation—in particular, the excessive use of some of the more artificial figures of rhetoric" (36). Intriguing as the detective-story approach to the characters may be, moreover, it is important to consider them on their own terms as artistic entities. Undoubtedly they are rooted in the *commedia dell'arte*, as shown by Oscar J. Campbell in an essay (1925, included in this collection) that has been signalled by Harry Levin and others as a "pioneering study" (Levin 117). Perhaps because the comic characters were conceived as the stock types of *cinquecento* comedy, relatively few critics have focused on them for their psychological makeup or dramatic function. In his 1938 book *Shakespearian Comedy*, H.B. Charlton pointed out deficiencies he saw in the play's characterizations in general. Strangely, he dismissed Armado while touting Sir Nathaniel as "a masterpiece in miniature" and Costard as "the most considerable character of them all" (274). Francesco Cordasco's brief study of Don Armado (1950) explained the character's complexity as the product of the many sources from which the character is drawn. In the same vein, S.C. Sen Gupta (1950) noted that "Don Armado cannot be identified with any particular eccentricity, linguistic or other. . . . It is easy to catalogue all the characteristics of Don Armado, but we do not know the core of personality from which they spring and draw their warmth and vitality" (92). In

Shakespeare's Early Comedies (1966), E.M.W. Tillyard flouted "common opinion" in declaring Armado and Holofernes "the leading characters" (164), as they are the leaders in the verbal excess that characterizes male adolescence, which Tillyard sees as the general theme of the play. Demonstrating "how brilliantly Shakespeare can diversify an inherited type" (167), Don Armado is "both a unique character and the eternal type of those for whom life is too much and who must somehow erect a barrier against it" (169).

Among the four pairs of lords and ladies, it is difficult to find more than superficial features to distinguish one from another as individuals. Only Berowne and the Princess stand apart in any significant way. The individuality of the Princess is explored in a chapter (included in this collection) from Irene G. Dash's 1981 book. According to Sen Gupta, "Berowne has a rich and varied individuality. If he is not as prominent as the greater creations of Shakespearian comedy, that is merely because there is no plot through which he can reveal himself; no wonder, therefore, that his most characteristic expression is through lyrical outbursts rather than through dramatic utterance or action" (93). John Palmer singled out Berowne as the subject of a chapter in his *Comic Characters of Shakespeare* (1947). He began by comparing Berowne to some of Molière's comic characters, the significant difference being that we merely laugh at Molière's characters whereas Berowne (and others of Shakespeare's comic characters) can be laughed at and loved at the same time: the more Berowne is mocked, the more he seems attractive. Berowne, according to Palmer, "is the first fine product of that imaginative process whereby Shakespeare identifies himself with the object of his mirth, thus combining in a single gesture of the spirit, detachment with sympathy, serene judgment with congenial understanding, the objectivity of a creating mind with an entire subjection of the imagination to the thing created" (25). Berowne was also the focus of Gates K. Agnew's 1968 article examining that character's progress through the action toward assuming the traditional role of youthful comic lover. Exploring "how the ambivalent attractiveness of Berowne is sustained" (41), Agnew elaborated on Berowne's three distinguishing attributes: his loyalty to his fellow votaries, his habitual self-assertion, and his mocking wit.

LANGUAGE AND STRUCTURE

Textual studies of *Love's Labour's Lost* abound. Not surprisingly, *explications de texte* have considerably outnumbered examinations of variants. James Bright's short 1898 piece in this collection exemplifies the kind of pointed attention to lines or phrases that the play has provoked. H.B. Charlton's 1917 article on "A Disputed Passage in *Love's Labour's Lost*" served its purpose in that most subsequent editions of the play followed his reasoning and restored the quarto and folio attributions of V.2.663 ("The party is gone") to Don Armado, rather than reassigning the line to Costard or treating it as a stage direction. Another close textual analysis, of the sort that actors and directors can put to use, is Weston Babcock's essay (1951) on the meaning of Rosaline's line (V.2.67): "So pertaunt like would I o'ersway his state." Citing a study that showed "pertaunt" to mean "partlet," Babcock arrived at his reading by examining the line in the context of the surrounding speeches, which contain several repetitions of the word "fool." An awareness of the almost identical pronunciation of "fool" and "fowl" in Elizabethan speech reveals the underlying humor in the sequence of speeches and helps us to "catch the very intonation and accent of the boy actor playing the part" (218). In the Arden edition, Richard David glossed the same line by citing a letter to the *Times Literary Supplement* (24 February 1945) from Dr. Percy Simpson, who changed "pertaunt" to "Paire-Taunt," the term for the winning hand in an obsolete card game. Numerous other lines and phrases have elicited similar close attention; some examples of the many that have appeared over the years in *Notes and Queries* are included in the Works Cited at the end of this introduction. Of special interest for its breadth of coverage is Herbert A. Ellis's book-length treatment of Shakespeare's wordplay in *Love's Labour's Lost* (1973). Categorizing words and phrases as either semantic puns or homophonic puns, he listed them alphabetically along with concise, lucid explanations of their meanings.

The play's emphasis on language as a concept (even as language also functions as the basic medium of artistic expression) places linguistic concerns in the forefront of critical studies from a variety of perspectives. Most have seen the play as an attack on artifice and excess in the use of language (and thus have labeled the comedy a satire). Kristian Smidt (1986) found romantic comedy giving way to satire as 'the great feast of languages' was "developed beyond the limits of mere topical ridicule and allowed to usurp a disproportionate part of the playing time as well as to recruit supernumerary contributors to the parade of affectations" (113). Robert Ornstein (1986) reconciled his linguistic approach with a comedic rather than satiric intention. The use of language, game-playing, and comic ironies are some of the devices by which the play's characters confront themselves—even as Shakespeare confronted his audience; these are the broad concerns of a book (1977) and two articles (1977) on *Love's Labour's Lost* by Louis A. Montrose. The "interdependence of language and the social order" (321) is the focus of James L. Calderwood's frequently-cited article (1965). As Shakespeare developed that theme, Calderwood notes, "we may see him passing from a sensuous enchantment with language, a wantoning with words, to a serious consideration of his medium, his art, and their relation to the social order" (318). In a similar vein, Harry Levin's article (1985) concluded with the important reminder that Shakespeare had to "commandeer artifice as a weapon against artificiality." The process was in a sense "his own courtship of the English language," allowing him the fun of having his cake while eating it during the "accession to artistic maturity" (129).

Walter Pater (1878, included in this collection) noted that many expressions in *Love's Labour's Lost* exhibit a "harmony with the half-sensuous philosophy of the Sonnets." In 1900 C.F. McClumpha signaled numerous examples of close correlation between lines or passages from the play and from the sonnets. Horace Howard Furness offered a small sampling of these in the Variorum Edition's appendix on the play's date of composition. Rosalie L. Colie (1974) juxtaposes this play and the sonnets, showing how both works manipulate conventions in a self-fashioning manner. Robert Giroux's *The Book Known as Q* (1983), an appreciation of the sonnets, devotes a chapter to their relationship to the play. And the prominent director Gerald Freedman, in his essay written especially for the present volume, shows how artistic instinct neatly dovetailed with scholarly inquiry on that subject.

The ties between *Love's Labour's Lost* and Euphuism have given rise to several explorations of the possible influence of John Lyly on this comedy. (It should be noted that if Edward De Vere, seventeenth Earl of Oxford, were accepted as the author, then the influence could be seen in the opposite direction; that is, "Shakespeare" would have influenced Lyly.) Among those who have examined the Shakespeare-Lyly connection with respect to *Love's Labour's Lost* are Hazleton Spencer (1940), G.K. Hunter (1962), David Bevington (1968), Barry Thorne (1970), and Martha Sue Hendrickson Herzog (1973). John Wilders (1977) shows how the play employs Lyly-like symmetry, social hierarchies, and debates that present opposing sides, but careful examination of this, "Shakespeare's most inconclusive comedy" (21), reveals that Shakespeare moves beyond Lyly's formal presentation of parallels and opposites to echo life with its ambiguities, gray areas, and lack of resolution.

The two songs at the end of *Love's Labour's Lost* have fascinated critics. Richmond Noble (1923) discerned their purpose as "to restore the spirit of comedy" at the end of the play with one last jab at pedantry; that satiric purpose was evident to him in way the songs are set up like an academic debate between the two birds as representatives of polarized views (34). Bertrand Bronson (1948) pointed out the paradox presented by the songs: the pleasures of springtime are mitigated by husbands' fear of being cuckolded, and the harshness of winter is compensated by the comfort of the fireside and a warm meal. The contrasts between the songs and within each song suggest "the age-old lesson of the imperfect and paradoxical condition of human felicity that is resident in this antiphony" (36). The full texts of both songs appear in this volume at the end of A.H. Moncure-Sime's 1915 essay on the play's music. Catherine McLay's article (1967, included in this collection) connected the songs to the meaning of the play as a whole. Robert G. Hunter (1974) also viewed the songs as integral to the play, arguing that their "broadly thematic" (55) function is to reconcile the conflict between linear time (leading to death) and cyclical time (a constant succession of death and rebirth). S.K. Heninger, Jr. (1974) analyzed the songs' function in terms of the play's structure: "Shakespeare stops the action at that point where a choice between an optimistic or a pessimistic ending must be made. He ducks this limiting choice . . . and emblematizes the intentional ambiguity by means of the closing song" (26). The narrative use of time and space gives way to the lyrical even as the songs continue the play's "pattern of contrasting opposites" (46).

Such uses of antithesis to structure the action as well as to create patterns within the whole (and to suggest thematic concerns) have inspired a number of twentieth-century aesthetic appreciations, including three of the most influential essays ever written on *Love's Labour's Lost*—those of Bobbyann Roesen, C.L. Barber, and John Dover Wilson. All three were published within a ten-year period, 1953–1962 [1963], and all three are included in this collection. Roesen, now better known as Anne Barton, wrote in 1953 of the opposition between the artificial and the real in the world of the play. The chapter on *Love's Labour's Lost* in C.L. Barber's seminal book, *Shakespeare's Festive Comedy* (1959 [1963]), demonstrates how far Shakespeare went "in the direction of making the piece a set exhibition of pastimes and games." In fact, he saw the play not as a story but as "a series of wooing games." The "holiday action" provides a kind of release and leads to recognition of limits required in the best interest of the community. John Dover Wilson's chapter from his book, *Shakespeare's Happy Comedies* (1962 [1963]), charmingly corroborated Harley Granville-Barker's earlier (1927) championing of *Love's Labour's Lost* as far more apt to delight the spectator in the theatre than the reader in the study. Wilson saw the play's patterns more in terms of parallelisms than contrasting oppositions, but he noted that "there are two elements in every pattern, balance and contrast as well as repetition and variation" (71).

Other critics too have explored dualities in the play's structure and patterns, especially as these may be linked to the theme. Ronald Berman (1964) opposed what is reasoned and what is instinctive in *Love's Labour's*

Lost and *The Taming of the Shrew*, concluding that "the protagonists of the comedies must vanquish their own sense of the reasonable to understand—or perhaps coexist with—the nature of things" (9). William Leigh Godshalk (1968) demonstrated how the intricate patterns in the play reify the delicate ordering of existence. In his 1962 article, Cyrus Hoy analyzed the comedic values of *Love's Labour's Lost* as derived from man's dual nature, which leads to a "discrepancy between the ideal and the reality, the intention and the deed" (31). The conflict between the imaginative conceits or fancies of the lords and what they are actually able to achieve is, to Joseph Westlund (1967), ultimately a conflict between artifice and nature. Malcolm Evans (1975) articulated the central duality as an opposition between the written and the spoken word, represented respectively by Mercury and Apollo. "The contending dualisms in the play" (170) are also a key element in William C. Carroll's 1976 book, *The Great Feast of Language in* Love's Labour's Lost:

> I believe this play can profitably be read as a debate on the right uses of rhetoric, poetry, and the imagination; extraordinarily self-conscious, the play ultimately exemplifies and embodies, in the final songs, what has only been discussed before. The term "debate" is justified by Shakespeare's use of the medieval *conflictus* between Spring and Winter at the end, but it defines a principle of structure in the play as well. The most typical method of structuring a speech or a scene is through a juxtaposition of opposites, a kind of literary counterpoint, usually in the form of obvious dualisms such as Spring and Winter or Nature and Art. A whole series of such debates takes place throughout the play. (8–9)

In *Shakespeare's Early Comedies*, E.M.W. Tillyard (1965) asked, "How does Shakespeare fabricate the delicate unreality of the park?" He noted references to "a bench in a manor-house, a 'curious-knotted garden,' a dairy (since Jacquenetta was 'allowed for the day-woman' (I.2.125), the 'steep up rising of a hill,' a deer, a school, a sycamore: things that make their impression but which do not add up to a district where real life goes on. Whatever the means, Shakespeare makes his park into a kind of Cloudcuckooland" (174). For Thomas McFarland (1972), the park is "truly a pastoral environment," a paradise of artifice and mock problems, an ideal world where there is no need of heroism, which is consequently ridiculed.

The abrupt change of mood effected by Marcade's highly theatrical entrance in the final scene has been as much admired by twentieth-century critics as it was disparaged earlier. Comments on that subject appear throughout the essays and reviews in this collection. Still, the fact that the "wooing doth not end like an old play" (V.2.866) occasions debate about Shakespeare's intention in breaking with the conventions of comedy. The subliminal power of traditional comic form probably conditions most readers and spectators to assume that the men have at last learned something about themselves and will indeed earn their happily-ever-afters. Others, however, signal the ambiguous ending as the very point of the play. "The main substance of the play is of uncertainties and irregularities," wrote Tillyard (178).

IMAGES AND THEMES

Caroline Spurgeon's trailblazing book on Shakespeare's imagery (1935) devoted a few pages to *Love's Labour's Lost*. In her view, the "dominating series" of images "is that of war and weapons, emphasizing the chief interest and entertainment of the play, the 'civil war of wits.'" She adds that words are "pictured throughout as rapier-like thrusts, arrows, bullets fired from a cannon or as combatants tilting with their spears at a tournament" (271). She also found "an unusual number of nature images, actually the highest number of any of the comedies" (275). Several critics have noted a surprising number of images of death, from Navarre's opening sentence to Marcade's announcement. Taking her cue from a turn of phrase in Don Armado's letter to the King—"that obscene and most preposterous event" (I.1.237), Patricia Parker (1993) explored a wealth of connotative meanings related to various kinds of inversions, high and low social class, and gender relationships. In terms of imagery, she found that "the play is filled with reminders of bodily functions . . . and body parts . . ." (472). In my own reading of the play for imagery, it was the references to "eyes" and "tongues" that seemed most compelling. Love strikes the young lords through the eyes, and their confidence in visual recognition of the loved one is shaken only when they mistakenly fasten upon the favors the ladies wear rather than on the women themselves. No sooner do the men fall in love than they must be expressing their love as extravagantly as possible, and the tongue is the metaphor for such expressions. However, the tongue's utterances are even less reliable than the judgment of the eye. The men's inability to keep the oaths they have sworn casts doubt on anything they may say, including their declarations of love.

The nature of love as understood during the Renaissance is the subject of Neal L. Goldstien's 1974 essay, which analyzed the play as "a vehicle for the discarding of the higher ideals of another age" (339)—Florentine Neoplatonism and Petrarchanism—which were the major components of the Renaissance vision of love. He found also that the songs of Spring and Winter "add another dimension to the tension between spirituality and sensuality" (349). In *Precious Seeing: Love and Reason in Shakespeare's Plays* (1987), Barbara L. Parker devoted a chapter to *Love's Labour's Lost* (81–98). She posited an identification of the self-seeking, morally blind love expressed by the lords with the Catholic doctrine of the treasure of merit ("buying" grace with good works), a doctrine rejected by Reformation theology as a commodification of grace and salvation. Conversely, the ladies, "impervious to flattery, gifts, and disguise" (94), represent the rational love (accompanied by charity) that is identified with Protestantism. Parker's compelling argument, well grounded in Elizabethan religious debate, illuminates several aspects of the play, including some specific line readings.

Since the 1970s there have been increasing numbers of studies of the relationships between the sexes as depicted in the play. J.J. Anderson's examination of the morality of *Love's Labour's Lost* (1971) considered differences in the behavior of the men and the women. "All of the men are irresponsible in that they sacrifice rationality, conscience, and feeling to wit" (58). The women, who expose and correct the men's faults, are "presented not as perfect, but as embodying norms of human conduct against which the aberrations of the noblemen are to be measured" (61). Kristian Smidt's close reading found that "the women are far unkinder than the men" and that their cruelty contains a degree of malice (103). In his 1981 essay (included in this collection), Peter Erickson analyzed the play in terms of its departures from conventional gender roles and how this affects those conventions as literary devices. In Erickson's view, the differences between the men and the women are serious enough to impede their ever achieving a harmonious union. David Bevington (1989) explored similarities in Lyly's and Shakespeare's male perceptions of "the female as the attractive yet baffling prize that seemingly cannot be attained or controlled" (2). Lacking self-knowledge, the men are afflicted with sexual anxiety, while the women (whose feelings for the men remain undeclared) enjoy control over the resolution of the action.

The "relationship between desire and power" was further explored by Mark Breitenberg in a 1992 essay. And John Turner (1990) focused on power games as an inevitable component of court life. Exploring competitiveness within the court, between the courts of Navarre and France, and between Navarre's court and its surrounding rural environment, he concluded:

> The history dramatized in *Love's Labour's Lost* holds the mirror up to the competitive life of a representative Renaissance court in all the exhilaration of its power and all the anxiety of its tensions; and it

traces those tensions to the unstable mixture of rivalry and fellow-ship structured into its competition, as it flourished internally between members of the same court, nationally between the court and the country it ruled and internationally between different courts. Life in such courtly circles was an exciting, melancholy affair, an opportunity and a trap from which there was no escape, a round of endless provisionality where the role of the new learning was only to improvise and where the individual's destiny lay lost beyond all individual control. (43)

Quite a different reason for the tensions exhibited by Navarre and his companions emerges in Ursula Hehl's psychological probing of the characters (1994). She noted in Navarre's dialogue and behavior the classic symptoms of a narcissistic personality disorder with its attendant "unconscious fear of failure" (55). From this perspective, she drew a clear distinction between the women, "who are characterized as mature and self-assured and as being furnished with well-developed superego structures," and the men, "whose psychic immaturity is reflected in the primacy they grant their own quickly-changing needs and desires" (66).

CRITICISM THAT INFORMS STAGE PRACTICE

A 1995 essay by Frederick Kiefer exemplifies critical writing at its best: research on and interpretation of primary sources to illuminate the text in a manner that may be put to practical application by theatre artists. On the assumption that "Shakespeare was inspired by the representation of the seasons in the pictorial arts of his time" (92), Kiefer examined sixteenth- and seventeenth-century iconographic representations of Spring and Winter as allegorical figures. This article includes several such illustrations and suggests that the most appropriate characters to reappear as Spring and Winter are Jaquenetta and Dull.

Before turning to the production history of *Love's Labour's Lost*, mention must be made of a piece of critical writing that probably had more influence than any other on subsequent staging of the comedy: Harley Granville-Barker's *Prefaces to Shakespeare*, originally published in 1927 and republished in 1946, 1963, and 1995. Writing from the point of view of the theatre practitioner, Granville-Barker acknowledged the difficulties this play poses for a theatre audience, but insisted that "there is life in it" (2). He pointed out that beyond the fun of "the gymnastics, the jargon and the antics" Shakespeare still had much to discover about the provision of conflict and balance and "the projection of character in action." *Love's Labour's Lost* thus forces the stage director to "consider carefully just what the carrying-power of this embryonic drama is, and how he can effectively interpret to a modern audience the rest of the play." Granville-Barker admitted that the theatregoer's spontaneous enjoyment will depend greatly upon "pleasant sights and sounds;" that is, "the verse and the pretty moving picture of the action" (9). He noted astutely that "the whole play, first and last, demands style" (11). Offering examples to show how the very "twists and turns" of the dialogue are "stage directions of the clearest sort" (19), he took to task modern editors who make textual "corrections" without regard for the requirements of the stage: "what is reasonable to a critic is not therefore natural to a playwright" (27). Finally, he grappled with the director's temptation to cut lines that the audience won't understand, concluding that one cannot "eviscerate a scene and expect to see no wound. . . . We must think of it all in terms of music, of contrasts in tone and rhythm and breaking of rhythm" (30). He placed his faith in the skill of the actor whose "adroit movement and the nice turning of a phrase" can convey the sense of a difficult passage. The impact of Granville-Barker's chapter on *Love's Labour's Lost* is noted in John Dover Wilson's 1962 essay (included in this collection).

LOVE'S LABOUR'S LOST IN PERFORMANCE

We know from the title page of the 1598 quarto that *Love's Labour's Lost* was originally performed no later than Christmas of 1597. From Walter Cope's letter (included in this collection), we know that the comedy was revived in 1604. Although there probably were earlier and/or intervening performances, no evidence of such has come to light. Nor do we know anything specific about the casting or staging of the 1597 and 1604 productions by the company with which Shakespeare was associated. However, Miriam Gilbert's 1993 book, *Love's Labour's Lost* (in a "Shakespeare in Performance" series), examines the demands of the play in terms of setting, costumes, and actors' movement and speech, convincingly relating those intrinsic demands to what we know of the conventions of the Elizabethan stage. In subsequent chapters, Gilbert offers in-depth analyses of productions of 1857, 1946, 1965, 1968, 1978, and 1984, as well as of the text of an anonymous adaptation, *The Students* (1762, included in this collection), for which there is no record of performance.

The earliest production about which we have any information is also the earliest recorded performance after that of 1604. In 1839, after more than two centuries of apparent neglect, *Love's Labour's Lost* was chosen by Madame Vestris to inaugurate her management of Covent Garden Theatre. Though widely regarded as a mistake of judgment, the choice was probably motivated by a desire to identify the company with England's great dramatic heritage yet offer some novelty. It also had the advantage of not depending upon a star performer and of allowing for some opulent costumes designed by J.R. Planché, an early advocate of historical accuracy in costuming. The opening curtain revealed a beautiful setting by Thomas Grieve: "a scene of surpassing grandeur—the stage representing the terraced portico of the palace of the King of Navarre, approached by a broad flight of steps, leading to spacious gardens laid out in the old French taste, forming a beautiful back-ground" (cited by Appleton 125). The entrance of the King and his com-panions was heralded by a retinue of seventeen guards, pages, and servants, according to the production's prompt book in the Folger Library (Gilbert 27–29). Similarly, the Princess and her ladies in their tent were surrounded by guards and pages. Eight musicians accompanied the Muscovites. The grand finale included three separate processions of shepherds and shepherd-esses, wild men, children, and emblematic figures. The opening performance was marred by the noisy demonstrations of theatregoers angered by the un-availability of one-shilling admissions to the gallery. Although the "shilling gallery" was reinstituted for subsequent performances, the play did not cap-ture the public's interest and left the repertoire after nine performances.

Eighteen years later, Samuel Phelps made a stage success of *Love's Labour's Lost* for nineteenth-century audiences. The production that opened on 24 October 1857 at Sadler's Wells Theatre was praised for "the beauty and gracefulness of the characters in a 'series of sparkling pictures,'" and for meticulous attention to detail in even the smallest roles and most insig-nificant props (Gilbert 34–35). According to Henry Morley's *Journal of a London Playgoer* (Salgado 115), this "comedy of leisure" ran "daintily and pleasantly" and served as "a relief to busy men in anxious times." Phelps himself played a lumbering Don Armado in delightful counterpoint to the tiny Miss Rose Williams as Moth. Medieval costumes, painted backdrops of verdant scenes, music, and processions added to the production's appeal. For the pageant of the Nine Worthies, a platform stage was pulled into the scene, and each Worthy was accompanied by a Banner Bearer. Spring and Winter were brought into the finale, each riding in a cart. After their verses, the orchestra played a march to underscore the parting bows and curtsies of the lords and ladies.

On the American stage, the earliest recorded performance of *Love's Labour's Lost* was at the Arch Street Theatre in Philadelphia in 1858. A comic opera based upon the play (text adapted by Henri Drayton to the music of various composers, including Verdi and Donizetti) was presented on 8 November 1859 in Drayton's New Parlor Opera House at 718–720

Broadway in New York. Of particular interest are two New York productions, in 1874 and in 1891, presented by Augustin Daly. The first opened at Daly's Fifth Avenue Theatre on 21 February, winning a rave review in the *New York Times*. The reviewer praised the "liveliness and action," the "illustrative ornamentation," and "singularly faultless rendering" by the cast, resulting in "an unquestionable success." William Winter's chronicle (1916) provides more precise details, including the fact that it was presented in six acts. The opulent scenery "really created an illusion of Nature." For the tableau of Spring at the end, there was "a silver fountain, deep vistas of luxuriant foliage, climbing vines, blooming flowers, mossy banks, and jutting rocks, with shepherd lads and lassies grouped in a radiance of changeful lights" (192–193). Both Winter and the *New York Times* reviewer signaled Charles Fisher's Don Armado. The latter commended "the braggart lover, with a make-up that will become dramatically historic," and Winter described him as "large, broad, stately in style, sapiently absurd and delightfully quaint." Daly's 1891 revival (*New York Times* review included in this collection) starred Ada Rehan as the Princess of France, while two cast members repeated their roles of seventeen years earlier: George Clarke playing Biron with "exuberant, sustained vivacity," and James Lewis as a "dryly whimsical and quaintly droll" Costard. Again, according to Winter, Daly gave the play "exceptionally beautiful" scenic settings and costumes. "The picture comprising the Princess and her Ladies, sitting beside the lake, listening to music, was one of exceptional loveliness" (194).

The first production of *Love's Labour's Lost* at the Shakespeare Memorial Theatre in Stratford-upon-Avon opened on 23 April 1885 under the direction of Charles Bernard. Amateur productions include one at St. James's Theatre in London on 2 July 1886 (review by Bernard Shaw included in this collection) and one at Bloomsbury Hall in London on 24 April 1904, presented by the English Dramatic Society under the direction of Nugent Monck. At the Shakespeare Memorial Theatre in 1907, F.P. Benson both directed and played Biron. Professional productions were given at the Old Vic in 1918 and at Birmingham Repertory Theatre in 1919. The Oxford University Drama Society presented the play in 1924. The Shakespeare Memorial Theatre revived it in 1925 and 1934, both productions directed by W. Bridges-Adams; Rachel Kempson played the Princess in the latter.

In 1920 Nugent Monck directed the first of three Norwich Players productions of *Love's Labour's Lost*; the subsequent ones were at the Maddermarket Theatre in 1930 and 1951. It was Monck's 1930 staging of it that directly inspired Tyrone Guthrie's 1932 production at Westminster Theatre, which led to Guthrie's being hired to direct it at the Old Vic in 1936.

Monck had experimented with combining pictorial beauty and simplicity of staging, using a permanent setting to avoid breaks for scene changes. Guthrie later wrote that "most of the good ideas in my production were culled from Monck's at Norwich" (Hildy 121). Guthrie recalled also that in those days Shakespeare's comic episodes were very "apt to be heavily overlaid with 'vaudeville' business," whereas Monck had taught him to treat those sequences "simply, realistically and sympathetically" (84). Guthrie's 1936 cast included several actors who later rose to prominence: Michael Redgrave as the King, Alec Clunes as Biron, and Alec Guinness as Boyet; Rachel Kempson was once again cast as the Princess.

Shakespeare's ever-tenuous relationship with French audiences was given a great boost by Jacques Copeau's landmark production of *Twelfth Night* at the Vieux Colombier in 1914. Thirty years later Copeau published an essay on *Love's Labour's Lost* in *Le Figaro littéraire* (published for the first time in English translation in this collection). Although Copeau himself never directed *Love's Labour's Lost*, that essay was undoubtedly a stimulus for the Paris production of the play which opened in January 1946 at the Odéon in an adaptation by J. Dapoigny (two reviews have been translated into English for this collection). Among those who saw the 1946 Paris production was the 20-year-old Peter Brook, who channeled its influence into his direction of the play in Stratford-upon-Avon later that year. Peter Brook's landmark production of *Love's Labour's Lost* opened at the Shakespeare Memorial Theatre on 26 April 1946 and became the surprise hit of the season, its success earning a 1947 revival. Among its noteworthy features were the Watteau-inspired stage pictures, the fantastical melancholy of Don Armado as played by Paul Scofield, and the daringly long pause and drastic change of mood when Marcade entered. Details of the production are provided in Gilbert (44–51), W.P. Shaw (38–44), and Leiter (339–40); Brook's own reminiscences are included in this collection. Gilbert also analyzes the influence of Brook's production on that staged by Hugh Hunt (with Michael Redgrave as Berowne) at the Old Vic in 1949 (51–53). In "the sweetness of its verbal music, its rich costume and youthful outlook," the play, in Hunt's view, makes "a special appeal to the romantic in us all." In his *Old Vic Prefaces*, Hunt evoked the final moments: "The last movement of this comedy of youth, when the great barge with its black flag, bearing the sorrowful Princess and her ladies, moved slowly away to the accompaniment of the song of spring, the gradual darkness shrouding the silhouette of Don Armado, the falling of a leaf from the summer trees, produced a sense of reverence in us all. . . . An owl hooted and the curtain fell" (2–26).

The first New York revival of *Love's Labour's Lost* since the Augustin

Daly production of 1891 was presented at City Center in 1953. In two reviews Brooks Atkinson deplored that cast's inability to speak Shakespearean lines, and assumed that director Albert Marre had resorted to "interpolating bits of hokum that are much too precious to be tolerable" in order "to divert attention from the performances." Among those bits were a vintage motorcar and Victrola, a croquet game, and cigarettes sneaked by the ladies when the men weren't looking. In 1956, the first post-Brook revival at the Shakespeare Memorial Theatre was the occasion for the Stratford-upon-Avon directorial debut of Peter Hall. The setting represented palace architecture more than a park, but the stylized French Renaissance costumes were superb. Other productions of the 1950s included one directed by Hugh Goldie at the Open Air Theatre in London's Regent's Park (1954), one directed by Riic Jacobs at Antwerp's Reizend Volkstheater (1954), one directed by Arthur Lithgow for the Antioch College Shakespeare Festival's fifth season, and a Polish-language production in Cracow during the 1958–59 season, in addition to numerous college and amateur productions in the United States and England.

The 1960s brought a number of important productions. James Sandoe's lively direction for Colorado Shakespeare Festival in 1961 stressed the satire of pedantry. At Stratford, Ontario, that season, Michael Langham melded pictorial beauty with exuberant comedy, while allowing Paul Scofield to reprise his legendary Armado and introducing the young Zoe Caldwell as Rosaline. At the Oregon Shakespeare Festival, where *Love's Labour's Lost* has been presented each decade since 1947, the 1962 revival is considered outstanding. Rod Alexander directed the "utterly enchanting nonsense" of a production "studded with deft little touches" (Prosser 453) and featuring Stacy Keach and Elizabeth Huddle as Berowne and Rosaline. John Barton directed the play for the Royal Shakespeare Company (RSC) in 1965, a production overshadowed by his 1978 version. His 1965 cast included Glenda Jackson (Princess), Janet Suzman (Rosaline), Tony Church (Holofernes), and Michael Pennington (Dumaine). Gerald Freedman directed his first of five productions of *Love's Labour's Lost* (see his essay in this collection) for the New York Shakespeare Festival in 1965, with sets by Ming Cho Lee and costumes by Theoni V. Aldredge. Comedy was stressed by director Philip Minor, who gave the play a contemporary setting, at Great Lakes Shakespeare Festival in 1967. Laurence Olivier directed the play for the National Theatre in London in 1968. Reviews were mixed with much attention devoted to the Christmas-card–like snow effect at the end. India was evoked in the music and design elements of Michael Kahn's 1968 production for the American Shakespeare Theatre in Stratford, Connecticut.

In the 1971 season at Colorado Shakespeare Festival, "some of the brightest moments in the fourteen years of the Festival were strung together in Edgar Reynolds's loving presentation of *Love's Labour's Lost.*" The costumes designed by Robert Dewitt Morgan, Jr. used a "dazzling variety of line and color" to give the effect of "love games through the ages" (Crouch 302). Mid–eighteenth-century costumes worked to good effect in the 1972 production at the Old Globe in San Diego, directed with compelling restraint by Eric Christmas. Also in 1972 Kenny McBain directed the play at the Aldwych Theatre in London. David Jones directed a "Mozartian" 1973 revival at the Royal Shakespeare Theatre. Robert Speaight admired the "dashingly Carolean" costumes, Timothy Dalton's "lovable" and "lively" Costard, and Tony Church's "*hispanidad* as Don Armado" (404). That production (with some cast changes) was presented on tour in 1975 at the Brooklyn Academy of Music and subsequently at the Aldwych Theatre in London for the 1975 World Theatre Season. Nicholas Pennell played Berowne under Michael Bawtree's direction at Stratford, Ontario, in 1974. The Guthrie Theatre in Minneapolis presented the play in 1974, directed by Michael Langham (see the reviews in this collection). John Barton's 1978 staging for the Royal Shakespeare Company is well represented in this collection by Barbara Hodgdon's essay. Among numerous other productions of the 1970s were those of The Acting Company (1976, directed by Gerald Freedman), Alabama Shakespeare Festival (1977, directed by Martin Platt), the Open-Air Theatre in Regent's Park (1976, revived 1977, directed by David Conville), and New Jersey Shakespeare Festival (1978, directed by Paul Barry).

The summer of 1980 saw *Love's Labour's Lost* included in the season lineups at the Old Globe in San Diego (directed by Jerome Kilty) and at Colorado Shakespeare Festival (directed by Daniel S.P. Yang). A French translation by Jean-Michel Déprats was presented under the direction of Jean-Pierre Vincent at Avignon. The 1983 American Players Theatre production is evoked in this collection by the interview with Theodore Swetz, who played Berowne. My own theatregoer's notes recall some elements of the RSC's 1984 production directed by Barry Kyle. Miriam Gilbert's book includes a full chapter on the 1984 BBC Television version, which is represented in this collection by Mary Z. Maher's review. Two reviews in this collection assess Gerald Freedman's 1988 production at Great Lakes Theater Festival, which was revived with some cast changes in 1989 (see Clive Barnes's review) at the New York Shakespeare Festival's Public Theater.

A 1990 RSC revival in Stratford-upon-Avon, directed by Terry Hands, featured Ralph Fiennes as Berowne and Amanda Root as Rosaline. 1991 saw a revival of Déprats's French version, staged by Andrzej Seweryn and performed by the actors in training at the Théâtre National de Chaillot. Georgia Shakespeare Festival offered an irreverent 1950s version in its 1992 season. In 1993, Michael Langham once again directed the play, this time at St. Clement's Church in New York, using actors who had graduated from the Juilliard School. In 1994 Nebraska Shakespeare Festival presented a visually charming *Love's Labour's Lost* with a very Spanish Don Armado.

Perhaps the best indication of the success of *Love's Labour's Lost* in recent decades is the number of times it is revived by Shakespeare festivals and other major theatre companies. For example, it was presented at the Old Globe Theatre in 1958–59, 1971–72, 1979–80, and 1988; at Colorado Shakespeare Festival in 1961, 1971, 1980, and 1989; at Oregon Shakespeare Festival in 1947, 1956, 1963, 1972, 1980, and 1988; at Utah Shakespearean Festival in 1969, 1976, 1986, and 1994; at the Open-Air Theatre in Regent's Park in 1935, 1936, 1953, 1962, 1976, and 1977. Such statistics are the more remarkable in that most of these theatres produce only two or three Shakespeare plays each season, thus making it impossible to get through the canon in a decade. *Love's Labour's Lost* has indeed become established, as Roger Warren observed, "as one of Shakespeare's major plays."

Works Cited

Acheson, Arthur. *Shakespeare and the Rival Poet.* London: John Lane, 1903.

Addenbrooke, David. *The Royal Shakespeare Company: The Peter Hall Years.* London: William Kimber, 1974 (pp. 8–11 on *LLL*).

Agnew, Gates K. "Berowne and the Progress of *Love's Labour's Lost,*" *Shakespeare Studies* 4 (1968), 40–72.

Akrigg, G.P.V. *Shakespeare and the Earl of Southampton.* Cambridge, MA: Harvard University Press, 1968 (chapter 3 of Part II, pp. 207–215, on *LLL*).

Allen, Shirley S. *Samuel Phelps & Sadler's Wells Theatre.* Middletown, CT: Wesleyan University Press, 1971.

Anderson, J.J. "The Morality of *Love's Labour's Lost,*" *Shakespeare Survey* 24 (1971), 55–62.

Anderson, Randall Louis. "Love's Labor's Lost" (review of Yale Dramatic Association production), *Shakespeare Bulletin* (Summer 1992), 23–24.

Andrews, Michael Cameron. "The Owl's 'Merry Note'," *Notes and Queries* (June 1984), 187–8.

Appleton, William W. *Madame Vestris and the London Stage.* New York: Columbia University Press, 1974.

Atkinson, Brooks. Reviews of *Love's Labour's Lost* at City Center, New York. *New York Times* (5 Feb. 1953), 20; (8 Feb 1953), 24.

Babcock, Weston. "Fools, Fowls, and Pertaunt-Like in *Love's Labour's Lost,*" *Shakespeare Quarterly* 2, no. 3 (July 1951), 211–219.

Babula, William. *Shakespeare in Production, 1935–1978: A Selective Catalogue.* New York: Garland Publishing, 1981 (pp. 152–161 on *LLL*).

Barber, C.L. *Shakespeare's Festive Comedy.* New York: World Publishing (Meridian Books), 1963 (chapter 5: "The Folly of Wit and Masquerade in *Love's Labour's Lost,*" 87–118).

Barnes, Clive. "Royal Troupe's *Love's Labour's Lost,*" *New York Times* (14 Feb. 1975).

———. "Youthful touch of tenderness," *New York Post* (28 Feb. 1989), 34.

Beckerman, Bernard. "Stratford (Connecticut) Revisited 1968," *Shakespeare Quarterly* 19 (1965), 376–80.

Berman, Ronald. "Shakespearean Comedy and the Uses of Reason," *The South Atlantic Quarterly* 63, no. 1 (Winter 1964), 1–9.

Berry, Ralph. *On Directing Shakespeare*. New York: Barnes and Noble, 1977.

———. "The Words of Mercury," *Shakespeare Survey* 22 (1969), 69–77.

Beyer, Beverly and Ed Rabey. "Love's Labours not lost on Southern Oregon," *Los Angeles Times* (16 May 1993), L7.

Bevington, David. "'Jack Hath Not Jill': Failed Courtship in Lyly and Shakespeare," *Shakespeare Survey* 42 (1989), 1–13.

———. *Tudor Drama and Politics: A Critical Approach to Topical Meaning*. Cambridge, MA: Harvard University Press, 1968.

Billington, Michael. "Love's Labour's Lost," *Manchester Guardian Weekly* (27 August 1978), 21.

Biswas, Dinesh. *Shakespeare's Treatment of His Sources in the Comedies*. Calcutta: Jadavpur University Press, 1971.

Boquet, Guy. Review of *Peines d'amour perdues*. *Cahiers élisabéthains* 41 (April 1992), 70–72.

———. Review of *Peines d'amours perdues*. *Cahiers élisabéthains* 42 (October 1992), 100–101.

Boughner, C. Daniel. "Don Armado and the *Commedia Dell'Arte*," *Studies in Philology* 37 (1940), 201–224.

———. "Don Armado as Gallant," *Revue Anglo-Américaine* 13 (1935), 18–28.

Bradbrook, Muriel C. *The School of Night: A Study in the Literary Relationships of Sir Walter Ralegh*. Cambridge: Cambridge University Press, 1936.

Brandes, Georg M.C. "Shakespeare's Conception of the Relation of the Sexes," trans. by William Archer. *William Shakespeare*. London: Heinemann, 1898.

Breitenberg, Mark. "The Anatomy of Masculine Desire in *Love's Labor's Lost*," *Shakespeare Quarterly* 43, no. 4 (Winter 1992), 430–449.

Bright, James W. "A Shakespearean Quibble," *Modern Language Notes* 13, no. 1 (January 1898), 38–39.

Bronson, Bertrand H. "Daisies Pied and Icicles," *Modern Language Notes* 63, no. 1 (Jan. 1948), 35–38.

Bullough, Geoffrey, ed. *Narrative and Dramatic Sources of Shakespeare*, Vol. 1. New York: Columbia University Press, 1957 (pp. 425–442 on LLL).

Calderwood, James L. "*Love's Labour's Lost*: A Wantoning with Words," *Studies in English Literature 1500–1900* 5 (Spring 1965), 317–332.

Campbell, Oscar J. "*Love's Labour's Lost* Re-Studied," *Studies in Shakespeare, Milton and Donne* (University of Michigan Studies in Language and Literature), 1925, pp. 3–45. Reprinted by Phaeton Press, New York, 1970.

Capell, Edward. "Introduction to Shakespeare," 1768. Reprinted in *Shakespeare, the Critical Heritage*, Vol. 5, ed. by Brian Vickers. Boston: Routledge and Kegan Paul, 1979 (pp. 317–318 on LLL).

Carroll, William C. *The Great Feast of Language in* Love's Labour's Lost. Princeton: Princeton University Press, 1976.

Chambers, E.K. "Introduction to *Love's Labour's Lost*," *The Red Letter Shakespeare*. London: Blackie, 1905. Reprinted in *Shakespeare: A Survey*. London: Sidgewick & Jackson, 1925.

Charlton, H.B. "The Date of *Love's Labour's Lost*," *Modern Language Review* 13 (1918), 257–266, 387–400.

———. "A Disputed Passage in *Love's Labour's Lost*," *Modern Language Review* 12 (1917), 279–285.

———. *Shakespearian Comedy*. London: Methuen, 1938 (pp. 266–298 on LLL).

Chukovski, Kornei. *Liudi i Knigi*. Moscow: Gosudarstvennoe Izdatelstvo Khudozhestvennoi Literaturi, 1960.

Clark, Eva Turner. *Hidden Allusions in Shakespeare's Plays*, 1931. 3rd revised edition, ed. by Ruth Loyd Miller. Port Washington, NY: Kennikat Press, 1974.

———. *The Satirical Comedy* Love's Labour's Lost. New York: William Farquhar Payson, 1933.

Coleridge, Samuel Taylor. *Coleridge's Essays and Lectures on Shakespeare and Some Other Old Poets and Dramatists*. London: J.M. Dent & Sons, Ltd., 1911 ("Notes on *Love's Labour's Lost*," pp. 71–76).

———. *Shakespearean Criticism*, ed. by Thomas Middleton Raysor, Vol. 2. London: J.M. Dent & Sons, Ltd., 1960 (comments on *Love's Labour's Lost* in The Fifth Lecture, pp. 76–79).

Colie, Rosalie L. *Shakespeare's Living Art*. Princeton: Princeton University Press, 1974 (chapter 1: "*Love's Labour's Lost* and the *Sonnets*," pp. 31–65).

Cookman, A.V. "*Love's Labour's Lost*," *The Times* (London, 29 April 1946), 6C.

Copeau, Jacques. "*Vain Labeur d'amour* ou les débuts de Shakespeare," *Le Figaro Littéraire* (18 August 1942), 3–4. Translated from the French especially for this Garland volume by Mari Pappas.

Cordasco, Francesco. *Don Adriano de Armado of "Love's Labour's Lost."* Bologna: Facolta di Lettere e Filosofia, La Universita, 1950.

Coursen, Herbert R., Jr. "*Love's Labour's Lost* and the Comic Truth," *Papers on Language and Literature* 6 (1970), 316–322.

Crouch, J.H. Review of Colorado Shakespeare Festival. *Shakespeare Quarterly* 22 (1971), 302–303.

Danks, K.B. "Love's Labour's Lost," *Notes and Queries* 193 (1948), 545.

Dash, Irene G. *Wooing, Wedding, and Power: Women in Shakespeare's Plays*. New York: Columbia University Press, 1981 (chapter 2 on *LLL*).

David, Richard. "Introduction," *Love's Labour's Lost* (The Arden Shakespeare). New York: Methuen, 1987.

Déprats, Jean-Michel. "Shakespeare in France," *Shakespeare Quarterly* 32 (1981), 390–392.

Doll, David M. "Shakespearean comedy defrosts" (review of Milwaukee Repertory Theatre production), *Milwaukee Downtown Edition* (20 January 1994).

Dowden, Edward. *Shakspere: A Critical Study of His Mind and Art*. London, 1875. Revised ed., New York: Harper & Brothers, 1881 (pp. 55–57 on *LLL*).

Ellis, Herbert A. *Shakespeare's Lusty Punning in Love's Labour's Lost* (Studies in English Literature, Vol. 81). The Hague: Mouton, 1973.

Erickson, Peter. "The Failure of Relationship between Men and Women in *Love's Labour's Lost*," *Women's Studies* 9 (1981), 65–81.

Evans, Malcolm. "Mercury versus Apollo: A Reading of *Love's Labor's Lost*," *Shakespeare Quarterly* 26, no. 2 (Spring 1975), 113–127.

Evett, Marianne. "Another winner, a feast worthy of the Bard himself" (review of Great Lakes Theater Festival production), *The Plain Dealer* (Cleveland, 9 May 1988), 5, 8–B.

Foster, William H. "About *Love's Labour's Lost*," *On-Stage Studies* 13 (1990), 100–104.

Freedman, Gerald. "Directing *Love's Labor's Lost*," *Love's Labor's Lost* (The New York Shakespeare Festival Series), ed. by Bernard Beckerman and Joseph Papp. New York: Macmillan, 1968, pp. 22–69.

Furness, Horace Howard, ed. *A New Variorum Edition of Shakespeare: Love's Labour's Lost*, 1904. Reprinted by Dover Publications, New York, 1964.

Furnivall, Frederick J. "Introduction," *The Leopold Shakspere*. London, 1877.

Fussell, E.S. "'Veal,' Quoth the Dutchman'," *Notes and Queries* 196 (1951), 136–7.

Fuzier, Jean. Review of *Love's Labour's Lost*. *Cahiers élisabéthains* 14 (October 1978), 123–124.

Ganong, Joan. *Backstage at Stratford*. Toronto: Longmans Canada, 1962.

Garebian, Keith. Review of *Love's Labour's Lost*. *Journal of Canadian Studies* 19 (Winter 1984/85), 139.

Gervinus, G.G. *"Love's Labour's Lost* and *All's Well That Ends Well," Shakespeare Commentaries,* trans. by F.E. Bunnètt. London: Smith, Elder, & Co., 1877. Reprinted by AMS Press, New York, 1971. Originally published in German in 1877.

Gilbert, Miriam. *Love's Labour's Lost* (Shakespeare in Performance). Manchester: Manchester University Press, 1993.

Gildon, Charles. "Remarks on the Plays of Shakespear: The Argument of *Love's Labour's Lost"* (pp. 308–313) in *The Works of Mr. William Shakespear* (Nicholas Rowe edition), Vol. 7. London: 1710. Reprinted by AMS Press, New York, 1967.

Giroux, Robert. *The Book Known as Q: A Consideration of Shakespeare's Sonnets.* New York: Vintage Books, 1983.

———. "This *Love's Labor's* Is a Labor of Love," *New York Times* (12 Feb. 1989), 5, 38.

Godshalk, William Leigh. "Pattern in *Love's Labour's Lost," Renaissance Papers* (1968), 41–48.

Goldstien, Neal. *"Love's Labour's Lost* and the Renaissance Vision of Love," *Shakespeare Quarterly* 25, no. 3 (Summer 1974), 335–350.

Gouhier, H. "Théâtre" (review of Paris production), *La Vie intellectuelle* 14, no. 3 (March 1946), 130–132. Translated from the French especially for this volume by Felicia Londré.

Granville-Barker, Harley. *Prefaces to Shakespeare.* London: Sidgwick & Jackson (First Series: includes *LLL*), 1927.

———. *Prefaces to Shakespeare,* Vol. IV. Princeton: Princeton University Press, 1963, pp. 1–37.

Gray, Austen K. "The Secret of *Love's Labour's Lost," Publications of the Modern Language Association of America* 39 (1924), 581–611.

Graziani, René. "M. Marcadé and the Dance of Death: *Love's Labour's Lost,* V.ii.705–11," *The Review of English Studies* 37, no. 147 (August 1986), 392–395.

Greene, T.M. *"Love's Labour's Lost:* The Grace of Society," *Shakespeare Quarterly* (Autumn 1971), 315–328.

Griffin, Alice. "The New York Shakespeare Festival 1965," *Shakespeare Quarterly* 16 (1965), 335–339.

Gussow, Mel. "How a Labour of Love Turns out Well for All," *New York Times* (11 March 1993), C20.

———. "The Romantic Roundelay of *Love's Labor's Lost," New York Times* (23 Feb. 1989).

Guthrie, Tyrone. *A Life in the Theatre.* New York: Limelight Editions, 1985.

Halliwell-Phillips, James Orchard. *Memoranda on 'Love's Labour's Lost,' 'King John,' 'Othello,' and on 'Romeo and Juliet'.* London: James Evan Adlard, 1879.

Hanreddy, Joseph. "Shakespeare's *Love's Labour's Lost," Prologue* (Milwaukee Repertory Theatre, January 1994), 1.

Harris, Laurie Lanzen and Mark W. Scott, eds. *Shakespearean Criticism* Vol. 2. Detroit: Gale Research, 1985.

Harvey, Nancy Lenz and Anna Kirwan Carey, eds. *Love's Labor's Lost: An Annotated Bibliography.* New York: Garland Publishing, 1984.

Hassel, R. Chris, Jr. "Love versus Charity in *Love's Labor's Lost," Shakespeare Studies* 10 (1977), 17–41.

Hazlitt, William. "Love's Labour's Lost," *Characters of Shakespear's Plays.* London: C.H. Reynell, 1817 (pp. 293–7).

Hehl, Ursula. "Elements of Narcissistic Personality Disorders in *Love's Labour's Lost," Literature and Psychology* 40, nos. 1 & 2, (1994), 48–70.

Heninger, Jr., S.K. "The Pattern of *Love's Labour's Lost," Shakespeare Studies* 7 (1974), 25–53.

Heraud, J.A. *Shakspere: His Inner Life,* etc. London, 1865.

Herzog, Martha Sue Hendrickson. "The Scoffer: Development of a Character Type by Lyly and Shakespeare." Ph.D. dissertation, University of Texas, Austin, 1973. *DAI* 34 (1974), 5912A–5913A.

Hibbard, G.R. "Introduction," *Love's Labour's Lost* (The Oxford Shakespeare), ed. by G.R. Hibbard. New York: Oxford University Press, 1990.

Hildy, Franklin J. *Shakespeare at the Maddermarket: Nugent Monck and the Norwich Players.* Ann Arbor: UMI Research Press (no. 41), 1986.

Hodgdon, Barbara. "Rehearsal Process as Critical Practice: John Barton's 1978 *Love's Labour's Lost*," *Theatre History Studies* 8 (1988), 11–34.

Horn, Robert D. "The Oregon Shakespeare Festival, 1956," *Shakespeare Quarterly* 7 (1956), 415–418.

Horobetz, Lynn K. "Shakespeare at the Old Globe, 1972," *Shakespeare Quarterly* 23 (1972), 405–407.

Hoy, Cyrus. "*Love's Labour's Lost* and the Nature of Comedy," *Shakespeare Quarterly* 13, no. 1 (Winter 1962), 30–40.

Hugo, François-Victor. *Oeuvres complètes de Shakespeare.* Paris, 1868.

Hulbert, Dan. "Elizabethan love enchants in '50s get-up," *Atlanta Journal Constitution* (16 June 1992), D1, 5.

Hunt, Hugh. *Old Vic Prefaces.* Westport, CT: Greenwood Press, 1974.

Hunt, Maurice. "The Double Figure of Elizabeth in *Love's Labour's Lost*," *Essays in Literature* 19 (Fall 1992), 173–192.

Hunter, G.K. *John Lyly: The Humanist as Courtier.* London: Routledge and Kegan Paul, 1962.

Hunter, Robert G. "The Function of the Songs at the End of *Love's Labour's Lost*," *Shakespeare Survey* 7 (1974), 55–64.

Jackson, Berners W. "Shakespeare at Stratford, Ontario, 1974," *Shakespeare Quarterly* 25 (1975), 395–399.

Johnson, Samuel. "Notes on *Love's Labour's Lost*," *Johnson on Shakespeare*, ed. by Arthur Sherbo, Vol. 1. New Haven: Yale University Press, 1968 (pp. 266–287).

Joslyn, Jay. "MRT's cast finds gold in *Love's Labour's Lost*" (review of Milwaukee Repertory Theatre production), *The Milwaukee Sentinel* (18 January 1994).

Kehler, Dorothea. "Jaquenetta's Baby's Father: Recovering Paternity in *Love's Labour's Lost*," *Renaissance Papers* (1990), pp. 45–54.

Kemp, Robert. "*Peines d'amours perdues* à l'Odéon" (review of Paris production), *Le Monde* (26 Jan. 1946), 7. Translated from the French especially for this volume by Felicia Londré.

Kerrigan, John. "*Love's Labour's Lost* and the Circling Seasons," *Essays in Criticism* 28 (October 1978), 269–287.

————. "Shakespeare at Work: The Katharine-Rosaline Tangle in *Love's Labour's Lost*," *The Review of English Studies* 33, no. 130 (May 1982), 129–136.

Kiefer, Frederick. "Spring and Winter in *Love's Labour's Lost*: An Iconographic Reconstruction," *Comparative Drama* 29 (Spring 1995), 91–107.

Knight, Charles. "*Love's Labour's Lost*," *Studies of Shakspere*, 1849.

Kodama, James Hisao. "Armado's 'You that way; we this way'," *Shakespeare Studies* (Tokyo, Shakespeare Society of Japan) 8 (1969–70), 1–17.

Lamb, Mary Ellen. "The Nature of Topicality in *Love's Labour's Lost*," *Shakespeare Survey* 38 (1985), 49–59.

Lambert, J.W. "Shakespeare for Pleasure," *Drama* (Autumn 1978), 12–13.

Lambin, G. "The Heir of Alanson, Katharine Her Name," *Shakespearean Authorship Review* (1959), 5–6.

Lambrechts, G. "'The Brief and the tedious of it': Note sur le texte de *Love's Labour's Lost*," *Etudes anglaises* 17, no. 3 (1964), 269–283.

Laroque, François. Review of *Love's Labour's Lost. Cahiers élisabéthains* 8 (October 1975), 79–80.

————. Review of *Peines d'amour perdues. Cahiers élisabéthains* (October 1980), 118–119.

Lee, Elizabeth. "Festival gives Bard 20th-century twist," Gwinnett (Georgia) *Daily News* (9 June 1992), 3.

———. "*Love's Labour's Lost* mismatches story and setting," Gwinnett *Daily News* (16 June 1992), F3.

Lee, S.E. "A New Study of *Love's Labour's Lost*," *The Gentleman's Magazine* 249 (July to December 1880), 447–458.

Lefranc, Abel. "Les Eléments français de *Peines d'amour perdues* de Shakespeare," *Revue Historique* 178 (1936), 411–432.

———. *Sous le masque de "William Shakespeare": William Stanley VIe Comte de Derby*. Paris: Payot. Tome I: 1918. Tome II: 1919.

Leiter, Samuel L., ed. *Shakespeare Around the Globe: A Guide to Notable Postwar Revivals*. New York: Greenwood Press, 1986. Section on *LLL*, pp. 335–354.

Levin, Harry. "Sitting in the Sky (*Love's Labor's Lost*, 4.3)," In *Shakespeare's "Rough Magic": Renaissance Essays in Honor of C.L Barber*, ed. by Peter Erickson and Coppélia Kahn. Newark: University of Delaware Press, 1985.

Lewis, Anthony J. "Shakespeare's *Via Media* in *Love's Labor's Lost*," *Texas Studies in Literature and Language* 16 (1974), 241–248.

Lloyd, W.W. *Critical Essays* (Singer's Second Edition). London, 1856.

Londré, Felicia. "Elizabethan Views of the 'Other': French, Spanish, and Russians in *Love's Labor's Lost*," *The Elizabethan Review* 3, No. 1 (Spring/Summer 1995), 3–20.

———. "The Flourish of All Gentle Tongues," essay in souvenir program for Nebraska Shakespeare Festival (1994), 10–11.

Looney, J. Thomas. *"Shakespeare" Identified*, 2 vols., 3rd revised, annotated edition, ed. by Ruth Loyd Miller. Jennings, LA: Minos Publishing, 1975.

"*Love's Labor's Lost*," *New York Times* (29 March 1891), 4.

"*Love's Labor's Lost* at the Fifth Avenue Theatre," *New York Times* (22 Feb. 1874), 5.

"*Love's Labor's Lost*: New plays worth seeing," *New York Times* (5 April 1891), 5.

"*Love's Labour's Lost*: New Theatre," *The Times* (London, 12 October 1949), 7.

Maher, Mary Z. "Moshinsky's *Love's Labor's Lost*" (review of BBC-TV production), *Shakespeare on Film Newsletter* 10, no. 1 (December 1985), 2–3.

Mastroianni, Tony. "Director leaves mark on *Love's Labour's Lost*" (review of Great Lakes Theater Festival production), *The Beacon Journal* (Akron, 12 May 1988), B7.

Matthews, William. "Language in *Love's Labour's Lost*," *Essays and Studies*, n.s. 17 (1964), 1–11.

McCauley, Mary Carole. "*Love's Labour's Lost* a Hanreddy triumph," *Milwaukee Journal* (17 January 1994).

McClumpha, C.F. "Parallels Between Shakspere's *Sonnets* and *Love's Labour's Lost*," *Modern Language Notes* 15, no. 6 (June 1900), 168–174.

McFarland, Thomas. *Shakespeare's Pastoral Comedy*. Chapel Hill: University of North Carolina Press, 1972 (chapter 2, pp. 49–77, on *LLL*).

McLay, Catherine M. "The Dialogues of Spring and Winter," *Shakespeare Quarterly* 18, no. 2 (Spring 1967), 119–127.

Mézières, A. *Shakespeare, ses Oeuvres et ses Critiques*. Paris, 1865.

Moncure-Sime, A.H. *Shakespeare: His Music and Song*. London, 1915.

Montégut, Emile. *Oeuvres complètes de Shakespeare*. Paris, 1867.

Montrose, Louis Adrian. *"Curious-Knotted Garden": The Form, Themes, and Contexts of Shakespeare's* Love's Labour's Lost. Salzburg: Institut für Englische Sprache und Literatur, 1977.

———. "'Folly, in wisdom hatch'd': The Exemplary Comedy of *Love's Labour's Lost*," *Comparative Drama* 11 (1977), 147–170.

———. "'Sport by sport o'erthrown': *Love's Labour's Lost* and the Politics of Play," *Texas Studies in Language and Literature* 18, no. 4 (Winter 1977), 528–552.

Morozov, P. "Bezplodniya Usiliya Liubvi," *Shekspir* 1 (1902, St. Petersburg), 114–121.

Muir, Kenneth. *Shakespeare's Comic Sequence*. Liverpool: Liverpool University Press, 1979 (pp. 35–42 on *LLL*).

Munro, John, ed. *The Shakspere Allusion-Book: A Collection of Allusions to Shakspere from 1591 to 1700*, Vol. 1. 1909. Reprinted by Books for Libraries Press, Freeport, New York, 1970.

Nakanori, Koshi. *Shakespearean Comedy: Its Structures and Techniques*. Tokyo: Kinokuniya, 1982. Translated from the Japanese especially for this Garland volume by Toru Iwasaki.

Noble, Richmond. *Shakespeare's Use of Song*. Oxford: Clarendon Press, 1923 (pp. 32–83).

Ogburn, Charlton. *The Mysterious William Shakespeare: The Myth and the Reality*, 2nd edition. McLean, VA: EPM Productions, 1992.

Ogburn, Dorothy and Charlton. *This Star of England*. New York: Coward-McCann, Inc., 1952 (chapters 16, 17, 18 on *LLL*).

Ornstein, Robert. "The Great Lakes Shakespeare Festival," *Shakespeare Quarterly* 18 (1967), 425–427.

———. *Shakespeare's Comedies: From Roman Farce to Romantic Mystery*. Newark: University of Delaware Press, 1986 (chapter 3, pp. 35–47, on *LLL*).

Palmer, John. *Comic Characters of Shakespeare*. London: Macmillan, 1947 (chapter on Berowne, pp. 1–28).

Parker, Barbara L. *A Precious Seeing: Love and Reason in Shakespeare's Plays*. New York: New York University Press, 1987 (chapter 5, pp. 81–98, on *LLL*).

Parker, Patricia. "Preposterous Reversals: *Love's Labour's Lost*," *Modern Language Quarterly* 54, no. 4 (December 1993), 435–482.

Pater, Walter. "On *Love's Labour's Lost*," *Macmillan's Magazine* 13 (December 1885), 89–91.

Perkin, Robert L. "Shakespeare in the Rockies: IV," *Shakespeare Quarterly* 12 (1961), 411–413.

Potter, Stephen. "Note on Stratford," *The New Statesman and Nation* (11 May 1946), 336–337.

Price, Thomas R. "*Love's Labour's Lost*," *Shakespeariana* 6 (July 1889), 292–297.

———. "Shakespeare's Word-Play and Puns: *Love's Labour's Lost*," *Shakespeariana* 7 (April 1890), 67–91.

Prosser, Eleanor. "Shakespeare at Ashland and San Diego," *Shakespeare Quarterly* 14 (1963), 449–454.

Ralli, Augustus. *A History of Shakespearian Criticism*, 2 vols. Oxford University Press, 1932. Reprinted by Humanities Press, New York, 1959.

Ranald, Margaret Loftus. "*Love's Labor's Lost*" (review of Theatre for a New Audience production), *Shakespeare Bulletin* (Summer 1993), 14–15.

Reiter, Amy. "Continuous Sonnets," *Theatre Crafts International* 27 (Jan. 1993), 9.

Richmond, Hugh M. "Shakespere's Navarre," *The Huntington Library Quarterly* 42, no. 3 (Summer 1979), 193–216.

———. *Shakespeare's Sexual Comedy: A Mirror for Lovers*. Indianapolis: Bobbs-Merrill, 1971 (pp. 64–83 on *LLL*).

Roesen, Bobbyann. "*Love's Labour's Lost*," *Shakespeare Quarterly* 4, no. 4 (October 1953), 411–426.

Salgado, Gamini. *Eyewitnesses of Shakespeare: First Hand Accounts of Performances 1590–1890*. London: Sussex University Press, 1975 (pp. 114–116 on *LLL*).

Saunders, John. *Notes on* Love's Labour's Lost (York Notes). Beirut: York Press, 1980.

Schlegel, Augustus William von. *Lectures on Dramatic Art and Literature*, trans. by John Black and revised by the Rev. A.J.W. Morrison. London: George Bell & Sons, 1879 (pp. 383–384).

Sen Gupta, S.C. *Shakespearian Comedy*. Calcutta: Geoffrey Cumberlege, Oxford University Press, 1950.

Shaheen, Naseeb. "Biblical References in *Love's Labour's Lost*," *Notes and Queries* (March 1991), 55–56.

Shaw, Bernard. "Love's Labour's Lost" in *Shaw on Shakespeare*, ed. by Edwin Wilson. New York: E.P. Dutton & Co., 1961 (pp. 118–120).

Shaw, William P. "Meager Lead and Joyous Consequences: RSC Triumphs among Shakespeare's Minor Plays," *Theatre Survey* 27 (May and November 1986), 37–67 (pp. 38–44 on *LLL*).

Shrimpton, Nicholas. "Shakespeare Performances in Stratford-upon-Avon and London, 1983–84," *Shakespeare Survey* 38 (1985) (pp. 211–213 on *LLL*).

Siler, Henry D. "A French Pun in *Love's Labour's Lost*," *Modern Language Notes* 60 (1945), 124–125.

Skura, Meredith Anne. *Shakespeare the Actor and the Purpose of Playing*. Chicago: University of Chicago Press, 1993 (pp. 88–95).

Smidt, Kristian. *Unconformities in Shakespeare's Early Comedies*. London: Macmillan, 1986 (chapter 5: "*Love's Labour's Lost* or the Revenge of the Shrews," pp. 80–119, 202–209).

Smirnov, A. "Bezplodniva Usiliya Liubvi," *Polnoe sobranie sochinenii*, vol. 2. Moscow: Isskustvo, 1957–60, pp. 542–545.

Smith, Peter D. "'Sharp Wit and Noble Scenes': A Review of the 1961 Season of the Stratford, Ontario, Festival," *Shakespeare Quarterly* 13 (1962), 71–73.

Snider, Denton J. "*Love's Labor's Lost*," *The Shakespearian Drama, a Commentary: The Comedies*. Sigma Publishing Co., n.d.

Sorenson, Fred. "'The Masque of the Muscovites' in *Love's Labour's Lost*," *Modern Language Notes* 50, no. 6 (December 1935), 499–501.

Speaight, Robert. "Shakespeare in Britain," *Shakespeare Quarterly* 16 (1965), 313–324.

———. "Shakespeare in Britain," *Shakespeare Quarterly* 20 (Autumn 1969), 440–441.

———. "The Stratford-upon-Avon Season," *Shakespeare Quarterly* 24 (Autumn 1973), 403–404.

Spencer, Hazleton. *The Art and Life of William Shakespeare*. New York: Harcourt Brace, 1940.

Spurgeon, Caroline F.E.. *Shakespeare's Imagery and What It Tells Us*. Cambridge: Cambridge University Press, 1935 (pp. 271–272, 275 on *LLL*).

Straat, Evert. "Wie Was Biron? Over Shakespeare's *Love's Labour's Lost*," *Maatstaf* 7 (1959–60, Amsterdam), 544–559.

Striar, Brian. "A Note on *Love's Labour's Lost* V.ii.417–418," *Notes and Queries* (March 1994), 33.

Swinburne, Algernon Charles. *A Study of Shakespeare*. London: Chatto and Windus, 1880.

Taylor, Rupert. *The Date of* Love's Labour's Lost. New York: Columbia University Press, 1932.

Temkine, Raymonde. "Avignon: Un Festival en transition," *Europe* 620 (Nov.-Dec. 1980), 197.

Thorne, Barry. "*Love's Labor's Lost* : The Lyly Gilded," *The Humanities Association Bulletin* 21 (1970), 32–37.

Tillyard, E.M.W. *Shakespeare's Early Comedies*. London: Chatto and Windus, 1965 (chapter 6: *LLL*, pp. 137–181).

Tofte, Robert. *Alba: The Month's Minde of a Melancholy Lover*, Reprint of the 1598 edition, ed. by Rev. Alexander B. Grosart. Manchester: Printed for the Subscribers (62 copies only), 1880.

Trewin, J.C. "Shakespeare in Britain," *Shakespeare Quarterly* 30 (Spring 1979), 154–155.

Turner, John. "*Love's Labour's Lost*: The Court at Play," *Shakespeare: Out of Court*, by Graham Holderness, Nick Potter, and John Turner. New York: St. Martin's Press, 1990.

Ulrici, Hermann. "Criticisms of Shakspeare's Drama: *Love's Labour's Lost—Two Gentlemen of Verona—All's Well That Ends Well*," *Shakspeare's Dramatic Art: And His Relation to Calderon and Goethe*, trans. by Rev. A.J.W. Morrison.

London: Chapman Brothers, 1846. Originally published in German in 1839.

Warburton, William. Essay in *The Works of Shakespear . . . collated . . . corrected and emended . . . by Mr Pope and Mr Warburton*, Vol. 2. London: J. and P. Knapton, 1747.

Wardle, Irving. "Olivier stages *Love's Labour's* with a spirit of gentle delirium," *New York Times* (22 Dec. 1968), 54.

Warren, Roger. "Shakespeare on the Twentieth-Century Stage," *The Cambridge Companion to Shakespeare Studies*, ed. by Stanley Wells. Cambridge: Cambridge University Press, 1986, pp. 257–272.

———. "A Year of Comedies: Stratford 1978," *Shakespeare Survey* 32 (1979), 208–209.

Watt, R.J.C. "Armado's *Fadge Not* in *Love's Labour's Lost*: The Case Against Emendation," *Notes and Queries* (September 1986), 349–50.

Wells, Stanley. "The Copy for the Folio Text of *Love's Labour's Lost*," *The Review of English Studies* 33, no. 130 (May 1982), 137–147.

Werstine, Paul. "The Editorial Usefulness of Printing House and Compositor Studies," *Play-Texts In Old Spelling: Papers from the Glendon Conference*, ed. by G.B. Shand and Raymond C. Shady. New York: AMS Press, 1984, pp. 35–72.

———. "Variants in the First Quarto of *Love's Labour's Lost*," *Shakespeare Survey* 12 (1979), 35–47.

Westlund, Joseph. "Fancy and Achievement in *Love's Labour's Lost*," *Shakespeare Quarterly* 18, no. 1 (Winter 1967), 37–46.

Whalen, Richard F. *Shakespeare: Who Was He? The Oxford Challenge to the Bard of Avon*. Westport, CT: Praeger, 1994.

White, R.S. "Muscovites in *Love's Labour's Lost*," *Notes and Queries* (September 1986), 350.

Wickham, Glynne. "*Love's Labour's Lost* and *The Four Foster Children of Desire*, 1581," *Shakespeare Quarterly* 36, no. 1 (Spring 1985), 49–55.

Wilders, John. "The Unresolved Conflicts of *Love's Labour's Lost*," *Essays in Criticism* 27, no. 1 (January 1977), 20–33.

Wilson, John Dover, C.H. *Shakespeare's Happy Comedies*. Evanston: Northwestern University Press, 1963 (chapter 3 on *LLL*, pp. 55–75).

Winter, William. *Shakespeare on the Stage*, 1916. Reprinted by Benjamin Blom, New York, 1969 (pp. 167–195 on *LLL*).

Wood, Roger and Mary Clarke. *Shakespeare at the Old Vic 1954–55*. London: Adam and Charles Black, 1956 (pp. 136–140 on *LLL*).

Yates, Frances A. *A Study of Love's Labour's Lost*. Cambridge: Cambridge University Press, 1936.

PART II

LOVE'S LABOUR'S LOST AND THE CRITICS

FROM *ALBA: THE MONTH'S MINDE*
OF A *MELANCHOLY LOVER*

Robert Tofte

LOVES LABOR LOST, I once did see a Play,
Ycleped so, so called to my paine,
Which I to heare to my small Joy did stay,
Giving attendance on my froward Dame,
 My misgiving minde presaging to me Ill,
 Yet was I drawne to see it gainst my Will.

This *Play* no *Play* but Plague was unto me,
For there I lost the Love I liked most:
And what to others seemde a Jest to be,
I, that (in earnest) found unto my cost,
 To every one (save me) twas *Comicall*,
 Whilst *Tragick* like to me it did befall.

Each Actor plaid in cunning wise his part,
But chiefly Those entrapt in *Cupids* snare:
Yet all was fained, twas not from the hart,
They seemde to grieve, but yet they felt no care:
 Twas I that Griefe (indeed) did beare in brest,
 The others did but make a show in Jest.

Yet neither faining theirs, nor my meere Truth,
Could make her once so much as for to smile:

Alba: The Month's Minde of a Melancholy Lover, divided into three parts. By R.T., Gentleman. London: Printed by Felix Kingston, for Matthew Lownes, 1598, p. 105. Reprint edited, with introduction and notes and illustrations by the Rev. Alexander B. Groshart, 62 copies only, printed for the subscribers, by Charles E. Simms, Manchester, 1880.

Whilst she (despite of pity mild and ruth)
Did sit as skorning of my Woes the while.
 Thus did she sit to see LOVE lose his LOVE,
 Like hardned Rock that force nor power can move.

To the Right Honorable the Lorde Vycount Cranborne at the Courte

Sir Walter Cope

Sir,

I have sent and bene all thys morning huntyng for players Juglers & Such kinde of Creaturs, but fynde them harde to finde, wherfore Leavinge notes for them to seeke me, burbage ys come & Sayes ther ys no new playe that the quene[1] hath not seene, but they have Revyved an olde one, Cawled *Loves Labore lost,* which for wytt & mirthe he sayes will please her excedingly. And Thys ys apointed to be played to Morowe night at my Lord of Sowthamptons, unles yow send a wrytt to Remove the Corpus Cum Causa to your howse in Strande. Burbage ys my messenger Ready attendyng your pleasure.

Yours most humbly,
Walter Cope

NOTE

1. Anne of Denmark (1574–1619), wife of James I of England.

Letter endorsed: 1604, Sir Walter Cope to my Lord. Hatfield House MSS. From *The Shakspere Allusion-Book: A Collection of Allusions to Shakspere from 1591 to 1700,* Vol. 1, revised edition edited by John Munro, 1909, reprinted by Books for Libraries Press, 1970.

REMARKS ON THE PLAYS OF SHAKESPEAR

THE ARGUMENT OF *LOVES LABOUR'S LOST*

Charles Gildon

The King of *Navarre* and some of his Nobles make a Vow of retiring from the World to their Books for three Years, and forswear the Conversation of all Women. But the King of *France*'s Daughter and some ladies her Attendants come in an Embassy from her Father to the King of *Navarre*, which obliges them to a Conversation with the Ladies, and that makes them all in Love; and endeavour after they have found out each other's Frailty and Breach of oath to win the Ladies to yield to love them. But they admit them to hope, on Condition they remain in the same Mind a Year, and perform certain Penances. This and the News of the *French* King's Death ends the Play.

Tho' I can't well see why the Author gave this Play this Name, yet since it has past thus long I shall say no more to it, but this, that since it is one of the worst of *Shakespear*'s Plays, nay I think I may say the very worst, I cannot but think that it is his first, notwithstanding those Arguments, or that Opinion, that has been brought to the contrary. *Perhaps* (says this Author) *we are not to look for his Beginnings like those of other Authors among their least perfect Writings. Art had so little, and Nature so large a Share in what he did, that for aught I know, the Performances of his Youth, as they were the most vigorous, and had the most Fire of Imagination in them, were the best. I would not be thought by this to mean, that his Fancy was so loose, and extravagant, as to be independent of the Rule and Government of Judgment; but that what he thought was commonly so great, so justly and rightly concerted in itself, that it wanted little or no Correction; and was immediately approv'd by an impartial Judgment at first Sight.*

Nicholas Rowe's edition of *The Works of Mr. William Shakespeare* was published in six volumes in 1709. In 1710 a seventh volume was added, which included Charles Gildon's "Critical Remarks on His Plays." A facsimile reprint was published by AMS Press, New York, 1967. The remarks on *Love's Labour's Lost* are on pp. 308–313 of Vol. 7.

But since this Gentleman has only given us a Supposition of his own, without confirming it with any convincing, or indeed probably Reason; I hope I may be permitted to throw in another *Perhaps* for the Opinion of Mr. *Dryden*, and others without offending him by the Opposition, I agree with him, that we have indeed in our Days seen a young Man start up like a Mushroom in a Night, and surprize the Whim of the Town into a momentary Reputation, or at least by a surprizing first Play (as Plays go at this Time) and in all his after Tryals give us not one Line, that might supply our Credulity with the least Reason to believe that he wrote the first himself. Thus *Love's last Shift* was an excellent first Play, and yet that Author after so many Tryals has not only never come up to his first Essay, but scarce to any thing tolerable, except in one, that like a Cheder Cheese was made by the Milk of a Parish.

But in *Shakespear* we are not considering those Masters of the Stage, that glare a little in the Night, but disappear in the Day; but fix'd Stars that always show their unborrow'd Light. And here the common Experience is directly against our Author; for all the Poets, that have without Controversy been Masters of a great Genius have rose to Excellence by Degrees. *The Wild Gallant* was the worst of *Dryden's* Plays and the first, and the *Plain Dealer* was the last of Mr. *Wycherly's*; *Otway*, the brightest and most Tragic Genius of our World, gave us three moderate Plays before the *Orphan* and *Venice Preserv'd*. And why we shou'd think, that *Shakespear* shou'd grow worse by Practice, I can find no shadow of a Reason from what is advanc'd. But—*the Performances of his Youth, as they were the most Vigorous, and had the most Fire, and Strength of Imagination in 'em were the best.*—But still this is begging the Question, and taking that for granted, which wants to be prov'd, *viz.* that the Productions of his Youth had the *most Fire and Strength of Imagination*, his *Fables* excelling all, that he ever wrote before. Nor can we think but that *Shakespear* was far from his Dotage when he Died at fifty-three, and had retir'd some Years from the Stage, and writing of Plays. But shou'd we allow what our Author contends for, his Supposition wou'd not hold; for the Play before us and all his most imperfect Plays have the least Fire and Strength of Imagination; and that Fancy, that is in them is almost every where independent of that *Rule of Judgment*, which our Author supposes him Master of. I am sure Judgment encreases with Years and Observation; and where *Shakespear* shews, that he is least Extravagant, 'tis plain he depends most on that *Rule of Judgment*. I confess the Terms are something Obscure and Equivocal; But I pretend not to enter into a Debate with him on this Head; all I have said being to justify Mr. *Dryden* and some others, who yet think, that we ought to look into *Shakespear's* most imperfect

Plays for his first. And this of *Loves Labour's Lost* being perhaps the most defective, I can see no Reason why we shou'd not conclude, that it is one of his first. For neither the Manners, Sentiments, Diction, Versification, *&c.* (except in some few places) discover the *Genius* that shines in his other Plays.

But tho' this Play be so bad yet there is here and there a Stroak, that persuades us, that *Shakespear* wrote it. The Proclamation, that Women shou'd lost their Tongues if they approach'd within a Mile of the Court, is a perfect penalty. There are but few Words spoken by *Jaquenetta* in the later End of the first Act, and yet the very Soul of a pert Country Lass is perfectly express'd. The several Characters of the King's Companions in the Retreat, is very pretty, and the Remarks of the Princess very just and fine, p. 404 and p. 425. *Longavile's* good Epigram furnishes a Proof, that these publish'd in this Volume are Genuine, and for that Reason I will transcribe it.

> *Did not the heavenly Rhetorick of thine Eye,*
> *'Gainst whom the World cannot hold Argument,*
> *Persuade my Heart to this false Perjury?*
> *Vows for thee broke deserve not Punishment.*
> *A Woman I forswore, but I will prove,*
> *Thou being a Goddess I forswore not thee.*
> *My Vow was Earthly, thou a Heavenly Love;*
> *Thy Grace being gain'd cures all Disgrace in me.*
> *Vows are but Breath, and Breath a Vapour is.*
> *When thou fair Sun, which on my Earth doth shine*
> *Exhal'st this Vapour-Vow, in thee it is.*
> *If broken then it is no fault of mine*
> *If by me broke; What Fool is not so Wise*
> *To lose an Oath to win a Paradise?*

The Discovery of the King's, *Longavile's*, and *Dumain's* Love is very prettily manag'd, and that of *Biron* by *Costard's* mistake, is a well contriv'd Incident. The whole indeed is a tolerable Proof how much in vain we resolve against Nature, nor is *Biron's Casuistry* amiss when he strives to salve their common Breach of Oath.

> *Of Delights.*
> BIRON. Why all Delights are vain, and that most vain
>   Which with Pain purchased does inherit Pain, *&c.*
>
> *Pag.* 393

On Study.
Study is like the Heaven's glorious Sun
That will not be deep search'd with saucy Looks;
Small have continual Plodders ever won
Save base Authority from other Books, *&c. ibid.*

Beauty.
Beauty is bought by Judgment of the Eye
Not utter'd by base Sale of Chapmen's Tongues, *&c.* 403

A pleasant Description of Cupid *of Love.*
This whimpled, whining, purblind wayward Boy,
This Signior *Junios* Giant-Dwarf Don *Cupid*,
Regent of Love-Rhimes, Lord of folded Arms,
The anointed Soveraign of Sighs and Groans;
Liege of all Loyterers and Malecontents;
Dread Prince of Plackets, King of Codpisses, *&c.*

p. 414.

Of a Wife.
＿＿＿＿ I seek a Wife;
A Woman that is like a *German* Clock,
Still a repairing; ever out of Frame, *&c. ibid.*

There is a pretty Account of Love *p.* 432. beginning

But Love first learned in a Lady's Eye, *&c.*

And on *Women's Eyes* there are some pretty Reflections, *p.* 433. beginning thus,

From Women's Eyes this Doctrine I derive,
They sparkle still the true Promethean Fire, *&c.*

And *Pag.* 460 is a good Reflection on a satyric biting Wit.

Notes on Shakespeare's Plays

Love's Labour's Lost (excerpts)

Samuel Johnson

I.1.31   DUMAIN. To love, to wealth, to pomp, I pine and die;
               With all these living in philosophy.

The stile of the rhyming scenes in this play is often entangled and obscure. I know not certainly to what "all these" is to be referred; I suppose he means that he finds "love, pomp, *and* wealth *in* philosophy."

I.1.75   BIRON.   while truth the while
               Doth falsly blind the eye-sight of his look

"Falsly" is here, and in many other places, the same as "dishonestly" or "treacherously." The whole sense of this gingling declamation is only this, that "a man by too close study may read himself blind," which might have been told with less obscurity in fewer words.

I.1.95   DUMAIN. Proceeded well, to stop all good proceeding.

To "proceed" is an academical term, meaning, "to take a degree," as "he *proceeded* bachelor in physick." The sense is, "he has taken his degrees on the art of hindring the degrees of others."

I.1.147   BIRON. Necessity will make us all forsworn
               Three thousand times within this three years' space:
               For every man with his affects is born:
               Not by might master'd, but by special grace.

From *The Plays of William Shakespeare* (1765) by Samuel Johnson, reprinted in *The Yale Edition of the Works of Samuel Johnson*, Volume 7: *Johnson on Shakespeare*, edited by Arthur Sherbo (New Haven: Yale University Press, 1968), excerpts from pp. 266–287. Reprinted by permission of Yale University Press.

Biron amidst his extravagancies, speaks with great justness against the folly of vows. They are made without sufficient regard to the variations of life, and are therefore broken by some unforeseen necessity. They proceed commonly from a presumptuous confidence, and a false estimate of human power.

II.1.104   PRINCESS. 'Tis deadly sin to keep that oath, my Lord;
            And sin to break it.
Sir T. Hammer reads "not" sin to break it. I believe erroneously. The Princess shews an inconvenience very frequently attending rash oaths, which whether kept or broken produce guilt.

II.1.222   MARIA. My lips are no common, though several they be.
"Several" is an inclosed field of a private proprietor, so Maria says, "her lips *are* private property." Of a Lord that was newly married one observed that he grew fat; yes, said Sir Walter Raleigh, any beast will grow fat, if you take him from the "common" and graze him in the "several."

IV.1.18   PRINCESS. Here—my good glass—take this for telling true
To understand how the princess has her glass so ready at hand in a casual conversation, it must be remembered that in those days it was the fashion among the French ladies to wear a looking glass, as Mr. Bayle coarsely represents it, "on their bellies"; that is, to have a small mirror set in gold hanging at the girdle, by which they occasionally viewed their faces, or adjusted their hair.

IV.3.2   BIRON. They have pitcht a toil, I am toiling in a pitch
Alluding to lady Rosaline's complexion, who is, through the whole play, represented as a black beauty.

IV.3.43   BIRON. Why, he comes in like a perjure, wearing papers
The punishment of perjury is to wear on the breast a paper expressing the crime.

V.1.2   NATHANIEL. Sir, your reasons at dinner have been sharp and sententious; pleasant without scurrility, witty without affectation, audacious without impudency, learned without opinion, and strange without heresy.
I know not well what degree of respect Shakespeare intends to obtain for this vicar, but he has here put into his mouth a finished representation of

colloquial excellence. It is very difficult to add any thing to this character of the schoolmaster's table-talk, and perhaps all the precepts of Castiglione will scarcely be found to comprehend a rule for conversation so justly delineated, so widely dilated, and so nicely limited.

It may be proper just to note, that "reason" here, and in many other places, signifies "discourse," and that "audacious" is used in a good sense for "spirited, animated, confident." "Opinion" is the same with "obstinacy" or *opiniatreté*.

V.1.11   HOLOFERNES. He is too piqued
To have the beard "piqued" or shorn so as to end in a point, was in our authour's time a mark of a traveller affecting foreign fashions: so says the Bastard in *King John*.

> I catechise
> My *piqued* man of countries.

V.1.89   ARMADO. with his royal finger thus dally with my excrement
The authour has before call'd the beard valour's excrement in the *Merchant of Venice*.

V.2.419   BIRON. Write, "Lord have mercy on us," on those three
This was the inscription put upon the door of the houses infected with the plague, to which Biron compares the love of himself and his companions; and persuing the metaphor finds the "tokens" likewise on the ladies. The "tokens" of the plague are the first spots or discolorations by which the infection is known to be received.

V.2.676   BIRON. Pompey is mov'd; more Ates, more Ates; stir them on,
                      stir them on.
That is, more instigation. Ate was the mischievous goddess that incited bloodshed.

V.2.767   PRINCESS. And in our maiden council rated them
                      At courtship, pleasant jest, and courtesy;
                      As bombast, and as lining to the time
This line is obscure. "Bombast" was a kind of loose texture not unlike what is now called "wadding," used to give the dresses of that time bulk and protuberance, without much encrease of weight; whence the same name is yet given to a tumor of words unsupported by solid sentiment. The Princess, therefore, says, that they considered this courtship as but "bombast," as

51

something to fill out life, which not being closely united with it, might be thrown away at pleasure.

In this play, which all the editors have concurred to censure, and some have rejected as unworthy of our poet, it must be confessed that there are many passages mean, childish, and vulgar; and some which ought not to have been exhibited, as we are told they were, to a maiden queen. But there are scattered, through the whole, many sparks of genius; nor is there any play that has more evident marks of the hand of Shakespeare.

LOVE'S LABOUR LOST, FROM LECTURES ON DRAMATIC ART AND LITERATURE

CRITICISMS ON SHAKESPEARE'S COMEDIES

August Wilhelm von Schlegel

Love's Labour Lost is also numbered among the pieces of [Shakespeare's] youth. It is a humorsome display of frolic; a whole cornucopia of the most vivacious jokes is emptied into it. Youth is certainly perceivable in the lavish superfluity of labour in the execution: the unbroken succession of plays on words, and sallies of every description, hardly leave the spectator time to breathe; the sparkles of wit fly about in such profusion, that they resemble a blaze of fireworks; while the dialogue, for the most part, is in the same hurried style in which the passing masks at a carnival attempt to banter each other. The young king of Navarre, with three of his courtiers, has made a vow to pass three years in rigid retirement, and devote them to the study of wisdom; for that purpose he has banished all female society from his court, and imposed a penalty on the intercourse with women. But scarcely has he, in a pompous harangue, worthy of the most heroic achievement, announced this determination, when the daughter of the king of France appears at his court, in the name of her old and bed-ridden father, to demand the restitution of a province which he held in pledge. Compelled to give her audience, he falls immediately in love with her. Matters fare no better with his companions, who on their parts renew an old acquaintance with the princess's attendants. Each, in heart, is already false to his vow, without knowing that the wish is shared by his associates; they overhear one another, as they in turn confide their sorrows in a love-ditty to the solitary forest: every one jeers and confounds the one who follows him. Biron, who from the beginning was the most satirical among them, at last steps forth, and rallies the king and

From Schlegel's 1808 lecture on Shakespeare's comedies, the twenty-fourth of thirty lectures on dramatic poetry given at Vienna and published as *Über dramatische Kunst und Literatur* in 1809–1811. This translation is by John Black, revised according to the latest German edition by the Reverend A.J.W. Morrison, *Lectures on Dramatic Art and Literature* by Augustus William Schlegel (London: George Bell & Sons, 1879).

the two others, till the discovery of a love-letter forces him also to hang down his head. He extricates himself and his companions from their dilemma by ridiculing the folly of the broken vow, and, after a noble eulogy on women, invites them to swear new allegiance to the colours of love. This scene is inimitable, and the crowning beauty of the whole. The manner in which they afterwards prosecute their love-suits in masks and disguise, and in which they are tricked and laughed at by the ladies, who are also masked and disguised, is, perhaps, spun out too long. It may be thought, too, that the poet, when he suddenly announces the death of the king of France, and makes the princess postpone her answer to the young prince's serious advances till the expiration of the period of her mourning, and impose, besides, a heavy penance on him for his levity, drops the proper comic tone. But the tone of raillery, which prevails throughout the piece, made it hardly possible to bring about a more satisfactory conclusion: after such extravagance, the characters could not return to sobriety, except under the presence of some foreign influence. The grotesque figures of Don Armado, a pompous fantastic Spaniard, a couple of pedants, and a clown, who between the whiles contribute to the entertainment, are the creation of a whimsical imagination, and well adapted as foils for the wit of so vivacious a society.

LOVE'S LABOUR'S LOST, FROM THE LECTURES ON SHAKESPEARE AND MILTON

Samuel Taylor Coleridge [reported by J. Tomalin]

The reason [Coleridge] considered *Love's Labour['s] Lost* as the first of Shakespeare's plays was that it afforded the strongest possible presumption that Shakespeare was not an ignorant man, and that the former part of his life had been passed in scholastic pursuits, because when a man began to write, his first work will bear a colour or tincture of his past life, provided he be a man of genius. . . .

What was the *Love's Labour['s] Lost*? Was it the production of a person accustomed to stroll as a vagabond about the streets, or to hold horses at a playhouse door, and who had contented himself with making observations on human nature? No such thing! There is scarcely a trace of any observation of nature in Shakespeare's earliest works. The dialogue consisted either of remarks upon what is grotesque in language, or mistaken in literature; all bore the appearance of being written by a man of reading and learning, and the force of genius early saw what was excellent, or what was ridiculous. Hence the wonderful activity of this kind in the first scene of *Love's Labour['s] Lost*. Such thoughts would never have occurred to a man ignorant and merely an observer of nature.

The King says to Biron—

> These be the stops that hinder study quite,
> And train our intellects to vain delight.

Biron replies—

Coleridge's 1811–1812 lectures on Shakespeare and Milton were delivered extemporaneously and reported by various people. This excerpt from the fifth lecture (given in December 1811 and reported by J. Tomalin) is from Coleridge's *Shakespearean Criticism*, Vol. 2, edited by Thomas Middleton Raysor (New York: Dutton, Everyman's Library, 1960), pp. 76–79. Reprinted by permission of Everyman's Library, David Campbell Publishers.

Why! all delights are vain—and that most vain,
Which, with pain purchased, doth inherit pain:
As painfully to pore upon a book
To seek the light of Truth, while Truth the while
Doth falsely blind the eye-sight of his look:
Light seeking light, doth light of light beguile.

Coleridge would venture to say that the two first lines of Biron's answer contain a complete confutation of Malthus's theory. Truly we had delights which pain alone could purchase, the continuance of pain, without giving the most distant prospect of good to be obtained from it. The concluding sentiment also received his highest eulogium, which compared the light of truth to the light of the sun, the gazing at which destroyed the sight.

This play in reality contained in itself very little character. The *dramatis personae* were only the embryos of characters. Biron was afterwards seen more perfectly in Benedict and Mercutio, and Rosaline in Beatrice, the beloved of Benedict. The old man Boyet came forward afterwards in Lafeu in *All's Well That Ends Well*. The poet in this play *[L.L.L.]* was always uppermost, and little was drawn from real life. His judgement only was shewn in placing the scenes at such a period when we could imagine the transactions of the play natural.

In former ages [existed] the courts of Love, which are now entirely forgotten and appear in themselves improbable; but in Shakespeare's time they were not so far removed, and it was only a pleasing effort on his part to revive the recollection of something not far distant.

But the play was most interesting as it exemplified Shakespeare's mind, when one of the characters, Longueville, objects to Biron—

Biron is like an envious sneaking frost
That bites the first-born infants of the spring.

A thousand times had the answer of Biron occurred to Coleridge in this age of prodigies, when the young Roscii of the times had been followed as superior beings, wonderment always taking place of sense. Nothing was valued according to the moral feeling it produced, but only according to its strangeness, just as if a rose could have no sweetness unless it grew upon a thorn, or a bunch of grapes could afford no delight to the taste unless it grew by some miracle from a mushroom.

Biron's reply was—

Well! say I am; why should proud summer boast
Before the birds have any power to sing?
Why should I joy in an abortive birth?
At Christmas I no more desire a rose
Than wish a snow in May's new fangled shows
But like of each thing that in season grows.

Coleridge wished the last line to be impressed on every parent in this wonder-loving age—*"but like of each thing that in season grows."*

But if they attended to it, he should not have seen so many miserable little beings taught to think before they had the means of thinking. One of them he had once seen walking about a room, and enquiring why she did so, she answered, "I do it for exercise, not for pleasure, but too much study will injure my health." This young old lady was aged about four years!

If parents constantly kept the last line in their view, they would not delight in hearing their infants reason when patience ought to be exercised in listening to their natural infantile prattle. . . .

. . .

Above all it should be recollected that [Coleridge] had taken the great names of Milton and Shakespeare rather for the purpose of illustrating great principles than for any minute examination of their works. . . .

LOVE'S LABOUR'S LOST, FROM LECTURES AND NOTES ON SHAKSPERE AND OTHER ENGLISH POETS

Samuel Taylor Coleridge

The characters in this play are either impersonated out of Shakspere's own multiformity by imaginative self-position, or out of such as a country town and a schoolboy's observation might supply,—the curate, the schoolmaster, the Armado (who even in my time was not extinct in the cheaper inns of North Wales), and so on. The satire is chiefly on follies of words. Biron and Rosaline are evidently the pre-existent state of Benedick and Beatrice, and so, perhaps, is Boyet of Lafeu, and Costard of the Tapster in *Measure for Measure;* and the frequency of the rhymes, the sweetness as well as the smoothness of the metre, and the number of acute and fancifully illustrated aphorisms, are all as they ought to be in a poet's youth. True genius begins by generalizing and condensing; it ends in realizing and expanding. It first collects the seeds.

Yet if this juvenile drama had been the only one extant of our Shakspere, and we possessed the tradition only of his riper works, or accounts of them in writers who had not even mentioned this play,—how many of Shakspere's characteristic features might we not still have discovered in *Love's Labour's Lost,* though as in a portrait taken of him in his boyhood.

I can never sufficiently admire the wonderful activity of thought throughout the whole of the first scene of the play, rendered natural, as it is, by the choice of the characters, and the whimsical determination on which the drama is founded. . . . This sort of story, too, was admirably suited to Shakspere's times, when the English court was still the foster-mother of the state and the muses; and when, in consequence, the courtiers, and men of rank and fashion, affected a display of wit, point, and sententious observation, that would be deemed intolerable at present,—but in which a hundred

Excerpted from Coleridge's 1818 notes on *Love's Labour's Lost,* taken from his *Lectures and Notes on Shakspere and Other English Poets,* edited by T. Ashe (London: George Bell and Sons, 1904), pp. 282–289.

years of controversy, involving every great political, and every dear domestic, interest, had trained all but the lowest classes to participate. . . .

Hence the comic matter chosen in the first instance is a ridiculous imitation or apery of this constant striving after logical precision, and subtle opposition of thoughts, together with a making the most of every conception or image, by expressing it under the least expected property belonging to it, and this, again, rendered specially absurd by being applied to the most current subjects and occurrences. The phrases and modes of combination in argument were caught by the most ignorant from the custom of the age, and their ridiculous application of them is most amusingly exhibited in Costard; whilst examples suited only to the gravest propositions and impersonations, or apostrophes to abstract thoughts impersonated, which are in fact the natural language only of the most vehement agitations of the mind, are adopted by the coxcombry of Armado as mere artifices of ornament.

The same kind of intellectual action is exhibited in a more serious and elevated strain in many other parts of this play. Biron's speech at the end of the fourth act is an excellent specimen of it. It is logic clothed in rhetoric; — but observe how Shakspere, in his two-fold being of poet and philosopher, avails himself of it to convey profound truths in the most lively images,—the whole remaining faithful to the character supposed to utter the lines, and the expressions themselves constituting a further development of that character:—

[Here Coleridge quotes Berowne's lines, IV.3.320–361.]

This is quite a study;—sometimes you see this youthful god of poetry connecting disparate thoughts purely by means of resemblances in the words expressing them,—a thing in character in lighter comedy, especially of that kind in which Shakspere delights, namely, the purposed display of wit, though sometimes, too, disfiguring his graver scenes. . . .

LOVE'S LABOUR'S LOST, FROM CHARACTERS OF SHAKESPEAR'S PLAYS

William Hazlitt

If we were to part with any of the author's comedies, it should be this. Yet
we should be loth to part with Don Adriano de Armado, that mighty po-
tentate of nonsense, or his page, that handful of wit; with Nathaniel the curate, or Holofernes the school-master, and their dispute after dinner on "the
golden cadences of poesy;" with Costard the clown, or Dull the constable.
Biron is too accomplished a character to be lost to the world, and yet he
could not appear without his fellow courtiers and the king: and if we were
to leave out the ladies, the gentlemen would have no mistresses. So that we
believe we may let the whole play stand as it is, and we shall hardly venture
to "set a mark of reprobation on it." Still we have some objections to the
style, which we think savours more of the pedantic spirit of Shakespear's time
than of his own genius; more of controversial divinity, and the logic of Peter Lombard, than of the inspiration of the Muse. It transports us quite as
much to the manners of the court, and the quirks of courts of law, as to the
scenes of nature or the fairy-land of his own imagination. Shakespear has
set himself to imitate the tone of polite conversation then prevailing among
the fair, the witty, and the learned, and he has imitated it but too faithfully.
It is as if the hand of Titian had been employed to give grace to the curls of
a full-bottomed periwig, or Raphael had attempted to give expression to the
tapestry figures in the House of Lords. Shakespear has put an excellent description of this fashionable jargon into the mouth of the critical Holofernes
"as too picked, too spruce, too affected, too odd, as it were, too peregrinate, as I may call it;" and nothing can be more marked than the difference
when he breaks loose from the trammels he had imposed on himself, "as
light as bird from brake," and speaks in his own person. We think, for in-

Originally published in Hazlitt's book *Characters of Shakespear's Play* (London: C.H.
Reynell, 1817), pp. 293–297.

stance, that in the following soliloquy the poet has fairly got the start of Queen Elizabeth and her maids of honour:—

> BIRON. O! and I forsooth in love,
>   I that have been love's whip;
>   A very beadle to an amorous sigh:
>   A critic; nay, a night-watch constable,
>   A domineering pedant o'er the boy,
>   Than whom no mortal more magnificent.
>   This wimpled, whining, purblind, wayward boy,
>   This signior Junio, giant dwarf, Dan Cupid,
>   Regent of love-rhymes, lord of folded arms,
>   Th' anointed sovereign of sighs and groans:
>   Liege of all loiterers and malecontents,
>   Dread prince of plackets, king of codpieces,
>   Sole imperator, and great general
>   Of trotting parators (O my little heart!)
>   And I to be a corporal of his field,
>   And wear his colours like a tumbler's hoop?
>   What? I love! I sue! I seek a wife!
>   A woman, that is like a German clock,
>   Still a repairing; ever out of frame;
>   And never going aright, being a watch,
>   And being watch'd, that it may still go right?
>   Nay, to be perjur'd, which is worst of all:
>   And among three to love the worst of all,
>   A whitely wanton with a velvet brow,
>   With two pitch balls stuck in her face for eyes;
>   Ay, and by heav'n, one that will do the deed,
>   Though Argus were her eunuch and her guard;
>   And I to sigh for her! to watch for her!
>   To pray for her! Go to; it is a plague
>   That Cupid will impose for my neglect
>   Of his almighty dreadful little might.
>   Well, I will love, write, sigh, pray, sue, and groan:
>   Some men must love my lady, and some Joan.

The character of Biron drawn by Rosaline and that which Biron gives of Boyet are equally happy. The observations on the use and abuse of study, and on the power of beauty to quicken the understanding as well as the senses, are excellent. The scene which has the greatest dramatic effect is that in which Biron, the king, Longaville, and Dumain, successively detect each other and are detected in their breach of their vow and in their profession of attachment to their several mistresses, in which they suppose themselves to be overheard by no one. The reconciliation between these lovers and their sweethearts is also very good, and the penance which Rosaline imposes on Biron, before he can expect to gain her consent to marry him, full of propriety and beauty.

[Here Hazlitt quotes the final exchange between Berowne and Rosaline, V. 2.917–947.]

The famous cuckoo-song closes the play: but we shall add no more criticisms: "the words of Mercury are harsh after the songs of Apollo."

ON *LOVE'S LABOURS LOST*

Walter Pater

Love's Labours Lost is one of the earliest of Shakspere's dramas, and has many of the peculiarities of his poems, which are also the work of his earlier life. The opening speech of the king on the immortality of fame—on the triumph of fame over death—and the nobler parts of Biron, display something of the monumental style of Shakspere's Sonnets, and are not without their conceits of thought and expression. This connection of *Love's Labours Lost* with Shakspere's poems is further enforced by the actual insertion in it of three sonnets and a faultless song; which, in accordance with his practice in other plays, are inwoven into the action of the piece and, like the golden ornaments of a fair woman, give it a peculiar air of distinction. There is merriment in it also, with choice illustrations of both wit and humour; a laughter often exquisite, ringing, if faintly, yet as genuine laughter still, though sometimes sinking into mere burlesque, which has not lasted quite so well. And Shakspere brings a serious effect out of the trifling of his characters. A dainty love-making is interchanged with the more cumbrous play; below the many artifices of Biron's amorous speeches we may trace sometimes the "unutterable longing;" and the lines in which Katharine describes the blighting through love of her younger sister are one of the most touching things in older literature.[1] Again, how many echoes seem awakened by those strange words, actually said in jest!—"The sweet war man [Hector of Troy] is dead and rotten; sweet chucks, beat not the bones of the buried: when he breathed, he was a man"—words which may remind us of Shakspere's own epitaph. In the last scene, an ingenious turn is given to the action, so that the piece does not conclude after the manner of other comedies—

This essay, apparently written in 1878, is from *Macmillan's Magazine* 53 (December 1885), 89–91. It appears also, with only minor spelling changes, in Pater's book *Appreciations: With an Essay on Style* (London: Macmillan, 1898), pp. 167–175.

Our wooing doth not end like an old play;
Jack hath not Jill:

and Shakspere strikes a passionate note across it at last, in the entrance of the messenger, who announces to the Princess that the King her father is suddenly dead.

The merely dramatic interest of the piece is slight enough—only just sufficient, indeed, to be the vehicle of its wit and poetry. The scene—a park of the King of Navarre—is unaltered throughout; and the unity of the play is not so much the unity of a drama as that of a series of pictorial groups, in which the same figures reappear, in different combinations, but on the same background. It is as if Shakspere had intended to bind together, by some inventive conceit, the devices of an ancient tapestry, and give voices to its figures. On one side, a fair palace; on the other, the tents of the Princess of France, who has come on an embassy from her father to the King of Navarre; in the midst, a wide space of smooth grass. The same personages are combined over and over again into a series of gallant scenes—the Princess, the three masked ladies, the quaint, pedantic King—one of those amiable kings men have never loved enough, whose serious occupation with the things of the mind seems, by contrast with the more usual forms of kingship, like frivolity or play. Some of the figures are grotesque merely, and, all the male ones at least, a little fantastic. Certain objects reappearing from scene to scene—love-letters crammed with verses to the margin, and lovers' toys—hint obscurely at some story of intrigue. Between these groups, on a smaller scale, come the slighter and more homely episodes, with Sir Nathaniel the curate, the country-maid Jaquenetta, Moth or Mote the elfin-page, with Heims and Ver, who recite "the dialogue that the two learned men have compiled in praise of the owl and the cuckoo." The ladies are lodged in tents, because the King, like the princess of the modern poet's fancy, has taken a vow

To make his court a little Academe,

and for three years' space no woman may come within a mile of it; and the play shows how this artificial attempt was broken through. For the King and his three fellow-scholars are of course soon forsworn, and turn to writing sonnets, each to his chosen lady. These fellow scholars of the King—"quaint votaries of science" at first, afterwards "affection's men-at-arms"—three youthful knights, gallant, amorous, chivalrous, but also a little affected, sporting always a curious foppery of language—are throughout the leading figures in the foreground; one of them, in particular, being more carefully depicted than the others, and in himself very noticeable—a portrait with somewhat puzzling manner and expression, which at once catches the eye irresistibly and keeps it fixed.

Play is often that about which people are most serious; and the humorist may observe how, under all love of playthings, there is almost always hidden an appreciation of something really engaging and delightful. This is true always of the toys of children; it is often true of the playthings of grown-up people, their vanities, their fopperies even—the cynic would add their pursuit of fame and their lighter loves. Certainly, this is true without exception of the playthings of a past age, which to those who succeed it are always full of pensive interest—old manners, old dresses, old houses. For what is called fashion in these matters occupies, in each age, much of the care of many of the most discerning people, furnishing them with a kind of mirror of their real inward refinements, and their capacity for selection. Such modes or fashions are, at their best, an example of the artistic predominance of form over matter; of the manner of the doing of it over the thing done; and have a beauty of their own. It is so with that old euphuism of the Elizabethan age—that pride of dainty language and curious expression, which it is very easy to ridicule, which often made itself ridiculous, but which had below it a real sense of fitness and nicety; and which, as we see in this very play, and still more clearly in the Sonnets, had some fascination for the young Shakspere himself. It is this foppery of delicate language, this fashionable plaything of his time, with which Shakspere is occupied in *Love's Labours Lost*. He shows us the manner in all its stages; passing from the grotesque and vulgar pedantry of Holofernes, through the extravagant but polished caricature of Armado, to become the peculiar characteristic of a real though still quaint poetry in Biron himself—still chargeable, even at his best, with just a little affectation. As Shakspere laughs broadly at it in Holofernes or Armado, he is the analyst of its curious charm in Biron; and this analysis involves a delicate raillery by Shakspere himself at his own chosen manner.

This "foppery" of Shakspere's day had, then, its really delightful side, a quality in no sense "affected," by which it satisfies a real instinct in our minds—the fancy so many of us have for an exquisite and curious skill in the use of words. Biron is the perfect flower of this manner—

A man of fire-new words, fashion's own knight

—as he describes Armado, in terms which are really applicable to himself. In him this manner blends with a true gallantry of nature, and an affectionate complaisance and grace. He has at times some of its extravagance or caricature also, but the shades of expression by which he passes from this to the "golden cadence" of Shakspere's own chosen verse, are so fine, that is is sometimes difficult to trace them. What is a vulgarity in Holofernes, and a caricature in Armado, refines itself in him into the expression of a nature truly and inwardly bent upon a form of delicate perfection, and is accompanied by a real insight into the laws which determine what is exquisite in language, and their root in the nature of things. He can appreciate quite the opposite style—

In russet yeas, and honest kersey noes;

he knows the first law of pathos, that—

Honest plain words best suit the ear of grief.

He delights in his own rapidity of intuition; and, in harmony with the half-sensuous philosophy of the Sonnets, exalts, a little scornfully, in many memorable expressions, the judgment of the senses, above all slower, more toilsome means of knowledge, scorning some who fail to see things only because they are so clear—

So ere you find where light in darkness lies,
Your light grows dark by losing of your eyes—

as with some German commentators on Shakspere. Appealing always to actual sensation from men's affected theories, he might seem to despise his learning; as, indeed, he has taken up his deep studies partly in play, and demands always the profit of learning in renewed enjoyment; yet he surprises us from time to time by intuitions which can come only from a deep experience and power of observation; and men listen to him, old and young, in spite of themselves. He is quickly impressible to the slightest clouding of the spirits in social intercourse, and has his moments of extreme seriousness; his trial-task may well be, as Rosaline puts it—

To enforce the pained impotent to smile.

But still, through all, he is true to his chosen manner; that gloss of dainty language is a second nature with him: even at his best he is not without a certain artifice; the trick of playing on words never deserts him; and Shakspere, in whose own genius there is an element of this very quality, shows us in this graceful, and, as it seems, studied, portrait, his enjoyment of it.

As happens with every true dramatist, Shakspere is for the most part hidden behind the persons of his creation. Yet there are certain of his characters in which we feel that there is something of self-portraiture. And it is not so much in his grander, more subtle and ingenious creations that we feel this—in Hamlet and King Lear—as in those slighter and more spontaneously developed figures, who, while far from playing principal parts, are yet distinguished by a certain peculiar happiness and delicate ease in the drawing of them—figures which possess, above all that winning attractiveness which there is no man but would willingly exercise, and which resemble those works of art which, though not meant to be very great or imposing, are yet wrought of the choicest material. Mercutio, in *Romeo and Juliet*, belongs to this group of Shakspere's characters—versatile, mercurial people, such as make good actors, and in whom the

Nimble spirits of the arteries,

the finer but still merely animal elements of great wit, predominate. A careful delineation of little, characteristic traits seems to mark them out as the characters of his predilection; and it is hard not to identify him with these more than with others. Biron, in *Love's Labours Lost*, is perhaps the most striking member of this group. In this character, which is never quite in touch with, never quite on a perfect level of understanding with the other persons of the play, we see, perhaps, a reflex of Shakspere himself, when he has just become able to stand aside from and estimate the first period of his poetry.

NOTE

1. Act V, scene 2.

Shakespeare's Word-Play and Puns

Love's Labour's Lost

Thomas R. Price *

Burby's quarto of 1598 speaks on its title-page of *Love's Labour's Lost* as "a Pleasant Conceited Comedie." The description suits well. For among all the plays this is the one in which the poet, free as yet from all constraint of serious thinking on any grave problem, has given the widest range to his love of the fantastic element in life and speech. Those critics are, indeed, very foolish that can see nothing but conceits in the comedy, and those readers are very stupid who fail to find the conceits pleasant. But, along with much daintiness in portrayal of character and large wealth of poetic effects, there is throughout the drama a youthful debauch of the poet in word-plays. In fact there is not perhaps in literature any other work of a great poet that contains within so small a compass so vast a variety of tricks with words. Of the eighteen characters, sixteen may fairly be called punsters, and the dialogue at all stages of the action is sparkling and flashing from all sides with puns.

Of these word-plays, which come so thick and fast as almost to blind observation, more than two hundred and fifty may be observed as noteworthy. The distribution of these two hundred and fifty among the sixteen characters is, for the study of Shakespeare's method in portraying character, so curious that it may be given in tabular form:

Nathaniel makes 1 word-play.

Jaquenetta	"	1	"
Longaville	"	4	"
Maria	"	5	"
Dull	"	6	"
Dumain	"	7	"
Katharine	"	11	"

From *Shakespeariana* 6, no. 67 (July 1889), 292–297.

Holofernes	"	13	"
The King	"	13	"
Armado	"	19	"
Boyet	"	20	"
Rosaline	"	20	"
Moth	"	22	"
The Princess	"	22	"
Costard	"	34	"
Biron	"	48	"

The only characters that do not play with words are the Forester and Lord Marcade. To them the poet gives the chance to say but a word, and they manage to say that word, simply and gravely, without a pun. The Forester, a bashful young man, country-bred, is awestruck by the Princess, perplexed and a little hurt by her punning upon his words. Lord Marcade, heavy with his message of death, delivers it with tender gravity (V.2.726).

Sir Nathaniel, the country-preacher, ventures shyly upon his single pun. He asks his idol, Holofernes, "where he will find men *worthy* enough to present the nine *worthies*" (V.1.131).

Jaquenetta's pun is a somewhat ingenious play on Armado's love-making. The Don proposes to her an assignation at the lodge. "That's *hereby*," she says (I.2.141). She means *hereby* to put him off without a serious answer; but Armado takes the adverb locally.

Longaville is Shakespeare's type of the tall, handsome, stupid soldier, the guardian of later fiction. He is honest and dull, the winner of woman's love by his good looks. He tries to catch from his society the fashion of word-play, but his puns are heavy and far-fetched, or utterly commonplace. When Biron inveighs so learnedly against learning, Longaville says:

He *weeds* the corn and still lets grow the *weeding*. (I.1. 95)

When Katharine twits him, in the masquerade, with his stupid silence, he explains his own lack of tongue by saying:

You have a *double tongue* within your mask. (V.2.244)

And, when she calls him calf, he answers with the coarse old play on *horns*:

Look how you *butt* yourself in these sharp mocks! Will you *give horns*, chaste lady? (V.2.251–2)

Of course, as Longaville is big and handsome and stupid, his Maria, who is not beautiful, is clever. Theirs is the sort of union by contraries that serves, in Galtonian phrase, to keep up among mankind its average of mediocrity. All Maria's puns are good. When Dumain offers her himself and his sword, she replies, dropping into French,

> No *point*, quoth I. (V.2.277)

When Rosaline taunts old Boyet with his domestic misfortunes, Maria tells him:

> You still wrangle with her, Boyet, and she *strikes at the brow*.
> (V.1.119)

When Boyet tries to kiss her, to take "pasture" "on her lips," she flashes out refusal:

> My lips are no *common*, though *several* they be. (II.1.223)

Finally, in taking leave of her tall lover, she makes on the double meaning of *long* a kind of half pun that is very tender and graceful. Her lover says of the twelvemonth's waiting:

> I'll stay with patience, but the time is *long*,

and she replies:

> *The liker you*, few taller are so young. (V.2.846)

Among this gay company of lords and ladies, bred to such skill in the use and abuse of words, Dull is the type of stolid and illiterate rustic, to whom words are a trouble and a snare. He is far from being a fool, a man of sane and direct understanding. But language is too much for him, and, when he has to use language, he gets his syllables badly mixed. Hence his puns are all of the illiterate kind. He misses the word he aims at, and sometimes he stumbles upon one that has a grotesque unfitness for its place. He *reprehends*, instead of *represents*, the person of the King (I.1.184). He orders Costard to be punished by cutting him off in prison from all *penance* (I.2.134). He takes Holofernes' Latin *Haud credo* for some kind of wild animal (IV.2.12). He turns Holofernes' learned *allusion* into *collusion* and *pollusion* (IV.2.43, 46). Only once is there conscious fun in him. When Sir

Nathaniel praises the "rare *talent*" of Holofernes, Dull says: "If a *talent* (=talon) be a *claw*, look how he *claws* him with a *talent* (IV.2.65).[1] (=*To claw, to tickle, to delight.*)

The puns of Dumain represent in Shakespeare's art a man of thin and poor character. He is pert and impudent, always ready with his small wit, but destitute of real humor and echoing and prolonging the jokes of more original minds. Once he puns obscenely, *yard* (V.2.674); once, when backed up by the King, he dares to gibe feebly at Biron:

> *Proceeded* well, to stop all good *proceeding.* (I.1.94)

All the rest of his puns are discharged at his inferiors, sure mark of a mean character. Holofernes says:

> Judas I am, *ycliped* (=called) Maccabaeus,

and Dumain breaks in with,

> Judas Maccabaeus *clipt* is plain Judas. (V.2.603)

Judas, when called *Jude,*

> stays for the latter end (*ass*) of his name. (V.2.630)

When Armado, playing Hector, is complimented on having too big a leg for his part, Dumain cries, "More *calf* certain" (V.2.644). And when Armado, in playing his part, distorts his countenance, Dumain mocks him:

> He's a god or a painter, for he *makes faces.* (V.2.649)

And Hector's "lemon stuck with *cloves*" is for Dumain "a *cloven* lemon" (V.2.655), surely the feeblest pun extant. Dumain is in love with Katharine, and their taste in puns is such as to make them a well-matched pair. For, although Katharine puns more freely than Dumain, her puns themselves are for the most part as superficial and feeble-minded as his. So the commonplace puns on *light*, in its many senses (V.2.20, 25, etc.), on *fair* (V.2.42), on *weigh* (V.2.27, etc.), on *calf* (V.2.248), are not worthy of noting. When Rosaline seems vexed at her foolish word-play, Katharine answers:

> You'll mar the *light* by taking it in *snuff* (=by getting angry at it). (V.2.22)

When Rosaline laughs at her pock-pitted face, Katharine replies bravely enough,

> Pox of that jest! and I *beshrew* all *shrows*. (V.2.46)

The Dutch word *veel* (=much) she puns with the French *veal* (calf), thus teaching us a lesson in 16th century pronunciation,[2] and out of her *veal* she gets as many puns as an Italian cook gets dishes. The best of them is when she tells Longaville

> Then die a *calf* before your *horns* do grow. (V.2.253)

The young and beardless Dumain is her calf-lover; and, laughing at his lack of beard, she says,

> I'll mark no words that *smooth-faced* wooers say. (V.2.838 and 829)

Her last words, however, her ambiguous promise to Dumain, contain her deepest play on words:

> Come, when the King doth to my lady come:
> Then, *if I have much love*, I'll give you some. (V.2.840)

The speech of the King is right kingly. Shakespeare's "matchless Navarre" was of gentle and gracious character, a man not prone to use his wit in gibe and buffoonery. Thus the form of word-play that he loves is the dainty antithesis of a word with itself in sound and sense. For example:

> "Let fame," he says, "*grace* us in the *disgrace* of death." (I.1.3)

So he tells Biron that his "oath is *passed* to *pass* away" from the sight of women (I.1.49). And he remonstrates against Biron's learned assault on human learning by saying:

> How well he's *read* to reason against *reading*. (I.1.93)
> So *extreme* and *extremely*. (V.2.750)

This habit of speech slides over by graceful transition into full-bodied pun. So he sends word to the Princess that

> Say to her, we have *measured* many miles
> To tread a *measure* with her on this grass. (V.2.184)

And when Rosaline brings her dance to soon to an end, he pleads with her for "more *measure* of this *measure*" (V.2.222).

The King's puns do not, however, always take this form. Some seem to be purely facetious. So, when Armado is playing Hector, the King says:

Hector was but a *Trojan* (=rogue, knave) in respect of this. (V.2.640)

Don Armado himself the King describes as

a man of *complements* (I.1.169),

meaning both *fine words* and *unusual accomplishments*. When the Princess comes to throw herself on his hospitality, the King says:

She must *lie here on mere necessity.* (I.1.149)

Worse still, when Costard seeks to escape his fate by swearing that Jacquenetta is no damsel but a maid, the King says:

The maid *will not serve your turn*, sir. (I.1.300)

For the credit of kingship, Navarre makes no other pun so wicked as this. On the other hand, he sometimes uses the pun in a poetic sense. When the Princess says that "her face was *clouded*," there is a pretty gallantry in the King's reply:

Blessed are *clouds* to do as such *clouds* do (=kiss her face). (V.2.204)

And he calls in each lord to sign his name to the oath, in order

That his own *hand* (=handwriting, signature) may strike his honour down
That violates the smallest branch. (I.1.29)

Notes

*Price also wrote a longer essay on the play, *Love's Labour's Lost*, *Shakespeariana* 7, no. 2 (April 1890), 67–91.

1. *Talon* and *talent* merged in sound by apocope of the final consonant (*t* after *n*), so common in English speech.

2. The pun on *beat* and *bait* (*Winter's Tale*, II. 3.91).

A Shakespearean Quibble

James W. Bright

Shakespeare who was master of all knowledges was, of course, also master of the science of Physics, as may be observed in the following remarkable line:

Light, seeking light, doth light of light beguile.[1]

Love's Labour's Lost I.1.77

From this, it would seem, it may be inferred that even before Newton's *Principia* the much later discovery of the "interference of light" had been "prevented" in a youthful composition of the bard. But if this supposition transgresses the limits of probability, it may be assumed that it is merely the corpuscular theory of light that is here darkly foreshadowed; in this case the interpretation of the line might be stated, following tradition, in something like the following manner: Any object in nature that is to be "studied" must be illuminated; if the object be already luminous, the illumination required for the investigation will so much surpass the object"s light as to make it relative darkness ("where light in darkness lies"). Sun-spots, to the observer looking at the full sun, appear black; but when the body of the sun is "screened," the spots, relieved of contrast, are found to be luminous. Now Shakespeare may be supposed to have had in mind the investigation of light itself, with an intimation of the notion that light consists of material substance, the notion which culminated in Newton"s corpuscular theory, and the substitution of "light" for "luminous object" would therefore render the preceding explanation of the line exact.

The discovery of this profound interpretation must warrant some indulgence in self-approbation, but the real purpose of this note is to level malice at the two commas in the line, which are found in almost all editions

From *Modern Language Notes* 13, no. 1 (January 1898), 19–20.

of the play, the Globe edition being a notable exception. These commas led Tieck to translate thus:

Licht, das nach Licht sucht, stiehlt dem Licht das Licht.

This must represent the sense which Shakespearean scholars have read into the line, but what that sense is has not been divulged. For my part, I cannot think of a meaning that would hold to the commas. Johnson said of the passage embracing the line in question: "The whole sense of this gingling declamation is only this, that a man by too close study may read himself blind," and this is correct; but if he has foreseen the destiny of a particular line of the text he would, no doubt, have singled it out for some such comment as this:

Light seeking light doth light of light beguile.

That is, the act of reading (light—"sight of the eyes"—seeking light—"seeking knowledge") deprives the eyes of sight.

NOTE

[The line in question is rendered thus in the Quarto edition:

Light feeking light, doth light of light beguyle:

And in the First Folio:

Light seeking light, doth light of light beguile:

Horace Howard Furness, editor of the New Variorium Edition of *Love's Labour's Lost* (1904) cited Bright and added his own opinion: "I think a hyphen should connect 'Light' and 'seeking.' It is this 'Light-seeking light' which is the nominative to 'doth.' The meaning, as I understand it, is: the eyes which are seeking for truth deprive themselves (by too much application) of the power of seeing." The current Oxford and Arden editions both omit all commas in the line. The New York Shakespeare Festival edition (1968) follows the Quarto and Folio in its placement of a single comma, and glosses the line: "sight seeking truth does eyes of sight cheat."—FHL]

Love's Labour's Lost, from *Shakespeare: His Music and Song*

A.H. Moncure-Sime

Love's Labour's Lost has been compared to Comic Opera. Its lyrical character is one of its most noteworthy features. The experts place it first of the plays of the rhyming period. In the form in which we now have it, it contains twice as many rhymed lines as blank verse, and probably in its original state the proportion may have been greater. While this Play only provides us with two songs, it contains an immense amount of doggerel and alternate rhymes. Dr Johnson thinks that a song has apparently been lost from Act III, sc.1, where the Author tells us there is singing. What a beautiful and comprehensive request is here made by Armado. "Warble, child"; (speaking to Moth) "make passionate my sense of hearing." None of the fine arts can subsist or give rapture, without passion. Hence mediocrity in painting, sculpture, or music, is more intolerable than in any of the other Arts. Music, when not of the best in form and execution, and without any high fervour or passion, is apt to be monotonous as the tolling of a bell or the antics of a clown.

There are a good many references to dances and an allusion to a notable ballad in this Play.

When Armado tells Moth to warble, the Page does so, and the air he sings is "Concolinel," the song which as suggested above has been lost.

> ARMADO: Sweet air!—Go, tenderness of years; take this key,
> give enlargement to the swain, bring him festinately hither.
> I must employ him in a letter to my love.
> MOTH: Master, will you win your love with a French brawl?
> ARMADO: How meanest thou? brawling in French?

From a section of Chapter 4 of *Shakespeare: His Music and Song* (London: K. Paul, Trench, Trübner, 1915), pp. 47–52.

MOTH: No, my complete master; but to jig off a tune at the tongue's end, canary to it with your feet, humour it with turning up your eyelids, sigh a note and sing a note, sometimes through the throat, as if you swallowed love with singing love, sometime through the nose, as if you snuffed up love by smelling love; with your hat pent-house-like o'er the shop of your eyes; with your arms crossed on your thin-belly doublet, like a rabbit on a spit; or your hands in your pockets, like a man after the old painting, and keep not too long in one tune, but a snip and away. These are compliments, these are humours; these betray nice wenches, that would be betrayed without these; and make them men of note—do you note me?—that most are affected to these.

The Brawl was one of several tunes to which the Country Dance was danced, whether in a ring, or "at length," like our "Sir Toby." Brawl was the English of the French "bransle" or "branle." Like the Allemande of Bach, "it containeth the time of eight, and most commonly in short notes."

The Canary was a fairly quick dance, and its rhythm was generally 6-8 time. There is no history of the name, but Skeat thinks it probably derived its name from the Canary Islands. This dance is referred to in two other Plays, and the allusions make clear the lively character of the dance.

It is in this Play that the only mention is made by Shakespeare of the Round country-dance, so loved by the rustics—the Hey, Hay, or Haye. The allusion is in Act V, sc. 1, where the account is given of the preparation for the Pageant of the Worthies. The Hay was a very lively, even boisterous dance. "The performers stood in a circle to begin with, and then 'wind round handing in passing until you come to your places'."

The Morrice, or Morris Dance was very popular in Shakespeare's time, and he introduces it into this Play—when Holofernes says to the country wench Jaquenetta, "Trip and go, my sweet." "Trip and Go" was one of the liveliest of morris-dances. Many of the old dances were sung, and Elson suggests that the very word "ballad" may have been derived from *ballare* (Italian), to dance. The old song-dances sometimes went by the name of "ballets."

The allusion which Shakespeare makes to one of the notable old ballads is in Act I, sc. 2, when Armado asks Moth if there is not a ballad of the King and the Beggar? Moth replies, "The world was very guilty of such a ballad some three ages since: but, I think, now 'tis not to be found; or, if it were, it would neither serve for the writing nor the tune."

Armado says he will have the subject "newly writ o'er," and he certainly kept his promise, for his declaration of love which follows is taken bodily from the old ballad, *A Song of a Beggar and a King*.

In sc. 2 of Act V we have two songs, one to be sung by Ver, the spring, and the other to be maintained by Hiems, winter. The former is well-known:

When daisies pied, and violets blue,
    And lady-smocks all silver-white,
And cuckoo-buds of yellow hue,
    Do paint the meadows with delight,
The cuckoo then, on every tree,
    Mocks married men; for thus sings he,
        Cuckoo;
Cuckoo, cuckoo: O word of fear,
Unpleasing to a married ear!

When shepherds pipe on oaten straws,
    And merry larks are ploughmen's clocks,
When turtles tread, and rooks, and daws,
    And maidens bleach their summer smocks,
The cuckoo then, on every tree,
    Mocks married men; for thus sings he,
        Cuckoo;
Cuckoo, cuckoo: O word of fear,
Unpleasing to a married ear!

And the latter is:

When icicles hang by the wall,
    And Dick the shepherd blows his nail,
And Tom bears logs into the hall,
    And milk comes frozen home in pail,
When blood is nipp'd and ways be foul,
    Then nightly sings the staring owl,
        Tu-whit;
Tu-who, a merry note,
While greasy Joan doth keel the pot.

When all aloud the wind doth blow,
    And coughing drowns the parson's saw,

And birds sit brooding in the snow,
    And Marian's nose looks red and raw,
When roasted crabs hiss in the bowl,
    Then nightly sings the staring owl,
        Tu-whit;
Tu-who, a merry note,
While greasy Joan doth keel the pot.

LOVE'S LABOUR'S LOST RESTUDIED

Oscar J. Campbell

Until very recently, *Love's Labour's Lost* has not received the critical attention to which its position in Shakespeare's dramatic work entitles it. It is probably his first comedy and often thought to be the first play that he wrote without collaboration. A thorough study of this drama might, therefore, be expected to reveal what Croce would call Shakespeare's "comic presuppositions." It might have discovered the bases of his entire comic technique. Such a genetic study might have simplified the history of Shakespeare's development as a writer of comedy and given it a coherence now lacking. It might even have thrown light upon his puzzling beginnings as a playwright.

No study of *Love's Labour's Lost* has cast such illumination upon Shakespeare's career. The comedy, rather, has been considered as a little apart from the straight course of his development, as a kind of experiment which yielded its author few permanent results either intellectual or technical. Moreover, a sort of unrecognized mystery has hung over this drama. No source for the plot has been discovered. To be sure, the scene is laid at the court of Henry of Navarre and the action is supposed to have been suggested by historical and social events in the life of that monarch, vaguely like those presented in the play. The style or dramatic manner of the play has been almost universally recognized as very like that of John Lyly. The dialogue has been thought to be in every way an approximation to that developed by Lyly, and the spirit and tone of the social life of the courtly ladies and gentlemen as depicted by both writers to be identical. One play of the earlier dramatist, in particular, *Endimion*, is believed to have furnished Sir Tophas and his page, Epiton, models for Armado and Moth. One other derived character appears,

Originally published in *Studies in Shakespeare, Milton, and Donne*, edited by Eugene S. McCartney. University of Michigan Studies in Language and Literature, Vol. 1 (1925), pp. 3–45.

Holofernes, the Latinizing pedagogue, who is a stock character in the six-teenth century comedy of France and Italy.

Except for these slight echoes of earlier comic practice, this drama, according to orthodox critical opinion, is Shakespeare's own invention,—his sustained travesty of contemporary court life, and of the fashions in speech and behavior that prevailed there. In this satire he adverts to incidents of current social and political life, and in it he directly satirizes figures well known in that world. In brief, *Love's Labour's Lost* has been regarded as Shakespeare's *Précieuses ridicules*.[1]

Some of the elements of this rounded theory have been called into question. The sceptics, for example, have pointed out that it was extraordinary that a young man who had come, but meagrely educated, from the provinces a few years before, should show, at the outset of his career, enough familiarity with the uses and temper of a court to satirize them before an audience composed largely of courtiers. This was pointed, but negative criticism. Recently, newly discovered facts about this play have yielded positive results and have made a partial revision of the traditional estimate necessary. Indeed, they have rendered a complete reëxamination of the comedy highly desirable.

The most important of these new truths is the discovery that the central fable of the play reflects faithfully some definite historical events which took place at the court of Henry of Navarre, at Nérac in 1578. This important discovery is due to the researches of M. Abel Lefranc, published in *Sous le masque de William Shakespeare*.[2] Inasmuch as the thesis of this book has prevented most American scholars from acquainting themselves with the sound historical investigations which it contains and which in no way depend upon the author's contention that the plays of Shakespeare were written by the sixth Earl of Derby, I shall review briefly his evidence on this question of historical fact.

Vague correspondences between the play and events at the contemporary court of Navarre had been recognized since 1880. In that year Sir Sidney Lee suggested[3] that the plot of *Love's Labour's Lost* reflected events occurring at the court of Henri Quatre in the year 1586. At that time Catherine de Medici, the dowager queen of France, journeyed to Saint Bris, with the ladies of her court, in an attempt to settle the perennial disputes between Henry of Navarre and the King of France. General similarities between the meeting of Navarre and the princess in the play and the historical interview at Saint Bris undoubtedly exist. The social atmosphere of the two is identical, but the political objects are utterly different.

Queen Catherine's expedition was concerned principally with an attempt to persuade Navarre to divorce his dissolute wife, Marguerite of

Valois, who had left her husband for fear of his resentment at her moral vagaries.[4] This accomplished, the dowager queen was to persuade Henry to marry Christine, a daughter of the Duke of Lorraine.[5] The expedition in Shakespeare's comedy is not concerned in the remotest degree with this project. Furthermore, the historical embassage was led by Catherine, then old and grievously afflicted with gout.[6] She is not a likely prototype of the lovely princess in *Love's Labour's Lost*, nor is her expedition a seed from which would grow naturally a comedy of amorous persiflage.

Now M. Lefranc shows that an expedition made to the court of Navarre in 1578 by Catherine and her daughter, Marguerite, is much more nearly like the fictitious one. The political object of this mission is identical with that in the play. It sought the settlement of the question of sovereignty in Aquitaine, which in the drama is accurately called "the dowry of a queen,"[7] and of a dispute over the payment of a hundred thousand crowns to Navarre by the King of France.[8] Furthermore, contemporary accounts of this diplomatic mission show that its social atmosphere was very like that presented in the play. Marguerite of Valois in her *Mémoires* herself describes the occasion as follows: "faisant la plupart de ce temps-là (quatre ou cinque ans que je fus en Gascogne) nostre séjour à Nérac, où nostre cour estoit si belle et si plaisante, que nous n'envions point celle de France, y ayant Madame la Princesse de Navarre sa soeur, qui depuis esté mariée à Monsieur le Duc de Bar mon nepveu, et moy avec bon nombre de dames et filles; et le Roy mon Mary estant suivy d'une belle trouppe de seigneurs et gentils-hommes, aussi honnestes gens que les plus galants que j'aye veu à la cour; et n'y avoit rien à regretter en eux, sinon qu'ils estoient huguenots."[9]

As one of the historians of the period remarks, the presence of the two queens transformed the town into a capital of the rank which it held in the reign of Henri d'Albret.[10] It is not strange, then for Marguerite to confess that the court was so brilliant that she and her ladies did not envy the life at the greater court in Paris.[11] These descriptions invoke the essence of the social atmosphere of the diplomatic mission in *Love's Labour's Lost*. In the play, as doubtless at Nérac, the diplomatic questions are early referred to the experts and the social gaiety is all that meets the eye. The diplomats become courtiers and the political aims of the ladies are completely hidden by the social brilliance which attends them.

The dramatic figures, too, have some curious personal traits in common with the historical personages whom they represent. Ferdinand of *Love's Labour's Lost*, as he now appears in the comedy, is obviously not Henry of Navarre, yet he inherits one of the monarch's foibles as a courtly lover. The princess describes a *billet doux* which she receives from Ferdinand as follows:

> As much love in Rime
> As would be cram'd up in a sheet of paper,
> Writ on both sides the leafe, Margent and all
> That he was fain to seale on Cupid's name.[12]

M. Lefranc reports[13] that an authentic original of one of Navarre's poems, *Charmante Gabrielle*, which was sent in the form of a letter to Gabrielle d'Estrées, presents these same characteristics. Strophes are written in the margin and the letter is sealed with the seal of which the word *Amor* forms the center.

Similarities of a like sort exist between the Princess of the play and Marguerite de Valois. It is significant for this identification that the Princess was obviously called "queen" in the early editions of the play. In the first quarto she is called "queen" a number of times;[14] and many of these designations are retained in the folio edition. Moreover, there are clear references in the comedy to journeys that Marquerite had made with her ladies in the years just previous to this historical visit to Nérac.[15] They have no dramatic point in their context and can be regarded as introduced only for the sake of "local color." M. Lefranc finds other rather cryptic references in the plays made clear by regarding them as adversions to events in the history of the entourage of Marguerite which are narrated in her *Mémoires*, or to actual conditions of life in the little court at Nérac.[16]

Taken in their entirety, these similarities between Shakespeare's comedy and historical conditions at the court of Nérac in 1578 during an embassy of Catherine, Queen Marguerite of Valois, and their ladies-in-waiting are completely convincing. The author of the fable of *Love's Labour's Lost* was evidently well acquainted not only with the spirit, but with the details of the life there.

One aspect of the picture, however, seems inharmonious with the facts of history. How could an author familiar with this gay life and undoubtedly also with the notorious love intrigues of the youthful Henry of Navarre, present him and his court as tinged with asceticism and determined intellectuality? The device of the oath, as I shall show later, may have been an invention necessary to solve a distinctly theatrical problem of the dramatist. However, in the solution of a technical problem an author must not destroy more important sorts of verisimilitude. As a matter of fact, the court at Navarre had the reputation among Englishmen of the time of being an exceedingly decorous place—a safe spot for the completion of the continental education of Protestant Englishmen. M. Lefranc calls attention to a letter written June 9, 1583, by Cobham, the English ambassador to the Court of

France, to Walsingham.[17] In this report he remarks that Navarre has furnished his court with distinguished gentlemen of his religion and reformed his house. He ends with this significant phrase: "There are divers special persons of quality of intention to resort to that Court, and others send their children, understanding the honorable order that is there observed."

To Cobham, at least, it would have seemed not improper to speak of Navarre's court as a "little academe." To the gay and licentious Marguerite de Valois this atmosphere of study seemed less admirable. She writes contemptuously to her husband, "Si j'osais dire, si vous etiez honete homme vouz quitteriez l'agriculture et l'humeur de Timon pour venir vivre parmi les hommes."[18] Such a woman would obviously enjoy thrusting herself and her flying squadron into such a world, with the deliberate purpose of enticing the students from their sobrieties into a society devoted to courtly love with all its artificial gallantries and barren felicities. At every point the knowledge of the court of Navarre during this expedition of 1578 reflected in *Love's Labour's Lost* proves to be, in the highest degree, intimate and accurate.

This hitherto unsuspected fact can be made to throw light upon the youthful Shakespeare's methods of composition from two angles. In the first place, we are able to say now what was, in effect, the source of this play and so we are able to determine by familiar methods of generic criticism what parts of this comedy are the product of Shakespeare's dramatic invention. In the second place, M. Lefranc's discovery may aid in the solution of some of the ever puzzling questions of Shakespeare's early relations to persons of the very highest social station and of the part they played in stimulating and directing his early literary activity. The second of these problems I shall discuss first, because it will be seen to have a bearing on determining what material the dramatist found ready to his hand when he began to write.

The first question that comes to mind is how could Shakespeare have possessed this accurate and detailed knowledge of life at Navarre's court.[19] We must dismiss at once the possibility of Shakespere's having himself been at the court at Nérac. In none of the wide journeys from Elsinore to Venice, postulated to explain fancied local color detected in his plays, has he been made to visit this little Protestant court. The chance of the poet's having had access to any printed account of such intimate details of social life at this court of Henry IV as *Love's Labour's Lost* reflects, seems equally remote. The remaining possibility[20] is that the information was given to him in some form by one of the many English gentlemen who in the age of Elizabeth made this court one of the principal places of sojourn on their *grands tours*.[21]

The peculiar nature of *Love's Labour's Lost* lends this theory plausibility. It was clearly not written for a popular audience. The form in which we now possess the drama is that which had been newly corrected for a court performance in the Christmas season of 1597–1598, but its original version was undoubtedly intended for a similar occasion. Professor Baker has presented effectively the reasons for believing that the essential character of the entire comedy was determined by a prospective courtly,—nay, royal—audience. He says, "The general attitude toward women, the sonneteering, and, above all, the eulogy of women which Biron utters near the end of Act IV, suggests strongly that originally, as in 1598, it may have been performed before the queen and her court, or that, as first written, it was given before an audience mainly composed of women. Throughout, the characters so much play with love rather than become its subjects, that one wonders whether it was not composed as a whole with a definite view of pleasing the Virgin Queen, who was such an adept in coquetry and was so fond of putting off her admirers just as they seemed nearest to the attainment of their wishes."[22]

Furthermore there is reason to suppose that the comedy was originally composed not for one of the professional companies, but for the children. An unusually large number of parts has been provided for boy actors. Moth, the Princess, her three ladies in waiting, Jaquenetta, and possibly Don Adriano de Armado, were roles to be played by boys.[23] Surely six, and possibly seven, parts were written for child-actors. This number is nearly twice as large as that usually provided for boys in Shakespeare's comedies. None of these figures, furthermore, has been excluded by any critics who have sought to reconstruct the hypothetical original version. Their presence, therefore, suggests that the play, as originally conceived, was written for the children, and so not for Shakespeare's company and its London stage, but for a special occasion.

In such a fête as the one conjectured above a gentleman of the court would have a special interest. He might be concerned as the host to the Queen on the occasion for which the play was planned, or he might wish the drama to advert allegorically to facts or projects in which he had a personal interest. Guesses as to the identity of such a person have been made. Professor Austen K. Gray[24] seeks to prove that the drama was devised at the instigation of Southampton as part of his entertainment for the Queen when he received her at Titchfield Park in 1591. He furthermore attempts to show that part of it is the young Earl's plea under the guise of an allegory to have his proposed marriage with Lady Elizabeth de Vere, Burleigh's granddaughter, postponed for at least a year. Southampton later obtained release from this undesired engagement through the payment of a round sum. The correspondences between the dramatic situation and this real one are close and entertaining; but however ingenious this sort of study, such facts as it seeks to establish are, I believe, now quite beyond proof. Such conjecture, however, serves to strengthen the plausibility of the view that the drama was composed under the eye of some gentleman of the court.

There is nothing intrinsically improbable in such a dramatic collaboration or cooperation between an actor-playwright and an Elizabethan gentleman, particularly in the construction of an occasional play. Hamlet's reception of the travelling players and, in particular, his discussion of dramatic composition with the first actor may be regarded as a realistic picture of an interesting phase of Elizabethan life.[25] Hamlet greets this player affectionately with "O my old friend" and discusses with him the play that was "caviare to the general" in such a way as to suggest that the actor was himself the author. Then he asks him to "study a speech of some dozen or sixteen lines" which he "could set down and insert" in one of their plays.[26]

In the frequent sojourns of travelling companies at the castles of nobility in Elizabethan times lay natural opportunities for the establishment of acquaintance and friendship between young literary nobles and talented actor-playwrights. At no time since have such occasions existed. The great concern of the Derby family for the drama, and particularly of the sixth Earl, whose interest as dramatist and patron M. Lefranc has abundantly established, is an example of an interest of which the scene in *Hamlet* is a dramatic picture. Shakespeare's later close friendship with Southampton is proof that he became the object of such an interest to one of the greatest nobles of his time. Such facts give us ample warrant for supposing that some travelled gentleman had established close enough relations with Shakespeare to induce the dramatist to use his personal reminiscences of the court of Navarre as a nucleus for his play.

From whatever source derived, this material would surely contain a description of the diplomatic mission, of its object, its methods, and its results. The Queen and her ladies would appear in the account with their atmosphere of graceful, half-sportive love-making and with their courtly badinage. The narrative, if true to history, would close not with marriages, nor with promised consummation of the half-playful wooing, but with the indicated success of the ladies' diplomatic mission and their regretful departure. The desire of the directing genius for an allegorical suggestion of some contemporary social situation may have determined other features of the play, such as the grouping of the lovers and the abrupt termination of the projects of the lovers by the surprising death of the father of the visiting princess.

Let us suppose, then, that Shakespeare received such a story from a source which must remain unknown. Upon this he was to build a comedy. To what events within the range of his experience would he most naturally turn, in order to find details which could give his play verisimilitude to an Elizabethan audience? The one obvious source for this sort of dramatic material was the entertainment given to Queen Elizabeth when she visited the country houses of the great lords of her kingdom. Shakespeare and his audiences would agree that in these elaborate and diversified Progresses were to be discovered the approved methods of honoring and amusing a sovereign. Catherine de Medici or Marguerite de Valois on the English stage would be expected to receive a similar form of entertainment from Henry of Navarre when she visited him at Nérac.[27]

The influence of these Progresses upon *Love's Labour's Lost* has been suggested before, but in an unfortunate manner. Efforts have been made to discover in the play reflections of one particular Progress. For example, Arthur Acheson in his recently published *Shakespeare's Lost Years in London*,[28] believes that *Love's Labour's Lost* reflects the events which took place at Cowdray House in August 1591[29] at the Honorable Entertainment given by Lord Montecuto *(sic)*. The evidence which he presents in support of this theory is not convincing. His thesis proves to be mere interesting conjecture. Indeed attempts to discover reflections of any one particular Progress in *Love's Labour's Lost* seem doomed to failure. However, the constructive dramatic principle of this comedy proves to bear close resemblance to that of a Progress, regarded as a dramatic type.

The Progresses of the Queen comprised a series of highly diversified sorts of out-of-door amusement, lasting from four to ten days. Modern students think of these shows as consisting mainly of spectacular classical and allegorical pageants, like the sumptuous water-fête at the Earl of Hertford's entertainment in 1591. They may also remember that there were masque-like shows in which Daphne or Pan appeared, or in which there was graceful dancing by Ceres and her nymphs before her Majesty. But in truth these features formed but a small part of the entire entertainment. Upon her arrival at the castle of her host the Queen is invariably greeted with some sort of oration; and verbal devices in prose and poetry pursue her wherever she walks. She hunts, in her youth riding to the hounds, in her more mature age shooting at the game from a covert. She is encountered by wild men.[30] She dines often in the walks of the garden, at tables sometimes as long as forty-eight yards. She is honored by the folk of the country-side, who present various forms of rustic and popular dramatic sport. She attends plays given by professional actors. All these forms of entertainment are presented out of doors, so that the Queen is constantly in some part of the park surrounding the castle of her host. When she is kept within doors by inclement weather, no pastime worth chronicling is offered to her. Just such a situation is presented in *Love's Labour's Lost*.

The first striking similarity of the play to the Progress lies in its setting. The scene of the entire play is the park of the King of Navarre. This, it will be noted, is not at all the pastoral wood which serves as the scene of *As You Like It*; nor is it the enchanted Arcadia of *The Tempest*. Furthermore the audience is constantly reminded by place notes[31] that the action is continuously laid in the park. The critic is indeed almost justified in conjecturing that the ascetic vows of the gentlemen were introduced to enable the poet to use the story of the visit to the court of Navarre and yet to keep all the action out in the purlieus of the castle. In this way he could give the comedy the first essential of a progress—the setting and the atmosphere of an English park.

Another peculiarity of this comedy may be attributed to its Progress-like nature. Critics have often noted the disproportionate length of the last two acts. Henry David Gray speaks of it as "a disproportion as amazing as it is unique in Elizabethan drama."[32] Various explanations of this fact have been given. Sir Sidney Lee thinks it a fault of the original writing—a youthful blemish. Professor Gray, on the other hand, believes that it is due to additions made to the play when Shakespeare revised it for presentation at court. These were largely made for the purpose of introducing the *Pageant of the Nine Worthies*.

A more satisfactory explanation for this apparent lack of proportion may be found in regarding the play as a drama intended to represent the events and the atmosphere of a royal Progress. Such dramatic disproportion as the critics have lamented would not have been noticed in this sort of comedy. It professed to be only a counterfeit presentment of a mere series of diverse entertainments. A division of such a sequence of scenes into acts was extrinsic to the nature of the play and clearly forced upon it when it was prepared for publication.

Furthermore, such a performance as that presented by the clownish figures was a conventional part of a prolonged Progress. I do not refer to the appearance of the people of the countryside in native costume in folk-dance and folk-song. Such picturesque entertainment was common.[33] But "countrie shows," either intentionally or inadvertently burlesques, were often presented. These inventions the courtly audience was supposed to receive, not with respect, but with raillery, like that rained upon Holofernes and his fellows. At least two shows of this sort are described by Laneham in his famous epistolary report of the Progress at Kenilworth. One was a mock nuptial celebration made a burlesque by the actors, who were louts or pretended to be. They presented their show with a portentous seriousness that aroused a gay spirit of ridicule in the audience, as the following extract from Laneham will show:

> Then followed the worshippful bride, led (after the countrie maner) between two auncient parishioners, honest toownsmen. But . . . ill-smelling was she: a thirtie-five yeer old, of colour broun-bay, not very beautiful indeed, but ugly, fooul, ill-favor'd: yet marveyloous faine of the offis, because shee hard say she woould dauns before the Queen, in which feat shee thought shee woold foot it az finely az the best.

It is exactly this combination of eagerness and ineptitude that makes Holofernes and his actors so amusing to the courtly audience in *Love's Labour's Lost*. Laneham's delight at this rustic fooling was fully as hearty as that of the ladies and gentlemen at the bombast of the *Nine Worthies*.

"By my Trooth," he exclaims, "twaz a lively pastime, I believe it would have moved sum man to a right merry mood, though it be toold him hiz wife lay a dying."

The hock-tide play presented on the same occasion by the men of Coventry led by one Captain Cox was received by the Queen in the same spirit of ridicule.[34] The first time that the folk played this pageant she was able to see but little of it. She therefore commanded that it be repeated on the following Tuesday "to have it full oout. Accordingly it waz prezented; whereat her Majestie laught well."[35] *The Pageant of the Nine Worthies* has been related to dramatic forms slightly different from these. It is well known that on the Progresses of the Queen the village schoolmaster or some equally self-important local functionary often prepared a show. Some of the crude plays of this origin have been thought to have suggested Shakespeare's burlesque in the pageants of Holofernes and Bottom.[36] But it is more probably that such burlesques as those presented at Kenilworth suggested to the playwright the dramatic propriety of making a similar form of comic entertainment an integral part of his stage version of a royal Progress.

The curious detachment from the rest of the play of the *Pageant of the Nine Worthies* and the men who enact it has been often unfavorably commented upon. Professor Baker remarks that an audience must take an entirely fresh start with the announcement of the play that Holofernes and his fellows are to present. He says, "The interests in the final act have been, so to speak, thrust in from the outside, rather than developed from elements of the story started in earlier acts."[37] Henry David Gray cannot accept this patchwork construction as evidence of Shakespeare's limitations, even at the outset of his career. He believes that the first edition of the play was shorter than that represented by the quarto of 1598, and that the *Nine Worthies* and the men who presented it were not a part of the original version. Holofernes and Nathaniel are abruptly introduced in the fourth act, because they are needed for the play, which has been rather loosely appended to the original comedy. Professor Gray asserts that "they have not the faintest excuse for being in the play, except to take part in the 1597 version of the masque."[38] But if the dramatic mould of *Love's Labour's Lost* be the essentially loose and episodic Progress, the late introduction of Holofernes and Nathaniel is natural and proper. Like the country folk in the burlesques presented at Kenilworth, their presence would not have been expected or tolerated until the time for their performance approached. Obviously the fortunes of the visiting Queen could not be involved in any plot-like fashion with these clowns. They were actors expected to appear only to furnish certain moments of amusement for their sovereign and then to vanish.

Light may be cast upon still another original and puzzling aspect of the comedy by considering it a dramatic initiation of a Progress. No satisfactory reason has been given for the unique and indeterminate ending of the drama.[39] When the ladies, at the moment of their departure, are sought in marriage by their lovers, they put them off for an entire year. This is an heretical ending for a romantic comedy, which never before had deliberately postponed love's felicity. Biron remarks the unconventionality of this close:

> Our wooing doth not end like an old play.
> Jack hath not Gill: these ladies courtesy
> Might well have made our sport a Comedy.[40]

But this ending is harmonious with the origin of the drama as here presented and to the type as here conceived. In the first place, the story of the visit of the two queens at Nérac offered just this sort of indeterminate ending. No marriages were arranged. Marguerite of Valois was already the King's wife. The expedition resulted in a treaty between Navarre and France; and the flying squadron of ladies, its diplomatic service rendered, departed. In *Love's Labour's Lost*, too, the Princess seems to have succeeded in her diplomatic mission. In her farewell to the King she says:

> Excuse me so comming so short of thankes
> For my great suite, so easily obtained.[41]

In the second place the Progresses of the Queen ended in the same way. However alluring the coquetry of Elizabeth and her ladies, however ardent the gallantry of the gentlemen, the imperial vot'ress passed on in maiden meditation fancy free. Therefore if *Love's Labour's Lost* had closed with the marriages of a typical romantic comedy, it would have departed in an important feature from the dramatic form which Shakespeare had chosen for it.

What hypothesis of the genesis and growth of *Love's Labour's Lost* have our studies up to this point enabled us to form? It occurred, we may suppose, to some Elizabethan gentleman that life at the court of Navarre, reflected at a moment when it was stirred into brilliant and picturesque movement by a famous visit of Marguerite of Valois and Catherine de Medici, would form an admirable foundation for an English court play. Whether his attraction was purely aesthetic or whether he saw in the possibilities of the situation an opportunity to make some personal plea in his own private interest, cannot now be determined. This idea became the property of Shakespeare. He believed that this situation would find its most suitable dramatic investiture in a play modelled on the royal Progresses of Elizabeth. It would be a new and piquant experience for the Queen to behold, as a spectator, the drama of a typical Progress, in which so many times she had been the central figure. Consequently as many as possible of the characteristics of these royal entertainments were preserved in the play. The scene of all the action was set in such a spacious park as surrounded many of the castles at which the Queen had been received. The play itself was not given any closely knit structure, but was deliberately planned as a chronicle of entertainments such as were provided for Elizabeth on successive days. The royal guest was given her inevitable opportunity to shoot deer from a covert. The gentlemen presented a merry anti-mask; the clowns, a burlesque show intended to provoke raillery. Finally there was a lyrical debate between the owl and the cuckoo and innumerable social conflicts of wit and dainty devices of speech and repartee. No one of these bits of entertainment in the Progress bore any intrinsic relationship to any other. Consequently Shakespeare felt no obligation to bind his dramatic pictures of such episodes any more closely together. They remain, as it were, a number of acts of the highest sort of Elizabethan vaudeville. Finally the Progress, as a dramatic form, would impose upon the playwright a kind of obligation to give his comedy an indefinite ending. The revels are over and the guests depart: "You that way; we this way."

In the Progress, therefore, we seem to have discovered the structural principle of *Love's Labour's Lost*. Other features of the play remain to be explained. They come from various sources. After the Progresses Shakespeare's most natural source for suggestions for the dramatization of his French story would be the plays of John Lyly, particularly the following comedies of court life: *Sapho and Phao, Endimion,* and *Midas.* Shakespeare's debt to these dramas in *Love's Labour's Lost* has often been assumed to be all-embracing. Bond expresses this opinion in the enthusiastic form of a special pleader. "In comedy," he says, "Lyly is Shakespeare's only model—and Lyly's influence is of a far more permanent nature than any exercised on the great poet by other writers. It extends beyond the boundaries of mechanical style to the more important matters of structure and spirit."[42] Professor Baker regards *Love's Labour's Lost* as a play constructed on the model of Lyly's work. He believes that it follows the earlier dramatist's method as it appears in his court comedies.[43]

In the latter statement there is much justice, if the critic be referring primarily to Shakespeare's style in this early play. The younger playwright may be said to have learned from Lyly the following important lessons, all of which he incorporated into *Love's Labour's Lost:*

1. How to present the intercourse of refined people conducted with the ease and grace of people to whom verbal ingenuity in conversation has become the supreme form of social delight.
2. How to write dialogue, most of it in prose, which is the proper conversation for such a group. It is always witty, brisk, and adorned with fancy and learning; it sometimes degenerates into a somewhat artificial wit combat.
3. How to make love the principal subject of this conversation, which is guided largely by the women who treat their lovers in a tantalizing, flippant manner.
4. How to lay so much emphasis upon dialogue that both plot and characterization become unimportant by comparison.
5. How to introduce many songs.

The influence of Lyly upon *Love's Labour's Lost* in all these respects is indisputable. The conversation of the ladies and gentlemen deals almost exclusively with love. Biron and Rosaline occasionally peer over their flying words to behold each other as man and woman. The others, however, are too completely engrossed in their verbal encounters for such human entanglements; they are blind mouths skilled only in the play of amorous words. This atmosphere of gay badinage is that of Lyly and the witty dialogue a mere echo of his.

The characters in this game of words are grouped somewhat as Lyly's are. The Princess is balanced by the King, and the three ladies, Rosaline, Maria and Katharine are wooed by the three gentlemen, Biron, Longaville and Dumain. In Lyly's plays the same sort of formalism often exists. In *Midas*, for example, there are three councillors, three pages, a group of ladies and a group of shepherds; in *Endimion* there are three pages, two councillors and two philosophers.

All of these elements appear in *Love's Labour's Lost* in greatly altered form. There they have been deepened until they form a somewhat definite comic view of life. Bond says, with warrant, that "there is, however, a humanity behind the trifling, the jokes and the affectations to which Lyly in his ripest work never attains."[44] In *Love's Labour's Lost* true love stories emerge, fitfully at least, from what would have remained in Lyly mere verbal trifling. Some critics, as has been noted, have seen in Shakespeare's comedy an "obvious satire on the notion that polite society, its sayings, and its doings was life in any real sense at all." All these differences serve to emphasize the fact that none of the structural elements of *Love's Labour's Lost* were derived from Lyly. His comedies were little more than manuals to which the younger dramatist referred for authentic details of proper courtly behavior.

Certain writers have believed Lyly's influence much more extensive. They maintain that most of the comic characters in Shakespeare's drama are copies of similar figures in Lyly. "The comic figures," says Baker, "except Costard and Jaquenetta, owe much both in the content and the phrasing of their speech to John Lyly."[45] Elsewhere Baker says that Shakespeare "presents somewhat caricatured figures of the day, in place of Lyly's exaggerated classic comic figures."[46] Bond says, a little more specifically: "The pretentious Sir Tophas, the ridicule of him by the pages, and his pairing with Bagoa, are the originals of the magnificent Armado, of his relation with Moth and his declension upon the country wench Jaquenetta."[47]

Shakespeare's imitation of Lyly in these respects seems very much more doubtful. Indeed upon examination these comic characters in *Love's Labour's Lost* prove to resemble the corresponding ones in Lyly only in the most general features.

The generally noted resemblances between Sir Tophas in Lyly's *Endimion* and Don Armado are the following:

1. They are both braggarts.
2. They are both in love with ill-favored rustic wenches.
3. The adventures of both reflect in humorous fashion the action of the main plot.
4. Each has, as an attendant, a derisive page or boy.

These similarities exist, but they are characteristics held in common by all the descendants of the Plautine and Terentian braggart soldier. Within the limits of that wide-spread tradition the two figures will be seen to differ so strikingly that it can be clearly shown that one is in no sense a model for the other, but that they attach themselves to the hoary tradition at quite different points. Sir Tophas is a farced *miles gloriosus*, a descendant of such exaggerated figures as Thersites in the English interlude of that name, sometimes attributed to John Heywood. His boasts are extravagant to the point of folly. He threatens to do bloody execution upon the mildest of God's creatures. He will slay the monster *Ovis*. "I will draw their guts out of their bellies," he shouts, "and tear the flesh with my teeth, so mortal is my hate."[48] He beholds two pages who he insists are wrens. Epiton, his boy, tells him that the objects are two lads. But Tophas replies, "Byrdes or boyes, they are both but a pittance for my breakfast."[49]

Now in the drawing of Armado no stress whatever is placed upon his grandiose boasting or such display of his military prowess. In fact, if he were not called "braggart" throughout the play, we should hardly recognize him as belonging to the *miles gloriosus* type. He is introduced rather as a voluble traveller, nice in his speech to the point of affectation. He speaks of himself as "Armado, a soldier, a man of travel, that hath seen the world."[50] Biron says:

> Armado is a most illustrious wight
> A man of fire, new words, fashions owne Knight.[51]

Ferdinand just a moment before has referred to him as

> A refined traveler of Spain
> A man in all the world's new fashion planted
> That hath a mint of phrases in his brain.

This figure is no swashbuckler and windy braggart, but a fop in manners and a virtuoso in speech.

This Armado in many of these important respects in which he differs from Sir Tophas and the *miles gloriosus* resembles the braggart as he had become conventionalized in the Italian popular comedy or the *commedia dell'arte*.[52] There, too, he was usually a Spaniard.[53] This transformation of the Latin braggart into a Spanish swashbuckler was a natural result of political conditions in Italy during the sixteenth century, when the Spaniards held much of the country as conquered territory. Their rule in many places, in Naples, for example, was cruel and repressive and provoked many uprisings and revolutions. The unpopular Spanish soldier quartered upon the unwilling Italian inhabitants was satirized by means of the age-old stage figure. Hence the *miles gloriosus* became the *Matamoros*. He was made to affect Spanish stateliness, to talk Castilian, and to adopt a vocabulary of magnificent high-sounding phrases.[54]

In this process of change most of the roughness and noisy extravagance of the role disappeared to be replaced by the polished extravagance of a gloved gentleman, who carries on his warfare with the utmost dignity and seriousness.[55] A contemporary pen-sketch of the character, reproduced by Rasi,[56] shows the figure to be in no sense grotesque in form or in his costume. His sword does not protrude behind at an absurd angle. His hat is embellished with two huge feathers, but he has no trace of the long pointed nose. On the whole he is a graceful gentleman overnicely clad.

Francesco Andreini, the most important impersonator of the *capitano* in the sixteenth century, was a captain of this sort, and became famous for the verbal virtuosity that he exhibited in his reading of the part. This Andreini was a contemporary of Shakespeare; he acted in the company of the Gelosi in 1571, 1574, 1576, 1599, and 1603–4 before the French court and in Paris at the Hôtel de Bourgogne.[57] He was so famous as an actor and a writer that an English actor and playwright of any intellectual curiosity could hardly have failed to hear of him and his work.

This actor-dramatist was a highly intelligent man, a member of a Florentine academy, and interested primarily in the entertainment he could afford by twisting *concetti* and every sort of literary allusion into the speech of his captain,[58] whom he called Capitano Spavento of Hell-Valley. These speeches were so much admired that he collected and published them in two different collections.[59] Of this braggart, as of Armado, it could be truthfully said that he had "a mint of phrases in his brain." At least it need surprise no one that the influence of a *commedia dell'arte* figure upon a farcical character like the *miles gloriosus* has been to refine it in much the same fashion in which Armado has been refined.

Shakespeare's figure certainly shows more points of relationship with this Italian re-creation than with Sir Tophas. It is, of course, probable that Shakespeare, like all literary artists, drew upon his personal experience when fashioning a character. He may have had his eye on the fantastical *monarcho*, a Spaniard who for years hung about the court of Elizabeth, when drawing Armado. However, the more we know of Shakespeare's sources, the more we realize that he usually had dramatic warrant for his so-called inventions—that his original conceptions were poured into dramatic moulds already cast. Such a rude mould existed in the Spanish braggart of the *commedia dell'arte*.[60]

Strong corroborative evidence of this origin can be found in the fact that each one of Don Armado's clownish associates in *Love's Labour's Lost* bears a close resemblance to a corresponding type-figure in the picturesque clown-group of Italian comedy. Such likenesses between characters as individuals, and as members of a conventionalized group, can hardly be fortuitous.

Before these points of similarity are indicated, a word should be said about the term "Italian comedy." This term is commonly applied to two types of drama: the *commedia erudita* or "learned" comedy, of which Gascoigne's *Supposes*[61] is the best known English example; and the *commedia dell'arte*, the professional or improvised comedy. The differences between the two in the essential qualities of plot and character were never very great. The same authors often wrote both sorts of comedy and brought the same literary conventions, the same notions of construction, and the same comic devices to both sorts of work.

The extent of the knowledge of *commedia erudita* in Elizabethan England can be fairly easily determined. That of the *commedia dell'arte* is obviously more difficult to fix. Yet the probabilities that this more popular form exercised an influence upon Elizabethan dramatists in general, and upon Shakespeare in particular, are strong.

The evidence in the records, of various sorts, of the presence of Italian actors and Italian companies in England during the later half of the sixteenth century has been often presented.[62] Payments were made by the Privy Council to Italians both singers and actors from 1550 on,[63] and there are occasional references in the Revels Accounts to representations by the Italian Players.[64]

The first notice of the appearance of an Italian company in England concerns a reward "gevin to the Italyans for serteyne pastymes that they showed before Maister Mear and his brethen"[65] in September 1573. This company apparently stayed on into the next year, because we find in the Revels Accounts various payments and furnishings and properties of some Italian actors who "followed the progresse and made pastyme first at Wynsor and afterwards at Reading."[66] The next Italian company apparently visited England early in the year 1576; at any rate the Treasurer of the Chamber paid "Alfroso Ferrabolle and the rest of the Italian Players"[67] for an entertainment presented at court on February 27, 1576. Finally, on January 13, 1578, the Privy Council ordered "The Lord Mayor of London to give orders that one Drousiano, the Italian, a commediante, and his companye may play within the Cittie and the liberties of the same between this and the first weeks of Lent."[68] This Drousiano was first identified by Collier as Drusiano

Martinelli;[69] and this identification has been accepted by practically all subsequent historians of Italian comedy. He was the brother of Tristano Martinelli,[70] the Arlecchino of the Gelosi. He was probably associated with this famous troupe himself, although there is no direct proof to establish this as a fact. However, this was the only company known to have been in France during the summer of 1577 and Italian players universally left some trace of their presence in France on their way to England. We can, therefore, say with assurance that Drusiano took certain members of this troupe across the Channel to perform before popular London audiences.[71] Later he took the leading roles in the Duke of Mantua's company of comedians.[72] The nature of the repertory of this company can be inferred from the plays acted by the Gelosi in Paris and by Drusiano's company while it was in Mantua. Besides the *commedia dell'arte*, he almost surely presented some of the *commedie erudite* written by members of the bourgeois academies to which many of the actors belonged.[73]

This company and others of a similar nature which probably followed it[74] evidently made a profound impression upon English authors and audiences. Nash's famous attack upon "the players beyond the sea" as "a sort of squirting baudie comedians that have whores to play women's parts— forbeare no immodest speech or unchast action that may procure laughter"[75] is but one of a score of references,[76] complimentary and, like this, condemnatory, made during the final quarter of the sixteenth century.

Indeed there is evidence to suggest that the comic dramaturgy of these years in England was permeated with the ideals of Italian comedy. Stephen Gosson in his *School of Abuse*,[77] and his *Plays Confuted in Five Actions*,[78] uses the term "comedies" and "Italian devices," or variations of this latter phrase, practically synonymously. His own comedy, an indiscretion of his youth, of which he heartily repents in his obscurantist maturity, he calls "a cast of Italian devices" with the title *The Comedie of Capitaine Mario*.

Plays, he is certain, came from the Devil, who first corrupted Englishmen by giving them wanton Italian books to read,[79] but "not contented with the number he hath corrupted with reading Italian bawdry, because all cannot read, presented us comedies cut by the same pattern." This trash is called "new-learning" by those which "bear a sharper smack of Italian devices in their heads, than of English religion in their hearts." "Compare London to Rome," he cried in *The School of Abuse*, "and England to Italy. You shall find the theatres of one, the abuses of the other to be rife among us." Repetition of more of these familiar passages should be unnecessary. Gosson's description of the constituent elements of comedy as he understands it fits Italian comedy best. "The Grounde Work of Comedies," he says, "is love cosenedge, flatterie, bawderie, slye conveyhance of whoredom; the persons cookes, queans, knaves, baudes, parasites, courtezannes, lecherous olde men, amorous young men." Allowing for the zealot's exaggeration, this passage might refer to either sort of Italian comedy, or even to that of Plautus or Terence; but taken in connection with the passage to be cited, it seems clearly intended as a description of the popular comedy.

The Devil, continues the implacable Gosson, seduces man by way of comedies, particularly through the eye, because he sendeth in "gearish apparell, maskes, vauting, tumbling, dancing of gigges, galiandes, morisces, hobbi-horses, showing of iudgeling castes."

The properties and devices here mentioned are of the very essence of the *commedia dell'arte*. The passage is primarily a description of the *lazzi* of the clowns with which the improvised comedy was replete. Moreover, it is highly probable that the word "maskes" in this context refers to the actual masks that the typical figures in this comedy wore. It obviously does not refer to the highly refined court show of the same name.[80] "Gearish apparell" obviously refers to costume and describes nothing so accurately as the fantastic parti-colored garments of the popular Italian comedy. "Maskes," Gosson opines, are equally designed to seduce the eyes of the vulgar. They must be, therefore, something related to "gearish apparell" and so probably the word refers to the grotesque half-faces which the clowns like Harlequin and Pulcinella habitually wore.

These passages tend to confirm our *a priori* judgment in this matter. Of the two sorts of Italian comedy one would expect the *commedia dell'arte* to have the more definite influence upon English drama.[81] Only those few literary comedies which were translated into English could have exerted any pervasive influence. The appeal of the *commedia dell'arte*, on the other hand, was largely independent of language. It flourished in nearly every capital and important city of the continent during the latter half of the sixteenth century. English travelling comedians are known to have played at the same places with Italian companies for prolonged periods. Before 1580, London had at least once submitted itself to the charm of the *commedia dell'arte*. Its appeal was striking, pictueresque, unique. Such plays, once seen, would be held securely in memory and all their comic devices cherished.

The historical facts adduced and such utterances as those of Gosson show that English dramatic life during the seventies and eighties of the sixteenth century was permeated by the form and spirit of the Italian comedy— largely of the popular sort. What reason is there to suppose that Shakespeare during the latter part of this period fell under the wide-spread influence of this striking comedy?

At the end of his career, Shakespeare knew well a certain type of Italian comic scenario. It has recently been shown that the story of *The Tempest* and many of its distinctive theatrical features are undoubtedly derived from a romantic type of *commedia dell'arte*.[82] A group of five scenarios, written down first in 1622, but representing much older traditions of the masked players, contains practically all of the constructive and distinctive histrionic features of *The Tempest*, in a combination which makes the evidence for their influence upon Shakespeare absolutely convincing. These newly discovered facts justify our assuming that by 1610 he had direct and specific knowledge of the *commedia dell'arte*. His general or traditional knowledge seems to have been much older. Specific allusions to the various Italian "masks" can be found throughout his work.[83] Even in the comedy under discussion Biron speaks of "some carry-tale, some pleseman, some slight zany."[84] These facts simply confirm what is an almost inevitable inference—that a young writer like Shakespeare, who throughout his career showed himself to be closely in touch with all the dramatic tendencies of his time, could hardly have failed, especially in the opening years of his career, to be aware of the spectacular action and striking stage figures of the *commedia dell'arte*. Its influence, perhaps next to that of Lyly, would be the most natural one to draw Shakespeare within its sphere. His clowns, indeed, would almost inevitably be related to that comedy of clowns. That the character of Armado should resemble the Spanish braggart of Italian comedy, then, and not the Latinate Sir Tophas of Lyly, need astonish no critic familiar with the European dramatic situation in the years when Shakespeare began to write for the stage.

All the points of likeness usually asserted as existing between Sir Tophas and Armado can now be recognized as traditions of the *capitano*. For example, Sir Tophas is said to be the prototype of Armado because he is forced to marry an ugly wench, Bagoa, just as Armado pairs with the country lout Jaquenetta. But this is one of the conventional ways of disposing of the *capitano*. Thus are his amorous conceit and amorous ambition broadly satirized. He is regularly either utterly humiliated and driven off in disgrace at the end of the play or he is married to some clownish and ill-favored female. Francesco Andreini, for example, in one of the discourses which he composed for this part of the *capitano* presents the plight of the *capitano*[85] who is married to the terrible fury Megara.[86] A less extravagant situation of this sort is that of Captain Crackstone in *The Two Italian Gentlemen*, an English adaptation of an Italian comedy.[87] This braggart woos the vulgar maid Attilia and apparently wins her. "How saist those Alice tittle tattle," he cries in the last lines of the play, "art thou content by love to be bound?"

Sir Tophas and Armado decline upon sorry wenches, then, because that amorous disaster is in the typical *capitano*'s part.

A relationship between Lyly's and Shakespeare's figure has been assumed because each is accompanied by a page, who ridicules the self-importance and the extravagant assumptions of his braggart master, particularly his role of love. But here again Sir Tophas and Armado have merely both inherited a common appendage of the *capitano*. He was invariably accompanied by such a servant. In the *commedia dell'arte* this fellow was one of the clowns, often Arlecchino, and his relation to his master was that of the page to Sir Tophas or to Armado. This figure, the zany, was originally the clown or mountebank, whose first requisite was the physical agility demanded for the performance of his *lazzi* or bits of horse-play. His brains in time came to be as swift as his muscles, because his function in the plot became more and more that of managing events in the interest of the *amorosa*. His quick wit was also shown more and more in puns, in word-play of all sorts, and in satiric repartee. He assumed so many forms and inherited so many characteristics of the *servus* of Latin comedy and resembled so closely the clown in native English drama that it is impossible to prove that a figure like Moth is a direct descendant of the zany attached to the *capitano*. However, the two belong to the same family, and it is reasonable to suppose that the servant would come from the same source as the master. If Armado came into English comedy as an Italian type, Moth probably had a similar origin.

A strong confirmation of this theory may be found in the fact that all the members of the subsidiary comic group have prototypes in the figures of the *commedia dell'arte*: Costard, the slow-witted rustic, in Pagliaccio, a similar heavy lout; Holofernes, in a figure with various names, charlatan, pedagogue, and pedant, with his speech habitually crammed with macaronic Latin and Bolognese riddles; Nathaniel, in the Parasite or *affamato*, who only in the *commedia dell'arte* is attached to the Pedant. Even Dull, English to the core in his particular form of conscientious stupidity, has a prototype in Italian comedy.

Costard's ancestor, a stupid rustic, appears in the earliest scenario that we possess.[88] There he evokes laughter only by his ridiculous clothing and rustic behavior,[89] and bears no relation whatever to the plot. The proper "business" for an actor presenting this character is explained in a dialogue about scenic performances composed between 1567 and 1590 by an actor-manager, Leone di Sommi.[90] His advice to the actor on this point is "If he plays a fool, besides answering off the point (which the poet will teach him by his words) he must be able to act the imbecile, catch flies, kill fleas, and do like foolish actions."

This rustic or fool first became an integral part of the bourgeois group who form the vehicle of the love plot, in the company of the Gelosi. He there usually bears the name of Pedrolino,[91] and is the servant of Pantalone. He is generally outwitted by the other servants, stupidly falls asleep at his post, or gets drunk with the *capitano* and his servant. In particular, he made himself ridiculous when encountering the principal zany and becoming involved in the toils of his wit. By the time of Barbieri's *Il Supplica*, written in 1634, the dramatic contrast between the two servants had become a thoroughly established dramatic convention and treated as such in this book of dramaturgy. Barbieri says, "The first servant provokes laughter by most subtle tricks and ready replies, the second by foolishness."

The dramatic contrast between these two servants Shakespeare did not develop strongly until he wrote *Two Gentlemen of Verona*. However, the possibilities of humor in such a contrast are suggested in *Love's Labour's Lost*. Costard, at any rate, is a very close equivalent of this Italian fool. Like his prototype described by Leone di Sommi, his humor is rustic behavior and the vice of mistaking the word or of answering off the point. Every time that he appears, he contributes bits of verbal misunderstanding like the following:

> ARMADO. Sirra, Costard. I will infranchise thee.
> CLOWN. O, marrie me to one Francis, I smell some l'envoy, some goose in this.[92]

The following dialogue illustrates the same point:

> BEROWNE. O my good Knave Costard, exceedingly well met.
> CLOWN. Pray you sir, How much Carnation Ribbon may a man buy for a remuneration?
> BEROWNE. What is a remuneration?
> COSTARD. Marrie, sir, halfe pennie farthing.[93]

Shakespeare naturally gave this Costard traits of English rustics, but the character is very clearly cast in the dramatic mould of the Italian figure.

Holofernes, another permanent member of the group of clowns, is also modelled on the very popular Italian figure of the pedant. Many critics, following the lead of Warburton, have attempted to see in this character Shakespeare's satire of some individual whom he knew and scorned. Warburton asserted without any apparent warrant that Holofernes was intended to represent John Florio.[94] Karl Elze makes the unsupported assertion that Shakespeare's pedant is a satirical picture of Thomas Hunt, the poet's teacher from 1572 to 1577.[95] Abel Lefranc, finding a manuscript play on the *Nine Worthies* by Richard Lloyd, the tutor of the sixth Earl of Derby, concludes that Holofernes is a comic portrait of this schoolmaster. Arthur Acheson believes that Holofernes represents Chapman and that "in the pedantry and verbosity of Holofernes he (Shakespeare) caricatures Chapman's style, and in the person of Holofernes excoriates Chapman himself."[96]

These theories, by no means all of the sort that have been advanced, besides being impossible of proof, ignore the existence of one of the most wide-spread and popular of the Italian stage conventions of the time—that of the pedant. The model from which the character was drawn was an international figure, the product of Renaissance culture. With the coming of the new learning the intellectual methods of the scholastics or medieval school-philosophers naturally became the objects of ridicule. This sort of scholar came to appear as an absurd combination of the rigid logician and formal rhetorician. In drama he was made to argue according to all forms of the syllogism—to concede the major and deny the minor. He fatuously came forward on all occasions with some general rule which he considered applicable to the particular case in hand.

Later the exaggerations of the humanist himself were made the object of satire—his confident and superior wisdom, which yet rendered him helpless in any difficult situation, and his motley tongue, half Italian and half Latin. He is particularly prone to use his learning in colloquies with people of the lower class, among whom he produces misunderstandings which fill him with rage. He usually falls in love, in which state his insatiable quotation of Latin maxims and classical precedents renders him particularly ridiculous. He is always cozened and misled, but he seeks to make his learning yield him comfort. He thinks of the great men of the past who have been pursued by misfortune and hopes that thought will bring him equanimity. Occasionally he is made a philosopher in words and a licentious hypocrite in fact. As such he is exposed and driven off the stage with scorn.

In Italian comedy, also, the pedant is usually the school teacher or tutor. In *Gl'Ingannati*[97] (1526), for example, one of the principal characters is Piero, the tutor of Fabrizio. In *The Two Italian Gentlemen*, Pedante, the tutor of Fidele,[98] enters "attired in a gown and cap like a schoolmaster." Both of these teachers fill their discourse with Latin and are particularly eloquent in that tongue before dolts who cannot understand them.

In *The Two Italian Gentlemen*, Attilia, the loutish maid, is the object of the pedant's attentions and is forced to listen to much incomprehensible Latin.

ATTILIA. I pray, Sir, what was it you sayde of love?

PEDANTE. Est Deus in nobis agitante calescimus illo.

I dare not tell you the meaning, lest I make your cheeks glow. This pedant, too, inserts Italian into his discourse with a freedom only once or twice attempted by Holofernes:

Andante allegramente, you are right under her window now

or

Oche cricca di vacche? What cattell have we heare?

To be sure, these Italian schoolmasters are in love and show their Latinate folly most completely in this situation.

Holofernes clearly belongs to this type.[99] He is a schoolmaster who "teaches boys the Horne-book." He apostrophizes good old Mantuan, whose Eclogues were a favorite text for study in the schools. Nathaniel, his parasite, praises his work as follows: "Sir, I praise God for you, and so may my parishioners, for their Sonnes are well tutor'd by you, and their Daughters profit very greatly under you; you are a good member of the Commonwealth."[100] Later in this same scene Holofernes says, "I do dine today at the father of a certaine Pupill of mine."

He crams his discourse with Latin and is outraged at the ignorance of the clowns who cannot understand him.

NATHANIEL. . . . but sir, I assure ye, it was a Bucke of the first head.
HOLOFERNES. Sir Nathaniel, haud credo.
DULL. 'Twas not a haud credo, 'twas a Pricket.
HOLOFERNES. Most barbarous intimation: yet a kind of insinuation, as it were in via, in way of explication facere, as it were replication, or rather ostentare, to show as it were his inclination after his undressed, unpolished, uneducated, unpruned, untrained, or rather unlettered, or ratherest unconfirmed fashion, to insert againe my haud credo for a dear.[101]

Holofernes is also keenly on the lookout for false Latin.

CLOWN. Goe to, thou hast it ad dungil, at the finger ends, as they say.
PEDANTE. Oh, I smell false Latin, dunghel for unguam.[102]

Furthermore he now and then falls into Italian as in his apostrophe to

Mantuan: "Ah good old Mantuan, I may speake of thee as the traveller doth of Venice, 'Venetia, Venetia, chi non te vede, no te pregia.'"[103]

The verbal affectations and flourishes of Holofernes in the use of his mother-tongue are of definite sorts. In the first place he shows his mastery of a vocabulary by uttering on every possible occasion a mass of synonyms. He says that the braggart is "too picked, too spruce, too affected, too odde, as it were, too peregrinat." He comments as follows on Don Armado's use of the term "posteriors of this day" for afternoon as follows: "The posterior of the day, most generous sir, is liable, congruent, and measurable for the afternoone: the word is well culd, chose, sweet and apt. I doe assure you."[104] He speaks of his own talent in making rhymes in the following way: "This is a gift that I have simple: simple, a foolish extravagant spirit, full of forms, figures, objects, ideas, apprehensions, motions, revolutions."[105]

In the second place, Holofernes indulges a passion for overingenious etymologies. He exclaims pompously, "But for elegancy, facility and golden cadence of poesie, caret. Ovidius Naso was the man. And why indeed Naso, but for smelling out the odoriferous flowers of fancy, the jerks of invention."[106] He answers Jaquenetta's "God give you good morrow, Master Parson," in the following jocose fashion: "Master Parson, quasi pers-on. An if one should be pierced, which is the one?"[107]

In the third place, he is sometimes given to false pronunciation. For example, he says to Nathaniel, after he has read the love letter, "You find not the apostrophas and so miss the accent. Let me supervise the cangenet" (canzonet).[108]

The following somewhat puzzling passage, in which Holofernes comments on Don Armado's pronunciation, is also an indication of bookish ignorance of the spoken idiom: "He clepeth a Calf; Caufe halfe, haufe; Neighbour vocabitur nebour: neigh abbreviated ne: this is abhominable, which he would call abbominable."[109] To assume that the pedant here is talking merely as a purist is to attribute to him a subtlety of humor not in harmony with his character as drawn elsewhere in the play. He is rather presented in this speech as a man essentially bookish, who has learned his words from a printed page, and is oblivious and contemptuous of their career in the living speech. His own mispronunciation of "abominable," based upon a false etymology, gives satiric emphasis to his ponderous ignorance of idiomatic pronunciation.

Now every one of these verbal affectations of Holofernes, with the necessary exception of his use of Italian, is a recognized convention of the pedantic doctor in the *commedia dell'arte*, and particularly of the role as played by Ludovico Bianchi of the Gelosi troupe. This *dottore*, generally called Graziano, is usually from Bologna, and his humors are exactly the same as those just catalogued. Rasi thus enumerates his foibles: "The doctor is always the invariable ignoramus and pedant, who utters wise saws in the inevitable mixture of macaronic Latin, foolish quotations and absurd etymologies. . . . Clear proof that the true type of Graziano had, in the eyes of the public, as distinctive and fundamental characteristics, ignorant pretension to learning, stupid etymologizing, grotesque mispronunciation of words and the buffoonery of Latin quotation."[110] Later Rasi mentions the doctor's penchant for synonyms and gives as an example the following: "Pero essend' tra un allegad et culigad la grazia, l'affabilita, la benignita, l'allegrezza," and so on for forty-eight synonyms.[111]

This doctor is a pedant, though not expressly so called. In Scala's Collection at least once the pedant is introduced by that name.[112] This Cataldo is also a tiresome Latinate pedant, but is primarily a hypocrite. Under cover of giving Isabella, the beautiful young wife of Pantalone, the counsel that she needs to keep her from betraying her husband with the captain, he attempts to seduce her himself. Isabella traps, and exposes him, and so holds him up to ignominy and ridicule. Cataldo is thus a sort of skeleton for Tartuffe. This aspect of the pedant was not uncommonly treated in Italian comedy. Indeed several passages in *Love's Labour's Lost* show that Holofernes was sometimes under the sway of similar wanton desires.[112] This Shakespearian pedant thus seems to exhibit most of the absurdities conventionally the humorous property of the *commedia dell'arte* pedant.

The attempt to find any specific dramatic figure who served as a definite literary prototype for Holofernes is probably futile. These characteristics of the *dottore* did not join in any figure before Holofernes in a combination enough like his own to furnish Shakespeare a serviceable model. In English literature before *Love's Labour's Lost*, the pedant played a comparatively insignificant role. Rombus in Sidney's *Lady of May* is one of the few. He exhibits many of the characteristics of the Italian type in his predilection for Latin quotation and his grandiloquence in his native idiom. However he is ridiculous principally because he is excessively prone to formal rhetoric and the forms of the syllogism. He is a belated scholastic. Churchill and Keller, in the article already cited,[114] suggest that Shakespeare might naturally have known the Cambridge University play *Paedantius*[115] and have used the comic protagonist there, as a model for Holofernes. However none of the similarities between the two lie in common deviations from the type figure, so that this assumption is hardly warranted. The pedant in *The Two Italian Gentlemen* is much more like Holofernes than either of these figures; doubtless because he bears a closer relationship to the Italian figure.

These facts pretty clearly establish the truth that Holofernes left a home in popular Italian comedy to travel with his clownish associates into Shakespeare's workshop. Naturally the English dramatist has transformed the figure in many ways. Some of his new traits may well have been derived from country schoolmasters whom he had known, but they never obscure Holofernes' relationship to the Italian type-figure.

Nathaniel is a parasite who, like hundreds of his prototypes from classical comedy down, flatters and toadies to the person to whom he attaches himself, so that he may satisfy his insatiable appetite for food.[116] It is only in Italian comedy, however, that the parasite attaches himself to the pedant. Moland[117] says that it is only in the *commedia dell'arte* that he is thus placed, but in *The Supposes* Pasiphilo divides his allegiance between Erostrato and the pedant Cleander.[118] Nathaniel is, of course, a character of very minor importance. Yet the slight indications that the author has given us prove that he is a representative of the parasite in the form that he came to assume in Italian comedy.

Even Dull has a prototype in the Italian comedy. A stupid magistrate was one of Francesco Andreini's most successful roles. In one of Bartoli's scenarii, *La Regina d'Inghilterra*, Trappola plays an officer with the same portentous stupidity as does Dull. In *The Two Italian Gentlemen*, described above, there is a representative of the same type-character in Sberri, captain of the watch. Examples could be multiplied. Even the presence of the multiform love story may be due to *commedia dell'arte* influence. There were nearly always, in these plays, a *prima donna* and a *secunda donna*. Each of these ladies had to be provided with a lover. Occasionally there was even a third lady who made a like demand of the author. This was in addition to the inevitable love-making among the servants and clowns. Shakespeare's multiform love stories in this comedy and elsewhere may be regarded as a natural expansion and complication of this structural feature of Italian comedy.

The *capitano*, upon examination, seems to have brought all of his Italian familiars with him into *Love's Labour's Lost*.[119] Certain members of this famous group had appeared in plays in English before this one, but this is the first English comedy in which the entire group appears as a veritable *société joyeuse*.

The young dramatist evidently felt that the clever courtly badinage of Lyly-like ladies and gentlemen, even when associated with a more natural and sincere love story than any that Lyly had ever presented, did not give enough comic substance to his play, which we have agreed to regard as a sort of dramatic progress. Accordingly, turning for material to the enormously popular characters of contemporary Italian comedy, he imported thence not isolated figures, but the entire group of clownish masks. Their mere presence gave his comedy a firm foundation for laughter. He forced them moreover to meet some of the structural needs of his drama, as when he assigned to them the presentation of the burlesque pageant of *The Nine Worthies*. Each one of them was also modified as a result of Shakespeare's observation of contemporary life, and perhaps occasionally by his impulse to satirize certain ridiculous individuals whom he knew. But the solidity of framework which this group gave his tenuously connected episodes and the perennial mirth which it aroused must have been their main recommendation to the young dramatist.

Love's Labour's Lost, therefore, proves to have had a somewhat complicated history of construction. The nature of the play shows clearly enough that even in its earliest form, it was connected in some way with the English court. Indeed its central plot reveals such an intimate familiarity with nearly contemporary events and social conditions at the court of Navarre as the author could scarcely have gained from his own personal experience. This fact points to Shakespeare's association with some gentleman of the court in the composition of this *Love's Labour's Lost*. Who he was or what his purposes were in this collaboration will probably never be known. To a student of Shakespeare's early methods of composition, these interesting personal questions are of only minor importance. Once given his central idea, the playwright invested it with vitality and diversity by bringing to it constructive principles and comic motifs from three sources clearly within the range of his knowledge—the progresses of Queen Elizabeth, the court comedies of John Lyly, and Italian comedy, particularly the *commedia dell'arte*.

We find Shakespeare then, at the outset of his career as a writer of comedy, not, as Bond asserts, having one master and one only—John Lyly. Nor do we find him working carefully in imitation of this one author in an effort to discover what qualities of his own would emerge during this process. Such a method is scarcely calculated to develop the great versatility in comic composition which Shakespeare shows early in his career. What he seems actually to have done is to have found dramatic suggestions for his own practice in many places. Fortunately his imagination kindled at many smouldering fires.

Moreover each one of his borrowed ideas he developed with a joyous creative exuberance. He was not to be satisfied with one love story in this play or even with two. He arranged four or five. He developed, intensified, and diversified Lyly's courtly conversation until it became a veritable dramatic symphony on the theme of Euphuistic speech. He introduced into it not single figures from Italian comedy, but all of the comic masks at once and made each one of them contribute his traditional humor, in a sublimated form, to the gorgeous progress given by the King of Navarre to his royal guests.

This imaginative abundance appears in all of Shakespeare's early plays—tragedies and historical. It is the temper of *The Comedy of Errors*, of *Titus Andronicus*, and of *Richard III*. May we not say it is the universally approved and natural method of all youthful genius?

NOTES

1. The facts are thus presented in Sir Sidney Lee's *William Shakespeare* (third revised edition, London, 1922), pp. 103ff.

2. *Sous le masque de William Shakespeare* (Paris, 1919), Vol. 2, pp. 17ff.

3. *The Gentleman's Magazine*, October, 1880.

4. There was also a declared intention to convert Henry from Protestantism, but that event can hardly have been expected.

5. Davila, *Memoirs of Civil Wars in France* (trans. London, 1758), I, pp. 505ff.

6. Ibid.

7. *Love's Labour's Lost*, II.1.8.

8. Cf. *Sous le masque*, Vol. 2, pp. 67ff.; also Batz-Trenquelleon, *Henri IV en Gascogne, 1553–1589* (Paris, 1885), pp. 75 and 122.

9. *Mémoires et lettres de Marguerite de Valois* (ed. par M.F. Guessard, Paris, 1842), p. 163 (Société de l'Histoire de France).

10. Batz-Trenquelleon, p. 129. [Henri d'Albret was Henri II of Navarre, father of Jeanne d'Albret, who became queen of Navarre and mother of Henri IV of France.—FHL]

11. *Mémoires*, p. 163.

12. *Love's Labour's Lost*, V.2.6–9.

13. *Sous le masque*, Vol. 2, p. 64.

14. II.4, once; IV.1, eighteen times; V.3, once. All of the eighteen of IV.1 are retained in the Folio.

15. II.1.60–65. There is a reference to a visit made upon her brother, the Duke of Alençon in 1578: cf. *Mémoires*, pp. 156–7. Berowne's "Did I not dance with you in Brabant once?" is a reference to a trip to Flanders made by Marguerite and her train in 1577: cf. *Mémoires*, pp. 88ff., particularly the ball referred to on page 97.

16. V.2.13ff. contains a reference to the death of Katharine's sister from unrequited love, which may be a recollection of the sad fate of Hélène de Tournon referred to in the *Mémoires*, pp. 110–114. The taunt (V.2.574) hurled at the actor playing Alexander: "You will be scraped out of the painted cloth," may refer to certain tapestries decorated with images of *The Nine Worthies* which we know hung in the royal apartments, sometimes at Pau and sometimes at Nérac.

17. *Calendar of State Papers. Foreign Series of the Reign of Elizabeth, June–January 1583* (London, 1913), p. 394.

18. It is interesting to remark that Berowne seems to refer to the King as Timon (IV.3.170ff.):

O me, with what strict patience have I sat
To see a king transformed to a Gnat,
And Critticke Tymon laugh at idle toyes.

19. Marlowe's knowledge of French history shown in *The Massacre of Paris*; Chapman's, shown in his five plays dealing with the same subject; or Dekker's and

Drayton's, undoubtedly exhibited in their plays on *The Civil Wars in France*, recorded by Henslowe, is not analogous to that of Shakespeare shown in *Love's Labour's Lost*. Their knowledge is of public political fact; Shakespeare's is of intimate personal incident.

20. Except, of course, the one sponsored by M. Lefranc that Shakespeare did not write the comedy.

21. Vid. sup. 5.

22. Baker, G.P., *The Development of Shakespeare as a Dramatist* (New York, 1907), pp. 107–108.

23. This fact is mentioned by Austen K. Gray in "The Secret of *Love's Labour's Lost*," *Publications of the Modern Language Association* 39 (Sept. 1924), 602.

24. Op. cit.

25. *Hamlet*, II.2.446ff.

26. In the play *Sir Thomas More*, Sir Thomas himself steps in and improvises a part for "Good Councell" until the fellow Luggins comes in to take the role.

27. Shakespeare could readily have obtained knowledge of the nature of these Progresses either through personal experience or through a perusal of the accounts of these fêtes, which were often printed within a year of their occurrence. For a comparison of the dates of the Progresses with those of the printed accounts, see Nichols's *Progresses*, passim.

28. *Shakespeare's Lost Years in London* (London 1920), p. 186.

29. Nichols, Vol. II.

30. For the meaning and tradition of this "wild man," cf. Chambers, *Mediaeval Stage* I, p. 182; also note 2.

31. Cf. Boyet's explanation of the King's reception of the ladies, II.1.91–94:

> He rather means to lodge you in the field,
> Like one that comes here to besiege his court
> Than seek a dispensation for his oath:
> To let you enter his unpeopled house.

Also II.1.181–183:

> You may not come, fair Princess, in my gates,
> But here without you shall be so received,
> As you shall deem yourself lodged in my heart.

32. Gray, Henry David, "The Original Version of *Love's Labour's Lost* with a conjecture as to *Love's Labour's Won*," *Leland Stanford Junior Publications*, 1918, p. 19.

33. Cf. The Earl of Hertford's Entertainment, Nichols, Vol. 2: "Three musicians under the window disguised in ancient country attire did greet her with a pleasant song of Coridon and Phyllida." In the Cowdray Entertainment (ibid.), we read the following: "on Thursday—in the evening the Countrie people presented themselves to her Majestie in a pleasant dance with taber and pipe."

34. Chambers (*The Mediaeval Stage*, Vol. 1, p. 155) points out the fact that the germ of this play is clearly a very old festival celebration, and, like hock-tide customs, found in many places throughout England. Its folk significance, however, had been entirely lost at this time and it was merely sport for the people and humor for the gentry.

35. Laneham, p. 25, in Nichols, Vol. 2.

36. Thorndyke, Ashley, "The Pastoral Element in the English Drama before 1605," *Modern Language Notes*, 1889, p. 230.

37. Op. cit., p. 112.

38. Op. cit., p. 15.

39. The only explanations are 1) that Shakespeare at this time, like all youthful genius, aimed at novelty of form (cf. H.D. Gray, op. cit., p. 14; also Grant White, quoted ibid.), or 2) that the play was written as a plea of Southampton to have his projected marriage postponed.

40. V.2.950ff.

41. V.2.811–812.

42. Lyly, John. *The Complete Works of John Lyly; Now for the First Time Collected and Edited from the Earliest Quartos with Life, Bibliography, Essays, Notes, and Index,* edited by R. Warwick Bond, Vol. 2 (Oxford: The Clarendon Press, 1902), p. 243.

43. Baker, op. cit., p. 114.

44. Bond, Vol. 2, p. 262.

45. Baker, p. 113.

46. Ibid., p. 114.

47. Bond, Vol. 2, 297.

48. *Endimion,* I. 11.

49. Thersites, when he catches sight of a snail, makes a similarly absurd remark:

But what a monster do I see now
Come hitherward with an armed bow?
What is it? Ah it is a sow.

50. V.1.103.

51. I.1.189–190.

52. Winifred Smith has noticed this general resemblance. She says ("Italian and Elizabethan Comedy," *Modern Philology* 5, 561), "Not less important is Shakespeare's Holofernes, whose name, manner of speech, and general imbecility place him far nearer to the Italian stage-type than to a possible village personage of Shakespeare's acquaintance."

53. Luigi Riccoboni says that the character was introduced into Italian drama comedy from Spanish drama; *Histoire du théâtre italien depuis la décadence de la comédie latine* (Paris, 1730), Vol. 1, p. 56. This statement, of course, ignores the obvious relation of this figure with its Latin prototype. Cf. also Scherillo, Michele, *La Commedia dell'arte in Italia* (1884), p. 96, and Lee, Vernon, *Studies of the Eighteenth Century in Italy* (1880), p. 235.

54. Contemporary Italian critics declared that the Spanish tongue was admirably suited to this verbal extravagance. Cecchini (*Frutti delle moderne commedie,* 1628) says, "Questa iperbolica parte par che suoni meglio nella spagnuola che nella Italiana lingua, come quella a cui vediamo esser più proprii a più domestici gl'impossibili."

55. Rasi, L., *I Comici Italiani; biografia, bibliografia, iconografia* (Firenze, 1897), Vol. 1, p. 63. "La maschera chiassona, urlona che atterrà un regimento di soldati con un semplice Guarda voi, ha ceduto il campo al gentiluomo, inguantato, levigato, compassato, che offre a tutti e non da al alcuno, che spara bombe colassali colla maggior calma e serietà del mondo."

56. Rasi, Vol. 1, p. 513.

57. Baschet, A. *Les Comédiens italiens à la cour de France sous Charles IX, Henri III, Henri IV, et Louis XIII* (1882), pp. 67ff.

58. Rasi, Vol. 2, p. 513.

59. Bevilacqua, Enrico, in *Giornale storico della letteratura italiana* 23, 87: "Egli cita spesso il Petrarca, l'Ariosto e il Tasso, cita il Marino, il Chiabrera, il Caporali, reporta in verso di Dante, sebbene per isbaglio dica che e del Petrarca, recorda molti scrittoti greci e latini."

60. Indeed in Elizabethan drama the term "braggart" came to be applied to this Armado type rather than to the traditional Miles. Braggardino in Chapman's *The*

Blind Beggar of Alexandria is such a creature; and Osric in *Hamlet* once in the first quarto (V.2) in a stage direction is called a "braggart gentleman." Shakespeare was probably not the first English dramatist to introduce this Spanish braggart to the Elizabethan stage. Basilisco in Kyd's *Soliman and Perseda* is a mixture of braggart and virtuoso in the use of inflated verbiage, as Bond has noted in his introduction to this play. Miss Smith ("Italian and Elizabethan Comedy," *Modern Philology* 5, 562) calls this Basilisco "the forerunner of Shakespeare's Armado and Parolles."

61. A free translation of Ariosto's *Gli suppositi*, appearing in 1575.

62. (a) Schücking, L.L., *Studien über die Stöfflichen Beziehungen der englischen Komödie zur italienischen bis Lilly*, Halle, 1901.

(b) Wolf, Max, op. cit., pp. 1–20.

(c) Smith, Winifred, *The Commedia dell'Arte* (1912), pp. 172ff.

(d) The latest and most complete account of Italian companies in England is to be found in Chambers, E.K., *The Elizabethan Stage* (1923), Vol. 2, pp. 261–265. This I follow rather closely.

63. *Acts of the Privy Council* Vol. 2, p. 88.

64. Edited by Feuillerat, A., *Documents Relating to the Office of Revels in the Time of Queen Elizabeth* . . . (London, 1903), pp. 225ff.

65. Murray, J.T., *English Dramatic Companies 1558–1642*, Vol. 2, p. 374.

66. Chambers (op. cit., p. 262) points out that "Queen Elizabeth was at Windsor on 11 and 12 July; on 15 July she removed to Reading and remained there to July 22."

67. Chambers suggests that this is probably a clerical error for Alfonso Ferrabosco, the first of three generations of that name attached to the English Court. Cf. Arkwright, G.E.P. *Notes on the Ferrabosco Family (The Musical Antiquary)*, Vol. 3, p. 221; IV, 42.

68. *Acts*, etc., Vol. 10, p. 144. Quoted by Smith, p. 175.

69. *History of English Dramatic Poetry* (1826), Vol. 3, p. 398, note.

70. Cf. Rasi, op. cit., under "Martinelli."

71. Dr. Furness, referring to the visit of this company, remarks (*Much Ado About Nothing*, Variorum Ed., Intro., p. xxvii) that it is evidence of "an intimate relationship at that early date between the English and the Italian stage, of which too little account is made by those who wish to explain Shakespeare's knowledge of Italian manners and names."

72. D'Ancona, Alessandro, *Teatro Montovano nel secolo XVI, Giornale storico*, Vol. 4, p. 37.

73. Winifred Smith, in "Italian and Elizabethan Comedy," *Modern Philology* 5, 557, says there there is no particular reason why the *Inganni* of Alessandro Piccolomini, which many have compared to *Twelfth Night*, may not have been given in London by the Italian actors.

74. Miss Smith (ibid.) says that Coryat in his *Crudities* (London, 1776, from ed. of 1611), Vol. 2, pp. 16, 17, must be alluding to such a company in his comment on a play he attended in Venice. "I saw women acte, a thing I never saw before, though I have heard it hath been sometimes used in London." Visiting Italians were the only ones who in those days could have had women actors in their troupes.

75. Nash, *Pierce Pennilesse* (1592, ed. Grosart), p. 92.

76. Cf. Smith, *Commedia dell'Arte*, p. 177; also Schücking, pp. 58ff.

77. For the text, see *The Shakespeare Society Publications*, No. 2, 1841.

78. For the text, see Hazlitt, *The English Drama and Stage under the Tudor and Stuart Princes: 1543–1664* (Roxburgh Library, 1859), pp. 157ff.

79. It is well known that the age of Shakespeare's youth was, as Schelling says (*Foreign Influences in Elizabethan Plays*, p. 49), "literally soaked in Italian literature and fiction."

80. The word was frequently used to mean a disguise or mumming. In the *Documents Relating to the Office of Revels 1559–60* one may read such entries as "A Maske of Patriarkes" and "A Maske of Italyen Women."

81. The almost universal knowledge of Italian among Elizabethan courtiers and gentlemen of distinction (cf. Schelling, *Foreign Influences in Elizabethan Plays*, p. 41) did not extend to the popular playwrights.

82. See Neri, Ferdinando, *Scenari delle maschere in Arcadia* (Città di Castello, 1913). Number I of *Documenti di storia letteraria italiana*, edited by Pietro Mattiacci, for the text. Cf. also Gray, Henry David, "The Sources of *The Tempest*," *Modern Language Notes* 35 (1920), 321.

83. He refers to Pantalone as "the old Pantaloon" in *The Taming of the Shrew*, III.1.37; as "the lean and slippered Pantaloon" in *As You Like It*, II.vii.158; as "the old Magnifico" in *Othello*, I.2.12. Cf. Smith, op. cit., pp. 178ff., where references of a similar sort by other Elizabethan dramatists are also collected.

84. *Love's Labour's Lost*, V.2.463.

85. *Le Bravure del Capitano Spavento . . . di Francesco Andreini da Pistoria Comico Geloso* (Venetia, 1607), Ragiomento ventesimo, pp. 134–141.

86. Cf. p. 138: "Quella notte tremo più volte l'Inferno, mentre ch'io rompeva lancie con la mia bella sposa, e per quanco io mi sapessi fare non hebbi gratia di renderla gravida di me, peresser ella troppo furiosa negli amorosi conflitte et per haver la matrice arsa, e bruciata."

87. *Il Fedela*, written by Luigi Pasqualigo.

88. In a description, written by Massuno Trojano, of an improvised comedy which he, as court choir-master, wrote for presentation at the Duke of Bavaria's wedding in 1568. Cf. Smith, op. cit., p. 70.

89. He is introduced "alla Cavajola." That is, he impersonated the peasant as he appeared in the "farse caviole," which represented the life of the folk in the southern Italian town of Cava. Cf. Torraca, F., *Il teatro italiano nei secoli XIII, XIV, XV* (Firenze, 1885), pp. 431ff.

90. Cf. Smith, op. cit., p. 70.

91. He inherits certain traits of a Pagliaccio of an earlier company and of a character called Bertoldino. Cf. the present author's *The Comedies of Holberg*, pp. 175 and 350.

92. III.2.

93. Ibid.

94. Variorium of 1821, p. 479: "By Holofernes is designed a particular character, a pedant and a schoolmaster of our author's time, one John Florio. . . ."

95. *William Shakespeare* (translated by L. Dora Schmitz, 1888), p. 37: "There is, probably, little doubt that the poet has immortalized Thos. Hunt as Holofernes."

96. Acheson, *Shakespeare and the Rival Poet* (1903), p. 83.

97. This play has been considered to be a possible source of *Twelfth Night*. Dr. Furness goes so far as to suggest that this might be one of the dramas brought to England by Drousiano in 1577–78 (*New Variorum Twelfth Night*, p. xxi). This play was also translated into Latin under the title of *Laelia* and presented at Queens College, Cambridge, in 1590 and again in 1598. Cf. Churchill and Keller, *Shakespeare Jahrbuch* 24 (1898), pp. 286, 291.

98. The characteristics of this pedant are important for our purpose, because he is one of a very few representatives of the Italian type who appeared in extant plays written before Shakespeare began to compose.

99. See note 52.

100. IV.2.

101. IV.2.10ff.

102. V.1.75–77.

103. In the Folio text this is written as gibberish: "Venice, venchie, que non te unde, que non te perreche." Theobald was the first to discern the Italian proverb in this hash. Scherillo (*La Via italiana nel seicento*, p. 336) finds this like similar speeches of the Dottore Gratiano, the pedant in the Gelosi company.

104. V.1.14–15.

105. V.1.87–90.

106. IV.2.80–83.

107. V.1.25. This speech is given to Nathaniel in the Folio, but obviously belongs to Holofernes, as Theobald was the first to see. After the first eighty lines of this scene there is much confusion in the attribution of speeches to Holofernes and Nathaniel. Fleay first (*Life*, p. 203) finds the origin of the confusion in the hurried retouching of the scene for a court performance. Later (*Anglia* 7, p. 229) he says that in the first draft of the play Holofernes was curate and Nathaniel the pedant. Dr. Furness (*Variorum*, p. 136) prefers the traditional scapegoats—the compositors or compositors' reader. I follow the attribution of the Cambridge editors.

108. IV.2.135.

109. V.1.24–26.

110. Rasi, Vol. 1, p. 407: "Il Dottore è sempre il solito ignorantone, saccentone, che sputa sentenze, con mescolanza inevitabile di latino maccheronico, di citazioni spropositate, di etimologie bislacche. . . . Segno evidente che il tipo vero del Graziano ebbe al cospetto del pubblico per base unica la saccenteria ignorante, la etimologia insula, la storpiature grottesca di vocaboli, la buffoneria delle citazioni latine."

111. Ibid., p. 412.

112. *Il Pedantee*, Giorno 31.

113. Compare the following speech of Holofernes: "Me hercule, if their Sonnes be ingennuous, they shall want no instruction. If their daughters be capable, I will put it to them. But *vir sapis qui pauca loquitur*." Numerous editors, beginning with Steevens and Malone, have caught a *double entendre* in these lines. In spite of good Dr. Furness's irritation at the ignoble minds of the critics, the double meaning seems to be in the text.

114. *Shakespeare Jahrbuch* 34 (1898), pp. 256ff.

115. Sir John Harington in his *Apology for Poetry*, written in 1591, speaks of the play, so that it was performed before this date.

116. Churchill and Keller (op. cit.) think that the presence of a second pedant Dromodotus in the school-comedy *Paedantius* proves that Shakespeare had this situation in this Latin play in mind when he introduced both Holofernes and Nathaniel into *Love's Labour's Lost*. Dromodotus is called Philosophus and is a scholastic ridiculously wedded to his medieval jargon. Nathaniel is not a second pedant; he is a lightly-sketched parasite of "affamato," as he was called in Italian comedy. Only in the confused attribution of speeches in Act IV, Sc.2, of the Folio text does he seem to be a second pedant.

117. *Molière et la Comédie Italienne*, 2nd ed., Paris, 1867.

118. *Supposes*, I.3: "I am of the householde with this scholer Erostrato [his rival] as well as with Domine Cleander; now with the one, and then with the other, according as I see their caters provide good cheere at the market."

119. Birowne enumerates them all except the constable (V.2.545), "The Pedant, the Braggart, the Hedge-Priest, the Foole, and the Boy."

LOVE'S LABOUR'S LOST

ONE OF SHAKESPEARE'S FIRST BOWS

Jacques Copeau

Too many clouds obscure the dialogue in this play. But sudden bursts of sunshine occur and set the characters, their feelings, their ideas, and their positions in the landscape into such lively relief and color that we become quite taken with them. Then would we like to catch hold of these amiable spirits, but they escape into the shadows and elude us.

It is from this perspective that Shakespeare's commentators regard this play, his first work, with something like spitefulness, and are more or less unanimous in their disparagement of it.

The play dates to 1590. Shakespeare is twenty-six years old when he writes it. His instrument, the English language, is still in a state of flux. There is no linguistic identity for the various provinces, nor any difference between court, city, and rural language. Nor between the spoken and the written, between the handwritten and the printed. The illiterate masses feel their way through these ambush-ridden terrains. They hear words and sentences; never do they see any.

Two things result from this. First, their auditory skills are highly developed and they are extraordinarily sensitive to the spoken word. Second, when their memory fails, however rarely that may happen, their imaginations leap to fill the gaps. They invent.

Thus, certain words, certain expressions are imprinted on their minds in erroneous form. Like children who don't know how to read, people construct false mental impressions that translate into spoken language through frequent errors, through ill-conceived applications to objects and ideas, all

Originally published as "*Vain Labeur d'Amour* ou les débuts de Shakespeare," *Le Figaro Littéraire* (18 August 1942), 3–4. Avec l'aimable autorisation du journal Le Figaro, Copyright Le Figaro 1994, par Jacques Copeau. Translated from the French especially for this collection by Mari Pappas.

of which strikes more educated ears as genuine wordplay, like puns.

It is easy to see how common man gets by in the domain of the "more or less." There he enjoys a margin of freedom to try his creative faculties. There he finds a point of departure for a purely verbal art where irregularities do not seem systematically and irritatingly gratuitous, as they do for us.

We know from a contemporary source that in the Elizabethan period enthusiasm for words was cultivated as a sport and as an art, according to well-established practice which imparted to pleasant conversation the tactics of a military battle.

It must be admitted that five-sixths of the text of *Love's Labour's Lost* is that very thing: a battle of words, a series of skirmishes—more or less brilliant, more or less insufferable—among "corrupters of words":

> The tongues of mocking wenches are as keen
> As is the razor's edge invisible,
> Cutting a smaller hair than may be seen
> Above the sense of sense; so sensible
> Seemeth their conference, their conceits have wings
> Fleeter than arrows, bullets, wind, thought, swifter things.

> (V.2.256–61)

It is expected that a boy and girl probe each other's intentions. It is natural that no mercy be shown in these exercises. They include sharp little pecks and great gnashings of teeth. We exhaust ourselves trying to give their voices the words of our language and our times. Those who stubbornly persist generally arrive at nothing more than exchanges of obscurities.

Let these children work themselves up to the point that the vocal cords upon which they rail ring false. Let them wear themselves out and unleash real nastiness at each other rather than holding back with zinging rejoinders. Tears are never very far away, as in Marivaux. Happily, in this case, the Princess is a princess of France, who presides as a kind of referee, when she herself is not engaged in sparring. She is there to correct lapses of taste and tact, to recall her ladies to propriety, or to congratulate those who best play the game.

From this multi-toned intensity, from this verbal false sublimity, from these endless comparisons borrowed from geography, astronomy, and mythology, from this metaphorization of the living universe by the dead writings of antiquity, there arises an atmosphere in which the artificial prevails, where the ornamental entwines, encrusts, and smothers the being of flesh and blood.

But it also happens that among so many expressions born of airy nothing if not out of idleness, glum counsel, and the impetus of aggressive *preciosité*, they discover a sentiment of honest origin, true and valid. It breaks free, rushes forth, and surfaces in a great gulp of air. It sparkles for an instant of extraordinary brilliance, then returns to nothingness. And we are left delighted and disappointed. Delighted to have picked up the echo of a poetry that is none other than that of the Sonnets. Disappointed to have been powerless to preserve it against an offensive return of pedantic affectation and excessive foppery.

Love's Labour's Lost bears a certain resemblance to *Much Ado About Nothing*. The Princess of France calls to mind by her grace, her decency, and her humanity the Countess Olivia of *Twelfth Night*. And the pageant of the Nine Worthies in the fifth act foreshadows *A Midsummer Night's Dream*. There we have what makes this comedy so precious to us. We find in it the born playwright serving his apprenticeship in his art. Here is what one of Shakespeare's finest critics, Harley Granville-Barker, called "his dramatic innocence."

"His dramatic innocence. . . ." We would like to linger with this beautiful phrase and extract from it all that it contains. Writers of genius have all left in their earliest efforts some sovereign traces and accents that the maturity of their talent, in far stronger and more balanced works, has never recovered. This is true especially of the dramatist. There is in theatrical talent, in aptitude for the stage, a large measure of predestination, of that which we call "the gift." There is also a measure, at least as important, of adjustment, of experimentation, of that which we call "craft." In the long run, the gift is completely debased by the craft. But how lucky we are to discover it, this gift, in a work absolutely lacking in experience and maturity, intact and in a state of innocence, still rough-hewn and full of itself.

First sign of innocence: disregard of theatrical formulae. The play, as it were, has no subject. And in terms of identifying the characters—whether or not the Princess of France is Catherine de Medici; the King of Navarre, Henri IV; Dumaine, the fat Duc de Mayenne; and little Moth named after the French ambassador LaMotte—we are not qualified to decide. All that we know is that if the comedy truly originated in 1590, it dates from the same year as the Battle of Ivry.

But let us leave history and endeavor rather to reconcile ourselves with poesy; that is to say, with Shakespeare. Shakespeare leads us into a French landscape:

Let fame, that all hunt after in their lives,
Live register'd upon our brazen tombs.

Thus begins the first act. A king, who is perhaps but a duke, decides to confine himself for three years within his court, together with three of his companions, and there to devote himself to austere studies, augmented by an appropriate dose of asceticism: little sleep, little nourishment, and no women. One of the three friends, Berowne, objects to the extreme rigor of the contract, protests that it cannot be observed, and that the edict, moreover, must necessarily be held in abeyance in view of the announced arrival of a beautiful princess, daughter of the king of France, accompanied by three maids of honor.

The ladies are already encamped nearby and pass the time composing verbal portraits. Maria, Catherine, and Rosaline know something of Longaville, Dumaine, and Berowne, having once been introduced to them. One suspects that these three little females realize they are susceptible as prey to those three males. And nothing is more pleasing than the comments by each of them about the lord who will presently press his attentions on her. First Longaville is "drawn" by Maria:

[Here Copeau gives the French version of II.1.40–78.]

Four ladies against four gentlemen: the quadrille is set. The author already resolves to exploit these four couples for every possible entanglement. He throws into the dance an extravagant Spaniard, a ridiculous parson, an ultra-pedantic schoolmaster, an idiot constable, a doltish yet cunning peasant, an impish page who sings and dances, which will suffice, the author thinks, to achieve all the elements of farce and comedy. And it is the alternated "entrances" of these diverse, contrasting characters that will suffice to give form to the work by maintaining its rhythm, movement, and interest.

And naturally, from the first encounter, the gentlemen and ladies attack one another reciprocally. "Did I not dance with you in Brabant once?" Berowne asks Rosaline. They move into position for this duel that lasts to the very end of the comedy and that is, in essence, the comedy itself.

Each of the lords is smitten by love. Each of the ladies decides to make a mockery of it. Each of the lords writes a love poem. We see them appear, one after the other: Berowne, the King, Longaville, Dumaine, each clutching a paper in hand and reading it to himself, believing himself to be alone. But Longaville unmasks Dumaine, the King unmasks Longaville, Berowne unmasks the King, and, when he has concluded his discourse, Berowne sees himself unmasked by the trio:

Sweet lords, sweet lovers, O! let us embrace.
As true we are as flesh and blood can be:

The sea will ebb and flow, heaven show his face;
Young blood doth not obey an old decree:
We cannot cross the cause why we were born;
Therefore, of all hands must we be forsworn.   (IV.3.210–5)

It remains only for them to conquer the lovely young women. This calls for a disguise. A conspiracy is launched. But Boyet, the Princess's steward, is there to expose and disclose:

[Here Copeau quotes the French version of V.2.82–118.]

And so, mockery for mockery. The four young ladies mask themselves and, to trick their suitors, exchange amongst themselves the love tokens they have received. Then, when the four suitors present themselves, disguised as Muscovites, themselves masked, and preceded by their little ambassador, the women execute a half-turn, as in a dance, turning their backs to the men. This doesn't deter these gentlemen from pressing their point. But a mere mask suffices to cause love to miss its mark. This very much debases love. And unfortunately—for us, at least—it culminates only in four duos alternating the usual double meanings, word games, and spoonerisms.

These characters are not very sensual. We rarely witness among them any signs of love beyond a kiss of the hand. Nor does the passionate chase seek anything other than a spiritual satisfaction. But all the same, these lively dialogues among eight masks, four of them rigged up in Russian style, decidedly possess a certain scenic intensity. They even achieve an aura of the fantastic. In order to depict them completely, we must not forget that the roles of women were played by young boys. And certainly this circumstance must have driven the author to seek the best of his effects in verbal virtuosity, considering that these boy-girls probably spoke in a pitch that gave these mouthed battles a particular vitality.

Everything concludes with an entertainment that occupies a large portion of the fifth act. It is a pageant of the "Nine Worthies," which is, fittingly, presented by the grotesque characters of the comedy. It is not only that the lilliputian page is charged with a role made to measure—Hercules!—but what is most emphasized here: the cruelty of the young lords toward the poor figures appearing before them in the improvised scene. Two or three of them gang up to silence the poor out-of-breath pedant. And he, before resolving to exit the scene, tells them piteously: "This is not generous, not gentle, not humble."

The final stroke is, in my opinion, totally remarkable. It is not unusual for Shakespeare to reach into his bag of tricks up to the very last moment. His comedies sometimes have not exactly multiple denouements, but several lulls, from which interest, surprise, or emotion rebound. And these gushes of poetry, these pulses from an inexhaustible source, possess a singular charm.

In this case, I do not know whether it is a question of extraordinary audacity or, more likely, tremendous innocence that translates into incredible nerve. The audience can decide. Everything that needs to be said has been said. The gallants have made honorable amends. The ladies are appeased. The buffoons have played the fools and spoken nonsense beyond measure. There is nothing left but to take a bow and ring down the curtain.

It is at this moment that the poet chooses to introduce a new character. A messenger, named Marcade. To make a speech? No. Look at this:

> *Enter Monsieur Marcade, a Messenger.*
> MARCADE. God save you, madam!
> PRINCESS. Welcome, Marcade,
> But that thou interrupt'st our merriment.
> MARCADE. I am sorry, madam; for the news I bring
> Is heavy in my tongue. The king your father—
> PRINCESS. Dead, for my life!
> MARCADE. Even so: my tale is told.

And, indeed, Marcade says nothing more. He fades from the picture.

Berowne enjoins the actors to retire, as "the scene begins to cloud." Utter silence. And how, at this point, can the play regain the appropriate tone that will carry us to the end of the comedy? The Princess addresses her steward:

> PRINCESS. Boyet, prepare: I will away tonight.
> KING. Madam, not so: I do beseech you, stay.
> PRINCESS. Prepare, I say. I thank you, gracious lords,
> For all your fair endeavors; and entreat,
> Out of a new-sad soul, that you vouchsafe
> In your rich wisdom to excuse or hide
> The liberal opposition of our spirits,
> If over-boldly we have borne ourselves
> In the converse of breath; your gentleness
> Was guilty of it. Farewell, worthy lord!
> A heavy heart bears not a humble tongue. . . . (V.2.719–29)

And in the refuge of this delicate veil of sadness, a new dialogue emerges between the pairs. Dialogue full of discretion and sensibility, through which the true feelings of the characters penetrate little by little. Both sides recognize that their words disguised them, that all this vain labor was deservedly painful and decidedly foolish. The ladies impose delays, proofs. And although this supreme moment is "a time, methinks, too short to make a world-without-end bargain in," we know that one day, an hour will come when the contract will be sealed.

Now the buffoons may return. They may again smile while singing a little song. When they have sung, the Captain will say: "You that way; we this way," and they will depart one and all, without further ado.

LOVE'S LABOUR'S LOST

Bobbyann Roesen (Anne Barton)

In a sense the play has ended; an epilogue has been spoken by Berowne and that haunting and beautiful kingdom created by the marriage of reality with illusion destroyed, seemingly beyond recall. In the person of Marcade, the world outside the circuit of the park has at last broken through the gates, involving the people of the play in its sorrows and grim actualities, the plague-houses and desolate retreats, the mourning cities and courts of that vaster country overshadowing the tents and the fantastic towers of Navarre. Yet before the final dissolution of that minute and once isolated kingdom of the play, when some of the characters seem already to have disappeared and the others are preparing sadly to journey into the realms beyond the walls of the royal close, there is granted suddenly a little moment of grace. In the waning afternoon, all the people of the play return to the stage and stand quietly together to hear the song which "the two learned men have compiled in praise of the Owl and the Cuckoo," a song into which the whole of that now-vanished world of *Love's Labour's Lost* seems to have passed, its brilliance, its strange mingling of the artificial and the real, its loveliness and laughter gathered together for the last time to speak to us in the form of a single strain of music.

> When daisies pied and violets blue
> And lady-smocks all silver-white
> And cuckoo-buds of yellow hue
> Do paint the meadows with delight. . . .

It is the landscape of the royal park that lies outstretched before us, a little world of thickets and smooth lawns, meadows and wooded hills. In the foreground, their appearance and speech as decorative and charming as

Originally published in *Shakespeare Quarterly* (1953), 411–426. Reprinted by permission.

the setting in which they have met to solemnize their vows of asceticism and study, stand four young men, Berowne, Dumain, Longaville, and that ruler of Navarre whose slender kingdom of foresters and dairy-maids, courtiers, pedants, and fools seems bounded by the park and its single, rustic village. Mannered and artificial, reflecting an Elizabethan delight in patterned and intricate language, Navarre's lines at the beginning of the play are nevertheless curiously urgent and intense.

> Let fame, that all hunt after in their lives,
> Live regist'red upon our brazen tombs,
> And then grace us in the disgrace of death;
> When, spite of cormorant devouring Time,
> Th' endeavor of this present breath may buy
> That honour which shall bate his scythe's keen edge,
> And make us heirs of all eternity.

With the King's first words, an expression of that peculiarly Renaissance relationship of the idea of Fame with that of Time and Death, a shadow darkens for a moment the delicate dream landscape of the park. Touched by this shadow, affected by its reality, the four central characters of *Love's Labour's Lost* enter the world of the play.

Fantastic and contrived as they are, those absurd vows to which the four friends commit themselves in the initial scene spring from a recognition of the tragic brevity and impermanence of life that is peculiarly Renaissance. For the people of the sixteenth century, the world was no longer the mere shadow of a greater Reality, the imperfect image of that City of God whose towers and golden spires had dominated the universe of the Middle Ages. While the thought of Death was acquiring a new poignancy in its contrast with man's increasing sense of the value and loveliness of life in this world, Immortality tended to become, for Renaissance minds, a vague and even a somewhat dubious gift unless it could be connected in some way with the earth itself, and the affairs of human life there. Thus there arose among the humanist writers of Italy that intense and sometimes anguished longing, voiced by Navarre at the beginning of *Love's Labour's Lost*, to attain "an immortality of glory, survival in the minds of men by the record of great deeds or of intellectual excellence. . . . "[1] At the very heart of the plan for an Academe lies the reality of Death, the Renaissance desire to inherit, through remarkable devotion to learning, an eternity of Fame, and thus to insure some continuity of personal existence, however slight, against the ravages of "cormorant devouring Time."

It is obvious, however, from the very beginning of the play, that the Academe and the idea of immortality which it embodies must fail. Less remote and docile than Dumain and Longaville, existing upon a deeper level of reality within the play, the brilliant and sensitive Berowne, a Chorus character throughout, first realizes how unnatural the vows are, how seriously they trespass, despite their three-year limit, against the normal laws of life and reality. The paradox of the Academe and the reason why its failure is not only understandable but absolutely necessary lie in the fact that this elaborate scheme which intends to enhance life and extend it through Fame and even beyond the boundaries of the grave would in reality, if successfully carried out, result in the limitation of life and, ultimately, in its complete denial. In their very attempt to retain hold upon life, the King and his companions, as Berowne alone understands, are cutting themselves off from it, from love, and the beauty of women, from all those simple sensuous pleasures of the world which have prompted the establishment of the Academe in the first place by making the "too much loved earth more lovely,"[2] and the thought of its loss in Death so unbearably grim.

Long before the appearance of those two delightful but sobering characters, Holofernes and Nathaniel, Berowne has seen the barrenness of learning that is divorced from life, the tragedy of those industrious men of science who find a name for every star in the western skies and yet "have no more profit of their shining nights / Than those that walk and wot not what they are." Even in the first scene of the play, before his love for Rosaline has made his perception deeper and more sensitive, Berowne realizes in some sense that the only way to deal with the bleak reality of Death and Time is to accept it, to experience as much of life's sensory loveliness as possible while the opportunity is still given. Implicit in his earliest lines is the knowledge, related somehow to the first group of the Sonnets, that "we cannot cross the cause why we were born," and although he agrees at last to take the oath, it is through him that we first sense the conviction expressed by the play as a whole that this idea of intellectual glory is an essentially sterile one, that the price exacted is too great to pay for a fame and a memory on earth that will soon be lost in the unimagined reaches of Time.

It was one of Walter Pater's most famous dictums that "All art constantly aspires towards the condition of music,"[3] and in his beautiful essay on "Shakespeare's English Kings" he asserted more particularly that "into the unity of a choric song the perfect drama ever tends to return, its intellectual scope deepened, complicated, enlarged, but still with an unmistakable singleness, or identity, in its impression on the mind."[4] Such a unity is evident throughout *Love's Labour's Lost*, and, indeed, the quality of the whole is very much that of a musical composition, an inexorable movement forward, the appearance and reappearance in the fabric of the play of certain important themes, forcing the harmony into a series of coherent resolutions consistent with each other and with the drama as a whole. Berowne has scarcely finished speaking before his assertion that "every man with his affects is born, / Not by might mast'red, but by special grace" is echoed in the structure of the comedy itself, with the entrance of Constable Dull and the reluctant Costard, the first to disobey the edicts of the new Academe.

The little episode which follows is not only significant of the trend of future action but, in itself, one of the most delightful moments of the play. As the King reads Armado's incredible accusation and Costard tries feebly to avert impending doom by making Navarre laugh, it becomes obvious for the first time how much enchantment the play holds for the ear, how subtly it combines highly individual idioms of speech into a single conversation. Love's Labour's Lost is a play of many voices, and much of its beauty grows from the sheer music of their rise and fall, the exploitation of their differences of quality and tone, accent and complication. Here in the first scene, the frank simplicity of Dull, the awed monosyllables of Costard, are placed by Shakespeare in a deliberate musical relationship with the studied sentences of Longaville, the fantastic style of Armado, and the more attractive elegance of Berowne, and the whole episode is given the quality of a polyphonic composition half artificial and half real.

Beyond its humor and fascination of language, the Costard scene has, of course, a more serious purpose in the play, a purpose virtually identical with that fulfilled by a scene in Measure for Measure. In the later comedy, Angelo appears in the opening scene of the second act in a role analogous to Navarre's in Love's Labour's Lost, and the old counsellor Escalus in one similar to Berowne's. The scheme of justice which Angelo would enforce in Vienna is as ridiculously inflexible, as ignorant of the nature of human beings as Navarre's Academe, and it is protested by Escalus. Not, however, until the sudden entrance of Constable Elbow, an Austrian cousin of Dull's, and Pompey, who can in some measure be compared to Costard, does it become completely obvious how impractical the system is, how helpless its high-minded idealism when forced to deal with real individuals, their private standards of morality and unpredictable human weaknesses. The fate of Angelo's justice is settled even before he himself has sinned agains it, in the process of that riotous contention between Elbow, Froth, and Pompey, and in the same way, Navarre's Academe has failed before he and his friends are actually forsworn, from the moment that the real and intensely individual figures of Costard and Dull appear in their respective roles as transgressor and upholder. Among the lower social levels of the park, life itself destroys the King's scheme almost in the moment of its foundation.

Walter Pater found *Love's Labour's Lost* particularly charming in its changing "series of pictorial groups, in which the same figures reappear, in different combinations but on the same background,"[5] a composition, for him, like that of some ancient tapestry, studied, and not a little fantastic. The grouping of the characters into scenes would appear, however, to have been dictated by a purpose far more serious than the mere creation of such patterns; it is one of the ways in which Shakespeare maintains the balance of the play world between the artificial and the real, and indicates the final outcome of the comedy.

There are, of course, huge differences in the reality of the people who walk and speak together within the limits of the royal park. From the artificial and virtually indistinguishable figures of Dumain and Longaville, never really more than fashionable voices, the scale of reality rises gradually towards Berowne, in whom the marriage of a certain remote and fantastic quality with the delightful realism which first recognized the flaws in the Academe reflects the comedy as a whole, and reaches its apogee in the utter substantiality and prosaic charm of Constable Dull, who could never in any sense be accused of retreating into unreality, or affecting an elegant pose. Again and again, characters from different levels along this scale are grouped into scenes in a manner that helps to maintain the delicate balance of the play world; thus, in the first scene, with the incredible idea of the Academe and the sophisticated dialogue of Berowne and Longaville, Costard and the bewildered Dull are employed in much the same way that the mocking voice of the cuckoo is in the glowing spring landscape of the closing song, to keep the play in touch with a more familiar and real world, as well as to indicate the ultimate victory of reality over artifice and illusion.

As the first act ends, this theme is repeated again, and the inevitability of future events made even more clear with the abandonment of the edicts of the Academe by the very individual who was responsible for the deliverance of Costard into the righteous hands of Dull, the intense and serious Armado. The grave figure of the Spanish traveller is one of the most interesting and in a sense enigmatic to appear in *Love's Labour's Lost*, and his sudden love for Jaquenetta is certainly the strangest of the five romances which develop within the park. Like Berowne, Armado is a very real person who is playing a part, but in his case it is far more difficult to separate the actor from the man underneath, and the pose itself is more complex than the fashionable role of Berowne. Even in his soliloquies, Armado seems to be acting to some invisible audience, and it is only in one moment at the end of the play that we are granted a glimpse of the man without the mask.

Romantic and proud, intensely imaginative, he has retreated into illusion much further than has Berowne, creating a world of his own within the world of the park, a world peopled with the heroes of the past, Samson and Hercules, Hector and the knights of Spain. Somehow, it is among these long-dead heroes that Armado really exists, rather than among the people of the play itself, and his bizarre language, so strange and artificial when placed beside the homely speech of Costard, was created for that remote, imaginative environment and possesses there a peculiar beauty and aptness of its own. A character with some of the isolation of Jaques, always separated from the gibes and chatter of Moth, he falls in love with Jaquenetta without accepting her as the real country-wench she is, but creates a little drama about the object of his passion in which his is the central role, and Jaquenetta appears in any likeness that he pleases, Delilah or Deianira. The illusion in which the real character of Armado lives has its own beauty and charm, but as the play progresses it becomes evident that this illusion is not strong enough to withstand the pressure of reality and must in the end be destroyed.

With the coming into the King's park of the Princess of France and her companions a new stage in the development of *Love's Labour's Lost* has been reached, and a theme we have not heard before begins slowly to rise in the musical structure of the play. Before the arrival of the ladies, it has been made clear that the Academe must fail, and it is no surprise when in the opening scene of the second act we find each of the four friends stealing back alone after the initial meeting to learn the name of his love from the obliging Boyet. As life itself breaks swiftly through the artificial scholarship of the court, the vitality of the play rises to an amazing height; the Academe is kept constantly before us, the reasons for its failure elaborated and made more plain, but at the same time, while the world of the royal park becomes more and more delightful, while masque and pageantry, sensuous beauty and laughter flower within the walls, it becomes slowly obvious that more than the Academe will be destroyed by the entrance of the ladies. Not only its scholarship, but the entire world of the play, the balance of artifice and reality of which it was formed, must also be demolished by forces from without the walls.

The Princess and her little retinue represent the first penetration of the park by the normal world beyond, a world composed of different and colder elements than the fairy-tale environment within. Through them, in some sense, the voice of Reality speaks, and although they seem to fit perfectly into the landscape of the park, indulge in highly formal, elaborate skirmishes of wit with each other and with the men, they are somehow detached from this world of illusion and artificiality in a way that none of its original inhabitants are. The contrived and fashionable poses which they adopt are in a sense less serious, more playful than those of the other characters, and they are conscious all the time, as even Berowne is not, that these attitudes are merely poses, and that Reality is something quite different. With them into the park they bring past time and a disturbing reminder of the world outside, and from them come the first objective criticisms which pass beyond the scheme of the Academe to attack the men who have formed it. Maria, remembering Longaville as she saw him once before in Normandy, criticizes in her first speech the unreality with which the four friends have surrounded themselves, and points out for the first time in the play the danger of attitudes which develop without regard for the feelings of others, of wit that exercises itself thoughtlessly upon all.

In the wit of the ladies themselves, it is a certain edge of reality, an uncompromising logic, which cuts through the pleasant webs of artifice, the courtly jests and elaborations in the humor of the men, and emerges victorious with an unfailing regularity. Unlike the women, the King and his companions play, not with the facts themselves, but with words, with nice phrases and antithetical statements, and when their embroidered language itself has been attacked, their courteous offers disdained as mere euphemisms, they can only retire discomfited. Even Berowne is utterly defeated when he approaches Rosaline with his graceful conceits.

> BEROWNE. Lady, I will commend you to mine own heart.
> ROSALINE. Pray you, do my commendations;
>   I would be glad to see it.
> BEROWNE. I would you heard it groan.
> ROSALINE. Is the fool sick?
> BEROWNE. Sick at the heart.
> ROSALINE. Alack, let it blood.
> BEROWNE. Would that do it good?
> ROSALINE. My physic says "ay."

Witty as Berowne, as agile of mind, Rosaline attacks his conventional protestations with a wit based on realism, a ridicule springing from a consciousness of the absurdity of artifice. That Berowne could be expressing a real passion in these artificial terms never enters her mind; he is merely mocking her, and she defends herself in the most effective way she can.

Berowne is, however, like the King, Dumain, and Longaville, suddenly and genuinely in love. The Academe has been thoroughly demolished and now, in the fourth act, Shakespeare introduces, in the characters of Holofernes and Nathaniel, reminders of what such a scheme might have led to, examples of the sterility of learning that is unrelated to life. As usual, Dull, surely the most delightful of that illustrious Shakespearian series of dim-witted but officious representatives of constabulary law, appears with them as the realistic element in the scene, the voice of the cuckoo which mocks, unconsciously, the intricate speech of the two pedants. Bewildered as usual, Dull shows here a quality of stubbornness we had not quite expected in him, maintaining stolidly against the fantastic perorations of Holofernes and Nathaniel that the deer killed by the Princess was "not a haud credo; 'twas a pricket." It is one of the most charming of his infrequent appearances, matched only by that little scene later in the play in which, utterly stupefied by the conversation which he has endured from Holofernes and Nathaniel at dinner, he sits mute and quiescent through all the arrangements for the pageant of the Nine Worthies, only at the very last, when roused by another character, entering the dialogue at all to offer us a personal performance upon the tabor, a talent as engaging and unexpected in Dull as song is in the Justice Silence of 2 *Henry IV*.

Unlike Dull, the schoolmaster and the curate are in some sense mere types, elements of a satire, but Shakespeare is after all not writing a treatise, and even though their absurdity is emphasized, the two have a certain charm of their own, and their interminable quibblings a faint and grotesque beauty. On a lower, less refined level, they reflect the love of words themselves that is visible throughout the play, reveling, not like Armado in the romance and wonder of the past, but in Latin verbs and bits of forgotten erudition, spare and abstract. As Moth says, "They have been at a great feast of languages and stol'n the scraps," and in their conversation the wisdom of ages past appears in a strangely mutilated form, the life drained from it, curiously haphazard and remote.

When in the third scene of Act Four, Berowne appears alone on the stage, we move from the two pedants to a higher plane of reality, but one in which artifice is still present. Berowne's love for Rosaline is becoming increasingly intense, and although he seems at first only to be adopting another pose, that of a melancholy lover, he is slowly becoming, as the play progresses, a more convincing and attractive figure, and his love more real.

> By heaven, I do love; and it hath taught me to rhyme and to be melancholy; and here is part of my rhyme, and here my melancholy. Well, she hath one of my sonnets already; the clown bore it, the fool sent it, and the lady hath it; sweet clown, sweeter fool, sweetest lady.

Often, beneath ornament and convention the Elizabethans disguised genuine emotion. Berowne's love for Rosaline is as sincere as Philip Sidney's for Stella, his longing as real as that of the unknown Elizabethan lover in Nicholas Hillyarde's strangest and most haunting miniature who stands in the attitude of a familiar poetic conceit, gaunt and disheveled, against a background of flames.

The episode which follows Berowne's introductory soliloquy is, of course, one of the finest in the entire play. It is the first of three scenes in *Love's Labour's Lost* which possesses the quality of a play within the play, formal in construction, somehow contrived, always beautifully handled. Here, above the whole scene, Berowne acts as spectator and as chorus, establishing the play atmosphere in his various asides, crying out upon the entrance of Longaville, "Why, he comes in like a perjure, wearing papers," or in a more general affirmation,

> "All hid, all hid"—an old infant play,
> Like a demigod here sit I in the sky,
> And wretched fools' secrets heedfully o'er-eye.

Throughout *Love's Labour's Lost*, the play is a symbol of illusion, of unreality, as it is in *A Midsummer Night's Dream*, and here it is employed to render the artificiality, the convenient but obvious device of having each of the four lovers appear alone upon the stage, read aloud the poem addressed to his lady, and step aside for the advance of the next one, not only acceptable, but completely delightful. In this play environment, a level of unreality beyond that of the comedy as a whole, the multiple discoveries are perfectly convincing, and the songs and sonnets read by the lovers the charming testimonies of a passion that is not to be questioned.

Through the comments of the spectator, Berowne, the scene is still, however, kept in touch with reality. From his wonderful, rocketing line upon the entrance of the King, "Shot, by heaven!" to the moment when he steps from his concealment in all the splendor of outraged virtue, Berowne's role is again analogous to that of the cuckoo in the closing song, mocking the lovers "enamelling with pied flowers their thoughts of gold,"[6] maintaining the balance of the play. When he actually appears among his shamefaced friends to chide them for this "scene of fool'ry," the play within the play ends, as the spectator becomes actor, and we return, with his beautifully sanctimonious sermon, to the more usual level of reality.

The sheer delight of the scene rises now towards its peak as, only a few lines after the close of the play scene, another and even more effective climax is built up. Costard appears with Berowne's own sonnet written to Rosaline, and suddenly the play rises into magnificence. "Guilty, my lord, guilty. I confess, I confess." Berowne has become more real and brilliant than ever before, and at the same time, his speech attains a power and a radiance new in the comedy, an utterance still fastidious, still choice, but less self-conscious, as he sums up for Navarre, Dumain, and Longaville all that Shakespeare has been saying long before, in the Costard scene, in the fall from grace of Don Armado.

> Sweet lords, sweet lovers, O let us embrace!
> As true we are as flesh and blood can be.
> The sea will ebb and flow, heaven show his face;
> Young blood doth not obey an old decree.
> We cannot cross the cause why we were born,
> Therefore of all hands must we be forsworn.

Following these lines, there is a deliberate slackening of intensity, and the scene descends for a moment into a completely artificial duel of wits among the King, Berowne, and Longaville, on a somewhat hackneyed conceit. Berowne's toying with the various meanings of dark and light is as artificial and contrived as anything we have heard from him earlier in the play, but from these lines the scene suddenly rises to its final climax in that speech justifying the breaking of the vows, which is without a doubt the most beautiful in the entire play. "Have at you then, affection's men-at-arms." Finally and completely, the Academe has crumbled, and it is Berowne, as is perfectly proper, who sums up all that the play has been saying up to this point in his exquisite peroration upon earthly love.

"Other slow arts entirely keep the brain, / And therefore, finding barren practisers, / Scarce show a harvest of their heavy toil." Holofernes and Nathaniel are indirectly brought before us, the symbols of learning divorced from life, and having thus disposed of scholarship, Berowne passes on to speak of Love itself, and the task of justifying his own perjury and that of this three friends. Gradually, his speech rises to a lyrical height unequalled in the rest of the play, his customary eloquence and delicacy of language transfigured and made splendid, the sincerity perfectly blended with the surviving mannerism. "And when Love speaks, the voice of all the gods / Make heaven drowsy with the harmony." With these two lines, the final climax of the scene has been reached, lines of an almost incredible beauty, sensuous and languid, their exact meaning a little puzzling perhaps, but communicating all that is necessary, in a realm beyond precise explanation.

After these lines, the speech loses something of its beauty, but its intensity remains and fires the King, Dumain, and Longaville. The action flares up suddenly in great, vibrant lines; "Shall we resolve to woo these girls of France?" "Saint Cupid, then! and, soldiers, to the field," and in a whirlwind of vitality and excitement the scene moves towards its close. "For revels, dances, masks, and merry hours, / Forerun fair Love, strewing her way with flowers." Yet, as is customary with Shakespeare, the scene ends quietly, with two thoughtful foreboding lines which are prophetic of what is to come in the next act. As though he turned back for a second, musingly, in the act of going off with the others, Berowne, as Chorus, remarks more to himself and that deserted little glade which was the scene of the play within the play than to his retreating friends, "Light wenches may prove plagues to men forsworn; / If so, our copper buys no better treasure," lines which despite their apparent gaiety are curiously disturbing.

With the beginning of that long, last act, a turning point in the action of the play has been reached. The Academe defeated by life itself on all levels of the park, one might expect that *Love's Labour's Lost* would move now, as *Much Ado About Nothing* does in its final act, into an untroubled close, a romantic ending like that of the Beatrice-Benedick plot. As we have in some sense been told by the title, and by the comments of the ladies, such an ending is, in this case, impossible. From the Academe theme the play now turns to the destruction of the half-real world within the royal park, a destruction which, in the actual moment in which it is accomplished, is unexpected and shocking, and yet has been prepared for and justified by previous events within the comedy. As we enter the fifth act, shadows begin to fall across the play world. Life within the park, its brilliance and laughter, mounts higher and higher, yet it is the winter stanzas of the closing song that this act suggests, and a new darkness, a strange intensity forces the harmony of the play into unforeseen resolutions. Vanished now are the untroubled meadows of spring, and the landscape acquires a realism that is somehow a little harsh.

> When icicles hang by the wall,
> And Dick the shepherd blows his nail,
> And Tom bears logs into the hall,
> And milk comes frozen home in pail,
> When blood is nipp'd and ways be foul. . . .

With Act Five, the thought of Death enters the park. The play opened, of course, under the shadow of death, the great motivation of the Academe, but after that opening speech of Navarre's, it vanished altogether, never appearing again even in the imagery of the play until the entrance of the ladies. Significantly, it is they, the intruders from the outside world of reality, who, first, in Act Three, bring death into the park itself. In this act, the Princess kills a deer, but in the lines in which the hunt is spoken of, those of Holofernes and the Princess herself, the animal's death is carefully robbed of any disturbing reality. After Holofernes has told us how "The preyful Princess pierc'd and pricked / A pretty, pleasing pricket," the fate of the deer is as unreal as the wooded landscape over which it ran. It might just as well have sprung to its feet and gamboled off when the forester's back was turned.

Not until Act Five does the death image become real and disturbing, and even here, until the final entrance of Marcade, it is allowed to appear only in the imagery, or else in the recollection by some character of a time and a place beyond the scope of the play itself, the country of France where Katharine's sister died of her melancholy and longing, or that forgotten antiquity in which the bones of Hector were laid to rest. Appearing thus softened, kept in the background of the comedy, it is nevertheless a curiously troubling image, and as it rises slowly through the fabric of the play, the key of the entire final movement is altered. In the mask scene, Berowne, half-serious about his love and that of the King, Dumaine, and Longaville, cries to the ladies,

> Write "Lord have mercy on us" on those three;
> They are infected; in their hearts it lies;
> They have the plague, and caught it of your eyes.
> These lords are visited; you and I are not free,
> For the Lord's tokens on you I do see.

and while the image is playfully treated still, it is surely a curious and grotesque figure, this marriage of love, the symbol throughout the comedy of life itself, with death. One cannot imagine such an image appearing earlier in the play, before the outside world, the echoes of its great plague bells sounding through desolate streets, the lugubrious cries of the watchmen marking the doors of the infected houses, began to filter obscurely through the little kingdom of the park.

It is the tremendous reality of death which will destroy the illusory world of Navarre as thoroughly as the gentler forces of life destroyed the Academe and the artificial scheme it represented, earlier in the play. At the very beginning of the fifth act, it is made apparent why this must happen, why it is completely necessary for the world of the comedy, despite its beauty and grace, to be demolished. The Princess and her gentlewomen have been discussing the favors and the promises showered upon them by the King and his courtiers, laughing and mocking one another gently. Suddenly, the atmosphere of the entire scene is altered with a single, curious comment, a kind of overheard aside, made by Katharine, upon the real nature of Love. Rosaline turns to her, and as she remembers past time and a tragedy for which the god of Love was responsible then, the scene suddenly becomes filled with the presence of death.

> ROSALINE. You'll ne'er be friends with him: 'a kill'd your sister.
> KATHARINE. He made her melancholy, sad, and heavy;
> And so she died. Had she been light, like you,
> Of such a merry, nimble, stirring spirit,
> She might have been a grandam ere she died.
> And so may you; for a light heart lives long.

Against such a memory of the reality of love, the Princess and her three companions place the fantastic protestations of Navarre, Berowne, Dumain, and Longaville. As we have seen, their love is genuine; it has made the character of Berowne immeasurably more attractive, caused him no little anguish of spirit, created that great speech of his at the end of Act Four. Beneath the delicate language, the elegance and the gaiety, lies a real passion, but the women from the world outside, where love has been coupled for them with death and reality, see only artifice and pose. The artificiality which has become natural to the four friends and the environment in which they live holds them from the accomplishment of their desire, for the ladies, hearing from Boyet of the masque in which their lovers intend to declare themselves, are unable to perceive in the scheme anything but attempted mockery, and in defending themselves, frustrate the serious purpose of the entertainment.

> They do it but in mocking merriment,
> And mock for mock is only my intent. . . .
> There's no such sport as sport by sport o'erthrown,
> To make theirs ours, and ours none but our own;
> So shall we stay, mocking intended game,
> And they well mock'd depart away with shame.

This masque scene is, of course, the second of the plays within the play, less delightful than the one before it, but immensely significant, the part of audience and commentator played in this instance by Boyet. As usual, the men are completely defeated by the ladies, the delicate fabric of their wit and artifice destroyed by the realistic humor of their opponents. Berowne, approaching the supposed Rosaline with a courteous request, "White-handed mistress, one sweet word with thee," is mercilessly rebuffed by the Princess—"Honey, and milk, and sugar; there is three"—and the charming illusion of the masque itself ruined by the satiric comments of Boyet who, unlike Berowne in the earlier play scene, actually insinuates himself into the unreal world of the entertainment, and totally upsets it.

Even when the exposure is complete and the men have asked pardon from their loves, the women think only that they have defeated a mocking jest directed against them, not that they have prevented their lovers from expressing a genuine passion. For the first time, Berowne reaches utter simplicity and humbleness in his love; his declaration to Rosaline at the end of the masque scene is touching and deeply sincere, but for her, this passion is still unbelievable, a momentary affectation, and she continues to mock her lover and the sentiments he expresses.

> BEROWNE. I am a fool, and full of poverty.
> ROSALINE. But that you take what doth to you belong,
> It were a fault to snatch words from my tongue.
> BEROWNE. O, I am yours, and all that I possess.
> ROSALINE. All the fool mine?

More sensitive, gifted with a deeper perception of reality than his companions, Berowne seems to guess what is wrong, and he forswears "Taffeta phrases, silken terms precise, / Three pil'd hyperboles, spruce affectation, / Figures pedantical . . . ," at least to Rosaline, but the rejection itself is somewhat artificial, and he remains afterwards with more than "a trick of the old rage."

The masque has failed, and Berowne's more direct attempt to announce to the ladies the purpose behind the performance and detect in them an answering passion has been turned away by the unbelieving Princess. At this point, Costard enters to announce that Holofernes and Nathaniel, Moth and Armado are at hand to present the pageant of the Nine Worthies, and the third and last of the plays within the play begins. As we enter this play scene, the vitality and force of the comedy reaches its apogee, but in its laughter there rings now a discordant note that we have not heard before. The actors themselves are, after all, no less sincere than Bottom and his troupe in *A Midsummer Night's Dream,* and they are a great deal more sensitive and easy to hurt. They are real people whose intentions are of the very best, their loyalty to their

King unquestioned, and although their performance is unintentionally humorous, one would expect the audience to behave with something of the sympathy and forbearance exhibited by Duke Theseus and the Athenians.

The only civil members of the audience in *Love's Labour's Lost*, however, are the ladies. The Princess cannot resist one sarcasm upon the entrance of Armado, but it is addressed quietly to Berowne, before the play itself begins, while Armado is engrossed with the King and obviously does not hear. Thereafter, every one of her comments to the players is one of interest or pity: "Great thanks, great Pompey," "Alas, poor Maccabaeus, how hath he been baited," "Speak, brave Hector; we are much delighted." The players have only the Princess to appeal to in the storm of hilarity which assails them, and it is only she, realistic as she is, who understands that a play is an illusion, that it is to be taken as such and respected in some sense for itself, regardless of its quality. Like Theseus in *A Midsummer Night's Dream*, she realizes somehow that "the best in this kind are but shadows; and the worst are no worse, if imagination amend them,"[7] and when she addresses the players she is wise and sensitive enough to do so not by their own names, which she has read on the playbill, but by the names of those whom they portray, thus helping them to sustain that illusion which is the very heart of a play.

In contrast to that of the Princess, the behavior of the men is incredibly unattractive, particularly that of Berowne. It is difficult to believe that this is the same man who spoke so eloquently a short time ago about the soft and sensible feelings of love, and promised Rosaline to mend his ways. Costard manages to finish his part before the deluge, and Nathaniel, although unkindly treated, is not personally humiliated. Only with the appearance of Holofernes as Judas Maccabaeus and Armado as Hector is the full force of the ridicule released, and it is precisely with these two characters that the infliction of abuse must be most painful. Costard, after all, is a mere fool; he takes part in the baiting of the others with no compunction at all, and Nathaniel throughout the comedy has been little more than a foil for Holofernes, but the village pedagogue is a more sensitive soul, and not at all unsympathetic.

Holofernes has his own reality, his own sense of the apt and the beautiful which, though perverse, is meaningful enough for him, and it is exceedingly painful to see him stand here on the smooth grass of the lawn, his whole subjective world under merciless attack, a storm of personal epithets exploding about him.

DUMAIN. The head of a bodkin.
BEROWNE. A death's face in a ring.

LONGAVILLE. The face of an old Roman coin, scarce seen.
BOYET. The pommel of Caesar's falchion.
DUMAIN. The carv'd bone face on a flask.
BEROWNE. Saint George's half-cheek in a brooch.

The laughter is unattractive, wild, and somehow discordant, made curiously harsh by the introduction of Berowne's "death's face," and it has little resemblance to the laughter which we have heard in the play before this, delicate, sophisticated, sometimes hearty, but never really unkind. When Holofernes cries at the last, "This is not generous, not gentle, not humble," he becomes a figure of real dignity and stature, restrained and courteous in the face of the most appalling incivility.

Meanwhile, around the pedagogue and his little audience the afternoon has been waning slowly into evening, long shadows falling horizontally across the lawn, and Boyet calls after the retreating Holofernes in a strangely haunting line, "A light for Monsieur Judas. It grows dark, he may stumble." A kind of wildness grips all the men, and though Dumain says in a weird and prophetic line, "Though my mocks come home by me, I will now be merry," Armado faces a jeering throng even before he has begun to speak. Of all the players, Armado is the one for whom we have perhaps the most sympathy. He is a member of the court itself, has had some reason to pride himself upon the King's favor, and has been good enough to arrange the pageant in the first place. The people represented in it are those who inhabit that strange world of his fancy, and one knows that his anguish is not alone for his personal humiliation, but for that of the long-dead hero he portrays, when he cries, "The sweet war-man is dead and rotten; sweet chucks, beat not the bones of the buried; when he breathed, he was a man." A little grotesque, as Armado's sentences always are, the line is nevertheless infinitely moving in its summoning up of great spaces of time, its ironic relation to the idea of immortality through fame expressed in the opening speech of the comedy. Not since the reference to Katharine's sister have we had such a powerful and disturbing image of death brought before us, death real and inescapable although still related to a world and a time beyond the play itself.

In the remaining moments of the play scene, the hilarity rises to its climax, a climax becoming increasingly harsh. During the altercation between Costard and Armado which results from Berowne's ingenious but unattractive trick, images of death begin to hammer through the fabric of the play. The painfulness of the realism grows as Armado, poor, but immensely proud, is finally shamed and humbled before all the other characters. For the first time in the play, the mask falls from Armado's face, and the man beneath it is revealed, his romanticism, his touching personal pride, the agony for him of the confession that in his poverty he wears no shirt beneath his doublet. Still acting, he tries feebly to pass off this lack as some mysterious and romantic penance, but the other characters know the truth; Armado knows they do, and the knowledge is intensely humiliating. The illusion of the role he has played throughout *Love's Labour's Lost* is destroyed for others as well as for himself, and he stands miserably among the jeers of Dumain and Boyet while complete reality breaks over him, and the little personal world which he has built up around himself so carefully shatters at his feet.

The other people in the play are so concerned with Armado's predicament that no one notices that someone, in a sense Something has joined them. His entrance unremarked by any of the other characters, materializing silently from those shadows which now lie deep along the landscape of the royal park, the Messenger has entered the play world.

> MARCADE. I am sorry, madam, for the news I bring
>   Is heavy in my tongue. The King your father—
> PRINCESS. Dead, for my life!
> MARCADE. Even so; my tale is told.

There is perhaps nothing like this moment in the whole range of Elizabethan drama. In the space of four lines the entire world of the play, its delicate balance of reality and illusion, all the hilarity and overwhelming life of this last scene has been swept away and destroyed, as Death itself actually enters the park, for the first time, in the person of Marcade. Only in one Elizabethan madrigal, Orlando Gibbons' magnificent "What Is Our Life?" is there a change of harmony and mood almost as swift and great as this one, and it occurs under precisely the same circumstances, the sudden appearance among the images of life in Raleigh's lyric of "the graves that hide us from the searching sun"[8] the memory of the inescapable and tremendous reality of Death.[9]

Clumsy, as one always is in the presence of sudden grief, the King can think of nothing to say but to ask the Princess "How fares your Majesty?" a question to which she, from the depths of her sorrow and bewilderment, gives no reply, but prepares with the dignity characteristic of her to leave for France. Now, the men come forward uncertainly, and first the King and then Berowne, clinging still to a world no longer existing, attempt to express their love in terms which had been appropriate to that world, terms at first still incomprehensioble to the women and then, at last, understood, but not altogether trusted.

As vows had begun the play, so vows end it. The King is assigned as his symbol of reality a "forlorn and naked hermitage" without the walls of the royal park, in the real world itself, in which he must try for a twelvemonth if this love conceived in the sunlit landscape of Navarre can persist in the colder light of actuality. For Dumain and Longaville, those shadowy figures, penances more vague but of a similar duration are assigned, and then at last, Berowne, shaken and moved to the depths of his being, inquires from Rosaline, who has been standing a little apart from the others, lost in thought,

> Studies my lady? Mistress, look on me;
> Behold the window of my heart, mine eye,
> What humble suit attends thy answer there.
> Impose some service on me for thy love.

Slowly, speaking with great care, Rosaline answers, and in the strangest and most grotesque of penances, Berowne is condemned to haunt the hospitals and plague-houses of the world outside the park, to exercise his wit upon the "speechless sick," and try the power of his past role, the old artificiality that had no concern for the feelings of others, that humiliated Armado in the play scene, the careless mocks of the old world, upon the reality of the ailing and the dying. "A jest's prosperity lies in the ear / Of him that hears it, never in the tongue / Of him that makes it." It was this reality of actual living that Berowne was unconscious of when he led the unthinking merriment of the play scene just past. Yet, at the end of the year, love's labors will be won for Berowne, and he will receive Rosaline's love, not in the half real world of the park, but in the actuality outside its walls. Thus the play which began with a paradox, that of the Academe, closes with one as well. Only through the acceptance of the reality of Death are life and love in their fullest sense made possible for the people of the play.

The world of the play past has now become vague and unreal, and it is not distressing that Berowne, in a little speech that is really a kind of epilogue, should refer to all the action before the entrance of Marcade, the people who took part in that action and the kingdom they inhabited and in a sense created, as having been only the elements of a play. It is a play outside which the characters now stand, bewildered, a little lost in the sudden glare of actuality, looking back upon that world of mingled artifice and reality a trifle wistfully before they separate in the vaster realm beyond the royal park. Through *Love's Labour's Lost*, the play has been a symbol of illusion, of delightful unreality, the masque of the Muscovites, or the pageant of the Nine Worthies, and now it becomes apparent that there was a further level of illusion above that of the plays within the play. The world of that illusion has enchanted us; it has been possessed of a haunting beauty, the clear loveliness of those landscapes in the closing song, but Shakespeare insists that it cannot take the place of reality itself, and should not be made to. Always, beyond the charming, frost-etched countryside of the pastoral winter, like the background of some Flemish Book of Hours, lies the reality of the greasy kitchen-maid and her pot, a reality which must sooner or later break through and destroy the charm of the artificial and the illusory.

For us, however, knowing how Shakespeare's later work developed, and how the play image itself took on another meaning for him, there is a strange poignancy in this closing moment, with its confident assertion of the concrete reality of the world into which the characters are about to journey, the necessity for them to adjust themselves to that reality. Later, in *As You Like It* and *Hamlet* Shakespeare would begin to think of the play as the symbol, not of illusion, but of the world itself and its actuality, in *Macbeth* and *King Lear* as the symbol of the futility and tragic nature of that actuality, "that great strage of fools."[10] Yet he must always have kept in mind the image as it had appeared years before in the early comedy of *Love's Labour's Lost*, for returning to it at the very last, he joined that earlier idea of the play as illusion with its later meaning as a symbol of the real world, and so created the final play image of *The Tempest* in which illusion and reality have become one and the same, and there is no longer any distinction possible between them. The world itself into which Berowne and his companions travel to seek out reality will become for Shakespeare at the last merely another stage, a play briefly enacted,

> And, like the baseless fabric of this vision,
> The cloud-capp'd towers, the gorgeous palaces,
> The solemn temples, the great globe itself,
> Yea, all which it inherit, shall dissolve,
> And, like this insubstantial pageant faded,
> Leave not a rack behind. We are such stuff
> As dreams are made on; and our little life
> Is rounded with a sleep.[11]

Notes

*Bobbyann Roesen has also published on Shakespeare as Anne Righter and as Anne Barton.

1. Nesca Robb, *Neoplatonism of the Italian Renaissance* (London, 1935), p. 45.
2. Sir Philip Sidney, *The Defence of Poesie*, in *The Complete Works of Sir Philip Sidney*, ed. Feuillerat (Cambridge, 1923), Vol. 3, p. 8.

3. Walter Pater, "The School of Giorgione," in *The Renaissance* (New York, n.d.), p. 111.

4. Pater, "Shakespeare's English Kings," in *Appreciations* (London, 1901), pp. 203–204.

5. Pater, "*Love's Labour's Lost*," in *Appreciations*, p. 163.

6. Sidney, "Astrophel and Stella, Sonnet III," in *Silver Poets of the Sixteenth Century*, ed. Bullett (London, 1947), p. 173.

7. *A Midsummer Night's Dream*, V.1.

8. Sir Walter Raleigh, "What Is Our Life?", in *Silver Poets of the Sixteenth Century*, p. 296.

9. Wilfrid Mellers, in a series of lectures given on "Elizabethan and Jacobean Music," Stratford-upon-Avon, July, 1952.

10. *King Lear*, IV. 6.

11. *The Tempest*, IV. 1.

THE FOLLY OF WIT
AND MASQUERADE IN
LOVE'S LABOUR'S LOST

C.L. Barber

> For revels, dances, masques, and merry hours
> Forerun fair Love, strewing her way with flowers.

It seems likely that when in *Love's Labour's Lost* Shakespeare turned to festivity for the materials from which to fashion a comedy, he did so because he had been commissioned to produce something for performance at a noble entertainment. There can be no doubt about this in the case of *A Midsummer Night's Dream*, though just what noble wedding was graced by Shakespeare's dramatic epithalamium no one has been able to determine.[1] But though nothing in *Love's Labour's Lost* points unambiguously out across the dramatic frame to an original occasion, the way the fairy blessing does at the end of the later comedy, the whole character of the piece marks it as something intended for a special group, people who could be expected to enjoy the recondite and modish play with language and to be familiar, to the verge of boredom, with the "revels, dances, masques and merry hours" of courtly circles. Part of the character of the piece can be laid to the influence of Lyly. To use fantastic elaboration and artifice like Lyly's would be a natural thing in addressing Lyly's select audience. And whether or not the original occasion was an aristocratic entertainment, Shakespeare made a play out of courtly pleasures. Professor O.J. Campbell, and more recently Professor Alice S. Venezky, have pointed out that the pastimes with which the French Princess's embassy is entertained, the dances, the masque of Muscovites, the show of the Nine Worthies, the pageant of Winter and Summer, are exactly the sort of thing which was a regular part of court life.[2]

Although he probably worked initially on commission, Shakespeare's professional interests naturally led him to produce a piece which could be used afterward in the public theater. So instead of simply building make-believe around an audience who were on holiday, as the authors of parts and shows for entertainments were content to do, he needed to express holiday in a way that would work for anybody, any day. Topical reference that might violate the privacy of the original occasion had to be avoided, or taken out by revision—hence, probably, the bafflement of efforts to determine what the original occasion was. And there had to be protagonists whose experience in a plot would define the rhythm of the holiday, making it, so to speak, portable. When one considers the theatrical resources Shakespeare commanded in 1594 or thereabouts, the company's skilled team of actors accustomed to play up to each other, and the dramatist's facility with dialogue and plot, what is striking about *Love's Labour's Lost* is how *little* Shakespeare used existing action, story, or conflict, how far he went in the direction of making the piece a set exhibition of pastimes and games. The play is a strikingly fresh start, a more complete break with what he had been doing earlier than I can think of anywhere else in his career, unless it be where he starts to write the late romances. The change goes with the fact that there are no theatrical or literary sources, so far as anyone has been able to discover, for what story there is in the play—Shakespeare, here and in *A Midsummer Night's Dream*, and nowhere else, makes up everything himself, because he is making up action on the model of games and pastimes.

"Lose our oaths to find ourselves"

The story in *Love's Labour's Lost* is all too obviously designed to provide a resistance which can be triumphantly swept away by festivity. The vow to study and to see no woman is no sooner made than it is mocked. The French Princess is coming; the courteous king acknowledges that "She must lie here of mere necessity." And so Berowne can gleefully draw the moral:

> Necessity will make us all forsworn
> Three thousand times within this three years' space;
> For every man with his affects is born,
> Not by might mast'red, but by special grace. (I.1.150–153)

We know how the conflict will come out before it starts. But story interest is not the point: Shakespeare is presenting a series of wooing games, not a story. Fours and eights are treated as in ballet, the action consisting not so much in what individuals do as in what the group does, its patterned movement. Everything is done in turn: the lords are described in turn before they come on; each comes back in turn to ask a lady's name; each pair in turn exchanges banter. The dancing continues this sort of action; the four lords and four ladies make up what amounts to a set in English country dancing. We think of dancing in sets as necessarily boisterous; but Elizabethan dancing could express all sorts of moods as one can realize from such a dance as Hunsdon House, at once spirited and stately. The evolutions in *Love's Labour's Lost* express the Elizabethan feeling for the harmony of a group acting in ceremonious consort, a sense of decorum expressed in areas as diverse as official pageantry, madrigal and motet singing, or cosmological speculations about the order of the universe. John Davies's *Orchestra*, which runs the gamut of such analogies, is a poem very much in the spirit of *Love's Labour's Lost*.

A crucial scene, Act IV, Scene 3, dramatizes the folly of release taking over from the folly of resistance. Each lord enters in turn, reads the sonnet love has forced him to compose, and then hides to overhear and mock the next comer. As the last one comes in, Berowne describes their antics as a game of hide and seek:

> All hid, all hid—an old infant play.
> Like a demigod here sit I in the sky
> And wretched fools' secrets heedfully o'er-eye.
> More sacks to the mill. O heavens, I have my wish!
> Dumain transform'd! Four woodcocks in a dish! (IV.3.78–82)

Having wound them into their hiding places one-by-one, Shakespeare unwinds them one-by-one as each in turn rebukes the others. Berowne caps the king's rebuke of Dumain and Longaville with:

> Now step I forth to whip hypocrisy. (IV.3.151)

But he too is betrayed by Costard, so that he too must confess

> That you three fools lack'd me fool to make up the mess.
> He, he, and you—and you, my liege—and I
> Are pickpurses in love, and we deserve to die. . . .
> DUMAINE. Now the number is even.
> BEROWNE.   True, true! We are four. . . .   (IV.3.207–211)

The technique of discovery in this fine scene recalls the *sotties* presented by the French fool societies on their holidays, where the outer garments of various types of dignified pretension were plucked off to reveal parti-colored cloaks and long-eared caps beneath.[3] The similarity need not be from literary influence but from a common genesis in games and dances and in the conception that natural impulse, reigning on festive occasions, brings out folly. Berowne summarizes it all with "O, what a scene of fool'ry I have seen!"

Such comedy is at the opposite pole from most comedy of character. Character usually appears in comedy as an individual's way of resisting nature: it is the kill-joys, pretenders, and intruders who have character. Molière's great comedies of character distortion, *Tartuffe*, *Le Misanthrope*, are focused primarily on the pretender or the kill-joy; the celebrants, those who can embrace nature, are generally on the periphery until the resolution. But with Shakespeare, the celebrants are at the center. And when merrimakers say yes to nature, taking the folly of the time, the joke is that they behave in exactly the same way: "More sacks to the mill." "Four woodcocks in a dish!" The festive comedies always produce this effect of a group who are experiencing together a force larger than their individual wills. Berowne hails it, when the treason of all has been discovered, with

Sweet lords, sweet lovers. O, let us embrace!
As true are we as flesh and blood can be.
The sea will ebb and flow, heaven shows his face;
Young blood doth not obey an old decree. (IV.3.214–217)

In the early festive plays, one touch of nature makes the lovers rather monotonously akin; they tend to be differentiated only by accidental traits. But Shakespeare gradually learned to exhibit variety not only in the way people resist nature but also in the way they accept it.

Already in *Love's Labour's Lost* Berowne stands out, not by not doing what all do, but by being conscious of it in a different way. Where clownish wit calls a spade a spade, Berowne calls a game a game. He plays the game, but he calls it too, knowing what it is worth because he knows where it fits within a larger rhythm:

At Christmas I no more desire a rose
Than wish a snow in May's newfangled shows,
But like of each thing that in season grows. (I.1.105–107)

It is Berowne who is ordered by Navarre to "prove / Our loving lawful and our faith not torn" (IV.3.284–285). The set speech he delivers is Praise of

Folly such as we have seen in Nashe. It is often quoted as "the young Shakespeare's philosophy," despite the fact that it is deliberately introduced as equivocation, "flattery for this evil . . . quillets, how to cheat the devil" (IV.3.288). In proving that it is women's eyes which "sparkle still the right Promethean fire" (IV.3.351), Berowne adopts the same mock-academic manner and uses many of the same genial arguments as Nashe's Bacchus, the same used later by Falstaff in proving sack "the first humane principle."[4] The high point of Berowne's speech has a fine lyric force as he pleads the case for the creative powers that go with release in love. Then as he moves into his formal peroration, he heaps up reduplicative sanctions in a recklessly punning way which keeps us aware that his oration is special pleading—true, yet only a part of the truth:

> Then fools you were these women to foreswear;
> Or keeping what is sworn, you will prove fools.
> For wisdom's sake, a word that all men love;
> Or for love's sake, word that loves all men;
> Or for men's sake, the authors of these women;
> Or for women's sake, by whom we men are men—
> Let us once lose our oaths to find ourselves,
> Or else we lose ourselves to keep our oaths.
> It is religion to be thus foresworn;
> For charity itself fulfills the law,
> And who can sever love from charity? (IV.3.355–365)

He has turned the word "fool" around, in the classic manner of Erasmus in his *Praise of Folly*; it becomes folly not to be a fool. After reciprocally tumbling men and women around (and alluding to the sanctioning fact of procreation), the speech concludes with overtones of Christian folly in proclaiming the logic of their losing themselves to find themselves and in appealing from the law to charity. But Berowne merely leaps up to ring these big bells lightly; there is no coming to rest on sanctities; everything is in motion. The groups are swept into action by the speech—holiday action. Longaville breaks off the game of the oration with

> Now to plain-dealing. Lay these glozes by.
> Shall we resolve to woo these girls of France?
> KING. And win them too! Therefore let us devise
> Some entertainment for them in their tents.
> BEROWNE. First from the park let us conduct them thither;

Then homeward every man attach the hand
Of his fair mistress. In the afternoon
We will with some strange pastime solace them,
Such as the shortness of the time can shape,
For revels, dances, masques, and merry hours
Forerun fair Love, strewing her way with flowers. (IV.3.370–380)

The final joke is that in the end "Love" does not arrive, despite the lords' preparations for a triumphal welcome. That the play should end without the usual marriages is exactly right, in view of what it is that is released by its festivities. Of course what the lords give way to is, in a general sense, the impulse to love; but the particular form that it takes for them is a particular sort of folly—what one could call the folly of amorous masquerade, whether in clothes, gestures, or words. It is the folly of acting love and talking love, without being in love. For the festivity releases, not the delights of love, but the delights of expression which the prospect of love engenders—though those involved are not clear about the distinction until it is forced on them; the clarification achieved by release is this recognition that love is not wooing games or love talk. And yet these sports are not written off or ruled out; on the contrary the play offers their delights for our enjoyment, while humorously putting them in their place.

It is in keeping with this perspective that masquerade and show are made fiascos. Of course, to put shows or masques on the stage effectively, things must go in an unexpected way. Benvolio glances at the hazard of boredom in planning the masque in *Romeo and Juliet*, a play written only a year or two after *Love's Labour's Lost*:

The date is out of such prolixity.
We'll have no Cupid hoodwink'd with a scarf,
Bearing a Tartar's painted bow of lath,
Scaring the ladies like a crowkeeper;
Nor no without-book prologue, faintly spoke
After the prompter, for our entrance. . . . (*Romeo* I.4.3–8)

One way to make pageantry dramatic is to have what is pretended in masque or game actually happen in the play. This is what Shakespeare did with the masque in *Romeo and Juliet*, where the conventional pretense that the masquers were strangers asking hospitality is used in earnest, along with the fiction that, once disguise is assumed, anything can happen.

BENVOLIO. Away, be gone; the sport is at the best.
ROMEO. Ay, so I fear; the more is my unrest. (*Romeo* I.4.121–122)

The other way to make masquerades dramatic is to have the fiction of the game break down, which is the way things consistently go in *Love's Labour's Lost*. Moth, drilled to introduce the Muscovite masquers, is just such a halting prologue as Benvolio scorns. And the masquers' dance scarcely gets started:

> ROSALINE. Since you are strangers, and come here by chance,
>   We'll not be nice. Take hands. We will not dance.
> KING. Why take we hands then?
> ROSALINE. Only to part friends.
>   Curtsy, sweet hearts—and so the measure ends. (V.2.218–221)

In breaking off the dance before it begins, Rosaline makes a sort of dance on her own terms, sudden and capricious; and clearly the other ladies, in response to her nodded signals—"Curtsy, sweet hearts"—are doing the same pirouette at the same time. The princess describes this way of making a variation on a theme:

> There's no such sport as sport by sport o'erthrown—
> To make theirs ours, and ours none but our own. (V.2.153–154)

Though there is a certain charm in this patterned crossing of purposes, it is itself too often predicted and predictable. The king and his company, returning without their Muscovite disguises after being shamed hence, are unbelievably slow to believe that they were "descried." Berowne especially ought not to take so long to see the game:

> I see the trick on't. Here was a consent,
> Knowing aforehand of our merriment,
> To dash it like a Christmas comedy. (V.2.460–462)

When the commoners in their turn put on the Show of the Nine Worthies, the lords have their chance to join the ladies in dashing it, and the Princess gives a rationale for enjoying another kind of comic failure:

> Their form confounded makes most form in mirth
> When great things labouring perish in their birth. (V.2.520–521)

If all we got were sports that fail to come off, the play would indeed be nothing but labor lost. What saves it from anticlimax is that the most important games in which the elation of the moment finds expression are games with words, and the wordplay does for the most part work, conveying an experience of festive liberty. It is all conducted with zest and with constant exclamations about how well the game with words is going. Wordplay is compared to all sorts of other sports, tilting, dueling—or tennis: "Well bandied both! a set of wit well played." Or a game of dice:

> BEROWNE. White-handed mistress, one sweet word with thee.
> PRINCESS. Honey, and milk, and sugar: there is three.
> BEROWNE. Nay then, two treys, an if you grow so nice—
> Metheglin, wort, and malmsey. Well run, dice!
> There's half a dozen sweets.
> PRINCESS. Seventh sweet, adieu.
> Since you can cog, I'll play no more with you. (V.2.230–236)

Besides this sort of repartee, another aristocratic wooing game is the sonneteering. The lords each "turn sonnet" (I.2.190); love produces rhyme by reflex. "I do love, and it hath taught me to rhyme," Berowne confides to the audience, holding up a paper.

The aristocratic pastimes with language are set against the fantastic elaborations of the braggart and the schoolmaster, Armado puffing up versions of Euphuistic tautology and periphrasis, Holofernes complacently showing off his inkhorn terms, rhetorical and grammatical terminology, even declensions and alternate spellings. To play up to these fantasts, there are Moth, a quick wit, and Costard, a slow but strong one. And there is Sir Nathaniel, the gull curate, who eagerly writes down in his table-book the schoolmaster's redundancies. Dull and Jaquenetta, by usually keeping silent, prove the rule of Babel. But even Dull has a riddle in his head which he tries out on the schoolmaster. The commoners normally speak prose, the lords and ladies verse; most of the prose is as artificial in its way as the rhymed, end-stopped verses. The effect is that each social level and type is making sport with words in an appropriate way, just as the lords' infatuation with the ladies is paralleled by Costard's and then Armado's attentions to Jaquenetta. "Away," says the schoolmaster, as he invites the curate to dinner, "the gentles are at their game, and we will to our recreation" (IV.2.171). And when they come from dinner, still babbling, Moth observes aside to Costard that "They have been at a great feast of languages and stol'n the scraps" (V.1.39).

This comedy is often described as a satire on various kinds of over-elaborate language. It is certainly true that the exhibition of different sorts of far-fetched verbal play becomes almost an end in itself. Armado is introduced as a buffoon of new fashions and "fire-new words." He and the schoolmaster do make ridiculous two main Elizabethan vices of style. But each carries his vein so fantastically far that it commands a kind of gasping admiration—instead of being shown up, they turn the tables and show off, converting affectation and pedantry into ingenious games. "Be it as the style shall give us cause to climb in the merriness," says Berowne in anticipation of Armado's letter (I.1.201). For a modern reader, the game with high or learned words is sometimes tedious, because we have not ourselves tried the verbal exercises on which the gymnastic exhibition is based. Even the princess and her ladies in waiting, when they talk in terms of copy-book letters, seem just freshly out of school:

> ROSALINE. O, he hath drawn my picture in his letter! . . .
> PRINCESS. Beauteous as ink—a good conclusion.
> KATHARINE. Fair as a text B in a copy-book.
> ROSALINE. Ware pencils, ho! Let me not die your debtor,
> My red dominical, my golden letter. (V.2.38–44)

This kind of thing does weigh down parts of the play; it is dated by catering to a contemporary rage, a failure rare in Shakespeare's works, and one that suggests that he was writing for a special audience.

But the more one reads the play, the more one is caught up by the extraordinary excitement it expresses about what language can do—the excitement of the historical moment when English, in the hands of its greatest master, suddenly could do anything. Zest in the power of words comes out particularly clearly in the clown's part, as the chief motifs so often do in Shakespeare. As Armado gives Costard a letter to carry to Jaquenetta, he gives him a small tip with big words: "There is remuneration; for the best ward of mine honor is rewarding my dependents." When he has gone out, Costard opens his palm:

> Now will I look to his remuneration. Remuneration—O, that's the Latin word for three farthings. Three farthings—remuneration. "What's the price of this inkle?" "One penny." "No, I'll give you a remuneration!" Why, it carries it! Remuneration. Why, it is a fairer name than French crown. I will never buy and sell out of this word.
> (III.1.137–144)

O brave new world, that has remuneration in it! But the clown's next exchange, with Berowne, promptly demonstrates that three farthings is three farthings still.

> BEROWNE. O my good knave Costard, exceedingly well met!
> COSTARD. Pray you, sir, how much carnation ribbon may a man buy
>   for a remuneration?
> BEROWNE. O, what is a remuneration?
> COSTARD. Marry, sir, halfpenny farthing.
> BEROWNE. O, why then, three-farthing worth of silk.
> COSTARD. I thank your worship, God be wi' you!
> BEROWNE. O, stay, slave; I must employ thee. (III.1.145–152)

Berowne has a letter of his own, for Rosaline, and he too gives money with it, a whole bright shilling: "There's thy guerdon! Go." Costard again opens his palm: "Gardon—O sweet gardon! better than remuneration! a 'levenpence-farthing better" (III.1.171–173). So words are good when they go with good things. By getting so literal a valuation of the words, Costard both imitates and burlesques the way his superiors value language.

Everybody in the play, however vain about themselves, is ready always with applause for another's wit. "Now by the salt wave of the Mediterranean, a sweet touch, a quick venew of wit," Spanish Armado exclaims in praise of Moth, appropriately using dueling terms. "Snip, snap, quick and home! It rejoiceth my intellect. True wit!" (V.1.61–64). Costard is equally delighted, after his own fashion:

> An I had but one penny in the world, thou shouldst have it to buy
> gingerbread. Hold, there is the very remuneration I had of thy master, thou halfpenny purse of wit, thou pigeon egg of discretion.
> (V.1.74–78)

Holofernes has the grace to applaud a pass of wit of Costard's, in a patronizing way, even though it turns against him a blunt thrust of his own, aimed at Jaquenetta:

> JAQUENETTA. God give you good morrow, Master Person.
> HOLOFERNES. Master Person, quasi pers-one. And if one should be
>   pierc'd, which is the one?
> COSTARD. Marry, Master Schoolmaster, he that is likest to a hogs-
>   head.

HOLOFERNES. Of piercing a hogshead! A good lustre of conceit in a turf of earth; fire enough for a flint, pearl enough for a swine. 'Tis pretty, it is well. (IV.2.84–91)

Holofernes is fascinated by a release in language he himself heavily fails to find. After his absurd alliterative poem, his gull Nathaniel exclaims "A rare talent." Dull throws in the dry aside: "If a talent be a claw, look how he claws him with a talent." But Holofernes has been carried away by the joy of creation:

> This is a gift that I have, simple, simple; a foolish extravagant spirit, full of forms, figures, shapes, objects, ideas, apprehensions, motions, revolutions. These are begot in the ventricle of memory, nourished in the womb of pia mater, and delivered upon the mellowing of occasion. But the gift is good in those in whom it is acute, and I am thankful for it. (IV.2.67–74)

Here, as so often in Shakespeare, the outlines of a caricature are filled in with the experience of a man: Holofernes has a rhapsody of his own, an experience of the "fiery numbers" Berowne talks about—strange as his productions may be.

WIT

In a world of words, the wine is wit. Festivity in social life always enjoys, without effort, something physical from the world outside that is favorable to life, whether it be food and drink, or the warmth of the fields when they breathe sweet. Exhilaration comes when the world proves ready and willing, reaching out a hand, passing a brimming bowl; festivity signals the realization that we *belong* in the universe. Now in wit, it is language that gives us this something for nothing; unsuspected relations between words prove to be ready to hand to make a meaning that serves us. All of the comedies of Shakespeare, of course, depend on wit to convey the exhilaration of festivity. But *Love's Labour's Lost*, where the word *wit* is used more often than in any of the other plays, is particularly dependent on wit and particularly conscious in the way it uses and talks about it. So it will be useful to consider general functions of wit as they appear in this comedy.

When Moth speaks of "a great feast of languages," Costard continues the figure with "I marvel thy master hath not eaten thee for a word; for thou are not so long by the head as honorificabilitudinitatibus; thou are easier swallowed than a flapdragon" (V.1.42–45).

This is excellent fooling, and sense, too. For the people in *Love's Labour's Lost* get a lift out of fire-new words equivalent to what a tavern-mate would get from swallowing a "flapdragon"—a raisin floating in flaming brandy. Eating words is apt because the *physical* attributes of words are used by wit: a witticism capitalizes on "external associations," that is to say, it develops a meaning by connecting words through relations or likenesses not noted or used in the situation until found. The "physical," for our purpose here, is whatever had not been noticed, had not been given meaning, until wit caught hold of it and made it signify. The exploitation of physical features of language is most obvious where the wit is forced, where what is found does not really do very well after all. Little or nothing is really found when Jaquenetta mispronounces Parson as "Person," and Holofernes tries to make an innuendo by wrenching: "Master Person, quasi pers-one. And if one should be pierc'd, which is the one?" By contrast, consider Berowne's zooming finale in the speech justifying oath breaking, where successive lines seem to explode meaning already present in what went just before:

> Let us once lose our oaths to find ourselves,
> Or else we lose ourselves to keep our oaths. (IV.3.361–362)

To appropriate physical relations of sound and position in language, so that it seems that language makes your meaning for you, as indeed it partly does, gives an extraordinary exhilaration, far more intense than one would expect—until one considers how much of what we are is what we can find words for. When wit flows happily, it is as though the resistance of the objective world has suddenly given way. One keeps taking words from "outside," from the world of other systems or orders, and making them one's own, making them serve one's meaning as they form in one's mouth.

In repartee, each keeps jumping the other's words to take them away and make them his own, finding a meaning in them which was not intended. So elusive yet crucial is this subject that it will be worth while to quote a passage of wit where much that is involved in repartee is almost laboriously exhibited. As constantly happens in this play, the nature of wit is talked about in the process of being witty, here by hunting and sexual metaphors:

> BOYET. My lady goes to kill horns; but if thou marry,
> Hang me by the neck if horns that year miscarry.
> Finely put on!
> ROSALINE. Well then, I am the shooter.

BOYET. And who is your deer?

ROSALINE. If we choose by the horns, yourself. Come not near.
  Finely put on indeed!

MARIA. You still wrangle with her, Boyet, and she strikes at the brow.

BOYET. But she herself is hit lower. Have I hit her now?

ROSALINE. Shall I come upon thee with an old saying, that was a
  man when King Pippen of France was a little boy, as touching the hit it?

BOYET. So I may answer thee with one as old, that was a woman
  when Queen Guinover of Britain was a little wench, as
  touching the hit it.

ROSALINE. "Thou canst not hit it, hit it, hit it,
  Thou canst not hit it, my good man."

BOYET. "An I cannot, cannot, cannot,
  An I cannot, another can."

COSTARD. By my troth, most pleasant. How both did fit it.

                              (IV.1.112–131)

To reapply or develop a given metaphor has the same effect as to reapply
or develop the pattern of sound in a given set of words. Costard's comment
descibes the give and take of the repartee by the sexual metaphor—which
the party go on to develop far more explicitly than even our freest manners
would allow. The point they make is that to use one another's words in banter is like making love; each makes meaning out of what the other provides
physically. They notice *in medias res* that there is the same sort of sequence
of taking advantage and acquiescing: the process of taking liberties with each
other's words goes with a kind of verbal hiding and showing. Boyet can go
especially far in this way because he is the safe elderly attendant of the royal
party of ladies, limited by his age and role to such peeping-Tom triumphs
as "An I cannot, another can." When there is a real prospect of going from
words to deeds, words are more dangerous. So when the ladies encounter
the lords, their game is to stand them off by denying them the "three sweet
words" for which the men ask to get started.

A single speaker can of course develop his thought by witty use of
verbal situations he himself lays out. Consider, for example, the soliloquy
in which Berowne, at the opening of the discovery scene, confesses that he
is in love:

The King he is hunting the deer; I am coursing myself. They have
pitch'd a toil; I am toiling in a pitch—pitch that defiles. Defile! a foul

word. Well, "set thee down, sorrow!" for so they say the fool said, and so say I, and I the fool. Well proved, wit. By the Lord, this love is as mad as Ajax: it kills sheep; it kills me—I a sheep. (IV.3.1–8)

This is almost dialogue in the way it moves, like repartee, from a statement to the reapplication of the statement to "prove" something. The process of setting up and exploiting verbal situations is less obtrusive in more successful witty talk, but crucial in giving an exhilarating sense of power. Berowne has some excellent couplets mocking Boyet:

> This fellow pecks up wit as pigeons pease,
> And utters it again when God doth please.
> He is wit's pedlar, and retails his wares
> At wakes and wassails, meetings, markets, fairs;
> And we that sell by gross, the Lord doth know
> Have not the grace to grace it with such show. (V.2.315–320)

How nicely the extension of the pigeon and pedlar metaphors goes with a complex pattern of alliteration, *pecks* to *pease* to *pedlar*, *wares* to *wakes* to *wassails*. It seems as though language had conspired with Berowne to mock Boyet. In such exploitation of the physical qualities of words, there are no hard and fast lines between wit and eloquence and poetry, a fact which is reflected in the broad Renaissance usage of the word wit. But one can observe that we now think of expressions as witty, rather than eloquent or poetic, when one is conscious of the physical character of the links through which the discourse moves to its meanings. And one must add that some of the wit in *Love's Labour's Lost* is, to our modern taste, tediously "conceited." The play occasionally deserved Dryden's strictures about Shakespeare's "comic art degenerating into clenches."

PUTTING WITTY FOLLY IN ITS PLACE

But though one cannot blink the fact the wit is often a will-o'-the-wisp, the play *uses* its witty extravagance, moves through it to clarification about what one sort of wit is and where it fits in human experience. There are a number of descriptions of the process of being witty which locate such release as an event in the whole sensibility. These usually go with talk about brightening eyes: typically in this play a lover's eyes catch fire just before he bursts into words. There is a remarkable description of the King's first response to the Princess which defines precisely a gathering up of the faculties for perception and expression:

BOYET. If my observation (which very seldom lies),
    By the heart's still rhetoric, disclosed with eyes,
    Deceive me not now, Navarre is infected.
PRINCESS. With what?
BOYET. With that which we lovers entitle "affected." (II.1.227–232)

Notice that Boyet does not answer simply "with love." Shakespeare is
out to define a more limited thing, a galvanizing of sensibility which may
or may not be love; and so Boyet goes round about to set up a special
term, "affected." He goes on to describe his observation of "the heart's
still rhetoric":

Why, all his behaviours did make their retire
To the court of his eye, peeping through desire. . . .
His tongue, all impatient to speak and not see,
Did stumble with haste in his eyesight to be;
All senses to that sense did make their repair,
To feel only looking on fairest of fair.
Methought all his senses were lock'd in his eye,
As jewels in crystal for some prince to buy,
Who, tend'ring their own worth from where they were glass'd,
Did point you to buy them along as you pass'd. (II.1.234–245)

This is extremely elaborate; but the dislocation of the language, for example
in "to feel only looking" (which bothered Dr. Johnson),[5] catches a special
movement of feeling important for the whole play, a movement of awareness into the senses and toward expression. The next step, from eye to
tongue, is described in Rosaline's account of Berowne.

            a merrier man
Within the limit of becoming mirth,
I never spent an hour's talk withal.
His eye begets occasion for his wit;
For every object that the one doth catch
The other turns to a mirth-moving jest,
Which his fair tongue (conceit's expositor)
Delivers in such apt and gracious words
That aged ears play truant at his tales
And younger hearings are quite ravished,
So sweet and voluble is his discourse. (II.1.66–76)

The rhythm here, even some of the phrasing, anticipate, in a sketchy way, the description of the enchanting power of the mermaid in *A Midsummer Night's Dream*:

> Uttering such dulcet and harmonious breath
> That the rude sea grew civil at her song,
> And certain stars shot madly from their spheres
> To hear the sea-maid's music. (*Dream* II.1.151–154)

There are a series of such descriptions of the Orphic power of musical discourse in the plays of this period, including Berowne's own climactic speech in this play. In Rosaline's lines, as elsewhere, there is a metaphor of conveying meaning out into language, perhaps with a glance at child-bearing in "delivers."[6] When Rosaline is characterized, in her turn, the power of nimble expression to free the heart of its burdens is charmingly described. Katharine contrasts her with a sister who died of Love. Love

> made her melancholy, sad and heavy,
> And so she died. Had she been light like you,
> Of such a merry, nimble, stirring spirit,
> She might 'a' been a grandam ere she died.
> And so may you; for a light heart lives long. (V.2.14–18)

The fullest description of this kindling into Orphic wit and eloquence, at the climax of Berowne's speech justifying folly, centers on the process of awareness moving out into the senses and powers:

> For when would you, my liege, or you, or you,
> In leaden contemplation, have found out
> Such fiery numbers as the prompting eyes
> Of beauty's tutors have enrich'd you with?
> Other slow arts entirely keep the brain,
> And therefore finding barren practisers,
> Scarce show a harvest of their heavy toil;
> But love, first learned in a lady's eyes,
> Lives not alone immured in the brain,
> But with the motion of all elements
> Courses as swift as thought in every power a double power
> Above their functions and their offices. (IV.3.320–332)

The speech is a perfectly fitting counter-statement to the ascetic resolutions with which the play began. The "doctrine" it derives from "women's eyes" is a version of the Renaissance cult of love as an educational force, especially for the courtier. But notice how little Berowne is concerned with love as an experience between two people. All his attention is focussed on what happens within the lover, the heightening of his powers and perceptions. He is describing a youthful response of elation; the mere sight of "the prompting eyes" of the tutor beauty is enough to whirl pupil love into an almost autonomous rhapsody:

> It adds a precious seeing to the eye:
> A lover's eyes will gaze an eagle blind.
> A lover's ear will hear the lowest sound
> When the suspicious head of theft is stopp'd.
> Love's feeling is more soft and sensible
> Than are the tender horns of cockled snails.
> Love's tongue proves dainty Bacchus gross in taste.
> For valour, is not Love a Hercules,
> Still climbing trees in the Hesperides?
> Subtle as Sphinx; as sweet and musical
> As bright Apollo's lute, strung with his hair.
> And when Love speaks, the voice of all the gods
> Make heaven drowsy with the harmony.
> Never durst poet touch a pen to write
> Until his ink were temp'red with Love's sighs.
> O, then his lines would ravish savage ears
> And plant in tyrants mild humility. (IV.3.333–349)

Can such delightful poetry, such rhapsody, be folly? There is a romantic response ready that would like to let go completely and simply endorse these lovely, vital lines. But the strength of Shakespeare's comic form is precisely that the attitude Berowne expresses can be presented as at once delightfully vital, *and* foolish. The foolishness is of a young and benign sort, in which the prospect of love sets off a rhapsody that almost forgets the beloved. Consummation in physical union of the sexes is not envisaged; the lady is involved only as her eyes start another sort of physical union by which the senses and powers are invested with amorous meaning.

The lords' quality of youthful elation and absorption in their own responses is what lays them open to being fooled as they are by the ladies

when they try to set about revelry wholeheartedly. The game they are playing, without quite knowing it, tries to make love happen by expressing it,
to blow up a sort of forced-draft passion by capering volubility and wit. A
remarkable set-piece by Moth describes an Elizabethan hep-cat version of
such courting: he tells Armado how to "win your love with a French brawl":

> . . . jig off a tune at the tongue's end, canary to it with your feet,
> humor it with turning up your eyelids; sigh a note and sing a note,
> sometime through the throat, as if you swallow'd love with singing
> love, sometime through the nose, as if you snuff'd up love by smell-
> ing love, with your hat penthouse-like o'er the shop of your eyes,
> with your arms cross'd on your thin-belly doublet, like a rabbit on
> a spit, or your hands in your pocket, like a man after the old paint-
> ing; and keep not too long in one tune, but a snip and away. These
> are complements; these are humours; these betray nice wenches that
> would be betrayed without these, and make them men of note—
> do you note me?—that most are affected to these. (III.1.11–26)

Such antics are more plebeian than the lords' revels, but tellingly alike in
purpose. The Princess and her ladies are not in any case the sort of nice
wenches to be betrayed. The ladies believe, indeed, rather too little than too
much. "They do it but in mocking merriment," says the Princess. "And mock
for mock is only my intent." When the men have been "dry-beaten with pure
scoff," Berowne eats humble pie in an effort to get started on a new basis:

> O, never will I trust to speeches penn'd
> Nor to the motion of a schoolboy's tongue,
> Nor never come in vizard to my friend,
> Nor woo in rhyme like a blind harper's song!
> Taffeta phrases, silken terms precise,
> Three-pil'd hyperboles, spruce affectation,
> Figures pedantical—these summer flies
> Have blown me full of maggot ostentation.
> I do forswear them; and I here protest,
> By this white glove (how white the hand, God knows!)
> Henceforth my wooing mind shall be express'd
> In russet yea's and honest kersey no's. (V.2.402–412)

Berowne abjures elaborate language, and it is for this alone that the lines
are usually quoted. Part of the point of them lay in criticism of affected style.

But a final, settled attitude toward such style has not been established. The lords' trusting in speeches penn'd, with three-piled hyperboles, has been part and parcel of trusting in the masquerade way of making love, coming in a vizard, in a three-piled Russian habit. And these pastimes are not being dismissed for good, but put in their place: they are festive follies, relished as they show the power of life, but mocked as they run out ahead of the real, the everyday situation. The point, dramatically, is that the lords had hoped that festivity would "carry it," as Costard hoped Armado's fancy word "remuneration" would carry it. Now they must start again, because, as Berowne's better judgment foresaw

> Light wenches may prove plagues to men forsworn:
> If so, our copper buys no better treasure. (IV.3.385–386)

Perhaps the most delightful touch in the whole play is the exchange that concludes Berowne's reformation, in which he playfully betrays the fact that his mockery of sophistication is sophisticated, and Rosaline underscores the point as she deftly withdraws the hand he has taken:

> And to begin: wench, so God help me, law!
> My love to thee is sound, sans crack or flaw.
> ROSALINE. Sans "sans," I pray you! (V.2.414–416)

Miss M.C. Bradbrook observes that "Berowne, who is both guilty of courtly artifice and critical of it, plays a double game with language throughout; the same double game that the author himself is playing. He runs with the hare and hunts with the hounds."[7] His control and poise in moving in this way goes with being able to call a game a game, as I have been saying. Another source of his mastery is the social perspective on the courtly pleasures which he gets by ironically dropping, at intervals, into homespun, proverbial speech. Of course there is a sort of affectation too in doing the downright in this way, and Berowne's humor recognizes that he himself is no common man. But he does get the power to stand apart from elegant folly by being able to say things like

> Sow'd cockle reap'd no corn,
> And justice always whirls in equal measure. (IV.3.383–384)

The roles of the commoners provide the same sort of perspective, especially the illiterate commoners, who almost always come out best in the exchanges. No sooner has the Duke proclaimed his "continent cannon" than Costard proves its absurdity by being taken with Jaquenetta:

> In manner and form following, sir—all those three. I was seen with her in the manor house, sitting with her upon the form, and taken following her into the park; which put together is in manner and form following. Now, sir, for the manner—it is the manner of a man to speak to a woman; for the form—in some form. (I.1.207–215)

"In some form," the truth about human nature comes out, despite the way Costard wrests the categories in a physical direction, or indeed because of this physical tendency. "I suffer for the truth, sir," is the swain's fine summary, "for true it is I was taken with Jaquenetta, and Jaquenetta is a true girl" (I.1.313–314). He is a thoroughly satisfactory "downright" style of clown, ironical about the follies of his betters half out of naïveté and half out of shrewdness. His role embodies the proverbial, homespun perspective Berowne can occasionally borrow. Moth, a pert page in the manner of Lyly, is less rich, but he too contributes comments which help to place what the lords are doing.

All of the commoners' parts, indeed, contribute to placing the festivities. Almost all of them make telling comments, even Holofernes, who has the courage, when he is mercilessly ragged as Judas in his Show of Worthies, to say "This is not generous, not gentle, not humble" (V.2.632). But comments are less important than the sense Shakespeare creates of people living in a settled group, where everyone is known and to be lived with, around the clock of the year. Though the different figures may have been shaped to some degree by examples in the *commedia dell'arte*—the braggart and his quick zani, the pedant, the parasite priest, the rustic clown—the group function together to represent "his lordship's simple neighbors." Through them we feel a world which exists before and after to the big moment of the entertainment, and we see the excitement of the smaller people about the big doings. Holofernes honors the Princess's success in hunting in strange, pedantical verse: "The preyful princess pierc'd and prick'd a pretty pleasing pricket" (IV.2.58). Schoolmasters in real entertainments often furnished shows; Sidney wrote out a part for a comically pedantic schoolmaster in making an entertainment for Elizabeth, "The Lady of the May," 1579. We see Armado courteously enlisting the help of Holofernes in designing "some delightful ostentation, or show, or pageant, or antic, or firework" (V.1.120). He understands, he says, that "the curate and your sweet self are good at such eruptions and sudden breaking-out of mirth." Their talk is absurdly affected, but it is also winningly positive and hopeful. Goodman Dull, "his grace's farborough," wants to take part too:

> HOLOFERNES. Via, goodman Dull! Thou hast spoken no word all
>   this while.
> DULL. Nor understood none neither, sir.
> HOLOFERNES. Alons! we will employ thee.
> DULL. I'll make one in a dance, or so; or I will play
>   On the tabor to the Worthies, and let them dance the hay.
> HOLOFERNES. Most dull, honest Dull! To our sport, away!
>
> (V.1.156–162)

Such a little scrap illustrates something that happens repeatedly in Shakespeare's festive comedies. Characters who might be merely butts also win our sympathy by taking part, each after his fashion, in "eruptions and sudden breaking-out of mirth" (V.1.121). This genial quality goes with dramatizing, not merely a story, nor merely characters, but a community occasion: "I'll make one," says a laggard Dull; "to *our* sport," says vain Holofernes.

When the show is actually produced, what we watch are not the Worthies but the people who are presenting them. Costard is self-respecting and humble enough to accept correction:

> *I Pompey am. Pompey surnam'd the Big—*
> DUMAIN. "The Great."
> COSTARD. It is "Great," sir.
>   *. . . I here am come by chance,*
> *And lay my arms before the legs of this sweet lass of France.*
>   If your ladyship would say "Thanks, Pompey," I had done.
> PRINCESS. Great thanks, great Pompey.
> COSTARD. 'Tis not so much worth. But I hope I was perfect.
>   I made a little fault in "Great." (V.2.553–562)

What poise and sense of proportion, from which the lords could learn something, is concentrated in "'Tis not so much worth"! When the poor curate, Sir Nathaniel, is non-plussed in trying to be Alexander the conqueror, Costard makes an apology for him that has become a by-word:

> Run away for shame, Alisander.
>   *[Sir Nathaniel stands aside.]*
> There, an't shall please you! a foolish mild man; an honest man,

look you, and soon dashed. He is a marvellous good neighbor, faith, and a very good bowler; but for Alisander—alas! you see how 'tis—a little o'erparted. (V.2.583–589)

Shakespeare presents a gulf fixed, and then spans it by touches like "and a very good bowler." It was part of his genius that he could do this; but it was also the genius of the society which he expressed and portrayed. As we have seen, festivities were occasions for communicating across class lines and realizing the common humanity of every level. And the institution of the holidays and entertainments was a function of communiity life where people knew their places and knew the human qualities of each in his place—knew, for example, that an illiterate Costard was more intelligent and more constructive than a polyliterate Holofernes.

Shakespeare can do without marriages at the end, and still end affirmatively, because he is dramatizing an occasion in a community, not just private lives. News of the French King's death breaks off the wooing game. In deferring the question of marriage, the princess says frankly but graciously that what has passed has been only "courtship, pleasant jest, and courtesy . . . bombast . . . and lining to the time . . . a merriment" (V.2.789–793). When the King urges that the suits be granted "Now at the latest minute of the hour," she can answer with common-sense tempered by goodwill:

> A time, methinks, too short
> To make a world-without-end bargain in.
> No, no, my lord! Your Grace is perjur'd much,
> Full of dear guiltiness; and therefore this:—
> If for my love (as there is no such cause)
> You will do aught, this shall you do for me: (V.2.797–802)

(Part of the delight of Shakespeare is that some of his people have such beautiful, generous manners! They can "do and say the kindest things in the kindest way.") So the king must spend a year in a hermitage to test his love. And Rosaline prescribes that Berowne must spend a twelvemonth visiting the sick, trying to make them smile by "the fierce endeavour of your wit." So he will have to recognize something beyond games and words, and learn the limits of a gibing spirit.

> Whose influence is begot of that loose grace
> Which shallow laughing hearers give to fools. (V.2.868–869)

The ladies' bizarre commands, by insisting that the men confront other types of experience, invite them to try separating their affections from the occasion to see whether or not their feelings are more than courtly sports. In the elation of the festive moment, the game of witty wooing seemed to be love: now comes clarification.

To draw the line between a pastime and a play is another way of marking limits. Berowne's final ironic joke shows how conscious Shakespeare was that he had made a play out of social pastimes, and one which differed from regular drama.

> Our wooing doth not end like an old play:
> Jack hath not Jill. These ladies' courtesy
> Might well have made our sport a comedy. (V.2.883–335)

Sport would have become drama if something had happened. Berowne almost says what Will Fool said of Nashe's pageant: "'tis not a play neither, but a show." *Love's Labour's Lost* is not a show, because the sports in it are used, dramatically, by people in a kind of history; it is comedy, precisely because Berowne can stand outside the sport and ruefully lament that it is only sport. Berowne's last line recognizes explicitly that to have brought these people from these festivities to the full-fledged event of marriage would have required a whole new development. The king observes hopefully about the unfinished courtship:

> Come, sir, it wants a twelvemonth and a day,
> And then 'twill end.
> BEROWNE. That's too long for a play. (V.2.886–888)

"WHEN . . . THEN . . ." — THE SEASONAL SONGS

The pageant and songs of summer and winter are the finale Shakespeare used instead of a wedding dance or masque; and they are exactly right, not an afterthought but a last, and full, expression of the controlling feeling for community and season. The songs evoke pleasures of the most traditional sort, at the opposite pole from facile improvisations. Nobody improvised the outgoing to the fields in spring or the coming together around the fire in winter. After fabulous volubility, we are looking and listening only; after conceits and polysyllables, we are told a series of simple facts in simple words:

> When daisies pied and violets blue
>   And lady-smocks all silver-white
> And cuckoo-buds of yellow hue

Do paint the meadows with delight,
The cuckoo then on every tree. . . . (V.2.904–908)

We have observed in connection with the songs in Nashe's seasonal pageant that the songs in Shakespeare's festive comedies are usually composed with explicit or implicit reference to a holiday occasion. The cuckoo and owl songs are cognate to such compositions, a very high order of poetry and of imaginative abstraction. We can briefly summarize Shakespeare's practice in composing festive songs to relate these in *Love's Labor's Lost* to simpler, more directly festive lyrics. When Silence suddenly sings out

Be merry, be merry, my wife has all,
For women are shrows, both short and tall,
'Tis merry in hall when beards wag all,
And welcome merry Shrovetide!
Be merry, be merry. (*2 H IV* V.3.35–39)

he is singing a traditional drinking song customarily used on the occasion which it names. Usually, however, Shakespeare wrote songs *like* those used on holiday but serving more exactly and richly his own imaginative purposes. For example, he developed from the women's vantage the same Shrovetide gesture, by which the sexes mock and dismiss each other, in the song that nettles Benedict in *Much Ado About Nothing*:

Sigh no more, ladies, sigh no more!
Men were deceivers ever,
One foot in sea, and one on shore;
To one thing constant never.
Then sigh not so,
But let them go,
And be you blithe and bonny,
Converting all your sounds of woe
Into Hey nonny, nonny. (*Much Ado* II.3.64–71)

How well this fits Beatrice's attitude—until the tide turns and she and Benedict experience a reconciliation all the more free-hearted for coming after their merry version of the war between men and women. The development of traditional moments of feeling into songs for particular moments in particular plays is of course a very complex process, sometimes random, and mostly beyond analysis. (No doubt Shakespeare did not think out what he was doing systematically; had he needed to, he could not have done what he did.)

One can see clearly enough where "It was a lover and his lass" comes from and how it fits into *As You Like It* at the moment (V.3) when love is about to be "crowned with the prime." So too with Feste's love song in the reveling scene of *Twelfth Night:*

> O mistress mine, where are you roaming?
> O, stay and hear! your true-love's coming,
>> That can sing both high and low. (*Twelfth Night* II.3.40–42)

The "roaming" here may be to the woods; the true lover commends himself simply for the festive accomplishments of singing high and low, and addresses his mistress simply as "sweet and twenty." What is mentioned and not mentioned gives the sense of neglecting individuality because of being wholly taken up in the festive moment, the "present mirth" and "present laughter." There is a deliberate variation from the expected in the fact that it is a love song, about spring pleasures, and not the within-doors drinking song that would go with Toby's Twelfth Night–style drinking party. This is noticed by the dialogue:

> CLOWN. Would you have a love song, or a song of good life?
> TOBY. A love song, a love song.
> ANDREW. Ay, ay! I care not for good life. (*Twelfth Night* II.3.36–38)

By a similar variation, it is songs of good life that provide the pattern for "Blow, blow thou winter wind," which is sung outdoors in the Forest of Arden.

> Then, heigh-ho, the holly!
> This life is most jolly. (*As You Like It* II.7.182–183)

is a crystallization of the mood of Christmas cheer, when it was customary for the men to sing songs in praise of the holly as their emblem, against songs by the women in praise of ivy: "Ivy is soft, and meek of speech."[8] This custom explains why the *As You Like It* chorus begins with a vocative: "Heigh-ho, sing heigh-ho, unto the green holly!" Shakespeare uses the gesture of groups singing in the hall together to express the solidarity of the banished Duke and his merry men in Arden. And he takes the Christmas feeling of mastering the cold by good life around a great fire and uses it to convey the exiles' feeling of mastering ingratitude by pastoral fellowship.

Now the spring and winter songs in *Love's Labour's Lost* primarily define moments in the year rather than particular festivals; they are a *débat*, conducted not by argument but by "praise of the Owl and the Cuckoo," as the debate between men and women could go forward by matching praises of the holly and the ivy. It seems clear, as Mr. Dover Wilson points out,[9] that Armado stage manages several disguised persons who form in two groups. The original stage direction reads "Enter all," and Armado presents pageant figures of Winter and Spring as well as of the two birds:

> This side is Hiems, Winter; this Ver, the Spring: the one maintained by the Owl, th' other by the Cuckoo. Ver, begin. (V.2.901–903)

On the title page of the early Tudor printing of *The Debates or Stryfes Betwene Somer and Wynter*,[10] Somer is shown as a gallant with a hawk; Wynter as an old man. Somer describes his antagonist with "Thou are very old, . . . go shave thy hair!" (Perhaps Shakespeare was thinking of the pageant figure in *Love's Labour's Lost* when he wrote of "old Hiems" in *A Midsummer Night's Dream*, II.1.109.) *The Debates* is a writing down of a kind of formal game of argument which had long been customary as a pastime at feasts. It is interesting in this connection that Armado introduces the songs as "the Dialogue that the two learned men have compiled in praise of the Owl and the Cuckoo." The interchange between Somer and Wynter frequently turns on the pleasures of the two seasons:

> WYNTER. I love better good wines and good sweet meats upon my
>   table . . .
> SOMER. Wynter, I have young damsels that have their breast white,
>   To go gather flowers with their lovers.

Wynter speaks of St. Martin's feast, when great and small drink wine. Somer answers with "the month of May," when there are "primroses and daisies and violet flowers" for "The true lover and his sweet leman," who "go home singing and make good cheer."

The magic of "When daisies pied and violets blue" and of "When icicles hang by the wall" is partly that they seem to be merely lists, and each thing seems to be dwelt on simply for itself; and yet each song says, in a marvelously economical way, where people are in the cycle of the year, the people of farm, manor, or village who live entirely in the turning seasons. The only syntax that matters is "When . . . then . . ."

When icicles hang by the wall,
    And Dick the shepherd blows his nail,
And Tom bears logs into the hall,
    And milk comes frozen home in pail,
When blood is nipp'd, and ways be foul,
Then nightly sings the staring owl:
        "Tu-who!
Tu-whit, tu-who!" a merry note,
While greasy Joan doth keel the pot.[11] (V.2.931–939)

Of course these songs are not simply *of* the world they describe, not folk songs; they are art songs, consciously pastoral, sophisticated enjoyment of simplicity.[12] Their elegance and humor convey pleasure in life's being reduced to so few elements and yet being so delightful. Each centers on vitality, and moves from nature to man. The spring song goes from lady smocks to the maidens' summer smocks, both showing white against the green of the season, from turtle cocks who "tread" to implications about people. The old joke about the cuckoo is made so delightful because its meaning as a "word," as a call to the woods, is assumed completely as a matter of course.[13] In the winter song, the center of vitality is the fire. (Wynter says in *The Debates*, "For me they make a great fire to cheer my bonys old." The fire is enjoyed "nightly," after the day's encounter with the cold. Gathered together "When roasted crabs hiss in the bowl," it is merry to hear the owl outside in the cold—his "Tu-whit, tu-who" come to mean this moment. Even the kitchen wench, greasy Joan, keeling the pot to keep it from boiling over, is one of us, a figure of affection. The songs evoke the daily enjoyments and the daily community out of which special festive occasions were shaped up. And so they provide for the conclusion of the comedy what marriage usually provides: an expression of the going-on power of life.

NOTES

1. See Chapter 6 [in C.L. Barber, *Shakespeare's Festive Comedy*], on *A Midsummer Night's Dream*.

2. O.J. Campbell, "'Love's Labour's Lost' Re-Studied," *Studies in Shakespeare, Milton and Donne*, U. of Michigan Pubs., Language and Literature, Vol. 1 (New York, 1925), pp. 13–20. Venezky, *Pageantry on the Elizabethan Stage*, pp. 70, 139, 158–161, and passim. Professor Venezky presents customary pageantry and the dramatists' use of it in a full, rounded way which brings out what was typical of the age in Shakespeare's practice.

3. Welsford, *Fool*, pp. 218–229. Miss Welsford discusses the general relations of the sottie to misrule and the masque in *The Court Masque, A Study in the Relationship between Poetry and the Revels* (Cambridge, 1927), pp. 376 ff.

4. See Chapter 4 of *Shakespeare's Festive Comedy*, pp. 67–73, for the relation

of Falstaff's praise of folly to that of Nashe's Bacchus. Berowne's points, and even his phrasing, are often remarkably close to Falstaff's: "abstinence engenders maladies" goes with Falstaff's "fall into a kind of male greensickness" (2 H IV, IV.3.100); "other slow arts entirely keep the brain" fits with "learning a mere hoard of gold kept by the devil, till Sack commences it"; "love . . . not alone immured in the brain . . . courses as swift as thought in every power" parallels "the sherris warms [the blood] and makes it course from the inwards to the parts extreme."

5. *A New Variorum Edition of Shakespeare*, ed. H.H. Furness (Philadelphia, 1904), p. 79. A few lines later we get a drastic collapse into a characteristic vice of this play, a kind of chop-logic with images:

I only have made a mouth of his eye
By adding a tongue which I know will not lie. (II.1.252–253)

This is bad taste, one of a number of places where the elaboration of fanciful paradox produces a result which can only be read abstractly: to form a physical image of a tongue in an eye spoils everything. An even more dramatic case is the draggle end of a wit combat over the beauty of Berowne's "black" lady, Rosaline.

LONGAVILLE. Look, here's thy love, my foot and her face see.
BEROWNE. O, if the streets were paved with thine eyes,
    Her feet were much too dainty for such tread. (IV.3.277–279)

To read Berowne's talk of walking on eyeballs with full imaginative participation "would be to experiment in mania," as I.A. Richards remarked about certain stanzas of Dryden's *Annus Mirabilis* in *Coleridge on Imagination* (New York, 1935), p. 95. But one can forgive such failures in so enterprising a writer as the young author of *Love's Labour's Lost*; he is trying everything.

6. This meaning Holofernes also develops in talking of wit "nourish'd in the womb of pia mater, and delivered" (IV.2.70–71).

7. *Shakespeare and Elizabethan Poetry* (London, 1951), p. 215.

8. Chambers and Sigwick, *Lyrics*, no. 138. See also nos. 139–141. The association developed in these songs is behind Titania's lines when she says

the female ivy so
Enrings the barky fingers of the elm. (*Dream* IV.1.46–47)

9. *Love's Labour's Lost*, ed. Sir Arthur Quiller-Couch and John Dover Wilson (Cambridge, 1923), p. 184. Mr. Wilson refers to Armado's remark to Holofernes, while they are planning the Show of the Nine Worthies: "We will have, if this fadge not, an antic" (V.1.154).

10. Ed. J.O. Halliwell-Phillips (London, 1860). The original printer was Lawrence Andrew; S.T. Coleridge estimates the original publication date as 1530.

11. The first "Tu-who," set out alone as a line, is not in the original texts, but was added by Capell in order that both songs might be sung to the same tune (*Variorum*, p. 318). Once a rhythm has established itself for everyone the way this one has, there is no point in pedantically restoring the original reading, though it may well be the correct one.

12. See Walter W. Greg, *Pastoral Poetry and Pastoral Drama* (London, 1906), pp. 1–8. I believe that "the sophisticated enjoyment of simplicity" is Sir Walter's phrase, but I cannot now find it in the fine introduction where he makes that point.

13. Bottom handles the old cuckoo joke just the other way:

The finch, the sparrow, and the lark,
    The plain-song cuckoo gray,
Whose note dull many a man doth mark,

> And dares not answer nay.
> For, indeed, who would set his wit to so foolish
> a bird? Who would give a bird the lie, though
> he cry "cuckoo" never so? (*Dream* III.1.133–139)

The stress on "who would give a *bird* the lie" separates men and nature with a comic literalness; and Bottom has a part of that right: one can worry too much. But the other part of the truth is in the *Love's Labour's Lost* song: that "cuckoo" is not just a bird's song—it is a "word of fear," because it means that all those flowers have sprung up, asking to be gathered.

LOVE'S LABOUR'S LOST

THE STORY OF A CONVERSION

John Dover Wilson, C.H.

The reputation of *Love's Labour's Lost* is one of the curiosities of dramatic history. In Elizabethan and Jacobean times it seems to have been among the more popular of Shakespeare's plays—at any rate in court circles. Sir Arthur Quiller-Couch and I suggested in our edition (1923) that it may have been first written for a private performance at Christmas 1593, possibly for Southampton and his friends. Certainly it was played before Queen Elizabeth at Christmas 1597, perhaps in revised form. But the opinion in which it was held emerges most clearly from the fact that during the Christmas season 1604–5, Burbadge picked it out for special recommendation as a play to be given at the Earl of Southampton's house before Queen Anne, declaring that "for wytt & mirthe" it "will please her exceedingly."[1] It is true that Shakespeare's company appears at this time to have been deliberately reviving old Elizabethan plays which James and Anne had not seen. But Burbadge's confidence in the attraction of *Love's Labour's Lost* is none the less remarkable, inasmuch as it was then ten or twelve years old, and is now regarded as essentially a topical play. Yet if the title-page of the second edition of the quarto (1631) is to be believed, it still held the stage after Shakespeare's death, being acted both at the Blackfriars and at the Globe. After that it just drops out. Nothing is known of it in the theatre for two hundred years, and though revivals took place during the nineteenth century, only three are recorded in this country and two in the United States, none of which seems to have been very successful.

As for its reputation among the critics, Dryden set the fashion, which is still to a large extent that of modern commentary. His *Essay on the Dramatic Poetry of the Last Age* (1672), in which he seeks to demonstrate the

Chapter 3 of *Shakespeare's Happy Comedies* by John Dover Wilson, C.H. (Evanston: Northwestern University Press, 1962), pp. 55–75. Reprinted by permission of Faber and Faber Ltd.

superiority in wit, language and conversation of his own times to that of Shakespeare, a superiority which he attributed to improvements in "gallantry and civility," includes *Love's Labour's Lost* among those plays which, he reminds his readers, "were so *meanly* written that the comedy neither caused your mirth, nor the serious part your concernment."[2]

This judgment was echoed a hundred years later by Dr. Johnson:

> In this play, which all the editors have concurred to censure, and some have rejected as unworthy of our Poet, it must be confessed that there are many passages *mean*, childish and vulgar; and some which ought not to have been exhibited, as we are told they were, to a maiden queen. But [he feels compelled to add] there are scattered through the whole many sparks of genius; nor is there any play that has more evident marks of the hands of Shakespeare.[3]

And there save for one exception the position stood in this country[4] until a few years ago. The exception, a remarkable one, is an essay by Walter Pater published in his *Appreciations* (1889), which comes very near to what I believe is the truth. He writes:

> The unity of the play is not so much the unity of a drama as that of a series of pictorial groups, in which the same figures reappear, in different combinations but on the same background. It is as if Shakespeare had intended to bind together, by some inventive conceit, the devices of an ancient tapestry and give voice to its figures.[5]

But Pater's was a voice crying in the wilderness of neglect and depreciation. The accusation of "meanness" which Dryden and Johnson both levelled at the play is based in the main upon the quantity of quibbling it contains. This is borne out by Dryden's condemnation of this fault in Ben Jonson, which occurs in the same essay. Jonson's wit, he declares, was excellent enough so long as he borrowed from the classics. But "when he trusted himself alone, he often fell into meanness of expression. Nay, he was not free from the lowest and most grovelling kind of art, which we call clenches, of which *Every Man in his Humour* is infinitely full; and, which is worse, the wittiest persons in the drama speak them."[6]

The puns he instances from Jonson, e.g. "Aristarchus" and "stark ass," "limbs of satin or rather Satan," are certainly "mean," if not "grovelling." But there is nothing of this sort in *Love's Labour's Lost*. Indeed, Shakespeare usually avoided what may be called the straight pun, Falstaff's notorious pun of "gravy" on "gravity"[7] being the exception that proves the rule. What he chiefly indulged in was, as we have seen above, rather the Quibble—a term that needs definition, and which I should define as a kind of word-play in which one character makes a remark or utters a word, and another immediately picks it up and uses it or replies to it in a different sense—even at times in two or three different senses. Such quibbling is one of the main roots of Shakespearian repartee, and there are pages of it in *Love's Labour's Lost*. This is how Boyet comments upon it:

> The tongues of mocking wenches are as keen
> As is the razor's edge invisible,
> Cutting a smaller hair than may be seen,
> Above the sense of sense; so sensible
> Seemeth their conference, their conceits have wings
> Fleeter than arrows, bullets, wind, thought, swifter things.[8]

And the description must be allowed true.

Take one example only: Katharine, masked and pretending to be Maria, who is the lady of Lord Longaville's choice, mocks that young gentleman, himself vizarded and disguised as a Muscovite. And the following dialogue then takes place, the main point of which is that, while he thinks she is Maria, she knows very well that he is Longaville. To encourage the bashful lover, she opens with

> KATHARINE. What, was your vizard made without a tongue?
> [This refers to the practice, still found in Christmas crackers, of making masks with long paper tongues which shot out at will.]
> LONGAVILLE. I know the reason, lady, why you ask.
> KATHARINE. O, for your reason! quickly, sir—I long.
> LONGAVILLE. You have a double tongue within your mask,
> And would afford my speechless vizard half.
> [In other words Katharine has the double (=deceitful) tongue that all women possess and is therefore ready to lend a tongue to him. But in saying "I long" Katharine had uttered the first syllable of Longaville's name and had thus "afforded his speechless vizard half" in another sense. It is this sense she now picks up in her reply, which is a multiple quibble, since it speaks the other half of his name, appears to applaud his jest by saying "Well!" after the comic pronuncia-

tion of contemporary Dutch or German merchants in London, and enables her to insult him at the same time.]

KATHARINE. "Veal" quoth the Dutchman. Is not "veal" a calf?

LONGAVILLE. A calf, fair lady?

KATHARINE. No, a fair lord calf.

[Longaville, finding himself getting the worst of it, now suggests a change of subject.]

LONGAVILLE. Let's part the word.

[Part = give up. Thus he means "Let's have done with this 'veal' business." Whereupon Katharine, pretending he means "let us divide or split the word 'calf,'" which would give the first two letters of her own name, retorts.]

KATHARINE. No. I'll not be your half [i.e., your better half].

Take all and wean it—it may prove an ox [i.e., a fool].[9]

With the mention of "ox" the quibblers have arrived at the goal of most Elizabethan jesting, viz. horns, and the dialogue drifts off into a series of jokes on the subject of cuckoldry, which to Elizabethans seems to have been as irresistibly laughable as the mother-in-law was to readers and spectators in Victorian England.

Such verbal ingenuity, fine-spun and carried forward from speech to speech, trivial as it may seem to us, undoubtedly cost Shakespeare much thought, and often embraced in *Love's Labour's Lost* a good deal of indelicate innuendo. Today we need elaborate commentary to understand it even in part. Could the Elizabethans follow it in the rapid give-and-take of the stage? We must suppose they did, otherwise Shakespeare would hardly have put himself to the pains of placing it in the mouths of his characters, which he does, not only in *Love's Labour's Lost*, but in play after play, until it reached its culmination in the sallies of Hamlet, anticly disposed.[10]

No doubt the sport had become stale by the time Dryden was writing. But he goes far astray in attributing Shakespeare's love of it to his lack of social opportunity. "In the age wherein those poets lived," he remarks, with the accustomed air of superiority which the Restoration writers assumed in speaking of their predecessors, "there was less of gallantry than in ours; neither did they keep the best company of theirs. . . . I cannot find that any of them had been conversant in courts, except Ben Johnson."[11] We should not perhaps pay too much attention to these words, seeing that they lead up to a paragraph dedicated to the praises of Charles II who "at his return . . . found a nation lost as much in barbarism as in rebellion; and, as the excellency of his nature forgave the one, so the excellency of his manners reformed the other."[12] In any event, the truth as regards *Love's Labour's Lost* was the exact opposite of what Dryden states. It was essentially a court play, could have been written only by one thoroughly "conversant" with the "wit, language and conversation," the manners and badinage of court life, and for that very reason among others, it fell rapidly out of favour, when the fashions changed. Hazlitt, who was too much taken with the figures in the underplot of the play to "set a mark of reprobation on it" as a whole, observed nevertheless that "Shakespear has set himself to imitate the tone of polite society then prevailing among the fair, the witty, and the learned, and he has imitated it but too faithfully."[13]

And there are two other features of the play, which must have contributed greatly to its popularity among the young noblemen and inns-of-court men for whom it was composed, but seriously detract from its reputation with posterity.

First, it was Shakespeare's most elaborate and sustained essay in satire and burlesque. It teems with topical allusions to persons known to the original audience—allusions bound to fade with the passing hour and with the fading memories of the persons concerned; never very explicit, even at the outset. Anything in the nature of direct lampooning of the great, however much out of favour at the moment, would be most inadvisable, so swift and sudden were the revolutions of Fortune's wheel at the court of those times. Hints were dropped—scattered broadcast indeed—and personal traits were perhaps aped upon the stage; but, if the spectators put two and two together and made five—that was their own look-out. As Jaques puts it in a later play,

> I must have liberty
> Withal, as large a charter as the wind,
> To blow on whom I please, for so fools have;
> And they that most are gallèd with my folly,
> They most must laugh; and why, sir, must they so?
> The "why" is plain as way to parish church:
> He that a fool doth very wisely hit
> Doth very foolishly, although he smart,
> Not to seam senseless of the bob: if not,
> The wise man's folly is anatomized
> Even by the squand'ring glances of the fool.[14]

And in the second place, *Love's Labour's Lost* is "a great feast of language." The English tongue was not only changing with unparalleled rapidity in the early nineties, at which period it was written, but the English people were peculiarly conscious of it. A fresh stream of words was pouring into the language, drawing its tributaries from many sources; all sorts of new experiments were being tried out, some of them high-flown and most egregious; and the effect of all this was the bewilderment of the uneducated, who made up the bulk of the nation, and the recreation of the educated, who found it in a game which they played with unflagging zest.

And of all the games played with the English tongue in the theatre of that age, *Love's Labour's Lost* was the most zestful, and must have seemed to contemporaries the most fascinating. It exemplifies and holds up to ridicule at least three distinct types of linguistic extravagance or corruption:

(a)   the stilted preciosity of court circles in Armado, whose pretentious eloquence is thus described by a rival rhetorician: "His humour is lofty, his discourse peremptory, his tongue filed, his eye ambitious, his gait majestical, and his general behavior vain, ridiculous and thrasonical. He is too picked, to spruce, too affected, too odd as it were, too peregrinate, as I may call it."[15]

(b)   then there is the pedantic affectation of Holofernes, the schoolmaster, who speaks the words just quoted, the affectation of the dictionary and the school-book of colloquies. His "epithets are sweetly varied" and his shadow the curate, who follows him about reverently with his table-book ready to "draw" at any moment for the noting down of the "singular and choice epithets" that fall from his lips, sums him up (by contrast) in his description of the unlettered Dull:

Sir, he hath never fed of the dainties that are bred in a book; he hath not eat paper, as it were, he hath not drunk ink; his intellect is not replenished, he is only an animal, only sensible in the duller parts:

And such barren plants are set before us that we thankful should be, Which we of taste and feeling are, for those parts that do fructify in us more than he.[16]

(c)   lastly there is Dull himself, and Costard the King's fool,[17] who represents the rustic misunderstanding and misuse, or the deliberate distortion by the jester, of the new wealth of words.

But if all this be so; if *Love's Labour's Lost* is replete with satirical hints about dead persons, some of them hardly known by name to scholars today, with parodies of fashions in speech demoded three centuries ago, and with three- or four-piled verbal ingenuities which can only be reconstructed (though hardly brought back to life) by the most laborious explanation—what possible significance or interest can it have for us in the twentieth century? To Charlton, who edited the play in 1917,

> It is deficient in plot and in characterisation. There is little story in it. Its situations do not present successive incidents in an ordered plot. . . . Four men take an oath to segregate themselves from the society of women for a term of years: circumstance at once compels them to a formal interview with four women; they break their oath. That is the whole story. . . . Clearly a story as simple as is this permits of little elaboration in the dramatic plotting of it. The oath is patently absurd. . . . Clearly it must be broken, and the only interest aroused is in the manner of the breach.
>
> All four men might forswear themselves in chorus, and have done with it; but by letting each lover try to hide his lapse from his fellows, a way is made for progressive revelations in the one scene of the play which is really diverting as a dramatic situation. . . . There are other scenes in which the actions and the words contribute equally to the theatrical interest; for example, that in which the men are led to a wrong identification of the masqued [sic] ladies; but they are accidental to the working out of the story, not really different in kind from the pageants, the masques, and the dances which make the padding of the play.
>
> But the worst consequences of the poverty of the story appear in the persons who perform it. The four courtiers could not but resemble each other in a wooden conformity; for they all have to do the same thing, and have all to be guilty of an act of almost incredible stupidity. . . . To the eye, at all events, the ladies of *Love's Labour's Lost* are a little more individualised than are the men; for being ladies, the colour of the hair and the texture of the skin are indispensable items in the inventory. . . . Yet under the skin, these ladies are as empty and as uniform as are their wooers. . . .
>
> No profound apprehension of life will be expected from *Love's Labour's Lost*. . . . So much and so little was Shakespeare when he began.[18]

So much and so little, one is tempted to retort, can one understand about a play when one has only read it in a book. And in saying this I am condemning myself. For in 1923, I, like Charlton, had edited *Love's Labour's Lost* and like him had therefore come to know it in no superficial fashion. We had both as it were eaten its paper and drunk its ink; and yet because we had never seen it upon the stage, or at any rate properly produced, we had missed the whole art and meaning of it. Truly, as Berowne says:

> Why, all delights are vain, but that most vain
> Which with pain purchased, doth inherit pain—
> As painfully to pore upon a book,
> To seek the light of truth, while truth the while
> Doth falsely blind the eyesight of his look.[19]

For two strenuous years I had purchased much delight from poring over the textual and topical and glossarial problems with which it teems, but without ever seeing the play as a play any more than Charlton had.

In 1927 Granville-Barker devoted one of his challenging prefaces to it, in which, after declaring that "there is life in it," that "it abounds in beauties of fancy and phrase, as beautiful today as ever," he made a valiant attempt to show that, with judicious cuts, the play was still worth a producer's pains. I read the preface with great interest, and with all respect due to its author, but I remained sceptical. For after all, the theatre had long ago given its verdict. The thing, I said to myself, was dead to the stage, quite dead.

And then, nine years after his *Preface* appeared, Granville-Barker was proved to be more right than even he can have dreamed possible. For in the summer of 1936 Mr. Tyrone Guthrie revived the play at the Old Vic, dressed it magnificently, put all his very considerable brains into the production, and revealed it as a first-rate comedy of the pattern kind—so full of fun, of *permanent* wit, of brilliant and entrancing situation, that you hardly noticed the faded jesting and allusion, as you sat spell-bound and drank it all in. It was a thrilling production, Shakespearian criticism of the best kind, because a real piece of restoration. The only thing wrong about it was that the critics, the plodding editors and the dictatorial professors had so infected the public with their bookish notions that no one went to see it. It was played to half empty houses for a fortnight or so, and taken off.

But I went, I saw, I was completely conquered; and I was not alone, for Alfred Pollard, my father in Shakespeare, went with me and was as completely conquered. I have had many memorable and revealing evenings with Shakespeare in the theatre—*Hamlet* in modern dress, *Othello* with Paul Robeson in the title role and Peggy Ashcroft as Desdemona, and so on, but none equal to this. For Mr. Guthrie not only gave me a new play, the existence of which I had never suspected, which indeed had been veiled from men's eyes for three centuries, but he set me at a fresh standpoint of understanding and appreciation from which the whole of Shakespearian comedy might be reviewed in a new light. The occasion had found the man, but the thing could probably not have happened earlier. *Love's Labour's Lost* had to wait until the whirligig of time brought both the pattern-play and a producer who believed in it once again into the English theatre.

I propose, therefore, to spend the rest of this chapter in discussing the play from the point of view of a spectator, not from that of an editor.

The first thing one notices about it in the theatre is its extraordinary vivacity; it was evidently written in the highest possible spirits, by a dramatist who was thoroughly enjoying himself, and knew how to make his audience enjoy themselves thoroughly also. If the actors catch this spirit of merriment and alertness, as they can hardly help doing, the spectators will be carried right off their feet from the outset; so much so that the sixteenth-century allusions will seem little more than pebbles in the eddying, yet never-ceasing ripples of the laughter. The critics insist that none of the characters is quite human—we shall see presently what is to be said about that—but at least they are one and all exceedingly bright and agile. Even "most Dull, honest Dull," the constable, catches the infection, feels that itching of the toes which all the rest display, so that his last words are

> I'll make one in a dance, or so; or I'll play
> On the tabor to the worthies, and let them dance the hay.[20]

The spirit of the whole is far more like that of a Mozart opera—quite an interesting comparison might be made with *Cosi fan tutte*—than anything we are accustomed to in modern drama.

But quotation will give a better idea of the pace of the play than mere description.

"Master," exclaims the page Moth, who dances about the portentous but magnificent Armado like a glistening speck of dust in sunlight, "will you win your love with a French brawl?"

> ARMADO. How meanest thou? brawling in French?
> MOTH. No, my complete master—but to jig off a tune at the tongue's
>   end, canary to it with your feet, humour it with turning up
>   your eyelids, sigh a note and sing a note, sometime through
>   the nose as if you snuffed up love by smelling love, with your
>   hat penthouse-like o'er the shop of your eyes, with your arms

crossed on your thin-belly doublet like a rabbit on a spit, or
your hands in your pocket like a man after the old painting—
and keep not too long in one tune, but a snip and away![21]

Prose—but what rhythm! The speaker's body and feet are constantly on the
move; he dances the brawl. "Snip and away" might be the play's sub-title.
Its structure may be mechanical, its plot feeble, its "apprehension of life"
shallow—as the critics allege—but it *goes*, goes with a swing and an impetus which, when seen on the stage, are irresistible. For sheer gaiety none of
Shakespeare's other comedies can beat it, not even the golden *As You Like
It* or that buck-basket stuffed full of fantastics, *The Merry Wives of Windsor*.

But "keep not too long in one tune," admonishes Moth, and so introduces us to the next outstanding quality of the play—its constant variety. This too can only be rightly appreciated in the theatre. What one first
notices is the varied play of colour, which my eyes first learned to feast upon
at the Old Vic performance. But I run ahead. To proceed more orderly, let
us first consider pattern and begin with the plot, of which all the commentators speak so scornfully. It is slight, though no slighter than that of some
of Shakespeare's other comedies, for it contains much more than has hitherto been allowed, and it constitutes the canvas upon which the rest of the
dramatic pattern is woven.

The King of Navarre and three sprightly young friends at his court
decide to devote themselves to study for three years. The decision takes the
form of the establishment of an academy which will embrace the whole court.

Navarre shall be the wonder of the world.

Such little academes were common enough at the time of the Renaissance. Hundreds of them were set up in the petty Italian courts in the fifteenth and sixteenth centuries.[22] And when the King tells us his reason for its establishment:

Let fame, that all hunt after in their lives,
Live registered upon our brazen tombs,

he gives utterances to yet another Renaissance commonplace. Had not Cicero
written "Trahimur omnes laudis studio, et optimus quique maxime gloria
ducitur?" and was not Milton, forty years later, still declaring that

Fame is the spur that the clear spirit doth raise
To scorn delights and live laborious days—

lines that exactly express the theme of *Love's Labour's Lost*, though from how different a standpoint!

We are not told the subject of study—but it is clearly philosophy, and Berowne's talk of star-gazing and the vow "to sleep but three hours of the night" points to natural philosophy, i.e. science, in its most popular form of astronomy. More stress is laid upon the kind of life the students are to lead, which is obviously stoical. They vow to fast once a week, to sleep but three hours out of the twenty-four, and to shut women out of the court altogether.

The last, of course, is what matters in the play. When it opens, the four men have just taken a solemn oath to observe this strict rule of life, and their oath is the pivot of the plot. "This oath," says Charlton, "is patently absurd." Of course; Shakespeare meant it to be. But it is at once more and less serious than Charlton perceived. More serious, because oaths were frequently taken by Elizabethans and meant much more in their life than they do to us, who except in a court of law seldom if ever bind ourselves in this fashion. Shakespeare's audience derived all the more fun, therefore, from watching the oath-takers becoming forsworn as they try to wriggle out of their solemn undertaking. Less serious, because Shakespeare makes it clear from the outset that the oath must be broken. And the comic idea of the play is the absurdity not only of the oath, but also of these academes which drive their votaries to tie themselves up into knots of the kind. And this, in turn, is symbolical of the absurdity of the purely academic view of life in general.

The play falls into two halves: (i) the retreat from Philosophy, (ii) the campaign for Love. At the outset, I have said, the oath has just been taken, and the fellow-students are about to "subscribe" their names to the schedule which embodies the terms of their undertaking; such subscription being a particularly solemn form of oath-taking. As they do so, Longaville and Dumaine reaffirm their intentions, but Berowne frankly expresses his scepticism, criticizes the whole scheme, and reminds the King that he cannot shut women out of his court, since the Princess of France is due to arrive with an embassy at any moment. Thus it is obvious from the beginning that it is impossible to live like stoics in a real world. And after this the academe rapidly crumbles. Costard, the unlettered swain, is naturally the first defaulter; but Armado is another. No sooner do the French ladies arrive than signs of weakness appear in the four students themselves. We next have Berowne's confession (all the more striking because unwilling) that he "that had been love's whip" was now love's slave. And the whole movement culminates in the delightful IV.3 in which each of the students gives himself away in the ears of the others, Berowne utters his great speech of recantation, and all, confessedly forsworn, determine to pursue their courtship *vi et armis*.

In the second half of the play, therefore, study is relegated to a subsidiary place: its claims and absurdities are represented by minor characters (pedant and curate) recently introduced into the drama (for this purpose). The main theme is the Love campaign, and the manner in which the four ladies constantly thwart the advances of the men. It is an elaborate flirtation (the word was unknown in this sense to Shakespeare) accompanied by masques, dances and an interlude. After many checks, the campaign is at last pushed home and victory seems in sight, when "at the latest minute of the hour" the cup is dashed from the lovers' lips by the news of the French King's death. The men are compelled to take a second vow and condemned to wait another year. This last defeat is one of the main points of the play, as its title *Love's Labour's Lost* indicates. The whole is then rounded off with the delightful mockery of the Cuckoo and the Owl, in which the learned men display their knowledge of life by translating the call of spring into a word of fear and the hoot of the owl into a merry note. There is a purpose behind all this, to which I shall return in my conclusion. For the moment, however, watch the patterning.

In the first place, the play is full of speech pattern. There is of course a great deal of rhyme in *Love's Labour's Lost*—so much so that many have thought it must be Shakespeare's earliest play, on the theory that the passage from rhyme to blank verse is one of the indications of his development in dramatic power. But the rhyme here, as in Dryden and Pope, is part of the wit; it adds just that touch of artificiality required for a pattern-play; it points the jest and gives the grace of an echo to the happy repartee. Without rhyme *Love's Labour's Lost* would lose much of its life and colour. But rhyme is not the only form of verse. When something serious shows through the glitter of the surface, blank verse is used. Thus Berowne, who laughingly defends his black mistress in rhyme, turns to blank verse in his great speech of recantation, while it is noticeable that little but blank verse is spoken after the entry of the messenger of death in V.2. An analysis of the whole play according to its use of rhyme, blank verse, and prose would be instructive. Glance a moment, for instance, at the opening scene. It begins solemnly; the King announcing the oath and the three courtiers giving their respective assents to it. Lines 1–48 therefore are in blank verse. Yet the whole thing is artificial, and, as we are intended to feel, a little comic: therefore the blank verse is end-stopped and the speeches terminate in couplets. Then, when Berowne makes his protestation, and the tone becomes lively, even flippant, the blank verse is dropped and the banter of the men, together with Berowne's mock rhetoric, is conveyed in couplets, quatrains and sonnets: a rhyme-pattern that forms a delightful accompaniment to the dialogue, something like the patter of feet on the floor in a Polish mazurka. And even when Costard and Dull enter at line 181 and prose begins, the patterning is not at an end, for Shakespeare writes his prose as well as his verse in patterned form in this play.

The structure of *Love's Labour's Lost* is of course a pattern also. The two parts are almost exactly equal in length, Berowne's recantation occurring about half-way through. But perhaps the most remarkable instance of parallelism in the two parts is in regard to the oaths. The oaths of the students at the beginning are offset by the oaths of the lovers at the end—with a significant difference, however. The students swear to follow the pagan stoical life for the sake of fame; the lovers are compelled to take *religious* vows as a penance for perjury and as a means of regeneration. And this system of repetition and echo is not confined to the main plot but is carried out in detail of all sorts throughout the play. For example in I.1, Costard's confession concerning Jaquenetta is followed by Armado's letter —both, though in different fashion, going over the same points. Or again, Armado's soliloquy in I.2 is matched by Berowne's in III.1; both have the same theme (contemptuous confession of Cupid's power) and both end with a promise of poetry. Or yet again, we have Armado's letter to Jaquenetta (franked by remuneration) contrasted with Berowne's letter to Rosaline (franked by a guerdon). Or lastly, take once more the famous recantation scene. Each of the four men in turn comes on to the stage, makes his confession of love and perjury, reads aloud his poem and hides himself as his successor appears. And when all have revealed their secrets in the view of their fellows, one by one they step forth again to denounce the perjurer who has last spoken, until at length Berowne the first comer and original spy springs down from his tree to denounce the lot, only to be himself unmasked by the entry of Costard and Jaquenetta with his incriminating letter to Rosaline. The scene winds itself up and unwinds itself again for all the world as if four boys were dancing and reversing about a maypole.

It would be idle to multiply examples, some of them of the subtlest character, so subtle that like the lesser variations upon a theme in music they are felt rather than perceived; suffice it to say that repetition with variations is one of the mainsprings of the play's structure.

But there is another, for there are two elements in every pattern, balance and contrast as well as repetition and variation. These are secured in *Love's Labour's Lost* chiefly by the grouping of characters, and by the shifting colour effects produced by the regrouping.

The play, we are told, is "deficient in characterization." But "characterization" is not one of the purposes of the play. Occasionally the persons fall into character, but as they do they tend to fall out of the pattern.

The minor characters are intended as types—the traditional types of the *commedia dell'arte*—not as rounded human characters at all, and Berowne tells us as much when he sums them up as the pedant, the braggart, the hedge-priest, the fool and the boy.[23] Charlton indeed declared Costard to be "the most considerable character" in the play and quotes as evidence Costard's oft-quoted words about Sir Nathaniel Alisander as the latter departs discomforted:

> There, an't shall please you, a foolish mild man—an honest man, look you, and soon dashed. He is a marvellous good neighbour, faith, and a very good bowler; but for Alisander, alas you see how 'tis—a little o'erparted.[24]

On the other hand, Granville-Barker, who had to think about stage-production and casting, comes to a very different conclusion, that Costard is (as Berowne calls him) "the fool," i.e. the official jester at the court of Navarre. And had it not been for the Alisander passage there would have been no doubt about it—the mask slips and accidentally reveals a face. For a moment Costard has stepped out of the stage design and become a man, as a Shakespearian Fool is in other plays.

As to the eight principals—the two groups of student lovers and mocking wenches, who "resemble each other in a wooden conformity," who "have all to do the same sort of thing," they constitute of course the most striking feature of the design and they do so the more effectively in that they provide the main element in the colour scheme.

The Elizabethan actors, saved all the cost of scenery and lighting which swells the bill of modern production, are known to have spent lavishly upon dress; and *Love's Labour's Lost*, which contains a sixteenth-century King and three attendant nobles, all in choice costume of similar though not identical cut and design; a French Princess with her three ladies also brilliantly tricked out in dresses of a quasi-uniform style (for when they mask they must look alike); the foppish old courtier Boyet; and "fashion's own knight," Don Adriano de Armado, with the page Moth at his heels, must have presented a perfect riot of colour and magnificence, to which the pedant and the curate, the patched fool, the frieze cloth constable and the ragged dairymaid acted as foils.

And the scenes are so arranged that the colour-scheme is constantly changing: the King and his lords are outblazoned by Armado and Moth, who after being contrasted with the simplicity of Dull, Costard, and Jaquenetta, are in their turn followed by the dapper Boyet and his bevy of dainty ladies. Next, the two main groups are brought together for the splendour of Navarre to confront the grace of France, and this first meeting is followed, of course, by many others. The encounters of the two groups are like dramatic minuets. In the Muscovite scene, indeed, we get what is obviously intended to represent, in a kind of comic ballet, opposing armies with heralds passing to and fro; the men masked and disguised as Russians, on one side of the stage, and the women, likewise masked and disguised by the interchange of "fairings,"[25] on the other. First Moth advances as "herald" for the men and after a vain attempt to deliver his "ambassage" retires in confusion. Then Boyet advances to the men and demands their intentions. This business is particularly effective on the stage, because though the two parties are only a few yards apart, the nimble Boyet runs backwards and forwards between them like a busy herald receiving and delivering messages; until at length the ladies line up, dress themselves by the right, make one pace forwards and speak to the enemy face to face.

So the kaleidoscope goes on, until suddenly, with the effect of a smashing hammer-stroke, there appears a figure clothed in black from head to foot. Death enters and the brilliant "scene begins to cloud."

The extraordinary impression left upon the audience by the entrance of the black-clad messenger upon the court revels was the greatest lesson I took away with me from the Guthrie production. It made me see two things— (a) that however gay, however riotous a Shakespearian comedy may be, tragedy is always there, *felt*, if not seen; (b) that for all its surface lightness and frivolity, the play had behind it a serious mind at work, with a purpose.

In conclusion then consider this purpose for a moment.[26] First there is the terrible portrait of a Renaissance schoolmaster, self-complacent, self-seeking, irascible, pretentious, intolerant of what he calls "barbarism," and yet himself knowing nothing but the pitiful rudiments, the husks of learning, which he spends his life thrusting down the throats of his unfortunate pupils. Holofernes moves upon Shakespeare's stage as the eternal type of pedant, the "living-dead man"[27] who will always be with us, because so long as there is a human race to be educated there will always be many to mistake the letter for the spirit.

It is a pity that *Love's Labour's Lost* is in parts so obscure, so topical. Else it might be commended without hesitation to the attention of all teachers, professors, and educationalists to be read once a year—on Ash Wednesday, shall we say?—for their souls' good. For we have here, not only in the figure of Holofernes, but in the play as a whole, Shakespeare's great onslaught upon the Dark Tower, the fortress of the enemies of life and grace and gaiety—

> The round squat tower, blind as the fool's heart,

the name of which is Pedantry. Against it he hoists the banner of Love, but though he talks much of ladies and their bright eyes, he means by love what Shelley means when he writes, "The great secret of morals is Love; or a going out of our own nature, and an identification of ourselves with the beautiful which exists in thought, action, or person, not our own,"[28] or what Rupert Brooke means when he tells Frederick Keeling that "his occupation is being in love with the universe."[29] Love for Shakespeare, in short, is a symbol of that passionate apprehension of Life, which sets all five senses afire and is the great gift of the poet and the artist to his fellows. And Berowne gives us the conclusion of the whole matter at IV.3.301ff.

> Why, universal plodding prisons up
> The nimble spirits in the arteries.
>
> .   .   .   .   .   .
>
> But love, first learnéd in a lady's eyes,
> Lives not alone immuréd in the brain,
> But with the motion of all elements,
> Courses as swift as thought in every power,
> And gives to every power a double power,
> Above their functions and their offices.
> It adds a precious seeing to the eye—
> A lover's eyes will gaze an eagle blind;
> A lover's ear will hear the lowest sound,
> When the suspicious heed[30] of theft is stopped;
> Love's feeling is more soft and sensible
> Than are the tender horns of cockled snails;
> Love's tongue proves dainty Bacchus gross in taste.
> For valor, is not Love a Hercules,
> Still climbing trees in the Hesperides?
> Subtle as Sphinx, as sweet and musical
> As bright Apollo's lute, strung with his hair;
> And when Love speaks, the voice of all the gods
> Make heaven drowsy with the harmony.
> Never durst poet touch a pen to write,
> Unless his ink were temp'red with Love's sighs.

1. Chambers, *The Elizabethan Stage* Vol. 4, p. 139; *William Shakespeare* Vol. 2, p. 332.

2. *Essays of John Dryden*, ed. by W. P. Ker (1926), Vol. 1, p. 165.

3. *The Plays of William Shakespeare*, ed. by Samuel Johnson (1765), Vol. 2, p. 224.

4. It is noteworthy that the young Goethe and his friends at Strassburg, rejoicing in Shakespeare, made a special study of *Love's Labour's Lost* both in translation and the original, delighting even in its "quibbles." See *Dichtung und Wahrheit*, Book 11 (1770–71).

5. Ed. 1907, p.163.

6. Dryden, op. cit., Vol. 1, p. 173.

7. *2 Henry IV*, I.2.160.

8. V.2.56–62.

9. V.2.241–50.

10. Cf. G.D. Willcock, op. cit., and *Hamlet* (New Cambridge) Introduction, pp. xxxv–xliii.

11. Dryden, op. cit., Vol. 1, p. 175; "Ben Johnson" is his spelling.

12. Dryden, op. cit., p. 176.

13. William Hazlitt, *Characters of Shakespear's Plays*, 1817.

14. *As You Like It*, II.7.47–57.

15. V.1.9–14.

16. IV.2.23–29.

17. See the discussion of Costard later in this essay.

18. H.B. Charlton, *Shakespearian Comedy* (1938), pp. 270ff.

19. I.1.72–76.

20. V.1.148–49.

21. III.1.8–21.

22. See for example *The French Academies of the Sixteenth Century* by Frances A. Yates, Warburg Institute, 1947.

23. V.2.539–40.

24. V.2.577–81.

25. V.2.2.

26. What follows is virtually a repetition of a passage from an essay on Shakespeare's Schoolmasters which I gave to the Royal Society of Literature in 1928.

27. The epithet belongs to another schoolmaster, Dr. Pinch, the pedant in *The Comedy of Errors* (V.1.242).

28. *Defence of Poetry*.

29. Edward Marsh, *Collected Poems of Rupert Brooke with a Memoir*, 1918, p. liv.

30. An anonymous emendation cited in the (old) Cambridge Shakespeare. The 1598 Q reads "head." "Heed"=what attracts attention; cf. I.1.82.

LOVE'S LABOR'S LOST
AND THE EARLY SHAKESPEARE

Alfred Harbage

After remarking that Sir Edmund Chambers, "the very pink of orthodoxy and paragon of caution," declines to recognize any date earlier than 1590–91 for Shakespeare's extant work, F.P. Wilson continues,

> The fact is that the chronology of Shakespeare's earliest plays is so uncertain that it has no right to harden into an orthodoxy, and perhaps we should do better to say that by 1592 he had certainly written *Henry VI* (all three parts), *Richard III, The Comedy of Errors,* probably *Titus Andronicus* and possibly *The Taming of the Shrew,* and that the earliest of these may have been written as early as 1588.[1]

The statement, like the delightful book in which it appears, is liberal in intention but it is tinged with the orthodoxy which it gently rebukes. As it proceeds from "certainly" to "probably" to "possibly," still excluding *Love's Labor's Lost,* it seems to sound an irrevocable doom. At the beginning of the eighteenth century *Love's Labor's Lost* was considered Shakespeare's first (and worst) play. At the end of the nineteenth, although "worst" was no longer a permissible word in Shakespearean commentary, the best Shakespeare scholars were convinced that "the first draft of the comedy must have been written when the author was a youth."[2] These "best scholars" were F.J. Furnivall, presiding genius of the New Shakespeare Society; F.G. Fleay, indefatigable analyst of versification and sundry clues; A.W. Ward, leading historian of the English drama; and Sir Sidney Lee, Shakespeare's "definitive" biographer. Their date for the play was 1587–90. "To *Love's Labor's Lost*," said Lee decisively, "may reasonably be assigned priority in point of

---

Originally published in *Philological Quarterly* 41, no. 1 (January, 1962), 18–36. Reprinted by permission.

time of all Shakespeare's dramatic productions."[3] This was the *old* orthodoxy. With equal decisiveness the best scholars of the present century have dated the play in the mid-nineties as one of the lyrical group. This is the *new* orthodoxy.

Orthodoxies are begotten of orthodoxies; firm stands on debatable issues are often assumed, at least in part, in reaction to preceding stands. Old opinions are recognizable as articles of belief. New opinions are easily mistaken for fact. Perhaps it is safest to remain moderate in faith.

One of the forces which have led to the re-dating of *Love's Labor's Lost* is the twentieth-century tendency to upgrade plays formerly regarded as unworthy such as *Titus Andronicus* and *Troilus and Cressida*; it is another brand snatched from the burning. In the eighteenth and nineteenth centuries it was considered poor and early. It is no longer considered poor, and hence (small value in this *hence*) no longer considered early. Scholars have insisted, and rightly, that it is poor only if judged by standards inapplicable to it. It is a coterie play, a "courtly" play, and stands naturally in contrast with the popular plays which have established in our minds the Shakespearean norm. So far so good. It is when we ask how a coterie play came to be written during the single interval when there were no coterie theatres (1591–98) that we detect a thinning of the ice. "Doubtless," says Kittredge, "the play was written for performance at court or at some great house."[4] The view is shared by Chambers ("suggests a courtly rather than a popular audience")[5] and by the two most ambitious of its modern editors, Dover Wilson ("written for a private performance in the house of some grandee")[6] and Richard David ("written for private performance in court circles").[7] This is a meager sampling of current affirmations—which are usually supplemented with suggestions of particular occasions in particular great houses where the play might have seen its birth.

Love's Labor's Lost thus joins the swelling list of plays for which private auspices of production are hypothesized: *Midsummer Night's Dream* for a noble wedding (with various weddings deemed appropriate), *Merry Wives* for an installation fête of the Order of the Garter (with several installations available), *Troilus and Cressida* for a feast at the inns of court (there were four inns and many feasts), and so on. The trouble is that there is nothing to support any of these hypotheses except the other hypotheses, now functioning as ghostly precedents. There is no supporting external evidence to prove that any regular play performed by any regular company, juvenile or adult, was originally written for a special occasion during the whole reign of Elizabeth and lifetime of Shakespeare. This total absence of evidence would be rather remarkable if such plays were as common in fact as they have become in theory. They are the kind of thing (as witness the entertainments offered during Elizabeth's progresses, and the masques at James's court) such as would have left records—in household accounts, in contemporary gossip, and on title pages. Instead we have records like the following:

> I have sent and bene all thys morning huntyng for players, Juglers & Such kinde of Creaturs, but fynde them harde to finde, wherfore Leavinge notes for them to seeke me, Burbage ys come, & Sayes ther ys no new playe that the quene hath not seene, but they have Revyved an olde one, Cawled *Loves Labore lost*, which for wytt & mirthe he sayes will please her excedingly. And Thys ys apointed to be playd to Morowe night at my Lord of Sowthamptons, unless yow send awrytt to Remove the Corpus Cum Causa to your howse in Strande. Burbage ys my messenger Ready attendyng your pleasure.[8]

The tone of this epistle conveys much truth about the theatrical world of the Elizabethans, who did not accord their great drama quite the respect that we do. That they were willing to accept for their private occasions plays from the regular repertories is proven by *many* records, of the royal court, the inns of court, and the "great houses." The Essex faction, even when in need of a propaganda piece in 1601, settled for *Richard II*, a back-number in the Chamberlain's Men's repertory. In 1599 Henslowe paid Dekker £2 "for the eande of Fortewnates for the corte."[9] He had already paid Dekker £7 for working over the play, which had been in some form or other part of the Admiral's Men's repertory since at least 1596. A company was willing to invest £2 in presumed royal gratitude, charging the sum against the modest fee they would receive for the court performance, but to buy and mount an entire play would have been another matter. And there is little to suggest that the court, the inns of court, or the great houses would have been willing to underwrite an entire production by professional actors, whose regular wares were available at fixed rates. Moreover, the writing and rehearsing of a play was a considerable undertaking, then as now, requiring more time than was normally available during preparations for a party. It does not follow that there was never a play *ad hoc*, but in view of the difficulties and the absence of records, it is clear that they could not have been common—not common enough surely to supply an easy explanation for the puzzling characteristics of every puzzling play. The burden of proof rests with those who resort to the explanation.

Love's Labor's Lost was duly performed for Queen Anne in 1605 after Burbage made his suggestion. It had probably been performed before Queen

Elizabeth under similar circumstances before its publication in 1598—"As it was presented before her Highness this last Christmas. Newly corrected and augmented By W. Shakespeare." The best scholars of the old orthodoxy naïvely read "newly corrected and augmented" to mean that Shakespeare had refurbished a play for the court performance much as Dekker had refurbished *Old Fortunatus*. Several duplicate passages in the text indicate cancels printed in error, and hence revision. The twentieth century has learned to read bibliographical evidence more subtly. The duplicate passages indicate revision in the course of original composition rather than in working over old matter; and the "newly corrected and augmented" may mean that there had been a "bad quarto" (now lost) just as there had been a bad quarto of *Romeo and Juliet* before the publication of the good quarto of 1599. True the latter reads "newly corrected, augmented, and amended," a slightly different thing, but we may admit the virtue of the suggestion.

Oddly enough, however, the new bibliographical findings do not in the least affect the old assumption that the 1598 quarto of *Love's Labor's Lost* represents an early play reworked, although they have seemed to do so to the finders. The duplicate passages indicate alterations during original composition, but only during composition of those parts of the play where they occur. Those parts *in toto* may be revisions, and as a matter of fact there is evidence (generally conceded) of revision of a different kind—structural revision, such as continues to suggest what the duplicate passages used to suggest. And although there may have been a "bad quarto," there is no reason to assume that it resembled the bad quarto of *Romeo and Juliet*, a debased version of the extant text. Since we are only hypothesizing it anyway, we may as well hypothesize something more on the order of *A Shrew*, *King Leir*, or the *Troublesome Reign*, or even a *good* version of an earlier form of the present play. Even a bad quarto precisely like that of *Romeo and Juliet* would not cancel the possiblility that the text it debased had itself been "newly corrected and augmented." That the 1598 quarto of *Love's Labor's Lost* was printed from the author's draft seems to me to have been proved,[10] but this draft may well have incorporated whole sheets from an earlier draft. Whereas the new findings do not really affect former assumptions, they seem (quaintly) to have prompted a compromise—to the effect that there *was* an early version but *less early* than formerly assumed. Perhaps it seemed wasteful to offer new data without offering new conclusions.

Of incalculable effect in the dating controversy has been Warburton's fatal surmise of 1747 that Holofernes in *Love's Labor's Lost* represents John Florio. Commentators worried this bone for a century and a half, then suddenly filled the air with dust in digging up rival bones. Warburton spoke with irritating certainty, and he was no intellectual giant; it is fitting that his state-ment should have aroused contempt in our times, but one wishes that the contempt had been directed at his mental processes rather than at their prod-uct. He should be blamed for the nature of his laboring rather than for his mouse. To him the fact that part of A resembled part of B meant that A was B. It means nothing of the kind, but neither do similar equations mean that A was really C or D or E or F, and so on endlessly. Actually, the suggestion that Holofernes is Florio is no worse, and considerably better, than most ri-val suggestions. None of the characters in *Love's Labor's Lost* resemble in other than a generic fashion (and not very much in that) any of the actual persons with whom they have been identified: King Philip, Bishop Cooper, Northumberland, Southampton, Perez, Lyly, Chapman, Ralegh, Harriot, Harvey, Nashe, etc. Not one of the episodes in the play resembles even ge-nerically the actual episodes in the Marprelate and Harvey-Nashe contro-versy, the Southampton marriage negotiations, the association of Ralegh with suspect intellectuals, etc. The methods used by the expounders of "topicali-ties" differ only in degree of recklessness from the methods used by Eva Turner Clark in proving that *Love's Labor's Lost* was written by the Earl of Oxford in 1578[11] or Abel Lefranc in proving that the earl was not Ox-ford but Derby.[12] The method is not that of beginning with a mystery and finding a clue, but of beginning with a clue and finding a mystery. None of the advocates of the rival interpretations have been able to convince one another, and all of them collectively should be unable to convince anyone who has passed an elementary course in logic.

So much in way of truth. Immediately we must recognize that most of the expounders have done sound scholarly work of other kinds, and that their work even in this kind is published under respectable auspices.[13] *Love's Labor's Lost* seems to act upon them as catnip acts upon perfectly sane cats, and possibly the fault lies in the play itself. Although its situations are con-ventional, there is a curious open-endedness about them which sends the fancies groping, and although all its jokes are explicable as jokes, some of them are so execrably bad as to create *hope* for ulterior meanings. And in-deed there are some few phrases associated with the persons and topics ad-duced. Shakespeare used the idiom of his day. There must be other phrases associated with other topics which happily lie too deeply buried for exploi-tation. Catch-phrases derived from current events do not mean that the writ-ing where they occur has to do with those events, and if the phrases appear in revised writing, they tell us nothing of original date and source of inspi-ration. Yet the sheer weight of the discussion of "topicalities," most of which date 1590–95, has created a sentiment or "climate of opinion" in favor of a date of original composition in the mid-nineties, even among those who reject the specific findings of the expounders. Perhaps they are unconsciously influenced by the dubious principle that where there is smoke there must be fire, or perhaps they are simply too charitable to remain impervious to so much earnest endeavor. Still a heap of fallacies has no more authority than any one of the fallacies comprising the heap; otherwise Shakespeare would surely be Bacon. The twentieth-century discussion of the "true meaning" of *Love's Labor's Lost*, heretical though it has seemed to conservative scholars such as Chambers and Kittredge, has nevertheless influenced their new orthodoxy in dating the play c. 1595.

It is time for more positive considerations. Anyone who maintains that the original version of the play was written between 1592 and 1597, and probably about 1595, must supply satisfactory answers to several questions. First of all, why does the play contain 228 lines of verse like the following?

> PRINCESS. What plume of feathers is he that indited this letter?
> What vane? What weathercock? Did you ever hear better?
> BOYET. I am much deceived but I remember the style.
> PRINCESS. Else your memory is bad, going o'er it erewhile.
> BOYET. This Armado is a Spaniard that keeps here in court,
> A phantasime, a Monarcho, and one that makes sport
> To the Prince and his bookmates.
> PRINCESS. Thou fellow, a word:
> Who gave you this letter?
> COSTARD. I told you—my Lord.
>
> (IV.1.93–100)

Nothing resembling such verse appears in *Richard II*, *Midsummer Night's Dream*, or *Romeo and Juliet*, the plays of the lyrical group. Indeed verse of this kind appears in quantity in only one other place in Shakespeare,[14] in Act I, scene 3 of *The Comedy of Errors,* and there has been viewed, at least by some, as a fossil of some quite early anterior version of the play.[15] It is hard to believe that, having adapted so perfectly to his purpose blank verse and the heroic couplet in the plays of the lyrical group (and in parts of *Love's Labor's Lost* itself) Shakespeare would have relapsed to doggerel, and considered it appropriate for the witty exchanges of royal and noble speakers. Dover Wilson, Chambers, and Kittredge have all spoken, justly, of the poetic facility of *Love's Labor's Lost* and the maturity of its blank verse. This means that they have been looking at less inconvenient passages than the one sampled above. Looking at such passages, A.W. Ward spoke of the "peculiarities, not to say crudities, of its versification,"[16] and W. J. Courthope of the resemblance to "the lumbering metre of the Moralities."[17]

Tumbling measures had been characteristic of the school drama of Nicholas Udall (*Ralph Roister Doister*, c. 1553); they persist in the chapel drama of Richard Edwardes (*Damon and Pythias*, 1565); and as late as 1581–84 appear in Peele's *Arraignment of Paris* performed by the Children of the Chapel while based in their theatre at Blackfriars. In fact the latter play, mingling as it does quatrains, heroic couplets, blank verse, etc., with old-fashioned doggerel, provides the nearest analogy we have to the commixture of measures in *Love's Labor's Lost*. Lyly's plays for the boy companies in the eighties were written in prose, but one can easily imagine other plays for these companies continuing in the manner of Peele and persevering in the use of tumbling measures until the end of the decade. Those who can just as easily imagine these measures being used by Shakespeare in a play written for the Chamberlain's Men in the mid-nineties should come to the assistance of the stubborn-minded. Chambers suggests that he was "experimenting" with their comic effect in *The Comedy of Errors*.[18] Was he still "experimenting" in 1595? Charlton's explanation does not strike me as helpful. In dismissing the doggerel as indication of an early date, he says "it is somewhat as if Shakespeare's metrical level at the period of *Hamlet* should be judged by reckoning the Player's declamation and the play within the play as the normal type."[19] But this is precisely my point. The tumbling measures in *Love's Labor's Lost* appear in no extraneous portions of the play, but in exactly those portions where we should expect to find verse of the "normal type."

My second question has to do with why Shakespeare should perversely have hit upon such a constellation of character-names as "Navarre," "Berowne," "Longaville," and "Dumain" for the members of his whimsical semi-Arcadian "academe" if the selection was made at any time later than August 1589. Before that date the choice was logical enough. The family of Navarre ruled in a small kingdom pleasingly associated in English minds with continental Protestantism, and the other names belonged to French noble houses important enough to be linked fictitiously with the "King of Navarre" in some never-never time when his name was Ferdinand, son of Charles. But after August 1589, the case was different. By edict of the deceased Henry III, the actual "Navarre" was now King of France, engaged in a death struggle with the League. The struggle was of crucial concern to the English. Three thousand English levies from London died in Navarre's cause in its first year. In 1591 the Earl of Essex was sent to assist him by besieging Rouen. In April of that year Essex banqueted with Navarre, Biron, and Longaville.

The latter two were no longer just any French lords, but Navarre's most important generals. "Dumain," in contrast, unless audiences had exercised heroic self-discipline in thought control, would have suggested du Maine or de Mayenne, brother of the Guise, and Navarre's formidable opponent. Then in July 1593 Navarre mightily offended Elizabeth and her nation by turning his religious coat and buying Paris "for a mass." It has been argued that such events made Shakespeare's character names "topical."[20] Rather they made the names a-topical or contra-topical. The author had been unlucky in his choice. Tucker Brooke has put the matter best:

> Doubtless Shakespeare first devised his fiction of Navarre and France at a period when it was possible to weave into it recent names and incidents [i.e. involving French embassies to Navarre in 1578–86] still too vague in their connotation for English auditors to jar against the playful spirit of the comedy . . . [but] to say nothing (virtually) of the military fame of the four gentlemen and associate Dumain in friendship with the rest, or alternatively to confuse Dumain with d'Aumont, would have affronted common intelligence if attempted very long after the death of Henry III (Aug. 2, 1589) had brought them all upon the centre of the political stage.[21]

It is hard to believe that *Love's Labor's Lost* could have been written or even performed in England between August 1589 and July 1593, or that its character names would have been voluntarily chosen between 1593 and 1598. Toward the end of the latter period they could have been tolerated in a revival. They were worked into the metrical pattern of a number of lines and would have been hard to excise. Besides, luck was running again with the author. After 1595 Navarre somewhat rehabilitated his name by making war on Spain and aligning himself again with the English. He and du Maine ceased to be enemies. But there would still have been small motive for associating four such portentous names in scenes of pastoral jollity even in 1596–98—and in referring only to a "war" in which Navarre had assisted the "King of France" and incurred certain expenses.

Some of those who have dated the original version of the play in the mid-nineties have been a little discomfited by the facts just reviewed. Dover Wilson admits the curious fact that in Shakespeare's play there is not the "slightest reference" to the war, and surmises that "in 1593 Shakespeare had worked over the manuscript of a 'French comedy' dealing with the incidents referred to [i.e. those of the 1578 French embassy to Navarre] and originally plotted by another dramatist somewhere in the eighties."[22] This does not make quite clear whether the "French comedy" envisioned was a comedy in French or a comedy abut France. If the first is intended, I know of no school of French drama of the time which discussed the affairs of the contemporary *haute monde*, using the names of actual lords. If the second is intended, I see no reason why it should have been "originally plotted by another dramatist" rather than Shakespeare himself. In any case "somewhere in the eighties" is something of a concession.

An elusive "French comedy" reappears in some curious remarks by W.W. Greg:

> Such adumbration of contemporary characters, particularly in an amiable light, is not exactly what we should expect after Henri IV had forfeited English sympathy by turning Catholic in the summer of 1593, and there are refernces in the play that point to a date later than this. It is possible, therefore, that Shakespeare worked on the basis of an earlier "French comedy" that drew upon sources not generally available; but even if that was the case, there is no necessity to suppose that he took from it more than the general situation together with a few names and incidental allusions.[23]

The phrase "not exactly what we should expect" strikes me as an understatement, and unless there are inferences in the passage that escape me, its end contradicts its beginning. Shakespeare, using a "French comedy," voluntarily selected from it those very names the involuntary selection of which the French comedy was originally hypothesized to explain. It seems to me simpler to suppose that he wrote his play about 1588–89 when the selection of the names was logical, and revised it about 1596–97 when the retention of the names was permissible.

My final question is, why should a play written for adult professionals in the mid-nineties so much resemble plays written for child professionals in the mid-eighties? The resemblance is not superficial. It is observable in content, form, and spirit. It seems highly suggestive that all the basic ingredients of the play became available in a cluster in the decade before 1588, and nothing that became available thereafter was used except incidental phrases. Although I agree with many students of the play, that the Holofernes-Nathaniel dialogues belong to the revision, my present point does not hinge upon this assumption.

This is no place to discuss in detail the "sources" of *Love's Labor's Lost*. Its central situation bears some relation to an actual visit in 1578 to Henry of Navarre at Nérac by Marguerite de Valois and her mother, Catherine

of France. The royal visitors were accompanied by *l'escadron volant* of ladies in waiting, and Aquitaine was discussed as part of Marguerite's dowry.
(The parallels with Shakespeare's play were first noted in a good article by
John Phelps in 1899[24] and not, as invariably stated, in a bad book by Abel
Lefranc in 1919.) The negotiations were of a kind to provoke continental
gossip, which seems to have reached the ears of Shakespeare, but they were
not epoch-making, and the interest in the gossip would not long have survived the more spectacular relations between France and Navarre of 1589
and later. By 1595 such gossip would have been very "old hat." The idea of
a Gallic contemplative retreat (associated wih Anjou rather than Navarre)
appears in de la Primaudaye's *French Academy*, translated into English in
1586. The stock characters of *commedia dell'arte*, which seem to have influenced the conception of Armado and Moth, not to speak of Holofernes
and Nathaniel, became known to the English through the visits of Italian
troupes to London before 1588.[25] The plays of Lyly whose specific influence
is discernible in *Love's Labor's Lost* were written between 1584 and 1588.
Lyly enthusiasts may have overstated the indebtedness, but it remains true
that in *Campaspe* there is an incipient philosophical "academy" and a conflict between love and kingly resolves. (In fact the claim of military austerity, or of friendship, or of philosophical detachment as opposed to the claim
of love between the sexes was a staple theme of the early "courtesy books"
as well as of the chorister drama for genteel audiences.) In *Gallathea* (III.1)
Diana's nymphs successively confess their broken vows and agree collectively
to succumb to passion; there is certainly some influence here upon the progressive revelations of recusancy in the most famous scene (IV.3) in *Love's
Labor's Lost*. In *Endymion* the Sir Tophas-Epiton-Bagoa triad shows more
than an accidental resemblance to the Armado-Moth-Jacquenetta triad in
Love's Labor's Lost. It would be phenomenal if so many reminiscences of
Lyly in Shakespeare were a delayed manifestation of 1595. And, finally, the
one plot ingredient that had been supposed conclusively to indicate a late
date[26] indicates nothing of the kind. The Gray's Inn revels of 1594, in which
there was a *conjunction* of Muscovite maskers and blackamoor torch-bear-
ers, has been strongly urged as a source of Shakespeare's play. But there was
just this conjunction in an actual court masque of 1510, and, more important, this masque was described in one of Shakespeare's favorite books,
Holinshed's Chronicles, 1587.[27] Combined with the actual visit of ludicrous
Russians to Elizabeth's court in 1583, this would have been suggestion
enough; and although the Gray's Inn revellers may have hit upon the device
independently, they may also have remembered it in *Love's Labor's Lost*:
they are as likely to have been Shakespeare's debtors as his creditors.

The structure of *Love's Labor's Lost* is radically different from that of typical Shakespearean comedy, and the difference is in the direction of Chapel and Paul's drama of the eighties—in the grouping and balancing of characters, the at-least-perfunctory deference to the "unities," the emphasis upon words at the expense of action, the use of scenes as set pieces rather than as links in an integrated plot. One must note also the large number of parts calling for non-adult actors (five women and a boy), and the absence of a professional court jester even in a comic court. So far as the spirit of the piece is concerned, one hesitates to be frank in the teeth of all that has been said about its adult suavity. It has been praised as representing the very acme of courtly grace, genteel manners, and sophisticated wit, but a reasonably objective reading, with attention to what the characters are actually saying, somewhat shakes one's faith. It is all in good fun, true enough, but the manners projected are atrocious and the characters uniformly barbarous. Their repartee consists largely in attacks upon each other's morals, intelligence, and personal appearance. When not reviling each other, they are reviling each other's sweethearts, whose complexions suggest to the speakers pockiness, dirt, shoe-leather, and other unsavory similes. Some of the retorts are brutal, and they by no means "abrogate scurrility." The one character whose manners achieve a minimal level of social decency is none other than the main butt of the piece—gentle Don Armado. The comic effect derives in the main from impudence, pertness, and animal spirits. In their offstage moments the "king" and his lords are visualized as tumbling about like frolicsome kids.[28] The atmosphere of boisterous juvenility is not a characteristic shared with the plays of Lyly, which are usually quite decorous, but it appears in chorister drama of a later period. I find it more congenial to imagine *Love's Labor's Lost* originally in the repertory of boy actors rather than of grown men.

That the play may have been written for children has been several times suggested, but there has been a singular reluctance to follow the idea home to its logical conclusion. A play originally written for boys would, we should suppose, originally have been produced by a chorister company in a "private" theatre if such a theatre were operating at the time when the play was written. But even those who have vigorously urged 1588–89 as the date of original composition, for instance F.G. Fleay and latterly T.W. Baldwin, have stopped short of such a suggestion.[29] Although Professor Baldwin claims too much for the idea of its only-rudimentary adherence to the alleged "five-act structure" as an indication of early date, and concedes too little about the late style and verbal allusions in parts of the play, neverthless his defence of his dating is often cogent.[30] The trouble is that, like Fleay, he claims the play for Strange's Men playing at the Cross Keys, and it is hard to think of *Love's Labor's Lost* in any form being produced at a converted inn as a rival attraction with a performing horse. None of the popular plays of the eighties resemble it in the least. A decade later, revised, somewhat humanized, and equipped with the sure-fire Holofernes and Nathaniel, it might have gone over as a novelty with a popular audience. Shakespeare himself had helped to educate such audiences in word-play: "We must speak by the card, or equivocation will undo us. By the Lord, Horatio, this three years I have taken note of it, the age is grown so picked that the toe of the peasant comes so near the heel of the courtier he galls his kibe." Still, we must remember that the play is never listed with his popular hits in its own time, and the only specifically indicated performances are those before Queen Elizabeth and Queen Anne.[31]

In 1588–89 there were facilities for such a play as *Love's Labor's Lost* in the commercial theatre of London. Although the Chapel Children had lost the first Blackfriars in 1584, they retained at least a shadowy existence. We hear of them on tour at Norwich in 1586–87 and at Leicester in 1590–91.[32] In 1594 two plays were published with identical inscriptions, "Played by the children of her Maiesties Chappell."[33] Although both seem considerably earlier than the year of publication, both contain writing later than 1584 when the Blackfriars ceased operating. However, the Paul's theatre provides the more interesting possibility. This remained open until 1590, generating plays which were good enough for occasional selection for performance at court. All we have of what must have been an extensive repertory is a few plays by John Lyly. We know positively that there were other plays and other playwrights. Let me propose that Shakespeare's *Love's Labor's Lost* in its original form was written for Paul's in 1588–89 and see what the hypothesis suggests.

The abruptness with which unmistakable allusions to Shakespeare in London begin to appear in 1590–93 creates the impression that his presence there, as distinct from the allusions, was also abrupt. Chambers seems to predicate a swift translation from Stratford to London in 1590, and an equally swift transformation of a provincial artisan or idler of twenty-six into an actor and playwright. In view of the general paucity of allusions to particular companies, plays, and playwrights in and before the period in question, the evidence will bear no such construction, and the probabilities are against it. Neither, in view of the circumstances, does the allusion to him as an "upstart crow" mean that he was *really* an upstart; and we know definitely that the work he himself called the "first heir" of his invention was not *really* the first. Those who predict for him an earlier career in the theatre try to trace back the ancestry of the Chamberlain's and Strange's companies and then postulate his association with such shadowy combinations of actors as emerge. This is better, but also vulnerable, since there was always much recruiting as well as realignment among acting groups. We do not know how Shakespeare became an actor: he may have joined a country troupe after he reached his majority; he may have come to London and haunted the theatres; he may have become a chapel boy in the household of a lord and been superannuated into the theatre. In 1582 Stephen Gosson speaks of actors "trained up from their childhood in this abominable exercise,"[34] and there is no lack of later evidence of chapel actors graduating into adult companies. As Hamlet says of the little eyases, "Will they not say afterwards if they should grow themselves to common players (as it is most like, if their means are no better), their writers do them wrong to make them exclaim against their own succession?" That Shakespeare himself may have walked this route has long been recognized as possible. We know that he was born in 1564, that he married and became a father in 1582–83, and that his wife bore him twins in Stratford in 1585. But marrying and even begetting twins are not exclusive occupations. His residence in Stratford from childhood may have been intermittent, and he may have been selected as a chapel child, as the gifted sons of plain people frequently were. It is not only the period between his production of twin children in Stratford in 1585 and his production of twin plays in London in 1590–91 that must be designated the "lost years."

As a chapel child, dwelling part of the time in a great house, part of the time behind his father's shop, Shakespeare would have gained that insight into two worlds which is one of his most striking characteristics. He would have continued with the education in Latin begun in the Stratford grammar school. As a youth he might have taught younger chapel boys, and guided them in the perfomance of plays. I wish now to bring together some scattered data which have never been satisfactorily explained and which may have some bearing on our subject. The solitary item in the "Shakespeare mythos" which scholars have been inclined to take seriously is John Aubrey's jotting, "He understood Latin pretty well: for he had been in his younger yeares a School-master in the Countrey."[35] There are several reasons for taking it seriously: the information came from Beeston, the son of a member of Shakespeare's own acting company; there is nothing scandalous about it such as would have appealed to Aubrey; there is nothing "generic" about it like the stories of deer-poaching and the like; and finally there is nothing in the least striking or colorful about it such as would suggest any reason for communicating it except the fact that it was true.

Now what does "School-master in the Countrey" suggest? To the American it suggests "country schoolmaster," perhaps evoking an image of Ichabod Crane. To the English I suspect that it suggests Nickleby's term of servitude in Dotheboys Hall, and perhaps the reference to the "charge-house on the top of the mountain" (V.1.58) where Holofernes presides would fortify this impression. I am ignorant of the various routes to the teaching profession in the sixteenth century, but I am inclined to believe that a regular "schoolmaster" would normally be a university graduate, and that the equivalent of an usher would only be found in a sizable school in a sizable town. My guess is that "in the Countrey" as Beeston or Aubrey would use the term would mean "in a country house"—the seat of a landed gentleman or nobleman. Here a non-university youth might quite well pass on such Latin as he had acquired to the more youthful recruits of the chapel, taking this load off the chaplain.

Chapels in the environs of London transformed themselves into regular acting companies, the occupants of "private" theatres. Chapels "in the country" sometimes went on theatrical tours. The "Earl of Oxford's Company" played at Bristol in 1581, "being I man and IX boys."[36] In 1581 Shakespeare was seventeen, "a codling when 'tis almost an apple: 'tis with him in standing water, between man and boy"; hence we might cast him either as the "I man" or one of the "IX boys" and remember that an association with Oxford's chapel could have landed him in 1584 squarely in the first Blackfriars theatre—as a coach and writer, of course, rather than as a juvenile actor. We may write off Oxford entirely (baleful name in Shakespearean speculation) and still recognize that Shakespeare may have penetrated the acting profession by almost growing up in it. We must always recognize that such an unusual man must have been an unusual boy and youth, and that there were "divers of worship" other than Oxford who could have brought him into the orbit of the Blackfriars and Paul's theatricals. With F.P. Wilson I fully agree that he must have known he was a poet from the first. I should go further and say that anyone who wrote plays like his of the early nineties, inferior though they may be when compared to his own later work, had nevertheless been writing plays for a considerable length of time.

Shakespeare lacked the family connections and the university degree of a John Lyly, such as might have put him in charge of a chapel company, but he could have served as a "Johannes factotum." Chapel masters had at one time acted with their boys, and occasional rôles in the plays of Lyly, such as that of Sir Tophas, suggest that the tradition of including an adult actor may have been maintained. Perhaps an adult who had been a chapel-boy actor would have been a useful adjunct about Paul's when long commercialization had rendered acting *infra dig* for the chapel master or the genteel entrepreneur associated with him. A good adult voice may have been useful too—and a good composer of drama of the time. Who wrote the songs for Lyly's plays, nearly all of which were excluded from editions during Lyly's lifetime? W. W. Greg's argument that Lyly did not write them is better than his argument that Dekker did.[37] Some of them are not only worthy of Shakespeare, but are much in his vein as in Dekker's, notably Appeles' song and Trico's song (V.1) in *Campaspe*. The latter reminds us of the concluding songs in *Love's Labor's Lost*, and contains phrases either repeated in or plagiarized from Shakespeare's own "Hark, hark, the lark."

The final unsolved puzzle I wish to mention is one of the strangest in our early dramatic history. Who was the subject of Spenser's lines in the lament of Thalia in *The Teares of the Muses*, registered in 1590 and printed in 1591 in *Complaints*?

And he the man, whom Nature selfe had made
To mock her selfe, and Truth to imitate,
With kindly counter vnder Mimick shade,
Our pleasant *Willy*, ah is dead of late:
With whom all ioy and iolly meriment
Is also deaded, and in dolour drent.

In stead therof scoffing Scurrilitie,
And scornfull Follie with Contempt is crept,
Rolling in rymes of shameles ribaudrie
Without regard, or due Decorum kept,
Each idle wit at will presumes to make,
And doth the Learneds task vpon him take.

But that same gentle Spirit, from whose pen
Large streames of honnie and sweete Nectar flowe,
Scorning the boldnes of such base-borne men,
Which dare their follies forth so rashlie throwe;
Doth rather choose to sit in idle Cell,
Than so himself to mockerie to sell.[38]

If Shakespeare suddenly appeared in the rôle of playwright in 1590, of course the lines could not refer to him. If he had been writing long enough for an interval to have occurred in his output just before 1590, the case is quite different. It is easy to say that Shakespeare was not the subject of the lines, but it is almost as easy to say that *no one* was the subject of the lines; it is impossible to name anyone writing joyous poetic comedy before 1590 with talent enough to command Spenser's respect. But there the lines stand, demanding an explanation; such comedies must have been written, or Thalia would have had nothing to lament. After canvassing the field, Chambers happily rejects his own suggestion of Dick Tarlton, then, in fault of better, hits upon John Lyly. But the lines do not suggest the literary personality of John Lyly, and Lyly was not inactive as a playwright in 1589–90; in fact he was involved in the Marprelate controversy; and it was the "scoffing Scurrilitie" and "shameless ribaudrie" of the plays of this controversy which led to the closing of Paul's and presumably to Thalia's lament. It is easy enough to guess what spate of comedies Spenser deplored; the difficulty lies in guessing what kindly comedies preceded them.

I am led to two reflections: first, that if anyone in his times was equipped to recognize Shakespeare's talents promptly, and to recognize their essential quality, it was Edmund Spenser; and second, that if Spenser's lines really did refer to Shakespeare, it would be the irony of the ages that the fact remains unconceded. After detecting allusions to Shakespeare in every likely and unlikely place, we would have failed to detect one in "our pleasant Willy . . . that same gentle Spirit." The idea of Shakespeare as the source of "streams of honnie and sweet Nectar" furnishes the first critical *cliché* that appears in authenticated allusions to his writing; and the idea of Shakespeare as one "whom Nature selfe had made To mock herself, and Truth to imitate" (i.e. that he was as true to nature as nature herself) furnishes the second critical *cliché* and the one which endured for a century and a half. Perhaps it is just too obvious to be believed.

No one in his right mind would wish to associate Shakespeare with the coterie theatres rather than the popular theatres, which produced the best drama of the era and where he obviously realized himself. But an apprenticeship in the coterie theatres would not have been disabling; players destined for the big leagues often begin in the little leagues. No one, either, would wish to part scholarly company with such men as E.K. Chambers, G.L. Kittredge, W.W. Greg, and F.P. Wilson in order to link arms with Furnivall and Fleay. Our twentieth-century "paragons of caution" have performed a great service in resisting "disintegration," super-subtle theories about ur-texts, progressive revision and the like. They have assumed, reasonably, that the existing texts of plays are the "original" texts or at least the ones most worth dating and discussing. But occasionally these scholars, useful though their stalwart skepticism has been, may have overstated their cases; and in their anxiety to shore up the wind-racked structure of Shakespearean scholarship, they may have boarded up certain doors.

I have proved nothing in this article, but I hope I have indicated why I should be sorry if the opinion that *Love's Labor's Lost* was first written in the mid-nineties should inexorably "harden into an orthodoxy." I think that this play is more likely than any other to suggest the avenues of investigation if there is ever to be a "break-through" in our knowledge of Shakespeare's theatrical beginnings. If I may resort once more to the jargon of our technological age, it is the only play, with the possible exception of the *Comedy of Errors*,[39] which contains "built-in" evidence of a date before 1590, along with hints of the original auspices of production.

NOTES

1. F.P. Wilson, *Marlowe and the Early Shakespeare* (Oxford, 1953), p. 113. The author on p. 121 passingly refers to *Love's Labor's Lost* as coming "soon" after the early plays and parodying their "artifices of style."

2. H.H. Furness, *New Variorum Edition* (1904), p. 337, quoting William Winter (1891).

3. *Life of Shakespeare* (London, 1898), p. 50. The statement remains unchanged in subsequent editions; cf. ed. 1917, p. 102, and others.

4. *Shakespeare: Complete Works* (1936), p. 193.

5. *William Shakespeare, A Study of Facts and Problems* (Oxford, 1933), Vol. 1, p. 338.

6. New Cambridge Edition (1923), p. xxxiv.

7. New Arden Edition (1951), p. 1.

8. Letter of Sir Walter Cope to Robert Cecil, Lord Cranborne, endorsed "1604" apparently for January 1605; cf. Chambers, Vol. 2, p. 332. (I am assuming that the letter refers to the performance noted in Chambers, Vol. 2, p. 331.)

9. *Henslowe's Diary*, ed. W. W. Greg (London, 1904–08), Vol. 1, p. 116.

10. This is the view of W. W. Greg, *The Shakespeare First Folio* (Oxford, 1955), pp. 219–223.

11. *The Satirical Comedy,* Love's Labour's Lost (New York, 1933).

12. *Sous le masque de William Shakespeare* (Paris, 1918–19), Vol. 2, p. 87–100.

13. The most conspicuous modern works on the "topicalities" since the speculations of F.G. Fleay, Arthur Acheson, and J.M. Robertson have been: Austin K. Gray, "The Secret of *Love's Labour's Lost*," PMLA 39 (1924), 581–611; John Dover Wilson, *Love's Labour's Lost*, New Cambridge Shakespeare (1923); Frances A. Yates, *A Study of* Love's Labour's Lost (Cambridge University Press, 1936); Muriel C. Bradbrook, *The School of Night* (Cambridge University Press, 1936). More conservative but bearing in the same direction is Rupert Taylor's *The Date of* Love's Labour's Lost (New York, 1932). A general endorsement seems to be given the speculative school by Richard David in his edition for the new Arden Shakespeare (1951).

14. There are a few quite brief patches of doggerel in *Two Gentlemen of Verona* and *The Taming of the Shrew*; elsewhere in Shakespeare's acknowledged plays there is only a scattered couplet or two, serving a specific whimsical purpose.

15. Allison Gaw, "The Evolution of the *Comedy of Errors*," PMLA 41 (1926), 620–666.

16. *History of English Dramatic Literature* (London, 1875), Vol. 1, p. 372.

17. *History of English Poetry* (London, 1895–1910), Vol. 4, p. (1903), p. 83.

18. Chambers, Vol. 1, p. 308.

19. H. B. Charlton, "The Date of *Love's Labour's Lost*," *Modern Language Review*, 13 (1918), 17.

20. Ibid. It does not follow that so good a scholar as H.B. Charlton still holds to views expressed in an article back in the times of the First World War.

21. The Yale Shakespeare edition (1925), pp. 129, 134.

22. New Cambridge Shakespeare, pp. 128, 130.

23. *The Shakespeare First Folio*, p. 219.

24. "The Source of *Love's Labour's Lost*," *Shakespeare Association Bulletin*, 17 (1942), 97–102. (This reprints from the *Baltimore Sun* the article of 1899; the author generously assumes that later publications represent independent discovery.) Other embassies to the court of Navarre have been mentioned as supplying suggestion, but none after 1586. Cf. Geoffrey Bullough, *Narrative and Dramatic Sources of Shakespeare*, Vol. 1, (London, 1957), pp. 425–442.

25. O. J. Campbell, "*Love's Labour's Lost* Restudied," *Studies in Shakespeare, Milton and Donne.* By Members of the English Department of the University of Michigan (1925). Professor Campbell's most telling points are that in the case of the *Capitano*, as Armado, the braggart is less a military swaggerer than a précieux; and that in the commedia dell'arte the *Affamato* (parasite) is attached to the *Dottore* (pedant) just as in *Love's Labour's Lost* Nathaniel is attached to Holofernes.

26. Rupert Taylor, op. cit., lays great emphasis on this "source."

27. Fred Sorenssen, "The Masque of Muscovites in *Love's Labour's Lost*," *Modern Language Notes*, 50 (1935), 499–501.

28. See the interesting passage V.2.90–118.

29. See Campbell, p.11; David, p.1. Charles Knight in the introductory notice to the play in his *Pictorial Edition of the Works of Shakspere* (London, 1839–43) proposes that the play was written in 1589 when Shakespeare "was a joint-proprietor in the Blackfriar's theatre" (Vol. 1, p. 76), but he seems, unfortunately, to have confused the second Blackfriars, acquired by the King's Men c. 1608, with the first Blackfriars, closed as a theatre in 1584.

30. *Shakespeare's Five-Act Structure* (University of Illinois Press, 1947), p. 635.

31. The second quarto, 1631, reprinting the play from the first folio "As it was acted by his Maiesties Seruants at the Blacke-Friers and the Globe" suggests a Caroline revival.

32. J. T. Murray, *English Dramatic Companies* (London, 1910), Vol. 1, p. 337.

33. *The Wars of Cyrus*, and Marlowe and Nashe's *Tragedy of Dido*.

34. *Plays Confuted in Five Actions* (1582), ed. W. C. Hazlitt, *English Drama and Stage* (London, 1869), p. 215.

35. Chambers, Vol. 2, p. 254.

36. Murray, *English Dramatic Companies*, Vol. 1, p. 345.

37. "On the Authorship of the Songs in Lyly's Plays," *Modern Language Notes*, 1 (1905), 43–52. What appears to be a debased version of Trico's song printed in Dekker's *Sun's Darling* in 1656 is taken by Greg to be the "original" version of the song printed in Lyly's *Six Court Comedies* in 1632; I cannot follow the reasoning.

38. Chambers, Vol. 2, pp. 186–187. Chambers also rejects as a reference to Shakespeare Spenser's lines in *Colin Clout's Come Home Again* (1591–95):

And there though last not least is *Aetion*,
A gentler shepheard may no where be found:
Whose *Muse* full of high thoughts inuention,
Doth like himselfe Heroically sound.

The last line suggests the heroic-sounding name "Shakespeare," and although Lee's ready acceptance of the identification seems a little uncritical, Chambers's ready rejection seems a little captious; the possibility remains open.

39. I think the two plays should be studied in tandem. The *Comedy of Errors* may have originally been chorister-company Plautine "contamination" with intrigues multiplied in the fashion of Lyly's *Mother Bombie*, then later supplied with its humanizing frame. W.W. Greg observes that some of the stage directions suggest "a set stage with three houses" (*The Shakespeare First Folio*, p. 200). Such suggestion of a localized or scenic stage is a characteristic of all eleven texts of chorister drama before 1590, and *Love's Labor's Lost* itself could have been set "in pastoral" as could some of the plays of Lyly. The allusion in the *Comedy of Errors* to France "armed and reverted, making war against her heir" (III.2.126) may belong to any time between August 1589 and July 1593, but signifies little if the text has been revised. A stronger link with *Love's Labor's Lost* is the fact that both texts share certain peculiarities and seem to have been set up from the same kind of copy. See Greg, p. 203 n.

The Dialogues
of Spring and Winter

A Key to the Unity of *Love's Labour's Lost*[*]

Catherine M. McLay

Despite the heretical ending of *Love's Labour's Lost*, an ending where "Jack hath not Jill" (V.2.865)[1] and the ritual marriage celebrations are denied or popstponed "too long for a play" (V.2.868), the drama does have its connections to the ritual origins of comedy in the concluding Songs or Dialogues of Spring and Winter.[2] Although there is considerable controversy over the dating of the play, it is generally agreed to be the product of at least two different periods, and there is indication that the songs belong to the 1597 additions.[3] Nevertheless, the songs are not merely tacked on to the completed play to bring it within the periphery of the usual comic definition. That they are functional, indeed that they hold a key to the interpretation of the central themes of *Love's Labour's Lost*, I hope to prove.[4]

The dramatic excuse for the Dialogues is admittedly weak. Introduced by the Braggart, they are presented as the conclusion to the interrupted Pageant of the Nine Worthies, which itself seems only to be justified by Berowne's remark: "'tis some policy to have one show worse than the king's and his company" (V.2.508–509). At first glance, the dialogues too seem digressive, for they have little direct connection with the events of the play. The opening stanza might easily fit the formula for a typical romantic spring lyric; it suggests that Shakespeare, newly in London, yearned for the freshness of Stratford in the spring:

> When daisies pied and violets blue
> And lady-smocks all silver-white
> And cuckoo-buds of yellow hue
> Do paint the meadow with delight.   (V.2.884–847)

Originally published in *Shakespeare Quarterly* 18, no. 2 (Spring 1967), 119–27. Reprinted by permission.

The chorus with its peculiar refrain, however, should make us pause to reconsider:

> The cuckoo then, on ev'ry tree
> Mocks married men; for thus sings he,
> > Cuckoo;
> Cuckoo, cuckoo: O word of fear,
> Unpleasing to a married ear! (V.2.888–892)

Now the significance of the cuckoo as an omen of adultery would be unmistakable to an Elizabethan ear, even in the middle of a lyric which seems to have for its only purpose the delightful conclusion of a light romantic comedy, as in *Twelfth Night*. But even before this, there are undertones which would unconsciously prepare an Elizabethan audience for a certain ambiguity in the tone and meaning, an ambiguity brought to the surface in the cuckoo refrain and the second stanza, and underlined by the subsequent inversion of the whole dialogue, where the Winter Song of the Owl becomes a "merry Note."[5]

Although the Spring Dialogue seems to deal solely with nature, there are certain elements of artificiality, Nature being described in terms of Art: the daisies are "pied" or artificially bred, and the meadows "painted,"[6] while the flowers are named metaphorically "lady-smocks" and "cuckoo-buds," both of which have sexual undertones. Neither lady-smocks nor cuckoo-buds were common plants; moreover, the former were *milk-white* (note the difference in connotation) and the latter not yellow at all.[7] In addition, the blue of the violets may be interpreted on two levels, since through a paradoxical inversion, blue had come in the Middle Ages to symbolize infidelity, cuckoldry, and folly.[8] This dual interpretation is further borne out in the second stanza, where the sexual undertones come to the surface in "Turtles tread, and rooks, and daws." If we examine the Winter Dialogue, however, we find no trace of the double-entendre which has been such a common device in the play as a whole. The surface romance has disappeared and, with it, the underlying sexual connotations. In its place, we have a dialogue of pure realism, marked by such phrases as "nipp'd," "foul," "greasy," and "red and raw" with its comic accentuation of the rhyme "saw."[9]

It becomes evident, in the Winter Dialogue, that we have a clear-cut example of comic inversion. Spring, complete with its accompanying romantic overtones, its spontaneity, freshness, and youth, is also the season of fear. Even the innocent simplicity of the birds and flowers reasserts this emphasis upon nature and natural copulation in opposition to the man-made conventions of marriage and fidelity. The season of love is at once the season of jealousy and folly, as symbolized by the cuckoo. On the other hand, the season of winter, associated with age and sterility, becomes the season of wisdom as represented by the owl. And if the cuckoo suggests the note of fear in disharmony with the whole mood of spring, it is the owl whose mournful "Tu-whit, Tu-who" becomes a "merry note." There is a peace and serenity in the last dialogue, with its acceptance of life as it is, which is missing in the gayer and more turbulent first stanzas.

Some readers may consider this interpretation of the Song Dialogue as too extreme, as attaching too complex a meaning to what is merely a sung dialogue in the mediaeval tradition of the debate of the seasons. In the remainder of this paper I hope to prove that these various suggestions and ambiguities are central to the meaning of the play, that the Song functions not only to bring the comedy to an appropriate and unified close, but also to summarize and draw together the basic themes and movements which have formed the dramatic fiber of the play's action. Like the Song, the play too moves from spring to winter, from art to nature, from illusion to reality. And the movement in the Song from the folly of the cuckoo to the wisdom of the owl has its counterpart in the handling of the several strands of the play's action, of its plots and subplots.

The dramatic balance of *Love's Labour's Lost* is maintained through the conflict of the two rival factions, the idealistic young students who have attempted to deny Life, and the practical young ladies. These two factions represent respectively, Art and Nature, and the identification is made quite explicit. The young scholars pledge themselves to a period of study and fasting:

> Our court shall be a little academe,
> Still and contemplative in living art. (I.1.13–14)

The Princess and her maidens are, on the other hand, aligned by Boyet on the side of Nature:

> Be now as prodigal of all dear grace
> As Nature was in making graces dear
> When she did starve the general world beside,
> And prodigally gave them all to you. (II.1.9–12)

The Princess completes the identification in her opposition to all things artificial, as implied by "painted":

> Good Lord Boyet, my beauty, though but mean,
> Needs not the painted flourish of your praise. (II.1.13–14)

And later, Berowne asserts: "Fie painted rhetoric! O! she needs it not" (IV.3.236). It is therefore fitting that the ladies should set up camp in the field while the young men alone belong to the court. Thus the dramatic opposition of the two factions is carried into the setting, and the ultimate victory of Nature is symbolized in Act II, by the transfer of the action from court to field.

The hunting scene of Act IV is central to the meaning of the play, for it is here that the ladies, like the Shavian Ann Whitefield, take over the role of pursuer. The underlying sensual implications of action and dialogue have been indicated by Eric Partridge in his *Shakespeare's Bawdy*, particularly in regard to the passage from lines 110 to 130, which he calls "one of the most greasy passages in the whole of Shakespeare."[10] Yet the nature of this debate, like that of the virginity debate in *All's Well That Ends Well*, is essential to the play's theme, which involves a movement from the artificial to the natural on its most basic, as well as its more refined, levels. For the park atmosphere and the hunt metaphor, taken on both levels, express the youth and fertility of Nature in the spring, an expression echoed later in the imagery of the final Spring dialogue. That many of the most bawdy passages are attributed to the virtuous heroines (and Shakespeare leaves no doubt that they, like his other romantic young heroines, *are* virtuous) is merely evidence of the comic inversion which pervades the play, and an accentuation of the natural vigor of the heroines, who represent the Life-force operating through Nature. Indeed we may carry the analysis one step further. The whole play may be seen as a satire, if a merry one, on Elizabethan artificiality, not only of language and manners but of romantic and courtly ideals. The Spring Song fits into this context. Both it and the hunt metaphor function to dispel conventional romantic illusions, to shock the audience into an awareness of nature and the natural premises of existence. It is not only the youths who are to benefit from the lesson taught by the "wise" Clown, "it is the manner of man to speak to a woman" (I.1.207–208).

Individually, the youths are prepared as early as Act III to admit that their challenge to Nature has failed (III.1.189–200), and even to concede the inevitability of Nature's victory, although their expression of this is as artificial as the Clown's was blunt:

> Yet I will love, write, sigh, pray, sue, and groan:
> Some men must love my lady, and some Joan. (III.1.201–202)

Nevertheless, it is not until the quadruple revelation scene of Act IV that they admit outwardly to the supremacy of Nature over man's artificial dictates, in a passage which indicates, by its natural use of imagery, their progress away from artificiality:

> Sweet lords, sweet lovers, O! let us embrace.
> As true we are as flesh and blood can be:
> The sea will ebb and flow, heaven show his face:
> Young blood doth not obey an old decree:
> We cannot cross the cause why we were born;
> Therefore, of all hands must we be forsworn. (IV.3.211–216)

But the process is not complete. And as is habitual in this play, whose central preoccupation is one of words, they fall back upon paradox to resolve their controversy:

> It is religion to be thus forsworn;
> For charity itself fulfills the law;
> And who can sever love from charity? (IV.3.360–362)

The central problem, however, still remains: to find the true nature of wisdom. It is no accident that "wit" is one of the most frequent words of the play and at the heart of the satire. As we have observed, it is not only Holofernes and Armado whose wit is mocked, for these serve chiefly as an intensification, a *reductio ad absurdum*, of the folly of the intellectuals themselves, on the stage and in the audience. Armado's "Assist me, some extemporal god of rhyme for I am sure I shall turn sonnet. Devise, wit; write, pen: for I am for whole volumes in folio" (I.2.173–175) is not the less hilarious because it may be seen, in retrospect, as an ironic parody on the sonnets of the young lovers.

The futility of Navarre's design is first exposed by Berowne, who, before the entrance of the ladies in Act II, operates as a natural balance to the Art school (I.1.55–69). Consequently, it is Berowne, who, early in the play, recognizes that there is an essential difference between Knowledge and Wisdom:

> Too much to know is to know naught but fame:
> And every godfather can give a name. (I.1.92–93)

It is not until the discovery scene of Act IV, however, that Berowne discovers that what men frequently call wisdom is, in reality, folly:

Then fools you were these women to forswear,
Or, keeping what is sworn, you will prove fools. (IV.3.352–353)

But in renouncing one illusion, the young men become prey to another: they renounce all for the sake of love and find in women the perfection of the world and a fit subject for study (IV.3.296–301). Nature again intervenes, and the folly of the young men (and of all young courtiers) is contrasted repeatedly with the wisdom of the girls:

PRINCESS. We are wise girls to mock our lovers so.
ROSALINE. They are worse fools to purchase mocking so. (V.2.58–59)

This contrast is dramatized effectively in the Russian disguise scene where the girls, informed by Boyet, "Cupid's grandfather" (II.1.255), are able to penetrate their lovers' disguise, while the lovers, blinded again by appearance, are again forsworn:

The ladies did change favours, and then we,
Following the signs, woo'd but the sign of she. (V.2.468–469)

In renouncing the artificiality which has been such a prominent characteristic of his style, Berowne reasserts the identification of the ladies with Nature and her wisdom:

Your capacity
Is that of Nature that to your large store
Wise things seem foolish and rich things but poor. (V.2.376–378)

But an understanding of reality has not yet been achieved, for at the opposite pole of Nature stands Death, and the entry of Marcade casts a shadow not only over the youths but also over the maidens as well. Until this point, Spring and Summer have held the center of the stage.[11] The youths have been associated by Berowne with Spring and, incidentally, with its folly: "'The spring is near, when green geese are a-breeding'" (I.1.97). The King's retort that Berowne is "like the envious sneaping frost / That bites the first-born infants of the Spring" (I.1.100–101), although it underlines the seasonal contrast of the imagery, is not to be taken seriously since Berowne is as unaware of Winter and Death as his companions. The ladies, in turn, are associated with the maturity and fertility of Summer in the rose image (V.2.293–297), which contrasts effectively with the "barren tasks" of the youths (I.1.47) and the "gelded" stage of Aquitaine (II.1.149). The analogy is carried still further, for the maidens share Summer's power as an agent of rebirth after the sterility of Winter:

> A wither'd hermit, five-score winters worn,
> Might shake off fifty, looking in her eye:
> Beauty doth varnish age, as if new-born,
> And gives the crutch the cradle's infancy. (IV.3.239–242)

The entry of Marcade marks the Winter period of the play, the period of suffering and purgation; however, there is promise that, if the young men fulfill their vows of penance, the ladies possess the power to restore the Spring-world to the "blossoms" of love:

> If this austere insociable life
> Change not your offer made in heat of blood;
> If frosts and fasts, hard lodging and thin weeds,
> Nip not the gaudy blossoms of your love,
> But that it bear this trial and last love;
> Then at the expiration of the year,
> Come challenge me. . . . (V.2.789–795)

But another theme has been suggested here. The seasonal metaphor has been used to suggest a new process, one beyond Nature and therefore Death. As Winter turns to Spring, age turns to youth and death to birth. Thus the entry of Winter in the fifth act suggests a passing out of the realm of nature and into a realm beyond, and the concluding song of the owl epitomizes Wisdom because it takes account not only of Life but also of Death. And so the apparently heretical ending of the play with the Winter Song is, in truth, an early statement of themes which Shakespeare was to develop very much later, in the Problem Comedies and the Late Romances, where the comedy passes beyond the suffering of the natural world and emerges in a New Heaven and a New Earth.

These major themes of the comedy, the movement from Art to Nature, from Illusion to Reality, from Folly to Wisdom, and from Spring to Winter, are accentuated and underlined through careful technical handling of the two sub-plots, embryonic though they may be. The Clown and Armado stand at the two opposite poles of comedy and incarnate between them the forces of the extreme natural and the extreme artificial which are struggling for the souls of the young men. For the Clown is the complete embodiment of the natural and uninhibited response to life, as Armado is of the egoistic and pedantic. The two are brought into dramatic juxtaposition in the opening scene, where the Clown comments on Armado's letter (I.1.227–254). The young men, associated to a certain degree with Armado, are to have the worst of the match, and it is not long before their ultimate fate is foreshadowed in the more comic, because more incongruous, fall of Armado: "I will hereupon confess I am in love; and as it is base for a soldier to love, so I am in love with a base wench" (I.2.54–56).

It is significant that Boyet, at the close of the hunt scene with its emphasis upon nature and natural copulation, should identify the Clown with the owl, even if ironically. For it is the Clown who puts his finger on the artificiality of the young scholars' design: "Such is the simplicity of man to hearken after the flesh" (I.1.215). And if Costard is the owl, there is little doubt as to who is the cuckoo, and our suspicions are confirmed when we hear of Jaquenetta's condition.[12] Thus in a highly ironic inversion, Folly becomes Wisdom and the "wise man" becomes the Clown;

> By my soul, a swain! A most simple clown!
> Lord, Lord, how the ladies and I have put him down! (IV.1.139–140)

> Ah! heavens, it is a most pathetical nit.[13] (IV.1.147)

Indeed it is Costard, the exponent of the natural, who is to provide the natural heir, if we are to believe Granville-Barker.[14]

The second sub-plot, introduced as late as Act IV, Scene 2, presents a new angle of affectation. The dialogue parodies, at one and the same time, the artificial and pedantic delight in words for their sound rather than their sense, and the ignorance of the "scholars" as to the most common meanings of the words they use, as "posteriors" of the day (IV.2.84–86). Again, the sub-plot functions as an accentuation of the main themes of the play. The Holofernes-Nathaniel dialogue juxtaposes once more the natural and the artificial in its use of language:

> The deer was, as you know, *sanguis*, in blood; ripe as the pomewater, who now hangeth like a jewel in the ear of *coelo*, the sky, the welkin, the heaven, and anon falleth like a crab on the face of *terra*, the soil, the land, the earth.[15] (IV.2.3–7)

Dull's misinterpretation of *haud credo* as an assertion that the deer is feminine gives Holofernes excellent opportunity for a tirade against those who cannot appreciate the finer points of the Latin tongue and, at the same time, maintains an emphasis on the male-female opposition which is essential to the main theme of the play. The delightful incongruity of the scene lies in its juxtaposition of the artificiality of learning with its ultimate sterility, and the fecundity of nature, carried unconsciously in the undertones of the dialogue. The sexual imagery of the play is further emphasized in Holofernes's metaphor of wit, the dry pedantic tone of the speech accentuating the contrast:

> This is a gift that I have, simple; a foolish extravagant spirit, full of forms, figures, shapes, objects, ideas, apprehensions, revolutions: these are begot in the ventricle of memory, nourished in the womb of *pia mater*, and delivered upon the mellowing of occasion. (IV.2.66–71)

The two sub-plots are interrelated not only in the association of the comic characters in the pageant which precedes the entry of Marcade, but also in the essential similarity of Armado and Holofernes, a similarity ironically pointed up by Holofernes himself in his description of Armado: "He draweth out the thread of his verbosity finer than the staple of his argument" (V.1.17–18). Again it is the Clown who can laugh at the foolishness of the seeming-wise who have "lived long on the alms-basket of words" (V.1.39–40). Even Dull, the fool's fool, puts a finger on the nature of their folly, although, characteristically, he is too dull to observe his own wisdom:

> HOLOFERNES. *Via*, goodman Dull! thou hast spoken no word all this while.
> DULL. Nor understood none neither, sir. (V.1.143–145)

And so, as we have seen, both main and sub-plots deal with the movement of the play from the artificial to the natural, from illusion to reality, from folly to wisdom. These themes are all present in the Spring-Winter debate, which functions, then, to draw together and unify them. But the Song does more than this. It introduces the problem of Time, which the whole play-world had neglected until the entry of Marcade. In the Spring-Winter debate, the cyclical nature of the seasonal metaphor carries us through the world of Winter and Death and into the new Spring. Thus the Song foreshadows the theme of the redemption which will form a major part of the action in *The Winter's Tale* and *The Tempest*. But only the seed is there. For Shakespeare, in the early years of his career, this theme would require a time "too long for a play" (V.2.868).

*This article was originally prepared for a graduate seminar in Shakespeare at the University of Toronto. The writer would like to thank Dr. F.D. Hoeniger of Victoria College for his encouragement and advice, both at the time of writing and during several revisions.

1. All quotations are from the New Arden text edited by Richard David (London: Methuen, 1951).

2. C.L. Barber discusses the relationship of the play to ritual comedy in his *Shakespeare's Festive Comedy* (Princeton University Press, 1959), pp. 87–118.

3. Richmond Noble, *Shakespeare's Use of Song* (Oxford University Press, 1923), p. 38. For a summary of the controversy over text and dating of the play, see R. David's introduction to the Arden text, pp. xvii–xxxii.

4. Richmond Noble, studying the text of the songs, concludes that they are digressive, having no close relationship to the theme (pp. 12–13). John Long, however, claims: "Shakespeare considered them [the songs] an integral part of the comedy" (*Shakespeare's Use of Music*, University of Florida Press, 1955, pp. 77–78). He notes the parallel between the language and imagery of the songs and the central theme of the play, "the ridiculing of pastoral conventions and exaggerated scholasticism" (p. 78). It is not part of Long's intention to examine the themes of the play and he does not do so. However, his conclusion is significant: "The relationship of the songs to the structure of the play appears to be so close that I would hesitate to label them extraneous songs. . . . They are a part of the setting and structure of the play. They serve, I think, for a final statement of the theme . . ." (p. 78).

It is interesting to note in the thesis of James Wey ("Musical Allusion and Song as Part of the Structure of Meaning of Shakespeare's Plays," Catholic University of America, Washington D.C., 1957) a close parallel between his intentions and my own. In both cases, the songs are seen to be highly relevant to the themes of the play as a whole, tying in action, characterization, and imagery, and rounding out the play dramatically and effectively. In addition, Wey is almost the only critic who observes the predominance of sexual reference and connotation in the songs, especially in the spring sequence which, he notes, concerns the theme of sexual activity and cuckoldry in contrast to the a-sexual activities of Winter where "greasy Joan" (interpreted sexually) turns from bleaching her summer smocks to a Winter of penance in the kitchen (p. 153). Wey also discusses the songs as "a gentle warning of the realities of married love" (p. 153), a restatement of the central theme of the play ("the fitness of the action to the time"), and a reflection of the "major imagistic motif . . . the opposition of light and darkness" (p. 155). He concludes that "the songs are like a microcosm of all the chief themes, motifs, actions of the play" (p. 167).

5. It is singular that almost all comments on the Spring Song, with the recent exception of Wey's, have insisted upon its freshness, innocence, and spontaneity. Tangible proof of this serious misconception is its assignment, in the eighteenth century, to Rosalind of *As You Like It* ! (Noble, p. 36). Only Noble and Bertrand Bronson, "Daisies Pied and Icicles," *Modern Language Notes*, 63 (1948), pp. 35–38, seem to note anything "unpleasant" in the song, and even they look no farther than the song of the cuckoo for this element. Noble considers the songs irrelevant in any case (see note 5 preceding), and Bronson, after speaking of the "vernal delights" of the opening lines, concludes that the Song is curious in that "the burden . . . falls upon a consideration which elsewhere in Shakespeare, as in life, makes toward tragedy" (pp. 35–36). He notes the structural parallel of the two songs, a "pretty" opposition between the "boding" note of the cuckoo and the perversely "merry" note of the owl, but finds in this reversal of roles only "a delightful surprise and reversal of the traditional 'debate' of the birds" (p. 37). If the Spring Song is as fresh and innocent as most seem to consider, one wonders why it is not included in the high school curriculum in Ontario, as is the Winter Song.

6. See Perdita's flower dialogue of *The Winter's Tale*, where Perdita rejects "pied" or artificially-bred flowers as products of Art rather than Nature. She also draws a parallel between artificial breeding in flowers and "painted" women (IV.4.78–103, especially 87–88 and 101–103).

7. Lever, J.W., "Three Notes on Shakespeare's Plants," *Review of English Studies*, new series 3 (1952), 117–20.

8. Huizinga, *The Waning of the Middle Ages* (London: Penguin Books, 1955). "By a very curious transition, blue, instead of being the colour of faithful love, came to mean infidelity too, and next, besides the faithless wife, marked the dupe" (pp. 273–274). In France, blue became the color of cuckolds and of "fools in general" (p. 274).

9. But see Wey (note 5), who interprets "greasy" in sexual terms and indicates that Winter is merely a period of arrested sexual desire.

10. Eric Partridge, *Shakespeare's Bawdy* (London: Routledge, 1947), p. 53.

11. Bobbyann Roesen notes that the hunting-scene marks the first entry of Death into the play, brought into the park by "the intruders from the outside world" but muted to remove "any disturbing reality," pp. 419–420 (*Love's Labour's Lost*, *Shakespeare Quarterly* 4 (1953), 411–26). Miss Roesen also notes the increase in the fifth act of imagery of disease and death which builds up to the entry of Marcade.

12. Granville-Barker comments: "It is surely clear—though, to many editors, it does not seem to be—that in the accusation poor Armado is most scandalously 'infamonized'! Where would be the joke else?" (*Prefaces to Shakespeare*, First Series, London: Sidgwick and Jackson, 1927), p. 46.

13. There is no doubt as to whom Costard refers in the second of these comments. The first might refer to Boyet who has just left the stage, but what, then, would be the point of the passage? R. David suggests that Armado has been present in an earlier draft of the scene (see footnote to this passage, Arden edition, p. 75).

14. See note 10 preceding.

15. J.A.K. Thomson, in pointing out the errors in "*sanguis*" and "*coelo*," remarks: "Shakespeare's knowledge of Latin was at any rate sufficient to tell him that these were errors. He must so mean that Holofernes does not know his own subject," p. 67 (*Shakespeare and the Classics*, London: Allen and Unwin, 1952).

LOVE'S LABOUR'S LOST

THE GRACE OF SOCIETY

Thomas M. Greene

The qualities of *Love's Labour's Lost* determine its limitations. The arabesques of wit, the elaborations of courtly artifice, the coolness of tone—these sources of its charm contribute to that brittleness and thinness and faded superficiality for which some critics of several generations have reproached it. For its admirers, a heavy stress upon these limitations is likely to appear irrelevant. But even admirers must acknowledge that, placed against its author's work, *Love's Labour's Lost* is distinguished by a certain slenderness of feeling, a delicate insubstantiality. It is most certainly not a trivial play, but its subtlety remains a little disembodied.

One source of that impression may be the play's lack, unique in Shakespeare, of any firm social underpinning. Not only is there missing any incarnation of responsible authority, any strong and wise center of political power, but there is equally missing any representative of a stable and dependable citizenry. There is nobody here who, however quirky or foolish or provincial, can be counted on, when he is multiplied enough times, to keep society functioning. Or if there is such a figure in the person of Constable Dull, we are struck with how very marginal a role his creator has permitted him. The patently comic figures—Armado, Holofernes, Costard, Nathaniel, Moth—are all too thin or specialized or socially peripheral to suggest any sort of living society. They may be contrasted with the mechanicals of *A Midsummer Night's Dream*, who, for all their splendid ineptness, do persuade us that a kind of Athenian proletariat exists. The earlier play may owe its peculiar airiness in part to a lack of that social solidity.

Yet despite its lack of a ballasted society, the play is really about "society," in a slightly different sense of the word. Its true subject is caught in

Originally published in *Shakespeare Quarterly* 22 (Autumn 1971), 315–328. Reprinted by permission.

an offhand remark by one of its funny men: "Society (saith the text) is the happiness of life" (IV.2.167–168).[1] The play does not challenge Nathaniel's text, however insubstantial its dramatic sociology. It is much concerned with society, and the happiness of life in society. If it does not present a living society in action, it presents and comments on configurations of conduct which sustain living societies in and out of plays. It is concerned with *styles*, modes of language and gesture and action which befit, in varying degrees, the intercourse of civilized people. And being a comedy, it is concerned with the failures of inadequate styles, since this is the perennial source of elegant comedy from Homer to Proust. Only at the end, and much more surprisingly, does it turn out to reflect the failure of all style.

To distinguish most sensibly the play's hierarchy of moral styles, one may adopt the vantage point of the Princess of France and her three attendant ladies. These four women, being women, cannot provide a strong political center but they do constitute a certain spirited and witty center of social judgment. In their vivacious and spontaneous taste, limited in range and depth but not in accuracy, each is a poised, a Meredithian arbitress of style. This power of discrimination is established by the first speech each lady makes on stage. In the cases of the three attendants, the speech consists in a sketch of the gentleman who is to become the given lady's suitor, and each speech, in its alert and finely qualified appreciation, does credit to the speaker as well as to its subject. Thus Maria:

> I know him, madam . . .
> A man of sovereign parts he is esteem'd;
> Well fitted in arts, glorious in arms.
> Nothing becomes him ill that he would well.
> The only soil of his fair virtue's gloss—
> If virtue's gloss will stain with any soil—
> Is a sharp wit match'd with too blunt a will,
> Whose edge hath power to cut, whose will still wills
> It should none spare that come within his power. (II.1.40, 44–51)

As regards the Princess, it is her modesty, her impervious disregard of flattery, the sense of proportion regulating her pride of birth, which betoken most frequently her moral poise. The Princess's first speech opens with a mild rebuke of the spongy Lord Boyet for his gratuitous compliments:

> Good Lord Boyet, my beauty, though but mean,
> Needs not the painted flourish of your praise. . . .

I am less proud to hear you tell my worth
Than you much willing to be counted wise
In spending your wit in the praise of mine. (II.1.13–14, 17–19)

She refuses coolly to be hoodwinked by the flattery her station conventionally attracts, with an acuteness which sets off the foolish egotism of the King.
His first speech, the opening speech of the play, is full of tiresome talk of
fame and honor, posturing predictions of immortality and glory. The
Princess's view of "glory" is plain enough after her quick disposal of Boyet,
as it is in a later scene when she laughingly dismisses with a tip an unwitting blunder by the forester. Indeed she follows that incident with reflections
which are painfully apposite to the King's foolish enterprise, even if they are
ostensibly and deprecatingly directed at herself:

And, out of question, so it is sometimes:
Glory grows guilty of detested crimes
When, for fame's sake, for praise, an outward part,
We bend to that the working of the heart. (IV.1.30–33)

This last phrase about bending to externals the working of the heart
touches very nearly the heart of the play. For *Love's Labour's Lost* explores
the relations of feeling and forms, feeling and language, feeling and the funny
distortions of feeling which our social experience beguiles us to fashion. The
four gentlemen, quite clearly, begin by denying the workings of their hearts
and libidos for the outward part of fame, just as Armado squirms from his
distressing passion for a girl who is outwardly—i.e. socially—his inferior.
The distinction of the ladies is that their feelings and their style, their outward parts, are attuned; they know what they feel and they are in control
of its expression. Although they are as quick to admire as the four gentlemen, they are slower to think they are falling in love. They are also, to their
credit, far clearer about the physiological dimension of their interest. The
freedom of their by-play about sex may have lost with time some of its comic
sprightliness, but next to the dogged Petrarchan vaporizings of their suitors
that freedom still emerges as the more refreshing and healthier mode of
speech. The four ladies are, in the best sense, self-possessed, although the
play does not try to pretend that the *scope* of their feelings or their experience is any wider than most girls'. An older person with no wider a scope
would risk the hollowness of the ambiguous, slightly sterile Boyet. The ladies are so engaging because their spirited and untested freshness is tempered
by instinctive good sense.

The roles of the gentlemen—Navarre and his three courtiers—are slightly more complicated. For they must justify to some degree the interest the ladies conceive in them. Longaville may not be quite the "man of sovereign parts" Maria says he is, but he must remain within hailing distance of that distinguished man she thought she saw and liked. We must always be able to assume that the gentlemen are salvageable as social animals and potential husbands, and need only the kind of education provided by laughter and the penances to which, at the close, they are assigned. But granting them a basic attractiveness, we have to confess that they resemble a little—in their deplorable affectations, their wayward rhetoric, their callow blindness to themselves—the caricatured figures of the sub-plot. There is a difference of degree, not of kind, between the doggerel of, say, Holofernes (IV.2.58–63) and the mediocrity of Dumaine's verses:

A huge translation of hypocrisy,
Vilely compil'd, profound simplicity. (V.2.51–52)

Like Holofernes, Armado, and Nathaniel, the gentlemen "have been at a great feast of languages and stolen the scraps"; all steal indifferently from a common alms-basket of words. They are failures as poseurs because their poses are never original, and as Holofernes himself is able to recognize, "imitari is nothing." The successive defeats of the gentlemen in their sets of wits with the ladies betray an ineptitude of social intelligence and style.

Shakespeare will tolerate cheerfully enough the fashionable inanities of sentimental rhetoric, but he sees the risk of mistaking rhetoric for real sentiment. It is the risk which anguished Pirandello, but it works in this more comical world to expose the gentlemen to their mistresses' ridicule. For the ladies, who are not all wise, know enough to distinguish language in touch with feeling from the language which does duty for feeling, or, more accurately, which papers over adolescent confusions of feeling. The ladies' rhetoric, cooler, more bracing, more alert than the lords', enlivened by the freedom of its casual license, finds a natural recreation in a kind of amiable flyting, a "civil war of wits." The ladies vanquish their suitors unfailingly in this civil badinage because they are, so to speak, in practice. The suitors are not, having attempted to exclude from their still and contemplative academy what they call "the world's debate." Or rather, they have allowed the debate to impinge only at second hand, as a recreative fancy and linguistic toy. They may hear, says the King, from Armado:

In high-born words the worth of many a knight
From Tawny Spain lost in the world's debate. (I.1.173–174)

Perhaps it is their unwillingness to be so lost—save in fantasy, through the mediation of high-colored language—which loses them the verbal battles under the banner of Saint Cupid. The play will end with a calendary debate, reminding us that nature itself, and the human lives it governs, are subject to the amoebean conflicts of the seasons.

The war of wits is "civil" in more meanings than one, since the term *civility* gathers up all of the play's central values. The term as Elizabethans used it embraced all those configurations of political and social and moral conduct which can render society the happiness of life. The gentlemen, in their cocksure unworldliness, have only bungling conceptions of civility, and for all their fumbling efforts toward urbanity, their parochial manners unflaggingly show through. The ideal is defined partly by its breaches: the ascetic breach represented by the academy's austere statutes; or the inhuman breach of the decree which would deprive an interloping woman of her tongue: "A dangerous law against gentility!" (I.1.129); or the inhospitable breach which denies the Princess welcome to the court of Navarre; or the rhetorical breaches of the gentlemen's poetastical love complaints; or the fantastical breach of the Muscovite embassy:

> Their shallow shows and prologue vilely penn'd,
> And their rough carriage so ridiculous. . . . (V.2.305–306)

or the final blunder which asks the bereaved Princess to listen still to her lover's suit. This variety of gaffes is filled out by the cruder affectations of the minor comic characters. Virtually all the men in the play violate, each in his peculiar way, the values of "civility," which meant at once civilization, social polish, government, courtesy, decorum, manners, and simple human kindness.

Of these various participant values, the play lays particular stress on the virtue of decorum, which becomes here a sense of the conduct appropriate to a given situation. Berowne's main charge against Navarre's academy appeals implicitly to that virtue:

> KING. Berowne is like an envious sneaping frost
> That bites the first-born infants of the Spring.
> BEROWNE. Well, say I am! Why should proud summer boast
> Before the birds have any cause to sing?

Why should I joy in an abortive birth?
At Christmas I no more desire a rose
Than wish a snow in May's newfangled shows,
But like of each thing that in season grows.
So you—to study now it is too late—
Climb o'er the house to unlock the little gate. (I.1.100–109)

Enterprise blossoms when, in Berowne's phrase, it is "fit in his time and place" (I.1.98); comedy wells up from the disjuncture of act and occasion. The lords' intuition of this great Renaissance virtue is blunted equally in their roles as students and as suitors, so that an especial irony tinges the King's summons to courtship:

Away, away! No time shall be omitted
That will be time and may by us be fitted. (IV.3.381–382)

That cry will receive an unwitting answer in Rosaline's fantasy:

O that I knew he were but in by th' week!
How I would make him fawn, and beg, and seek,
And wait the season, and observe the times. . . . (V.2.61–63)

and finds another faint echo later in the Princess's rejection of Navarre's last plea:

KING. Now at the latest minute of the hour
        Grant us your loves.
PRINCESS. A time methinks too short
        To make a world-without-end bargain in. (V.2.796–798)

This fault of abusing season and "time" is implicitly caught up in Berowne's incoherent apology for the misconduct of himself and his companions, whose errors he ruefully confesses to have sinned against decorum.

Your beauty, ladies,
Hath much deform'd us, fashioning our humours
Even to the opposed end of our intents;
And what in us hath seem'd ridiculous—
As love is full of unbefitting strains,
All wanton as a child, skipping and vain . . .

Which parti-colored presence of loose love
Put on by us, if, in your heavenly eyes,
Have disbecom'd our oaths and gravities,
Those heavenly eyes that look into these faults
Suggested us to make them. (V.2.765–770, 775–779)

The key words are "deform'd," "unbefitting," and "misbecom'd," suggesting offenses against that value of propriety which had not yet, in the sixteenth century, become the fossilized austerity we have learned to deplore.

The relationship of Berowne to the ideals of civility is rather more complex than his fellows', since he understands so much more than they without ever saving himself from their muddles. He has traits in common with Shaw's John Tanner: both are brilliant, ineffectual talkers who never quite learn how useless are even their best lines. Berowne for all his brilliance is easily put in his place by the securer wit of Rosaline. But despite his frustrations he remains the most original, interesting, and complicated character in the play. He is insincere from the outset; he knows of course that he will sign the articles of the academic oath, even as he calls attention to himself by pretending to refuse. He plays with life, and his life is a play within the play. It is the last word he speaks, in the famous regretful line that gives us—had we been so obtuse as to miss it—the key to his character:

That's too long for a play. (V.2.887)

Ironist, sophist, scoffer, he has one small, delusory faith: he believes in language, and it fails him. He is almost saved by his capacity to laugh at himself, but not quite; his worst muddle is his last, when he tries to chasten his rhetoric before the fact of death, and cannot shake his inveterate cleverness:

We to ourselves prove false,
By being once false for ever to be true
To those that make us both—fair ladies, you. (V.2.781–783)

To themselves they do indeed prove false, and to the motto that "Honest plain words best pierce the ear of grief" (V.2.762).

Berowne's teasing dilettantism is not up to death—nor (more surprisingly?) is it up to sex. His sexuality, like his fellow suitors', is visual, not to say voyeuristic. Their obsession with the eye transcends the Petrarchan cliché; it betokens their callow and adolescent virginity. It is symptomatic that the most sleazy joke the gentlemen permit themselves has to do with looking;[2] when the ladies' talk is bawdy, they refer to the more relevant organs. Their ribaldry is the cleaner. None of these women would say of her lover what Berowne is so foolish to admit:

> O, but her eye! By this light, but for her eye,
> I would not love her; yes, for her two eyes. (IV.3.10–12)

And again later:

> From women's eyes this doctrine I derive.
> They sparkle still the right Promethean fire:
> They are the books, the arts, the academes,
> That show, contain, and nourish all the world.
> Else none at all in aught proves excellent. (IV.3.350–354)

This fascination is echoed in the rhetoric of the other suitors, and enters the plot with the misleading exchange of favors:

> The ladies did change favours; and then we,
> Following the signs, woo'd but the sign of She. (IV.3.468–469)

The sign of She! That is always the object of immature desire. To know and love the complex living creature takes more time and a wiser heart.

The comedy of the gentlemen's sentimental inadequacies is reflected obliquely in the comedy of their inferiors. This reflection receives dramatic expression in Costard's mistaken interchange of Berowne's poem with Armado's letter. The confusion suggests a common element which we recognize as the vice of affectation, a vice which is only a few degrees more marked in the style of Armado and spills over into humor. One might almost say that we are invited to share Costard's error. But from another perspective the gentlemen as gallants emerge from the contrast with even less credit than the ostensible clowns. Costard at least represents the closest thing to good sense in the flights of folly of the opening scene; through his malapropising nonsense a few primitive truths are sounded which shatter all the foregoing silliness about asceticism:

> Now sir, for the manner—it is the manner of a man to speak to a
>   woman. (I.1.212–213)
> Such is the simplicity of man to hearken after the flesh. (I.1.219–220)

Armado of course is more closely parallel to the gentlemen because, unlike Costard, he fancies himself to be in love. Armado is the most suggestive of the comic figures and one of the richest of any in Shakespeare's early comedies, although his potentialities are not consistently developed. There is a resonance to his humor which is lacking, say, in the humor of his fellow pomposity, Holofernes. This is because Shakespeare invests Armado's grandiloquence with a touch of melancholy. We are allowed to catch a bat's squeak of pathos behind the tawny splendor, and a lonely desire for Jaquenetta behind the clumsy condescension to her. The pathos is really affecting when he must decline Costard's challenge and confess his shirtlessness, infamonized among potentates. Nothing so touching overshadows the presentation of the gentlemen. Armado's courtship is more desperate, more clouded, and more believable.

A conventional reading of the play places the main turning point at the end of the fourth act, with the four-fold exposure of the quondam academics and their abjuration of study in the name of Saint Cupid. But to read in this way is to be taken in by the gentlemen's own self-delusions. For their apparent conversion is at bottom a pseudo-conversion, the exchange of one pretentious fiction for another, and we are meant to view ironically their naive release of enthusiasm, as we view Caliban's "Freedom, high-day!" The Muscovite embassy represents the culmination of the gentlemen's clumsy posing, their inept sophistication, and their empty formalism. Never yet in the play have manner and mien been quite so far from feeling, and we learn merely that courtship as performance can be just as silly as the performance of monastic seclusion. The real turning point begins with Berowne's second abjuration and its potentially deeper renunciation of rhetorical affectation.

> Taffeta phrases, silken terms precise,
> Three-pil'd hyperboles, spruce affectation,
> Figures pedantical—these summer flies
> Have blown me full of maggot ostentation.
> I do forswear them. . . . (V.2.406–410).

Berowne underestimates the difficulty of the sacrifice, as Rosaline finds a way to suggest, but we are allowed to hope that the seed of understanding has been planted. Indeed the remaining action of this rich last scene—almost a one-act play in itself—can be regarded as a progressive and painful exorcism of the gentlemen's pretenses and pretensions. The first step involves a humiliating sincerity.

KING. Teach us, sweet madam, for our rude transgression
  Some fair excuse.
PRINCESS.   The fairest is confession.
  Were you not here but even now, disguis'd?
KING. Madam, I was. (V.2.431–434)

That step leads to the further humbling discovery of the exchanged favors
and mistaken identities, and that, in turn to the puzzling but clearly important episode of the Worthies' pageant.[3]

The intrusion of this interlude, so cruelly and even pathetically
routed at the climax of the action, has troubled more than one reader,[4] and
indeed it is not easily justified by our common standards of daily morality. Yet I think that Shakespeare has given us a key to its interpretation, a
key which no critic to my knowledge has noticed. The essential point is
the reluctance of the gentlemen to watch the pageant, chastened as they
already are at this point by their sense of their own absurdity. Yet in fact
they do watch. The exchange is notable that immediately precedes this
ambiguous entertainment:

KING. Berowne, they will shame us. Let them not approach.
BEROWNE. We are shame-proof, my lord; and 'tis some policy
      To have one show worse than the King's and his company.
KING. I say they shall not come.
PRINCESS. Nay, my good lord, let me o'errule you now.
      That sport best pleases that doth least know how:
      Where zeal strives to content, and the contents
      Dies in the zeal of that which it presents.
      Their form confounded makes most form in mirth
      When great things labouring perish in their birth.
BEROWNE. A right description of our sport, my lord. (V.2.512–522)

The clumsy pageant will imitate uncomfortably the fumbling Muscovite
masquing. The analogy is painfully close, as both the King and Berowne are
alert enough to perceive. The Princess's wise insistence on the performance—
"That sport best pleases that doth least know how"—creates a small moral
dilemma for the lords which they resolve by mocking their own unwitting
mockers. They recognize, not without a certain rueful courage, that the pageant represents a quintessential parody of their own offenses against propriety; so they choose to follow Boyet in turning upon that parody as though
to exorcise their own folly. The telling line is Dumaine's:

> Though my mocks come home by me, I will now be merry.
>
> (V.2.637–638)

Unforgivable in itself, the routing of the pageant is dramatically right as ritual action, as a symbolic rejection of a mask beginning to be outworn. Indeed only the savage shame one feels toward an unworthy part of one's self could motivate the gentlemen's quite uncharacteristic cruelty.

Considered in this way, the ridicule of the pageant needs no palliation, and yet two palliative observations can be made. The first is that the ridicule is not heaped equally on all five performers. Moth as Hercules remains silent while presented by Holofernes-Maccabaeus and is allowed to leave the stage after the six-line presentation without any interruption. Costard is interrogated twice and corrected once at the outset, but is then heard out quietly, thanked by the Princess and complimented by Berowne. Nathaniel fares somewhat worse, but the most scathing ridicule is reserved for the two most outrageous (if charming) pomposities, Holofernes and Armado. This careful apportioning of embarrassment is not accidental, nor is the circumstance that the two most harried victims achieve individually their finest and simplest moments under fire. Holofernes' reproach is his last line and his one stroke of quiet dignity:

> This is not generous, not gentle, not humble. (V.2.632)

Armado, the richer character, is vouchsafed by his creator a felicity close to eloquence:

> The sweet war-man is dead and rotten. Sweet chucks, beat not the
> bones of the buried: when he breathed, he was a man. (V.2.666–668)

and by the end something like a transformation seems to be operating even upon his stiff and shallow playing-card magnificence. ("For mine own part, I breathe free breath. I have seen the day of wrong through the little hole of discretion, and I will right myself like a soldier"—V.2.731–734). He too will serve a penance like his betters.[5] Thus the lash of comic criticism chastens with bitter success all the surquedry of this dramatic world. Thus all men are taught, with Nathaniel, not to o'erpart themselves.

The final and most telling chastisement appears with the entrance of Marcade, who brings the fact of death. Even a few minutes earlier, this fact would have shattered the play; now it can be borne. Heretofore death has been itself rhetorical, as in the very first lines:

> Let fame, that all hunt after in their lives,
> Live regist'red upon our brazen tombs
> And then grace us, in the disgrace of death. . . . (I.1.1–3)

Then an abstract unreality, death now is a particular event. No one of the characters has the emotional depth fully to command a rhetoric commensurate with the event, but in the speeches following Marcade's entry three degrees of rhetorical inadequacy can be distinguished. The Princess falls short only in the reserve with which she receives her bereavement, a reserve which betrays no feeling and risks the appearance of coldness. Otherwise she is sensible, brief, even, briskly courteous, alert to the relative inconsequence of all the badinage that has preceded. In contrast the poverty of the King's rhetoric is painfully manifest:

> The extreme parts of time extremely forms
> All causes to the purpose of his speed. . . . (V.2.749–750)

a rhetorical failure because it cannot conceal the underlying poverty of sympathy or even of decent respect. In essence, the King is making a request which is shockingly improper—that his courtship not be neglected because of her loss—and perhaps it is his consciousness of this indecorum that produces such monstrous linguistic convolutions and elicits her wryly polite answer:

> I understand you not. My griefs are double. (V.2.761)

Berowne's essay at a valediction, as we have seen, opens with a gesture toward the proper simplicity but winds up with an equally inappropriate contortion. Berowne at least recognizes the rhetorical problem; the lesson of *his* failure seems to be that habits of feeling and language are not quickly overcome. Earlier he had confessed:

> Bear with me, I am sick.
> I'll leave it by degrees. (V.2.417–418)

The degrees do indeed come slowly.

In the light of the lords' inadequacies before the fact of death, the penances set them by the ladies constitute a kind of final prodding toward maturation. Berowne's will test the relevance of his dilettantish jesting to human suffering[6] and thereby purge perhaps the frivolity of his ironies. In these closing moments of the last scene, one has the impression of the comedy turning back upon itself, withdrawing from those modes of speech and laughter which have in fact constituted its distinctiveness. Pater is surely right when he suggests that the play contains "a delicate raillery by Shakespeare himself at his own chosen manner"[7]—at least of the manner chosen for this work. The raillery has been there throughout, diffused and subtle, but now at the end it has become something more serious and has determined the conclusion. Could this final verdict have been introduced in the later version, "newly corrected and augmented," as the title page of the 1598 quarto informs us? The judgment on Berowne comes to seem like a judgment on the slenderness of a certain moral style that has been outgrown.

There could be no greater mistake than to conclude from this judgment that Shakespeare disliked rhetorics and forms, patterns of words and of experience. He was not, needless to say, in favor of the crude expression of raw passion. He knew that society, the happiness of life, depends on configurations and rituals. He represented the Muscovite masquing to be silly not because it was artificial but because, in his sense of the word, it was not artificial enough; it was "shallow" and "rough" and "vilely penned." This being so, one may ask whether Shakespeare did not provide within the play an instance of authentic artifice, and the answer is that he did provide it, in the form of the two concluding songs. If we regard the presentation of these songs literally, as a part of the pageant they are designed to conclude, then their artistic finish is out of place. But if we regard them as rhetorical touchstones by which to estimate the foregoing funny abuses of language, they form an ideal ending. In their careful balance, elaborate refrain, and lyric poise, the songs are artificial in the good old sense, but in their freshness and freedom from stale tradition, they blithely escape the stilted modern sense. They violate the cliché preference of spring to winter and adumbrate a finer decorum; they "like of each thing that in season grows." They like of each thing, but not conventionally or sentimentally; the "unpleasing" word of the cuckoo sounds in the spring, while the wintry cry of the owl is "merry." Joseph Westlund points out suggestively that the more attractively "realistic" world of Hiems lies further from the effete world of the play itself, and closer to the experience the gentlemen must come to face.[8] The winter song achieves a mingling of the lyrical and the humbly truthful which none of the courtly poetasters in Navarre could manage.

"The words of Mercury are harsh after the songs of Apollo," concludes Armado (V.2.940). A recent editor paraphrases:

> i.e., let us end with the songs, because clever words of the god Mercury would come harshly after the songs of Apollo, the god of poetry.[9]

Such may well be Armado's meaning, but his words can bear an ulterior construction. He might be taken to mean that the songs we have just heard, with their bracing directness, are to the rest of the play and its pseudo-golden poetry as Mercury is to Apollo. From the narrow world of neo-Petrarchan sentiment, the experience of the songs may well seem "harsh," since they treat of cuckolds and red noses and frozen milk. With that adjective in our ears, Armado ends the comedy: "You that way, we this way" (V.2.941). Who is "you"? The actors on the other side of the stage? Or we in the audience, who must leave the theater and exchange one set of conventions and disguises for another, less tractable to laughter?

Society may be, ideally, the happiness of life, but the end of the play has not placed us in it. Perhaps Nathaniel's text is fallacious. But by one very faint, almost surreptitious means, Shakespeare seems to me to remind us repeatedly of the possible felicity into which society can flower. This means is the unusual frequence and special prominence accorded the word "grace"—the word, we remember, with which the opening sentence plays (I.1.1–3, quoted above). As the play continues, the many extensions and intricate variations of "grace" in all its meanings are explored with deliberate subtlety. In no other play by Shakespeare is the address, "Your Grace," to a sovereign so alive with suggestiveness. The Princess is represented explicitly and emphatically endowed with "grace," from the first mention of her:

> For well you know here comes in embassy
> The French king's daughter with yourself to speak,
> A maid of grace and complete majesty. . . . (I.1.135–137)

and again at her first appearance, in Boyet's injunction:

> Be now as prodigal of all dear grace
> As Nature was in making graces dear
> When she did starve the general world beside
> And prodigally gave them all to you. (II.1.9–12)

The Princess's grace has something to do presumably with the comely carriage of her physical bearing, but also with a certain courtesy and sweetness of manner which transcend the body. As the multiple meanings of the word quietly exfoliated, educated Elizabethan playgoers may have remembered the quality of *grazia* in Castiglione's *Cortegiano*, that indefinable air which represents the courtier's supreme distinction, and which is repeatedly and emphatically opposed to affectation.[10] Such an echo could only heighten the ironies of the honorific "Your Grace" addressed to the King, and indeed on one occasion his fitness for it is indirectly questioned:

> Good heart, what grace hast thou thus to reprove
> These worms for loving, that art most in love? (IV.3.153–154)

The word in these contexts signifies a virtue a person can possess, but other contexts remind us that it is something that can be given to another. It is what lovers want, as Longaville's poem shows:

> Thy grace being gain'd cures all disgrace in me. . . . (IV.3.67)

and what the ladies determine to refuse:

> And not a man of them shall have the grace,
> Despite of suit, to see a lady's face. (V.2.128–129)

> No, to the death we will not move a foot;
> Nor to their penn'd speech render we no grace. . . . (V.2.146–147)

Grace is what a wit desires from his audience, perhaps meretriciously:

> For he hath wit to make an ill shape good,
> And shape to win grace though he had no wit. . . . (II.1.59–60)

> Why, that's the way to choke a gibing spirit,
> Whose influence is begot of that loose grace
> Which shallow laughing hearers give to fools. . . . (V.2.867–869)

but it is also the very ability to amuse:

> He is wit's pedlar, and retails his wares
> At wakes and wassails, meetings, markets, fairs;
> And we that sell by gross, the Lord doth know,
> Have not the grace to grace it with such show. (V.2.317–320)

These last passages suggest the paradoxical openness of this ability to perversion or manipulation, and other usages imply the same double-edged danger:

239

Folly, in wisdom hatch'd,
Hath wisdom's warrant, and the help of school,
And wit's own grace to grace a learned fool. (V.2.70–72)

But all these failures, real or potential, of the virtue never quite suppress the
hope which the word embodies: the hope for felicitous human conversation.
And although the hope is firmly rooted in the affairs of this world, at least
one usage holds the word open briefly to its theological sense:

For every man with his affects is born,
Not by might mast'red, but by special grace. (I.1.152–153)

That is Berowne on the resilience of human passion, to be echoed later by
his flip cynicism: "God give him grace to groan!" (IV.3.21). Is it fanciful to
think that the word is introduced deliberately, to enrich its resonance still
further, in the invitation of Holofernes to Nathaniel?

I do dine to-day at the father's of a certain pupil of mine,
where, if (before repast) it shall please you to gratify the
table with a grace, I will . . . undertake your ben venuto . . .
I beseech your society.
NATHANIEL. And thank you too; for society (saith the text) is the
happiness of life. (IV.2.159–168)

Here, just below the amusing surface, two or three meanings of the word
seem to coalesce.

The grace of entertainment, the grace of love, the grace of wit, the
grace of civility—*Love's Labour's Lost* is about the pursuit of all these fragile
goals. Its opening adumbrates the need of some ulterior, metaphysical principle to "grace us in the disgrace of death," though the principle of fame
proposed there is quickly forgotten. The reader may ask what means the play
holds out to us to confront that disgrace, since in fact we are forced at the
end to consider it, and the disgrace also of "the speechless sick" and "the
pained impotent." Perhaps the upshot is a wry surrender and such a devalu-
ation of grace as Kökeritz teaches us to find in the irreverent play of *The
Comedy of Errors* on the word's Elizabethan homonym:

Marry, sir, she's the kitchen-wench, and all grease. (III.2.96–97)[11]

But *Love's Labour's Lost* is not, in the analysis, devaluative, and in a sense its object is to live with the best sort of grace—with enlightened intercourse between the sexes, with gaiety and true wit, with poise, taste, decorum, and charity. The ending does not discredit this object, even if it acknowledges the helplessness of wit before suffering, and even if it extends the realm of grace to unexpected social strata. For the play does not leave us with the Princess; it leaves us with a pun on greasy Joan who keels the pot.

We can be grateful to the playwright for not attempting to put on stage the truly enlightened society. He leaves that achievement where it belongs, in the indefinite future, not altogether remote, but much too long for a play. In 1598 he was beginning to outgrow comedy as he knew it, and to question the truth of a comic resolution. Shortly he would reach his own Twelfth Night, an end to merriment. At the end of this comedy, we hardly know where we are, as Berowne goes off to the hospital and the King to a naked hermitage, and Armado to his plow, and the Princess to her loss, all off to the world's debate, and we are left with our former mirth a little suspect, and are signalled to leave, almost enigmatically: "You that way, we this way."

NOTES

1. Quotations from Shakespeare are from the edition of George Lyman Kittredge (Boston, 1936).

2. BEROWNE. O, if the streets were paved with thine eyes,
    Her feet were much to dainty for such tread!
    DUMAINE. O vile! Then, as she goes, what upward lies
    The street should see as she walk'd overhead. (V.3.278–281)

3. Still another step, just preceding and accompanying the pageant, is the reconciliation of Berowne to Boyet, upon whom Berowne has vented considerable irritation during this scene in two extended speeches (315–334, 459–581). The second speech (concluding bitterly "You leer upon me, do you? There's an eye / Wounds like a leaden sword.") is met with a surprisingly soft reply:

BOYET.   Full merrily
Hath this brave manage, this career, been run. (V.2.481–482)

That courtesy, a bit unexpectedly magnanimous and suggestive of a generosity beneath Boyet's mockery, elicits in turn Berowne's retirement from the quarrel:

Lo, he is tilting straight! Peace! I have done. (V.2.483)

and anticipates the warmer rapprochement a few moments later:

Well said, old mocker. I must needs be friends with thee. (V.2.552)

"Tilting straight" is generally taken to mean "tilting immediately"; it would make more sense if it better fit Boyet's actual speech, and motivated better Berowne's retirement. In any case, the acceptance of Boyet, with his more "realistic" and tougher wit, by Berowne (and by extension his companions) is not without psychological and thematic importance.

4. To cite two recent critics:

> In contrast to that of the Princess, the behaviour of the men is incredibly unattractive, particularly that of Berowne. It is difficult to believe that this is the same man who spoke so eloquently a short time ago about the soft and sensible feelings of love, and promised Rosaline to mend his ways. . . . The laughter is unattractive, wild, and somehow discordant . . . and it has little resemblance to the laughter we have heard in the play before this, delicate, sophisticated, sometimes hearty. But never really unkind. (Bobbyann Roesen, "*Love's Labour's Lost*," *Shakespeare Quarterly* IV [1953]), 422–423.

> After this defeat, and especially after Berowne's self-criticism one might expect the men to begin acting with more discretion and self-consciousness; but any such expectation proves false, for in the pageant of the Nine Worthies, which breaks in on the men's defeat, their behaviour attains to a new degree of crudity. (E.M.W. Tillyard, *Shakespeare's Early Comedies* [New York, 1965], pp. 147–148).

5. "I am a votary: I have vowed to Jaquenetta to hold the plough for her sweet love three year" (V.2.892–894).

6. Just as death has been an abstraction, so disease has heretofore served Berowne as a source of witty imagery:

> Light wenches may prove plagues to men forsworn. (IV.3.385)

> Write "Lord have mercy on us" on those three.
> They are infected, in their hearts it lies;
> They have the plague, and caught it of your eyes. (V.2.419–421)

7. Walter Pater, *Appreciations* (London, 1913), p. 166. Pater is speaking specifically here of the style of Berowne; the larger context deals with the "foppery of delicate language" as it is toyed with throughout the play.

8. "All the wooers must learn to be patient, to wait out the full seasonal cycle which the songs represent. . . . The gaudy blossoms of Ver, the wonderful artifice of wit and wooing, are to be tried by the rigors of winter—of experience in the real world." "Fancy and Achievement in *Love's Labour's Lost*," *Shakespeare Quarterly* 18 (1967), 45.

9. The Signet edition of *Love's Labour's Lost*, ed. John Arthos (New York and Toronto, 1965), p. 146.

10. "Sarà adunque il nostro cortegiano stimato eccellente ed in ogni cosa averà grazia, massimamente nel parlare, se fuggirà l'affetazione." Baldassare Castiglione, *Il Cortegiano, con una scelta delle opere minori*, ed. Bruno Maier (Turin, 1955), p. 129.

11. Helge Kökeritz, *Shakespeare's Pronunciation* (New Haven, 1953), p. 110.

The Failure of Relationship Between Men and Women in *Love's Labor's Lost*

Peter B. Erickson

For all its comic charm, *Love's Labor's Lost* presents an extraordinary exhibition of masculine insecurity and helplessness. While the veneer of male authority is brittle and precarious from the outset, female power is virtually absolute. This startling reversal of the expectation that men control women gives the play its capacity to disquiet us. By setting up such a marked inequality in their respective power, Shakespeare creates a gap between men and women which cannot be bridged. My thesis is that this fixed gap enables Shakespeare to explore dramatically the conventions of female domination and male humility which had become established in love poetry. I propose to examine the psychology of male and female stereotypes expressed in the men's poetry in order to show how this psychology creates a barrier which keeps the men and women apart.

The play's first scene quickly exposes the pretensions of masculine idealism and the fear of women which underlies it. The King's opening 23-line speech is too circumspect to mention directly the need to avoid women. But, as the speech moves from aspiration to prohibition, a discordant note enters and the tone becomes defensive. It remains for Berowne to reveal the fine print in "those statutes / That are recorded in this schedule here" (I.1.17–18): "But there are other strict observances: / As not to see a woman in that term . . ." (I.1.36–37). Berowne brings out the contrast between the grandness of the King's project of creating "a little academe" (I.1.13) and the narrowness of the means by which it is to be achieved. The spirit behind the plan is shown to be largely negative: the essential impulse is to construct a haven for masculine purity based on the exclusion of women. By implication, women are associated with "cormorant devouring Time" (I.1.4), the enemy originally named by the King. (Berowne's later claim that women

Originally published in *Women's Studies* 9 (1981), 65–81. Reprinted by permission of The Gordon and Breach Publishing Group.

"nourish all the world" (IV.3.350) is not strong enough to dislodge the fear of nonnurturant, "cormorant devouring" women.)

The King's utopian scheme is thoroughly discredited before it gets started. Berowne has already made the counter-statement in justification of love (I.1. 80–83), which anticipates his celebration of love in Act IV, scene 3. Though Berowne goes along with the King's plan, the damage has been done: we can no longer believe in the "little academe." The plan is so instantly undercut that it may seem that Shakespeare does not take it seriously or that it is a momentary aberration unrelated to the rest of the play. I believe it is crucial to see that the men's subsequent and predictable attraction to the women does not totally dissolve the initial dream of avoiding women. The relationships between men and women remain problematic in a way which derives from the King's original stance. The utopian scheme had cast woman in the role of the outsider.[1] By virtue of the role, women are given the power to be disruptive. This disruptive capacity is precisely what Shakespeare goes on to dramatize. His next step is to bring on stage the Princess who, in effect, originates in the King's legislation defining woman as the outsider. Of course the men fall in love, but they do so with ambivalence. Shakespeare maintains a tension between the irresistible attraction to the women and the apprehensiveness which made the King want to exclude the women in the first place. This tension leads to an impasse which is confirmed by the ultimate failure of relationship between men and women at the end of the play. The original desire to avoid women is ironically fulfilled by the women's denial of the men's suit and by the administering of penances.

The King's response to Berowne's reminder about the visit from the Princess is feeble: "What say you, lords? Why, this was quite forgot" (I.1.141). He seeks to escape the contradiction in which he finds himself by diversion. The King's sudden renewal of energy as he contemplates Armado— "One who the music of his own vain tongue / Doth ravish like enchanting harmony" (I.1.166–167)—shows that he is not aware, as we are, of the way this description applies to himself. The last word in the first scene is given to Costard, who has previously defended his violation of the King's law by asserting that "it is the manner of a man to speak to a woman" (I.1.209–210). In its comic way, Costard's final claim—"I suffer for the truth, sir" (I.1.311)—has a noble ring which contrasts favorably with the inflated nobility of the King's opening speech. The King himself will soon "suffer" for this "truth," and the verb proves to be apt.

The Princess appears on the scene at the beginning of Act II. She has come on political business for her father, a man who is emphatically weak: "decrepit, sick, and bed-rid" (I.1.138). Her first act shows her to be strong, self-confident, and poised as she firmly puts the officious Boyet in his place:

> Good Lord Boyet, my beauty, though but mean,
> Needs not the painted flourish of your praise:
> Beauty is bought by judgment of the eye,
> Not utt'red by base sale of chapmen's tongues. (II.1.13–16)

This speech sets the tone for the general action: the women will mock and reject the "painted flourish" of the four lords. In the assessment of their counterparts which follows, the women focus on the men's wit and begin their self-appointed task of challenging it (II.1.47–51, 59–60, 69–76). The battle of wits is also to be a battle of the sexes—the sexual lines are drawn prior to the first encounter as the separation of the men and women into two distinct groups is emphasized;

> He rather means to lodge you in the field,
> Like one that comes here to besiege his court,
> Than seek a dispensation for his oath,
> To let you enter his unpeopled house. (II.1.85–88)

The Princess's submissiveness—"while we attend, / Like humble-visag'd suitors, his high will" (II.1.33–34)—is only apparent. She places the King on the defensive: "The roof of this court is too high to be yours, and welcome to the wide fields too base to be mine:" (II.1.92–94). And, in short order, she places him in a double bind; "'Tis deadly sin to keep that oath, / And sin to break it" (II.1.105–106). Later, she will use this bind to refuse the King after his change of heart: "This field shall hold me, and so hold your vow: / Nor God, nor I, delights in perjur'd men" (V.2.345–346). The blend of virtue, wit and power is unbeatable and insures the women's predominance.

The men's inability to achieve relationship with the women can be seen in part as a result of the failure of their language. Berowne's tour de force in Act IV, scene 3 proving that women are the source of education is burdened with the same facility and posturing as the King's original outline of academe. Like the King's opening speech, Berowne's counter-statement is a verbal construction which cannot be put into action because of a disparity between means and end. In the new plan advanced by Berowne, the principal means by which they are to make contact with the women is poetry, but their poetry becomes an obstacle rather than a bridge since it leads, as C.L. Barber points out, to an "absorption in their own responses":

But notice how little Berowne is concerned with love as an experience between two people. All his attention is focussed on what happens within the lover, the heightening of his powers and perceptions . . . the prospect of love sets off a rhapsody that almost forgets the beloved. Consummation in physical union of the sexes is not envisaged. . . .[2]

Relative to the other lords, Berowne is more witty and more perceptive about his wit. However, he is no match for the woman who can exhaust his wit and bring him to a rueful admission of defeat:

> Here I stand, lady, dart thy skill at me,
> Bruise me with scorn, confound me with a flout,
> Thrust thy sharp wit quite through my ignorance,
> Cut me to pieces with thy keen conceit; (V.2.396–399)

Even Berowne's recantation of "Taffeta phrases, silken terms precise, / Three-pil'd hyperboles, spruce affectation, / Figures pedantical" (406–408) can be easily criticized on linguistic grounds:

> BEROWNE. Henceforth my wooing mind shall be expressed
> In russet yeas and honest kersey noes.
> And to begin, wench, so God help me law!
> My love to thee is sound, sans crack or flaw.
> ROSALINE. Sans "sans," I pray you. (V.2.412–416)

His most direct approach to Rosaline having been parried, Berowne is soon reduced to: "my wit is at an end" (V.2.430). The problem here is not simply that Berowne learns his lesson too late, but rather that, given his circumstances, he cannot learn the lesson at all.

Berowne is trapped by the women in the double game he has been playing. His comrades give Berowne the task of celebrating love, but he also retains his earlier role as supplier of ironic deflation. Berowne tries to reconcile these two positions by yielding to love with a comic self-consciousness that he is striking a conventional pose. He is aware that the men's poetry is "pure, pure idolatry" (IV.3.73), but he is unable to act on this awareness and helplessly gives in to the humor which short-circuits awareness. Berowne's playful self-mockery is not equivalent to critical perspective. The way in which he is compromised can be shown by contrast with the women's responses to the poetry at the beginning of Act V, scene 2. They have no trouble seeing it unequivocally for what it is: "as much love in rhyme / As would be cramm'd up in a sheet of paper, / Writ a' both sides the leaf, margent and all . . ." (V.2.6–8). Berowne, by comparison, is caught in a closed linguistic system from which there is no way out since he must simultaneously affirm and deny it as, for example, when he uses "painted rhetoric" (IV.3.235) to renounce such rhetoric.

Unlike the men, the women do not become victims of rhetorical inflation. While the men are stymied by the overblown hollowness of their language, the women demonstrate the potency of language. This difference between the men and the women's relation to language helps to account for the play's final impasse. Shakespeare goes out of his way to give the women the superior position which guarantees their consistent triumph. Not only do the women have a more effective wit, they also have the advantage in terms of plot when Boyet provides them with advance warning of the men's masque: "Arm, wenches, arm! encounters mounted are / Against your peace" (V.2.82–83). In Act IV, scene 3, Berowne had been strategically placed to observe his three "fellow scholars" reveal their violation of academe's statutes. This eavesdropping motif is continued as Berowne along with the others is observed by Boyet: "Warily / I stole into a neighbor thicket by, / And overheard what you shall overhear:" (IV.3.93–95). The play is clearly on the women's side. When Berowne realizes "the trick an't" (IV.3.460), he directs his anger particularly at Boyet, an anger which takes the specific form of threatening Boyet with the emasculation he himself may feel reduced to: "Die when you will, a smock shall be your shroud" (IV.3.479). Earlier he had glanced at Hercules' enslavement by Omphale: "To see great Hercules whipping a gig" (IV.3.165).

Armado's letter to Jacquenetta addresses the issue of power in a primitive, comic way. He acknowledges his inferiority by elevating the woman above himself: "More fairer than fair, beautiful than beauteous, truer than truth itself, have commiseration on thy heroical vassal" (IV.1.62–64). But Armado then reverses this standard posture of the male lover dependent on the mercy of his beloved when he assumes the role of King Cophetua who "overcame" the beggar Zenelophon: "I am the king, for so stands the comparison; thou the beggar, for so witnesseth thy lowliness" (IV.1.78–80). The tension between Armado's two positions as vassal and king is expressed as he goes on to review the various possible approaches to Jacquenetta: "Shall I command thy love? I may. Shall I enforce they love? I could. Shall I entreat thy love? I will." (IV.1.80–82). After appearing to settle on courteous obeisance as the appropriate mode, Armado revises his stance in a postscript which makes his submission contingent on her cooperation:

Thus dost thou hear the Nemean lion roar
'Gainst thee, thou lamb, that standest as his prey;
Submissive fall his princely feet before,
And he from forage will incline to play.
But if thou strive, poor soul, what art thou then?
Food for his rage, repasture for his den. (IV.1.88–93)

Armado's poetic threat of sexual assault is ironically circumscribed by the larger context, for Costard's mistake has put the letter in the hands of the group led by the Princess, whom we have just seen "play the murtherer" (IV.1.80). The sport of killing the deer places her in the roles of the virgin huntress Diana and of the cruel Petrarchan lady: "now mercy goes to kill" (IV.1.24).[3] The metaphorical application to relations between men and women is made explicit by the Princess's comment: " . . . and praise we may afford / To any lady that subdues a lord" (IV.1.39–40).

Because Costard mixes up the two, we are invited to see Berowne's message to Rosaline as parallel with Armado's to Jacquenetta. The two men share the automatic equation of being in love with writing poetry. Armado's love soliloquy ends with a flourish of poetic inspiration: "Assist me, some extemporal god of rhyme, for I am sure I shall turn sonnet. Devise, wit, write, pen, for I am for whole volumes in folio" (I.2.183–185). Berowne, at the conclusion of his soliloquy, resigns himself to the same poetic task: "Well, I will love, write, sigh, pray, sue, groan" (III.1.204). Although Berowne's poem is more refined than Armado's, it displays a similar concern with the relative power of lover and beloved. Berowne adopts the stance of poet: "Well learned is that tongue that well can thee commend" (IV.2.112). He is willing to take modest credit for his reverence for the lady: "Which is to me some praise that I thy parts admire" (IV.2.114). But he is emphatically humble about the hierarchy implicit in the relationship and attempts to mitigate the potential danger in which this hierarchy places him:

Thy eye Jove's lightning bears, thy voice his dreadful thunder,
Which, not to anger bent, is music and sweet fire.
Celestial as thou art, O, pardon love this wrong,
That sings heaven's praise with such an earthly tongue. (IV.2.115–118)

The poems of the other three men which follow deploy the same motif of a drastic imbalance of power in favor of the lady. In the King's case, for example, worship is reduced to pleading with a lady who is all but inaccessible: "So ridest thou triumphing in my woe" (IV.3.34). And, when Berowne is forced by his comrades to confess that, like the others, he is in love ("guilty, my lord, guilty"—IV.3.201), he presents his worship of Rosaline as an exaggerated prostration:

> . . . Who sees the heavenly Rosaline,
> That (like a rude and savage man of Inde),
> At the first op'ning of the gorgeous east,
> Bows not his vassal head, and strooken blind,
> Kisses the base ground with obedient breast? (IV.3.217–221)

In principle, the power of the poet-lover is equal to the lady's. The "doctrine" which Berowne "derives" from the eyes of women grants their total control:

> They sparkle still the right Promethean fire;
> They are the books, the arts, the academes,
> That show, contain, and nourish all the world. (IV.3.348–350)

Yet, though the nourishment is indispensable, the male poet has an essential role as interpreter of this experience. The beloved is the source of the lover's "double power" (IV.3.328), but the lover goes on to use this unusual power in his own powerful way:

> Never durst poet touch a pen to write
> Until his ink were temp'red with Love's sighs:
> O then his lines would ravish savage ears
> And plant in tyrants mild humility. (IV.3.343–346)

The poet is necessary to the lady because, through his art, he can give expression to her gift. Hence Berowne balances the line "Or women's sake, by whom we men are men" (IV.3.357) with "Or for men's sake, the authors of these women" (IV.3.356). The trouble with this image of mutability is that it is wishful thinking. At this point in the play, we have already seen the paltry products of the men's poetic efforts. Contrary to Berowne's theory, their poems have demonstrated the men's powerlessness rather than the complementarity of the sexes.[4] When he turns from his long speech on love to the practical matter of wooing, Berowne puts aside "these glozes" (IV.3.367) about the ideal harmony between the sexes and warns bluntly: "but be first advised, / In conflict you get the sun of them" (IV.3.365–366). Berowne's fear that the women will get the better of them is hinted in the scene's final speech: "Light wenches may prove plagues to men forsworn" (IV.3.382).

The masque of the Muscovites does prove to be the men's undoing. I think it is important to see the connection between the poems and the subsequent masque. In the poems, the men fashion their poses of worship and submission. In the masque, they attempt to act out these poses. The "penn'd speech" (V.2.147) which Moth is unable to finish delivering provides a direct link with the earlier poems. He recites the same platitudes about the women's divinity and the men's need to appeal to it—"Out of your favors, heavenly spirits, vouchsafe . . . / Once to behold with your sunbeamed eyes" (V.2.166, 169). The humor of the situation—which is considerable!—is that the women are present to respond: thus a dimension is added which the "dramatic situation" of a poem, monopolized as it is by the male voice, does not permit. The women turn their backs in implicit mockery of Berowne's notion about women's eyes as the source of poetic inspiration. After Moth's failure, the men in their Russian disguises labor to explain their mission. Berowne in particular repeats the language of obeisance:

> Our duty is so rich, so infinite,
> That we may do it still without accompt.
> Vouchsafe to show the sunshine of your face,
> That we (like savages) may worship it. (V.2.199–202)

By this time in the play, the women's deflation of this rote gesture comes as a welcome relief and serves as a partial exorcism. The women's refusal to dance implies a rejection of festivity based on the poetic conventions the men bring to it. The men depart thoroughly rebuffed, only to return for further "mockery merriment" (V.2.139) at their expense. It is as if Shakespeare's drama reveals the crippling psychological implications of the "pure idolatry" of women dictated by the sonnet mode. By creating dramatic characters who try to live out the standardized lyric assumptions about the respective roles of men and women,[5] Shakespeare shows that this hierarchical conception of masculine and feminine roles is unworkable. The men are placed in a no-win situation, and the vital contact between men and women cannot take place. But there is nowhere to go from this discovery since it involves a demonstration that the conventions have rendered impossible relations between men and women. Hence, the frustration, humiliation, and anger felt by the men are a necessary underside to the humor of their exposure.

The princess's final explanation of the women's motive carries with it a note of apology:

I thank you, gracious lords,
For all your fair endeavors, and entreat,
Out of a new-sad soul, that you vouchsafe
In your rich wisdom to excuse, or hide,
The liberal opposition of our spirits,
If overboldly we have borne ourselves
In the converse of breath—your gentleness
Was guilty of it. (V.2.729–736)

Talking among themselves however, the women had earlier been more candid about their "liberal opposition":

That same Berowne I'll torture ere I go.
O that I knew he were but in by th' week!
How I would make him fawn, and beg, and seek,
And wait the season, and observe the times,
And spend his prodigal wits in bootless rhymes,
And shape his service wholly to my device,
And make him proud to make me proud that jests!
So pair-taunt-like would I o'ersway his state
That he should be my fool and I his fate. (V.2.60–68)

Without discounting the playful surface, I think it is clear that the "torture" envisioned here is a psychologically convincing description of the women's approach. Certainly they are far from being benign, passive educators whose eyes silently instruct and inspire the men. In *A Midsummer Night's Dream*, Helena's complaints expose the poetic reflex by which men "vow and swear and superpraise my parts," "call me goddess, nymph, divine and rare, / Precious, celestial" (III.2.153, 226–227). Unlike Helena, the women in *Love's Labor's Lost* are given the power to revenge the conventions which artificially elevate them. They do so by taking advantage of the superior position in which the convention places them to force the men to "fawn, and beg, and seek." The women's action is legitimate because it involves turning back on the men their own pathetic subservience: the men are given what they deserve. However, the women's capacity to "pair-taunt-like . . . o'ersway his state" also confirms men in the worst fears about women which the convention has led the men to expect. In a self-fulfilling prophecy, the men's experience with the women proves what the clichés of their poetry taught about women's omnipotence and inaccessibility. Women have the power to dominate (they control the games), to withhold (they refuse to give themselves at the end), and to punish (they administer the final penances).

The separateness of the sexes is not an idea which is briefly proposed for academe and then discarded, but a motif which persists throughout the play. This separateness is emphasized by the way the men and women act in patterned units of four rather than as individuals. As "forsworn lords," the men renounce the original dream of a brotherhood of "fellow scholars" (I.1.17). Yet the brotherhood remains surprisingly intact. Its new form is the united masculine front of "soldiers" of "Saint Cupid" (IV.3.363). The bonds among the men are fashioned especially by the fraternal voyeurism of Act IV, scene 3 when they catch one another with love poems. In this moment, the lords have unwittingly activated the key law of academe:

> *Item*, If any man be seen to talk with a woman within the term of
> three years, he shall endure such public shame as the rest of the
> court can possibly devise. (I.1.129–132)

The elaborate theatricality of Act IV, scene 3 answers to just this notion of "such public shame as . . . the court can possibly devise." The crucial element in this shame is its being made "public." Only such publication can fulfill the King's wish for "sweet fellowship in shame" (IV.3.47). The shame paradoxically becomes a cause for rejoicing: "Sweet lords, sweet lovers, O, let us embrace!" (IV.3.210). The men's excitement suggests that they are more preoccupied with their own shame within the masculine group than with love directed outwards toward the women. This impression is also conveyed by the competition over who has the best woman (IV.3.226–277): the primary involvement here is with one another rather than with the women. Boyet offers a picture of the kind of cameraderie which love induces in the men as they prepare for the masque:

> With that all laugh'd, and clapp'd him on the shoulder,
> Making the bold wag by their praises bolder.
> One rubb'd his elbow thus, and fleer'd, and swore
> A better speech was never spoke before.
> Another, with his finger and his thumb,
> Cried, '*Via*! we will do 't, come what will come.'
> The third he caper'd, and cried, 'All goes well.'
> The fourth turn'd on the toe, and down he fell.
> With that they all did tumble on the ground,
> With such a zealous laughter, so profound,

That in this spleen ridiculous appears,
To check their folly, passion's solemn tears. (V.2.107–118)

In the hilarity of this scene, we can feel the nervousness behind the giggling. The laughter had been elicited by a joke about not fearing women: "The boy replied, 'An angel is not evil; / I should have fear'd her had she been a devil'" (V.2.105–106). The outburst of laughter confirms the fear. In their anxiety, the men turn inward to gain whatever support masculine solidarity can provide, but turning inward makes it all the more difficult to reach out to the women.

The final irony is that men in the end get the isolation from women which the vision of academe had originally asked for, but this isolation is now unwished for and set forth on the women's terms. Academe had incorporated an ideal of discipline which proved comically unenforceable. For example, the King changes the penalty imposed on Costard from "a year's imprisonment" (I.1.287) to "fasting a week with bran and water" (I.1.301), and Armado subsequently "enfranchises" him (III.1.120). The women redefine the idea of discipline and force the men to take it seriously. Following a strict application of courtly-love convention, the men become Christian knights undergoing purgation by performing good deeds in the service of a distant lady. Berowne had glibly conflated love and charity: "And who can sever love from charity?" (IV.3.362). He must now learn the difference between them in order to earn his "reformation" (V.2.869).

Love's Labor's Lost invokes the resources of festivity, but is unable to actualize them. The happy ending cannot be achieved as the play admits through the voice of Berowne:

Our wooing doth not end like an old play:
Jack hath not Gill. These ladies' courtesy
Might well have made our sport a comedy. (V.2.874–876)

Comedy cannot contain and transmute the difficulties which have emerged in the relations between men and women. These relations cannot be concluded and are not simply suspended for one year, but are fundamentally unresolved. Although the two songs represent in compressed form the one-year postponement and evoke the fulfillment of the seasonal cycle, they do not provide an adequate substitute for the failed closure: the pastoral trick of "putting the complex into the simple" will not work here.[6] Because their "harmony is essentially verbal,"[7] the songs recapitulate the men's characteristic predicament of being unable to translate verbal construct into action.

Shakespeare also blocks the release which the lords' scapegoating of the lower characters tries to forge. The men are conscious of the parallel between the masque of the Muscovites and the masque of the Nine Worthies: "'tis some policy / To have one show worse than the King's and his company" (V.2.512–413). The lords desperately mock the lower characters to make up for the mocking they received from the women: "Though my mocks come home by me, I will now be merry" (V.2.634–635). This effort does, however, boomerang. Berowne's penance in particular is a stern rebuke to such abuse of wit:

> ROSALINE. You shall this twelvemonth term from day to day
>   Visit the speechless sick, and still converse
>   With groaning wretches; and your task shall be,
>   With all the fierce endeavor of your wit,
>   To enforce the pained impotent to smile.
> BEROWNE. To move wild laughter in the throat of death?
>   It cannot be, it is impossible: (V.2.850–856)

Berowne's macabre punishment is a stark emblem for the limits of comedy.

The only evidence of connection between men and women is the Armado-Jacquenetta relationship.[8] But this tenuous fulfillment is treated as an embarrassment:

> COSTARD. She's quick, the child brags in her belly already. 'Tis yours.
> ARMADO. Dost thou infamonize me among potentates? Thou shalt die.
>   (V.2.676–679)

The lords do their best to stimulate the rivalry between Costard and Armado, to provoke an outbreak of violence: "More Ates! more Ates! stir them on, stir them on!" (V.2.688–689). It is as if the lords cannot tolerate this news of consummation and need to see Armado punished for it. It takes the abruptly chastening announcement of the death of the Princess's father to restore order (V.2.715–725).

The father's death is often seen as the introduction of realism in keeping with the pastoral motif of "Et in Arcadia Ego."[9] In accordance with my reading of the play as the breakdown of the relationship between men and women and of the triumph of the latter, I suggest an additional significance for the death of the father. Though the *pater ex machina* makes the father's presence strongly felt, it also continues his earlier image as "decrepit, sick, and bed-rid" by advertising his weakness and, indeed, his terminal absence. Because the unqualified control possessed by the women throughout the play has implicitly endangered patriarchal power, the climactic announcement about the father serves as a reassertion of patriarchal authority, and as a warning and protest against its demise. But, at the same time, the father's death symbolically confirms this demise. Marcade's message functions as an alarm for which the answering rescue is not forthcoming. It is true that this is the first time in the play the Princess has been upstaged, and that she complies to the extent of submitting herself to a year of mourning (V.2.807–810). Nonetheless, she remains in charge. Her "taming"[10] is nominal rather than definitive and conclusive. On the evidence of the play, we have every reason to feel that the Princess's sudden access of obedience is temporary and that male control remains threatened.

This continuing instability blocks the harmony and reassurance normally offered by comic closure. A genial resolution is prevented not only because the women retain essential power, but also because, despite their declarations of love for the women, the men remain strongly bonded to one another. Their homoerotic impulse has been ruthlessly mocked, but it is conspicuously not replaced by marital ties. The play thus exhibits in a stark, rudimentary way the problematic tension between the two: the awkward ending signals an uneasy stasis in which neither homoerotic nor heterosexual bonds can be affirmed. As I have argued elsewhere,[11] *As You Like It* affirms both, and does so by a patriarchal design which gives priority to male bonds over male-female relationships. Duke Senior provides an ultimate center of strength, which reconnects male solidarity with political power. By contrast, the death of the invalid father in *Love's Labor's Lost* is a resonant symbol because it is an analogue for the powerlessness of the four lords. Hence, whereas male bonding in *As You Like It* is dramatized as idealistic and dignified in the highest pastoral fashion, in *Love's Labor's Lost* male alliance is presented as plangent, foolish and embarrassing.

Notes

1. Leslie Fiedler develops the idea of the woman as "stranger" in *The Stranger in Shakespeare* (New York, 1972), pp. 43–45. See also his brief treatment of *Love's Labor's Lost* on pp. 27–33.

2. *Shakespeare's Festive Comedy* (Princeton, 1959), pp.106–107.

Holofernes' scholarship is not entirely useless since it indirectly gives us the key to the Princess's identity as the slayer of the deer.

HOLOFERNES. Dictynna, goodman Dull, Dictynna, goodman Dull.
DULL. What is Dictynna?
NATHANIEL. A title to Phoebe, to Luna, to the moon. (IV.2.36–38)

Dull's knowledge of deer lore is also useful. His insistence that the deer is a "prickett" (IV.2.12, 21, 48) unwittingly links up with the wordplay on "prick." He thereby makes the Princess's killing of the deer verbally equivalent to castration and provides another context for the men's uneasiness with women.

4. Spenser's sonnet 75 is an instance where the woman's power is balanced by the equal strength of the man: the poem effectively insists upon the poet's ability to convey immortality upon the lady. More often however, Renaissance sonnets immortalize the poet's self-abasement when the beloved refuses to respond. Many of Shakespeare's sonnets to the young man are written in this familiar mode of abjection.

5. Rosalie Colie's discussion of *Othello* in terms of testing lyric stereotypes by putting them into dramatic form can be usefully applied to *Love's Labor's Lost*. Colie describes this dramatization of sonnet convention as a process of "unmetaphoring." Though the consequences are not so drastic as in *Othello*, Shakespeare is nonetheless engaged in a similar kind of unmetaphoring in *Love's Labor's Lost*. See "*Othello* and the Problematics of Love" in *Shakespeare's Living Art* (Princeton, 1974).

6. The phrase is William Empson's: *Some Versions of Pastoral* (London, 1935), p. 23.

7. Anne Barton, Introduction to *Love's Labour's Lost* in *The Riverside Shakespeare*, p. 177. Barton's earlier work on the play appeared under her maiden name: Bobbyann Roesen, "*Love's Labour's Lost*," *Shakespeare Quarterly* 4 (1953), 411–426.

8. We should therefore recognize "the foolish wisdom of his melancholy union with Jaquenetta" as Richard Cody puts it in *The Landscape of the Mind* (Oxford, 1969), p. 124.

9. Erwin Panofsky, "Et in Arcadia Ego: Poussin and The Elegaic Tradition," *Meaning in the Visual Arts* (New York, 1955).

10. I take the term from the title of another early comedy in which an overt struggle for domination between men and women produces a conspicuously awkward ending. See Coppélia Kahn's recent account of the play as a critique of "male dominance": "this play satirizes not woman herself in the person of the shrew, but *male attitudes toward women*" [italics in original]. "*The Taming of the Shrew*: Shakespeare's Mirror of Marriage," *The Authority of Experience: Essays in Feminist Criticism*, ed. Arlyn Diamond and Lee R. Edwards (Amherst, 1977), pp. 84–100.

11. In "Sexual Politics and the Social Structure in *As You Like It*," *Massachusetts Review* 23 (1982), 65–83, I develop a more sustained comparison of the respective endings of *Love's Labor's Lost* and *As You Like It*, and delineate the patriarchal strategy by which, in the latter play, Shakespeare circumvents the disharmony of the former.

OATH-TAKING

Irene G. Dash

> A time methinks too short
> To make a world-without-end bargain in. (V.2.788–89)[1]

In *Love's Labour's Lost*, Shakespeare employs oaths to reveal how men and women characters perceive the meaning of truth and honesty. During the play, oaths increase in seriousness, progressing from the extravagantly humorous pledge of Act I when the King of Navarre and his men swear not to see women for three years; to the more moderate vow of Act IV, when the gallants plan to woo and win "these girls of France"; to the proposals of marriage of the last scene. Women constitute the subject of men's vows, although the men swear first to reject women, then pledge to pursue them, and finally to marry them. The ironic progression suggests that since the oath-takers are men, Shakespeare is mocking the male tradition of oath-taking, insisting that it be linked with honesty. In contrast, the Princess of France and the women of her court reject the offers of marriage of the King and his courtiers, refusing to be bound by this timeless oath. One of the men objects that this is no way to end a comedy. Thus Shakespeare presents a woman's point of view on honesty and truth, endowing the play with a significance that goes beyond the limits of the comic world.

The play opens at the court of the King of Navarre moments before he and his men sign a vow to dedicate themselves solely to the pursuit of learning:

> Our court shall be a little academe,
> Still and contemplative in living art. (I.1.13–14)

Chapter 2 of *Wooing, Wedding, and Power: Women in Shakespeare's Plays* (Columbia University Press, 1981), pp. 9–30, 257–258. Copyright © 1981. Reprinted with permission of the publisher.

He promises present fame and future immortality, confident that these immodest rewards will accrue naturally to the court. "Navarre shall be the wonder of the world" (I.1.12). The King assumes his men share his aim, particularly the quest for fame. They need only dedicate themselves to study and abjure the company of women for three years. Of the three courtiers, two—Longaville and Dumain—comply, even relishing the idea of self-sacrifice.

> I am resolved, 'tis but a three years' fast:
> The mind shall banquet, though the body pine (I.1.24–25)

exclaims Longaville. Dumain is even more extravagant in his pledge:

> To love, to wealth, to pomp, I pine and die,
> With all these living in philosophy. (I.1.31–32)

However, Berowne, the third man of Navarre's court, protests. Rational and quick-witted, he finds the terms antithetical to the whole spirit of education. Moreover, he believes them too harsh:

> . . . not to see a woman in that term,
>
> .   .   .   .
>
> And not be seen to wink of all the day—
> When I was wont to think no harm all night,
>
> .   .   .   .
>
> O, these are barren tasks, too hard to keep. (I.1.37–47)

Berowne would prefer to be excused from the pledge, explaining by most ingenious arguments that he "swore in jest" (I.1.54). His sophisticated reasoning and his rhetorical gifts set him apart from the others. He challenges the King's "study's godlike recompense" (I.1.58) with his own interpretation:

> Study is like the heaven's glorious sun,
> That will not be deep search'd with saucy looks;
> Small have continual plodders ever won,
> Save base authority from others' books. (I.1.84–87)

He describes those things most worth enjoying:

> At Christmas I no more desire a rose
> Than wish a snow in May's new-fangled shows;
> But like of each thing that in season grows. (I.1.105–7)

Nevertheless, he capitulates when Navarre insists on a written oath to confirm the verbal pledge. "You swore to that, Berowne, and to the rest" (I.1.53). Otherwise, "Well, sit you out; go home, Berowne; adieu" (I.1.110). Almost childlike in his petulant persistence, Navarre demands total compliance. And so, threatened with exclusion from the group, the courtier relents. Peer approval overrides reason. He will not break his oath:

> . . . I have sworn to stay with you;
> . . . I'll keep what I have sworn. (I.1.111, 114)

Oaths, whether reasonable or not, link the men. But the play questions the wisdom of such bonding. And the Princess, Rosaline, Katharine, and Maria are the chief challengers.

The extraordinary opening vow permits exploration of the values men and women place on oaths. Unlikely to strut across the stage with swords or magnanimously offer kingdoms for a pledge, women make seemingly colorless vows that lack bravado: vows of marriage. But they are timelessly binding, world-without-end bargains that will alter their lives. The women reject oath-taking as a method of confirming a temporary agreement, skeptical about the morality of vows too easily made and broken. When, for example, in the last act, the King asserts, "The virtue of your eye must break my oath" (V.2.348), the Princess of France objects, "You nickname virtue; vice you should have spoke, / For virtue's office never breaks men's troth" (V.2.349–50). The close relationship between "truth" and "troth" as well as between "troth"—to pledge one's word—and "troth" in the phrase "to plight one's troth" in marriage cannot have been lost on Shakespeare's audience. What makes the play unusual is that its ending confirms the women's skepticism.

Moments after being signed, that opening vow meets its first challenge when Berowne reminds Navarre of the forthcoming diplomatic visit of the Princess of France. She is to negotiate the "surrender up of Aquitaine / To her . . . father" (I.1.137–38). As we later discover, disagreement exists about the terms of an earlier treaty. But the immediate problem is oath-breaking. What now of an oath forbidding speech with a woman, or of that first decision in the written proclamation that Berowne reads: " 'no woman shall come within a mile of [the] court . . . on pain of losing her tongue' " (I.1.119–22)? Shakespeare exaggerates the terms for the sake of comedy. However, his later development of the character of the men and women around this basic plot reveals his genius. At this moment in the comedy, Navarre concedes that he must do something and so decides to bend his oath, welcoming the women to the park surrounding the palace but permitting them no entrance to the palace itself.

The argument is joined. The men must confront the women; vows must face honest appraisal.

> I hear your Grace hath sworn out house-keeping:
> 'Tis deadly sin to keep that oath, my lord,
> And sin to break it. (II.1.104–106)

The Princess observes his dilemma. Lack of hospitality ("housekeeping") had not been anticipated. A simplistic oath that seemed merely a rejection of women—debasers of men's higher goals—now turns sinful. Navarre had ignored the possibility of women as equals.

Writing of the reluctance of men to grant women equality, John Stuart Mill observes that it reflects a fear of living with an equal. To support his thesis of women's potential, he cites the training of princesses, their subsequent abilities as rulers, and the effect of this training on their self-esteem:

> Princesses, being more raised above the generality of men by their rank than placed below them by their sex, have never been taught that it was improper for them to concern themselves with politics; but have been allowed to feel the liberal interest natural to any cultivated human being in the great transactions which took place around them, and in which they might be called on to take a part.[2]

The Princess of France is such a woman.

She sets the tone and provides the example for the women who accompany her. As her father's envoy to the court of Navarre, she must negotiate a delicate political solution. But this role as emissary does not compromise her. Nor does it suggest that her father adversely governs her life, as do some of the fathers in Shakespeare's plays. Rather, like the princesses mentioned by Mill, she has gained by this training. Her father has supported her strength and endorsed her as a person. Her language throughout the play and her attitude toward herself and others clearly indicate her independence. The closing scene confirms the portrait when news of her father's death arrives, interrupting the merriment. Politically and economically independent, she is a woman who knows herself.

Her independence and its exhilarating effect on her women have seldom been discussed in critism.[3] Instead, historical parallels for her, the King of Navarre, Berowne, Dumain, Longaville, and others have preoccupied critics. The tendency has been to justify her on a historical basis rather than a human one. However, the Princess, whose freedom is unique, expresses ideas common to women but seldom spoken. Samuel Taylor Coleridge, who found traces of Shakespeare's later genius in this early comedy, observed: "True genius begins by generalizing and condensing; it ends in realizing and expanding."[4] Shakespeare's method for developing the Princess's character reveals this early genius. He particularizes her trait of honesty; she demands it of herself as well as others. And he never destroys her self-awareness and self-identification as a woman.

But the play is seldom seen and the remarkably outspoken Princess infrequently heard. She is the victim of eighteenth-century editing and of bias against outspoken, independent women. Durng its early years, Love's Labour's Lost was performed at court, both Queen Elizabeth's (1597 or 98) and James's in January 1605.[5] Records of performances also indicate that it appeared "at the Blacke-Friers and the Globe" sometime before 1631.[6] It was quite popular in Shakespeare's time, but its subsequent stage history has been bleak. The promptbooks of the nineteenth century and the one attempt at converting Love's Labour's Lost to an opera in the eighteenth century provide clues to its infrequent performance. Those works owe their shape to Alexander Pope, whose edition of Shakespeare's plays first appeared in 1723. Because of Pope's fame, his edition had great influence on attitudes toward the plays and on their form in the theater. Deciding that a passage was too raucous, outspoken, or imperfectly written, Pope would move it out of the text and place it in small print at the bottom of the page. The result in many cases was a divided page. Because of Pope's skill as a writer, the text at the top could be read without interruption. One hardly realized what had happened unless one looked at an asterisk and then turned to the small type at the bottom. The effect on the play and on the balance among characters was tremendous. Some works profited from Pope's insights; others suffered.[7] Love's Labour's Lost was among the latter. It became a thin comedy whose story line alone survived.

Although most later editors rejected Pope's edition and his method, the text, printed by the famous J. Tonson, remained in print. In 1773, when David Garrick thought he would try a production of Love's Labour's Lost if it could be converted to an opera, the adaptor Edward Thompson worked from a Pope text.[8] In 1939, when Madame Vestris produced the play, Pope's work still provided the skeletal basis for the cuts.[9] Vestris herself played Rosaline. The Princess's role was greatly abbreviated. Lines with sexual connotations as well as those that establish the Princess as a strong character disappeared.

Samuel Johnson, commenting on the play in his edition of 1765, indicates the general feeling of the age:

> In this play which all the editors have concurred to censure, and some have rejected as unworthy of our poet, it must be confessed that there are many passages mean, childish, and vulgar; and some which ought not to have been exhibited, as we are told they were, to a *maiden queen*. But there are scattered, through the whole, many sparks of genius; nor is there any play that has more evident marks of the hand of Shakespeare.[10] (italics mine)

As a result of this protective attitude toward women, many of the lines with sexual connotations, or lines that are direct and bawdy, were omitted. Unfortunately, many of these lines also help to establish the character of the Princess as a strong woman undisturbed by direct language. Three equally self-assertive women accompany her. Although less clearly defined, they too speak with directness. But the Princess is chief among them. Controlling both power and wealth, she is sovereign over herself. Original in her thinking, she is unafraid and undominated. She laughs at the Petrarchan tradition that dictates praise of a woman's beauty and insists on truth even in examining her own thoughts. Was she the product of her age—an age when a maiden queen, fearing no censure of her laughter, could listen and enjoy the language as well as the portraits of women in this comedy?

Direct and abrupt, the Princess's opening speeches offer the first clue to her character. She will insist on honesty, reject flattery, and dismiss flowery, unsubstantiated words, recognizing their hollowness. She listens to Boyet, the male adviser accompanying her party, as he praises her many endowments:

> Be now as prodigal of all dear grace
> As Nature was in making graces dear,
> When she did starve the general world beside
> And prodigally gave them all to you. (II.1.9–12)

Relying on Petrarchan conceits—mannerisms used in the poetry of the period—Boyet meets a sharp reprimand. His speech functions theatrically, triggering a response and offering an incisive character drawing of the Princess:

> Good lord Boyet, my beauty, though but mean,
> Needs not the painted flourish of your praise:
> Beauty is bought by judgment of the eye. (II.1.13–15)

Refusing praise that seems unrealistic, she insists that beauty may be easily observed and does not need words to create what is not present. This early reference to her own physical appearance is exploited later in her tests of the honesty of others. Now she merely mocks Boyet's use of obviously worn forms of flattery:

> I am less proud to hear you tell my worth
> Than you much willing to be counted wise
> In spending your wit in the praise of mine. (II.1.17–19)

She fails to convince him. With a last flourish, he leaves as her emissary to the King: "Proud of employment, willingly I go" (II.1.35). The Princess faults him once more: "All pride is willing pride, and yours is so" (II.1.36). Compared with Navarre, who was introduced as a man ambitiously seeking eternal fame, she has been introduced as a woman wary of fame and aware of the pitfalls of pride.

Shakespeare's technique for revealing her character differs from that used with the men. Berowne attempted to dissuade Navarre from his foolish vow. The Princess is never in conflict with her women. Rather, the dramatist parades a series of different men from different economic groups before her. With each she debates the meaning of truth; and each encounter further reveals her point of view.

Intellectually she resembles Berowne. Like him, she enjoys exploring and exploiting verbal meaning. Like him, she delights in philosophical development of an idea. However, the Princess, even when she tends to hypothesize or, introspectively, analyze her own actions, seldom forsakes reason for peer loyalty. Berowne, despite his brilliant argument against Navarre's academy, ultimately capitulates. The Princess, however, does not yield to the pressures of others.

Virginia Woolf, in *A Room of One's Own*, suggests that a woman of independent income eventually develops an independent perspective. No longer angry or afraid, she can see the defects in the education of men just as she knows that there have been defects in her own education. Woolf describes the healing power of economic freedom and independence:

> Indeed, I thought. . . . I need not hate any man; he cannot hurt me. I need not flatter any man; he has nothing to give me. So imperceptibly I found myself adopting a new attitude towards the other half of the human race. It was absurd to blame any class or any sex, as a whole. . . . Their education had been in some ways as faulty as my own. It had bred in them defects as great.[11]

The Princess of France has this clarity and lack of animosity. When she discovers that she must camp in the park surrounding the court, she accepts and respects the King's orders. She does not, however, accept the wisdom of his choice of life style.

Upon meeting him later in this scene (II.1), she follows the same pattern of close word analysis that she used with Boyet. To the King's "Fair Princess, welcome to the court of Navarre" (II.1.90), she responds by examining every word but "Princess":

> "Fair" I give you back again, and "welcome" I have not yet.
> The roof of this court is too high to be yours, and welcome to
> the wide fields too base to be mine. (II.1.91–94)

Continuing, she explores the meaning of "teach." Although couched in modesty—"To teach a teacher ill beseemeth me" (II.1.108)—her speeches are spattered with words revealing her own intellectual training: "knowledge," "ignorance," and "wise."

Shakespeare includes political as well as social skills in his characterization. She knows her mission and intends to acquire the rights to Aquitaine by proving that her father had returned "The payment of a hundred thousand crowns" (II.1.129). Indulgently, the King rehearses the terms, concluding with:

> Dear Princess, were not his requests so far
> From reason's yielding, your fair self should make
> A yielding 'gainst some reason in my breast,
> And go well satisfied to France again. (II.1.149–152)

But the Princess knows the background of the agreement. She cites documents that go back to the time of Navarre's father. It is unnecessary to review the terms of the agreement here; it is sufficient to know that the Princess's just grasp of the details of a treaty proves her acumen. She is more than a social creature sent to appease the King through the exercise of charm. She is a competent administrator. Navarre must change his estimate.

This brief encounter with him not only enhances the portrait of the Princess, it also emphasizes the disadvantages she faces because of her sex. Despite her economic and political power, she is reduced to the status of an outsider. The equality that should exist between the men and women does not. Handicapped, the women rely on honesty to deflate and combat the men. Whereas in Act I rustics, a pedant, and a clown mimic and burlesque the main action, suggesting the folly of the nobles, in Act II the entrance of the women signals the major contrast. Meeting the men in the Park of Navarre, each woman wins a silent admirer. Two—Berowne and the King—attempt light, insincere conversation. Each is rebuffed for dishonesty and superficiality. Conventional forms are laughed at by unconventional, free women.

"You shall be welcome, madam, to my court" (II.1.95), avers the King when he first meets her. "Conduct me thither" (II.1.96), responds the Princess. But, because of his oath, he cannot. "Did not I dance with you in Brabant once?" (II.1.114) asks Berowne. "Did not I dance with you in Brabant once?" (II.1.115) responds Rosaline. "I know you did," the annoyed Berowne replies (II.1.116). "How needless was it then to ask the question" (II.1.117). She has forced him to admit the foolishness of conventional patterns of conversation between men and women. She has also pinpointed dishonesty. But some of their conversation falls to the bottom of the page in Pope's and later acting editions.[12] And most of the frank joking among the women after the departure of the men also joins the small print.

Flattery may sometimes defeat honesty just as honesty weakened the men's oath. For women, flattery usually concentrates on physical beauty although, as a recent writer observed, "The average woman—and that means a good 95 percent of them—is not beautiful in the way the culture pretends."[13] A realist, the Princess knows this. At the close of the first scene between the men and the women, Boyet reports to her: "All eyes saw his [Navarre's] eyes enchanted with gazes" (II.1.247). But she refuses to be lulled or beguiled by such words. Instead, her physical appearance often provides the test for honesty.

Her drive for forthright appraisal of her not-too-attractive self extends from men of the court to men of another social class. Two opportunities occur in quick succession at the beginning of Act IV: her short interview with the Forester, and her light response to Costard.[14] In the first, the Forester directs her to an excellent vantage point for shooting deer:

> Hereby, upon the edge of yonder coppice,
> A stand where you may make the fairest shoot.
> PRINCESS. I thank my beauty, I am fair that shoot,
> And thereupon thou speak'st the fairest shoot.   (IV.1.9–12)

Once again she picks up the allusion to her appearance, this time creating a difficulty for the Forester by intentionally misreading his line. Unfairly, perhaps, she insists that he choose between honesty and flattery. To his, "Pardon me, madam, for I meant not so" (IV.1.13), she quickly acts astonished,

"What, what? First praise me, and again say no? / O short-liv'd pride! Not fair? alack for woe!" (IV.1.14–15). The poor Forester, completely confused, attempts to adopt the proper stance. "Yes, madam, fair" (IV.1.16), he retracts. But the Princess will not accept his answer:

> Nay, never paint me now;
> Where fair is not, praise cannot mend the brow.
> Here (good my glass), take this for telling true:
> Fair payment for foul words is more than due. (16–19)

The Princess has made her point. The way she looked to herself in her "glass" was the standard she would use to test the truth of others' statements. The speech also forms an important link to the beginning of the play. In her reference to "short-liv'd pride" she reminds us of that first scene when Navarre sought to create the "wonder of the world" and dreamed of immortal fame.

But Pope moved most of this exchange and the one that follows to the bottom of the page. And when the play finally arrived on the stage in the mid-nineteenth century, many of these same lines were excised. The major woman's role, instead of belonging to the Princess, went to Rosaline.[15] Because she is paired romantically with Berowne, critics mistakenly consider her his equivalent among the women. Dark-haired, alert, bright, with many of the play's good lines, she nevertheless does not parallel him. Instead, the Princess of France, paired with Navarre romantically, most resembles Berowne. For she is intellectually and verbally the most gifted of the women.

The second example of the Princess relating honesty to a description of her own person occurs in a confrontation with one of the play's rustics. Searching for the proper addressee of a letter, Costard barges onto the scene. When he asks for the "head lady," he learns only that she is the "highest." Unwilling to accept what might be a double meaning, he persists until assured, "The thickest and the tallest" (IV.1.47). "The thickest and the tallest! . . . / Are not you the chief woman? You are the thickest here" (IV.1.48–51). For the third time, she has chosen to measure honesty by statements about her physical size. The thickest and the tallest, she is a woman who knows herself not "slimly" but well.

In Costard, the play's Clown, Shakespeare creates a character who tries people's patience. Their varying responses to him offer a measure of their personalities and their self-control. Early in the play, for example, listening to the King's reading of a letter, Costard constantly interrupts. Eventually, Navarre orders, "Peace! . . . No words" (I.1.226, 229). Later, Berowne's outbursts are less restrained. Attempting to retain the Clown's attention, Berowne explodes: "Why, villain, thou must know first" [before you can act] (III.1.159). But this reprimand does not inhibit Costard who, most repectfully, continues on his own tangent. "I will come to your worship tomorrow morning," he promises. Berowne despairs: "It must be done this afternoon. Hark, slave, it is but this" (III.1.160–163). Finally, in Act IV, Costard's errors so embarrass Berowne that he swears, "Ah! you whoreson loggerhead, you were born to do me shame" (IV.3.200), and exclaims, "Will these turtles be gone?" (IV.3.208).

Compared with the hostility expressed by words like "villain," "slave," "loggerhead," "turtle," and "fool," the Princess's language shows remarkable restraint. Reminding Costard of his errand—the delivery of the letter—she insists he focus on his business, "What's your will, sir? What's your will?" (IV.1.52). Her directions to the Clown illustrate her characteristically tenacious concentration on the business at hand, revealed as early as her first scene when she sent Boyet on his way rather than allowing him time for chatter and flattery. Her equable "sir" indicates her patience and self-control. Nevertheless, when she expresses annoyance with Costard, critics tend to misread her actions. The most recent example is Richard David's comment: "Obviously the Princess is snubbing Costard for his impertinence." David then adds a cryptic reference to an earlier editor, "Furness makes a doubt of it."[16] To understand David, one must turn to the early twentieth-century *Variorum* where Horace Howard Furness asks: "In these words of the Princess may there not be detected an impatient eagerness to cut short Costard's rather uncomplimental references to her figure?"[17] What had been quizzical wondering becomes definite assertion. Was David influenced by Furness? The critic attributes vanity to the Princess, whereas the text implies the opposite. David's comment seems to reflect the editor's bias rather than the dramatist's intention and creates an unnecessary inconsistency in characterization. Thus may traditional notions of female behavior inhibit understanding of one of the women characters. Basically, the exchange with Costard is the last and most direct indication of the Princess's seeking honesty in description of her own person.

Shakespeare next develops his portrait on a more complex level, extending the test for honesty from the physical to the intellectual and the philosophical. And, finally, the value of Boyet to the Princess becomes apparent. For it is he, not the Forester, who challenges her statements. And it is he who acts as a refracting glass for the varied facets of her nature. When, following her exchange with the Forester, she ruminates on the vanity of the human quest for fame, Boyet wonders at her honesty. Speaking of fame, she says:

As I for praise alone now seek to spill
The poor deer's blood, that my heart means no ill. (IV.1.34–35)

Boyet, thus far primarily a flatterer, alertly probes her words:

> Do not curst wives hold that self-sovereignty
> Only for praise' sake, when they strive to be
> Lords o'er their lords? (IV.1.36–38)

I am calling your bluff, he insists. To him, her seeming humility isn't quite sincere. Women, too, in a very different context, seek praise, just as Navarre in Act I hoped for fame and immortality. But women's fame, unfortunately, is built on their wishing to be "lords o'er their lords."

Again, truth triumphs. The Princess agrees that, yes, indeed, "praise we may afford / To any lady that subdues a lord" (IV.1.39–40). Her answer characterizes a feminist's awareness. She does not smile at his innuendo. Nor does she modestly disagree that women have no aspirations to fame. Aware of the male world in which she moves—and made more aware by Navarre's foolish vow—she applauds any success, however slight, that women may achieve. The exchange between her and Boyet illustrates the dramatist's remarkable insight into the mind of a woman and his ability to create, as Pope observed, characters as "Individual as those in Life itself."[18] The nuances in this portrait testify to the importance of the Princess as the most fully defined of the woman characters. She is Berowne's intellectual counterpart.

Criticism of the play, however, has overlooked their resemblances. Concentrating on the romantically paired couples, it has lost sight of the variations among the women. Rosaline, because she is linked with Berowne, receives the greatest attention. But Shakespeare has invented two different types of pairing—the intellectual and the romantic. In this play they are not interchangeable. Taking their cue from the world they know, however, the critics acknowledge only the latter. Edward Dowden and H. H. Furness, for example, offer two interpretations. After crediting the women with clearer insight than the men, Dowden writes:

> And yet the Princess, and Rosaline, and Maria, have not the entire advantage on their side. It is well to be practical; but to be practical, and also have a capacity for ideas is better. . . . Berowne is yet a larger nature than the Princess or Rosaline. *His* good sense is the good sense of a thinker and of a man of action. When he is most flouted and bemocked, we yet acknowledge him victorious and master; and Rosaline will confess the fact by and by.[19]

Although Dowden mentions the Princess and Maria, he sees the major pairing as that between Berowne and Rosaline. His "by and by" takes us out of the play and into the world beyond the theater, a world where women do not set the rules. Neither the play's open-ended conclusion nor the Princess's "capacity for ideas" has relevance in such criticism. Dowden responds to the text less as a scholar and more as a man influenced by the contemporary culture.

H.H. Furness also found Berowne superior to Rosaline but arrived at his conclusion by comparing Berowne and Rosaline to other romantic couples in Shakespeare's plays. In that context, Rosaline proves weaker than other women, whereas Berowne proves superior to other men. Through a complex process of analysis and comparison of sets of romantic pairs, the editor conclusively proves Berowne's superiority to Rosaline.[20] But a close study of the text reveals that Berowne's equivalent in strength is not Rosaline—with whom he is romantically coupled—but the Princess of France.

The play continues to explore the relationship between oaths and truth. In Act IV, the first oath is challenged when the men individually—but overheard by one another—sigh for the different women of France: Navarre for the Princess: "'O queen of queens, how far dost thou excel / No thought can think, nor tongue of mortal tell' " (IV.3.39–40); Longaville for Maria: "Ay me, I am forsworn!" (IV.3.45); and Dumain for "O most divine Kate!" (IV.3.81).

Berowne's unmasking is more extreme. He is the victim of Costard's inattention to details. The letter meant for Rosaline is misdelivered and falls into Navarre's hands. Read aloud for all to hear, it forces Berowne to acknowledge that his bond with the others has become a broken vow. He then proposes: "Sweet lords, sweet lovers, O, let us embrace!" (IV.3.210). He forces them to confront the truth, but not for long. They now demand he exercise his rhetorical skill and intellectual ability to "prove / Our loving lawful, and our faith not torn" (IV.3.280–281). In one of the longest and most magnificent speeches in the play, he convinces them that their former oath—to pursue study and lead the celibate life—was "Flat treason 'gainst the kingly state of youth" (IV.3.289). Joyously, he weaves supports for his earlier thesis.

So effective is his argument that the men once more turn to oath-taking. They have learned little. Having forsaken one course of action, they swear once more, revealing their inability to temper enthusiasm with reason. Nor has the persistent Navarre, whose extravagant speech characterized the earlier movement of the play, learned to temper optimism with caution. "Saint Cupid, then! and, soldiers, to the field!" (IV.3.363), he rallies them. To Longaville's query, "Shall we resolve to woo these girls of France?" the King, who deals in absolutes, confidently asserts "and win them too" (IV.3.368–369). He is still a man unaware of the character of the Princess.

Like the first set of vows, the second, although more reasonable, is similarly immoderate. This time the men do not plan seclusion and a life of scholarship, but action on a field of battle—specifically the wooing of the women. The King proposes entertainments. Once again, he moves with extreme self-confidence. Not scholars in a study, they are to be soldiers in the field. They have shifted from the introverted to the extroverted life. Nevertheless, once again their goal is total victory and therefore unbalanced: not fame on their gravestones, but success in the Park of Navarre. It is they, not the women, who first invent the games to be played, the tricks to be practiced in a masquerade. Their masculine egos in command, all but Berowne assume victory. He alone is skeptical:

> Light wenches may prove plagues to men forsworn;
> If so, our copper buys no better treasure. (IV.3.382–383)

The text's lines, although consistent in their definition of character, prove a problem for Richard David, who comments: "Berowne's note of warning here comes in rather inharmoniously after his magnificent address of loyalty to Love."[21] But Berowne's verbal pyrotechnics have little to do with his underlying beliefs, as was evident in the first scene. His major role is as spokesman for the men, being the most brilliant and poetic among them. Actually the speech indicates that at least one of the men of Navarre's court has an understanding of the dignity and individuality of the women whom they plan to woo.

Resembling the Princess, the women express both their approval of the men and their skepticism about the male dedication to a cause—whether "academe" or women. "O that I knew he were but in by th' week!" (V.2.61), exclaims Rosaline of Berowne.

> A huge translation of hypocrisy,
> Vildly compiled, profound simplicity.[22] (V.2.51–52)

is Katharine's evaluation of the verses of Dumain while Maria expresses her doubts by desiring that the pearls sent by Longaville be longer and the letter shorter. Her comment, too, is relevant. Deriding the "fool'ry in the wise" (V.2.76) as an attempt "to prove, by wit, worth in simplicity" (V.2.78), she is expressing what the audience felt at the close of Act IV when listening to the men's rather simplistic approach to wooing.

Having sent gifts and flowery words to the women, the men expect easy acceptance. Instead, convention is once again challenged. The men, having decided to mask as Muscovites, encounter masked women. Masks meet masks. Truth, like the true identity of the women, is not easily uncovered. The wooers must rely on external symbols of the women behind the masks. But the women have exchanged gifts with one another. Again the men take oaths to convince the women as well as themselves of their serious intent. Each man pledges undying love to a masked symbol.

The dramatist once again suggests the weakness of oaths as proof of conviction. For the men have wooed the wrong masked women. "The King is my love sworn," exclaims Rosaline, who had posed as the Princess (V.2.282). "And quick Berowne hath plighted faith to me" (V.2.283), returns the Princess. Although the women graciously admit, "There's no such sport as sport by sport o'erthrown" (V.2.153), the scene furnishes another example of the danger of swearing, and prepares the way for the final exchange.

In the scene of reconciliation after the Muscovite adventure, Berowne faces his most difficult moment in the play. For he is uncertain whether to reply in words and fancy phrases or whether, in the method of the women, to resort to honesty. To Rosaline's challenge, "Which of the vizards was it that you wore?" (V.2.385), Berowne retorts with questions. "Where? when? what vizard? why demand you this?" (V.2.386). He begins to close the plot's circle.

"Necessity will make us all forsworn / Three thousand times within this three years' space" (I.1.149–150), he had said in Act I after joining the others in oath. In Act V, he merely laments: "Thus pour the stars down plagues for perjury" (V.2.394). Doubly perjured, in fact, are the men: first, for having forsworn their original oath; second, for having pretended no knowledge of the Muscovites. And they will be further perjured before the comedy ends. For oath-taking is a habit difficult to break.

The oath-maker confronts the truth-sayer in Act V. Navarre still believes in his invulnerability. To the Princess's warning, "When she shall challenge this [your overture], you will reject her" (V.2.438), the King swiftly answers with an oath, "Upon mine honor, no" (V.2.439). His self-confidence persists. Not daunted by her "Peace, peace, forbear: / Your oath once broke, you force not to forswear" (V.2.439–40), he continues to consider himself wiser than the woman who warns him. With bravura, he exclaims, "Despise me when I break this oath of mine" (V.2.441). "I will" (V.2.442), she answers simply. When the plot unfolds, the revelation of the exchange of tokens leads to yet another forswearing. The Princess's warnings anticipate her closing words of rejection: "No, no, my lord, your Grace is perjur'd much, . . . / Your oath I will not trust" (V.2.790, 794).

What type of character is the King, and what leads him to these excessive displays? We know that he is interested in fame in the present as well as the future, fame that will survive the grave. Moreover, he is at the opening of the drama fairly certain that he can achieve this fame through dedication to study. We also learn from Boyet very early in the comedy that Navarre is a man of great reputation. Later, in the King's opening encounter with the Princess, we note his self-confidence, his certainty that he, rather than she, knows the proper path for the man of wisdom. Countering her criticism of his actions with questions of a political nature, he challenges her in the area where, supposedly, he is the wiser. Nevertheless, his wisdom lacks sensitivity and intellectual depth.

In the last scene, the dramatist draws together the two strands—oath-taking and truth-telling—that weave through this comedy. The news of the death of the King of France is a clever device for joining these elements. Once again, Navarre functions as antagonist, providing the background against which the Princess's varied talents sparkle. While she is thinking of her father and of returning to her kingdom, the King is thinking of himself. To her declaration, "I will away to-night," he responds, "I do beseech you stay" (V.2.727–728). But he goes beyond that. He makes an offer of marriage that she doesn't understand:

> And though the mourning brow of progeny
> Forbid the smiling courtesy of love
> The holy suit which fain it would convince,
> Yet since love's argument was first on foot,
> Let not the cloud of sorrow justle it
> From what it purpos'd; since to wail friends lost
> Is not by much so wholesome-profitable
> As to rejoice at friends but newly found. (V.2.744–751)

Navarre's speech reveals an awareness of the tenuous relationship between them while at the same time minimizing, and thus distorting, the closeness of the ties between father and daughter. The dramatist cunningly gives lines to Navarre that establish a semantic parallel that does not exist, thereby emphasizing the intellectual ineptness of the King and the superiority of the Princess. She, on the other hand, unable to believe that a proposal of marriage could occur at this moment, thinks that she has suddenly lost her ability to comprehend subtle verbal meanings. For a person who has treasured her intellectual agility, this is a double blow. Not only is she bereft of father, but also of wit. "I understand you not, my griefs are double" (V.2.752), she admits.

Her intellectual counterpart, Berowne, then steps in, suggesting that "honest plain words best pierce the ear of grief" (V.2.753). Because this second parallel has seldom been recognized by critics, Berowne's sudden intervention has been questioned. Samuel Johnson believed that the speech was "given to a wrong person."[23] Johnson suggests giving the first line (752) to the Princess; the next several, beginning "And by these badges," to the King. But Shakespeare's distribution of these lines supports the methods he has developed throughout the comedy of contrast, comparison, and parallelism to help define the portrait of the Princess.

When she does understand Navarre's meaning, she brings those two faculties—a keen mind and a desire for honest words—to her speech:

> We have receiv'd your letters full of love;
>
> .   .   .   .
>
> . . . rated them
> At courtship, pleasant jest, and courtesy,
>
> .   .   .   .
>
> But more devout than this in our respects
> Have we not been. (V.2.777–783)

Thus does she evaluate the antics they have enjoyed. She then moves to the more complex question of oaths. Unlike Berowne who, though intellectually aware of the folly of Navarre's plot, had allowed peer pressure to override reason, the Princess remains true to her intellectual self. To the King's "Now at the latest minute of the hour, / Grant us your loves" (V.2.787–788), she responds:

> A time methinks too short
> To make a world-without-end bargain in. (V.2.788–789)

And she suggests that he not perjure himself again. Evaluating the type of oath now being asked of her, she knows that it requires more than a moment's consideration.

If Shakespeare was unsuccessful in retaining the comedic tone, as some critics have argued, he was remarkably successful in creating, although in sketch form, the portrait of an independent woman. Writing at a time when new perceptions of women were challenging the old, the dramatist molded a character who was individual, one who drew her strength from understanding herself—a woman functioning in a man's world and questioning that world's values.[24]

In a play where vows are made and broken, Shakespeare questions this approach to swearing by introducing the vow of marriage at a serious moment in the action. Marriage is a vow whose implication women know. It will inhibit their independence; it will tie them forever. "A world-without-end bargain" implies a sense of eternity, that which the King, in the first scene, had craved through learning. The phrase has a grandeur beyond the confines of the comic world. If such bargains are not to be broken, by brilliant talk, ingenious reasoning, and clever turns of phrase, new rules for oath-taking must be found.

Truth, vows, and eternity coalesce in the comedy's last moments. Ending as it does with "Jack hath not Jill," but with the promise of reconsiderations of the men's proposals a year later, the play asks for new attitudes toward women. It suggests seeing them as full, complex individual characters. Although a romantic comedy, the play is an exploration of the meaning of words as a key to perceiving truth, particularly those words— swear and oath—which often govern our future lives.

NOTES

1. The text used throughout is *The Riverside Shakespeare*, G. Blakemore Evans, textual ed. (Boston: Houghton Mifflin, 1974). For the sake of clarity, the square brackets appearing in the Riverside text have been eliminated. When used in this essay, square brackets indicate interpolation by the author.

2. John Stuart Mill, "The Subjection of Women," in *Essays on Sex Equality* (University of Chicago Press, 1970), p. 189.

3. A notable exception is the excellent book by William C. Carroll, *The Great Feast of Language in "Love's Labour's Lost"* (Princeton University Press, 1976).

4. Samuel Taylor Coleridge, *Shakespearean Criticism*, Vol. 1 (Harvard University Press, 1930), p. 92.

5. Edmund K. Chambers, *William Shakespeare* (Oxford: The Clarendon Press, 1930) Vol. 1, pp. 331, 338; Vol. 2, pp. 330–32.

6. Ibid., Vol. 1, pp. 332, 338.

7. See chapter 6 of *Wooing, Wedding, and Power* by Irene G. Dash.

8. Folger Prompt *LLL* 1. See also George Winchester Stone, Jr., "Garrick and an Unknown Operatic Version of *Love's Labour's Lost*," *Review of English Studies* 15 (1939), 323–328.

9. Folger Prompt *LLL* 2.

10. Samuel Johnson, *Johnson on Shakespeare*, Vol. 7 (Yale University Press, 1968), p. 287.

11. Virginia Woolf, *A Room of One's Own* (Harcourt, Brace & World, 1929), p. 38.

12. Warburton's edition of 1747 retains Pope's cuts. See Irene Dash, "Changing Attitudes towards Shakespeare as Reflected in Editions and Staged Adaptations of *The Winter's Tale* from 1703 to 1762" in chapter 6 of *Wooing, Wedding, and Power*.

13. Una Stannard, "The Mask of Beauty," in Vivian Gornick and Barbara K. Moran, eds., *Women in Sexist Society* (New American Library, 1972), p. 193.

14. Alexander Pope reduces IV.1.11–40 and 42–52 to small type at the bottom of the page thus eliminating most of this exchange. *The Works of Mr. William Shakespear*, Vol. 2 (J. Tonson, 1723–25), pp. 122–123.

15. Folger Prompt *LLL* 2, 8, 3, and 6. [According to Charles H. Shattuck, *The*

Shakespeare Promptbooks (University of Illinois Press, 1965), p. 233, no. 6 is a Daly 1874 book.] See also George C.D. Odell, *Shakespeare from Betterton to Irving*, Vol. 2 (Dover, 1966), pp. 187, 202–203, 222, 278. William Winter, in *Shakespeare on the Stage* (Moffatt & Yard, 1916) observes, "The comedy was produced in London for the first time in more than 240 years on September 30, 1839, at Covent Garden when Eliza Vestris (Mrs. Charles Mathews) began management of that theatre," with Vestris playing Rosaline and "the beautiful Louisa Nisbett as the Princess," p. 184. But note also that some shift of emphasis must have occurred when Ada Rehan became leading actress of Daly's company because she had the role of the Princess and Edith Crane, who was less famous, played Rosaline, p. 194.

According to Marvin Spevak, *Concordance to the Works of Shakespeare* (Georg Olms, 1968–70), Berowne has 15.23 percent of the speeches, 22.09 percent of the lines; Navarre has 11.14 percent of the speeches, 11.20 percent of the lines; the Princess of France has 9.90 percent of the speeches, 10.25 percent of the lines; Rosaline has 6.28 percent of the speeches, 5.97 percent of the lines.

16. Richard David, ed., *Love's Labour's Lost* (Arden Shakespeare Paperbacks, 1968), p. 62.

17. Horace Howard Furness, ed., *A New Variorum Edition of Shakespeare*, Vol. 14 (J.B. Lippincott, 1871–1955), p. 117.

18. Pope, *Works of Shakespear*, Vol. I (J. & P. Knapton et al., 1747), pp. ii–iii.

19. Edward Dowden, *Shakespeare: His Mind and Art* (London, 1875), p. 62. Reprinted in Furness, *Variorum Shakespeare*, Vol. 14, p. 362.

20. Furness, *Variorum Shakespeare*, Vol. 14, p. xix.

21. David, *Love's Labour's Lost*, p. 110.

22. "Vildly" means "vilely" and "simplicity" is often interpreted as "foolishness."

23. Johnson, *Johnson on Shakespeare*, Vol. 7, p. 285.

24. Lawrence Stone, *The Crisis of the Aristocracy 1558–1641* (Oxford University Press, 1965), pp. 610–70 and passim.

THE COPY FOR THE FOLIO TEXT
OF *LOVE'S LABOUR'S LOST*

Stanley Wells

The most thorough all-round investigation of the textual problems of *Love's Labour's Lost* remains that carried out by J. Dover Wilson for his Cambridge edition first published in 1923. Since then, some of his basic assumptions about the nature and transmission of dramatic texts have been discredited; and other scholars have made more detailed studies of limited aspects of the play's early printings. As a result, Dover Wilson's theories are not fully accepted, and he himself disowned some of them in his second edition of 1962. Nevertheless, his statements of problems and analyses of evidence are often still valuable even if we cannot endorse his deductions from the evidence; and it will be the argument of this article that in one important respect he came closer to the truth than, in later life, he and others believed.

There is no disagreement that the papers from which the first Quarto of 1598 was printed were in an unpolished state, and Wilson's demonstration (though not his explanation) of this remains valid. The evidence lies principally in imperfectly cancelled passages and in confused and inconsistent speech-headings. It is not necessary to my present purpose to restate the problems in any detail, but it may be helpful to recall that the worst of them are concentrated in Act II, Scene 1, and that in this scene, as printed in the Quarto, there is considerable confusion about which of the ladies is being wooed by Berowne and which by Dumain. Berowne has two flirtatious interchanges, the first with Katharine, the second with Rosaline. When Dumain enquires about the lady who has taken his fancy, he is told she is Rosaline; when Berowne makes his enquiry, he is told she is Katharine. Yet the remainder of the play makes it clear that Berowne woos Rosaline, and Dumain Katharine.

Originally published in *The Review of English Studies*, New Series 33, no. 130 (May 1982), 137–147. Reprinted by permission of Oxford University Press.

Wilson's explanation, indebted to both Capell and H.B. Charlton, requires so much effort to understand that a reader who masters it is predisposed to reward himself with belief. It rests on the hypothesis that Shakespeare originally intended the ladies to be masked; thus "Katharine" means "Katharine disguised as Rosaline;" and when Berowne and Dumain ask for names, each points to the wrong lady. But, still according to Wilson, Shakespeare decided to use masking again in Act V, Scene 2, so cancelled it here, inefficiently marking Berowne's interchanges for deletion and altering the names wrongly and inadequately. Wilson's explanation is challenged—rightly, I believe—by John Kerrigan in an article printed in this issue of the *Review of English Studies*.[1] I agree with him that the confusion is much more likely to originate in Shakespeare's failure to decide on names for the ladies.

It is also universally agreed that a copy of the 1598 Quarto was used by the compositors who set up the next edition of the play, in the Folio of 1623. They followed the Quarto in many errors; but they departed from it, too, at many points. Wilson classifies the variants thus:

1. two deliberate additions, namely of the word "Song" to the stage-direction at the head of III.1., and of the words 'You that way; we this way', which are placed in the mouth of Armado at the very end of the play;

2. a quantity of changes in the speech-headings, most of which are clearly deliberate and not misprints;

3. some 250 dialogue variants, many of them incorrect or trivial in character, many obvious press-corrections, but also some definite and intelligent improvements.[2]

Wilson was of the opinion that changes in the first two of these categories were "clearly beyond the scope of a compositor, and must be due to alteration by some agent outside the printing house." As they were "apparently far too casual for a literary editor they can be readily explained as the haphazard jottings of someone reading through the text in preparation for theatrical performance, for example in order to make out fresh players' parts and a 'plot'." The "Song" was "patently a sign-post insertion by prompter or stage-manager;" the play's last words are "virtually a fresh stage-direction."

In an attempt to decide whether the changes were made "at Shakespeare's instigation or with his approval," Wilson considered the changes in speech prefixes, remarking that they are "almost wholly confined to II.1, the scene which contains the Rosaline-Katharine tangle that has puzzled all editors and would naturally puzzle one engaged in making out players' parts."[3] So he conjectures "how the prompter, as we may call him, set to work in an attempt to render actable a scene which could not be acted if he followed the Quarto text before him." His conclusion is that the Folio presents a "clumsy, though actable version," that Shakespeare "was not consulted," and "that the changes were made for some performance when he was not present to explain his own text." On the basis of this, he decides that it is "in the highest degree unlikely" that Shakespeare "had anything to do with the 254 dialogue variants." Some of them are compositorial in origin; others "must be assigned to the playhouse scribe," but his pen was "as ever casual and haphazard in its operation." This last observation Wilson illustrates by remarking that, though the Quarto "contains twenty-one instances of the word 'God'," in the Folio it "is only once altered to 'Ioue' in deference to the statute against profanity."

Brilliant though Wilson's analysis in many ways is, it suffers from a failure to consider precisely the likely relationship between the Quarto and theatrical manuscripts. His discussion is vitiated by a deficiency which continues to exercise undue influence over editorial theory and procedure. This is the failure to make adequate allowance for the further stage or stages in both compositon and transmission which must have been necessary to produce from foul papers a satisfactory text for performance, and a prompt-book to regulate performance. The term "foul papers" itself implies recognition that another manuscript, in a more finished state, must have existed. The possibilities are these: the author himself made a fair copy, tidying the play up as he went along, and this was used as a prompt-book; the author made a fair copy which was transcribed by someone else and used as a prompt-book; and (least likely) someone else made sense, somehow, of the foul papers, transcribing and editing them, perhaps with the author's assistance, to form a prompt-book. It is evident that by whichever method the prompt-book was arrived at, it would have differed in various ways from the foul papers—or from a printed text derived from them. It is evident too that the differences could have included indifferent as well as substantive variants: that, to give an example germane to my argument, there could easily have existed a manuscript, written after the foul papers, in which speech prefixes, whether standardized or not, existed in a form differing from that used in the foul papers, while still referring to the same character: that, for example, Armado, who is also called Braggart in the Quarto prefixes, and so, presumably, in the foul papers, might in a later manuscript have been intituled, nominated, or called Braggart at points where in the earlier version he had been called Armado.

There is no dispute that manuscripts later than foul papers must have existed. The fallacy lies in supposing that the printed version of foul papers, which is so important to us, had any importance as a working tool for a dramatic company. Wilson considers that alterations to speech prefixes in Q1 "were clearly made in the playhouse, and made, we think, by someone whose interest was rather in the players' parts than in the prompt-book." But there is no conceivable reason why someone in Shakespeare's playhouse should have used a Quarto representing an unfinished state of the play when he could have had access to a later version of the text, in which the foul papers were brought to a state in which they could have been used for performance. (This procedure might, admittedly, have been resorted to by someone in a playhouse other than Shakespeare's trying to make sense of an imperfect printed text; but if so, his annotations must be presumed to have had no authority except, possibly, memories of the play in performance.[4]) Nor would we expect such a text to have been provided for the Folio by Heminges and Condell. It is not, however, primarily on these grounds that Wilson's theory has been criticized. W.W. Greg rejected the hypothesis of a playhouse annotator, while agreeing that the Quarto text had "received some editorial attention" before being used as copy for the Folio.[5] He thought there was nothing in the changes "that would be beyond the scope of an intelligent press reader," though he permitted himself the quip that "there is elsewhere little to justify the assumption of the presence of such a person in Jaggard's office." He notes "a rather unsuccessful attempt to reduce speakers' names to order," remarks somewhat casually that "there may have been some emendation," and considers that "A single substitution of 'Ioue' for 'God' (V.2.316) is slender evidence for any connection with the stage." The additions at the end of the play are "the editor's desperate attempt to fit the final words of Q into the structure of the play." Greg's conclusion is categorical: "F was printed from Q without reference to any playhouse authority."

This scepticism, reducing the situation to one of comforting simplicity, sounds authoritative; it proceeds, of course, from a sounder grasp of basic principles than Wilson had displayed in 1923. But what evidence is there for Greg's dogmatic conclusion? He gives no sign of having conducted a detailed re-examination of the evidence, but simply picks on a few variants which Wilson had argued emanated from outside the printing-house and asserts that this is an unnecessary hypothesis. However, his position is not as far removed from Wilson's as might appear. Both assume an annotator; Wilson postulates one working specifically for theatrical performance, Greg, one working purely in the printing-house. Neither Wilson nor Greg attributes any authority to the annotator's alterations. Some other scholars have concurred. For example, Alfred Harbage, in the Pelican edition, says that the Folio is "probably without independent authority," and the play's most recent editor, G. Blakemore Evans (in the Riverside edition, 1974), appears to follow Greg in writing that F "is essentially a reprint of Q1, such corrections as it affords, even in speech-prefixes, being within the scope of any intelligent printing-house editor."

Nevertheless, suspicion has been voiced from time to time that a playhouse manuscript may have been consulted. Indeed, as early as 1939 Peter Alexander stated this as fact: "The Folio reprints the Quarto: this is natural, since Heminge and Condell must have known the authority of Burby's edition. They had it checked, however, as certain changes in stage-directions and speech-headings show, with a stage version in their possession."[6] But Alexander did not argue his case, and has gone largely unheeded. Greg himself admitted that his own contrary conclusion is "rather surprising. We can only suppose that the editors, knowing that the 'bad' quartos had been replaced by others printed from Shakespeare's own manuscripts, were content to leave it at that without looking farther into the texts." R.W. David, in his Arden edition of 1951, remarked that none of the Folio improvements was "beyond the scope of an experienced printer. . . . Of the two major alterations, the Folio's 'That were to climb o'er the house to unlock the gate' (I.1.109) is ill-fitting and flat beside the Quarto's 'Climb o'er the house to unlock the little gate'; and the extra line 'You that way; we this way' . . . has presumably been the extra line added to make possible an orderly *Exeunt*. It has charm—it may be Shakespeare's; but, like the other improvements, it is well within the capacity of an intelligent prompter or stage-manager." This suggests a suspicion that the addition was made by someone connected with the theatre rather than with the printing-house, but not that a manuscript was consulted. It veers, that is, towards Wilson rather than Greg.

C.J. Sisson, in his edition of 1954, seems to be following Greg in his references to merely "minor editorial changes"; yet in his *New Readings*,[7] he argues strongly, though on purely critical grounds, for the appropriateness and authenticity of the Folio text's concluding words: "There is no more skilful or pleasing conclusion to a comedy in all Shakespeare." This is at the opposite pole from Greg's opinion on this point, and might be construed as a tacit rebuttal of it. J.K. Walton takes the implications of this to their logical conclusion by pointing out that it implies "reference to a manuscript—presumably a prompt-book"; his own conclusion is that "some very casual reference was made to the prompt-book in preparing the quarto copy for F."[8]

It would seem, at least on the evidence of their published work, that none of the scholars who have expressed themselves on the subject since

Dover Wilson has examined the evidence except on the assumption that the best way to discover whether a manuscript was consulted is to assess the quality of the Folio's divergences from the Quarto. The aim has been to discover whether any of the Folio's readings could be judged so superior to the Quarto's as to be beyond the capacity of an annotator without access to a manuscript. Attention has focused on a limited number of variants, above all the play's last few words in the Folio text. Judgment of them has proved highly subjective. Those who see no great merit in them are content, like Greg, to assume that they, and all other variants, have no independent authority. The others attribute authority to them, and so are forced to the assumption that before being reprinted the Quarto had been partially revised by someone with access to an authoritative manuscript, or who, at the very least, knew the play in the theatre.

It is obvious that the presence in a reprinted text of variants—or more convincingly additional passages—of indisputable authority means that a manuscript must have been consulted. An example is provided by the Folio text of *Titus Andronicus*, printed from Quarto but adding an entire scene, previously unprinted but generally agreed to be by Shakespeare. The Folio text of *Love's Labour's Lost* affords nothing so decisive. The only addition to the dialogue worth remarking—'You that way, we this way'—is both so short and so conspicuous that it might, for once, have derived from memory rather than a manuscript. The variants are mostly interior, indifferent, or of only arguable superiority. But it is possible that correction from a manuscript would produce variants which are identifiable as having derived from a manuscript while not being conspicuously superior.

And so it is, I believe, with *Love's Labour's Lost*. The evidence lies primarily in the fact that many of the alterations to the Quarto seem not necessarily improvements but totally inexplicable except on the hypothesis that someone has had access to a document which he believed to be of superior authority to the Quarto, and which he followed, at times, without concerning himself about the reason for its variants. For example, Armado is named by an abbreviation of *"Braggart"* in all except the first of his many speeches in Act I, Scene 2, although Q does not use this term for him, in dialogue, stage directions, or speech prefixes, until the opening direction of Act III, Scene 1. Why should the compositor or annotator have made this alteration?[9] Wilson supposes that an annotator, working through the play and coming to Act III, Scene 1, then turned back and, on his own initiative, altered the prefixes in the earlier scene. I find it far easier to suppose that the annotator was using an independent manuscript in which the prefixes differed, and that he altered them on the assumption that Braggart and

Armado were not the same person. It would have been perfectly easy for Shakespeare, making a fair copy from his foul papers, to use the generic rather than the personal name. There are other instances of indifferently variant speech prefixes. At I.1.302 and 306, Quarto's "*Fer.*" becomes "*Kin.*" The same happens (with minor variants) at II.1.129, 158, 163, and 167, and at II.1.179 "*Na.*" becomes "*Kin.*" These alterations might be independently derived, but they carry less weight, as the evidence that Ferdinand is the King of Navarre was readily available from the Quarto itself. It is less easy to see why a printing-house editor should have altered Quarto's "*Ros.*" (II.1.182, 184, 186, 188, 190, and 192) to "*La. Ro.*"

A more interesting category of variants is that of substantively changed prefixes. In Act I, Scene 1, the interrogation of Costard is carried out by the King, except that one line—296—is ascribed to "*Ber[owne].*" In F1, this is given to "*Fer.*" Of course, this might easily be a misprint. Yet it could be a deliberate correction. Interestingly enough, both the (Old) Cambridge and the New Variorum editions follow F1 without recording Q1's variant; Dover Wilson, Kittredge (1936), Richard David, Peter Alexander (1951), C. J. Sisson, and Alfred Harbage (Pelican, 1963) do the same—that is, they appear to be accepting the Folio reading without realizing that it is an emendation. Blakemore Evans and John Arthos (Signet, 1965) accept F1, recording the Quarto variant. So if F1's reading is a misprint, it is a lucky one, being accepted by all modern editors. But if it is a deliberate alteration, it is likely to have been made on authority, since it is not self-evidently necessary. At II.1.79, "*Ma.*" replaces "*Lord.*" I can see no reason why this change should have been made without authority. On the other hand, it is easily imagined as part of a simple process of reducing the number of supernumeraries. The opening direction calls for "*three Lordes,*" but the only one of any importance is Boyet. The Princess addresses them collectively at II.1.37, and one replies, briefly: "*Longauill* is one." Their only other function is at line 79, where one says "Heere comes *Boyet.*" Yet the scene continues for close on another 200 lines, during which two spare lords might have been regarded as an embarrassing extravagance. It is easy to suppose that the scribe who was annotating the Quarto found the line reallocated in his manuscript, and that it was part of a process of writing the lords out of a scene in which they were felt to be redundant.[10]

This supposition is supported by the fact that even in the text as printed, the lords rapidly dwindle away; as Wilson notes (II.1.39), "These 'Lords' of the Princess are very shadowy persons. 'Lor.' has two speeches, of three words each, in II.1.; 'her Lordes' are given a second entry in IV.1. (Head); in V.2. they are completely forgotten." A similar instance of substantive variation unlikely to have been made without authority is at IV.1.3, where Q's "*Forr[ester].*" becomes "*Boy[et].*" The attribution to Forester is not self-evidently wrong; yet reallocation to Boyet is perfectly possible, especially as the Forester has not yet been identified in the dialogue. Indeed, Wilson adopts this, failing to record the variant (I suspect he was using as a working text the Old Cambridge edition, which here follows F), as do Kittredge, Alexander, Sisson, and Harbage.

The most interesting substantive alterations of prefixes relate to the textual tangle in Act II, Scene 1. At line 53, "*Lad.*" becomes "*Lad. 1.*" This might easily be compositorial. But at line 64, "3 *Lad.*" becomes "*Rossa.*" (as Wilson failed to notice); this is correct, but far from obvious from the printed text. At lines 115–127, "*Rosa[line].*" replaces "*Kath[arine].*" This again is, by general agreement, correct. Wilson assumes that the alteration was made because the corrector knew what only later becomes apparent, "that Rosaline was the name of Berowne's lady" (p. 131). It might just as well derive from a manuscript. The most puzzling change in the entire play comes in the second interchange between Berowne and Rosaline, lines 181–193 ("Ladie I will commend you to my none hart. . ."). Here, all the man's speeches except the last are ascribed to "*Boy.*"[11] There seems no possibility that the speeches should have been reallocated to Boyet or that this could be the result of a compositor's misreading of printed copy. It is conceivable as a manuscript misreading; that is, a playhouse scribe might have misread "*Ber.*" as an abbreviation of Boyet (who speaks shortly before and after this exchange), and the annotator of the Quarto could have unthinkingly, if incompletely, "corrected" his copy. At line 218, "*La. Ma.*" for "*Lady Ka.*" may be accidental, but at the end of the scene comes a clearly deliberate, if half-hearted, attempt to improve on Q1; there, the ladies' speeches are headed respectively "*Lad.*," "*Lad. 2,*" "*Lad. 3,*" "*Lad.*," and "*Lad.*"; F1 reads "*La. Ro.*," "*Lad. Ma.*," "*Lad. 2,*" "*La. 1,*" "*Lad. 2.*" The identity of the speakers is not self-evident. The Folio identification of "*Lad. 2*" with Maria does not correspond with Q's "2 *Lad.*" (line 56), who must be Katharine. The Folio's readjustments seem beyond the call of duty for a compositor; I find it easier to imagine them as the annotator's corrections based on an alternative authorial copy (fairer than that used for Q, though still not "fairest of fair") than as editorial tinkering.

One other prefix variant may be relevant. At II.1.21, in the middle of a speech by the Princess, F1 adds the prefix "*Prin.*" Wilson's explanation is lame: his annotator, noticing "the irregular *Queene*" as the prefix at the beginning of the speech, "scrawled the more correct *Prin.*, but so carelessly that the F compositor took it for a second speaker and attached it to line 21, near which it probably stood in the margin." But the scene's first twenty lines are made up of recapitulation and compliments.[12] The line (21) before which the otherwise redundant prefix is added—"You are not ignorant all telling fame . . ."—would make a strong opening to the scene; and I suggest that the annotator derived his prefix from a manuscript in which the opening lines had been marked for omission. The Folio actually omits III.1.85–93—the first run-through of "The Fox, the Ape, and the Humble-Bee"; this may be accidental, as the following lines make little sense without the omitted ones.

My conclusion is that the Quarto from which the Folio was printed had been compared with a manuscript, and that this manuscript was one which presented the play in a form closer to that in which it was performed than the foul papers from which the Quarto was printed. Nevertheless, the fact remains that a great many important and self-evident errors remain uncorrected in F. The annotator was indeed, in Wilson's words, "casual and haphazard." If it should seem surprising that someone who took the trouble to do the job at all, nevertheless did it so efficiently, we can only respond that this is part of a regular pattern in the preparation of Quarto copy for the Folio.[13] Moreover, there appears to be a discernible pattern to the Folio alterations. The first changes in the Folio which might derive from manuscript authority are on Folio page L2^v; there are no discernible Q1 errors in speech prefixes before then. Changes continue to occur until IV.1.3 (*Boy.* for *Forr.*), at the foot of L5. Anything approaching systematic collation with the manuscript seems then to have ceased. On L5^v the Folio adds a necessary *Exeunt* (IV.1.108), a change which might have been made by an attentive compositor without reference to a manuscript. The alteration of "God" to "Jove" on M4 (V.2.316) also could be compositorial. More interesting is "manager'" for "nuage" on M5 (V.2.482), which, however, could easily reflect consultation of the manuscript by a compositor or proof-reader faced with apparent nonsense. The annotator seems to have resumed his task only on the last page of the play, printed on the second column of M6^v. Between L5^v and M6^v we find a series of serious errors in speech prefixes which the Folio reproduces without alteration (including the notorious Holofernes-Nathaniel confusion, beginning on L6). This pattern has no relationship to the stints of the Folio compositors or the order of printing; all three compositors set pages with variants and pages without variants. In short, it appears that the annotator began by checking speech prefixes and stage directions in Q1 against a manuscript, with reasonable thoroughness; then, about half-way through the play, stopped, stepping ahead to the last page. If someone wished to give the appearance of having corrected the whole text, it would be a wise precaution to check for any variants on the last page. The annotator's laziness may be reprehensible, but recognition of this pattern of variants at least makes his conduct comprehensible. It is also possible that some or all of the alterations are post-Shakespearean: the title-page of the second Quarto, of 1631, refers to performances at the Blackfriars, which Shakespeare's company did not acquire till 1608.

The consequence for an editor is that all the Folio variants have to be considered potentially authoritative. But the haphazard nature of the annotator's methods means that some alterations cannot be adopted because they may seem to form part of a sequence of revisions only imperfectly recorded. For instance, the alteration of "*Lord*" to "*Ma.*" at II.1.79 carries little conviction unless the redundant lords are also written out at ll. 37–39. The fact that there is some reason to suppose that this happened in performances by Shakespeare's company will be of interest to a director but cannot properly influence the editor. On the other hand, the reattribution of the Forester's line to Boyet at IV.1.3 is of purely local significance. Many editors have adopted it. There is some reason to believe that they have done so without realizing that it was an emendation of their control-text, but an editor with this information might still regard it as a superior and acceptable reading, whether he took "*Forr.*" as a misreading of "*Boy.*," or the ascription to Boyet as an improvement upon Shakespeare's original intention.

When Folio's revisions make sense of passages which seem nonsensical in Q, they naturally deserve particularly serious consideration. The most conspicuous example is at the play's ending. The Quarto reads, without speech prefix, "The wordes of Mercurie, are harsh after the songs of Apollo." Folio adds the speech prefix "*Brag.*" (i.e. Armado), the closing words "You that way; we this way," and the direction "*Exeunt omnes.*" The editor may feel that some mystery remains—why is Q as it is?—but is likely, like most of his predecessors, to accept the Folio version as, at least, a workable ending, whether or not he shares Sisson's conviction that it is the most skilful and pleasing conclusion to any of Shakespeare's comedies.

NOTES

1. Pp. 129–136.
2. Wilson omits to mention other clearly deliberate additons, e.g. of "*Exit*" at I.2.136, "*Exeunt*" at IV.1.108, and "*Exeunt omnes*" at the end. There is also a substantial omission, III.1.85–93. There is no particular reason to suppose that these changes were made on external authority, though the first is interesting. It follows the words "Fare you well," spoken by Dull. Editors usually reject it, and certainly it could easily be an independent, mistaken deduction from the dialogue. Yet it could be right if we interpret the words "Come, Jaquenetta, away," spoken by Costard in Q and F but attributed by Theobald and later editors to Dull, as Costard's instruction to

Jaquenetta to leave, not a request for her company. Note: References to *Love's Labour's Lost* are to the facsimile of Q1, Shakespeare Quarto Facsimiles No. 10 (Oxford, 1957). Quotations from Dover Wilson are from his New Shakespeare edition (1923).

3. This is something of an exaggeration. Wilson failed to notice at least three substantive variants outside Act II, Scene 1.

4. Evidence for use of Quartos as prompt-copies is given by C. J. Sisson, "Shakespeare Quartos as Prompt-copies," *Review of English Studies* 18 (1942), 129–143. He admits that "There is no certain usage" of printed plays as prompt-copies "by any company of its own plays in quarto form" (p. 143).

5. Greg's views are quoted from *The Shakespeare First Folio* (Oxford, 1954), p. 223; they are essentially the same as those expressed in his *The Editorial Problem in Shakespeare* (Oxford, 1942).

6. *Shakespeare's Life and Art* (1939, rept. 1944), p. 87.

7. *New Readings in Shakespeare*, Vol. 1 (Cambridge, 1956), p. 124.

8. *The Quarto Copy for the First Folio of Shakespeare* (Dublin, 1971), p. 234.

9. It is worth remarking Fredson Bowers's conclusion that, on the evidence of *All's Well That Ends Well*, "however much compositors may have styled text to suit their own spelling and punctuation habits, the movement toward normalizing the dramatic appurtenances such as stage-directions and speech-prefixes was slight" ("Foul Papers, Compositor B, and the Speech-Prefixes of *All's Well That Ends Well*," *Studies in Bibliography* 32 [1979], 81). Furthermore, although Act I, Scene 2 was set after Act III, Scene 1, it was by a different compositor (Charleton Hinman, *The Printing and Proof-Reading of the First Folio of Shakespeare*, Vol. 2 [Oxford, 1963], p. 405).

10. An alternative explanation is that Q1's *Lord* is a mistaken expansion of an abbreviation for *Lady*, meaning Maria, and that this mistake had been corrected in the manuscript from which the Quarto was annotated.

11. John Kerrigan supposes that this results from the annotator's remembering "no more parleying for Berowne but much teasing for Boyet" (*The Review of English Studies* n. s. 33, May 1982, 135). This relates to his theory that the lines were not spoken at this point in the play.

12. Interestingly enough, one sentence—"Beautie is bought by iudgement of the eye, / Not vttred by base sale of chapmens tongues"—is twice echoed later: "Where faire is not, praise cannot mend the brow" (IV.1.17), and "To thinges of sale, a sellers prayse belonges," (IV.3.240).

13. Of the eight plays "where the F text was printed from quarto copy but where variants between quarto and Folio are few," J.K. Walton writes: "Despite the fact that prompt-books must have been available, generally speaking only casual reference was made to them in preparing the quarto copy" (op. cit., pp. 230, 245).

THE STRUCTURE OF
LOVE'S LABOUR'S LOST

Koshi Nakanori

Some of Shakespeare's works have long been neglected and only recently come to critical attention. *Love's Labour's Lost* is a typical example, illustrating most vividly the fluctuations in Shakespearean criticism.

Aside from Richard Burbage's opinion, contemporary to the play and praising its "wytt" and "mirthe," the general tone of its critical history since the Restoration has been negative, although parts of the play were occasionally commended. Until the twentieth century, most critics considered the play a failure or an immature piece. William Hazlitt went so far as to declare: "If we were to part with any of the author's comedies, it should be this."[1]

Even in the age of adaptations, *Love's Labour's Lost* earned only one such compliment, the anonymous *The Students*, published in 1762, but never performed. It was not until the 1830s that the original version of the play returned to the stage along with other plays of Shakespeare.

The main reason for this disregard is the play's structural defect; that is, its lack of substantial plot. Four young men swear to reject women's company and to devote themselves to scholarly life but easily give up their resolution upon meeting four young ladies. They approach the ladies in disguise and try to woo them, but end up being ridiculed. Such a flimsy main plot is accompanied by a subplot no less trifling. Critics also charge that the pedantic language is unnatural and too extravagant, not suitable for the action or the characters. As for characterization, the play is not totally devoid of impressive characters, yet they are a far cry from Hamlet or Falstaff. Thus, *Love's Labour's Lost* came to be regarded as the playwright's earliest experimental work and different from the later comedies.[2] It is argued from the way the characters enter and exit that the play

From Koshi Nakanori, *Shakespearean Comedy: Its Structures and Techniques* (Tokyo: Kinokuniya, 1982). Translated from the Japanese especially for this collection by Toru Iwasaki.

should be seen as a sort of masque.³ Indeed, it was staged as a musical comedy in 1919.

A diametrically opposed view has gained momentum in the latter half of this century. In this new view, the play is a mainstream Shakespearean comedy, or at least its prototype, certainly not of the alleged minor status. In place of the time-honored concept of romantic comedies, C.L. Barber introduced the "festive" viewpoint and tried to apply it to all Shakespearean comedies. In this perspective, *Love's Labour's Lost* is a typical festive comedy.⁴ P.G. Phialas argues that the critics have mistaken a difference in degree for one in kind. Relative weight placed on each component may vary, but the entire makeup of the play is clearly the same as that of the other Shakespearean comedies.⁵

These two recent approaches are different in that the former deals with the play's deep structure, while the latter engages in a thematic or moralistic analysis. Both of them, however, emphasize common features that the play shares with the other comedies. On the other hand, the play's language has been attracting increasing attention recently, and many papers try to reevaluate the play from this angle. What was once a cause for critical disregard has turned into an object of admiration. Although as a romantic comedy reminiscent of medieval romance, *Love's Labour's Lost* is no match for *Twelfth Night* and *As You Like It*, I contend that structually the play has unmistakable features of Shakespearean comedies. Even the play's language is not essentially different, though it is entangled with the action in an exceptionally complicated manner due to the disproportionately large emphasis placed on it. I would like to elaborate on my thesis by noting at the outset the check and balance between the two conflicting forces—especially the one working on a structural level—that can be observed throughout Shakespearean comedies.

Such forces operate as the plot unfolds. What is common among many Shakespearean plays and especially marked in his early comedies is a pattern in which the plot movement virtually comes to a halt in much of a scene and shifts to a gallop in the few remaining lines. In *Love's Labour's Lost* this pattern appears in Act I, Scene 2, wherein Armado and Moth converse. The only thing that is revealed in the first 120 lines of their conversation is that despite his pledge with the King and the lords to three years of scholarly life, Armado has fallen in love with Costard's sweetheart Jaquenetta. It is not until the last part of the scene that she is described in detail. Before that, the audience has no choice but to enjoy the scene as it is: light-hearted wordplay (mainly puns) and a song. And as Costard enters the scene, the plot unfolds quickly. A similar pattern is observable in the latter half of Act

I, Scene 1, of *Two Gentlemen of Verona*, when Proteus talks with Speed, and also in the final act of *The Merchant of Venice*, when Lorenzo and Jessica talk in the moonlight.

Rather than see such stagnation and activation of the plot movement as a rhythm inherent in the plot itself, we should take it as the coexistence of narrative thrust and an entertainment factor. In other words, Shakespearean comedies harbor two conflicting forces: a centripetal (converging) force driving the story forward and a centrifugal (diverging) force indulging the audience in whatever merriment a particular moment offers. This coexistence is not limited to the level of the scene. The centrifugal factor is found on a smaller scale, for instance, as song and dance and wordplay, or on a larger scale as the carefree life in the timeless "Forest of Arden," which takes up much of the play. In *Love's Labour's Lost* the conflicting forces are relatively apparent. So, the charge that the play lacks plot must be reconsidered from this viewpoint.

Three dramatic traditions predominated when Shakespeare began his career as a playwright: medieval moralities, classical tragedy and comedy, and the romance. Moralities and interludes were still performed. The London stage was very much alive with various types of plays including dramatizations of myths and romances by John Lyly and Robert Greene, tragedies written in blank verse by Christopher Marlowe and Thomas Kyd, and Anglicized classical comedies like *Ralph Roister Doister*. Among them it was probably the dramatized romances that Shakespeare most consciously drew upon, partly because that was the most popular type of comedy at the time, and partly because throughout his career—from early comedies like *The Two Gentlemen of Verona* through middle comedies to late plays like *Pericles* and *The Winter's Tale*—we can vividly see the influence of romances. Even *The Comedy of Errors*, which is usually considered to have been modeled mainly on a classical comedy, has been seen by one critic as inspired by the framing romance of the breakup and reunion of a family.[6]

A romance generally has a complicated plot ranging widely in time and space, in which strange things happen in succession. A girl pursues in disguise her estranged lover who got away, and survives numerous difficulties to be reunited with him in the end. A family blown apart by a storm comes together after more than a decade. A chaste wife is persecuted by her jealous husband. Such stories were popular in those days.

The influence of the Roman comedies on Shakespeare was significant as source material rather than as an operational dramatic tradition. It is characteristic of Roman comedies, especially those by Terence, that the plot is closely connected with characterization. The plot somehow derives from characterization, and there is little action independent of the plot.

Moralities (though they are not necessarily comedies) naturally have actions with a certain didactic orientation.

A comedy, as long as it drew upon these three traditions, was created on a progressive principle, and scenes irrelevant to the plot development had no place in it. The dramatic traditions that Shakespeare's flexible and comprehensive mind employed, however, were not limited to those three. Other native traditions—miracles and chronicle plays—must also be taken into account. Among the many kinds of influence (including staging methods) that these plays had on Shakespeare, the most important one for our concern is the emphasis on scenes rather than on plot. While the play as a whole relates a history or unfolds a portion of a character's life, the scenes are not necessarily connected in an organic manner, nor was it unusual for a role to be played by several actors. That Shakespeare adopted such a scene-oriented creative principle is apparent when we turn our eyes from his histories to tragedies like *Hamlet*, not to mention his comedies.

Depending upon the distribution of emphasis—either on plot development or on individual scenes—various combinations result. What further complicates the matter is the influence of the courtly and popular festivals and entertainments. If we call them "festive elements," the theatre itself is a festive element in our life. Shakespeare came to integrate festive elements into his theatre, largely due to the circumstances of his age. As C.L. Barber and other critics have pointed out, in addition to obvious festive elements like songs, dances, and plays-within-plays, Shakespeare's comedies often contain an experience in which the characters are temporarily released from reality and return with an insight into society and human nature. And this type of experience is characterized by haphazardry rather than by a clear direction.

These various elements meet in Shakespeare's genius, and the chemistry produces an organism called play. The product as a whole keeps balance while each part of it contains conflicting forces.

Returning to *Love's Labour's Lost*, we find that the story unfolds along two different axes. One is a thematic development: the King of Navarre and his lords wrongfully defy human nature when they forswear interaction with women, and they come to realize their folly through their contact with the outside world. Instead of restoring natural affection, however, they overly idealize or idolize love, and must face another correction. After they go through several stages, the play ends with a hope of happy marriages. Such a thematic thread may well be spun from impressions of the play. It is also justified, considering the way Shakespeare was to write his later comedies.

When the plot unfolds along such a thematic line, each scene or episode is drawn along by a centripetal force.

The other direction concerns theatrical language and entertainment-related expressions abundantly found in the play. They may introduce a scene or episode, or drive the story on to the next scene or episode.

> BEROWNE. All hid, all hid; an old infant play.
> Like a demi-god here sit I in the sky,
> And wretched fools' secrets heedfully o'er-eye. (IV.3.74–76)

> .   .   .   .

> HOLOFERNES. . . . . To our sport, away! (V.1.146)

> .   .   .   .

> PRINCESS. There's no such sport as sport by sport o'erthrown,
> To make theirs ours and ours none but our own:
> So shall we stay, mocking intended game,
> And they well mock'd, depart away with shame. (V.2.153–156)

While these lines call for entertainment, the motive for doing so often seems arbitrary. Sometimes it looks as though entertainment was needed only to further the plot.

The structure of *Love's Labour's Lost* should be analyzed along this line. Berowne asks: "But is there no quick recreation granted?" (I.1.159). The King mentions Armado in reply, and immediately enter Dull and Costard with a letter from Armado. The audience has the impression that the comical exchanges between these clownish characters are the very sport Berowne has just requested. The same pattern can be observed in *A Midsummer Night's Dream*. At the beginning of the play, Theseus orders Philostrate to make necessary arrangements to while away the time merrily until his wedding. As soon as the order is given, Egeus comes with his daughter to seek justice from the Duke. Then begins a panoramic revel lasting till the wedding day.

A Midsummer Night's Dream unfolds before the Duke as a revel performed by the Athenian youths, the mechanicals, and the fairies. And at the same time, unwittingly involving the members of court as participants, it forms itself as a celebratory play. The same structure applies to *Love's Labour's Lost*. The subplot unfolds as an entertainment called forth by the King and his lords, and the main characters join in to amuse the Princess of France and her ladies with their Russian disguise and the pageant of the Nine Worthies. Finally, the concentric structure of the play reaches another sphere involving the Princess and her ladies, and completes itself as a festive comedy. (In this case, it does not matter whether the play was written for a special occasion.) In a play with such a structure, each scene or episode is regarded as a part of the entertainment, introduced haphazardly, neither based on characterization nor thematic necessity. A scene ends just as a game does: the disguise exposed or an outside force interrupting the revel (i.e., a messenger reports the death of the French King in V.2).

Love's Labour's Lost is thus constructed on the two conflicting forces, centripetal and centrifugal. Yet the relation between the two forces must be an ambiguous one, considering that a more mature comedy has a harmonious atmosphere. These two forces, while seemingly directed in opposite courses—and, indeed, working thus on the surface—ultimately have the same function. Many of Shakespeare's comedies share a pattern in centripetally developing the plot or story. Alone and away from the ordinary world, the hero or heroine faces a physical and psychological crisis, and somehow survives to be rewarded with a happy marriage. This pattern could be generalized further into Northrop Frye's formula. After going through a crisis, there is a restoration of identity of the main characters and the society in which they live. It happens to describe then the same type of human experience enacted during a festival or entertainment. There we are released voluntarily or automatically from the rules of and the protection provided by our daily life, and after going through an intensive experience in the relationship newly formed in nature, return home. And by the homecoming the ordinary world is infused with new energy, just as in a Shakespearean comedy the society is revitalized by a marriage.

In Shakespearean comedies, each scene or moment has a tendency to fade spatially into the festive world, just as it unfolds temporally along the plot line, both expressing the same human experience. This is unique to Shakespeare and not observable, for instance, in Molière's satirical comedies. There, individual characters are deposed to restore social order, and plot is closely related to characterization in its centripetal progress. The more emphasis is placed on individual characters, the less room is left for a comedy to accommodate festivity. In Shakespeare's comedies, on the other hand, restoration of social order is definitely secondary to restoration of individual characters. In a few exceptional works like *The Merry Wives of Windsor*, which do not center on the common human experience mentioned earlier, the festive element derails the action. In a typical Shakespearean comedy, however, as long as the overall harmony is not disturbed, the festive element adds to the richness of the play. *Love's Labour's Lost* elucidates this mechanism all the more clearly because it has no definite sources.

Love's Labour's Lost is a festive play also in terms of language. At the outset, the King of Navarre calls for the three young lords to subscribe to the agreed-upon pledge that for a three-year period they renounce women's company and other worldly desires and devote themselves to studies. Unlike the other two who sign immediately, Berowne complains. Is study to be sought at such pains? Can we expect a reward proportionate to the pains? It's unnatural in the first place: I do not desire a rose at Christmas any more than I wish snow in May:

> Light seeking light doth light of light beguile:
> So ere you find where light in darkness lies,
> Your light grows dark by losing of your eyes. (I.1.77–79)

He argues against study in such highly rhetorical language replete with alliterations and rhymes that we want to quip with the King:

> How well he's read, to reason against reading! (I.1.94)

This irony corresponds with another in the middle of Act V, Scene 2, the climax of this play in terms of language. After their elaborate scheme to woo the ladies is exposed and fails completely, Berowne states his resolve on simplicity in a highly rhetorical language. Instead of employing "taffeta phrases, silken terms precise / Three-pil'd hyperboles, spruce affectation, / Figures pedantical" (V.2.406–407), he says,

> Henceforth my wooing mind shall be express'd
> In russet yeas, and honest kersey noes! (V.2.413–414)

After all, *Love's Labour's Lost* cannot break the spell of language. We feel that Shakespeare, while casting a cynical eye at indulgence in language, cannot escape the trap himself. Indulgence in language, of course, is not confined to the author, but can be found in every character. This play has many instances where, in response to someone uttering a sharp aphorism or making a witty reply, another in the company praises it or makes a note of it.[7] Indeed, as Moth says: "They have been at a great feast of languages and stolen the scraps" (V.1.33–34). It is not too much to say that *Love's Labour's Lost* is a feast of language through and through. The other plays of Shakespeare also abound in linguistic appeal and wordplay, but this play is unique in that most speeches throughout the play are given some twist by the speakers consciously or unconsciously, and that the words are inseparable from characterization, and they combine to form the action of the play.

The twists in the speeches and wordplay range widely from puns to witty exchanges, but they agree in being a free departure from the context and a free association of meanings. Ambivalent words shift from one meaning to the other and sometimes mix both meanings. Distorted or nearly lost, their meanings become mere sounds or even mere length (honorificabilitudinitatibus). Words become tennis balls to bounce among the speakers, dice to be cast among the players. In such ways, words continually overcome the stagnation of fixed meanings and are revitalized by new associations. For people who do it consciously, this process involves constant relaxing of rigidities and keeping themselves flexible. Thus it may be said to parallel the festive experience, which, as noted before, proceeds from liberation to rebirth.

In the very first scene of the play, the votaries' pledge is no sooner made than broken. We can attribute the cause of the failure not to the visit of the French Princess and her ladies, but to the pledge itself. The rhetorical expressions in Berowne's speech noted above may serve to emphasize that the pledge is a hollow one from the start. According to Rosalie Colie, the action of *Love's Labour's Lost* lies in the process by which conventional doctrine or expressions are exposed to be artificial and unnatural, and are replaced by seemingly more realistic doctrine or expressions.[8] For instance, the idea that an academic paradise can be created by excluding women was already out of fashion at the time, and it naturally falters in the play all too easily. To cover up their defeat, Berowne brings up another stereotype (this time, Petrarchan), which again harbors a self-destructive element. It is the Princess and her ladies who respond to it from a realistic point of view and materialize it on the stage. The moment the King's group meets that of the Princess, their words become the target of criticism.

> KING. Fair Princess, welcome to the court of Navarre.
> PRINCESS. 'Fair' I give you back again, and welcome I have
> not yet. (II.2.90–92)

Here she takes his mere formalities literally and retorts in a sarcastic manner—a device Shakespeare is to employ repeatedly in his later works. The more the men elaborate their speech, the more suspicious the women become, for the men's expressions of love are perceived on the level of wordplay. This attitude is illustrated in the battle of wit between Rosaline and Katharine over the various meanings of "light" at the beginning of V.2. Love letters fall into the wrong hands and the masked lovers woo the wrong ladies, stage actions ironizing hollow amatory speech. If love letters and amatory talk are mere words after all, it does not matter from whom to whom they are addressed. Of course, the letters of Berowne and Armado function differently in the plot, but in terms of expression, both of them signify their affection and are therefore interchangeable.

Similarly, the subplot casts a cynical light on the unnatural pledge and the exaggerated expressions of affection of the King and Berowne. Immediately after they subscribe to the pledge, Constable Dull brings Costard before them with Armado's letter reporting that he caught Costard secretly meeting Jaquenetta in defiance of the King's proclamation. The King faces the first test of his resolution. He gives Costard a sentence ordering him to "fast a week with bran and water" (I.1.280). Berowne comments in an aside: "These oaths and laws will prove an idle scorn" (I.1.288). Costard complains: "I suffer for the truth, sir; for true it is I was taken with Jaquenetta, and Jaquenetta is a true girl" (I.1.302–304). Although he is placed in the custody of Armado, Costard acts without any restraint in the later development of the plot. Furthermore, his words come to have a sharper satirical effect than he intended, as his custodian falls in love with Jaquenetta and the proclamation is invalidated by the bad faith of the proclaimer. Costard's function is retained in the latter half of the play, as Jaquenetta's pregnancy brings into relief the hollowness of the love of the youths in the main plot. The subplot involving *commedia dell'arte* stock characters burlesques the main plot and engenders a similar atmosphere through the theme of love and language. It is a typical example of the function of double plot in Shakespearean comedies.

Don Armado is a pivotal figure for the double plot. That he and Berowne are deliberately contrasted is clear from the way they both fall in love against the pledge they made, and the way they soliloquize at the end of Acts I and III respectively. It is also clearly shown in their language. Yet while Armado, who "hath a mint of phrases in his brain" (I.1.163), indulges in rhetoric as he is reputed to do, he also shows clumsiness in his response to Moth's wit and he can only behave brusquely with Jaquenetta. This is probably due to his function as Berowne's foil, which he also fulfills with his comically embellished love letter. We should also note that he functions as a funhouse mirror: in laughing at Armado, the courtiers see their own follies reflected in him. The most marked characteristic, shared only by Berowne and Armado among all the characters, is that while they cannot resist their feelings of love, they also know the defects of their lovers.

ARMADO. I do affect the very ground, which is base, where her shoe,
which is baser, guided by her foot, which is basest, doth tread.
BEROWNE. A whitely wanton with a velvet brow,
With two pitch-balls stuck in her face for eyes;
Ay and by heaven, one that will do the deed
Though Argus were her eunuch and her guard.
And I to sigh for her! to watch for her!
To pray for her! (III.1.186–190)

This ambivalent attitude of disillusioned indulgence is the most fundamental one that pervades Shakespearean comedies. It has a similar function to ambivalent words which cannot be pinned down to one meaning
or another.

In the pageant of the Nine Worthies, the worlds of the courtiers, the
French nobility, and the commoners are merged. And just as the festivity
reaches a climax, a messenger arrives to report the death of the King of
France. This sudden blow is a reminder, along the thematic line of language,
that the "russet yeas and honest kersey noes" of Berowne and others are still
too artificial. It also serves an important purpose of changing the mood of
the play. It often happens in Shakespearean comedies that the mirthful action suddenly assumes a serious tone at, or very close to, the denouement.
Besides being a sobering artistic device, it contextualizes the festive world
in the society, be it artificial or natural.

At the end of *Love's Labour's Lost*, at least, the frivolous love of the
youths is placed in the context of human nature and the real society: the ladies will marry them if they can renounce playful language and keep the
flame of their love burning. And the closing song of the cuckoo and the owl
wraps it all up in an even larger perspective. The song consists of four stanzas—two dealing with spring and the other two with winter—and sounds
as if it enveloped the artificial world in the cycle of nature. We should also
note that the song, as sung (and perhaps danced) by Holofernes and other
characters in the subplot, reflects the mood of the entire play in its comical
effect. Finally, in terms of its ironical structure—amorous spring causes jealous husbands to worry, whereas harsh winter has its share of warm domes-
ticity—the song parallels the entire play.

NOTES
1. William Hazlitt, *Characters of Shakespeare's Plays* (Oxford: The World's
Classics, 1817), p. 241. Hazlitt goes on to evaluate the characters, and as each one of
them is difficult to leave out, he concludes, "we may let the whole play stand as it
is," with the reservation that he objects to the play's pedantic style.

2. For example, H.B. Charlton, *Shakespearean Comedy* (London 1938); Alfred Harbage, "*Love's Labour's Lost* and the Early Shakespeare," *Philological Quarterly* 41 (1962), 18–36.

3. Harley Granville-Barker, *Prefaces to Shakespeare: First Series* (London 1927).

4. C.L. Barber, *Shakespeare's Festive Comedy* (Princeton 1959), pp. 87–118.

5. P.G. Phialas, *Shakespeare's Romantic Comedies* (Chapel Hill 1966), pp. 65–101.

6. Leo Salingar, *Shakespeare and the Tradition of Comedy* (Cambridge 1974), pp. 66–67.

7. III.1.129; IV.2.60; V.1.16; V.2.29.

8. Rosalie L. Colie, *Shakespeare's Living Art* (Princeton 1974), pp. 31–50.

M. Marcadé and the Dance of Death

Love's Labour's Lost v.2.705–711

René Graziani

M. Marcadé is the courtier who brings news of her father's death to the Princess of France—a father role, incidentally, even more oblique than that in the *Merchant of Venice*. Although Marcadé makes no other contributions to the play, R.W. David is right in observing the "powerful effect of Marcadé's entrance . . . not only as a superb *coup de théâtre* but as setting up an ever present pressure of reality throughout the rest of the play.[1] He should appear, of course, in full mourning.

Only lately has Marcadé attracted real attention. Early editors merely emended the spelling of his name from Quarto and Folio "Marcade" to Macard (Rowe, Pope, Theobald, Hanmer, Warburton, and Johnson), Mercade (Capell), and Marcadé (Keightley), this last correctly I believe.[2] W.W. Greg used the particularity of the name to support a hypothesis of an earlier form of the play: "M. Marcadé, who appears . . . . in place of the usually anonymous messenger, must certainly have had an earlier history."[3] Most recently an ingenious explanation connecting Marcadé and Mercury presented itself independently to two critics, this with the added attraction of expanding the significance of the enigmatic last words of the Quarto: "THE WORDS OF MERCURY ARE HARSH AFTER THE SONGS OF APOLLO." In a 1978 *Times Literary Supplement* article Anne Barton argued that Shakespeare was deliberately appropriating the comically ignorant mispronunciation Markedy for Mercury which had been perpetrated by the Cobbler in *The Cobbler's Prophecy*, a play by Robert Wilson performed perhaps in 1589/90 and printed in a quarto edition in 1594, that is four years before the publication of *Love's Labour's Lost* in 1598.[4] She went on to link the two plays by topics, such as court and country, soldier and scholar (very conventional ones to be sure) and by

Originally published in *The Review of English Studies* 37, no. 147 (August 1986), 392–395. Reprinted by permission.

their shared moral concern over attitudes of contempt. Nevertheless her basis for relating the two plays is primarily the verbal resemblance of Markedy and Marcadé. A questionable point here is whether Wilson's malapropism could have been picked up by an audience years later, however discerning or how much of a coterie they were, and then in such a differently sombre setting. Again, does a little laugh here at the cobbler's error fit in with anything we know of Shakespeare, or reflect any similar practice of allusive naming by other dramatists? With no more evidence to go on, it seems extravagant of her to claim that Markedy "was clearly established as a synonym, a kind of alias, for Mercury." The same criticism applies to J.M. Nosworthy's identical, independent proposal of the Markedy/Marcadé derivation in "The Importance of Being Marcade" since he does not add substantially to the evidence either.[5] The point that Mercury was a messenger and guide to the underworld is true, but has no weight in linking Marcadé and Markedy. However, Nosworthy does usefully recall the "pointed ambiguity" of other minor figures with significant names such as Seyton and Eros.

Marcadé's name in fact succinctly reflects his function of bringing the news and the atmosphere of death to the ballooning high spirits of the young nobles. This name had somehow displaced, at least for one writer who describes the work, the original name of the Dance of Death in the cloisters of the Cemetery of the Innocents in Paris, the Dance of Macabré. This was Noël du Fail in his learned Rabelaisian stories, the *Contes d'Eutrapel* (Rennes, 1585).

Early usage of the original and correct name "Macabré" (its derivation and significance still an unsettled matter) was attached generically to a dance of death, but later it seems to have been exclusively applied to the particular representation in the cloister of the Innocents and attributed as a personal name to a Doctor Macchabré, envisaged as the presenter-preacher for the Dance. This name was correctly transmitted through the many editions of the verses and woodcuts of the Paris Dance published from 1485 through 1589, although it never established itself in any other locality in France, Germany, Italy, Spain, England, or elsewhere. At this time, moreover, there could have been no "authority" for it. It was only in the latter part of the nineteenth century—the date also for use of the word macabre—that scholars from Mone to Gaston Paris established its authenticity, mainly from a usage of 1376 by Jehan le Febvre. Another Parisian keeping a journal in the early fifteenth century gets the name of the Paris Dance wrong at the first mention, but corrects "maratre" to "macabre" when he names the dance again. Puzzlement over the name led to early variants; the most popular explanation was that it meant the dance of the Maccabees; another evoked St Macarius.[6] What Noël du Fail was doing was establishing, I think for the first time, the popular modern explanation, that the name was that of the *inventor* of the Innocents' murals. Emile Mâle has effectively quashed the intrinsic value of such an explanation by asserting that medieval works were *not* named after artists, but one can see that in du Fail's time it seemed an excellent one. I assume that because Macabré was not (and is not) a French surname, du Fail substituted Marcadé, and that this may have fitted equally well with whatever traces of a name there were left on the cloister walls.

Du Fail mentions the alchemist Nicolas Flamel who had added some features to the Cemetery of the Innocents which everyone flocked to see:

> . . . et sur tout on les voit par bandes et regiments comment estourneaux, se promenans au Cloistres sainct Innocent a Paris avec les trespassez et secretaires des chambrieres visitans la dance Marcade, Poete Parisien, que ce savant et belliqueux Roy Charles le quint y fit peindre, ou sont representées au vif les effigies des hommes de marque de ce temps la, et qui dansent en la main de la mort.[7]

In England the original name still clung to memories of the old Dance of Paul's in the Pardon churchyard even though its actual figures and inscriptions had all been destroyed in 1549 in the interests of the reformation in religion (the building materials were removed to make Somerset House):

> About this Cloyster, was artificially & richly painted, the dance of Machabray, or dance of death, commonly called the dance of *Pauls*; the like whereof, was painted about *S. Innocents* cloister, at *Paris* in *France*: the meters or Poesie of this daunce were translated out of French into English by Iohn Lidgate, Monke of Bery & with ye picture of Death leading all estates, paynted about the Cloyster: at the special request and dispence of *Ianken Carpenter*, in the raigne of Henry the 6. . . .
>
> In the year 1549, on the tenth of Aprill the said Chappell, by commaundement of the Duke of Summerset, was begun to bee pulled downe, with the whole Cloystre, the daunce of Death, the Tombes, and monuments: so that nothing thereof was left, but the bare Plot of ground, which is since converted into a garden for the Pety Canons.[8]

Stow's account was printed in 1598, the year the quarto of *Love's Labour's Lost* appeared. The fact that English and French names for the Dance differed may indeed have piqued interest and prompted speculation in some minds. At all events the correspondence of Dance Marcadé to Shakespeare's Marcadé and his news of death seems too striking to be ignored.

Further verbal and conceptual links tend to be marginal but should be mentioned. Thoughts of the Dance of Death may inform some phrases used by Rosaline and Berowne. As she sentences him to spending a year of jesting to the sick in a hospital (surely a macabre touch catching the spirit of the dance's humour), she defines him as "a man replete with mocks . . . Which you *on all estates* will execute," squaring with the basic estates framework of the Dance. Berowne instantly jumps on the enormity of the paradox in this realistic-romantic labour imposed on him: "To move wild laughter in the throat of death!" Berowne has to learn to mend his mocking ways, of course, but there are indications that Shakespeare is himself being increasingly drawn to a spirit of comedy in tune with that of the dance macabre, where laughter engages with death, tragedy, and horror, albeit the development is one that goes far beyond plucking *memento mori*s out of the popular tradition. Yet Shakespeare does not shrink from the simpler links with that tradition reflected in such figures as Yorick, Barnardine, and Cloten, or in the habit of personifying death, strongest in the early histories, but still meaningful as the "fell sergeant, Death" in the virtual triumph of Death that is Hamlet's experience. In *Love's Labour's Lost* the change of mood imposed by Marcadé does not settle finally on death, however, but on comic correction of behavior too precious and self-congratulatory to be a good foundation for wedlock. This must rest on something firmer if, as *Ver* and *Hiems* sing, horns are not to be Jack's lot or mere drudgery Joan's.

This explanation of Marcadé means disconnecting him from the Mercury of the play's last line. But perhaps attempts to fathom these enigmatic words will proceed all the better for not being so cluttered by the Marcadé/Markedy suggestion.

NOTES

1. *Love's Labour's Lost*, ed. Richard David (rept. 1960), p. xvi.
2. Ibid., ed. H.H. Furness (1904), p. 3.
3. W.W. Greg, *The Shakespeare First Folio* (Oxford, 1955), p. 224.
4. *Times Literary Supplement* 24 Nov. 1978, pp. 1373–1374.
5. *Shakespeare Survey* 32 (1979), 105–14.
6. D. Th. Enklaar, *De Dodendans. Een Cultur-Historische Studie* (Amsterdam, 1950), pp. 126–131, and Robert Eisler, "Danse Macabre," *Traditio*, 4 (1948), 187–225; also L.P. Kurtz, *The Dance of Death and the Macabre Spirit in European Literature* (New York, 1934), passim.
7. *Oeuvres Facétieuses de Noël du Fail* Vol. 1, ed. J. Assézat (Paris, 1874), Chapter 10, p. 328.
8. John Stow, *The Survey of London* (1598), pp. 264–265.

Jaquenetta's Baby's Father

Recovering Paternity in *Love's Labour's Lost*

Dorothea Kehler

When Longaville first sees Maria, he asks Boyet, "Pray you, sir, whose daughter?" "Her mother's, I have heard" (II.1.201–202),[1] quips Boyet, in effect withholding the information Longaville seeks—Maria's paternity. Boyet's witticism intimates that establishing paternity is chancy. Faulconbridge, the Bastard in *King John*, reminds John that the paternity of "all men's children" is a secret that lies in their mothers' keeping (I.1.63); and, coincidentally, Maria of *Love's Labour's Lost* turns out to be "an heir of Falconbridge" (II.1.205).

Variations on Boyet's jest appear in other Shakespearean comedies. In *Taming of the Shrew* the pedant replies to the question "Art thou his [Lucentio's] father?" with "Ay, sir, so his mother says, if I may believe her" (V.1.32–34). In *Much Ado* Don Pedro, seeking to identify Hero, remarks to Leonato, "I think this is your daughter," to which Leonato retorts, "Her mother hath many times told me so" (I.1.104–105). In *The Tempest* Prospero tells Miranda that he was once Duke of Milan. Astonished, Miranda asks, "Sir, are not you my father?" "Thy mother was a piece of virtue, and / She said thou wast my daughter . . ." answers Prospero (I.2.55–57).[2] That a man should assume his paternity on the word of "a piece of virtue" is not surprising. But if, as in *Love's Labour's Lost*, the source of his belief is the word of his rival, one he has earlier "taken with the manner" (I.1.202–203), that is, caught in the act, neither he nor the audience should overlook the possibility of deception.

Love's Labour's Lost is notable for a spate of cuckoldry jokes and for an open ending involving the main characters and inviting questions about closure among their lower-ranking counterparts. Nevertheless, critics persist in overlooking the possibility that Costard is and has been deceiving Don Armado for some months before the play opens. Only a few critics

Originally published in *Renaissance Papers* (1990), 45–54. Reprinted by permission.

come near to suspecting Costard. Harley Granville-Barker is not convinced that Jaquenetta is pregnant—"it may all be a joke"—but "If there were a guilty party, we might rather suspect Costard, who did 'confess the wench.'"[3] Ronald Berman, while using the term *"in flagrante"* and recognizing the triangle, nevertheless asserts "that Jaquenetta proves eventually to be pregnant by the pedant [Armado]."[4] Herbert A. Ellis, aware of "Costard's having been taken *in coitu* with Jaquenetta, a wench of questionable probity,"[5] pursues the point no further. And Louis Adrian Montrose almost acknowledges Costard's possible paternity: "Whether Costard's accusation against him be true or false, Armado's composure . . . is thoroughly confounded."[6] Montrose continues:

> The original stage direction, "Berowne steps forth" . . . can be interpreted as indicating a collusion between Berowne and Costard to slander Armado. Armado's penance, however, makes tacit confession to the accusation of his paternity. This aspect of the plot has much greater significance as Armado's act than as Costard's fabrication.[7]

I believe that considerable significance inheres in the opposite view. I am making a case either for Armado's being deceived, or for his consciously deciding to woo the mother of his competitor's child, in order to uncover a radical subtext for *Love's Labour's Lost*. In that subtext not only are male/female and menial/non-menial binarisms reversed but also the stigmas attaching to cuckoldry and female promiscuity disappear.

The play encourages us to detect deception. Marriages are not forthcoming among the aristocratic couples because the lords have delayed making forthright declarations of their love; Berowne's description of Rosaline offers an explanation for such delay: she is "one that will do the deed / Though Argus were her eunuch and her guard" (III.1.198–199). Since Berowne has no particular reason to suspect Rosaline, we may understand that he fears being cuckolded by any woman and that a woman is suspect merely because she *is* a woman.[8] Certainly, both direct and indirect allusions to cuckoldry and other modes of sexual deception (including the deception of women by men) abound in *Love's Labour's Lost*. My count yields twelve passages aside from the final cuckoo song[9]—enough to awaken suspicion regarding Costard's easy attribution of paternity to Armado. Such an accusation seems all the more suspicious in light of Armado's difficulty with arithmetic—"I am ill at reck'ning, it fitteth the spirit of a tapster" (I.2.40–41)—and Costard's stubborn refusal to grant Berowne's premise that "three times thrice is nine":

COSTARD. Not so, sir, under correction, sir, I hope it is not so.

.   .   .   .

BEROWNE. How much is it?

COSTARD. O Lord, sir, the parties themselves, the actors, sir, will
show whereuntil it doth amount. (V.2.489–500)

The next "party" Costard speaks of is Jaquenetta; he interrupts Hector's
"The party is gone" with "Fellow Hector, she is gone; she is two months
on her way. . . . Faith, unless you play the honest Troyan, the poor wench
is cast away. She's quick . . ." (V.2.671–676). The blurring of the number
of Worthies in the pageant with the term of gestation—all the more blurred
for Armado, bemused by numbers—emphasizes the uncertainty of when
Jaquenetta became pregnant and, more important, by whom. Our acceptance
of the braggart soldier's fatherhood, seemingly self-evident, may rest upon
no more than Costard's clever choice of verb: "the child brags in her belly
already. 'Tis yours" (V.2.676–677).

Bearing on this argument is the interpretation of Armado's considered response, some fifty lines after his immediate response to Costard's accusation—threatening Costard with death for conferring infamy upon him.
Upon further reflection Armado says, "For mine own part, I breathe free
breath. I have seen the day of wrong through the little hole of discretion,
and I will right myself like a soldier" (V.2.722–725). Editors have reached
no consensus on the meaning of this passage. Warburton, Heath, and
Steevens are all at odds with one another.[10] A division of opinion is still reflected in the split between Evans's Riverside reading: "I now perceive my
wrongdoing and will make honorable amends"; and Harbage's Pelican reading: "I have caught on to the fact that I am abused ('to see day through a
little hole' was proverbial for 'to be no fool')."[11] If Harbage is correct, then
the question of why Armado feels himself abused becomes crucial. Is he angered by public exposure, or does he, unlike the critics, suspect that Costard
is attempting to escape responsibility for producing Jaquenetta's interesting
condition? Having himself apprehended Costard, does he in fact know that
Costard could very well be the father? Does he know that Costard has been
more successful "in the manor-house" (I.1.206) than he (Armado) has been
"at the lodge" (I.2.135) and that he himself could not possibly be the father?

Ellis, whose labors in the linguistic netherlands of the play have been
prodigious, believes that through a homophonic pun on "following," Costard claims to have had intercourse with Jaquenetta. He argues that "*follow* was pronounced like *fallow* 'to plough', and that, figuratively, meant
'to copulate with.'"[12] Ellis points to the following lines:

COSTARD. I was seen with her in the manor-house, sitting with her
upon the form, and taken following her into the park, which,
put together, is in manner and form following. Now, sir, for
the manner—it is the manner of a man to speak to a woman;
for the form—in some form.
BEROWNE. For the following, sir?
COSTARD. As it shall follow in my correction, and God defend the right!
(I.1.206–214)

Additionally, Ellis hears "park" as a pun on "pock" as in venereal disfiguring and "right" as a pun on "rite" or sex act.[13] It is only right, therefore, that
we take Costard's confession—if it is a confession—into account as we try
to decide whether Don Armado intends "to right himself like a soldier" by
doing the right thing by Jaquenetta or by fighting Costard for defaming him.

These are not the only passages alerting the audience to possible
treachery within the Jaquenetta-Armado-Costard triangle. Early in the play
Costard brings Jaquenetta's sexual status into question:

COSTARD. . . . I deny her virginity; I was taken with a maid.
KING. This maid will not serve your turn, sir.
COSTARD. This maid *will* serve my turn, sir. (I.1.296–299, my emphasis)

Moreover, Jaquenetta mocks Armado cruelly. J.J. Anderson notes that in Act
I, scene 2, she "turns every one of Armado's remarks against him."[14] This
is the only time Jaquenetta speaks to Armado; she never speaks *of* him. Her
amiability toward Costard stands in stark contrast. Significantly, Berowne
later characterizes Jaquenetta and Costard as "turtles" (that is, turtledoves;
IV.3.208). We would say lovebirds. Armado misses the point of Moth's song,
which generates suspicion of women:

If she be made of white and red,
Her faults will ne'er be known,
For blush in cheeks by faults are bred,
And fears by pale white shown:
Then if she fear, or be to blame,
By this you shall not know,
For still her cheeks possess the same
Which native she doth owe. (I.2.99–106)

What solace Moth has for Armado in this scene is, as Neal L.

Goldstien observes, ambiguous: "He seeks comfort in his pain from his page Moth, who cites Samson and Hercules as great men who have been in love. The Spaniard's foolishness keeps him from grasping the fact that these are figures who were deceived by love."[15] In fact, Moth is convinced that Armado misjudges Jaquenetta. In an aside, he implies her prior seduction by calling her "a hackney" (III.1.32), that is, a whore. She is again associated with promiscuity by Costard, who suspects Armado's intention to "enfranchise" him. Costard seems to fear being married off to Jaquenetta—to "one Frances," to "some goose" (III.1.120–122), both slang terms for whore.

Costard is undoubtedly ready to mate if not to marry. His physical endowments, metonymically certifying his ability to sire a child, are never in question. Holofernes determines that "this swain (because of his great limb or joint) shall pass Pompey the Great . . ." (V.1.127–128), and Berowne confirms the wisdom of Holofernes' choice: "Greater than great, great, great, great Pompey! Pompey the Huge!" (V.2.685–686). Costard's English name gives him another advantage over his Spanish rival, for as Costard's countrymen defeated the Armada, so Costard promises to defeat Armado in love. Further support for Costard's having falsely accused Armado of fathering Jaquenetta's baby is the fact that, because the lords forswear their oaths, a major part of the play's action deals with love's perjury and betrayal. Forms of the word "perjury" are used thirteen times in Love's Labour's Lost.

Composed before the development of blood tests to establish the likelihood of paternity, the play insists that hierarchical and patrilineal systems remain vulnerable to female subversion due to the nature of the reproductive process. Shakespeare explores some class and gender implications of this circumstance in his rendering of Armado's love. Armado is due for a major comeuppance. His letter to Jaquenetta, in which he represents himself as king and her as beggar, is absurdly arrogant: "I *profane* my lips on thy foot, my eyes on thy picture, and my heart on thy every part" (IV.1.84–86, my emphasis). Equally unattractive is the letter's "poetic threat of sexual assault"[16] in "But if thou strive, poor soul, what art thou then? / Food for his rage, repasture for his den" (IV.1.92–93). If "Armado is a convex mirror held up to the court, . . . [who] reflects, grotesquely, the folly of the lords,"[17] then three years of wooing and working for (but not necessarily winning) a woman whose child may or may not be his can be seen as a symbolic corporal punishment; Armado, the whipping boy, pays not only for his own élitism and attempt to intimidate but also for the wrongheadedness of the gallants, who are protected from greater mortification by their rank.[18]

Similarly, by taunting Armado as she does in Act I, scene 2, and then putting him on probation, Jaquenetta becomes a mirror of the ladies. Moreover, if she is pregnant by Costard, then Armado is, for lack of a better term, a pre-marital cuckold, and Jaquenetta's behavior is a lower-class actualization of *expected* aristocratic behavior; for, as Berowne states the case, Rosaline will "do the deed / Though Argus were her eunuch and her guard." While the ladies retain their chastity, metonymically through Jaquenetta suspicion breeds the event.[19]

Issues of class may explain why Armado must endure a longer probationary period than the lords. Armado's three-year term of labor is appropriate not because he broke or sought to break a foolish, externally imposed vow of celibacy. Rather, it is just that he "hold the plough" (V.2.883–884) because of his Harold Skimpole-like existence. More parasite than braggart soldier, Armado neither works nor fights. He travels, and his journeys end in courts where he can live off a flair for the extravagances of language. Holding the plough for Jaquenetta's love will be an exercise in productivity, a counterpart to Jaquenetta's reproductivity. Rather than suffering humiliation for lack of a shirt (V.2.710), he will soon be able to earn a shirt.

Since the surface of the play must remain "class-bound,"[20] the heaviest penalty falls on a Spaniard whose rank is unspecified and whom critics group with the "low" characters. Nevertheless, by virtue of his title (Don), his association with the lords, his page Moth, and the world of courtly fantasy he constructs for himself, he appears to be a gentleman, perhaps a knight, albeit an impoverished one.[21] For Armado, desire proves stronger than the ideology of class, stronger than the ideology of male dominance. At the end of the play, writes Erickson of the Princess, "patriarchal authority is presented as weak or nonexistent, precariously exposed or threatened."[22] Although an uneducated rustic, now barefoot and pregnant, Jaquenetta exerts a power over Don Armado that is even more striking than that of the ladies over their social equals. Jaquenetta's role is especially remarkable because she is the only "maid" in Shakespeare to breach the code of female chastity and lose nothing by it.[23] Shakespeare's slandered-lady plays (*Much Ado, Othello, Cymbeline,* and *Winter's Tale*) are ideologically conservative in that, although the lady's reputation is redeemed, the code remains in place. Here, on the other hand, at least the possibility exists that, unburdened by moral pretensions, Jaquenetta slept with one or more men (perhaps Armado, perhaps not), was proposed to by Armado, and provisionally rejected him in favor of single parenthood. Eventually, she may have received his letter and decided he was a fool. Conceivably, she always preferred Costard. At any rate, the ladies' rejection of the lords parallels Jaquenetta's bid for a more extreme version of independence.

The shadow text that haunts the received reading is constructed of such subversive challenges as these to status quo thinking. Cuckoldry jokes may be more than just jokes; instead, there is the chance of genuine deception due to male competition for sexual favors and reluctance to take responsibility for the consequences of sex. No less subversive, in a class-conscious, patriarchal society Armado ennobles himself by remaining the milkmaid's votary, no longer a braggart but a man brave enough to accept the ignominy other men fear.[24] Disturbing even now, judging from its total absence from the criticism, is the possibility that Jaquenetta herself does not know who the father of her child is—a reminder that paternity may not be recoverable.

This being so, should Jaquenetta give birth to Jacaranda, who grows up lovely as a tree, surely someday a young man will ask, "Pray you, sir, whose daughter?" Not unexpected might be the reply, "Her mother's, I have heard."

NOTES

1. All Shakespeare citations are from *The Riverside Shakespeare*, ed. G. Blakemore Evans et al. (Boston: Houghton Mifflin, 1974).

2. A similar joke appears in *1 Henry IV*, where Falstaff, playing the king, addresses Hal: "That thou art my son I have partly thy mother's word . . ." (II.4.402–403).

3. Granville-Barker, "*Love's Labour's Lost," Prefaces to Shakespeare* Vol. 4 (Princeton: Princeton University Press, 1946), p. 34.

4. Berman, "Shakespearean Comedy and the Uses of Reason," *South Atlantic Quarterly* 63 (1964), 3.

5. Ellis, "*Shakespeare's Lusty Punning in* Love's Labour's Lost *with Contemporary Analogues* (The Hague: Mouton, 1973), 189.

6. Montrose, *"Curious-Knotted Garden": The Form, Themes, and Contexts of Shakespeare's* Love's Labour's Lost, Salzburg Studies in English Literature 56 (Salzburg: Institut für Englische Sprache und Literatur, 1977), p. 117.

7. Montrose, p. 211, n.15, citing *LLL* V.2.664.

8. Leslie A. Fiedler suggests that in Shakespeare's personal mythology the Academy is a paradise of men and that *Love's Labour's Lost* can be read as "a new version of the Fall of man, in which woman and the serpent are identified with each other and Adam is condemned to leave the garden arm in arm with his temptress—if she will have him" (*The Stranger in Shakespeare* [New York: Stein and Day, 1972], p. 30).

9. At I.1.201–203; I.2.123–124; II.1.201–202; III.1.22–25, 30–33, 120–122, and 198–201; IV.1.111–118 and 125–130; IV.3.334–335; V.1.61–70; and V.2.252–253. Where the bawdy allusion is not immediately apparent, see Ellis.

10. Quoted in Horace Howard Furness, ed., *A New Variorum Edition of Shakespeare:* Love's Labour's Lost (Philadelphia: J.B. Lippincott, 1904), p. 298, n. 796.

11. At V.2.713–715 in Alfred Harbage, ed., *Love's Labour's Lost*, in *William Shakespeare: The Complete Works*, The Pelican Text Revised (Baltimore: Pelican, 1969).

12. Ellis, p. 132.

13. Ellis, pp. 172 and 186–187.

14. Anderson, "The Morality of *Love's Labour's Lost*," *Shakespeare Survey* 24 (1971), 57. Oddly, Joseph Westlund cites this passage as evidence of Armado's triumph over Costard after acknowledging that "Costard's momentary success with Jaquenetta suggests that the swain is more direct, and thus more effective, than the lords" ("Fancy and Achievement in *Love's Labour's Lost*," *Shakespeare Quarterly* 18

[1967], 39). Westlund forgets that a "momentary success" is all that is required to make a baby.

15. Goldstien, "*Love's Labour's Lost* and the Renaissance Vision of Love," *Shakespeare Quarterly* 25 (1974), 347.

16. Peter B. Erickson, "The Failure of Relationship Between Men and Women in *Love's Labour's Lost*," *Women's Studies* 9 (1981), 71.

17. John Kerrigan, ed., "Introduction," *Love's Labour's Lost* (New York: Penguin, 1982), p. 26. Kerrigan adumbrates the links between Armado and the lords on pp. 25–26.

18. My thanks to Bethany Sinnott of Catawba College for pointing out similar conflicts between élitism and desire in *As You Like It* (Touchstone and Audrey) and *Measure for Measure* (Lucio and Kate Keepdown).

19. See Marilyn L. Williamson's important article on lower-ranking characters who enact behaviors not allowed the superiors whom they double ("Doubling, Women's Anger, and Genre," *Women's Studies* 9 [1982], 107–119).

20. John Kerrigan, "*Love's Labour's Lost* and the Circling Seasons," *Essays in Criticism* 28 (1978), 283.

21. Armado's provenance may suggest low comedy in that he derives from *commedia dell'arte*'s Spanish Miles Gloriosus, Capitano Spavento del Vall'Inferno (Richard David, ed., "Introduction," *Love's Labour's Lost* [London: Methuen, 1956], p. xxxi). Yet William C. Carroll writes, "In Armado, Shakespeare seems to have found the perfect representative of a bygone era of knights, chivalric romances, and flamboyant grandiloquence" (*The Great Feast of Language in* Love's Labour's Lost [Princeton: Princeton University Press, 1976], 47).

22. Peter B. Erickson, "Sexual Politics and the Social Structure in *As You Like It*," *Massachusetts Review* 23 (1982), 79.

23. *Henry VI*'s Queen Margaret and *King John*'s Lady Faulconbridge are wives; Cleopatra is Ptolemy's widow.

24. The King of France could have served as an example of an iconoclast of another sort, having empowered his daughter as his plenipotentiary.

ARMADO AND COSTARD
IN THE FRENCH ACADEMY

PLAYER AS CLOWN

Meredith Anne Skura

The Taming of the Shrew, framed as theater by its Induction, is almost certainly earlier, but the pageant in *Love's Labour's Lost* is the first Shakespearean inner play proper. Since the players' roles call for comedians in the modern sense, their entry here marks the first confrontation in the canon between King and Clown and establishes Shakespeare's opposition between the player and the aristocratic world of heroes from whom he begs alms.[1] Ferdinand, King of Navarre, is the "great man" in *Love's Labour's Lost* and though he may have "sworn out house-keeping" (II.1.103), he cannot escape from his duty as host, either to the visiting princess or to the players who help him to entertain her. And when the motley players in *Love's Labour's Lost* perform their Pageant of Worthies, they gain access not only to Navarre's academic retreat in his country house, surrounded by its "curious-knotted garden" (II.1.242), but to the entire world of manly aristocratic heroics which it represents. This is a world shaped by the ideology of honor and driven by the heroic thrust toward "fame" as a means of establishing an eternal name, and transcending all that is base and shameful in mortality. It naturally encourages the rituals and "activities that are most integral to the whole idea of aristocracy—leading troops in a patriotic war against the King's enemies."[2] This world had been the first object of Shakespeare's dramatic attention in the "heroical histories" of the first *Henriad*, which opens with the death of Henry V and the funeral proclaiming "death's dishonorable victory" (*1H6* I.1.20), and is dominated by Talbot's effort to fight on in Henry's name and transcend death through heroic fame.[3] Talbot's project in *Henry VI, Part One* is symbolized by his devotion to the rituals of the Order of the Garter, with its implicit opposition

From Chapter 4 of *Shakespeare the Actor and the Purpose of Playing* by Meredith Anne Skura (University of Chicago Press), pp. 88–95, 269–272. © 1993 by the University of Chicago. Reprinted by permission.

between heroic fame and cowardly shame: "*Honi soit qui mal y pense.*" His failure is signaled by the rituals of the aristocratic hunt when Talbot, who was accustomed to penetrating enemy cities, at last finds himself surrounded by the French and "bounded in a pale" like "a little herd of England's timorous deer, / Maz'd with a yelping kennel of French curs" (*1H6* IV.2.45–47).

Love's Labour's Lost might not seem at first to belong in such company, but it continually alludes to the heroic tradition drawn not only from the English chronicles which furnished the plot of *Henry VI*, but also from the lives of the famous "Worthies"—beginning with Hercules, whose labors supply the title of *Love's Labour's Lost*.[4] Similarly, both in its structure and its major concerns, *Love's Labour's* mirrors Shakespeare's *Henry VI, Part One*. Certainly Navarre's men see themselves as members of the illustrious company of departed heroes like *Henry VI's* St. George and Henry V. *Love's Labour's Lost* is an oddly death-conscious comedy; and, scholars though they are, Navarre and his fellow votaries fancy themselves above all to be chivalric warriors battling against "the huge army of the world's desires" in order to transcend "death's dishonorable victory," as it was called in *Henry VI*, or "the disgrace of death," as it is called here (*LLL* II.1.3, 10; *1H6* I.1.20). And just as their serious work drives them to stalk the elusive "fame that all hunt after all their lives," in their leisure they devote themselves to the aristocratic hunt, seen as appropriate entertainment for a royal princess. The play refers insistently to the hunting party which provides the first occasion for the "bookmen" to mingle with the Princess's entourage. There Navarre spurs his horse hard upon the hill and reveals his "mounting mind." Indeed the whole play is cast as a reversible "hunt," and Navarre and his men meet a fate like Talbot's. The love-struck Berowne complains, "The king he is hunting the deer; I am coursing myself: they have pitched a toil [set a snare for the deer]; I am toiling in a pitch" (IV.3.1–2).[5] Meanwhile the Princess jokes about the deer she kills and, as she prepares to shoot her bow, likens herself to a "curst wi[fe]" who "subdues a lord" (IV.1.36, 40).[6] Navarre and his votaries had entered boldly commanding that "fame, that all *hunt* after in their lives, / Live register'd upon our brazen tombs" (I.1.1–2); italics added). Now the hunters are hunted and the suitor-shooters shot.

Navarre's aristocratic ideals thus run exactly counter to the base, effeminate pastime of playing,[7] and the players here are mere foils showing that Navarre's heroic ambition turns out to be no better than the "Pageant of Worthies," where everyone is "o'er-parted." Military prowess in early modern Europe was indeed spectacle—nowhere more visibly so than in the French wars from which Shakespeare took the names of Navarre and his men (and to which he may already have alluded in *Henry VI, Part One*).[8]

Shakespeare was not alone in mustering his grandeur for his stage. Marlowe had made fun of soldiers who march in garish robes like players in *Edward II* (1592–93 [1592]), and one reason for the reluctance of the players in *Histriomastix* (1598–99 [1599]) to go to war is the fear that the soldiers would steal their "playing parrell" and "strout it in the field" (286)—a joke that loses its point unless soldiers were already known for strouting. The popularity of Braggadocchio suggests that they were.[9] Even when not parodied, the soldier was represented as an actor on display for spectators, subject to the actor's extremes of fame and shame.[10]

Shakespeare's glorious soldier, heroic Talbot himself, is introduced on display, high in a tower where he has been "watched . . . even these three days" (*1H6* I.4.16) by the master gunner below. For Talbot, fame and success in war entail a physical display of prowess, so that he can terrify the French, whose "whole army stood agaz'd on him" (*1H6* I.1.126). Similarly, when failure threatens Talbot, it threatens in the form of public shame when the French witness his inability to live up to his role. Recounting his captivity in France, what Talbot most deplores is the shame of public exposure:

> In open market-place produc'd they me
> To be a public spectacle to all:
> Here, said they, is the Terror of the French,
> The scarecrow that affrights our children so.

And Talbot directs his heroic fury not at his captors but at his audience:

> Then broke I from the officers that led me,
> And with my nails digg'd stones out of the ground
> To hurl at the beholders of my shame. (*1H6* I.4.38–45)[11]

Later he is almost trapped by the Countess, who locks him within her walls and laughs at his heroic pretense; and before he finally dies the general of the encircling French forces announces that "these *eyes*, that *see* thee now well coloured, / Shall *see* thee wither'd, bloody, pale and dead" (*1H6* IV.2.37–38; italics added).[12] Appropriately enough, Talbot sees death itself as an audience, "Thou antic Death, which laugh'st us here to scorn" (*1H6* IV.7.18).

But the comparison which likens a soldier to an actor works the other way too. Navarre and his men are struggling with precisely the ambition and its discontents that lead people—including Armado and company—to the stage. We have heard the twentieth-century actor described as "a soldier going into battle,"[13] and heard about his "warlike energy" and "gladiator instinct." The sixteenth-century *Hamlet*, the most theatrical of Shakespeare's plays, pairs the soldier and actor as well, when Hamlet compares himself first to a player, then to the soldier Fortinbras, and when at the end he is carried "like a soldier to the stage" (*Ham.* V.2.401).[14] Not long before *Hamlet*, Shakespeare's most heroic soldier, Henry V, had encouraged his warriors into the breach by telling them to *act* like tigers, while the Chorus of that play encouraged the audience to strain and work like soldiers.[15]

In *Love's Labour's Lost*, therefore, Navarre's sense of himself as a warrior, as well as his search for fame and immortality, provide a model as well as an antitype for theatrical ambition.[16] Navarre's world represents everything drama aspired to in its proudest claims. More than ten years would pass before John Davies would complain that players "weene they merit immortalitie," and thirty before Massinger's Roman actor could claim outright that he played for "glorie, and to leave our names / To after times."[17] But the grandiose fantasies of twentieth-century actors—that acting can make contact with the past or recreate life—were already inscribed in the praise topoi used by Thomas Nashe and Thomas Heywood in their defenses of Renaissance drama. Drama, for these men, was almost synonymous with a pageant of worthies that both recognized and created heroic immortlity. We have already had occasion to cite Nashe's famous testimony to the power of *Henry VI*, which we might see as Shakespeare's own "Pageant of Worthies":

> How it would have joyed brave *Talbot* . . . to think that after he had lyne two hundred years in his Tombe, hee should triumphe again on the stage and have his bones newe embalmed with the teares of ten thousand spectators at least . . . who, in the Tragedian who represents his person, imagine they behold him fresh bleeding.[18]

Nashe concludes with a less well-known but even more sweeping claim for all drama: "There is no immortalitie can be given a man on earth Like unto Playes."[19] Heywood's emphasis is on the power the play has over the audience, but he too insists on the way in which theater goes beyond creating mere "shadows" or "forms": "To see a souldier shap'd like a souldier, walke, speake, act like a souldier: to see a *Hector* all besmered in blood, trampling upon the bulkes of Kinges. . . . To see as I have seene, *Hercules*, in his own shape hunting the Boare, knocking down the Bull . . . Oh, these were sights to make an *Alexander!*"[20] Webster's *Excellent Actor* (1615) makes the same claim: "A man of deepe thought might apprehend, the Ghosts of our ancient *Heroes* walk't again, and take [the player] (at severall times) for many of them."[21] Neither Nashe, Heywood, nor Webster really believes in reincarnation; just as the same complaints turn up again and again in the antitheatricalist tracts, resurrection had clearly become part of the standard defense of drama. Yet there is something in their praise that sounds like Macbeth's awe at the line of eight real kings raised up in the witches' show (*Mac.* IV.1.111, stage direction)—or like the scholars struck with admiration at Faustus's ability to raise Alexander and his paramour from the dead "in their own shapes" (*Dr. Faustus* IV.1[1233]).[22] Faustus's opening complaint in Marlowe's play was that no human doctor could raise the dead; apparently in some minds the players could.[23] If nothing else, the player was the one who brought a play to "life," and the idea of resurrection, as we have seen (chap. 2 of the book from which this essay is taken), inhabited the language of the theater.

Perhaps then, the pageant of dead white male worthies in *Love's Labour's Lost* serves as parodic displacement not only of Navarre's overblown aspirations but also of Shakespeare's own theatrical aspirations in *Henry VI*—just as Pyramus and Thisbe would soon parody his efforts at romance in *Romeo and Juliet*. In any case the pageant certainly serves to expose the proud beggars in *Love's Labour's Lost* who arrange to perform it for the king. Shakespeare devotes an unusually large proportion of lines and even whole scenes to these characters, whom Berowne dismisses as a crew of walking stereotypes from the *commedia dell'arte*—"the pedant, the braggart, the hedge-priest, the fool, and the boy" (V.2.536)—but who are remarkably well developed as individuals.[24] They include the flamboyant Spaniard Armado, his page Moth, and Costard, retainers who have been invited into the academe to provide "sport" for the bookmen. They are joined by the local villagers, the pedant Holofernes, his Parasite, Nathaniel the Curate, and Constable Dull, who help put on the pageant. The players run the gamut from narcissistic would-be stars to less-talented hired (in this case drafted) men, just as Quince's troupe does in the Athens of *A Midsummer Night's Dream* and as London companies did. Preparations for this performance may provide a glimpse of what went on in Elizabethan performances, though we have no way of knowing whether the power struggles among actors here, the preference for typecasting, the threat of stage fright, and the rudeness of the audience are models for, or nonsensical distortion of, professional practice.

In any case the performance gives a glimpse of would-be actors as Shakespeare saw them. Most revealing among these actors is the group's leader, Armado, another version of Shakespeare's proud beggar. Though he is a braggart soldier by stereotype, Armado has a good deal of the braggart player about him. He resembles Robert Greene's equally spruce and arrogant player in *Groatsworth of Wit*. Greene's player boasts to Roberto that he can make "a prettie speech," and reports that he had "terribly thundred" the twelve labors of Hercules on stage, in a role not very different from those in the pageant.[25] Even Holofernes, a vain man himself, sees through Armado's similar bombast:

> his humour is lofty, his discourse peremptory, his tongue filed, his eye ambitious, his gait majestical, and his general behaviour vain, ridiculous, and thrasonical. He is too picked, too spruce, too affected. . . . I abhor such fanatical phantasimes, such insociable and point-devise companions. (V.1.9–13, 17–19)

Armado's sensitivity however distinguishes him from Greene's unworthy charlatan and makes him an important indicator of Shakespeare's attitude toward actors. Armado's pride is not only a matter of social pretense, but an involvement with self and self-image that suggests something like what we now mean by narcissism. He is as concerned with emotional as with sartorial style, and he cannot even fall in love without playing a role. When Jaquenetta steals his heart Armado desperately seeks "some mighty precedent" to shore up his battered sense of self: "Comfort me, boy," he asks his clever page, "What great men have been in love?" (I.2.60–61). And, like Richard III, if Armado is proud and thrasonical, he nonetheless finds himself in humiliating pursuit of a most unlikely woman. Like Richard with Lady Anne, Armado veers between brazen self-assertion and abject submission, claiming to be the Nemean lion to Jaquenetta's lamb, the King to her Beggar—then vowing at the end to hold the plow three years for her.

Armado is awed both by his female audience—as Navarre and his men are by theirs—and by the king for whom he organizes the Pageant of Worthies. He is a fawning courtier thoroughly concerned with pleasing his audience and, like all Shakespeare's later players, he feels an exaggerated, even childlike, deference for his lord and patron. For him, self-esteem is inseparable from Navarre's approval. When he learns that "the king would have me present the princess, sweet chuck, with some delightful ostentation" (V.1.102–104), he takes it as sign that his theatrical duties have "singled [him out] from the barbarous" (V.1.73). He never suspects that he has been included in the festivities as mere sport, and is assumed to be no better than a "Monarcho" or court fool.[26] If we take his unwitting innuendoes seriously, Armado finds an almost obscene pleasure in serving Navarre and being his "familiar":

> Sir, the king is a noble gentleman, and my familiar, I do assure ye, very good friend. For what is inward between us, let it pass . . . for I

must tell thee, it will please his grace, by the world, sometime to lean upon my poor shoulder, and with his royal finger, thus, dally with my excrement, with my mustachio; but, sweet heart, let that pass. . . . some certain special honours it pleaseth his greatness to impart to Armado, a soldier, a man of travel, that hath seen the world: but let that pass. The very all of all is, but, sweet heart, I do implore secrecy, that the king would have me present the princess, sweet chuck, with some delightful ostentation, or show, or pageant, or antic, or firework. (V.1.87–104)

As he prepares a pageant for "The posteriors of this day" (V.1.80–81), Armado, with unconscious camp, elaborates the king's patronage into an indecent fantasy of something "inward" between them as the king's "royal finger" dallies with Armado's excrement.

Before the pageant is over—or rather interrupted, as nearly all Shakespeare's inner plays are—Armado and his fellows experience the extremes of egotism and shame inherent in a player's life. Some of them are truly "shame-proof" (Berowne's wishful claim; V.2.508): Holofernes begins the project ridiculously overconfident about his worthiness to play three Worthies, and nothing that happens during the performance can faze Costard, who walks off barely containing his delighted "I hope I was perfect" (V.2.554), despite the audience's rudeness to him. But when the audience is unrelenting in its seemingly motiveless malignity toward the poor players, others fall apart. Holofernes, like Tomkis's "fresh player" or T.G.'s "bashful" player, is literally put "out of countenance."[27] Nathaniel is so afflicted by the audience's scorn—"A conqueror, and afeared to speak!" (V.2.573–574)—that he forgets his lines and must "run away for shame" (V.2.574). He responds to their rejection just as Boyet predicts the would-be lovers will respond to the ladies' rejections: "Why, that contempt will kill the speaker's heart, / And quite divorce his memory from his part" (V.2.149–150). The men attack not only the acting but the very shape and odor of the actors' bodies, taking advantage of their physical vulnerability: Nathaniel smells; Holofernes' face is too thin like a "death's face"; and (spoken sarcastically) Armado's "leg is too big" in the "calf" and the "small" (V.2.562, 607, 631–634). If Armado's devotion to the King evokes the familial fantasies modern actors describe, his experience during the performance itself suggests the modern actor's sense of being held at bay by Canetti's baiting crowd. The players become scapegoats. "Only the savage shame one feels toward an unworthy part of oneself," Thomas Greene notes, "could motivate the gentlemen's . . . (quite uncharacteristic) cruelty."[28] It is a telling analysis of audience psychology.

In the end, Armado, insulted in his effort to present Hector, suffers the worst reversal. Like Navarre claiming to be heir to all eternity, Armado has staged a heroic drama and attempts (à la Nashe and Heywood) to bring dead heroes to life. But instead the pageant turns into an unheeded memento mori, a "death's face in a ring," as Berowne calls Holofernes (V.2.607). When "Alexander" comes on stage to announce that, "when in the world I lived, I was the world's commander" (V.1.557), his words only remind the audience that in the world he does not live any longer. Then too, Armado's play, as much as Navarre's own efforts, is interrupted by the messenger from France announcing the death of the Princess's father. More painful for Armado than the metaphysical failure of his fictional pageant, is the real-life defeat that it accompanies. Costard interrupts "Hector" in midspeech and accuses Armado of getting Jaquenetta pregnant. "Dost thou infamonize me among potentates?" Armado cries (V.2.670), ready to fight for his honor; and the bookmen crowd around to laugh not at Hector but at Armado. The poor Spaniard endures an almost literal realization of the actor's fear of being naked in front of an audience, when Costard challenges him to strip to his shirt and Armado is forced to admit, shamefully, that he has none ("I go woolward for penance"; V.2.701–702). The man who played Hector, and who identified with the King when he quoted the ballad of "The King and the Beggar" to Jaquenetta, is humiliated in front of his King. He is a portrait of the actor as vulnerable narcissist.

But Shakespeare's satiric thrust in *Love's Labour's Lost* is aimed more at the aristocrats than the actors; even their attack on the players reflects back on themselves. The joke is not so much on the clownish players as on Navarre and his men, whose plans are interrupted when Marcade breaks up the play. Besides, *Love's Labour's Lost* exudes a confidence and delight in itself as theater which contradicts its mockery of the pageant. Its self-assurance emerges not least in the way it teases its offstage aristocratic audience, both by inviting their complicity in the play's dense allusiveness and private jokes, then refusing them the expected happy ending, and by suggesting that they are as unsatisfying an audience as Navarre and his fellows.

NOTES

1. Jack Cade in *Henry VI, Part Two* comes earlier, but he does not meet with the king himself.
2. G.K. Hunter, "Bourgeois Comedy: Shakespeare and Dekker" in *Shakespeare and His Contemporaries*, ed. E.A.J. Honigman (Manchester: Manchester University Press, 1986), p. 3.
3. David Riggs, *Shakespeare's Heroical Histories* (Cambridge: Harvard University Press, 1971), describes the heroical ideal the plays embody and rework.

4. Both the chronicles and the Worthies also contributed to the "prentice literature" aimed at and consumed by seventeenth-century adolescents. The apprentices "conceived of themselves as possessing the manly virtues displayed on the battlefields of France and of the Holy Land . . . and with the romantic virtues of Johnson's *Nine Worthies.*" The latter was a prentice version of the famous heroes, celebrating nine London prentices all of whom made good. Steven R. Smith, "The London Apprentices as Seventeenth-Century Adolescents," *Past and Present* 61 (1973), 149–61.

5. Berowne's playful conceit, at least when applied to lovers rather than actors, was hardly unique to Shakespeare. At about the same time that Berowne was onstage, Arden in the anonymous *Arden of Faversham* (1585–92 [1589]) has a premonitory dream before his wife murders him:

> This night I dreamed that being in a *park*,
> A *toil* was *pitched* to overthrow *the deer*,
> And I upon a *little rising hill*
> Stood whistly watching for the herd's approach.
> Even there, methoughts, a gentle slumber took me. . . .
> But in the pleasure of this golden rest
> An ill-thewed foster had removed the toil,
> And rounded me with that beguiling home
> Which late, methought, was pitched to cast the deer.
> With that he blew an evil-sounding horn,
> And at the noise another herdsman came
> With falchion drawn, and bent it at my breast,
> Crying aloud, "Thou art the game we seek."

Arden of Faversham, ed. Martin White (New York: W.W. Norton, 1982), 6.6–19 (italics added).

6. Two scenes later Holofernes evokes the hunt again for us, when he reads his "extemporal epitaph on the death of the deer," which begins, "The preyful princess pierc'd and prick'd a pretty pleasing pricket," and notes how "the dogs did yell" bringing the pricket down (IV.2.47–48, 55, 58). Hers is only a playful preyfulness, but the bantering which accompanies it suggests a parallel between the Princess's attack on the deer and the French attack on Talbot. The phrase "in blood," found both in Holofernes' poem and in the description of Talbot's predicament, is another link between the two. See also Holofernes' unusual reference to Diana as "Dictynna" (IV.2.35)—a name Ovid uses only when calling her "hunter of deer."

7. The incompatibility was being explored on the stage at the time. In *Histriomastix*, for example, the traditional opposition between soldier and scholar becomes a conflict between soldier and player when the Captain comes to press the players into service: "What?" the Captain cries, "Playes in time of Warres? hold, sirra / Ther's a new plott," and remains unconvinced when one of the players explains, "'Tis our Audience must fight for us, / And we upon the stage for them." *Histriomastix*, in *Plays of John Marston*, 3:285–286.

8. For several years, across the channel, Navarre's namesake, Henri the "white plume of Navarre," (compare Armado, that "plume of feathers": IV.1.95) had become a folk hero to the English by challenging the Catholics on the French throne. Essex, a man with an eye for self-preservation, used Henri's wars to act out his expensive dreams of chivalric glory, with his old-fashioned knights errant "armed like the antique figures shown on old tapestries, with coats of mail and iron helmets . . . going into battle to the sound of bagpipes and trumpets"; Anthony Esler, *The Aspiring Mind of the Elizabethan Younger Generation* (Durham: Duke University Press, 1966), p. 93.

9. Less derogatory was the new military genre in painting which deemed soldiers worthy subjects for artists. See J.R. Hale, *Artists and Warfare in the Renaissance* (New Haven: Yale University Press, 1991).

10. When King John besieges Angiers in Shakespeare's *King John*, for example, the citizens standing on the city walls are like an audience "in a theater, whence they gape and point / At [King John's] industrious scenes and acts of death" (*KJ* II.1.375–376).

11. The rest of his scenes are dogged by shame: "let Talbot perish with this shame" (*1H6* III.2.57), he cries when defeat seems likely; he and his son speak of "shame" three times (and infamy once) in seventeen lines when they meet; his fellow soldiers speak of his "shame" after he is gone. This obsessive sense of shame has a biblical flavor about it, and does actually echo the prophetic wrath in Jeremiah, where an angry God shames his people for their "abominations": "For the greatness of thine iniquity (are thy skirts discovered and thy heels made bare) . . . therefore will I discover thy skirts about thy face, that thy shame may appear...." (*Jer.* 13:22) Talbot not only suffers from a sense of shame as physical exposure; he tries to inflict it on his enemies as well. He punishes the coward Fastolfe by publicly stripping off his garter in a technically accurate but nonetheless unhistorical defrocking ceremony. And his showiest victory in France is the attack on Orleans in which the French, as Alençon says, were "shamefully surprised" (*1H6* II.1.65). There Talbot roused "the Dauphin and his trull" from "drowsy beds" (*1H6* II.2.28, 23) so that they come running on stage "in their night clothes" (*1H6* stage directions after II.1.38), and then, as another stage direction says, "fly, leaving their clothes behind them" (*1H6* stage directions after II.1.7). He revenges his earlier shame by exposing his enemies.

12. His opponent throughout the play, Joan of Arc, threatens—though she fails to effect—a similarly fatal gaze: "O were mine eyeballs into bullets turned / That I might shoot them at your faces!" (*1H6* IV.7.79–80).

13. Stuart W. Little and Arthur Cantor, *The Playmakers* (New York: W.W. Norton and Co., 1970), p. 90.

14. Fortinbras, it turns out, is marching for no more than a "fantasy" or a "trick of fame" (*Ham.* IV.4.61)—hardly better than the First Player caught up in his "fiction" or "dream of passion" (*Ham.* II.2.246); while by contrast the player can make himself into Pyrrhus, a potent soldier.

15. See Chapter 5 and Afterword of the book from which this essay is taken.

16. Heroic drama was also the medium used by dramatists to compete with one another. George Peele, Robert Greene, and Thomas Kyd all tried to out-Tamburlaine Christopher Marlowe—and thus were exploring not only a national ideology but a much more pragmatic trade war.

17. John Davies, *Microcosmos* (1603) in *The Complete Works of John Davies of Hereford*, ed. Alexander B. Grosart (Edinburgh University Press, 1878), Vol. 1, p. 82; Philip Massinger, *The Roman Actor* (1626), ed. William Lee Sandidge (Princeton: Princeton University Press, 1929), 4.1.31–32.

18. *Pierce Pennilesse His Supplication to the Divell*, in *The Works of Thomas Nashe*, ed. Ronald B. McKerrow (Oxford: Basil Blackwell, 1966) Vol. 1, p. 212.

19. Ibid.

20. Thomas Heywood, *Apology for Actors* , B3v–B4r.

21. John Webster, *An Excellent Actor*, cited in E.K. Chambers, *The Elizabethan Stage* (Oxford: Clarendon Press, 1967) Vol. 4, p. 258.

22. Like Faustus, the magician John a Kent (who is even more than Faustus a figure for the dramatist) can "from foorth the vaultes beneathe, / call up the ghosts of those long since deceast"; Anthony Munday, *John a Kent and John a Cumber* (1587–90 [1589]), ed. Muriel St. Clare Byrne, Malone Society Reprints (Oxford University Press, 1923) 5, lines 108–109. Shakespeare's magician-dramatist Prospero claims that "graves at my command / Have wak'd their sleepers, op'd, and let 'em forth" (*Tem.* V.1.48–49), although we never see any such thing.

23. D.J. Palmer claims that Shakespeare also "resurrected" Henry V in that king's eponymous play; D.J. Palmer, "Casting Off the Old Man: History and St. Paul in *Henry IV*," *Critical Quarterly* 12 (1970), 267–83. This seems even truer in the con-

text of the full cycle of history plays, which began with Henry V's death in *Henry VI, Part One* (1592) and ended with the live Henry's greatest triumph in *Henry V* (1599).

24. The proportion may have been even larger in an earlier draft. Editors have suggested that a scene with Armado and Moth is missing, and that the original play lacked the lengthy Muscovy fiasco which fills out the aristocratic plot. For a summary of the discussions see Richard David, ed., *Love's Labour's Lost*, Arden Shakespeare (London: Methuen, 1968), pp. xxii, xxi. The degree of character development is such that scholars continue to search for the historical originals of the mechanicals as well as for those of the aristocrats.

25. Robert Greene, *Greenes Groatsworth of Wit*, in *The Life and Complete Works in Prose and Verse of Robert Greene*, ed. Alexander B. Grosart, The Huth Library (London: Hazell, Watson, and Viney, 1881–83), Vol. 12, pp. 131–132.

26. A Spaniard in post-Armada England, Armado is already branded as an inferior "other."

27. Thomas Tomkis, *Lingua* (1607). "Bashful player" is in T.G[ainsford]., *Rich Cabinet*, in W.C. Hazlitt, ed., *The English Drama and Stage under the Tudor and Stuart Princes 1543–1664* (London: Wittingham and Wilkins, 1869), p. 230.

28. Thomas Greene, "*Love's Labour's Lost*: The Grace of Society," *Shakespeare Quarterly* 22 (1971), 323.

Elizabethan Views of the "Other"

French, Spanish, and Russians in *Love's Labour's Lost*

Felicia Hardison Londré

The abundant use of foreign settings and characters throughout Shakespeare's canon provides us with a basis for conjecture about his own perspective on various nationalities, and perhaps that of Elizabethans in general. Admittedly, it may not always be possible to distinguish between the dramatist's personal biases and his appropriation of popular prejudices for dramatic effect. While he was not above caricaturing foreigners (for example, the Welsh Sir Hugh Evans and the French Dr. Caius in *The Merry Wives of Windsor*),[1] Shakespeare often demonstrates a more sophisticated international outlook than what we know to have been the popular Elizabethan sense of the differences between the English and other peoples.[2] *Love's Labour's Lost* serves as an excellent text for examining his depiction of foreigners, because it brings together French lords and ladies, a Spaniard, noblemen masquerading as Russians, and some comic lowlife figures who seem to have wandered into the French royal preserve from an English village.[3] At the same time, an understanding of England's relations with France, Spain, and Russia from the 1570s to the 1590s can illuminate some of the oddities in this charming but perplexing play.

During the reign of Edward VI (r. 1547–53), England was inundated with French Huguenots and other foreign Protestants seeking refuge from persecution. Many of the French stayed on into the reigns of Mary (r. 1553–58) and Elizabeth I, finding employment as tutors and teaching principles of humanism along with the French language. To the English, French culture set an unattainably high standard of excellence.[4] French was the language of choice for many English courtiers, according to observers as early as 1550 and as late as 1591.[5] The English nobility of the late sixteenth cen-

Originally presented at the Twelfth World Congress of the International Federation for Theatre Research, Moscow, Russia, 8 June 1994. First published in *The Elizabethan Review* 3, no. 1 (Spring 1995), pp. 3–20.

tury also employed numerous French riding masters, French dancing masters, French cooks, and French instructors in the (Italian) art of fencing. French imports included wines, manuals of needlework, and—most notably—fashionable apparel.[6] French visitors to the English court were treated with every courtesy. It was in the best interests of Queen Elizabeth (r. 1558–1603) to maintain good relations with France, especially in view of the Vatican's efforts to promote a Spanish invasion of England. To that end, Elizabeth prolonged for thirteen years the negotiations for a marriage between herself and a member of the French (Catholic) royal family. Even after her ally Henri de Navarre suddenly converted to Catholicism in July 1593 (in his immortal words, "Paris vaut une messe"), Elizabeth maintained their alliance, though she vented her feelings in a mildly chastising letter to him: "It is dangerous to do evil, even for a good end."[7]

Most Elizabethans did not share in the cordial sentiments of the Queen and her court toward the French. Indeed, Hoenselaars claims that "the influx of foreigners during the second half of the sixteenth century placed a heavy burden on the native economy and coupled nascent national awareness with a strident form of popular xenophobia."[8] With reference to the 1590s, he notes further that "xenophobia and clashes between Englishmen and foreigners may have been rampant among the lower and middle classes at times; but in learned circles and among the aristocracy the exchange of culture and ideas thrived in an atmosphere of cordiality."[9] Shakespeare's history plays, according to Cumberland Clark, "reflected the national prejudice against France born of centuries of struggle,"[10] and they appeal to a "crude . . . patriotism."[11] Thomas Nashe's comment in *The Unfortunate Traveller* (1587) typifies the English commoner's view of the French: "What is there in France to be learned more than in England, but falsehood in fellowship, perfect slovenry, to love no man but for my pleasure, to swear 'Ah par la mort Dieu,' when a man's hams are scabbed."[12] Estienne Perlin, a French priest who spent two years in England and Scotland, published his observations in Paris in 1558. He reported that "the people of this nation hate the French to death, considering us their old enemies, and universally call us *France shent, France dog,* that is to say 'despicable Frenchman,' 'French dog,' and also call us 'whoreson,' 'villain,' 'son of a bitch,'. . . It annoys me that these peasants, in their own country, spit in our faces, whereas when they come to France, they are honored and revered like little gods; that is, the French prove themselves to be open-hearted and noble-spirited."[13]

The image of the French that comes across in *Love's Labour's Lost* accords more closely with the courtly attitude than with that of the populace. With respect to Spaniards and Russians, there seems to have been less divergence between the aristocrat's and the commoner's view of the "other": Spain was the arch-enemy, and the Russians could safely be regarded as figures of fun. Even so, in consideration of vicissitudes in English foreign policy during the reign of Elizabeth I, the date of composition of *Love's Labour's Lost* is pertinent. Its date, moreover, is germane to our interpretation of Shakespeare's treatment of the French characters in the play. In his groundbreaking studies of the historical background to *Love's Labour's Lost*, the French scholar Abel Lefranc pointed out that the play is, "in fact, the representation of a scintillating episode in our history. . . . The events that form the basis for the play occurred precisely between 1578 and 1584. . . . The very substance of the play, far more than previous scholars have imagined, is impregnated with quite recognizable French elements. . . . Indeed, the work stands as testimony that the dramatist had a virtually impeccable and absolutely amazing acquaintance with aspects of France and Navarre of the period that could have been known to only a very limited number of people. . . . One is led to suspect that the author, whoever he was, must have sojourned for a time at the court of Henri de Navarre and of Marguerite de Valois."[14] If Lefranc is correct—and there is, indeed, other evidence linking the play to the early dates that he specifies—then the play offers not so much an image of "Frenchness" as an ordinary Elizabethan would have perceived it, but rather some specific portraits of individual members of the nobility who happened to be French.

Our *terminus ad quem* for the dating of *Love's Labour's Lost* is the 1598 publication of the Quarto edition. We know by its title page that this was a revised version. That page reads: "A Pleasant Conceited Comedie called, Loves labors lost. As it was presented before her Highness this last Christmas. Newly corrected and augmented By W. Shakespere. Imprinted at London by W.W. for Cutbert Burby. 1598." Further indications of revision include the repeated lines in IV.3 (lines 292–314 are echoed in lines 315ff.); a similar redundancy in V.2;[15] and the use of generic names (King, Braggart, Boy, Clown, Constable, Pedant, Curate) in some scenes for the characters named Ferdinand of Navarre, Don Armado, Moth, Costard, Dull, Holofernes, and Nathaniel in other scenes.[16]

The dating of the earlier version or versions of *Love's Labour's Lost* must be conjectured according to topical references in the text. Numerous internal references point to 1578 as the original date of composition,[17] and this is corroborated by the external evidence that *The Double Maske: A Maske of Amasones* and *A Maske of Knights* was presented at court on 11 January 1579 to honor the French envoy Simier, whose coming had been announced three months earlier.[18] Described in the records of the Court

Revels as "an entertainment in imitation of a tournament between six ladies and a like number of gentlemen who surrendered to them," *The Double Maske* may well have been the Ur-*Love's Labour's Lost*.[19] A piece depicting French ladies and knights engaged in a combat of wit would certainly have been considered appropriate entertainment for Simier and his entourage. Of the internal evidence, most compelling is the fact that Euphuism—of which *Love's Labour's Lost* is universally acknowledged to be a textbook example—was a courtly fad in 1578–79, and even a year or so later the play's witticisms and in-jokes about that linguistic affectation among members of the court would have been quite stale. Earlier in 1578 the Queen had made a progress during which Thomas Churchyard presented a pageant of Nine Worthies, apparently just as ineptly as the one we see in *Love's Labour's Lost*.[20]

In France that same year, the Duc d'Alençon gave an elaborate entertainment which included soldiers masquerading as Russians.[21] Pierre de la Primaudaye's *L'Académie française*, a treatise on four young gentlemen of Anjou who spend their days in self improvement through study, exercise, and moral conversation, was published in French in 1577 and may be considered a probable source for the play.[22] And of particular significance is the "scintillating episode" to which Lefranc alludes: on 2 October 1578, Marguerite de Valois met with her husband, Henri de Navarre, after a two-year separation. She had travelled to the south of France with her "flying squadron" (*escadron volant*) of attractive maids-of-honor for the reunion in Nérac, but religious factionalism was so intense at the time that the Protestant husband and his Catholic wife could not safely reside in the same city, a situation echoed in the exclusion of the Princess from Ferdinand of Navarre's court in *Love's Labour's Lost*. Another concern of Henri de Navarre and Marguerite was her unpaid dowry, against which he was holding parts of Aquitaine; this too parallels the business discussed by Ferdinand of Navarre and the Princess in the play.[23] Despite these problems, the encounter was celebrated with various festivities and entertainments, including some held outdoors in the lovely park of the chateau de Nérac. Lefranc notes that textual allusions to the park that is the setting for *Love's Labour's Lost* evoke the milieu just as Marguerite de Valois describes it in her memoirs.[24] Her memoirs record also that "the King my Husband being followed by a handsome troupe of lords and gentlemen, as honorable as the finest gallants I've ever seen at court; and there was nothing less than admirable about them, except that they were Huguenots."[25] Even the "Nine Worthies" figure prominently in the gathering at Nérac. The royal chateaux at Pau and at Nérac were furnished with two series of large tapestries depicting the Nine Worthies. French court records show that in November 1578 one complete set of these tapestries was transported from Pau to Nérac, presumably for the enjoyment of Marguerite, her mother, and her maids of honor.[26] That Shakespeare had these tapestries in mind when he wrote the play is evident in Costard's reproach to Sir Nathaniel for his poor performance as Alexander the Great (V.2.569–570): "O! sir, you have overthrown Alisander the conqueror. You will be scraped out of the painted cloth for this."

There is some evidence testifying to an interim revision of *Love's Labour's Lost* between 1578 and 1598, probably in 1592.[27] A confusing attribution of lines in II.1 of the Quarto raises the possibility that an earlier version had "only three pairs of lovers."[28] This squares nicely with the fact that the names of Maréchal Biron (Berowne) and Duc de Longueville (Longaville) were well known in England even before 1591, when Elizabeth sent troops under the Earl of Essex to aid the cause of Henri IV of France, but the Duc de Mayenne (Dumain) remained Henri's foe until 1593.[29] Thus, the intermediate version—making the original six generic pairs of ladies and gentlemen (Amasones and Knights) into three couples with specific personal names—would have been written before 1593, leaving the incorporation of Dumain and Katharine for the version published in quarto in 1598. What we have then is a comedy originally written as a playful spoof of Euphuism combined with a tribute to the French manners and fashions that were so admired at the English court in the 1570s; later revised to tie the attractive leading characters to actual historical figures who were sympathetically regarded by the English (possibly even using their real names, judging by the fact that the Princess of France is occasionally listed as Queen in the Quarto); and finally revised—to make the politically sensitive identities less obvious to the man in the street, while further amusing the court by giving Ferdinand and his fellow oath-takers their comeuppance at the end of the play—after 1593, when Henri de Navarre converted to Catholicism, forswearing his Protestantism. As Berowne comments in IV.3.359: "It is religion to be thus forsworn."

Numerous other details in *Love's Labour's Lost* betray Shakespeare's firsthand knowledge of personalities and circumstances at the French court.[30] There were, for example, at the court of Henri IV actual people with the same names as secondary characters in the play: Antoine Boyet, minister of finance; de La Motte, a squire like his namesake Moth; and Marcadé.[31] Lefranc notes that "the art of rhyming was practiced at the court of Navarre perhaps more than at any other: Marguerite de Valois composed many love poems, as did Henri."[32] The infamously amorous Henri de Navarre also had a habit of writing his love poems on both sides of the page with verses filling the margins, folding them like letters, and drawing around the wax seal an emblem signifying a kiss.[33] Thus the Princess describes the letter she has received from Ferdinand: ". . . as much love in rhyme / As would be cramm'd up in a sheet of paper, / Writ o' both sides the leaf, margent and all, / That he was fain to seal on Cupid's name" (V.2.6–9). A few lines later, Katharine speaks of her sister, who died of love; this too has its historical counterpart in the death of the lovely young Hélène de Tournon at Brabant in the summer of 1577, as recounted in the memoirs of Marguerite de Valois.[34] These are but a few of the many specific allusions and brain-teasing references clearly intended for the amusement of a coterie audience. From this we might generalize that in the writing of *Love's Labour's Lost* Shakespeare was not thinking of the French characters as national types, but as avatars of individuals known to members of Elizabeth's court.

According to Cumberland Clark, the "anti-French feeling" of the Elizabethan chronicle plays and of "the English nation as a whole" manifests itself in the imputation of three chief faults to the French: treachery, fickleness, and cowardice.[35] *Love's Labour's Lost* does imply fickleness in the French king and his three lords who first break their oaths "not to see ladies" for three years, and who later swear oaths to the wrong women.[36] However, unlike the patriotically motivated history plays, this comedy geared to courtly sensibilities offers largely sympathetic portrayals of the French. The four couples are physically attractive, well-mannered, quick-witted, and act with the best of intentions. Even the business dealings between Ferdinand and the Princess are conducted with the utmost grace (II.1.128–178). It is possible, however, that some of the same qualities that delighted the audience at court could have taken on quite different overtones in the popular perception. The banter of the ladies among themselves, egged on by Boyet, in IV.1 is so ribald that Costard, upon hearing it, marvels: "O' my troth, most sweet jests! most incony vulgar wit; When it comes so smoothly off, so obscenely as it were, so fit" (IV.1.143–144). Such "sweet vulgarity and smooth obscenity" is seen as very French by the nineteenth-century German critic G.G. Gervinus,[37] and it is possible that the average Elizabethan may have taken a similarly jaundiced view of fine ladies speaking smut. At the same time, the French characters' self-conscious displays of refined rhetoric and manners would have struck the level-headed average Englishman as excessive. Yet if excess of refinement is regarded as a fault, it must be admitted that such matters are relative. Among the upper-class characters, it is the Princess's attendant Boyet who truly demonstrates affectation of speech and manners pushed to the extreme. Indeed, Berowne describes him as "the ape of form, monsieur the nice . . . Honey-tongu'd Boyet" (V.2.325, 335). The irony of seeing Boyet as an exemplar of French excess is that the character was undoubtedly intended to be a caricature of Sir Philip Sidney, whose relationship with Edward De Vere, seventeenth Earl of Oxford, was colored by considerable animosity, especially after their oft-reported "falling out at tennis"[38] in September 1579. Sidney's affectation was well known at court. Furthermore, he blatantly plagiarized lines from both Edmund Spenser and Edward De Vere for a pastoral he presented at Wilton. Sidney's habit of literary theft (many of his poems are verbatim translations from the French of Ronsard and Desportes)[39] undoubtedly inspired Berowne's description of Boyet:

> This fellow pecks up wit, as pigeons pease,
> And utters it again when God doth please.
> He is wit's pedlar, and retails his wares
> At wakes, and wassails, meetings, markets, fairs. (V.2.315–318)

Thus, Boyet—on balance the only less than sympathetic French character in *Love's Labour's Lost*—was, to the knowing audience at court, not representative of a Frenchman at all. Unquestionably, Shakespeare wrote *Love's Labour's Lost* from a courtly perspective, and the court's attitude toward France was cordial, at least during the period from 1578 to 1593. Could the play's 1598 publication (the first printed play to bear the name "William Shake-speare") have been a calculated step taken under Elizabeth's encouragement? She would have realized that the ordinary Englishman would view it as satire on the effete, frivolous, Catholic French. This would serve to reinforce Protestantism among the citizenry while she herself, above the fray, could maintain strong diplomatic ties with France.

England's attitude toward Spain was considerably less ambiguous. The English people hated Spain even when their queen, Mary Tudor (Elizabeth's older half-sister) was married to Philip of Spain (the future Felipe II). During Elizabeth's reign, Spain controlled the New World, Portugal, the Kingdom of Naples, the Duchy of Milan, and the Low Countries, including the commercial port of Antwerp. The Pope was urging Felipe II to employ his nation's huge "invincible" galleons in an attack on England, and thus Elizabeth sustained her tenuous alliance with France (even after Anglo-French diplomatic relations were seriously shaken by the slaughter of 30,000 Huguenots in the St Bartholomew's Day massacre in 1572) as a means of gaining time to build up England's naval force. According to Cumberland Clark, English hatred of Spain was "at once racial, imperial, commercial, and religious."[40] Anti-Spanish feelings are evident in the persistent English literary stereotype of the Spaniard "which comprises most of the vices and shortcomings known to man," according to William S. Maltby. "When the Spaniard has the upper hand, his cruelty and hauteur are unsupportable. When reduced to his proper stature by some unimpeachably nordic hero, he is cringing and mean-spirited, a coward whose love of plots and treacheries is exceeded only by his incompetence in carrying them out."[41] The English view of Spain as a "cruel and barbarous nation"[42] was corroborated by the 1583 publication of an English translation of the *Brevissima Relación de la Destrucción de las Indias* (1542) by Bartolomé de las Casas, chronicling the shocking acts of cruelty perpetrated by Spaniards against the innocent natives of the New World. Elizabeth herself sanctioned English anti-Hispanism with the official publication of her propagandistic *Declaration of the Causes Moving the Queen of England to Give Aid to the Defence of the People Afflicted and Oppressed in the Lowe Countries* (1585), which described the bloodthirstiness of Spanish troops in the Netherlands.[43] England's defeat of the attacking Spanish Armada in 1588 marked the high point of anti-Spanish feeling in England, and pamphleteers duly sensationalized the event. By exaggerating the size of the invading fleet, an implication of Spanish incompetence was added to Spain's reputation for inhuman barbarism.[44]

Given the vehemence of those attitudes, it seems surprising that Don Armado, the "refined traveller of Spain" (I.1.162) in *Love's Labour's Lost*, should be such a complex character in whom there is no imputation of villainy and very little of cowardice. Certainly, he is a ridiculous figure, a source of amusement for the courtiers and the butt of many jokes, verbally one-upped even by his diminutive squire Moth. Yet Ferdinand's description of him bears little relationship to either the official or the popular Elizabethan conception of Spaniards:

> A man in all the world's new fashion planted,
> That hath a mint of phrases in his brain;
> One who the music of his own vain tongue
> Doth ravish like enchanting harmony;
> A man of complements, whom right and wrong
> Have chose as umpire of their mutiny:
> This child of fancy, that Armado hight,
> For interim to our studies shall relate
> In high-born words the worth of many a knight
> From tawny Spain, lost in the world's debate. (I.1.163–172)

The qualities attributed to him here are: fashionable (Euphuistic) verbal display, conceit, courteous manners with perhaps an element of affectation, punctiliousness about the rules governing affairs of honor (duelling), high birth or good breeding, and a patriotic delight in bragging about little-known Spaniards. This largely sympathetic description undoubtedly survives from the 1578 version of the play, not only because of its reference to Euphuism as a "new fashion," but also because Elizabeth was then stilll concerned with buying time for an English naval buildup by keeping diplomatic channels open with Felipe II.[45] The more ridiculous attributes of the character may well have been added after the 1588 defeat of the Armada, at which time his name would have been changed from Braggart to Armado.

Gustav Ungerer has proposed that Don Armado is based upon a highly visible Spanish turncoat, Antonio Pérez, who had lost his post as chief minister under Felipe II through his own treacherous attempt to undermine relations between the Spanish king and his half-brother, Don John of Austria. Pérez escaped to Europe where he carried out a propaganda war of revenge against Felipe II, arriving in England, on a mission for Henri de Navarre, in April 1593. Ungerer analyzes various ways in which Pérez resembled Armado: both are Spanish; both write letters in Senecan prose style; both are described as "peregrinate" and "odd"; Armado's relationship with Jaquenetta resembles that of Pérez with Doña Juana Coello.[46] The description of Don Armado in V.1.9–14 apparently applied recognizably to Pérez: "his humour is lofty, his discourse peremptory, his tongue filed, his eye ambitious, his gait majestical, and his general behavior vain, ridiculous, and thrasonical. He is too picked, too spruce, too affected, too odd, as it were, too peregrinate, as I may call it." However, before we extend this commentary from Pérez to Spaniards in general, it must be noted that these lines are spoken by Holofernes, who is, if anything, even more ridiculous a character than Don Armado.[47]

It is important to remember that the figure of the braggart soldier or *miles gloriosus* originated in Roman comedy and became a staple of the Italian *commedia dell'arte*, where it was traditional to depict the swashbuckling *capitano* as a Spaniard, perhaps in part because the foreign accent served as an added source of humor for Italian audiences. O.J. Campbell traces the evolution of the *capitano* in the Italian comedy, showing how "most of the roughness and noisy extravagance of the role disappeared to be replaced by the polished elegance of a gloved gentleman, who carries on his warfare with the utmost dignity and seriousness."[48] Campbell rightly notes that Shakespeare's Don Armado is "no swashbuckler and windy braggart, but a fop in manners and a virtuoso in speech."[49] He further points out that the most famous of all Italian *commedia dell'arte capitanos* was Francesco Andreini, who was well known for his incorporation of literary conceits into his speeches. Andreini had, like Don Armado, "a mint of phrases in his brain" (I.1.164). As a member of the Gelosi company, Andreini performed before the French court in 1571, 1574, 1576, 1599, and 1603–04.[50] It is probable that Edward De Vere, seventeenth Earl of Oxford, saw the performances when he was visiting the court in Paris in 1576. Only three *commedia dell'arte* troupes are known to have visited Elizabethan England (in 1573, 1576, and 1578), and records of their performances are limited to London and to the court on progress. Yet most scholars agree with Richard David's recognition of the play's debt to the *commedia dell'arte*. He states: "Armado would have been impossible without the Captain and his kin."[51]

Other theories have been put forth to tie Don Armado to various known personages. In IV.1.99–101, Boyet says: "This Armado is a Spaniard, that keeps here in court; / a phantasime, a Monarcho, and one that makes sport / To the prince and his book-mates." Monarcho was a real person, a half-crazed, vainglorious Italian hanger-on at Elizabeth's court. Among the writers who recorded his antics was Thomas Churchyard.[52] Eva Turner Clark emphasizes a political subtext to the play: she sees Don Armado as representative of Don John of Austria and Jaquenetta as Mary Stuart, Queen of Scots, who intrigued with Don John against Elizabeth.[53] Some have seen both Don Armado and Holofernes as caricatures of John Florio, a prominent Italian resident in England.[54] Finally, Armado is seen by Oxfordians as one facet of the probable author of the play, Edward De Vere, seventeenth Earl of Oxford, who had been transformed into an "Italianated" Englishman during his European tour of 1575–76. Garbed in the latest fashions from the continent and leading the Euphuist faction at court in a "show-off" use of language, Oxford often functioned as a self-mocking "court jester" for Elizabeth.[55] The point of identifying all these optional prototypes for Don Armado is to suggest, again, that the character does not necessarily or primarily represent a Spaniard or a Spanish national type. As Cordasco observes: "For the spectator, Armado was the contemporary Spaniard; for the initiate, he was undoubtedly much more."[56]

When it comes to the Muscovites (a synonym for Russians) in *Love's Labour's Lost,* there can be no question that the portrayal is a caricature. The Muscovite sequence is a set piece, a masking dance, in which Ferdinand and friends assume stereotypical traits to pass themselves off as exotic foreigners. Their entrance is cued by a trumpet, and they are preceded by blackamoors. The costume references are sparse: "disguised like Russians, and visored" (V.2.157), "in shapeless gear" (V.2.303), and "in Russian habit" (V.2.368). The original intent of the four lords toward the ladies is to "with some strange pastime solace them" (IV.3.373), to pave the way to Love with "revels, dances, masks, and merry hours" (IV.2.375). Boyet reports to the ladies that "their purpose is to parle, to court and dance" (V.2.122). We learn also from Boyet that the men have taken the trouble to teach Moth to speak with a Russian accent and to adopt a certain style of movement: "Action and accent did they teach him there; / 'Thus must thou speak, and thus thy body bear'" (V.2.100). Presumably the disguised men adopt the same accent and movement, for Rosaline later recalls "their rough carriage so ridiculous" (V.2.306). Before they even appear, the Princess decides that "they do it but in mockery merriment" (V.2.139); and when they leave, she says: "Twenty adieus, my frozen Muscovites" (V.2.265). Returning to the ladies as themselves, the lords seem genuinely surprised that the ladies saw through their disguises (V.2.385–395). All these indications suggest that Elizabethan convention ascribed some readily recognizable traits to Russian nationals.

Russia had been "discovered" by the English only in 1553, when a ship commanded by Richard Chancellor left an Arctic expedition to seek refuge in the White Sea; Chancellor then accepted the Tsar's invitation to visit Moscow. A Russia Company was chartered the following year to exploit opportunities for trade between the two realms. "By the end of the century," according to Lloyd E. Berry and Robert O. Crummey, "Elizabeth's subjects had accumulated a store of experience of Muscovite life and customs far richer than that of any other European nation."[57] Travellers' reports available to Elizabethan readers were: accounts of the voyages of Richard Chancellor in 1553, Anthony Jenkinson in 1557, George Turberville in 1568–69, and Sir Thomas Randolph in 1568–69, all published by Hakluyt in 1589; Giles Fletcher's important work, *Of the Russe Commonwealth*, describing his year in Russia, 1588–89, published in 1591. (The *Travels* of Sir Jerome Horsey, based upon his visits and years of residence in Russia between 1573 and 1591, existed only in manuscript until 1856.) Despite differences in tone (due to the different personalities of the observers), these documents are consistent in their descriptions of Russian character, lifestyle, manners, and dress. The Elizabethan travellers all viewed the Russians as backward, rude and cruel to one another, hard-drinking, and adulterous. Fletcher, for example, noted "their manner of bringing up (void of all good learning and civil behavior). . . . [T]he whole country is filled with rapine and murder. They make no account of the life of a man. . . . As for the truth of his word the Russe for the most part maketh small regard of it so he may gain by a lie and breach of his promise."[58] The observation about Russian lying[59] might perhaps seem pertinent with reference to the lords who forswear their oaths. Rosaline's comment on the "Muscovites" after their exit— "gross, gross; fat, fat" (V.2.268)—accords with Fletcher's description of the

Russians: "they are for the most part of a large size and of very fleshy bodies, accounting it a grace to be somewhat gross and burly, and therefore they
nourish and spread their beards to have them long and broad."[60] Some excerpts from the verse epistles of George Turberville will further indicate what
Shakespeare envisioned for the masque of Muscovites:

> The Russie men are round of bodies, fully fac'd,
> The greatest part with bellies big that overhang the waist,
> Flat-headed for the most, with faces nothing fair
> But brown by reason of the stove and closeness of the air.
>
> .   .   .   .
>
> Their garments be not gay nor handsome to the eye:
> A cap aloft their heads they have that standeth very high,
> Which *kolpak* they do term. They wear no ruffs at all.
> The best have collars set with pearl, *rubashka* they do call.
> Their shirts in Russie long, they work them down before,
> And on the sleeves with colored silks two inches good or more.
> Aloft their shirts they wear a garment jacketwise
> High *odnoriadka*; and about his burly waist he ties
> His *portki*, which instead of better breeches be;
> Of linen cloth that garment is, no codpiece is to see.
>
> .   .   .   .
>
> And over all a *shuba* furr'd, and thus the Russie goes.[61]

Like the French and Spanish references in *Love's Labour's Lost*, the
Muscovite sequence is rooted in actual circumstances known to members
of the English court. According to Horsey, Tsar Ivan IV ("the Terrible") was
contemplating a proposal of marriage to Elizabeth in 1571. Although nothing
came of that impulse, Ivan IV continued to dream of marriage to an English-
woman, preferably a close relative of the "virgin queen." An English doctor at his court described Lady Mary Hastings, daughter of the second Earl
of Huntingdon, and the tsar determined to make her his wife, even though
he was still married to his seventh wife. To that end, he sent Fyodor Pisemsky
as envoy extraordinary to negotiate the marriage and to bring back a portrait of the lady. Pisemsky arrived in London in September 1582, but it was
the following May before he was able to see Lady Mary.[62] Horsey described
the encounter: "Her majesty caused that lady to be attended on with divers
great ladies and maids of honor and young noblemen, the number of each
appointed to be seen by the said ambassador in York House garden. She put
on a stately countenance accordingly. The ambassador, attended with divers

other noblemen and others, was brought before her ladyship; cast down his countenance; fell prostrate to her feet, rose, ran back from her, his face still towards her, she and the rest admiring at his manner. Said by an interpreter it did suffice him to behold the angel he hoped should be his master's spouse; commended her angelical countenance, state, and admirable beauty. She was after called by her familiar friends in court the empress of Muscovy."[63] Thus, in *Love's Labour's Lost*, when Longaville exclaims "O sweet Maria, empress of my love!" (IV.3.53), the courtly audience would have remembered Mary's missed opportunity to be empress of Muscovy and enjoyed a good laugh.

And again we see that—even though Ferdinand, Berowne, Longaville, and Dumain assume stereotypical traits that would identify them as Russians in the popular imagination—setting the play in its true historical context yields references to specific individuals and circumstances known to the court, and the comedic value of these in-jokes must have far outweighed that of facile caricature when performed for its intended audience. The inescapable conclusion is that while Shakespeare may not have been averse to having public playhouse audiences find humor in broad ethnic and national stereotypes, he was primarily writing for the more refined sensibilities of a coterie audience.

NOTES

1. It should be noted that Shakespeare's use of caricature could be said to encompass his fellow Englishmen, such as the tavern lowlife surrounding Falstaff. Typical of the many observations on English character that are found in Shakespeare's work is Falstaff's comment: "It was always yet the trick of our English nation, if they have a good thing, to make it too common" (*Henry IV, Part 2*, I.213–214).

2. See, for example, Marienstras, pp. 101–103; Hoenselaars, p. 32.

3. Campbell demonstrates that Don Armado as well as the English types (Costard, Holofernes, Nathaniel, and even Dull) have their origins in the stock figures of the Italian *commedia dell'arte*; see especially pp. 33–43 of his article.

4. According to Lee, for example, "in some forty French provincial towns printing presses were at work without intermission from the earliest years of the sixteenth century, and were in constant process of multiplication in the hundred years that followed. . . . There is nothing in the annals of the English Renaissance which can compare with this diffusion of intellectual energy and ambition" (p. 26).

5. Jacques Peletier du Mans, *Dialogues de l'Ortographe* (1550); Mellema (1591); both cited by Lee, p. 44.

6. Lee, pp. 47–53.

7. Perry (her translation of Elizabeth's French), p. 297.

8. Hoenselaars, p. 27.

9. Ibid., p. 52.

10. Cumberland Clark, p. 136.

11. Ibid., p. 138.

12. Lee, p. 50.

13. From Perlin's *Description des royaulmes d'Angleterre et d'Ecosse* (Paris, 1558), cited by Lee, pp. 59–60: "Les gens de ceste nation hayent à mort les Francoys, comme leurs vielz ennemis, et du tout nous appellent *France chenesve, France dogue,*

qui est à dire 'maraultz François', 'chiens François', et autrement nous appellent *orson*, 'villains', 'filz de putring'. . . . Il me desplait que ces vilains, estans en leur pays, nous crachent à la face, et eulx, estans à la France, on les honore et revere comme petis dieux; en ce, les Francois se monstrent francs de coeur et noble d'esperit." The English translation in the text is my own, as are other translations from the French, unless otherwise attributed.

14. Lefranc's two-volume work *Sous le masque de William Shakespeare* (1919) includes an extensive analysis of *Love's Labour's Lost*. The statements cited here are from his 1936 article on the play, pp. 411–412, 414–415.

15. According to David, the redundant lines are "clearly an early draft, somehow left uncancelled by Shakespeare although he had written new lines for Rosaline and Berowne, and borrowed from the old for Dumain and Katharine" (p. 180, note to lines 809–814).

16. See David, p. xxii.

17. Will Shakspere of Stratford-upon-Avon would have been only fourteen years old in 1578, but it is hoped that the reader will examine the evidence objectively. It must be stated from the outset that this author brings an Oxfordian perspective to this study; that is, my research over the years has forced me, as a matter of intellectual honesty, to accept Edward De Vere, seventeenth Earl of Oxford (1550–1604) as the most likely author of the plays and poems published under the pseudonym William Shakespeare.

18. Simier's mission was to negotiate a marriage between Queen Elizabeth and the Duc d'Alençon, brother of Henri III (r. 1574–89) and brother-in-law of Henri de Navarre, the future Henri IV (r. 1589–1610). The latter, a close friend of Edward de Vere, seventeenth Earl of Oxford, is generally acknowledged to have been the model for the character of Ferdinand of Navarre in *Love's Labour's Lost*. Among the textual references to the envoy Simier's suit on behalf of François, Duc d'Alençon is Costard's line (III.1.119): "O! marry me to one Frances—I smell some l'envoy, some goose in this."

19. Eva Turner Clark, p. 136; Ogburn, p. 173.

20. Thomas Churchyard, *A Discourse of the Queenes Maiesties entertainment in Suffolk and Norfolk: with a description of many things then presently seene* (1578). See comments on this event by Wikander, pp. 6, 29, 32. See also Eva Turner Clark, 243. Churchyard, an associate of Edward de Vere, seventeenth Earl of Oxford, may have been the model for the character of Costard (Ogburn, p. 198).

21. Ogburn, p. 195.

22. T. Bowes's English translation, *The French Academie*, was published in 1586; see excerpts in Bullough, pp. 434–435.

23. Eva Turner Clark, pp. 183–184.

24. Lefranc (1936), p. 412.

25. Marguerite de Valois, p. 163.

26. Lefranc (1936), pp. 425–426.

27. In 1592, Queen Elizabeth visited Oxford University in violation of her own 1561 statute forbidding the lodging of women on the premises of a college or cathedral; she had done this only twice before, in 1564 and in 1566. Thus she was guilty of an "oath forsworn" like Ferdinand and friends in the play. Performed at court, the play would have amused the Queen with its gently mocking reminder that she, like the Princess in the play, must be refused admittance to certain precincts (Eva Turner Clark, pp. 142–143).

28. See David, p. xx.

29. Civil war was at its height in France in 1589–94. In II.1.224–226 of the play, the Princess obliquely alludes to France's wars of religion when she tells her ladies that "this civil war of wits were much better us'd / On Navarre and his bookmen, for here 'tis abused."

30. Edward De Vere spent time at the French court in the first months of 1575 and again in March and April of 1576. There he formed friendships with Marguerite

de Valois and Henri de Navarre, the future "Reine Margot" and Henri IV. The warmth of the relationship between the latter and Oxford is evident in a letter (5 October 1595) to Oxford from the French king. The text of that letter is given in French and English in Eva Turner Clark, pp. 131–132.

31. Lefranc (1919), Vol. 2, p. 60; in his 1936 article Lefranc argues for the overlapping identification of Boyet with Marguerite de Valois's chancellor Guy du Faur Pibrac (1529–84), a political opportunist of rare eloquence, who also accompanied her to Nérac in 1578.

32. Ibid., p. 62.

33. Ibid., pp. 64–65.

34. Ibid., pp. 74–9; see also Lefranc (1936), pp. 422–425.

35. Cumberland Clark, p. 139.

36. Henri de Navarre was a notorious womanizer, a trait which earned him the nickname le Vert-Galant. His mistresses included Jacqueline de Bueil (Contesse de Moret), Corisande (Contesse de Gramont), Charlotte des Essarts (Contesse de Romorantin), Antoinette Guercheville, Henriette d'Entragues, Esther Imbert, Charlotte of Montmorency, and most importantly, Gabrielle d'Estrées.

37. G.G. Gervinus, *Shakespeare Commentaries* (1877); cited by Cumberland Clark, pp. 145–146.

38. *Hamlet* II.1.58.

39. Looney, Vol. 1, pp. 248–250.

40. Cumberland Clark, p. 214.

41. Maltby, p. 6.

42. Ibid., p. 20.

43. Ibid., p. 55.

44. Ibid., pp. 76–8.

45. In a letter dated 20 December 1577, Elizabeth wrote to Felipe II: "We beg very affectionately that all suspicions may be banished from between us, if any such have been raised by the arts of wicked men with the object of destroying that close friendship which we enjoyed in our earlier years." On 16 March 1578, Elizabeth received Felipe II's ambassador Don Bernardino de Mendoza, who had been instructed that Felipe II hoped to have Elizabeth "on our side and that as a friend and sister she will turn her arms as she promises to do, to our support" (Perry, pp. 233–234).

46. Ungerer, Vol. 2, pp. 377–392.

47. The intermediate revision of the play undoubtedly made Holofernes into a caricature of the pedant Gabriel Harvey, who publicly praised his benefactor Edward De Vere, seventeenth Earl of Oxford, while privately satirizing him in verses that much resemble the speech by Holofernes quoted here. Note that as the scene continues Holofernes appears to be won over by Armado (whom some have seen as De Vere's mocking self-portrait). It is significant that in the pageant of the Nine Worthies, Holofernes is cast as Judas (Looney, Vol. 2, p. 244).

48. Campbell, p. 24.

49. Ibid., p. 23.

50. Ibid., p. 25.

51. David, p. xxxi.

52. Churchyard was a longtime servant of Edward De Vere, seventeenth Earl of Oxford. See David, p. 67, for further references to Monarcho.

53. Eva Turner Clark, pp. 157, 161.

54. Sells, p. 212.

55. In that capacity, Oxford's relationship to Elizabeth is echoed in that of Feste to Olivia and the Fool to King Lear. Among the many clues associating Oxford with Don Armado is the name itself: Armado is an anagram of "O drama"; that is, "O[xford's] drama" (Ogburn, p. 196). There is also much of Oxford in both Berowne and Longaville; Berowne's speeches incorporate the identifying "O" almost to excess.

56. Cordasco, p. 6.

57. Berry and Crummey, p. xiii.

58. Giles Fletcher in Berry and Crummey, p. 245.

59. For an interesting analysis of Russian lying, see Edmund Wilson, *A Window on Russia* (Farrar, Straus and Giroux, 1972), pp. 203–206.

60. Fletcher, p. 241.

61. Turberville, "To Parker," in Berry and Crummey, p. 81.

62. Payne and Romanoff, pp. 406–409.

63. Berry and Crummey, p. 301; see also Bullough, p. 442. According to Payne and Romanoff, Lady Mary was at first intrigued by the idea of becoming an empress, but, after learning more about Ivan the Terrible, begged Queen Elizabeth to get her out of the situation. Elizabeth directed Pisemsky to explain to the Tsar that Lady Mary's ill health would not permit her to make the difficult journey to Moscow (p. 409).

Works Consulted

Berry, Lloyd E. and Robert O. Crummey, eds. *Rude & Barbarous Kingdom: Russia in the Accounts of Sixteenth-Century English Voyagers*. Madison: University of Wisconsin Press, 1968.

Bullough, Geoffrey, ed. *Narrative and Dramatic Sources of Shakespeare*, Vol. I. New York: Columbia University Press, 1957. *Love's Labour's Lost*, pp. 425–442.

Campbell, Oscar J. "*Love's Labour's Lost* Restudied," *Studies in Shakespeare, Milton and Donne*, ed. by Eugene S. McCartney. New York: Phaeton Press, 1970 (originally published 1925), pp. 1–45.

Clark, Cumberland. *Shakespeare and National Character*. New York: Haskell House Publishers, Ltd., 1972 (originally published 1932).

Clark, Eva Turner. *Hidden Allusions in Shakespeare's Plays*, 3rd revised edition, ed. by Ruth Loyd Miller. Jennings, LA: Minos Publishing, 1974 (first published in New York, W.F. Payson, 1931).

———. *The Satirical Comedy* Love's Labour's Lost. New York: William Farquhar Payson, 1933.

Cordasco, Francesco. *Don Adriano de Armado of* Love's Labour's Lost. Bologna: Facolta di Lettere e Filosofia, La Universita, 1950.

Cross, Anthony G. *The Russian Theme in English Literature: From the Sixteenth Century to 1980*. Oxford: Willem A. Meeuws, 1985.

Dallington, Robert. *The View of Fraunce*. Shakespeare Association Facsimiles No. 13, with an Introduction by W.P. Barrett. London: Humphrey Milforde, Oxford University Press, 1963 (originally published by Simon Stafford, 1604).

David, Richard. "Introduction," *Love's Labour's Lost* by William Shakespeare (The Arden Edition). London: Methuen, 1987, pp. xiii–xliv.

Frey, Albert R. *William Shakespeare and Alleged Spanish Prototypes*. New York: AMS Press, Inc., 1971 (originally published by Press of the New York Shakespeare Society, 1886).

Gervinus, G.G. *Shakespeare Commentaries*, trans. by F.E. Bunnett. New York: AMS Press, Inc., 1971 (originally published by Smith, Elder, 1877).

Graham, Winston. *The Spanish Armadas*. Garden City: Doubleday, 1972.

Hoenselaars, A.J. *Images of Englishmen and Foreigners in the Drama of Shakespeare and His Contemporaries*. Rutherford, NJ: Fairleigh Dickinson University Press, 1992.

Hunter, G.K. "Elizabethans and Foreigners," *Shakespeare Survey* 17 (1964), 37–52.

Lambin, Georges. "The Heir of Alanson, Katharine Her Name," *Shakespeare Authorship Review* (1959), 5–6.

———. *Voyages de Shakespeare en France et en Italie*. Geneva: Librairie E. Droz, 1962.

Lee, Sidney. *The French Renaissance in England: An Account of the Literary Relations of England and France in the Sixteenth Century*. New York: Octagon Books, 1968 (originally published by Clarendon Press, Oxford, 1910).

Lefranc, Abel. "Les Eléments français de 'Peines d'amour perdues' de Shakespeare," *Revue historique* 178 (1936), 411–432.

———. *Sous le masque de "William Shakespeare": William Stanley, VIe Comte de Derby*, 2 tomes. Paris: Payot et Cie., 1919.

Lievsay, John L. *The Elizabethan Image of Italy*. Ithaca: Cornell University Press (Folger Booklets on Tudor and Stuart Civilization), 1964.

———. "Shakespeare and Foreigners" in *William Shakespeare: His World, His Work, His Influence*, Vol. I, ed. by John F. Andrews. New York: Charles Scribner's Sons, 1985.

Looney, J. Thomas. *"Shakespeare" Identified*, 2 vols., 3rd edition, ed. by Ruth Loyd Miller. Jennings, LA: Minos Publishing, 1975.

Maltby, William S. *The Black Legend in England: The Development of Anti-Spanish Sentiment, 1558–1660*. Durham, NC: Duke University Press, 1971.

Marienstras, Richard. *New Perspectives on the Shakespearean World*, trans. by Janet Lloyd. New York: Cambridge University Press, 1985 (originally published as *Le Proche et le lointain*, Les Editions de Minuit, 1981.)

Ogburn, Dorothy and Charlton. *This Star of England*. New York: Coward-McCann, 1952.

Payne, Robert and Nikita Romanoff. *Ivan the Terrible*. New York: Thomas Y. Crowell, 1975.

Pearson, Hesketh. *Henry of Navarre: The King Who Dared*. Westport, CT: Greenwood Press, 1976 (originally published by Harper & Row, 1963).

Perry, Maria. *Elizabeth I: The Word of a Prince: A Life from Contemporary Documents*. London: The Folio Society, 1990.

Ralli, Augustus. *A History of Shakespearian Criticism*, Vol. I. New York: The Humanities Press, 1959 (first published by Oxford University Press), 1932.

Sells, A. Lytton. *The Italian Influence in English Poetry: From Chaucer to Southwell*. Bloomington: Indiana University Press, 1955.

Shakespeare, William. *Love's Labour's Lost,* ed. by R.W. David. London: Methuen (The Arden Shakespeare), 1987.

———. *Shakespeare's Plays in Quarto: A Facsimile Edition of Copies Primarily from the Henry E. Huntington Library*, ed. by Michael J.D. Allen and Kenneth Muir. Berkeley: University of California Press, 1981.

Ungerer, Gustav. *A Spaniard in Elizabethan England: The Correspondence of Antonio Perez's Exile*, 2 vols. London: Tamesis Books, 1974.

Valois, Marguerite de. *Mémoires et Lettres de Marguerite de Valois*, ed. by M.F. Guessard. Paris: Société de l'Histoire de France, 1842.

Wikander, Matthew H. *Princes to Act: Royal Audience and Royal Performance, 1578–1792*. Baltimore: Johns Hopkins University Press, 1993.

REVIEW OF THE DRAMATIC STUDENTS AT ST. JAMES'S THEATRE

Bernard Shaw

A performance of *Love's Labour's Lost* is a sort of entertainment to be valued rather for Shakespear's sake than for its own. The Dramatic Students did not tempt many people into the St. James's Theatre on the sultry afternoon of 2nd July by the experiment; and it is perhaps as well that they did not, for their efforts bore much the same relation to fine acting as the play does to *Antony and Cleopatra*. They failed not only in skill and finish, but in intelligence. Having gathered from their study of the play that they must all be very amusing and in desperately high spirits, they set to work to produce that effect by being obstreperous in action, and in speech full of the unnatural archness by which people with no sense of humor betray their deficiency when they desire to appear jocund. Though they devoutly believed the play a funny one, they did not see the joke themselves, and so, ill at ease in their merriment, forgot that dignity and grace may be presumed to have tempered the wit of the gentlemen of the Court of Navarre, and the vivacity of the ladies of the Court of France. In some scenes, consequently, the performance was like an Elizabethan version of *High Life Below Stairs*. I shall say nothing of the feminine parts, except that they were all unfortunately cast. The men were better. Mr. G.R. Foss as Boyet and Mr. Frank Evans as Holofernes were quite efficient; and Mr. Lugg as Costard, though as yet a raw actor and prone to overdo his business, enlivened the performance considerably by his fun and mimetic turn. He sang "When Icicles Hang by the Wall" with commendable spirit, and with the recklessness of a man who has got the tune on his ear and considers that it is the conductor's business to keep the band with the singer, which poor Herr Schoening tried gallantly to do, with more or less success. Mr. Bernard Gould and Mr. de

Originally published in *Our Corner* (1 August 1886). Reprinted by permission of The Society of Authors on behalf of the Bernard Shaw Estate.

Cordova, as Biron and Armado, were next best; but they made very little of their large share of the best opportunities of the afternoon. Mr. Gould's gaiety lacked dignity and variety: he swaggered restlessly, and frittered away all the music of his lines. His colleague looked Armado, but did not act him. Mr. de Cordova is always picturesque; but his elocution, correct as far as it goes, is monotonous; and the adaptability and subtlety which go to constitute that impersonative power which is the distinctive faculty of the actor are not at present apparent in him. His qualifications, so far, are those of an artist's model: he has yet to make himself an actor.

The play itself showed more vitality than might have been expected. Three hundred years ago, its would-be wits, with their forced smartness, their indecent waggeries, their snobbish sneers at poverty, and their ill-bred and ill-natured mockery of age and natural infirmity, passed more easily as ideal compounds of soldier, courtier, and scholar than they can nowadays. Among people of moderate culture in this century they would be ostracised as insufferable cads. Something of their taste survives in the puns and chaff of such plays as those of the late H.J. Byron, and even in the productions of so able a writer as Mr. Gilbert, who seems to consider a comic opera incomplete without a middle-aged woman in it to be ridiculed because she is no longer young and pretty. Most of us, it is to be hoped, have grace enough to regard Ruth, Lady Jane, Katisha and the rest as detestable blemishes on Mr. Gilbert's works. Much of *Love's Labour's Lost* is as objectionable and more tedious. Nothing, it seems to me, but a perverse hero-worship can see much to admire in the badinage of Biron and Rosaline. Benedick and Beatrice are better; and Orlando and Rosalind much better; still, they repeatedly annoy us by repartees of which the trivial ingenuity by no means compensates the silliness, coarseness, or malice. It is not until Shakespear's great period that began with the seventeenth century that, in *Measure for Measure*, we find this sort of thing shown in its proper light and put in its proper place in the person of Lucio, whose embryonic stages may be traced in Mercutio and Biron. Fortunately for *Love's Labour's Lost*, Biron is not quite so bad as Mercutio: you never absolutely long to kick him off the stage as you long to kick Mercutio when he makes game of the Nurse. And Shakespear, though a very feeble beginner then in comparison to the master he subsequently became, was already too far on the way to his greatness to fail completely when he set himself to write a sunny, joyous, and delightful play. Much of the verse is charming: even when it is rhymed doggrell it is full of that bewitching Shakespearean music which tempts the susceptible critic to sugar his ink and declare that Shakespear can do no wrong.

The construction of the play is simple and effective. The only absolutely impossible situation was that of Biron hiding in the tree to overlook the king, who presently hides to watch Longaville, who in turn spies on Dumain; as the result of which we had three out of four gentlemen shouting "asides" through the sylvan stillness, No. 1 being inaudible to 2, 3, and 4; no. 2 audible to No. 1, but not to 3 and 4; No. 3 audible to 1 and 2, but not to No. 4; and No. 4 audible to all the rest, but he himself temporarily stone deaf. Shakespear has certainly succeeded in making this arrangement intelligible; but the Dramatic Students' stage manager did not succeed in making it credible. For Shakespear's sake one can make-believe a good deal; but here the illusion was too thin. Matters might have been mended had Biron climbed among the foliage of the tree instead of affixing himself to the trunk in an attitude so precarious and so extraordinarily prominent that Dumain (or perhaps it was Longaville), though supposed to be unconscious of his presence, could not refrain from staring at him as if fascinated for several seconds. On the whole, I am not sure that *Love's Labour's Lost* is worth reviving at this time of day; but I am bound to add that if it were announced to-morrow with an adequate cast, I should make a point of seeing it.

REVIEW OF *LOVE'S LABOR'S LOST* AT DALY'S THEATRE

For the closing of a Winter term marked by uncommon activity, steadfast adherence to high artistic aims, and well-deserved prosperity, Mr. [Augustin] Daly last evening put forward on the stage of his theatre a well-arranged version of Shakespeare's earliest comedy—probably his first play—*Love's Labor's Lost*. The revival of this dainty, whimsical, fantastic work, never hitherto produced by any American manager except Mr. Daly, is intended to last a fortnight only. The actors of Daly's Theatre will start upon their annual tour of other cities after Saturday, April 11. But the luxury, costliness, and splendor of the production entitle it fairly to a hundred nights' run, and the refinement and good taste shown in every detail, and the beauty of the rendering of the poetry, ought to be potent enough to make it last a thousand.

Love's Labor's Lost is not one of the master's greatest works. It is not, indeed, great in any sense. It is merely, to employ the old phrase used to describe it in the first quarto, a "merry conceit." Of plot it has little, and that a palpable artifice; its humor, though still appreciable, is antique; much of its sentiment is elusive. But it has the touch of commanding genius. It could not be mistaken for the work of Greene or Shirley. Its elaborate euphemisms, manifestly intended to gently travesty the manner of John Lyly—the dramatist most esteemed by the Court of Elizabeth in Shakespeare's young manhood—have a poetic quality one must seek for in vain in the works of that pompous versifier.

There is little depth in its character drawing, and no complexity. Even gallant Biron, who speaks common sense as well as flowery sentiment, is not a man we get to know well. The sumptuous Princess of France and the gracious King of Navarre are little more than ingeniously devised puppets,

From the *New York Times* (29 March 1891), 4.

349

magnificently clothed, gifted with musical speech, but without real feeling. Rosaline is a younger, shadowy Beatrice, but without the heart of Beatrice. There is not a note of pathos in the play. But it has the buoyant grace of youth, the delicate fragrance of the Spring. Its charm is irresistible, and twice in his honorable career our foremost theatrical manager has proved the wise commentators of the ages wrong by showing that it is a good play—one worthy of good acting, worth seeing, worth the attention and labor of any manager not bent upon following the noisy common herd in their search of the trivial and the vulgar.

The production of *Love's Labor's Lost* at Daly's Theatre last evening was brilliantly successful. The house was crowded. A distinguished audience accepted the performance eagerly with many manifestations of delight.

In its pictorial features the production is a worthy rival of the representations of other Shakespearean plays on this stage. Indeed, no handsomer setting of a play by Shakespeare was ever seen in this country—or in any other, probably. Every picture is a noble example of the scene painter's art. The finest skill of the electrician and the mechanical workers of the theatre is employed to produce the spectacular effects with which the production abounds, never, however, to the lessening of the higher aesthetic effect striven for by a company of well-trained actors. The incidental music, rendered by many voices, is appropriate and beautiful. In the last act there is a dissolving view. The frozen landscape of Winter changes to an ideal view of Spring, and incidentally the icicle song and the cuckoo song—which belong to this play and not to *As You Like It*—are sung by John McCauley and Kitty Cheatham. The closing picture recalls the now famous Paul Veronese tableau in *The Taming of the Shrew*, but it has more depth and greater variety than that. The other views in the park and about the palace of Navarre, by sunlight and moonlight, are richly suggestive, excellent in design, harmonious in coloring. The scenery was painted by James Roberts and Lafayette Seavey. The costumes were designed by Hamilton Bell.

The play has been arranged in four acts, and the text has been carefully scanned, with reference to the best authorities. Of course it has been greatly reduced, in the sentimental passages and the comic interludes as well, but more of it could be spared. The piece, as it was presented last night, dragged in the middle of the third act—just before the bright passages of wit known to the students of Shakespeare as the orchard scene. Mr. Harry Edwards is a good actor, but he has no such fund of personal humor as William Davidge had, and his Holofernes is a performance more pedantic than the pedantry that person is intended to satirize. Mr. Leclercq looks like Sir Nathaniel, and would be acceptable if, like Juliet in the balcony, he would speak, yet say nothing. The long scene between these two might be further shortened without lack of reverence.

While in the mood for objections, just a word of protest may be uttered against the too demonstrative horse-play of the Nine Worthies episode. There were "groundlings" in Shakespeare's day whose ears the deviser of stage entertainments was compelled to tickle. There are hosts of them today, but you cannot touch them with Shakespearean comedy even when it is combined with horse-play. Horse-play is here used in its literal sense. The meaning of the word is aptly illustated in the comic pageant.

Miss Rehan as the Princess of France is regally beautiful, and she lends to the flowing verse, with its juvenile rhymes, the matchless melody of her voice. She has little more to do, but the very best actor should not always have the very best part. Mr. Drew is perhaps less happy as the whimsical King of Navarre; he is not beautiful, in his straight Florentine wig and beard, but he renders his share of the text with his accustomed taste and skill.

The best parts in the piece fall to the lot of Mr. George Clarke as Biron, Miss Edith Crane as Rosaline, and Mr. Sidney Herbert as Armado. Of these Mr. Clarke, a thoughtful and finished artist, gains the greatest triumph. He received the only individual curtain call last night for his rendering of Biron's glowing tribute to the power of love, a discreet and effective example of elocution.

Mr. Herbert has personal humor and a keen understanding, but he has not yet the authority, the mellowness of speech, the breadth of style needful to play Armado as Charles Fisher played the part. His performance is neat and well considered, but no deeper in meaning and scarcely richer in humor than the nimble, sprightly performance of Armado's page, Moth, by Miss Ethel, which was warmly applauded last night. Miss Crane's acting as Rosaline may have a definite artistic purpose. She is a pretty woman.

Mr. Lewis lends his fund of dry humor to the part of Costard, Miss Cheatham is Jaquenetta, Mr. Wheatleigh is Boyet, and the other parts are in competent hands. The ensemble is perfect. This production of *Love's Labor's Lost* is commended to the public attention. The play cannot often be seen, is worth seeing, and all its poetic beauty, buoyant spirits, humor, and sentiment are preserved.

IMITATIONS

THE STUDENTS, 1762

Horace Howard Furness

In 1762 there was published in London *The Students. A Comedy Altered from 'Shakespeare's Love's Labour's Lost, and Adapted to the Stage.'* The author is unknown, which is probably merciful. Genest says that it does not seem "to have been ever acted,"[1] which is certainly merciful.

The Prologue concludes with the assertion that—

> All *Congreve's* wit, the polish'd scenes require,
> All *Farquhar's* humour, and all *Hoadly's* fire.
> Our bard, advent'ring to the comic land,
> Directs his choice by *Shakespeare's* happier hand;
> *Shakespeare!* who warms with more than magic art,
> Enchants the ear, whilst he instructs the heart;
> Yet should he fail, he hopes, the wits will own,
> There's enough of *Shakespeare's* still, to please the town.

The *Dramatis Personae* reveal that Holofernes and Sir Nathaniel are not included in this "enough," and that Costard becomes a "Clown belonging to the King," and Jaquenetta one of the Princess's Ladies.

The first positive alteration on which "our bard" ventures is to represent the Princess and her Ladies as resolved to "practice all their little arts" to rouse Navarre and his friends from the "lethargy" of a "life so dull, and so unsociable" as that which they have sworn to follow. Rosaline enters eagerly into the plan, and announces that

> we'll teach our eyes to glance,
> Our tongues to rail; sometimes a sudden blush

Published as an appendix in *Love's Labour's Lost: A New Variorum Edition*, edited by Horace Howard Furness (J.B. Lippincott Co., 1904), pp. 378–380.

Shall damask o'er our cheeks, as if surprised
We had been caught with gazing at them:
Then we'll be coy, and difficult of speech,
Then free and affable, to commend their studies;
Till we perceive, we've touch'd their gentle hearts,
And then—I need not tell the rest.

When, however, Navarre and his companions visit the princess, the sight of Biron seems to have put to flight from Rosaline's mind all these excellent maxims. Mark the following gay and sprightly dialogue:

ROSALINE. Pray, sir, what's your study?
BIRON. Books, madam. What a face! what eyes!
ROSALINE. Sir!
BIRON. Yes, madame, there is undoubtedly much rational amusement
    in books. Study polishes our manners, enlarges our ideas,
    improves—What a delicate shape!
ROSALINE. Sir!
BIRON. Study, I say, madam, improves our understanding, calms our
    passion, sweetens the afflictions of life. In short, fair lady,
    love refines the man. Love—
ROSALINE. Love! Sir, you mean study—ha! ha! ha! but we are observed.
BIRON. Ah me!

"Our bard" follows Shakespeare in giving another short conversation between Rosaline and Biron, in which the vivacious lady responds to Biron's exclamation that he is "sick at heart":

ROSALINE. Study is an excellent medicine.
BIRON. What, how to win your favour?
ROSALINE. No, abstinence, and the pale midnight lamp,
    Will cure this raging fever in your blood.
BIRON. For once I'll follow your advice, so fare you well.
    Exit.

This seems to be one of the turning points of the comedy. Biron in mistrust of Rosaline's love determines to visit the Princess's pavilion in disguise. He waylays a Clown, named Timothy Clod (his name is not in the *Dramatis Personae*) who is carrying home to Costard a suit of clothes. This suit Biron purchases from Timothy, and, disguised in it, acts as the messenger of the Duke, Dumain, and Longaville in carrying their letters and sonnets to the Princess's pavilion. There is, of course, neither letter nor sonnet for Rosaline, and the disguised Biron "makes free to listen" to the confessions of love for the Duke and his companions made by the Princess and her ladies, and also to the teasing speeches when they twit Rosaline about her neglected state, and also to Rosaline's attempt to laugh off her chagrin.

In the fifth act there is no announcement of the death of the Princess's father, and when the Duke, Dumain, and Longaville (Biron is present still disguised as Costard) demand the loves of the girls of France, they are put off, as in Shakespeare, with a twelvemonth's penance. Then it is that Biron proves the hero of the hour; doffing his disguise, he confounds the ladies by bringing home to them their own confessions of love which he had overheard. Turning to Catherine, he asks, "Can you deny this charge?" Then ensues the following dialogue:

> CATHERINE. Biron, I know
>> Your humour is as keen as polish'd steel,
>> But wit, my lord, may over-shoot itself.
> BIRON. Then each man to his mistress [the logical connection of
>> thought is not here quite apparent] and he that cannot win
>> her, deserves her not. Rosaline, your hand!
> ROSALINE. But not my heart.
> BIRON. Nay, prithee, child, no affectation now—
>> Believe me too, I am a fickle swain,
>> I am not used to love whole months or years.
> ROSALINE. A man, my lord, who cannot love a year,
>> Is ne'er entitled to a woman's love;
>> A man, my lord, who will not be a slave
>> To all the fickle humours of a woman,
>> Now cringing, fawning, begging, suing, praying,
>> Now dying, sighing, languishing, despairing,
>> Can never hope to win a woman's love.
> BIRON. Have mercy, Lord—how mad these women are!
> ROSALINE. These, Sir, and twenty other things like these,
>> So strange and so fantastical we are,
>> You must endure with patience.
> BIRON. I must—
>> Madam, farewell, I humbly take my leave;
>> I shall offend no more—

ROSALINE. Nay, Biron, stay—
    I meant—
BIRON. And I mean too—
ROSALINE. What! what! my lord!
BIRON. Never again to think of womankind.
ROSALINE. Perhaps, Sir—
BIRON. Madam, speak on—
ROSALINE. Cannot you guess?
BIRON. I have no judgment, madam, in divining.
ROSALINE. Perhaps—I was joking.
BIRON. Then, madame, your hand, and with your hand your heart;
    To France I will attend you.

No one will begrudge, I think, the time spent in reading the wooing, just quoted, so robust, and, withal, so arch. But any more time devoted to this stuff, the present Editor does feelingly begrudge; his purpose in offering the foregoing abstract is attained if he may thereby crush every emotion of envy which might otherwise be awakened over his possession of this deservedly scarce play.

NOTES

1. P. Genest, *The English Stage, 1660–1830* Vol. 10 (Bath, 1832), p. 180.

REVIEW OF *PEINES D'AMOUR PERDUES* AT THE ODÉON

FROM LE MONDE

Robert Kemp

A King and three Jacks, clever lords. . . matched by four "Queens."
Shakespeare's comedy is a deck of cards. After dealing us the eight faces and
briefly shuffling them, he sets about getting them properly paired. At the
same time, it's like a quadrille, or like dancing wind-up toys, or like . . .
whatever you like.

It's well known that this piece of whimsy is the key element in Abel
Lefranc's case against the man from Stratford. If this royal court is truly that
at Nérac, if this King is our Henri IV and this Princess our effervescent
Margot, how could the young, unlettered, working-class Shakespeare, unfamiliar with France and its courtly poetry, have contrived such highly refined repartee and have made the gentlemen babble at such length? And how
could he . . . but let's not get carried away on that subject!

I've resolved to make a shameful confession! Despite the number of
times I've tackled this famous play, both in English and in translation, I've
never succeeded in reading it all the way through. My most energetic resolutions always dissolved in irritation. Oh, I don't deny that the dialogue has
its grace notes, its sensuous charms, its Euphuism, and its caricature. I admit that it's a sprightly ballet of wits. It can evoke a bit of Don Quixote,
maybe some Gongora, maybe Marot, and can even take you by surprise with
some touches of Marivaux. And yet. . . I couldn't do it.

So I reserved a ticket for the Odéon, for M. Dapoigny's adaptation,
his pruning, his delicate surgery. And the show, while not totally enraptur-
ing, does amuse and lifts one's spirits. We see privileged people under a clear
sky expressing their lightweight philosophy, their idle chat honed and pol-

Originally published as *"Peines d'amour perdues* à l'Odéon," *Le Monde* (26 January
1946), 7. Translated from the French by Felicia Londré especially for this volume.
Reprinted by permission of *Le Monde*.

ished to a fine sheen, dressed as appetizingly as fresh fruits, with young faces and mellifluous voices.

Alongside the eight dancers of the quadrille are the buffoons, and there is the culminating pageant which foreshadows that of *A Midsummer Night's Dream*. And the dancing peasants are as sanitized as those of the *opéra-comique*.

M.R. Peignet painted the fresh green bowers and white balustrades, not so much inspired by nature itself—certainly not by nature as it exists in Gascony—as designed for vibrant upholstery fabric; it's bracing to the eye. The King's white suit, the strawberry and currant reds of the jerkins, the dresses trimmed in rainbow colors, all gaily put on a display. M. Gaston Girard (Biron) is the best actor. But I wouldn't detract from the others: Messieurs Guillet, Morange, Gallon; the delightful Costard, M. Raoul Henry. Nor from the ladies: Mesdames Dargent, Harmina, Coeur; Mlle. Cardi as Jacquenetta, and above all, Mlle. Janeval as the tiny page, Moth.

I could not have been very bored last night if I'm so full of praise this morning! And I almost forgot the music, with its sixteenth-century resonances, by M. Cadou.

Review of *Peines d'amour perdues* at the Odéon

From *La Vie intellectuelle*

Henri Gouhier

Love's Labour's Lost appeared in 1598 with the notice: *newly corrected and augmented*. It is generally accepted that the original version of the play is Shakespeare's first work and would have been performed around 1591. The text that we know thus represents a revision. From it M. Jacques Dapoigny has made a "free adaptation" for the Odéon.

Very free, indeed. The comedy is closely tied to a historical situation chosen to suit the interests of its contemporaries. Mme. Longworth-Chambrun evokes a Shakespeare writing his play for an England that was becoming "increasingly interested in France, in the wake of the alliance negotiated with Henri IV," naming his characters "after names that were becoming known through the gazettes": Biron, Longueville, du Maine, friends of the king of Navarre. And then, "thanks to new treaties of commerce, the public's interest in Muscovy was awakened," so Shakespeare gave them a Russian interlude. His criticism of puffery targeted a well-known figure in London, and pedantry was mocked in the person of an Italian scholar, Giovanni Florio, here given a name borrowed from Rabelais: Holofernes.[1] Certainly, the French theatregoing public of 1946 isn't going to find much fun in those aspects of *Love's Labour's Lost*.[2] But what remains will suffice to justify this adaptation and even a more faithful adaptation: this Act V is as much the product of the translator as it is of the author.

A king and three friends decide to devote themselves to study for three years. They renounce all the pleasures of the world as well as interaction with women. The daughter of the king of France arrives, charged with a diplomatic mission. Three maids of honor accompany her. Our humanist scholars become more human than the statutes of their Academy allow. It all con-

---

Originally published as "Théâtre," *La Vie intellectuelle* 14 (March 1946), p. 131. Translated from the French especially for this volume by Felicia Londré. Reprinted from *La Vie intellectuelle* by permission of Les Editions du Cerf.

cludes with the promise of four marriages after the test of one year's time. It also ends with songs. A very "Renaissance" style comedy, *Love's Labour's Lost* leads us into a cosmopolitan world, mocking pedantry in the name of naturalness and a contemplative ideal in the name of nature.

This is one of the best productions staged by the Odéon since the Liberation, though it might have been better not to orient the adaptation and the staging toward Second Empire–style operetta. M. André Cadou's music sets the appropriate "Renaissance" tone. Given my reservation, it must be said that the costumes are pretty, the stage business delightful, and the performances superior to those we've been seeing.

Notes

1. *Shakespeare, acteur-poète* (Paris: Librairie Plon, 1926), pp. 86–87, 127 ff., 243–244.

2. The title is based on an Italian proverb: *Parler d'amour, c'est peine perdue* (To speak of love is labour lost).

From *The Shifting Point*

Peter Brook

One of the first productions of Shakespeare that I did was *Love's Labour's Lost*, and at that point I felt and believed the work of a director was to have a vision of a play and to "express" it. I thought that's what a director was for. I was nineteen or twenty. I had always wanted to direct films, and in fact I started in films before going into the theatre. A film director shows his pictures to the world, and I thought a stage director did the same in another way. . . .

When I did *Love's Labour's Lost*, I had a set of images in mind which I wanted to bring to life, just like making a film. So *Love's Labour's Lost* was a very visual, very romantic set of stage pictures. And I remember that from then all the way through to *Measure for Measure* my conviction was that the director's job, having found an affinity between himself and the play, was to find the images that he believed in and through them make the play live for a contemporary audience. In an image-conscious time, I believed designing and lighting to be inseparable. . . .

. . . When I directed Shakespeare's *Measure for Measure* in 1956, I thought the director's job was to create an image which would allow the audience to enter into the play, and so I reconstructed the worlds of Bosch and Brueghel, just as I had followed Watteau in directing *Love's Labour's Lost* in 1950 [sic]. It seemed to me then that I should try to produce a striking set of fluid pictures to serve as a bridge, between the play and the audience.

When I studied the text of *Love's Labour's Lost*, I was struck by something that seemed to me to be self-evident, but which at the time seemed to be unheard of: that when, at the very end of the last scene, a new, unexpected character called Mercade came on, the whole play changed its tone entirely.

From *The Shifting Point: Theatre, Film, Opera, 1946–1987* (New York: Harper & Row, 1987), pp. 78, 11–12. Reprinted by permission of Harper & Row, Publishers.

He came on bringing death. And as I felt intuitively that the image of the Watteau world was very close to this, I began to see that the reason that the Watteau *Age of Gold* is so particularly moving is that although it's a picture of springtime, it's an autumn springtime, because every one of Watteau's pictures has an incredible melancholy. And if one looks, one sees that in Watteau (unlike the imitations of the period, where it's all sweetness and prettiness) there is usually a dark figure somewhere, standing with his back to you, and some people say he is Watteau himself. But there's no doubt that the dark touch gives the dimension to the whole piece.

And it was through this that I brought Mercade over a rise at the back of the stage—it was evening, the lights were going down, and suddenly there appeared a man in black. The man in black came onto a very pretty summery stage, with everybody in pale pastel Watteau and Lancret costumes, and golden lights dying. It was very disturbing, and at once the whole audience felt that the world had been transformed.

ARMADO'S "YOU THAT WAY; WE THIS WAY"

James Hisao Kodama

The English Department of Gakushuin University chose *Love's Labour's Lost* for its thirteenth annual Shakespearean production, which was given on sixteenth and seventeenth of May, 1968. This choice was rather strange, because the play does not come within the usual repertory of Japanese students' theatrical groups. Most probably, it had never before been presented by Japanese actors, either professional or amateur, either in the English language or in a Japanese translation.

We met with many difficulties. Among them, not the least was the interpretation of the last sentence of the play:

> The Words of Mercurie,
> Are harsh after the songs of Apollo:
> You that way; we this way.[1]

There was a time when the attention of scholars was focussed on the possible topical allusions in *Love's Labour's Lost*, and we can now get fairly adequate knowledge of the background of the play from such books and articles as H.B. Charlton's "The Date of *Love's Labour's Lost* (1918),[2] Austin K. Gray's "The Secret of *Love's Labour's Lost*" (1924),[3] Rupert Taylor's *The Date of* Love's Labour's Lost (1932),[4] and Frances A. Yates's *A Study of* Love's Labour's Lost (1936).[5] We may add Professor M.C. Bradbrook's *The School of Night* (1936)[6] in which her elucidation of the intellectual milieu of the day is very inspiring. We now know that Berowne, Longaville, and Dumain—three young noblemen who make an oath to study in seclusion for three years—are named after the French lords who were fighting for or

Originally published in *Shakespeare Studies* 8 (Tokyo: Shakespeare Society of Japan, 1969–70), 1–17. Reprinted by permission.

against Henry of Navarre. We now know that there is a great possibility that Armado is a portrait (or caricature) of either Sir Walter Raleigh, Gabriel Harvey, or a Spaniard named Antonio Pérez.[7] These pieces of knowledge, though valuable in themselves, cannot help us much in the production of the play. Nowadays we cannot expect audiences to be able to apprehend the subtle relationship between Navarre, Berowne, Longaville, and Dumain on the stage and the historical personages in the French civil wars of the sixteenth century. Many will be embarrassed to understand why Sir Walter Raleigh, whom we know as the introducer of tobacco to the Old World, should be satirized under the form of Armado the Braggart. I believe this unfamiliarity of the audience with such matters is not very different in England or in Japan. After all, the play was written more than three and a half centuries ago.

It seems to me that the recent studies of the play lay special emphasis on its closing scene. Probably this new interest among the critics goes hand in hand with the revival of this play on the stage since the crucial days of the 1930s. In the gathering storm which foreboded the approach of disaster for the world, people became more susceptible to the fear of the ominous intruder who might at any moment come and snatch away their life and mirth.[8] Shakespeare writes in one of his sonnets that "Love's not Time's fool."[9] At the opening of this play, Shakespeare lets Navarre declare a challenge to the tyranny of all-devouring Time.

> Let fame, that all hunt after in their lives,
> Live register'd upon our brazen tombs,
> And then grace us in the disgrace of death;
> When, spite of cormorant devouring Time,
> Th' endeavour of this present breath may buy
> That honour which shall bate his scythe's keen edge. (I.1.1–6)

But Fame in this sense will depart from him, and Time will make a fool of him within two hours' traffic on the stage. If anything attracts modern minds to this satirical court-play of the 1590s, it will be the sudden entrance of Death in the midst of the gorgeous and youthful merriment in the court of Navarre.

In the student production at Gakushuin University, the announcement of the death of the King of France was emphasized by the sudden darkening of the stage and the Princess's fainting.

The Princess soon recovers, but to the disappointment of the King of Navarre and his followers, she makes up her mind to return home soon, and orders a sudden departure.

KING. How fares your majesty?
PRINCESS. Boyet, prepare: I will away to-night.
KING. Madam, not so; I do beseech you, stay.
PRINCESS. Prepare, I say. . . .
　　　　. . . Farewell, worthy lord!
A heavy heart bears not a humble tongue. (V.2.716–727)

The love-game has suddenly come to an end. There will be no more teasing and bantering. The time for love's verdict has come.

We know what kind of sentences are given to Navarre, Berowne, and the two other lords in this assize. Navarre is to go to "some forlorn and naked hermitage,"[10] and remain there for one year, discarding all the pleasures of the world. He should not spend his time in the pursuit of the vainglorious fame by being a scholarly king. He is not allowed to laugh away his time by thinking himself a better person than such a braggadocio as Don Adriano de Armado.[11] He must not belittle others. He himself must be belittled. Contemplation and contrition are to be his ordeal.

Berowne's trial will be a little different. He too is assigned one year's penance before he can sue for the hand of Rosaline; but, his is not a year of seclusion. Instead, he is ordered to spend one year in a hospital, visiting "the speechless sick," and pleasing "groaning wretches" by his witty conversation.[12] He is ordered to use his ready wit, which has hitherto been a pride to himself and a deadly weapon against his neighbors, to give consolation to the sick and the forlorn.

Dumain and Longaville are to endure one year's penance and patience, too. Such sentences are passed in the court of love's justice, and the session is closed. It is highly satirical that the play, which opens with the prosecution of Costard for having transgressed the proclamation against love, ends with the passing of judgment on the King and his peers by their lovers. The honorable judges of the beginning of the play are now standing as defendants in front—and at the mercy—of these beautiful judges.

At the beginning of the play, these lords believed that they should cast off amorous desire in order to devote themselves to study. But now they are obliged to realize that they must be purged of their vanity and selfishness before they may enter the garden of love.

Our perspective will not be complete if we ignore the fact that Shakespeare was conscious of the long tradition of courtly love when he wrote this play. We are not certain how far he was immersed in this tradition. Sometimes he seems to have enjoyed its conventional feminine supremacy quite naïvely. Many times he was a heretic, and critical of the formalism of love courtesies. Still, his belief in the purifying power of romantic love lasted to the end of his dramatic career. In *Love's Labour's Lost*, though the courtships meet with abrupt interruption due to the arrival of sad news, the spirit of romance never dies; for instead of accepting their votaries' professed love, the ladies give them ordeals of love and make them go on a pilgrimage to fulfill severe conditions in order to be worthy lovers to them.[13]

It is a misleading, though not utterly mistaken, idea that the theme of this play is the recovery of men's natural instinct, for the verdicts which the ladies pass on their lovers seem to me as unnatural as the young men's oath to study three years without meeting any women. Not to see a lover for one year may appear to be an unbearable self-punishment to modern eyes. To prohibit the access of her lover for one year—that is to say, to endure his absence for one year—appears no less absurd an act than the rules of Navarre's little academe. Unless we admit the undercurrent of the romantic tradition in this play, we are unable to understand its meaning.

The ladies are wise in giving reasons for their decision. The Princess says,

> If frosts and fasts, hard lodging and thin weeds,
> Nip not the gaudy blossoms of your love,
> But that it bear this trial and last love;
> Then at the expiration of the year,
> Come challenge me, challenge me by these deserts,
> And, by this virgin palm now kissing thine,
> I will be thine. (V.2.791–797)

She is well aware that Time will exercise a sobering effect on the fanatical excitement of a lover's mind and cool off the heated impetuosity of his desire; she also is aware that Time is not so cruel as to take away her maidenly beauty within this short period.

And Rosaline proves to be a better wit than Berowne when she says,

> A jest's prosperity lies in the ear
> Of him that hears it, never in the tongue
> Of him that makes it. . . . (V.2.851–853)

She continues her speech, and challenges him to try if his jokes have any power to gladden the ears of sick persons.

> . . . then, if sickly ears,
> Deaf'd with the clamours of their own dear groans,

Will hear your idle scorns, continue then,
And I will have you and that fault withal;
But if they will not, throw away that spirit,
And I shall find you empty of that fault,
Right joyful of your reformation. (V.2.853–859)

Whether the patients that lie sleepless on the beds in a hospital will find solace in his talk or not remains, of course, beyond the reach of our knowledge. But we can surely smile when we paint on the canvas of imagination the figure of Berowne, perplexed as to how to make the saddest patient laugh by the skill of his wit and shrewdness. And his reply to Rosaline, though resolute and audacious, sounds quite comical.

A twelvemonth! well, befall what will befall,
I'll jest a twelvemonth in an hospital. (V.2.860–861)

It is necessary to notice the use of the rhyming couplet here. Berowne has been frustrated but not overcome. He is the first to own his defeat but the last to give up his resistance. He tries to turn his defeat into a jest. See the use of rhyme in the following conversation:

PRINCESS. Ay, sweet my lord; and so I take my leave.
KING. No, madam; we will bring you on your way.
BEROWNE. Our wooing doth not end like an old play;
    Jack hath not Jill: these ladies' courtesy
    Might well have made our sport a comedy.
KING. Come, sir, it wants a twelvemonth and a day,
    And then 'twill end.
BEROWNE.   That's too long for a play. (V.2.862–868)

His nimble spirit of joking will never leave him. I expect he will remain a satirist and humourist till the end of his life. Whether he will be successful in his courtship, or remain a bachelor for life does not matter much to me— but this is indeed a story "too long for a play."

What I should like to ask is whether the ladies are wiser than the young lords. Certainly they are the winners; they become the judges in the court of love's justice; but it does not necessarily mean that their state is any better than their lovers', for the next moment, there enters on the stage one more love-sick knight, Don Adriano de Armado, who tells them that he is going to marry a country girl.

This declaration of Armado's should be presented on the stage as impressively as that of Marcade, for it is the opening of one more phase in the finale of this comedy. His speech is short, but effective.

> I will kiss thy royal finger, and take leave. I am a votary; I
> have vowed to Jaquenetta to hold the plough for her sweet love
> three year. (V.2.872–874)

Mathematically, three years' service is three times as long as the one year's penance which the young lords have promised to their lovers; and that length will be sufficient to make up for the breaking of their common oath to keep out of the company of women for three years. At the last moment, the ladies and the lords are surpassed by the resoluteness of this bragging knight.

More important is the fact that Armado is most probably going to marry Jaquenetta without delay—she is already "two months on her way."[14] I do not know whose child she is going to geve birth to.[15] But certainly he is happy, for happiness chiefly depends upon what he himself thinks the matter to be. I believe the Elizabethan audience also took this marriage as a triumph, and not as a punishment. I understand that marriage is not always a happy ending in Shakespearean comedies; for instance, at the end of *Measure for Measure*, Lucio the Braggart is forced to marry a woman who is his mistress and the mother of his illegitimate child. He is discouraged, and complains in vain,

> Marrying a punk, my lord, is pressing to death, whipping, and
> hanging. (V.1.528–529)

But the tone of the finale of *Love's Labour's Lost* is quite different from the gloomy *dénouement* of that dark comedy. In this play that ends with the antiphony between Spring and Winter, the punishment named "Marriage" can hardly enter. Most of us feel happy when Armado the Bridegroom serves as chorus-master to this antiphony.

He introduces the singers to the ladies and the lords:

> This side is *Hiems*, Winter, this *Ver*, the Spring; the one
> maintained by the owl, the other by the cuckoo. (V.2.881–882)

From this description, we may infer fairly certainly that the two groups of country folk are symmetrically situated on the stage, dividing it into the right and the left. Suppose that the right side is occupied by *Hiems*, and left by *Ver*. Armado, when he introduces *Hiems*, probably stands on the right side of the stage; then, he moves to the left side, where he introduces *Ver* to all. There he orders, "*Ver*, begin!" (V.2.883). And the song of "Spring" begins.

> When daisies pied and violets blue
>> And lady-smocks all silver-white
> And cuckoo-buds of yellow hue
>> Do paint the meadows with delight,
> The cuckoo then, on every tree,
> Mocks married men; for thus sings he,
>> Cuckoo;
> Cuckoo, cuckoo: O word of fear,
> Unpleasing to a married ear! (V.2.884–892)

A lovely song with pastoral beauty—yet Moth may call it "a dangerous rhyme"[16] because of its uncanny reference to "cuckoo" and "word of fear, / Unpleasing to a married ear!"

Then comes the song of "Winter."

> When icicles hang by the wall,
> And Dick the shepherd blows his nail,
>> And Tom bears logs into the hall,
> And milk comes frozen home in pail,
> When blood is nipp'd, and ways be foul,
> Then nightly sings the staring owl,
>> Tu-whit;
> Tu-who, a merry note,
> While greasy Joan doth keel the pot. (V.2.902–910)

Here is described the hard and severe life of poor shepherds. The father and son are working outdoors, while the housewife, Joan, is cooking their supper indoors. The coldness is overwhelming; still, we are certain that the fire in the hall where Joan cooks will never go out, and the logs will never run short as long as Tom works. Moreover, they will remain happy and healthy till they grow old.

Before this song begins, Armado may have crossed the stage so as to conduct the *Hiems* group, standing to the right of the stage. And this, I presume, is the position where he speaks his last and enigmatic words:

The Words of Mercurie,
Are harsh after the songs of Apollo:
You that way; we this way.

Who can boast that he knows the true meaning of this riddling sentence? In the First Quarto of this play which was published in 1598, this sentence was printed in larger type than the rest of the text, and the last part "You that way; we this way" was lacking. J. Dover Wilson in his New Cambridge edition of the play (1923) followed suit, and printed "The words of Mercury are harsh after the songs of Apollo" in larger type. His commentary reads,

> . . . the compositor would hardly have troubled to take out a fresh case of type unless he had a strong leading in his "copy." No one has explained the sentence hitherto; and we make no attempt, beyond suggesting that words, written in a large hand at the end of Shakespeare's manuscript, may conceivably have been a comment on the play by someone to whom he had lent it for perusal.[17]

In the revised second edition of 1962, however, he dropped his hypothesis that the last part might be a "comment on the play" by someone else, and inserted instead Sir E.K. Chambers"s commentary that these words may be "the beginning of an epilogue or of a presenter"s speech for a following mask,"[18] as well as Professor Schrickx"s theory that "Mercury" (Hermes) stands for Chapman"s hermeneutic philosophy.[19] If the latter be the case, "the sentence is a hinted comparison between the crabbed obscurity of Chapman and the limpidity of Shakespeare," J. Dover Wilson deduced.[20]

In the New Arden edition of the play (1951), Mr. Richard David is also careful in editing this sentence. He follows the New Cambridge edition and adopts the First Quarto reading. He says, "the Folio addition [i.e., "You that way; we this way"] was perhaps made by the stage-manager to ensure a tidy *Exeunt*."[21]

There are, nevertheless, several scholars to whom "You that way; we this way" appears to belong to the genuine text. Thus Professor John R. Brown writes,

> Armado has been forced to forget his fanciful, self-created nobility and to recognize a plain man's desire for a plain "Maid," the "base wench," Jaquenetta (I.2.62 and 139–140). This leads him to find his

true degree in society, for, after he has attemped to play his part as a Worthy, he leaves the stage to follow the plough with the "simple" folk: "You that way," he seems to tell the courtiers, and "we this way."[22]

And he gives the following footnote to this part.

These words occur only in the Folio; some editors consider them to be an unintelligent correction of the abrupt conclusion of the Quarto text, but, if the ideal of order is recognized in this play, their appropriateness may attest their authenticity.[23]

I doubt whether Professor Brown has paid due regard to the fact that Armado's pledge "to hold the plough for her sweet love" lasts only for three years.[24] After the lapse of this length of time, he may come back to the court to be a courtier once again. But this is a small point here. What is of importance is the fact that Professor Brown sees the figure of Jaquenetta standing beside Armado on the stage, for if we follow his interpretation, "we" chiefly means here "Jaquenetta and I." If we are right in our supposition that Armado is standing to the right of the stage and near the *Hiems* group, it will also be right to suppose that Jaquenetta belongs to that singing group—is probably the prima donna of the group. That she is among the members who sing ". . . while greasy Joan doth keel the pot," seems to me suggestive, because, though she may now appear young, gay, and slender, she surely has every qualification for becoming a "greasy Joan" when she grows to be a middle-aged housewife.

What is meant by "You that way; we this way"? Let us first examine the meaning of "you" and "we" in this context.

First, is it possible that they mean "the French Princess and her retinue" (i.e., you) and "the King of Navarre and his subjects" (i.e., we). The Princess has already ordered departure (V.2.717), and is just about to start (V.2.862), when Armado comes in with the country folk. It is natural that the end of the songs should be the time for their leaving. But there remains the question whether a courtier of such low rank (or a courtier no more) as Armado can give directions to the train of the French Princess. Boyet may do it,[25] but anyone who dares to do it had better be prepared for the ensuing resentment of the King of Navarre and his peers—and perhaps of the French Princess and her maids of honor, too.

Secondly, they may mean "the courtiers" (i.e., you) and "the common people" (i.e., we). This is probably the most popular interpretation, and the one which was adopted by the late Dr. Shōyō Tsubouchi in his Japanese translation of this play (1926). The problem remains. If the words indicate their exeunt according to their class-divisions, it is improper that the order should be given by one who belongs to the lower class. Berowne may do it, but Armado may not do it without unnaturalness. Besides, the courtiers are, in fact, in two groups, and the group of the French Princess is to leave Navarre presently. It is more natural that not only the noblemen but also the commoners of Navarre should see them off.

Thirdly, they may mean "the *Ver* group of singers" (i.e., you) and "the *Hiems* group of singers" (i.e., we). This interpretation avoids the clumsiness of Armado's being the director of all those present on the stage. The common folk have come on the stage by Armado's order, and there is no reason why they should not depart also by his order. Still, it seems to me highly problematic that the commoners would disappear from the stage earlier and leave the nobility unattended, which would surely weaken the stage-effect of the last scene. If we take this interpretation and want to avoid this defect, only one conceivable solution is left. Let the French ladies and Navarrese lords retire during the songs. But then, what is meant by "The words of Mercury are harsh after the songs of Apollo"?

The fourth interpretation is to take the words as a kind of epilogue spoken directly to the audience. Then, "you" means "the audience," and "we" means "the actors." And the meaning of the sentence is, "It is a pity that we should say 'Good-bye' after the play. Please go back home, as we retire into the greenroom."

There remains one more interpretation; and we adopted it in our annual Shakespeare production of 1968. We took "you" to indicate the four pairs of noble ladies and lords. We took this "we" to mean only "Jaquenetta and Armado." The contrast between those four pairs and this couple is manifest. The Princess and the ladies have given orders to their lovers to keep one year's penance, and are going to leave them. Their intention to return "mock for mock" (V.2.140) has been fulfilled. It is really true that "There's no such sport as sport by sport o'erthrown" (V.2.153). They have been proved to be clever girls and the complete winners of their love-games—but, alas! how quickly their victory loses its lustre when Armado the new bridegroom stands on the stage, side by side with his bride, Jaquenetta. In the 1968 production, we clothed her in a simple, rustic wedding dress.

Unfortunately we were obliged to omit the song of "Winter" because of the shortage of time and cast. The country folk appeared on the stage where the French Princess and her ladies were seated on the right-hand side while the lords occupied the left-hand side. Boyet stood just behind the Princess. The singers gathered behind these courtiers, and sang "When daisies Pied and violets blue. . . ." Then the music of the song of "Winter" was played, and a simple ring-dance followed. First, the Princess and the King, hand in hand, came forward to the front of the stage, made obeisance to the audience, then to each other, and parted; they were followed by Rosaline and Berowne, Maria and Longaville, and Katharine and Dumain. Then Boyet came forward and made a deep bow. The music ended.

At this moment, Armado stepped forward, hand in hand with Jaquenetta, from behind the nobility, as far as the middle of the stage, and shouted— shouted because the audience had already started applauding—"The words of Mercury are harsh after the songs of Apollo." Here he paused, and then they walked across the stage to the right wing, where they stopped. Armado turned his back toward the audience, and raising his arms forward and parting them horizontally as if he were really separating the French ladies from the Navarrese lords, cried to them, "YOU THAT WAY!" And then, taking the arm of his bride, he once again cried, "WE THIS WAY!" They stepped down from the stage to the gangway in the pit, and disappeared among the audience—presumably to their new home.

The moment they did this the house was filled with laughter. The curtain fell.

Our intention in this production was first, to pursue the theme of outmatching. In the triple eavesdropping scene in Act IV, Scene 3, Dumain is outmatched by Longaville; both are outmatched by the King, who in turn is outmatched by Berowne. But Berowne himself is vanquished by the unexpected arrival of Costard. Moreover they are all overpeered by Boyet, who we know has been taking a nap somewhere near the site of this eavesdropping scene, and has overheard their Muscovy masque scheme in advance.[26]

In the last scene, the King and the other lords are easily conquered by the Princess and her ladies, but the ladies and all are overwhelmed by the information that the King of France is dead, as well as by the surprising news of the marriage of Don Adriano de Armado with a country wench.

Secondly, we wished to establish a close identity between ourselves and Armado. He is vain, pedantic, and cowardly; but we are all somewhat vain, somewhat pedantic, and somewhat cowardly. Like Armado who falls in love with Jaquenetta, we are likely to be infatuated with worthless and ignorant mates—mates who are just as worthless and as ignorant as ourselves.

Armado is proud of his behaviour, of his talents, and of his knowledge. But from the start he is treated only as a source of diversion by the King and his peers.[27] He gets disgraced in his duel with Costard. His is not an honorable role. Still, when the curtain fell, the audience at our Gakushuin

Production of 1968 clearly understood that the winner came last and his name was Don Adriano de Armado.

Afterwards, one of the audience told me that, when she heard Armado's last words, "You that way; we this way" in the theatre, she thought they were adlibbed by the actor. As soon as she went home, she found, to her surprise, that they are in Shakespeare's original text! I was glad that she had not used either the New Cambridge or the New Arden Shakespeare. Otherwise, she would have believed that we had audaciously sullied the genuineness of Shakespeare's text.

N. B.: The production of *Love's Labour's Lost* in 1968 was directed by Miss Hiroko Fuse (now Mrs. Abe) who was a senior, under the guidance of Mr. Takayuki Hara of Tōhō Theatrical Company and myself. Mr. Masahiko Takahashi who played Berowne and Mr. Tomonori Fujii who played Armado are now on their way to becoming professional actors.

NOTES

1. This passage is quoted from the First Folio. All other quotations from *Love's Labour's Lost* are from the New Arden edition, edited by Richard David (1951).
2. *Modern Language Review* 13 (1918), 257–266, 387–400.
3. *Proceedings of the Modern Language Association (PMLA)* 39 (1924), 581–611.
4. New York, 1932, 1966 (reprinted).
5. Cambridge, 1936.
6. *The School of Night: A Study in the Literary Relationships of Sir Walter Ralegh.* Cambridge, 1936.
7. Cf. Gustav Ungerer's *Anglo-Spanish Relations in Tudor Literature* (Bern, 1956); Robert Gittings's *Shakespeare's Rival* (London, 1960).
8. Tyrone Guthrie produced this play in 1932 (Westminster), and in 1936–37 (Old Vic); W. Bridges-Adam in 1934 (Stratford-upon-Avon). The Open Air Theatre staged it in 1935, 1936, and 1943. In 1946, Peter Brook successfully presented it on the stage at Stratford-upon-Avon; it deeply influenced J. Dover Wilson (cf. The New Cambridge edition of *Love's Labour's Lost*, 2nd edition, 1962, p. lxii; "*Love's Labour's Lost*: The Story of a Conversion" in *Shakespeare's Happy Comedies*, London, 1962, pp. 55–75). Hugh Hunt produced this play in 1949 (Old Vic); his *Old Vic Prefaces: Shakespeare and the Producer* (London, 1954) contains his valuable comments on this production.
We should never forget the influence of Sir Harley Granville-Barker's inspiring preface to this play, which was published in 1927 (*Prefaces to Shakespeare*, 1st series).
9. Sonnet 116.
10. V.2.785.
11. Cf. I.1.160–177.
12. V.2.841–842.
13. Cf. John Vyvyan's *Shakespeare and the Rose of Love* (London, 1960), and *Shakespeare and Platonic Beauty* (London, 1961); Karl F. Thompson's "Shakespeare's Romantic Comedies" (*PMLA* 67 1952, 1079–1093).
14. V.2.662.
15. Costard says, ". . . she's quick; the child brags in her belly already: 'tis

yours." (V.2.666–667) But bragging in the mother's belly does not testify that it is Armado the Braggart's child. How far can we trust Costard in this?

16. I.2.101.

17. p. 185.

18. E.K. Chambers, *William Shakespeare: A Study of Facts and Problems*. 2 vols. Oxford, 1930. Vol. 1, p.338.

19. W. Schrickx, *Shakespeare's Early Contemporaries: The Background of the Harvey-Nashe Polemic, and* Love's Labour's Lost. Antwerp, 1956.

20. p. 189.

21. p. 196 n.

22. *Shakespeare and His Comedies*. London, 1957. pp. 132–33.

23. Ibid., p. 133 n.

24. Cf. V.2.873–874.

25. The words have no speech-head. So, it is thinkable that they belong to some other person than Armado.

26. V.2.89–125.

27. See note 11.

Love's Labor Reviewed as Mozart-Like

John H. Harvey

Presented by the Guthrie Theater, Minneapolis, MN. Opened 3 July 1974. *Direction*: Michael Langham. *Set*: John Jensen. *Costumes*: Desmond Heeley. *Lighting*: Duane Schuler. *Music*: John Cook. *Muscovite dance*: Fran Bennett. *King of Navarre*: Peter Michael Goetz. *Berowne*: Kenneth Welsh. *Longaville*: Ivar Brogger. *Dumaine*: Mark Lamos. *Costard*: Lance Davis. *Don Adriano de Armado*: Nicholas Kepros. *Moth*: John Newcomb. *Jaquenetta*: Sheriden Thomas. *Princess of France*: Patricia Conolly. *Rosaline*: Maureen Anderman. *Katharine*: Katherine Ferrand. *Maria*: Valery Daemke. *Holofernes*: Ken Ruta. *Nathaniel*: Frank S. Scott. *Boyet*: Jeff Chandler. *Musicians, villagers, diplomats, etc.*: Jared Aswegan, Dennis Babcock, Drew Birns, J. Stephen Crosby, Robert Engels, Brian Grivna, James Harris, Henry J. Jordan, Gary Martinez, Jill Rogosheske, William Schoppert, Cleo Simonett, David Straka, Linda Sultze.

If the Guthrie Theater's *King Lear* is a triumph of majestic tragedy, *Love's Labor's Lost*, which opened Wednesday night, is a jewel of youthful laughter, love, and language.

Director Michael Langham seems to see a kinship between this work and Mozart in its gayety, its wit, its parody of love's extravagances ("Cosí fan tutte"), its winged arias and its clouded ending, so like Mozart's sudden, delicate plunges into melancholy.

And, as Mozart's best operas also require, he and his company have given it style, polish, and a beautifully meshed ensemble. John Jensen's set and Desmond Heeley's costumes, too, have given it the colors and airiness of a bright summer day.

The symmetrical love affairs between the King of Navarre and his three companions and the Princess of France and her three ladies are an amiable bit of puppetry. Amusing though this main plot is, and virtuosic though Shakespeare is in juggling it, it cannot alone sustain the play without the comic characters—the schoolmaster Holofernes, the curate Nathaniel,

Originally published in the *St. Paul Dispatch* (4 July 1974), 3. Reprinted with permission of the *St. Paul Pioneer Press*.

the groom Costard, the constable Dull and the grandiloquent Spaniard, Don Adriano de Armado. And the fast-tongued, precocious page Moth. All of these, each in his own way, are keenly played and beautifully filled out.

The conclusion is a master stroke. The conventional happy ending would have been too pat, too expectable. So the playwright holds out the promise of one, but delays it.

And on the Guthrie stage there is the first fall of summer leaves and Don Adriano wraps his cloak around him against the sudden chill in the air.

Of the four young men, Berowne has the lion's share of soaring lyricism, and fine opportunities for verbal jousts with Rosaline in a Beatrice-Benedick foreshadowing. Kenneth Welsh plays the part brilliantly, and Maureen Anderman's Rosaline is a worthy foil for him.

Patricia Conolly bestows fine dignity, wit and spirit on the Princess, and Peter Michael Goetz gives warmth to the somewhat stilted King. The other lovers—Mark Lamos and Katherine Ferrand, Ivar Brogger and Valery Daemke—give life and gloss to their parts too.

Don Adriano's haughty absurdity and the convolutions of his elabo-

Michael Langham directed Love's Labour's Lost *at the Guthrie Theater in Minneapolis in 1974, in a setting by John Jensen, with costumes by Desmond Heeley and lighting by Duane Schuler. The four lords were played by (left to right) Ivar Brogger as Longaville, Peter Michael Goetz as the King of Navarre, Mark Lamos as Dumaine, and Kenneth Welsh as Berowne. Photograph courtesy of the Guthrie Theatre Company.*

rate Euphuistic speech are marvelously handled by Nicholas Kepros, who makes him a memorable and endearing figure—a cousin, perhaps, of Don Quixote.

Round-eyed, bobbing Lance Davis is an excellent, bouncy Costard; John Newcomb's Moth is the sort of smart kid on the Lord High Executioner's little list; and Oliver Cliff is a juicily bumbling Dull.

Then there are Ken Ruta, a member of the original 1963 company, whose rancidly pedantic Holofernes makes his return welcome indeed; Macon McCalman as a gently, sweetly dim Nathaniel, and Sheriden Thomas's lively Jaquenetta.

If the Guthrie's other productions are anywhere near in the class of its first two, this will be a banner season.

REVIEW OF *LOVE'S LABOR'S LOST* AT THE GUTHRIE THEATER

Mike Steele

For his second offering of the new Guthrie season, Michael Langham has given us a great summer bon-bon, an utterly charming rendition of *Love's Labor's Lost* that is the triumph of this or any season.

It's a production which succeeds in being stylish while still pulling out the stops; it's a verbal dance brimming with wit and warmth, the excessiveness and the delights of youth.

It's a youngish play by Shakespeare celebrating the coming of age of the English language and of England itself. It was a period of an enormous expansion of expressiveness coming on the wings of a new-found pride and consciousness among the sixteenth-century English. Concomitant with discovery was excess and Shakespeare delights in satirizing, gently and warmly, the excesses of his countrymen.

As a consequence, the language of the play—much of it obscure now—draws from many influences, from the French especially and the German and the once dominant Latin of academe. Shakespeare clearly took delight in his puns and wordplays, his courtly floridity and his rural verbosity, all melded together with musicality.

He teasingly incriminates the excesses of this time of discovery. The King of Navarre has set up his own academy where his court must, for three years, give up life's pleasures—including women—to pursue study and contemplation. Shakespeare immediately brings in the Princess of France and her court, with one lovely lady evenly matched with each distraught man, to show the absurdity of such an approach and the nonutility of knowledge when it's used only for vanity and fame.

He elaborates marvelously on that theme with the introduction of

From *The Minneapolis Tribune* (5 July 1974). Reprinted by permission of the Minneapolis *Star Tribune*.

Frank S. Scott as Nathaniel takes center stage as Alexander the Great in the Pageant of the Nine Worthies, which is presented for the lords and ladies in Act V. Michael Langham directed this 1974 production at the Guthrie Theatre in Minneapolis. John Jensen designed the set and Desmond Heeley designed costumes. Photograph courtesy of the Guthrie Theatre Company.

Holofernes, a pedant clinging to Latinisms, unable to conquer the pronunciation of the new English. And he gives us the fantastic Spaniard Armado, who creates huge dishes of language to elevate his stature, yet is constantly confounded by his juvenile page, Moth. And he gives us the rural bumpkin, Costard, who is all human nature and little learning yet the wisest of all as he pursues life's pleasures.

There's a warning here about the perversion of truth and love when study becomes an end in itself and mere erudition is confused with truth, but mostly it's a high comic romp.

Langham has created here an opera-ballet of words, flowing and cohesive and clear, a context in which the excessive, obscure, and unfamiliar create no stumbling blocks to understanding.

And the cast is superb at clarifying Shakespeare's wordplays and metaphors through the intonations and stresses and physicality of delivery.

The performance reinforces my feeling that this year's company is the strongest yet seen on this stage. Kenneth Welsh's Berowne is outstanding— a wise, romantic, sardonic courtier capable of complex mood changes even within a given speech.

Patricia Connoly as the Princess of France is always a knowing, warm, but strong-willed lady. Maureen Anderman is a splendid Rosaline, girlish but intelligent.

Nicholas Kepros continues a superb season as Armado, dressed out as a Don Quixote figure, pathetic in his way and all the funnier for it as he chases the uncatchable. Ken Ruta returns to the Guthrie after too long an absence with a remarkable balancing act as the pedant Holofernes, a *commedia* figure babbling scholarly doggerel, tilting between high comic satire and low comic farce with agility.

Lance Davis is a wide-eyed Costard having great fun dashing after all that's base, spewing out all the wondrous wisdom of the natural free spirit.

Jeff Chandler as the foppish Boyet pranced, twitted, and schemed through the role with wondrous agility. Beyond this, there are too many to mention. Both courts are wonderful—led by a solid Peter Michael Goetz performance as Navarre. John Newcombe's Moth is clear and charming. Sheriden Thomas is excellent as Jaquenetta.

Desmond Heeley has had equal fun with the costumes, a pastiche moving from the pastoral elegance of Fragonard to such clever sight gags as the Quixotic Armado's outfit and the pedant's *commedia* suit. Only John Jensen's set goes awry and it goes far awry, a nauseous green that conquers the beautiful costumes and leaves all kinds of encumbrances about the stage to ruin the physical flow. But it's a glorious romp that tickles and tugs and delights.

Review of the Royal Shakespeare Company

Michael Billington

I suspect John Barton's favourite season is the period when summer glides into autumn. In his beautiful production of *Love's Labour's Lost* at the Royal Shakespeare Theatre in Stratford-upon-Avon the leaves are just beginning to fall from the Ralph Koltai trees, there is a slight nip in the air and the evening shadows lengthen on the grass. And that idea of seasonal transition reflects Barton's vision of the play: as a *corrective* comedy about four young men whose lives are likewise at a turning point.

The usual tendency is to treat the play as a high-spirited verbal romp upon which death dramatically intrudes. But Barton is much more interested in the idea of intellectual arrogance and posturing romanticism being brought down to earth. Michael Pennington's Berowne, dressed in the monkish habit of a penitent, urges his fellow-courtiers who have all withdrawn from the world to study: "Let us once lose our oaths to find ourselves"; but Barton reminds us oaths must be kept, vows respected.

As a result, the ending of the play takes on an unusual poignancy. There is a chilling moment during the village pageant of the Nine Worthies when Berowne cruelly seizes a flag borne by Don Armado and careers around the stage with it only to find Rosaline desperately trying to wrest it off him. Thus when Rosaline later condemns Berowne to visit the "speechless sick" and "enforce the pained impotent to smile" she is making the punishment fit the crime. Jane Lapotaire delivers these rebukes to Berowne with gravity and weight; and the ending of the play becomes for once not a conventional dying fall but a real punishment of intellectual pride.

Within that moral framework, however, Barton still finds a lot of social accuracy and genuine fun. His productions have an almost novelistic detail: here, for instance, we are reminded that the Princess of France is of

From *The Manchester Guardian Weekly* (27 August 1978), 21. © *The Guardian*.

royal stock and that her ladies are expected to shine her shoes and impress pearl ornaments on her dizzy coiffure. And that attention to detail is carried over into the language. With its high-flying satire on Euphuistic conceits, this play is nothing if not verbally complicated. But I think it is indicative of the way modern RSC productions make us *listen* that the biggest laugh of the evening comes when the curate, Sir Nathaniel, is paying homage to the pedantic Holofernes and dubs him "learned without opinion." Any *Love's Labour's Lost* that can raise the roof on that has clearly got its audience by the ears.

As always at Stratford, the company also seems to grow with the season.

Rehearsal Process as Critical Practice

John Barton's 1978 *Love's Labour's Lost*

Barbara Hodgdon

John Barton's most recent *Love's Labour's Lost* with the Royal Shakespeare Company opened in August 1978 to rousing, though not unanimous, critical acclaim. Intriguingly, almost without exception, enthusiastic as well as dissenting reviewers noted that what they saw and heard differed from their expectations of the play they thought they knew. Writing in the Sunday *Times*, John Peter went further, characterizing Barton's performance text as "one of those productions which re-draw the map of a play."[1]

Those words aptly describe my own perception of Barton's rehearsal process during the summer of 1978. As an observer of that process, I kept a log in which I recorded the company's day-to-day exploration of Shakespeare's playtext, what amounted to their working conversations.[2] Documenting such a collaborative effort encompasses a *bricolage* of discourses: chronicle history; the voices of individual participants; anecdote; those signs of thought occcuring both inside and outside the rehearsal room; the observer's own voice, a kind of chorus.[3] In what follows, I want to transform that interweave of voices into a necessarily selective description of a Shakespearean playtext at work in the theatre; and, in so doing, I want to privilege process over product.[4] What interests me especially here is recuperating some features of this production's rehearsal life in order to examine what this kind of performance work contributes, not only to our understanding of the playtext but also to what we mean by "the play."

The Text

The actors begin work with a text (John Dover Wilson's New Cambridge edition) cut by approximately 400 lines.[5] Although this number of cuts is

---

Originally published in *Theatre History Studies* 8 (1988), 11–34, along with eight production photographs. Reprinted by permission.

slightly heavier than usual for a Royal Shakespeare Company production, behind them lies a practical question: how much text is necessary in order to tell the story? Barton's initial playing version removes what he views as overly repetitive, decorative, or excessive word-play which does not advance the understanding of either character or situation: thus, for example, Berowne's "Light, seeking light, doth light of light beguile" (I.1.77), as well as the next six lines, disappear. Other cuts sharpen a "set of wit" or an exchange (especially those between Moth and Armado), remove intrusive obscurities (such as some features of Holofernes' circumlocutions), or make a long speech more completely alive (Berowne's IV.3 justification for breaking the oath loses 25 lines [293–415]—those, according to most editors, that belong to an earlier version and "should have" been cancelled in revision).[6] Here, the idea is to compensate for what Barton views as Shakespeare's over-writing, to remove topical allusions lost to us and to ration verbal fooling so that the audience will listen. Lines from the Quarto (included in most readers' texts), such as the exchange between Berowne and Katharine (II.1.116–125),[7] go in order to privilege the Folio's text's more complexly focused dynamic—the confrontation between Rosaline and Berowne ("Did I not dance with you in Brabant once? . . . How foolish was it then to ask the question" [II.1.111–116]). Similarly, especially in the wit exchanges, occasional lines are rearranged, even reassigned, based on the rationale that swapping lines within formal verbal patterns helps both to differentiate characters and to develop and strengthen character relationships. As rehearsals begin, Barton presents all cuts as conditional; finally, some 100 lines are restored either to support an actor's felt need for additional text in order to move from thought to thought or to retain the closural energy of a rhyme. Early on, for example, Michael Pennington (Berowne) argues for retaining the "Light, seeking light" passage on the grounds that he (as well as some audience members) will miss it and that it both initiates a recurrent motif and completes a rhyme.

Much more striking than these cuts and minor rearrangements are several transpositions. In II.1, Barton moves the exchange between Rosaline and Berowne about hearts and knives (II.1.178–191) to follow Boyet's exit with the other women, so that it caps the scene with a little coda that foregrounds their relationship and emphasizes both their attraction to each other and their opposition. And again, in V.2, lines belonging to Rosaline (II.1.61–67) are re-placed to precede Boyet's entrance (1.78), highlighting her desire to make Berowne her "fool" and to distinguish her attitude from those of the other women. Neither change is revolutionary: Barton had used the first in his 1965 production; David Jones's 1973 production also re-placed the exchange (though in a slightly different position) to stress the Rosaline-Berowne relationship.[8] But Barton's most significant—and unusual—transposition occurs later in V.2. He moves lines 343–356, an exchange between the King and the Princess, to directly follow the Berowne-Boyet "duel" (ending with V.2.483), which makes the conflict between the King and the Princess the end rather than the beginning of an intricate intellectual and emotional structure. It is *this* "fair fray," not the antagonism between Berowne and Boyet, that Costard interrupts with news of the Worthies' pageant.

Overall, these changes tighten the play's narrative structure and sharpen its psychological relationships; both are strategies designed to help actors make a complex verbal surface both alive and intelligible in the theatre.[9] Nevertheless, making such choices evokes the traditional debate between textual purists and theatrical practitioners. Even those who acknowledge that cuts and rearrangements may sharpen a play or give it a fresh voice tend to qualify their statements by suggesting that even though the cut playtext works in the theatre, it is not "the real thing"—that is, such versions do not faithfully reconstruct *the* text of readerly desire or dream. Demystifying this perceived threat is long overdue. As I have argued elsewhere,[10] critical and theatrical practice share similar methodologies and processes of selection which suggest that they are more similar than different. Although the scholar-critic likes to believe that her or his reading process consistently includes "the whole play" (with *all* its words, in their "original" order), any critical reading of a play re-constructs a selective text which often ignores—and sometimes effectively erases—large sections of text. This is not called cutting, however; it is called making an argument. But it *is* cutting, and it is done in a surreptitious rather than a forthright way. For both critical readings and performance texts, who does the cutting, and for what purposes, constitute additional factors affecting perceptions of "textual responsibility." Nevertheless, the issue of *playing* a "full text" remains the ideal, even in the light of contemporary textual scholarship—particularly that concerning multiple-text plays, such as *King Lear*[11]—which suggests that the playtext is mutable, subject to change from its very inception, open to processes of adaptation and co-creation in the theatre as well as in the mind.

FIRST REHEARSAL DAY

The impact of casting choices surfaces at once, as Barton spends the morning working first with Boyet (Alan Rickman) and the Princess (Carmen du Sautoy), two of the most ambiguously drawn characters. Both have positions of authority—not only in terms of class status but insofar as both are controlling figures in many scenes. Of the two, Boyet presents problems for everyone in the play, not exclusively for the actor who plays him. *Who* he is seems to be missing from the text, which contains no deep character clues: the only clear hint is that, like most of the people in the play, he enjoys verbal play. Other evidence includes two comic, unsuccessful attempts at love (II.1.216–224 and IV.1.107–115) and the lift he gives to scenes—important but puzzling clues to the man. It is often Boyet who sets up the games of verbal facility; each time he enters a situation, he pushes the story forward. But his character raises a number of questions. Why do the women feel so safe with him? Have they chosen him as chaperone-advisor or has he been chosen for them by the Princess's father? How old is he? Certainly the women do not seem to read him as sexually attractive (or threatening); rather, they mock him. For Barton, he is closest to *As You Like It* 's Jaques but lacks his melancholy and plays a more functional role in the narrative. Whereas Barton sees the character as a tough advisor, Rickman is fascinated by the games-player, the "Monsieur Nice" bits of his persona; searching for a visual image that expresses his sense of the character, Rickman conjectures a Boyet all in black with red hair—an eccentric masked in conventional dress and role. (At a later rehearsal, Ian Charleson [Longaville] suggests that Boyet is "an absolute stylist," a man who cannot cope with human relationships; rather, he likes to watch the pairing-off from a distance.) Barton departs from a theatrical tradition of avuncular, arguably homosexual Boyets in casting Rickman: can this younger actor handle Boyet's extreme self-consciousness of himself as a phrase-maker? He puts Rickman to work on the "sycamore" speech (V.2.89–118), urging him to separate its functions—simple telling or report, self-consciously "found" words or phrases and rhymes.

Director and actor circle each other; Rickman asks questions; Barton volunteers information and invites comments, orienting the actor toward his role and toward one strategy for working with the language. Now, he works briefly with Carmen du Sautoy, pointing out that, although Rosaline and Berowne are easy to discover, the Princess is as elusive as Boyet. Initially, the actress seems a bit uncomfortable, even vulnerable; strikingly, her initial responses to her role embody the qualities that Barton will later stress in the Princess. Barton calls du Sautoy's attention to the opening of II.1; he mentions that Shakespeare often gives the first speech, in a scene where royalty are present, to the royal personage, yet here Boyet, not the Princess, speaks first, suggesting that she may be hesitant or unwilling to take control. Although du Sautoy asks first how old she is, her real concern is whether what Boyet implies—that she is beautiful—is true, since what she says deflects, even contravenes, his flattery. Barton smiles, avoiding an answer, except to indicate that he may cut some of the lines about the Princess's beauty [he does not]. A bit impatiently, du Sautoy then asks about her attitude toward Navarre, and Barton suggests that the Princess falls in love with him at first sight (and he with her) but that neither reveals that love through speech or reads the other's responses as love.

Both Rickman and, to a lesser extent, du Sautoy represent some departure from traditional casting; working first with these actors signals more than the director's wish to welcome (or indoctrinate) them to the company. Barton's decision to privilege these usually subsidiary roles both widens the possibility of creating ensemble relationships and de-emphasizes Rosaline and Berowne's usual "star" status. A further casting choice, which might be described as revolutionary, confirms Barton's desire to play against aristocratic stereotypes: Richard Griffiths will play the King of Navarre. A somewhat stout actor, Griffiths is not built to play romantic leads; his work with the company has been primarily as a comic—this season he played Trinculo in *The Tempest* and Pompey in *Measure for Measure*—or in so-called character roles, often middle-aged to old men. Offstage, he wears glasses—as he will (like the Princess) in this production. What lies behind this seemingly quirky decision? Small-talk in rehearsals reveals that Barton himself played Navarre at Cambridge; some speculate that he has chosen Griffiths not so much as a latter-day surrogate of himself but as a deliberate contrast to his own persona. Three somewhat unconventional choices, dictating—or at least inviting—a particular interpretative strategy. How will these actors inscribe themselves within their characters? What will be the effect on the overall ensemble in influencing, even prescribing, the course of this production as well as its eventual reception?

First All-Company Meeting

Ralph Koltai, the designer, shows the cast a model of the set—a rather small rectangular raked platform framed by a "naturalistic" park, indicated by huge leafy branches that hang over the back two-thirds of the stage. A tree branch bent to form a rustic bench (left center of the platform acting area) and two park benches placed in the wooded upstage area are its only "furniture." Koltai describes his set as "an acting area in front of a three-dimensional painting" and identifies the set designer's problem, for this play, as avoiding "a set about a tree." (Berowne will climb a ladder-like support placed just at the proscenium opening, stage right.) The set design also, I think, represents a response to or reaction against the set Barton chose for his 1965 production: tall, tangled, dark-green yew hedges that, according to one reviewer, overwhelmed the play, announcing at the outset "a solemn recognition of death's inevitable demands."[12] Koltai's light, spare set—

artificial foreground platform and naturalistic background—seems well suited for revealing the double life of the playtext. The platform encourages the presentational display of soliloquies as well as pageants, of quiet revelations as well as loud deceptions; in the shady upstage area, characters can retreat into poses or tableaux, effectively becoming scenic elements themselves. Whereas many past productions of the play have conformed to Harley Granville-Barker's view of it as an Elizabethan artifact which needs to be staged, costumed, and played for elegance and "style,"[13] Barton wants to counter the clichés he feels every Shakespearean play develops in the theatre. Rather than bowing to the Watteau-like preciosity of tradition, the costumes will have a loosely Elizabethan silhouette and will be rather homespun: the courtiers in brownish-blacks, greys and whites, with small individualizing touches in texture—cloaks for the women, monks' robe-like garments for the men, the country people all in brownish tones. (Jane Lapotaire [Rosaline] protests, "Oh dear, I had hoped for a pretty frock.") And, although Barton sees the play as taking place in an ambiguous season, he also notes that its narrative as well as metaphoric movement is from Spring to Winter; thus the lighting will run the gamut of the seasons, with separate lighting plots to further define and distinguish the platform acting area and Koltai's upstage "romantic painting."

Now Barton sketches out his vision of the play's overall shape: a melancholy, countrified first half (the Interval will occur following IV.3, the sonnet scene) and—accommodating the Muscovites' and the play-within-the-play's dress-up performances—a bubbly, upbeat second half. At first, this seems to me as well as to the actors to counter—even reverse—what he has just described as its narrative and metaphoric structure. But no one questions him at this point as he talks about the play's intimate focus on relationships and about the need to find varying sizes and moods for its situations and to orchestrate these carefully. Finally, Barton's thinking about the location and function of clues for developing characters and situations, for defining characters' relationships to one another and for individual characters' attitudes toward language becomes explicit: "Think Chekhov, not Elizabethan." At first the actors read this as a prescriptive comment aimed at placing an overlay of nineteenth-century meanings on the play; one asks why Barton has not chosen to "do" the play in the nineteenth century. The answer comes immediately: "Because the text is Elizabethan." He explains further with references to *Othello*, which he once (in 1971–72) set in the nineteenth century. That play has textual qualities which make such a setting appropriate: aside from Othello's own language, the text is fairly plain, relatively free of metaphor; amid the social milieu, especially the emphasis on rank and caste, is entirely compatible with Victorian culture. But *Love's Labour's* insistent foregrounding of verbal artifice locates it as "incontrovertibly Elizabethan." Yet, like Chekhov's plays, it rings changes on a single situation, is basically static, and has a similarly "enclosed" atmosphere. And because the linguistic surface functions as a kind of verbal disguise, masking feeling and an ability to speak one's true thoughts, Barton sees his analogy with Chekhov as a useful strategy for approaching both the play's narrative process and the rehearsal process—as a means of situating the actors; energizing their imaginations; urging them, as they approach their roles, to discover a naturalistic reality beneath the contrived surface of the text. The next step, he acknowledges, is more difficult: adapting those discoveries to the non-naturalistic demands of the text—not only in linguistic terms but also in terms of its comic mechanisms.

MEN AND WOMEN: CHOREOGRAPHING ROLES

The first full days of rehearsal focus on establishing a group identity for both the men and the women. Beginning with the men, Barton works on shaping their initial appearances in order to reveal both individual characters and relationships within the group. As the actors discuss the attitudes of the men toward the oath (I.1) and the King's attitude toward each, their comments reveal their own assumptions about playing *Love's Labour's* initial situation as slick, camp, and purely comedic. Immediately, Barton rejects this as an easy answer and points out that the King's first speech signals a potentially tragic move—the rejection of worldly life—and that in order to make the situation read as comedy, it is necessary, as in farce, to play the men's rather adolescent commitment to the idea of study as deadly serious rather than simply to play the men as foolish courtiers. All save Berowne seem earnestly willing to cloister themselves away, yet the ending suggests that they know very little of "real life"; instead, they only have ideas about it. Barton does not suggest a read-through but puts the scene on its feet immediately, choreographing a long traveling entrance for the men (examining the place where they'll spend the next three years, studying) and attempting to establish a meditative stillness that will set up Berowne's refusal to take the oath. To-day—and consistently hereafter—he permits the actors to create their own blocking, relying on their own instincts to give scenes an informal, natural physical shape which he later sharpens and formalizes.

To find further character evidence—and, not incidentally, to begin to link the stages in the characters' growth—that will help the actors think about the opening, Barton moves directly from I.1 to IV.3, the sonnet scene, justifying his rather extensive cuts by saying that it is the most highly verbal moment of the play and must be thought of in terms of the overall shaping to come.[14] Looking briefly at the sonnets each man speaks, Barton points out their cues for character: Longaville's stresses rational argument, not lyric; Dumain's is full of sentiment, melancholy and pining; the King's is too long (Griffiths points out that it looks as though it's been "infinitely rewritten" and that this absentminded-professor of a King—here, a sidelong glance at Barton—has worked hard on it but can't get it right). Several days later, when they rework the opening scene, Longaville has become measured, deliberate, earnest; Dumain (Paul Whitworth) teeming, quick, impulsive; Navarre desperately dissatisfied with his verses. And when Berowne begins to argue about taking the oath, they all exchange a look ("ah, here we go again"); impatiently, the King cuts him off with "Your oath is passed." But Berowne's "What *is* the end of study?" puts the King on the spot; he hasn't thought of an answer, and Pennington uses this to energize Berowne's argument further until, sensing that his friends may turn against him, he finally does swear.

With the women, Barton's strategy differs slightly. When they ask about their relationships with one another and especially about the extent to which they defer to the Princess, Barton indicates that they are both a group—a sort of all-female assault on the court of Navarre—and individuals. Maria and Katharine seem to be close friends whereas Rosaline is something of a loner, with the Princess only somewhat set apart, largely because of her rank. In response to questions about whether the women are already in love—Jane Lapotaire notes that what Rosaline says here differs greatly from her attitude at the end—Barton turns to IV.1 to examine the moments where the Princess talks with the Forester and then to point out several bits of text later in the play which provide character clues for the other women. Most of IV.1's opening exchange, with its repetitive, teasing play on the Princess's "fairness," seems straightforward enough and is later shaped to show the Princess trying out a courtly exchange about beauty with the painfully honest Forester. (Barton's rationale for retaining the unnecessary [to the narrative] exchange with the Forester is that it is one of the few places where court and country meet: such moments form one sort of cohesive structuring for the play.[15]) Then the Princess has a puzzling meditative speech about shooting deer, though her "heart means no ill" (IV.1.21–35). Carmen du Sautoy notices that the Princess's first words—"Was that the King . . . ?"—indicate that she is "looking for Kings everywhere"; responding to her questions about the references to shooting, Barton suggests it as a metaphor for wooing, points out the quick turns through which the Princess justifies "the kill" and invites her to think about the speech as an unsuccessful attempt to mask her love for the King. Then, moving briefly to V.2, where the women are joking about the favors they have received, Barton notes the Princess's ambiguous attitude: first, she decides to mock the men and then, following the Muscovites' masque, she seems at a loss and seeks Rosaline's advice. For further clues to the relationships he has spoken of, Barton calls attention to the opening of V.2, where Rosaline accuses Katharine of not being friends with Cupid because he killed her sister (see V.2.10–28 for the exchange) and asks her to build a serious, melancholy mood. "*Is* Rosaline a 'light wench' [as Katharine calls her here]?" asks Lapotaire. And Barton points to her vow, a bit later on—"That same Berowne I'll torture ere I go"(V.2.60)—and to how his transportation of the rest of her speech will help to set her attitude slightly apart from those of the others.

Now Barton returns to II.1 and outlines the basic situation: that Boyet and the women have come to do a job—to deliver a diplomatic document—not to be wooed, that this is the Princess's first embassage, and that the scene is about waiting to go into the court. Varying the physical pattern he established for the men, he asks Boyet to enter first and for the women to follow, each coming from a different spot, stage left. Apparently displeased (perhaps realizing that having Boyet enter first contravenes the order of Shakespeare's stage direction?), Barton now asks the women to precede him. The pattern that emerges: an annoyed Princess enters quickly and immediately sits on the log bench; Rosaline wanders in more slowly and deliberately chooses a more comfortable seat on the bench; Maria (Sheridan Fitzgerald) and Katharine (Avril Carson) enter together and stand, looking around. Economically, their movements provide details of their characters and of their relationships; following them, Boyet can more easily set himself apart and function as a visual anchor for the group as he explains to them (and to the audience) their reason for being there. Very quickly, Barton returns to IV.1, blocking an entrance whose pace contrasts with this one. The Princess enters on a long, slow downstage travel from upstage center and the others follow her in a series of brisk, broken moves that gather them into an upstage group, giggling at her interest in the King, her unfamiliarity with hunting, and her preoccupation. It is Rosaline who breaks from that group, moving downstage to the Princess and leading her out of her reverie about shooting, fame, praise, and the heart. Lapotaire suggests that the moments are like those in Woody Allen's *Annie Hall* where the characters say one thing but think another (their thoughts revealed in the film's sequence by subtitle), and du Sautoy points out that the Princess, in mentioning "the working of the heart," exposes her desires.

A later rehearsal exploits what the actors have developed here—the Princess's feelings about the King and her unawareness of her own naiveté—

to energize the letter-reading moments which follow, largely by giving value to the women's reactions to Boyet's reading rather than having him read the entire text of the letter as a set piece or performance. The letter thus becomes a guessing game, with Boyet asking a series of questions which the women vie to answer. "Who came?" All but the Princess answer, "The King!", and she looks away. But when Boyet asks, "The captive is enriched—on whose side?" and the Princess answers, "The King's!", the others mock her, chiming in together with "The beggar's." The joke of reading aloud the letter seemingly meant for Rosaline thus turns against the Princess; "The catastrophe is a nuptial—on whose side?" (again, "The King's") climaxes their communal joke. Now Boyet kneels, as though playing the King (who will also kneel to the Princess later in V.2, as will Berowne to Rosaline), on "Shall I entreat thy love?" and the women, catching on, sigh in unison on "my heart on thy every part." The Princess then covers her embarrassment with "What plume of feathers is he that indited this letter?" and breaks away from the group. The reworking of the letter gives added point to her early exit—to be alone, to recover her composure—as well as preparing for the shift from a mood of shared community to the more brittle wit exchanges and comments that conclude the scene.

Composing Beginnings and Endings

Barton follows this ensemble and character work with II.1.90–212—the first meeting between the women and men. The group begin to think about the scene in terms of what it *ought* to be—a careful courtly welcome—in order to measure the extent to which the playtext departs from that ideal: the King is shy and awkward; the Princess behaves rather badly—and both keep their advisors (each a brilliant and witty person) close. Barton again stresses the importance of these two characters; the situations they create—the vow, the embassage that interrupts and challenges that vow—form a spine for the play's action. Here, their meeting erupts into an argument over the question of rights to Aquitaine and the repayment of monies lent by Navarre's father to the Princess's father. Richard Griffiths asks if he's missed something or if he's correct that these issues never come up again, and Barton reassures him that indeed everyone forgets about them, including Shakespeare. The moments are worked to clarify two values: attraction and opposition. Even though their first meeting is set within a public scene about politics, it is primarily, in Barton's view, a love scene: he suggests that both the King and the Princess are shy and nervous and that each, though irritated at the other's reactions, falls in love but fears rejection. Barton points out that the text setting up the previous scenes with each group alone has been heavily

Alan Rickman as Boyet peruses Don Armado's misdelivered letter in IV.1 of the 1978 Royal Shakespeare Company production directed by John Barton. Also shown are Carmen du Sautoy as the Princess, Jane Lapotaire as Rosaline, Sheridan Fitzgerald as Maria, and Avril Carson as Katharine. Photo reprinted by permission of The Shakespeare Birthplace Trust.

rhymed; now, however, the playtext shifts into blank verse. There are only two rhyming couplets until the first exit of the King with his "scholars," yet even those have a more naturalistic feel than those couplets formalizing "sets of wit." Again—as in I.1 and the earlier section of this scene with the women—the situation is about waiting, about wanting to know something. Throughout, questions arise: Is the Princess beautiful? When the women talk about the men, are they already in love with them? What details separate Navarre and the Princess, Rosaline and Berowne, from the others? How similar or different is this scene from the ending? And again Barton moves between two ways of working: giving actors suggestions and listening to their own dialogue and questions, and being extremely prescriptive about some elements of a scene's shaping, particularly in terms of varying the pace and build of juxtaposed scenes. His strategy not only avoids monotony (for which some criticized his 1965 production)[16] but also helps to retain an improvisational feel, countering the contrivance and artificial texture of the language.

Clearly, initial work on these moments further reveals Barton's desire to foreground Navarre and the Princess, but some of the values he wishes to stress obviously lie between the lines, in the realm of conventional subtext or, alternatively, in thoses "white spaces" on the page which remain open to actors' choices. In a later rehearsal, the actors find a moment—just after the Princess's request, "Vouchsafe to read the purpose of my coming, / And suddenly resolve me in my suit" (II.1.108–109)—to pause and register their attraction to each other in silence. The King turns upstage to read the letter as a way of coping with his feelings, while the Princess crosses to the downstage bench, faces the audience, and deliberately removes her glasses. Following this relatively intimate, nearly naturalistic (and "added") moment, Barton works the men's individual returns to question Boyet about the women as a series of mechanical quick turns; similarly, he shapes the exchanges between Boyet and the women which follow for concentrated energy, communal friendship, and flippant ease, permitting the transposed lines between Rosaline and Berowne (II.1.179–191) to set up a taut coda for this first confrontation between the men and the women. Whereas the jack-in-the-box returns of the men foreground the comedy's mechanism, the Rosaline-Berowne confrontation is alert with sexual innuendo. Barton suggests that the two speak a kind of code, that each finds the other deeply provocative, that they want to play a whole scene together but cannot because there is no time: Berowne needs to be surreptitious because he is violating the oath; the other women or Boyet may return to see Rosaline. Pennington and Lapotaire explore alternatives for their physical behavior. Lapotaire suggests (1) exiting and returning to catch Berowne looking after her, (2) crossing up right to wait for Berowne, and (3) simply sitting on the bench until he enters. The first takes too long; the second creates no suspense; the third is too stable. All overweight the moment, pre-signaling its importance. What later developed from this initial exploration combined the first and third choices. Rosaline swings around the stage, preparing to leave, and seems to see Berowne lurking in the stage-right bushes. Instead of following the other women, she seats herself, one arm resting casually along the bench's upper limb—the very picture of carefully arranged relaxation. Berowne reveals himself and greets her: they remain at opposite sides of the stage, using their language, alternately, to attract and repel one another. And as they leave the stage—Berowne at right and then Rosaline at left—each pauses to glance after the other, initiating a shorthand joke that all the men and women will use to register their desire for one another. Barton hopes that the repetition will not only read but also (as it does, in performance) draw an audience's complicit laughter.

But before the shaping I have just discussed occurs, the rehearsal leaps from the first meeting of the men and women to the moments when the men "return in their proper habits" (Wilson's editorial stage direction) after the Muscovite masque (V.2.311–484, including Barton's transposition) and the

King questions Boyet about the Princess. Boyet asks for a read-through of the revised text, pointing out how the transition foregrounds the relationship of the King and Princess and gives the issue of oath-breaking a stronger focus. Part of the longest scene in the canon, this situation turns the II.1 meeting on its head, yet the action does not reach a climax, and the relationship between Navarre and the Princess is just as prickly and uneasy as it is at their first meeting. As he puts the scene on its feet, Barton is searching for ways to clarify the difference between the characters' expressions of mockery and serious anger. At first, the men act fidgety and impatient, waiting for the women. Once the women enter, as a group, the men attempt to break them from their phalanx for a dialogue, which results in their own foolishness being exposed. Out of early blocking comes the need to formalize Berowne's confession/repentance (V.2.394–415), giving it air and space on the stage so that his speech, Rosaline's chiding, and his reply have uninterrupted focus. Barton suggests choosing between making what he sees as a thinking speech private or public and letting movement reflect that choice. What results combines both: apart from her at first, Berowne approaches Rosaline on "honest kersey noes" but is then sent away by her comment, "Sans 'sans,' I pray you." The moment builds toward and then sets up a series of tonal dissolves; the first problem involves getting Navarre and the Princess back in focus. Since Rosaline and Berowne have played their exchange apart, Barton directs Navarre and the Princess to stand close together, down center, and to deliver their lines (V.2.431–441) facing out, keeping an extremely formal tone. Then that tone shifts when Rosaline exposes the King's oath-breaking to the Princess. The King does not understand: Berowne must explain, Boyet comment, Berowne give up, "Peace, I have done." Because some transition is needed here, Barton asks the women to laugh at the men's confusion, which forms a useful bridge to the transposed section of text, for the King can read the laugh as a hopeful cue on which he can invite the Princess to his court. But again his courtly invitation blows up in his face as the Princess replies explosively, in real anger. The quick charge of electricity, even at a first rehearsal, pleases Barton: "An odd bit but a smashing bit," he says, satisfied with the work.

By juxtaposing beginnings and endings, Barton shows the actors the emotional distance they must travel and begins to map the similarities as well as the differences between opening and close and to underscore the stages in the character's emotional and intellectual journeys. Now he moves to the exchanges following Mercade's entrance; later he works out a wild game of keep-away with Jaquenetta's dish clout that masks Mercade's entrance until he catches the object and throws it to the ground.

In the first rehearsal of this part of the final scene, all kneel to the new Queen of France, and then the women rise and move instinctively toward her. In the silence, she steps away from the others, alone with her thoughts and grief. Someone recalls that Elizabeth II, in Africa when George VI died, first knew of ther father's death when she was addressed as "Your Majesty." Here, it is Navarre who attempts to break into her silence with "How fares your. . . majesty?" "This is the most gorgeous bit of the play," says Barton, "because here we see the center of the people, not the witty facade; here the roles go to a different level." The key emotive phrase comes from the Princess: "your gentleness / Was guilty of it." Only at the last does the Princess fully realize the King's tenderness, his extreme self-consciousness about proposing in public. At first Barton isolates each couple, but later he stresses the scene's ensemble relationships by describing the moment as a public symphony with eight instruments arising from the couples' earlier communal feeling.

Barton suggests that the Princess's "We have received your letters" speech, which describes how the men have acted and how the women read their actions, is hard for her to say, because she is admitting that they received the letters, played the game and thought the men's wooing "a merriment." But it is not until Rosaline's line, "We did not quote them so," that the *labours* of love are lost—and nearly so, the loves. The men start to go— in what turns out to be a false exit when the King turns back: "Now, at the latest minute of the hour, / Grant us your loves." As in her IV.1 meditation, the Princess's "A time methinks too short / To make a world-without-end bargain in" is a personal speech rising out of a more public moment. It begins naturalistically, becomes increasingly formal, and moves toward an ending rhyme, a textual rhythm which is echoed by the King as well as the others. Barton uses the formalizing change in the verse to cue the stage patterning: in a more sober echo of II.1's slick mechanism, he blocks the mass proposals as artificial rather than naturalistic, isolated exchanges. Then, countering the energy and projection of this mass wooing, the Rosaline-Berowne exchange that begins "Studies my lady?" shifts toward a more intimate style, toward what Barton sees as the most important moment in the play—one that must, in performance, keep earning itself.

In rehearsal, the exchange moves from one where the actors share a full embrace on "And I will have you" to one that begins in quiet gravity and ends with sober pain—and with no embraces. Rather, Rosaline kneels by a dejected Berowne and lightly touches his face as she says, "throw away that spirit, / And I shall find you empty of that fault, / Right joyful of your reformation." He ruefully accepts her task: "well; befall what will befall, /

I'll jest a twelvemonth in an hospital." As Pennington spoke these lines in rehearsal, giving "hospital" its modern pronunciation and avoiding the expected rhyme with "befall," I heard, as though for the first time, how the verse itself disappoints, refuses easy closure, promised union.

LISTENING TO THE LANGUAGE

Barton's own program note for his 1965 *Love's Labour's Lost* spoke of the need to take apart the various stylistic elements of the text and find a harmony among them. Apparently, however, that notion resulted in what one reviewer described as a minimized degree of stylistic variation and what another summarized as measured, weighty delivery that burdened lines with irrelevantly direct emotion and with "vocally showy" verse speaking which, especially in the last act, "weight[ed] dramatic implication at the cost of rhythmical and metrical coherence."[17] Although Barton asserts that the play is never very far away from song and dance, obviously he is now striving to explore its various tunes and gestures, to reveal both the harmonies and discords in the language and to distinguish between them—not only during daily rehearsals but also on "Sonnet Saturdays," where together the company explore particular speeches in minute detail.

For Barton, the language *is* the play: making Shakespeare's words *work*—come alive in the theatre—is his special territory.[18] In this play, everyone speaks in heightened language, often obviously enjoying both sound and sense; finding a way to justify that love of words in acting terms—to make people from these beautiful words—is the actors' central problem. Several precepts about finding a playing style for *Love's Labour's* variety of rhetorical artifice become clear early on. First, Barton stresses relishing the artificiality and advises the actors to think of rhyming as a part of the characters' consciousness; he suggests that discovering why a character rhymes at a particular moment will help to differentiate between several levels of artifice. The men, for example, use rhyme to impress the women (and each other), to attempt to convince them of the depths of their passion. Their rhymes are consistently more elaborate, less direct, than those of the women. Berowne and Holofernes rhyme because they admire verbal skill. And all the characters seem to use rhyme to play one-upmanship games, especially in the "sets of wit" which trace a spurring, heightened rhythm of exchange throughout the play, tinselling the more naturalistic flow of the blank verse speeches. If, in the a/b/a/b rhymes shared between speakers, the first speaker remains unaware that he or she is setting up a rhyming quatrain, then it becomes witty and funny both for the actor and for the character (as well as for the audience) to gradually reveal that slick surface for what it is. In acting terms, rhyming moments need to express huge delight and have a light, technical crispness: Barton advocates playing the rhythms at a canter, like nursery rhymes, energizing occasional lines with physical action in order to make the rhyme accessible to the audience. Time after time, he stresses "serving up" a rhyme by putting energy into it to point the thought and to avoid running on to the next line. If thirty to forty lines become highly energized, they will justify a pause or point a change in rhythm. But he warns against pausing within rhyming sections, which produces a naturalistic feel: essentially, he is inviting, even requiring, the actors to play two styles at once, to combine naturalistic gesture and highly stylized verbal delivery. Quatrains seem more difficult for the actors to master than rhyming couplets, which are more down-to-earth, direct, biting: Rosaline, Barton suggests, uses them masterfully (as, of course, do others) to drive a point home. Half-rhymes function as interruptions in what can risk becoming doggerel, and Barton advises holding down the actors' tendency to turn these into full rhymes for comic reasons, which can generate the impression that the speaker is wringing the neck of the verse in order to prove that it's funny.

Barton's approach to using the rhyme echoes his earlier statements about the way it serves as a verbal disguise, as a series of postures that mask feeling. He stresses that the rhymes must earn the great serious speeches in blank verse—notably those in V.2, where the language styles set each other off brilliantly. In spite of the predominantly slick surface of the play, Barton maintains that only rarely does the text reveal the concentrated, jeweled elegance commentators tend to foreground; like other Shakespeare texts, this one changes frequently, moving from extremely formal to more naturalistic means. Clearly he will measure his own success with this performance text in terms of how well the company can ring the changes form rhyme to blank verse: for him, the unique quality of *Love's Labour's* verbal texture *is* that change.

Shaping the Ending

Every Shakespearean playtext has, it seems to me, at least one central problem that governs the play's realization in the theatre. With *Love's Labour's Lost*, that problem—which is enhanced by the multiple closings that override each other in the long final scene—is how to avoid not only anticipating the ending but also turning the entire structure into a play *about* an ending. As the actors work, first, with individual sections of the final scene and, then, with integrating all its shifts of tone and mood, Barton's initial puzzling statement about the play's overall emotional shape—melancholy to joyful—begins to make strategic sense. Again, he seems to be responding to adverse comments about the 1965 production by simplifying his earlier presentational means. B.A. Young, for example, had objected to the elaborate staging of both the masque and the pageant. The pseudo-Russians arrived on a float big enough to hold them all, as well as a five-piece band; the Worthies entered on a "vast double-decker shandrydan"; and large wicker models of the cuckoo and the owl, with the band behind them, presided over the ending.[19] Although the intent seems to have been to find a way to make the Worthies' show "larger" than the Russians' appearance and to support and re-enforce the final verses with visual means, the effects seemed not only exaggerated but imposed.[20] This time, Barton makes deliberate efforts to counter a "heavy" ending; to avoid sentimentality; to keep physical and intellectual energy high, both in the Muscovites' masque and the Nine Worthies' show; and to sustain for as long as possible the expectation that the usual comic resolution will prevail. Achieving balance and flow among the counterpointed elements of the ending occupied much of the rehearsal period; here I describe some highlights of that work.

The first time the actors rehearse the Muscovite entrance (V.2.158ff.), Barton remarks that this is the most difficult bit to stage, largely because it requires trust of the comic mechanism and staging that keeps the scene going so that there is no time for the audience to ask questions about *why* it is happening. Its initially wooden shape seems far distant from what he wants to achieve—*bravura con brio* spaghetti-Western Russians and a sense of as much mystery, ceremony, and melodrama as possible. Although Barton maintains that trusting Shakespeare's mechanism always works, the scene is not working, largely because the actors are attempting to fit in all the implied blocking in the text, such as taking hands and beginning to dance. Trying to solve the problems, Barton asks the actors to take the dialogue as fast as possible. What this makes clear is that Rosaline controls the dynamics of the scene and that the King, attempting to follow her lead, becomes a gibbering wreck. Identifying this verbal power shift as essential to the scene suggests how further work can capitalize on the high energy of what Griffiths calls the "seducer-rapist Muscovites." The men approach the women with highly organized, clearly patterned movement, which is then so undercut by the women's "keen mockery" that holding hands as well as their planned dance literally doesn't have *time* to work, and they attempt to save face in a quick and noisy exit, accompanied with several "bangs!"

The next morning, the rehearsal room prop table is filled with voluminous black capes, old *Troilus and Cressida* helmets, bows, clubs, guns, balalaikas, swords, and an enormous wineskin. Delighted as children, the men put on bits of costume: they are indeed marvelous ill-favored Muscovites, playing at dressing up. Following Barton's suggestion that they begin with a few vaguely Russian yelps, the scene begins quite slowly, the actors reworking the earlier blocking as Barton coordinates each move, setting it tight to the verbal rhythms in an attempt to retain improvisational energy. Apparently pleased with the barbaric quality of the earlier yelps, Barton suggests another round of them after Berowne's "Nothing but peace and gentle *w*isitation." As though on some prearranged cue, the men fall to their knees; grunting, moaning, and snorting, they turn into creeping sex maniacs, moving slowly and inexorably across the stage toward the women, falling at their feet, pushing them behind the stage-left bench. This invasion of vaguely reptilian Muscovites, looking like giant turtles dressed for Hallowe'en, has come as a complete surprise: the room rocks with laughter.

The released delight energizes the rest of the session: the actors work quickly, building bits of business. On "Play music, then," Dumain tries frantically to get his balalaika into position but he is too late, and the others show their annoyance. Navarre, still on his knees, sings, "Vouchsafe some motion to it" and "But your legs should do it." "We'll not be nice—take hands" brings the King to his feet, prompting a momentary tableau, which Barton formalizes into a picture, a freeze-frame of potential harmony before Rosaline's "We will not dance" breaks apart. When the women finally agree to chat, responding to the King's pleading, his "I am best pleased with that" becomes an aside to the rehearsal-room audience as he rises wearily to talk apart wih Rosaline. Boyet's "The tongues of mocking wenches" speech is blocked upstage center (later, he lounges on the bench), a clearly ironic comment on the scene which, like Holofernes' words in IV.2.70–77, touch on the mystery of imagination revealed in language.[21] As the group breaks for lunch, Barton warns the women not to lace their bodices too tight. He is still smiling. So are we all.

On another morning—designated for work on the Worthies' Show—the giant hobby horses from Barton's 1972 *Richard II* are grazing comfortably in the upstage park as we come into the rehearsal room. Costard (Allan Hendrick) is given a small wooden hobby horse, which encases him completely, and a small band—Dull (David Lyon) on drum, the Forester (Dennis Clinton) on horn and cymbals, and Jaquenetta (Ruby Wax) on tambourine—accompany his gallop "along this coast" with improvised toots, drum rolls and clangs, as well as some horse-hoof sound effects provided by Stephen Dobbin, the assistant stage manager, with two wooden blocks. Sir Nathaniel (David Suchet) enters completely encased in one of the huge horses, only a part of his nose and mouth showing in an oversize helmet. He carries props from a previous *Troilus and Cressida*—a fifteen-foot pennant lance and an enormous shield. As Nathaniel dries in his role—repeating "When in the world I lived, I was the world's commander"—he goes into a soprano register and begins to sink, very slowly, into the floor, horse and all, shield askew, lance descending. We all explode with laughter that turns to tears—even Barton seems surprised by this response to conditions he has obviously set up. At lunch, Suchet is still pleased with himself: "Do you think he'll let me keep it in?" he asks.

Suchet's initial invention paves the way for those that follow: Holofernes' entrance, also wearing a horse, must obviously differ in some way, and Paul Brooke executes several decorative circles and a pirouette on the edge of the platform, treating his horse as though it were a bustle. Once he steps onto the platform, Dumain strokes Holofernes' horse and Longaville produces a lump of sugar, but the horse bites him. ("You must be careful," says Barton, "These horses upstage a man.") Although the business was cut before the production reached performance, it illustrates how Barton encourages playing excessive responses to the text and then pulling back to shape and refine what the actors produce. The danger, obviously, lies in creating so much comic detail for its own sake that telling the story gets lost. What Barton wants from each entrance here is a romantic quality, with Armado's Achilles (Michael Hordern) as a climax, accompanied by a shimmer of percussion from the rustic band. What characterizes the pageant initially is the attempt to do it—both for the actors and for the characters they play. The scene has an elaborate balance of tonalities: it must juggle the Worthies, the men's heckling attacks, and the women's responses to their mockery. Central to the show, Barton suggests, is the Worthies' sense of their own worth; they approach their play with honesty and high (sometimes self-inflated) seriousness. Though individually each may realize that the show risks failure, each should speak and act without apology, without embarrassment. On the surface, the pageant becomes a rural entertainment which the women treat as a divertissement and which the men react to as an interruption to their wooing, so that their two kinds of teasing—gentle and vicious—grow from their expectations of what they want to happen. In shaping the scene, Barton attempts to point their differing attitudes so that the audience will be able to recognize the women's playful irony and the men's more callous condescension from earlier moments.

In staging the play's coda—the cuckoo and owl songs—Barton is more than usually prescriptive. And, although 1965 reviewers puzzled over why the final songs were spoken, not sung,[22] he is convinced that they should be spoken and stresses Armado's reference to them as a *dialogue* (V.2.881). He wants Holofernes and Nathaniel to speak very slowly and quietly. For Barton, the most important thing about the verses is that the two pedants have composed them *together*; what he wants to achieve here is a brief moment of harmony, with the whole company echoing the bird calls, before the final separation of the men and women. He warns Suchet and Brooke not to perform the verses by submitting to their insistent rhythm but rather to remain consistently aware of shifting the tempo and gathering the rhythm toward a marked change in the third stanza, capped by the fourth. Because Barton senses that the mixture of melancholy and sharp sounds here echoes the overall "sound" of the play, he urges the actors to play the lines for storytelling and argument and to avoid sentimentalizing their delivery.

The first time the coda is played in rehearsal, it falls into place as a moment of desirable, even necessary, ease that *does* risk sentimentality. Barton re-blocks the moments so that Nathaniel and Holofernes sit on the log rather than standing. Now the countrymen encourage their listeners to join in: the rustics respond with "Cuckoo" (the brash Costard with "Cuckold"): Jaquenetta and Costard with hissing owl noises, which are taken up by the others, resonating echoes that, in performance, are re-echoed by a "real" off-stage owl hooting in the still night. Everyone looks up, the owl sings again, and Nathaniel says happily, "a merry note." Armado's voice drops to a whisper as he says goodbye, "You that way; we . . . this way." The rustics quietly back away; the men and women separate, glancing for the last time at one another; the lights dim; Armado strums his lute, humming the song about the King and the beggar maid. Jaquenetta lies under a bush downstage left; a warm light glows on her as she silently plays "he loves me, he loves me not" with a leafy branch. The aged knight steps toward her, then slowly moves upstage, the gentle sound of lute and voice fading with the light.[23]

As with so many of Shakespeare's plays, *Love's Labour's Lost* has tempted both its director, John Barton, and its by now distant observer, to extend its time; to continue—beyond the text of the play, beyond the text of the rehearsal process—to tell its story.

EPILOGUE

Like an author's working drafts or an artist's cartoon, the rehearsal offers a preliminary array of artistic decisions, some of which never become part of the performance text. Often, in shifting from the rehearsal room to a larger stage space, much—and especially the carefully worked-out features of intimate relationships—can be swallowed up. In the case of Barton's *Love's Labour's Lost*, however, rehearsal process and performance text retained striking correspondence; the way of working on the play not only became one with its final playing style but also influenced its critical reception. Although no critic suggested an analogy with Chekhov, many implied it by noting how closely observed and orchestrated details revealed, for the first time in their memories, real people rather than an assortment of Euphuistic speakers arranged in confectionary poses. The play about which Granville-Barker had long ago said, "Our spontaneous enjoyment will hang upon pleasant sights and sounds alone, sense and purpose apart," had been replaced by a "corrective comedy" which revealed, in Michael Billington's words, "intellectual arrogance and posturing romanticism being brought down to earth"—a play where the final suspension of comic closure took on "gravity and weight" to become "not a conventional dying fall but a real punishment of intellectual pride."[24] If *Love's Labour's Lost* represented, for its 1590s audiences, one text among many which reproduced—and critiqued—the artifices of courtly patronage, John Barton's rehearsal strategies together with his resulting performance text offer an analogous model of critical practice, a contemporary re-reading of the Elizabethan social sphere Shakespeare's play constructs.

*   *   *   *   *

CREDITS FOR *LOVE'S LABOUR'S LOST*, ROYAL SHAKESPEARE COMPANY, 1978

First performance 8 August 1978

The Court of Navarre
Ferdinand, King of Navarre .... Richard Griffiths
Longaville .... Ian Charleson
Dumain .... Paul Whitworth
Berowne .... Michael Pennington
Don Adriano de Armado .... Michael Hordern
Moth, his page .... Jo James
The French Embassage
Princess of France .... Carmen du Sautoy
Boyet, Chamberlain to the Princess .... Alan Rickman
Maria .... Sheridan Fitzgerald
Katharine .... Avril Carson
Rosaline .... Jane Lapotaire
Mercade, a messenger .... Alan Cody
The Local Inhabitants
Dull, a Constable .... David Lyon
Costard, a Clown .... Allan Hendrick
Jaquenetta, a Country Wench .... Ruby Wax
A Forester .... Dennis Clinton
Holofernes, a Schoolmaster .... Paul Brooke
Sir Nathaniel, a Curate .... David Suchet

Directed by John Barton
Designed by Ralph Koltai
Lighting by Nick Chelton
Music by James Walker
Company Voice Work by Cicely Berry

1. John Peter, Sunday *Times*, 13 August 1978, 35.
2. I am grateful to Maurice Daniels for arranging observer status with the Royal Shakespeare Company.
3. Examples of such published documents include Charles Marowitz, *The Act of Being: Towards a Theory of Acting* (New York: Taplinger Publishing, 1978), which includes an *Othello* casebook, documenting his rehearsal process; Kenneth Tynan, ed., Othello: *The National Theatre Production* (London: Rupert Hart-Davis, 1966); David Selbourne, *The Making of* A Midsummer Night's Dream (London: Methuen, 1982); Sally Beauman, *The Royal Shakespeare Company's Centennial Production of* Henry V (Oxford: Pergamon Press, 1976); Judith Cook, *Shakespeare's Players* (London: Harrap, 1983) and *Shakespeare's Women* (London: Harrap, 1980); Anthony Sher, *Year of the King* (London: Chatto and Windus, 1985); and Philip Brockbank, *Players of Shakespeare* (Cambridge: Cambridge University Press, 1985).
4. The emphasis on process in, say, Peter Brook's rehearsals (see G. Banu, ed., *Brook*, Vol. 13 in *Les Voies de la Création Théâtrale* (Paris: Centre National de la Recherche Scientifique, 1985) and John Russell Brown's *Free Shakespeare* (London: Heinemann, 1974) and *Discovering Shakespeare* (London: Macmillan, 1981) is echoed by current theoretical concerns that foreground the signifying processes of texts through semiotic, marxist, and psychoanalytic approaches.
5. All line references are taken from John Dover Wilson's edition of *Love's Labour's Lost* (Cambridge University Press, 1923 [rpt. 1969]).
6. See, for example, Wilson, pp. 105–107.
7. In the Folio, the exchange is between *Boyet* and Rosaline, with the last line assigned to Berowne. Although editors may well be right in conjecturing that this involves a compositor's error in speech assignment, the alternative reading is worth thinking about, for it has an extremely complex dynamic. It makes Boyet a wooer, and puts Boyet and Berowne in opposition for Rosaline. The exchange thus serves not only to dismiss Boyet as a suitor but also makes extremely good sense of his final line to Berowne, "Farewell to me, sir, and welcome to you."
8. See the prompt copy for Jones's performance text. The Shakespeare Centre Library, Stratford-upon-Avon.
9. Barton's changes and rearrangements to *Love's Labour's Lost* are on a much smaller scale than those in, say, the Peter Hall-John Barton 1963–64 playing version of the three *Henry VI* plays and *Richard III* called *The Wars of the Roses* or in his more recent production of *King John* (1974). See John Barton and Peter Hall, *The Wars of the Roses* (London: BBC, 1970); prompt copy for *King John* at The Shakespeare Centre Library, Stratford-upon-Avon.
10. "Parallel Practices, or the *Un*-Necessary Difference," *The Kenyon Review* 7, no. 3 (Summer 1985), pp. 57–65.
11. See, for example, Gary Taylor and Michael Warren, *The Division of the Kingdoms: Shakespeare's Two Versions of* King Lear (Oxford: Oxford University Press, 1984) and Steven Urkowitz, *Shakespeare's Revision of* King Lear (Princeton: Princeton University Press, 1980).
12. John Russell Brown, *Shakespeare Survey* 19 (1966), pp. 116–117.
13. Harley Granville-Barker, *Prefaces to Shakespeare*, Vol. 4 (Princeton: Princeton University Press, 1946), pp. 1–37. Entries in the Garland bibliography that cite reviews of past productions indicate that many are judged precisely on how well they evoked a sense of "Elizabethan-ness" (see Nancy Lenz Harvey and Anna Kirwan Carey, comps., Love's Labour's Lost: *An Annotated Bibliography* [New York: Garland Publishing, 1984]). The program for Barton's production reproduces photographs of some previous productions; one of the effects is to suggest that the mise-en-scène of Barton's production differs substantially from those pictured.

14. Barton cut thirty-six lines in addition to lines 293–315, the "duplication" within Berowne's long justificatory speech. See Wilson, pp. 105–108.

15. Transforming my rehearsal log into this text has omitted much, notably Armado and those Costard refers to as the "true folk," whose scenes received as much careful attention to developing relationships as those I do describe. Holofernes and Nathaniel, bound together by their admiration of books and learning, their skill and facility with words, became a comic team; Dull their marvelously taciturn straight man. Costard's excitement at being around such splendid beings, his peasant cunning (especially with remunerations) and his own love for words gave his primarily functional role as go-between particular flair. Michael Hordern's Armado, which began as a broad comic caricature ("Do I play him as funny?" was his first question to Barton), developed into a melancholy, dignified yet absurd old soldier, puzzled by his irresistible attraction to Jaquenetta's wisely innocent "country wench." Barton worked out a pre-show—the local country people sweeping leaves to clear the stage—as a kind of homage to Beerbohm Tree's *Rip Van Winkle* and because he liked the idea of people working in an otherwise very "posh" and courtly play.

16. *The Times*, 8 April 1965, 114.

17. *The Times*, 8 April 1965, 114; John Russell Brown, pp. 113–116.

18. See John Barton, *Playing Shakespeare* (London: Methuen, 1983) for further details on Barton's way of working with Shakespeare's texts.

19. B.A. Young, *Financial Times*, 8 April 1965.

20. Ian Richardson, David Jones's 1973 Berowne, spoke (at the University of Nebraska, Omaha, where the Royal Shakespeare Company was in residence in 1975) of the difficulty the cast experienced with making the two shows, the Muscovites and the Nine Worthies, as well as the moments surrounding them, different in degree and tone.

21. Cf. Theseus in *A Midsummer Night's Dream* V.1.2–22.

22. *The Times*, 8 April 1965, p. 114.

23. I am grateful to Miriam Gilbert for sharing with me her description of a performance of Barton's production.

24. Granville-Barker, pp. 1 and 9; Michael Billington, "*Love's Labour's Lost*," *Guardian* 14 August 1978.

From a Theatregoer's Notebook

The RSC's *Love's Labour's Lost*

Felicia Hardison Londré

Matinee performance of *Love's Labour's Lost*, 7 September 1985, directed by Barry Kyle, the Royal Shakespeare Company at the Barbican Theatre, London.

The opening scene was played on the apron before a black drop. The King (Kenneth Branagh) and his three friends each sat at a small Edwardian desk, each with a green-shaded lamp, books, etc. They were costumed in Edwardian black suits, Berowne's very slovenly. Each inscribed his name in a ledger as he vowed to devote himself to three years of study; Berowne (Roger Rees) merely scrawled a big B. Then they settled down to their studies, but this was very perfunctory: the King shuffling the books on his desk, Berowne drawing on a canvas, etc.

The black drop rose to reveal a pale, idyllic landscape filling the stage. The set (designed by Bob Crowley) was done all in off-white and very pale beige. With the raising of the drop, the groundcloth was spread forward from the setting to cover the forestage in white with a scattering of white and beige leaves. At stage right were a statue of Eros, a statue of Apollo, and a sundial, all on pedestals. Stage left was forested with a dozen white umbrellas on poles about twenty feet high. There was also a patio-style umbrella table. Three or four irregularly shaped mirrors in the floor looked like puddles of water. Beyond the low stone wall that bounded the playing area were painted curtains with muted landscapes in green and gold. At first these were seen through gauzy white curtains, beautifully lit (lighting design by Brian Harris), but as the men began falling in love, the white curtains were raised, perhaps to suggest the veils lifting from their eyes. For the transitions, peasant women—one of them having an especially beautiful soprano voice—sang melancholy folk melodies (music composed by Guy Woolfenden).

Casting a beautiful black actress (Josette Simon) as Rosaline gave a special boost to Berowne's lines like "she is born to make black fair"

(IV.3.257). All four women had several changes of costume, but they always wore white, ivory, or cream gowns with elegant Edwardian lines. The men wore black academic robes until they caught each other with their love poems. Berowne's speech urging them to give in to their impulses was beautifully delivered and led to the climactic flinging of their academic robes into a pile on the ground. They jumped up and down on the robes, then ran offstage, and were next seen in white Edwardian suits.

The sequence in which the King and lords overhear each other's poems in turn was quite inventively staged. Berowne jumped up on the pedestal with Eros and made his shape conform to that of the headless statue. The King rolled under the garden bench and placed a potted plant—"this bush"—in front of his face as he lay there. Longaville (James Simmons) jumped onto the umbrella table, opened the umbrella, and tilted it to shield himself from Dumaine's view.

The low-life characters were not treated as very earthy. It was a restrained approach, especially by Don Armado (Richard Easton). The best of them was Holofernes (Christopher Benjamin), whose exquisite interpretation of that difficult role was funny and touching within the compass of the character's pomposity. His line, "this is not generous, not gentle, not humble," was utterly moving, coming after the subtle but clear deflation of his ego in public.

The 1985 Royal Shakespeare Company production was directed by Barry Kyle and designed by Bob Crowley, with lighting by Brian Harris. Kenneth Branagh (seated) played the King of Navarre. At the far left and right are Josette Simon as Rosaline and Roger Rees as Berowne. Photo reprinted by permission of The Shakespeare Birthplace Trust.

"Like a demi-god here sit I in the sky, / And wretched fools' secrets heedfully o'er-eye," says Berowne in IV.3 as he eavesdrops on the other three lords. Here Roger Rees perches on a statue in the setting designed by Bob Crowley. Photo reprinted by permission of The Shakespeare Birthplace Trust.

Moth (Reuben Purchase), played by a boy, interpreted his lines beautifully, but I thought that the characterization was too heavy. This was caused partly by his costuming in a uniform with lots of gold braid, making him a mini-Don Armado; it was a sort of glorified bellhop uniform on a rather chunky boy. Boyet (John Carlisle) too had perfectly clear and credible line readings, but his character tended to fade into the scenery as he made no attempt to bring out the comedy in the role.

The Muscovites were also done in a restrained manner: more or less "realistic" court uniforms, wigs and beards quite different in color from the men's own. Berowne did a head-bobbing tic as the Muscovite. The women simply pulled down thick white veils from their wide-brimmed hats and put on gloves, so it was indeed impossible to tell which one was the dark-skinned Rosaline.

A small wagon stage was trundled out for the pageant of the Nine Worthies. The pageant performers had clearly put a lot of effort into their little show. The entrance of Marcade, all in black, stepping through the little wagon stage of the Worthies, brought a most effective, instant change of mood.

All in all, I thought Barry Kyle's direction was excellent, if somewhat restrained. Roger Rees's Berowne may be said to have stolen the show, because he was the one who pushed back the boundaries of restraint. He really was a scamp with a soul, who clearly learned his lesson in the end.

During the owl and cuckoo songs, led by the beautiful soprano voice, both songs quite melancholy and sweet-sounding, some white leaves began falling from the flies, and one by one the white "tree" umbrellas closed (no visible mechanism). The effect was lovely, lovely, very plaintive and haunting.

Moshinsky's *Love's Labor's Lost*

Mary Z. Maher

Although Elijah Moshinsky has made his reputation directing grand opera, he is clearly a favored director in the BBC-TV/Time-Life "Shakespeare Plays" series, having been hired to work under two different executive producers (Shaun Sutton and Jonathan Miller) to direct a number of the most challenging plays: *All's Well, Cymbeline, Merchant of Venice, Coriolanus,* and *Love's Labor's Lost.* I was fortunate enough to sit in the production booth at the BBC Television Centre in Wood Lane on this latter production and to watch Moshinsky work. *Love's Labor's Lost* was video-recorded June 30–July 6, 1984.

The most striking feature of Moshinsky's directorial skill is his painterly inclination, his distinctly visual style. *Love's Labor's Lost* was the only play of the series where the production design did not conform to BBC period guidelines and which could be said to have had a stylized directorial concept, *à la* Watteau. Obviously, Moshinsky was to be given his head on this particular play.

In *Love's Labor's Lost,* Moshinsky pays elaborate attention to costume detail, not only to shades and hues of color but also to texture and line in fabric. There was one scene where the Princess and her court in pastel dresses looked like giant bulbous peonies on the lawn. There was another scene with the women dressed for the hunt in camel-colored wool gabardine skirts, dark green jackets, and miniature tri-cornered hats.

Naturally, this focus on visual beauty dictates minute adjustment of lighting. Moshinsky underlit (strong lighting coming from the floor of the set) much of the production to get molded three-dimensional looks on actors' faces.

Originally published in *Shakespeare on Film Newsletter* 10 (December 1985), 2–3. *Shakespeare on Film Newsletter* is now incorporated in *Shakespeare Bulletin,* which granted permission to reprint the piece.

He also shot through gauze to create a romantic softness in line and color. In fact, everything in the studio is fair game for Moshinsky's roving camera—an unusual piece of furniture, a grouping of candles, a reflection in a mirror. He will take extra time to work an interesting visual idea into a production.

"Shooting" is perhaps not exactly the right word for the kind of television directing that Moshinsky does. The more traditional director will shoot in large scenic sequences of seven to twelve minutes. Moshinsky shoots in smaller segments, often forty-five seconds to twelve minutes, and then crafts the final tape in the editing room, making sure that development shots, front angles, reverses, and special stills are interwoven in a film-like sequence of cutting and blending for visual effect. His way is "finding" the play through various camera angles. He will often cut pieces of Shakespeare's smaller lines (entrances and exits, for example) because he realizes that these stage directions written for a theater space would overdefine action if used on video, which has capability for closeups and visual selection.

Moshinsky's purpose carries over into his style when working with actors and technical crews. He seldom uses the intercom system to critique or coach actors; he goes down to the studio floor and privately "visits" with them, a technique which has the advantages of saving ego and insuring precise communication. With his technical crew, he delegates work in a quiet, authoritative way. The production of *Love's Labor's Lost* was characterized by efficiency, a positive leadership style, and good cheer—important qualities in a teamwork endeavor. Henry Fenwick, journalist on the Time-Life BBC plays and writer of extensive accounts of productions in the BBC Shakespeare text series, said that most of the series' directors further theater through television. Elijah Moshinsky has the objective of furthering the craft of television in order to make it an art form.

ANOTHER WINNER, A FEAST
WORTHY OF THE BARD HIMSELF

REVIEW OF *LOVE'S LABOUR'S LOST*,
PERFORMED BY THE GREAT LAKES THEATER FESTIVAL
AT THE OHIO THEATRE ON PLAYHOUSE SQUARE

Marianne Evett

When the curtain of pale-green fronds goes up on *Love's Labour's Lost* at the Ohio Theater, it reveals an elegant springtime world, potent as May and redolent of the innocent luxury of *Brideshead Revisited*.

Gerald Freedman, who directed, continues his string of winners with his most polished and beautiful Shakespeare production yet, featuring a handsome young ensemble full of silliness and grace.

This early comedy has its problems because all its characters are in love with words, playing with them like so much Silly Putty, stretching and bouncing them around. In our own word-gray times, it's hard to keep up. Yet some of the jokes must have been told around the cave fire, and a talented comic crew help us get a good many more that depend on words no longer current. You have to pay attention, but it's worth it.

The young King of Navarre and his three friends swear off women for three years of study and fasting. But hardly is the ink dry on their vows than the Princess of France shows up with her ladies on a diplomatic mission, and the young men begin working at their roles as lovers with as much energy and as little common sense as they had shown as scholars. Meantime, a group of local fools, headed by the schoolmaster and a resident melancholy Spaniard, pursue (among other things) the maid, a dishy blonde.

It's hard to single out performances because everybody is very good. Ray Virta as the King seems a natural leader, but insecurity bubbles under his unwitting arrogance (was Prince Charles a model?); as his friend Dumaine, Spike McClure combines mischief with a baby's wide eyes and rosebud mouth.

Don Reilly plays the sharp-tongued Berowne, whose habit of mocking gives him the idea he is wiser than the others. Reilly risks alienating us

---

From *The Plain Dealer* (Cleveland, 9 May 1988), 5B, 8B. Reprinted by permission of *The Plain Dealer*.

by playing him relatively cool and cynical, but in Act II, he lets us see a young man whose pride and loss of control in the situation have deeply upset him— and the interpretation engages us. All the lords have to grow up.

The ladies, on the other hand, are in touch with reality, underlined by all the earthy jokes they tell. (Some of their fooling seems tedious, however.) Gloria Beigler has a sweet gravity as the Princess, fully aware of the responsibilities of her regal position.

Reno Roop's performance as the melancholy Spaniard is high comedy; he enters in a somber whirlwind of cape, black hair, and anguished eyes like an El Greco—and then he speaks with a bit of a lisp. An extravagant poseur, he is still an innocent, and thus appealing as a child playing dress-up. Steve Routman is a wonderfully impudent Costard; Joseph Costa leers wittily as a greasy pedant, and Bernard Canepari is funny as a cigar-chomping constable, aptly named Dull.

Freedman directs with his usual clarity of line, even in the play's thicket of words, so that we see the depth under the humor. It is, after all, a play about what fun it is to be young, as well as about our need to grow up. At the end, when grim news puts an end to the unfinished revels, the love affairs are only beginning, and everyone, clowns included, has learned something. The change in tone seems to me to begin a little too soon, nearly stopping the show the clowns are putting on, but it makes sense.

The set (John Ezell), costumes (James Scott), and lighting (Natasha Katz) are ravishing; John Morris's music, which segues wittily from Elizabethan to jazz, adds a dimension.

Director Leaves Mark on *Love's Labour's Lost*

Review of *Love's Labour's Lost*, Performed by the Great Lakes Theater Festival at the Ohio Theatre on Playhouse Square

Tony Mastroianni

Determining a director's contribution to a play's success is frequently a matter of guesswork—and don't let any critic tell you otherwise.

But there are times when a director's stamp is unmistakable, when a text is enhanced and illuminated in a way that has nothing to do with the actors.

Consider the Great Lakes Theater Festival production of *Love's Labour's Lost* at the State Theatre at Cleveland's Playhouse Square. Directed by Gerald Freedman, the play is almost a living textbook on the subject of direction.

I am not referring to the 1930s setting, which is more cosmetic than cosmic and which makes no substantive changes in the play.

It is in subtler and more important ways that Freedman's work is clearly stamped.

This is best shown in the ending. Shakespeare's stage directions (none of which was ever very elaborate) are simply "exeunt omnes" (all exit).

This suggests that a stage filled with actors is simply emptied with everyone departing at once. Undoubtedly it has been done this way, with characters looking a little awkward as they wait for the curtain line.

Of the four couples in this production, only Rosaline and Berowne are left on stage, with Armado off to one side. The other three couples have wandered off, the women having put their would-be lovers on hold for a year and a day.

Berowne is a man who uses wit both as weapon and armor. Rosaline is strong-willed and quick-witted herself. Neither has quite broken through to the other, although each is receptive.

They sit with their backs to each other. Each moves a hand, groping

From *The Akron Beacon Journal* (Ohio, 12 May 1988), p. B7. Reprinted by permission of *The Akron Beacon Journal*.

to touch the other's hand. Rosaline is about to take his hand when she is touched on the shoulder by another character, given a sign that she must hurry and leave.

Berowne reaches and finds nothing, but at this moment Rosaline turns on an impulse, rushes back and kisses him lightly. A suddenly radiant Berowne gets up, goes after her, and they embrace briefly.

There are no lines for this in the text, no indication in the stage directions. This silent scene is sentimental and romantic, the only instance of sentimentality in a play that is about romance but that derides it with wit. But the pairing off of the four couples during the play is clearly romantic on Shakespeare's part, and the director's final scene is a grace note. The play has gone full circle. We know that all will be well.

There are other directorial touches, bits of stage business, some of them obvious, some merely entertaining.

When the four young men disguise themselves as Russians, they do a Cossack dance—not just a few steps but a real performance. When they vow to avoid women, a servant removes the statue of a nymph from the fountain and replaces it with a telescope.

Other matters are more subtle, but subtle or obvious, they help a play that needs help.

Love's Labour's Lost is a difficult play with wit that is often more literary than dramatic. The speech and manners of the time are the subjects for its humor. But it is a worthwhile play, an early and brilliant example of Shakespeare's ability to mix low and high comedy.

This play requires direction that is more than just competent.

The actors perform with a high degree of competence. Don Reilly and Ellen Jane Smith are all they should be and then some as Berowne and Rosaline. Ray Virta and Gloria Biegler as the king of Navarre and the princess of France are strong enough to hold their own in a play that naturally drifts in the direction of the wittier lovers.

Steve Routman as Costard is a flesh-and-blood character as well as a superb clown, and Reno Roop brings the right amount of humanity to Armado. Julia Gibson as Jaquenetta is fascinatingly believable as a country wench who could turn any man's head.

As for the 1930s setting—handsome in itself without being intrusive—it is different from but not an outright denial of the original. There are no jarring anachronisms, unless a saxophone bothers you. Pretend it's a lute.

Imagine that Shakespeare has been mixed with a bit of F. Scott Fitzgerald and that Jay Gatsby is probably throwing a party at his place down the road. Then sit back and enjoy.

YOUTHFUL TOUCH OF TENDERNESS

REVIEW OF *LOVE'S LABOR'S LOST*
AT THE PUBLIC THEATER

Clive Barnes

As so often on Shakespearean matters, it was Harley Granville-Barker who said the most sensible thing about *Love's Labor's Lost* when he wrote: "Here is a fashionable play; now, by three hundred years, out of fashion."

Granville-Barker then, as was his custom in his Shakespeare "Prefaces," proceeds to give the most valuable advice, here on the staging of this early, almost heartless, desperately fantasticated, parodistic comedy.

It is advice that Gerald Freedman—in his production of the play which last night clocked in at No. 7 in Joseph Papp's Shakespeare canonic marathon at the Public Theater's Newman Theater—has either taken to heart or did not need.

Freedman—himself apparently approaching the play for the third time as director—has caught its measure most exquisitely, making a silk purse out of a scholar's ear.

Taking to heart the play's mood of fashionable mockery, and heeding the lengthening shadows of its final dying fall, Freedman has thrust the play into some Anglo-Ruritania of this century's early '30s.

The shuttlecock resonances here evoked are wonderfully helpful to the fabric and intent of the play. We have had so many Shakespearean productions that played indiscriminate ducks and drakes with Shakespeare's times and places.

But here modern dress has a classic purpose—not to remind us, as if any reminder were needed, of the "universality" of Shakespeare, that crutch of modish directors, but to transform the play's original fashionable text into a fashion closer to our own comprehension and understanding.

From "On the Town," *New York Post* (28 February 1989), 34. Reprinted with permission from the *New York Post*.

To be sure, we either get, or miss, the outlandish puns with some irrelevant portion of our senses. But the sensibility of the piece, the concept of harsh, callow youth having its foolish fling before the onset of life's maturity, is made as immediate as a newsflash from our soul.

This contemporaneity not only enables the kids to behave like upper middle-class oafs from Terence Rattigan endowed with a touch more wit, but also permits Shakespeare's clowns to emerge with a certain kindly glow.

A difficulty of the play is that these clowns—so obtuse through most of the play—at the end, during the scene of the Nine Worthies, become fools of warmth, winning our compassion. Revealing them throughout as the class-enemies of the giddy, gilded doomed playboy generation, Freedman gives the play a very special cohesiveness.

The setting by John Ezell cunningly and cannily suggests the placing for an Anouilh comedy of rosy manners, and John Morris's music admirably complements the action, with only James Scott's costumes—the very idea of a '30s gentleman having a blazer-crest sewn onto a dinner jacket!—missing in period feel.

So far the Shakespeare marathon has been something of a parade of stars, a parade not bad in itself, but a whit lacking perhaps in confidence.

This *Love's Labor's Lost* is a brilliant, virtually starless night—but with some of the best acting the Shakespearean round has so far vouchsafed us.

William Converse-Roberts's cynical common sense as Berowne makes that hero a master of charming expediency, and the clowns, particularly Richard Libertini as a finely muddled grandee of a Don Armado, the coarse learning of Joseph Costa as Holofernes, and the amiable sycophancy of Ronn Carroll's Sir Nathaniel, are beautifully done.

Indeed, here I should have mentioned, P.J. Ochlan's perky Moth, Steve Routman's wiseboy Costard, Steve Ryan's sweetly impenetrable Dull, Julia Gibson's pert and pouting Jaquenetta, and, in a different part of the woods, John Horton's waspishly avuncular Boyet.

The rich young things, Converse-Roberts apart, are probably by intention altogether less attractive, although Christine Dunford makes a knowingly charming, and queenly, Princess of France.

And throughout, Freedman has set his whirligig spinning merrily—concentrating on the famous set pieces, such as the love-letter disclosure scene, and the Muscovite deception, but also giving an air of mad gaiety mingled with great sadness to a play too often wrongly dismissed as a mere giddy thing of youth, with little humanity to speed it to our hearts.

ON DIRECTING *LOVE'S LABOUR'S LOST*—FIVE TIMES*

Gerald Freedman

In the fall of 1992, I directed my fifth incarnation of Shakespeare's *Love's Labour's Lost*. Each production had a different cast, different settings and costumes, and each has pleased audiences and critics. My first had been for the New York Shakespeare Festival in 1965, my second for The Acting Company in 1974 (touring until 1976), my third for Great Lakes Theater Festival in 1988, my fourth for the Public Theatre in New York in 1989, and my fifth—when I could choose whatever I wanted to direct—was at North Carolina School of the Arts.

Why five productions of *Love's Labour's Lost*? Certainly, there are better known and arguably greater comedies in Shakespeare's canon. But many things about it interested me. It asks for a cast of young actors, demanding ensemble playing rather than a star turn or a duo of standouts, and its plot offers love relationships of real immediacy for young lovers. Then too, the play's formidable problems of language and verse-speaking are swept along by currents—one might say torrents—of emotional behavior. And the sometimes arcane comedy and wit are subsumed in rich characterizations. The foibles and fashions of these character types still carry the day.

To put it in modern show-business vernacular, *Love's Labour's Lost* "works." This means that actors find it playable and audiences find it funny and touching. Its comedy derives from satire and hoary vaudeville turns and from Shakespeare's deep sensitivity to the foolishness of humankind both in and out of love. It is overflowing with musical language and verbal horse-play and generosity of spirit. Its final scene is transcendent. I sometimes wonder if Shakespeare wrote another of equal humanity and compassion until *The Tempest*. Although that is an extravagant claim, the final scene in production merits such praise. If, as it seems, this was one of Shakespeare's earliest plays (though perhaps not his first), all his plangent genius was already in evidence. The rest of his work only deepened and widened and exposed landscapes of feeling and experience and intuition that seem already imbedded in the coruscating theatrical colors of this last scene.

Before I go forward in an effort to document my experience with the play and, particularly, my growth in appreciation of Act V, Scene 2, let me go back a few steps. I do not pretend to be a scholar in my approach to *Love's Labour's Lost*. My first and subsequent experiences with it have been pragmatic, based upon my theatrical instincts that have honed in the popular theatre, on Broadway, in regional theatres, and in outdoor festival production in New York's Central Park. What has been arresting and rewarding to me was to find out in subsequent research how much of my naïve, innocent instinct about the play has been corroborated by scholarship. And yet my discoveries are truths about the play that are best discovered in a rehearsal situation in a theatre. A production always puts a different "spin" on the facts that only actors working in concert can contribute. A production stamps a play with an authority that only actors and audience fulfill.

In 1989, as I embarked on my fourth encounter with *Love's Labour's Lost* (as part of the New York Shakespeare Festival/Public Theatre Shakespeare Marathon), I was interviewed for the *New York Times* by the well-known writer and publisher Robert Giroux. Mr. Giroux had been enthusiastic about my earlier production (in 1965 for the New York Shakespeare Festival), and I was eager to share with him my new-found sense of a strong correspondence between the Sonnets and *Love's Labour's Lost*. It was clear to me that they *had* to have been written at about the same time, as there were so many overlaps of sentiment, language, and feeling. Mr. Giroux seconded my enthusiasm and passion of discovery by gently and tactfully revealing that he had written a book on that very subject ten years earlier. Titled *The Book Known as Q*, it is an extraordinarily well-reasoned book that reads like a detective story. Rather than being embarrassed or chagrined by this information, as perhaps I should have been, I was elated that my instinct was now shored up by scholarship.

As Mr. Giroux points out in his book, *Love's Labour's Lost* was the *only* play of Shakespeare's that was "never performed during the Restoration, or in the eighteenth and early nineteenth centuries" (133). This is all but inexplicable today when one experiences a veritable glut of productions. It had acquired a bad "rep" as an artificial, all-but-unproducible play, with tongue-twisting language and incomprehensible comedy. But I find its artificiality and complex language to be among its most enduring attributes, and it seems to me that the charge of incomprehensibility stems from a misunderstanding of its strengths and content. Shakespeare, many scholars averred, had clearly not written the last scene, as its sudden change in tone indicated poor craftsmanship—or else some hack had written the earlier scenes and Shakespeare was called in to give it a gloss. In fact, as anyone who has produced the play will tell you, the shift in tone is one of the most deft and most daring shifts accomplished in dramatic literature; it is prompted by the core idea of the play, rather than being added on. It is implicit in Navarre's first speech:

> When spite of cormorant devouring Time,
> Th' endeavor of this present breath may buy:
> That honour which shall bate his scythe's keen edge,
> And make us heirs of all eternity. (I.1.4–7)

Only a life of true value can outlast the ravages of Time, and only in the penultimate moment do the young people in the play understand. Only then do they come in contact with and become affected by a true sense of time and commitment.

This is the glory of Shakespeare's craft and insight (genius): this sudden cloud that dims the false glare of high spirits and hormones that have generated the games and wordplay. The king desperately tries to detain the Princess of France with

> Now at the latest minute of the hour,
> Grant us your loves. (V.2.778–779)

The Princess replies:

> A time methinks too short
> To make a world-without-end bargain in. (V.2.780–781)

If this is early Shakespeare, when did he ever write lines that were more poignant, beautifully poised, and succinct?

Berowne is verbally cut down by the witty and sharp Rosaline. He vows to give up his gift of gab in eschewing

> Taffeta phrases, silken terms precise,
> Three-pil'd Hyperboles, spruce affectation,
> Figures pedantical, these summer flies
> Have blown me full of maggot ostentation. (V.2.406–409)

Was there ever a character in Shakespeare more gifted in self-awareness and self-satire than Berowne? One with such audacity to proclaim and condemn

Gerald Freedman directed his third of five productions of Love's Labour's Lost at Great Lakes Theater Festival in 1988. He set the production in the early 1930s, a time when "appearance meant everything." Shown here are Ellen Jane Smith as Rosaline, Spike McClure as Dumain, Mark Hymen as Longaville, Ray Virta as Ferdinand, and Don Reilly as Berowne. Photo by Roger Mastroianni, courtesy of Great Lakes Theater Festival.

the fault while committing it! This is writing of the highest order. One wonders how it could have been missed or misunderstood for centuries.

Perhaps the initial barrier lies in the subplot of the outrageous comic characters. At first reading, the language of Holofernes, Don Armado, and even Costard seems not merely obscure, but impenetrable. When one looks at the behavior and relationships, the layers of confusion begin to fall away. The characters are obviously indebted to classic types of the *commedia dell'arte*. Shakespeare even refers to them as the pedant (Holofernes), the braggart soldier (Armado), the pretty boy (Moth), and so on. But already, in this early play, Shakespeare is addicted to seeing his clowns in three dimensions instead of the conventional two. Though this leads to some confusion in the case of a Shylock, it seems a stroke of genius here. In a few telling phrases—a sentence—a word—he gives the fools in this play dimension, after first subjecting them to ridicule, low comedy routines, and sometimes brutal satire.

Shakespeare parades Holofernes' pomposity like a honking goose on its way to the barnyard, his erudition trailing behind him in the uneven cadence of unruly goslings. Shakespeare exposes him, with all his fatuous lust, to the nubile and innocent temptations of Jaquenetta. If Holofernes is a bullying Oliver Hardy, he is paired, in Nathaniel, with the much-abused Stan Laurel, as when Holofernes utters an aside that speaks volumes of subtle, sarcastic torment: "Priscian, a little scratched, 'twill serve." And yet Shakespeare redeems Holofernes in one searing exchange in 5.2. He gives Holofernes the last word after the brutal and cruelly adolescent treatment he receives from the young lords:

This is not generous, not gentle, not humble. (V.2.623)

In performance, this is a stinging rebuke that gets a huge laugh, and then a hushed follow-through of appropriate chastisement when the rude conduct is so acutely acknowledged.

In another line, and in preparation for the ending, there is one more moment, a beat, that prepares us for the so-called abrupt change of tone in this comedy. Don Armado has been laughed at, insulted, satirized, used as the butt of jokes and low-comedy routines, and yet Shakespeare, with his deep sense of character in the round, has him fearlessly interrupt the farcical play-within-the-play by chastising the sassy lords once more, to defend the character of Hector:

The sweet war-man is dead and rotten.
Sweet chucks, beat not the bones of the buried.
When he breathed, he was a man. (V.2.653–655)

Shakespeare is able to restore Don Armado's dignity and humanity at the expense of the young lords.

This hush presages the deeper and more complex silence that follows Marcade's announcement: "I am sorry, madame, for the news I bring is heavy in my tongue. The King your father—," but the Princess snatches the news from midair. She does not allow him to finish: "Dead, for my life!" In one direct, unadorned statement, Shakespeare elevates this silly, affectionate comedy into another sphere of mature realignment, and the young lords are transformed. The Princess, with this action, at this unexpected moment, brilliantly echoes Rosaline's sharp wisecrack in a retort to Berowne earlier in the scene: "It were a fault to snatch words from my tongue."

One despairs at a first reading of the comic scenes. What does the Latin mean? Is the Italian supposed to be funny? What am I missing in the reading of the letters? What is really going on in the scene with so many characters on stage? Is there any sense behind "the fox, the ape, and the humble bee"? (I think I found one answer in production.) Most often the sense is revealed in the behavior and not the words, although the words add an additional layer of comedy. One comes to recognize standard comic routines that have been around since Greek and Roman comedy, that existed in the rough-and-tumble burlesque, and that are still seen in television sitcoms.

Because the content dictates the form, the several productions I directed were substantially the same. But each time, my appreciation for the text deepened. For my first production, which I directed when I was in my early thirties, I characterized the essence of the play as the "game" of love. In my last production, I saw it as the "truth" of love. The dark underside of the play's content had overtaken the sunny superficial activity of the play's events in my consciousness.

The decor differed in four of the productions, although there were some constants. The play is about affluent, carefree, clever, and intelligent young people whose fun is abruptly interrupted and inexorably changed by the cloud of death. An appropriate period setting must suggest a time of national high spirits and vigor about to be shadowed by darker events. My first production (which featured some wonderful, then unknown, actors including Lee Grant, Jane White, Michael Moriarty, and Richard Jordan) was set in Jacobean England and performed amidst the natural splendor of New York's Central Park. The details of Olmsted's bridges and gardens found a natural extension onto the stage as they are all based upon gothic motifs.

The production for the Great Lakes Theater Festival was updated in decor to the early 1930s, before the clouds of World War II darkened the national spirit. It was suggestive of the wit and wisdom of *Brideshead Revisited*, and the clothes suggested a fashionable upper-class garden party.

My most recent production was played by student actors in contemporary clothes in an abstract setting, in a 400-seat theatre at the North Carolina School of the Arts. Because the play is largely concerned with language and words, I thought it would be an interesting idea to make the subject of the play the environment of the play. Language is used as ornament and entertainment, as an end in itself rather than as a means of direct communication. It is the point of the play: actions speak louder than words, which often obscure true intent and sincere feeling. Therefore, the designer and I created an outdoor park of oversized, three-dimensional letters spelling out the title of the piece. The actors interacted with the letters. They moved them around to spell out other words; they stood and sat on them; they perched in or on a letter. The letters were freestanding. A few were like oversized blocks that have an alphabet character or color on each surface, like a child's set of building blocks. In other words, the set mirrored and was the mediuim of the subject: wordplay.

It didn't seem to make a difference whether the audience was the polyglot, multiracial, multilayered gathering in Central Park or the educated, footnoted spectators of the college circuit. In every case, the audience response was identical. The laughs, the silences of hushed suspense, all came at the same places. Shakespeare caps it all with the astonishing lyrical outburst of the final song. When appropriately set to music, the lyrics mirror in every nuance the beauty, lyricism, lighthearted comedy, rustic charm and sweet sadness of the previous five acts. It is one of Shakespeare's most compelling and beautiful songs. And then, in a last brilliant stroke, Shakespeare acknowledges his achievement:

> Don Armado. The Words of Mercury
> Are harsh after the songs of Apollo:
> You that way, we this way. (V.2.922–923)

Note

*Gerald Freedman, artistic director of Great Lakes Theater Festival and dean of the North Carolina School of the Arts, wrote this essay especially for this volume.

On Designing *Love's* *Labour's Lost*—Twice*

John Ezell

Love's Labour's Lost is a play that cannot be paraphrased scenically. It is centered on language more than any play I've ever designed, and it is not easy to create a visual equivalent for language itself.

The dramatic imagination need not be tied down to literal readings of references to tents pitched for the ladies or the threshold that Costard has tripped over. Indeed, whether a scene takes place within the cloistered walls of Navarre's "little academe" or outside the gates through which the Princess of France may not pass is not a matter of geographic rigidity. Shakespearean space is telescopic. As Margaret Webster observed, "where the actor is—there is the place." The place is determined by the magnetic pull of verbal energy. An actor leaves by one gate and comes in another, thereby moving from one locale to another. Shakespeare shifts the place to the actor rather than shifting the actor to the place. Synecdochically, a part represents the whole, the whole represents each part.

My first task as designer of *Love's Labour's Lost* was to find the architectonic structure under the play's efflorescent poetic allusions. What I discovered was that the structure of Shakespeare's workshop, the Elizabethan stage itself, is embedded in the text. Prepositions like *within, without, up, down, in, out* provide the clues. The structural dynamic of the Elizabethan stage informs the writing—even if the play was originally performed in a banqueting hall at court and even when it is transferred to other spatial configurations in the modern theatre.

If you look at the two settings I have designed for *Love's Labour's Lost* —the first for Gerald Freedman's 1988 production at Great Lakes Theater Festival (later transferred to the New York Shakespeare Festival as number seven in Joseph Papp's Shakespeare Marathon), the second directed by Melia Bensussen in the Helen F. Spencer Theatre for the University of Missouri-Kansas City professional theatre training program in 1994—you see

John Ezell designed the setting for Gerald Freedman's 1988 production at Great Lakes Theater Festival, which became the basis for the 1989 production at the New York Shakespeare Festival. Ezell's original rendering is done in soft shades of blue-green. Photo courtesy of John Ezell.

two very different interpretations of the court of Navarre. But if you look through the façades of time, texture, and temperament for each setting, you discover what is essentially the structure of the Globe Theatre. You might say that I started with something like a sculptor's armature and then fleshed it out. In fact, despite great differences in feeling and complexion, my designs for *Othello* at the Shakespeare Theatre in the Folger and for *Titus Andronicus* at Great Lakes Theater Festival made fundamentally the same use of space.

In IV.3 of *Love's Labour's Lost*, the King and lords enter the garden one by one, and each in turn eavesdrops on the romantic ruminations of the next. Berowne says: "Like a demi-god here sit I in the sky" (IV.3.76), as he looks down upon "four woodcocks in a dish." Logic demands an upper level on which Berowne may "stand aside," an inner below where the King may "step aside," and two side entrances through which Longaville and Dumain may enter and subsequently "step aside." Berowne's characterization of the stage below him as a "dish" is reminiscent of the Chorus's description in *Henry V* of the theatre as a "wooden O." The armature of the Elizabethan stage fits these plays like a glove.

Once the Elizabethan armature is in place, we can depart from the Tudor complexion of the Elizabethan stage. A specific setting can be devised to give the play a historical, metaphorical, and emotional context all its own. Both Jerry Freedman and Melia Bensussen wished to set the play in a historical period for which the *Zeitgeist* would be analogous to that of the text. Jerry's analog was the 1930s as expressed in fashions, manners, customs, attitudes, and gestures. This is, of course, not the only way to proceed with Shakespeare in the late twentieth century. For example, one might apply a conscious metaphor as a commanding image. But neither Jerry nor Melia found it useful to attempt to subsume the metaphorical meanings of this play in a dominant commanding image. Despite its youthful intransigence, *Love's Labour's Lost* is far too complex and much too subtle to be easily summarized.

The *Love's Labour's Lost* set must have a sense of enclosure. Gerald Freedman's production used a damp, fertile garden surrounding a two-story neoclassical glass conservatory. (Although it was never my conscious intention to make it so, the design of this pavilion suggested a three-tiered wedding cake to some observers.) In any case, this architectural confection, covered with fermenting moss, seemed to be falling into ruin, a victim of time and prolific vegetation. At center stage, a fountain featured statues of three graces, soon to be replaced by instruments of science in tribute to the young lords' vows of abstinence. Beneath its playful exterior, the setting conveyed a vague sense of danger; the roses in this garden were spiked with thorns.

In Melia Bensussen's production too, it was clear that nature would prevail over manmade forms. Her garden was surrounded by thick stone walls, but the conscious stability of the architecture was challenged by an enormously twisted tree growing up through the structure of the inner above. (This effect was directly inspired by an ancient tree I saw growing through the crumbling retaining wall of an old colonial consulate just across from Hong Kong Cultural Center.) Melia's *point de repère* was the romantic *oeuvre* of Fragonard and Boucher, those masters of fashionable dalliance, for whom the study of antiquities became an instrument of escape from the tyranny of standard eighteenth-century social convention. Our staging marked the ritual nature of each of the four seasons—from "daisies pied and violets blue" in spring, to "oaten straws and summer smocks," to autumn's "all aloud . . . wind," to the "icicles . . . by the wall" and "birds . . . brooding in the snow" of winter—vividly recalling the evolution of what Suzanne Langner has called the "feeling form." There was an almost pageant-like progression from the warm Italianate golds and amethyst of Fragonard's *Fête at Saint-Cloud* to the deep blues and jade of *The Fête at Rambouillet*, underscored by the drift of blossoms, fruit, foliage and, finally, snow.

Though the settings I designed for Jerry and Melia were very different in appearance and atmospheric quality, both emphasized tensions between artifice and nature. In Melia's production, the changing seasons—from spring to summer to autumn to winter—served as a metaphor for the progress of life, from callow adolescence to beyond maturity. Within that progression are two theatrical explosions, the masque of Muscovites and the masque of the Nine Worthies. In Jerry's 1930s approach, the audience knows that everyone is on the brink of World War II. Berowne is undoubtedly killed in the war before the year is up.

Love's Labour's Lost has a dark inner lining that I find appealing. The merciless sarcasm inflicted by the young lords upon the amateur actors' performance of the pageant of the Nine Worthies is much more insulting and less good-natured than the jibes of the courtiers during the comparable performance of Pyramus and Thisbe in *A Midsummer Night's Dream*. And whereas *A Midsummer Night's Dream* ends with three weddings and a blessing of the house, the ending of *Love's Labour's Lost* is emotionally ambivalent, to say the least.

Each of Shakespeare's plays seems to follow an arc, sometimes steep and at other times gradual. The apogee of each arc functions like a pivot and is marked by dramatic contrasts in the use of verse and prose. Sometimes the pivotal moment comes early, as in the first act of *King Lear;* the scene of Lear's abdication and rejection of Cordelia is followed by a long unwinding of the consequences of his actions. Richard III shares his most private thoughts with the audience until the pivotal moment of his coronation midway through the play, after which he is less inclined to communicate with us directly. It's crucial for the designer to find the pivot, because the complexion of the play changes there.

After the pivot in *Love's Labour's Lost* (the report of the Princess's father's death), everyone lingers to finish the entertainment, but it's in a different key. We get spring and winter, Ver and Hiems, and then the heartbreaking "you that way, we this way," reminding us that for each coming together there must, inevitably, come a parting. Like bad news at a picnic, the ending is wildly asymmetrical and, alas, all too much like life.

NOTE

*John Ezell is Hall Family Foundation Professor of Theatre at the University of Missouri-Kansas City, resident designer for Missouri Repertory Theatre, and associate artistic director of Great Lakes Theater Festival. He wrote this essay especially for this volume.

LOVE'S LABOR'S LOST

Randall Louis Anderson

Presented by The Yale Dramatic Association at Yale Repertory Theatre, New Haven, CT. February 21–23 and 26–29, 1992. Directed by Rosey Hay. Set by Matthew Moore. Costumes by Karen Ngo. Lighting by Jeremy Stein. Sound by Erich Stratmann. Original music by Chris Beck. With Leo Marks (King of Navarre), Josh Newman (Longaville), Matthew E. Wulf (Dumain), Alessandro Nivola (Berowne), Robert Davenport (Don Armado), Xeni Fragakis (Mote), Adam Drucker (Boyet), Jenny Lord (Princess of France), Nadine A. George (Maria), Jordana H. Utter (Katharine), Laura Goldschmidt (Rosaline), Newton Kaneshiro (Marcade), Daniel Shiffman (Dull), James Waterston (Costard), Anne B. Johnsos (Jacquenetta), Cebra Graves (Forester), Adam Kingl (Holofernes), and Rasmus Johansen (Sir Nathaniel).

*   *   *

Once each year, Yale College's oldest and largest theatre organization, known informally as the Dramat, has access to the University's main stage, the Yale Repertory Theatre. Designed to optimize its annual opportunity, the Dramat's philosophy for this production—that the choice of an accomplished director was more important than the play selected—was rightly rewarded by the effort of Rosey Hay (whose credits include work with RSC and NYSF). Although a notoriously difficult play to stage effectively, when thoughtfully directed *Love's Labor's Lost* can offer (*contra* Dr. Johnson and Granville-Barker) much more than a dense tissue of inaccessible witticisms. In my eyes, Hay's sophisticated interpretation merited the same praise that John Dover Wilson bestowed on Tyrone Guthrie's 1936 Old Vic *Love's Labor's Lost*: she "gave me a new play, the existence of which I had never suspected," and "set me at a fresh standpoint of understanding and appreciation" (*Shakespeare's Happy Comedies* [Evanston: Northwestern UP 1962], 64). I exchanged my own shortsighted expectations of an anachronistic artifact from Shakespeare's immaturity for awareness of a social and psychological commentary capable of engaging a modern audience.

Originally published in *Shakespeare Bulletin* 10 (Summer 1992), 23–24. Reprinted by permission.

The most striking example of this production's refreshing approach was provided by Don Armado. Before the house lights went down and throughout I.1, keen eyes, focused downstage right, caught Armado asleep within the perimeter of Navarre's Academe (a decaying, grey stone wall), bundled against the autumn chill (suggested by a few barren saplings and dried leaves and cold, blue-filtered light). At the beginning of I.2, Mote led the still drowsy Armado to center stage, where the page tenderly shaved the fantastical Spaniard and replaced the worn blanket draped over his shoulders with a tattered, threadbare jacket that sagged under the weight of what appeared to be campaign medals. While his venerable profile was reminiscent of recent attempts to incarnate Don Quixote in Don Armado (such as in Michael Langham's offering at Stratford, Ontario, in 1984), his attire betrayed his homelessness and, by extension, suggested his emotional desperation; this Armado did not step out of a Velásquez canvas as much as he stepped in from the streets of New Haven.

Hay's production was beleaguered by no latent political agenda, but the resonance of the image was unavoidable. It immediately lent this dispossessed Armado an air of vulnerability that kept the audience on his side throughout the play, and, before his duel with Costard, it added particular poignancy to his admission "The Naked truth of it is, I have no shirt."

Robert Davenport's Armado also revealed uncommonly believable depth of feeling; he did not descend into caricature. When left alone at the end of I.2, for example, he dropped arthritically to one knee and, steadying himself with his sword-cane (an interesting symbolic representation of Armado's geriatric brand of chivalry), lovingly, longingly kissed the spot where Jacquenetta's foot had rested. This proved a touching prologue to the speech that followed: "I do affect the very ground . . . where her shoe . . . doth tread." In sharp contrast to the staging of Armado's affections, Berowne's face was derisively pushed to the forest floor when in IV.3 he inquired, rhetorically, who "Kisses [not] the base ground" for Rosaline? Thus the fundamental difference was displayed between the desperate—yet authentic—devotion of the old and the hollow fancies of the young.

The court parties of Navarre and France were refugees from the Jazz Age. Their costuming (which culminated in long cocktail dresses and white tie and tails for Act V) effectively underscored their youthful exuberance and suggested a certain shallowness and selfishness of desire as well as the premium they would attach to studied stylishness (reflected poetically by the young men's fashionable participation in the sonneteering craze). In conjunction with the sensibilities implied by the costuming, Hay's selection of *Love's Labor's Lost* was (as she remarked to me) all the more suitable for the

Dramat because it employed a youthful cast that did not have to stretch far to display the behavior patterns of its characters. The program notes usefully cited, as the production's credo, John Keats's definition of adolescence as that time during "which the soul is in ferment, the character undecided" and from whence proceeds "all the thousand bitters which men must necessarily taste"—certainly an appropriate description not only of the play's but also of the players' transformation.

Such self-subverting ferment of soul was featured from the play's start. The King's breathless excitement when advertising his Academe's edicts was quickly defused by the failure to think through the implications of his impetuous resolve: he searched his companions' faces for sympathy when proclaiming with embarrassment the French embassage "was quite forgot." The collective inconstancy of the young men was celebrated when the academic robes eagerly assumed in I.2 were more eagerly shed with the exhortation "Saint Cupid, then! and, soldiers, to the field!" In this production, the court of France appeared much more malignant to, rather than maligned by, the games of Cupid. These were tough, headstrong women who meant business when resolving "the gallants shall be task'd"; their self-confidence—which sometimes bordered on self-righteousness—was fully apparent to the audience when rationalization turned declaration: "There's no such sport as sport by sport o'erthrown."

Even had the women of France not been as formidable as they were, the two pageants in V.1 gave the men of Navarre plenty of rope with which to hang themselves. The Muscovite embassy—complete with fur *shapki* and *gopak* dancing—begged the return of "mock for mock," down to Boyet's mimicking of Navarre's affected accents ("Notink but peace and gentle wisitation"). The spectacle of the nine worthies used the stage quite effectively: at first there was some integration between the court parties, but the groups became physically polarized as the jests became more abusive. The King was the last to linger on the ladies' side, but his pained expression did not cloud his companions' faces. Eventually, the play's gender gap was spatially, as well as temperamentally, realized.

Set against the self-conscious court parties were the indigenous folk of Navarre: Dull convincingly displayed eponymous density, Sir Nathaniel answered Holofernes's pedantry with fits of narcolepsy, and Holofernes himself, supercilious *in extremis*, relished occasional, violent visits to his snuffbox while ferreting out false Latin. But the most engaging locals by far were the two who, with Armado, completed the play's love triangle. Anne B. Johnsos's Jacquenetta exuded fertility and raw sexual energy, coupling an attractive innocence with an unexpected aggressiveness: her response to

Armado's promise to visit her at the lodge was to pull his hand deep into her lap when exclaiming "That's hereby." James Waterston's Costard clearly enjoyed his carefree life style, but he hardly lived up to Berowne's abusive indictment of him as a "loggerhead."

This was the most cunning Costard imaginable; regardless of his hopelessly limited vocabulary (Waterston's reinflections of *remuneration* and *guerdon* provided a delightful revision of the notion that sound makes an echo to the sense), he proved quite capable of subverting the practiced linguistic posturing of the *billets doux*. The confusion of Armado's and Berowne's letters was wholly premeditated, which Waterston revealed by hitting the side of his head in mock surprise when producing from his pocket the letter he knew was truly intended for Rosaline. With the pruning of all the bawdy banter after IV.1.106 and the reducing of Costard's closing speech in that scene to a self-reflexive couplet—"O' my troth, most sweet jests! most icony vulgar wit; / When it comes so smoothly off, so obscenely as it were, so fit"—he assumes full responsibility for the undoing of Armado and Berowne so he can enjoy Jacquenetta with impunity. After an extended, groping embrace of her in IV.3, he lacerates Navarre with his indignation: "Walk aside the true folk, and let the traitors stay."

By putting Costard in control of the play's *dénouement*, this production disclosed one view of love's labor that is lost in less searching interpretations; although the play relies so heavily on stylized language, it ultimately asserts the inefficacy of that language to insulate one from the realities of life. Here the prolixity of the court parties masked their mutual fears of feeling too much; the prolixity of Armado masked his anxiety that no one might feel anything for him in return (which is in evidence to the end: he is left alone, weeping, after Jacquenetta sings Winter's song). In the instance of the court parties, reality—mortality—intrudes with Marcade, and adolescence is abandoned according to the Keatsian formula. The comedy's discomfiting closure, however, was further problematized by Armado's frailty: it was unlikely he would live to see the end of his three years' penance (for paternity that clearly was not his). When Armado addressed the closing stage direction to the audience—"You that way: we this way"—we were reminded that theatre cannot substitute for human reality but certainly can make us more sensitive and reponsive to it.

Continuous Sonnets

Amy Reiter

Designer Kandis Cook describes the language in *Love's Labour's Lost* as both a floating champagne bubble which cannot land and a piece by Mozart which must not be interrupted. So when director James Macdonald called on her to design the set and costumes for Manchester's Royal Exchange Theatre production of Shakespeare's play, which opened in mid-September [1992], she was careful not to invade the purity of the language with her design.

"It's continuous sonnets," says Cook. "I designed so that you could concentrate on the language, so that what you were visually picking up was actually introducing you into the rhythm of it. It was really important that we didn't obstruct with visuals what we were trying to listen to."

Cook put a grass turf circle at center stage with two gangways of natural brick on either side. "When they were on the grass turf you couldn't hear any movement except the rustling of material," says Cook. "It was designed so that you could actually hear the language."

The clothes were designed with the same goal in mind. Cook says, "I put it around 1640, and then I stretched it. I didn't want to bog everybody down with a period look which is heavier, in fact, than the language." Costuming the fantastical Spaniard Armado, for instance, whom Cook calls "a periodless person, extremely sentimental and romantic," she used clothing from all different times.

Cook created the costumes for the princess and her three attending ladies with an even lighter hand. "It was a sort of ethereal look," she says. "The women had to appear totally magical. When they arrive, they completely throw the young scholars; they are not able to think straight for the rest of the play. They're all wearing layers of silk taffeta, silk organza, silk

Reprinted from *Theatre Crafts International* 27 (January 1993), 9, with permission of Entertainment Technology Communications Corporation; copyright 1993. Information: http://www.etecnyc.net.

royal, and georgette; they're very, very light." The princess herself was granted additional heavenly sparkle with a bodice and a long train of intricately appliqued bead-work.

The palette for the four women was equally ethereal. Cook dressed them in what she terms "a very, very soft champagne kind of ivory, pale, pale pastel, kind of pink-peachish type skin-tone color." She added soft mauve tints in the cream to prevent glare under the lights (designed by Ace McCarron). "They came in like a massive cloud, billowing with this material that just kind of fused together. They were really like a four-headed spirit coming into the space when they appeared and then they broke into four separate components."

LOVE'S LABOR'S LOST

Margaret Loftus Ranald

Presented by Theatre for a New Audience at St. Clement's Church, New York, NY. March 6–April 3, 1993. Directed by Michael Langham. Set by Douglas Stein. Costumes by Ann Hould-Ward. Lighting by Matthew Frey. Sound by Jim van Bergen. Music by Alexandra Harwood. Choreography by Jill Beck. Fights by J. Allen Suddeth. With Zachary Ehrenfreund (Navarre), Gregory Poretta (Longaville), Trellis Stepter, Jr. (Dumain), Alec Phoenix (Berowne), Peter Jacobson (Dull), Mark Niebuhr (Costard), Michael Rudko (Don Armado), Kathleen Christal (Moth), Frani Ruch (Jaquenetta), Eric Swanson (Boyet), Christina Haag (Princess), Enid Graham (Maria), Linda Powell (Katharine), Melissa Bowen (Rosaline), Francis E. Hodgins (Sir Nathaniel), Samuel Baird (Holofernes), Bruce Racond (Marcade), Lisa Dove (Photographer), and others.

*   *   *

A curious sense of autumnal loss pervaded Michael Langham's production of Shakespeare's wittiest early comedy. Signaled by the set and sustained by the slow-paced dialogue, this directorial perspective overwhelmed the play's coruscating wit. Perhaps Langham underestimated the intelligence of his audience and therefore had his players labor puns or witticisms in order to gain understanding from the uninformed. Or this approach may have been chosen to facilitate communication with the high school audiences to which this company has a special mission. Whatever the reason, the dialogue, which ought to have sparkled, became rather leaden, while the initial renunciation of all feminine company had a world-weariness about it that few later moments were able to redeem.

The ravages of death and time were emphasized in the standing set, which provided a gazebo reminiscent of the Sultan Ahmet Fountain of Istanbul, surmounted by a weathervane of Father Time or even Death. A shrouded urn stage left recalled Poussin's sarcophagus with its motto "Et in Arcadia Ego," while the central stump of a felled mature tree increased the funereal quality of this faux-cerebral pastoral world. Later, the urn was

Originally published in *Shakespeare Bulletin* 11 (Summer 1993), 14–15. Reprinted by permission.

replaced by a statue of Cupid, once the young men fell in love, and the statue remained onstage as an ironic icon as they reluctantly accepted their purgatorial year of waiting. The shocking intrusion of real life through the death of the Princess's father, which finitely (or perhaps infinitely) postpones matrimonial fulfillment, was vitiated by the melancholy ambiance that counterpointed any merriment. The lute and cello music by Alexandra Harwood reinforced the mood. Even the useful program notes contributed to it, beginning with the fall of Constantinople and continuing with the Puritan opposition to the theatre.

Overall, the spirit of fun was missing here, even in the deliberately satiric and comic "lowlife" characters. Slapstick was blessedly minimal, but the "feast of words" was undigested, and *honorificabilitunidinitatibus* was masticated rather than flourished. Anthony Dull, all too well named, looked inappropriately like a member of the G & S Constabulary, while Costard was mildly catatonic and Jaquenetta merely blowsy. In short, laughter was minimally extracted from the audience, whose profoundly serious respect was maximal, so that the wit generally became marmoreal. Holofernes and Nathaniel simply seemed irrelevant here, but then the bite of the original personal satire is almost irrecoverable, and so to some extent is Shakespeare's heady delight in and experimentation with a newly developing literary language.

I found myself desperately trying to find a reason to laugh, waiting for the fun to begin, and finally welcoming the exuberant Muscovite interlude as a piece of escapism that had been too long absent from this somewhat spent stage world. Here the spirited drums and musical accompaniment gave the audience its only opportunity for shedding inhibitions with a good laugh. For the first time, the young Navarrese noblemen threw themselves heartily into action in this showpiece Russian dance complete with flashing swords and folkloric kick line. It was a deliciously parodic piece, choreographed by Jill Beck and performed with the precision of the real thing.

Anachronistically, there was also some comic solace in the sight-gag of the invisible roving photographer recording important events for posterity with flash and drumbeat. It drew its first laugh at the swearing ceremony, as everyone momentarily "froze," and recurred throughout the performance as a means of emphasis, for example, to heighten the entrance of the Princess and her retinue. The problem was that this device coarsened both the comic action and the verbal wit. I did enjoy Boyet's stage business in his diplomatic mission between the ladies and gentlemen (conducted with the solemnity of a military negotiation) and the use of handholds in the backstage wall as a tree for overhearing the love sonnets.

The assemblage of ladies, composed of contrasting personalities and distinguishable ethnic backgrounds, was more interesting than the posturing men. Christina Haag showed a good sense of comedy of manners as the Princess-controller of her lovelorn ladies, who occasionally fell into affectation. The hunting scene opened at a faster clip, but then the wit declined into overstatement—"a pretty pleasing PRICK-et"—or high-speed racing—so that the "hundred SoreL" went glimmering. Certainly the women had a better sense of the ridiculous than their men, who needed a great deal of instruction in the art of living and loving.

Perhaps the mixture of periods in this production created a thematic dislocation both onstage and in the audience. The style could best be described as Edwardian eclectic, and the ladies had the best of the bargain in their triple changes of dress and flattering hats. The Princess wore pale floating gowns, and I particularly liked Rosaline's sophisticated gold-striped opening costume. The young men were all in contrastingly colored three-piece suits of World War I undergraduate vintage, in the King's case with a knightly sash. Then, after taking their oath of eremitical study on the King's sword, they were ceremonially invested in varied brown-toned academic gowns, again an autumnal note rather than one of youthful idealism. But as "Muscovites," their costuming literally shone. I was puzzled, however, about the military-looking French diplomat in Act I and the Paris policeman who arrived to announce the death of the King of France.

The cast spoke the lines with intelligence and understanding, indicating perhaps their general Juilliard training, probably under Langham, and incidentally proving that standard stage American is an admirable vehicle for the Shakespearean line. They clearly understood the nature and the quality of their verbal acts but were too calculatedly cerebral in firing off their witty "invisible bullets" in this early treatment of the "merry war" between the sexes. The young men remained very callow in love—hardly the products of the court of the legendary Marguerite—and one wondered why the ladies bothered with them. As usual in the comedies, the women had the common sense, but I had the nagging feeling that these young men would never measure up. The final "cuckoo" song offered a genuine possibility of unfulfillment or infidelity rather than "a world-without-end bargain." That Jack would never have Jill seemed likely—but then what would happen to the women?

Something was missing at the heart of this production. In a play where rhetoric competes with pedantry, quibbles with malapropisms, and eloquence rides high above all, one should not complain that the production fell short of verbal brilliance. But this flawed production certainly proves the necessity of matching mood and matter to take full advantage of the play's richly multilayered tragicomic texture. At the moment, *Love's Labor's Lost* may well be "caviare to the general." Still, this production offers only some hints of its joyous, romantic, and stimulating possibilities.

Shakespeare, Half of Creation

Reminiscences of Don Armado*

Péter Huszti

Stratford! Green lawn, fresh-cut grass, weeping willow, plants, barges, preening swans, a theatre, a church, tortuous streets—on which he walked! A half-timber house—where he was born! Chairs, beds, kitchen utensils, pens, books: things we want to believe, and so we do believe that each of them belonged to him. A small town, which he escaped from, and later escaped back to, and there finished his life. Shakespeare's country!

Could he have known that this land would all become known as his, just as theatres, companies, and festivals are named after him?

Could he have known that centuries later the greatest excitement for directors, actors, actresses, and audiences anywhere in the world would be to perform his dramas, to listen to them, to see them?

Could he have lived a life encompassing as much as he knew about the world? About love, friendship, hate, jealousy, desires, dreams, politics, and power. About youth, age, boys, girls, men, women; about us. If a Shakespeare play cuts such a big doorway into life, and a major Shakespeare role cuts so deeply into the actor, what if he had actually struggled through the events of those tragedies and comedies in his life? Oh, God!

In the opinion of the great Hungarian poet Sándor Petőfi, Shakespeare is half of Creation. And I have come to realize that one who thinks about Shakespeare thinks about life, and one who thinks about life is thinking about the self.

The moment I first knew I was an actor and the most important stations in my life as an actor belonged to Shakespeare. As a green student actor, I had already started to flirt with the Master. On that little practice stage, I fearlessly tackled the maddening story of Macbeth, I had a turn as Petruchio in a short scene opposite a long-legged girl, and I got to strut and fret my hour upon the stage as Malvolio. But I was only twenty and understood nothing.

The third year of training got me a student actor's backstage pass and the chance to appear on the stage of the Madách Theatre. Whether it was set with the castle at Elsinore or the forest in *As You Like It*, it seemed so vast.

And then there were so many figures created out of dirt and sunshine, into whose skins I have slipped, and who have slipped under mine. Of them all, the most interesting were the roles provided by the great Shakespeare. With them I have walked the most dangerous paths. With them I suffered and struggled most, and fell the farthest and flew the highest. Through them I learned the most about life, and I started to know myself.

How many hot, crazy, magical, dreadful nights he gave me! On midsummer night, as Demetrius, overcome by the love potion, I ran up and down in ecstasy in the woods outside Athens. In *Troilus and Cressida*, honest Hector—whose tragedy was precisely his clarity—lent me his fortitude. Petruchio and I met again, and once again he swept me into a painful, strange, cruel comedy, using the latest techniques of "mind-clearing" to find some accommodation with the stubborn Kate. The rich, abundant, and sorrowful story of *Twelfth Night*—a play in which the Poet's magic touch can instantly transform an ecstatic roar into numbing silence—gave me my favorite alter ego: Sir Toby Belch, who longs for friendship and love, and kills his bitterness in wine, beer, brandy, and wild carousing. Hamlet and Iago. Heaven and earth! In monumental stories that shake heaven and earth I came dangerously too close. The cruel story of King Lear, who became wise in his madness, who became a man through suffering, coursed through me and forced me to see myself.

Seventeen years ago I was that "fantastical Spaniard," Don Adriano de Armado. For 150 nights the story of *Love's Labour's Lost* brought from the audience gurgles of delight, rapturous applause, roaring laughter, and the sudden silence of embarrassment. After all this time I remember vividly the tingling, forgiving flow of love coming from the darkness of the auditorium to reach my gallant gentleman who again and again set out to fight the battle of love. His energy still penetrates my body and soul.

Before I go into that story, I must pause to repeat the commonplace that the theatre exists to serve the audience. We play to the audience, with them, for them, and—often, more importantly, especially when it's Shakespeare—representing them. It's actually impossible to play Shakespeare without the participating presence of the audience. Their eagerness before the opening curtain, their laughter, weeping, applause, and silence are part of the joy of being an accomplice in the action. Our audiences in Budapest and throughout Hungary have the impudence and insight to expose themselves bravely to daring approaches, thereby giving their directors and actors the impetus to attempt new interpretations. This is the audience that claims Shakespeare for their own, crowning him eternal king of the Hungarian stage regardless of social or political systems or various fashions and movements with names ending in "-ism."

To tackle the comedies of Shakespeare is a formidable task. For the actor, it is a journey fraught with peril, through a jungle of mysteries and pitfalls, orchids and snakepits. What is the true nature of Shakespeare's comedies? They might be described as airy, sweet, ethereal. But for all their poetry, virtuoso wit, and lightness, they are at the same time quite earthbound. There is in them coarse humor, overheatedness, filthy talk, slushy erotics, and savageness. There is cruelty in the battle of the sexes. Just when one becomes entranced by the lightness and sparkle, then all hell breaks loose. In the sun-drenched groves of the comedies, there are springs smelling of brimstone and poisonous gases, spouting chaos and dark impulses. The poisonous gases cause the tawdry pieces of clothing to fall dramatically while smiles sag on cheeks and grins slushy with booze get cruelly frozen. Now perfidy, lies, hypocrisy, conceit, and stupidity stand out in the same light. What has always grabbed me in Shakespeare's comedies is this bitterness. No matter whether I played Demetrius, Petruchio, or Sir Toby Belch, my thoughts were always loitering about the suspicion that Master William probably knew these people so well that it was dangerous for him. Perhaps he knew more than he should. We don't like knowing so much about ourselves. Such a degree of self-knowledge might exceed our endurance.

During the weeks of preparation for *Love's Labour's Lost*, I was surprised at the abundance of less-than-enthusiastic—and sometimes forthrightly hostile—essays that had been published on this comedy. There was a wide range of unfavorable opinion: An extremely bad play! Nothing but fiction and diction! Literary concentrate! A big, lively nothing! Only Berowne, a distant spiritual relation of Petruchio and Mercutio, was granted some absolution; he might evolve into Benedict or prefigure the spirit of Prince Hal or even that of the Prince of Denmark. But no one put in a good word for my awkward Don Armado, at least not in the essays I read. That might be the very reason for my becoming so involved in his character. That is what fueled my enthusiasm to take a firm stand for him. One of my professional quirks may have been born of my encounter with Don Armado. The actor—dare I say it?—sometimes functions as a solicitor. The actor solicits the audience's acceptance of the character. Every absurd figure acts in accordance with some inner order. Each is right in his or her own way, so the actor must take this character's truth into himself and put faith in it. The actor has no choice but to fight stoutly for the character's view, even when it is proved false. To identify with sin is a game of peril. And how often this game has put me into the defendant's dock, into awkward situations difficult to clear up.

At the first reading rehearsal I didn't have the faintest idea how this "dog comedy" would be staged, what my awkward Don Armado would look like, how he would speak, move, love, and suffer. Like it or not, I was about to live the life of this chap, whoever he was. Then, following the usual procedure that is—thank God!—standard practice in the theatre, we put aside essays and began to rehearse. We began to explore this story of love, jealousy, desires, dreams, and tottering people, each defending our own truth. How my gestures or emphases developed and gave birth to my character I cannot clearly recall. My misty recollection of my funny guy of the past is of a thickheaded, shy crank, who is clumsy, cautious, and posing, who exerts himself to avoid stumbling and as a result trips over his own foot. In his mind his actual failures become heroic deeds, and these become the subject of epics he can sing about himself after picking himself up and dusting himself off. Though everybody laughs at him, he becomes me, and I am dead earnest in speaking his every word, his every sentence. Similarly, he takes seriously everything that happens to him or others. On the side, I was always drawing windmills in my script as reminders of some spiritual source under the name and mask of Don Quixote. This probably would not have bothered the Master, since he regularly helped himself to elements from well-known stories and showed no sign of guilty conscience.

As a start, I committed a brave falsification, which might elicit serious objections. Don Armado's choking, jealous letter of "denunciation," which in the text is carried by Dull was in our production delivered by Don Armado. Stammering, stuttering, sniveling, I handed it over to the king. It was crucial that I be the one to report personally the upsetting event, the revolting "porno" scene that I had witnessed: my secret love Jacquenetta fornicating with a guy of low rank. It was at this point, at the very beginning, that everything became confused for my melancholic, gallant gentleman. The lyrical poet, the ordained priest of enthusiasm, the lunatic general of peace goes mad in front of everyone and becomes a fool of love.

That stricken state served as the basis on which to reanimate the figure's body and soul. My clumsy military uniform coat reaching to the ground, my feathered Spanish hat, rusty sword, riding gauntlet with holes in it, fine handkerchief, laces and ribbons, the faded red rose, and slips of paper with love sonnets were all the belongings of the lonely soldier with the soul of a lyric poet. These are the props of a middle-aged man longing to love and be loved, seeking friendship, emotionally still a teenager. He is a being so lonely, so defenseless, desiring so much to belong to someone and something, that it is easy for him to be hurt, to be driven mad.

Even in this bitter comedy, everything revolves around love. Loud-mouthed bragging, firebrand love letters, frightened evasions, frisky flirtations, jealous spying—all aim at one thing: to conquer the heart of the beloved "she." As if contemplating my youth, I remember in a muddled way the events and places of the play. The forest where we chased each other, bushes that hid us when we fornicated, a board fence that served to protect me, castle gates that opened creakily and swung shut with a loud bang behind me, raging storms and gales, blasting trumpets and screaming bugles have all infiltrated my private memory. No matter how far in the past those sounds recede, the memory of them can still fluster me. The realm of the imagination created by Shakespeare is closer to living reality than the tangible world. While the important streets, houses, stairs of my youth fade with passing time, something from Don Armado's world made a permanent impression on me. When Don Armado stepped into my shoes, something determining happened, something that had an impact on my whole life.

The brilliant punchline of the parallel-action plot is definitely the amateur performance of Holofernes's dreadful play of the Nine Worthies. Presenting theatre within the theatre is always a peculiar experience for

Péter Huszti played Don Adriano de Armado at the Madách Színház in Budapest. Photo courtesy of Péter Huszti.

actors and audience, especially when it includes a mockery of actors' zeal. But in our production, the "staff meeting" in which the performance is planned (Act V, Scene 1) was every bit as enjoyable as the payoff. In that scene, we insolently let our own experiences sneak into the discussion; that is, experiences my fellow actors and I had all had in confrontations with small-minded politicians in charge of culture, dull bank officials, and ministry employees who bore a grudge against the theatre. Then came our pageant, and all hell broke loose at last. The audience screamed with laughter to the point that we could scarcely continue. Even objects played an active part in undermining the Nine Worthies. The folding screens toppled over, swords broke, helmet visors resisted being raised or lowered, curtains sagged, torches ceased burning when light was necessary and shone obstinately when it should have been dark. The riff-raff band, playing completely off key, struck up a tune at an inappropriate moment. And finally all of the stage trappings collapsed, burying all the zealous dilettantes beneath it. On top of the failures in his private life, his disappointments in love, Don Armado was pulled down as an artist too. Desires, dreams, and hopes miscarried. However, the fatal stab was still ahead. No sooner had I risen to my feet again than Costard, who stole my love, challenged me to a duel in the presence of the king and the whole court, fixing the condition that the duel be fought with both parties in their shirts, as befits real gentlemen. Tension filled the room. What a horrible moment for me! In this hard, stunning silence, I pondered whether I had to admit that I was unable to protect my honor, unable to accept the challenge of my opponent, unable to remove my military coat and fight in a shirt, because the dreadful truth was that . . . I had no shirt. There was a sudden burst of laughter both on the stage and in the audience. Then I was stripped of my coat, left standing half naked and defenseless in front of my beloved king, my lost love, and the whole court. Everything went black in front of my eyes. The world ceased to exist. *Finita la commedia!*

At that moment, every single night, as if by the sudden touch of a magic wand, the audience's laughter subsided. For youngsters and elderly people alike, this cruel joke, this awkward, unnecessary humiliation exceeded everybody's tolerance. So the miracle was accomplished. That's enough, thank you.

Shakespeare is most gratifying at times like that, when I succeed in getting close, body and soul, to those sitting in the auditorium. Conversations after the performance showed me that the stories of Hamlet, Othello, King Lear, Petruchio, Sir Toby Belch, Oberon, Hector, and Don Armado were not mere fairy tales to them. They must have recognized something from life and learned something about themselves. Thus Shakespeare's comedies and tragedies can be considered cruel courses in life, which instruct us in getting acquainted with others and with ourselves at the same time.

At the end of each performance of *Love's Labour's Lost*, we came to the front of the stage, piled up our props, the fake jewelry, the lopsided hats, the broken swords, the faded flowers. With sweat smudging the makeup on our faces, we crooned a tune of love, which is to conquer everything. But I scarcely heard the tune, so enchanted was I with watching people who sat like children, their cheeks red from laughing, their eyes filled with tears, stretching out their hands towards us a bit timidly, but hopefully. . . . Hey, Mr. Shakespeare! You teach us the most dreadful truths through your plays. The higher you take us, the greater our fall will be when you bring your dreams and magic to an end. It happens after each comedy, each tragedy, each rehearsal, each performance. Hey, Mr. Shakespeare in front of the altar of Stratford! Take care of us! Pay attention to us!

NOTE

*Péter Huszti, one of Hungary's leading stage and screen actors, has been a member of the Madách Színház theatre company in Budapest since 1966. He wrote this essay especially for this volume.

THE "OTHERNESS" OF THE FOREIGNER IN CONTEMPORARY PRODUCTIONS OF *LOVE'S LABOUR'S LOST*

Daniel J. Watermeier

The truism articulated by Gary Taylor—that "we find in Shakespeare only what we bring to him or what others have left behind; he gives us back our own values"[1]—suggests that a given Shakespeare production will tell us as much about the director and/or that theatre's audience as it does about Shakespeare; and by extension, a study of productions of a Shakespeare play in a particular period or country should reveal something about that cultural context. With its interesting mix of non-English characters, *Love's Labour's Lost* virtually invites its interpretive artists to display their attitudes towards foreigners by stressing or stylizing real or imagined national traits in the French lords and ladies, in the Spanish Don Armado, and in the lords disguised as Muscovites. One might especially expect such a tendency within the context of the postwar trend of "contemporizing" Shakespeare's plays through modern costumes and decor and through character interpretations that evoke actual contemporary figures or widely recognizable types from contemporary film or literature or society at large, particularly in the spheres of politics, business, and entertainment. A survey of postwar English and American productions, however, does not yield any clearcut pattern of prejudices or even very strong tendencies to objectify the foreign characters as recognizably different or "other" from the beholder.

American and British attitudes in the postwar period towards the national types portrayed in *Love's Labour's Lost* are in some respects not dissimilar from the attitudes of Elizabethans. There remains, for example, despite longstanding political alliances, a certain antipathy between the English and the French, and perhaps even between Americans and the French—a complex love-hate relationship, an admiration but also wariness

---

An earlier version of this paper was presented at the Twelfth World Congress of the International Federation for Theatre Research, Moscow, Russia, on 8 June 1994.

of the "other." The attitude is frequently projected in cartoon and cinema caricatures of "typical" Frenchmen—caricatures which range from bumbling clowns with bizarre French accents (Inspector Clouseau in the *Pink Panther* movie series, for example) to snobby aristocrats or smarmy playboys who disdain English and Anglo-American culture. (Two recent American films featuring Gérard Depardieu—*Green Card* and *My Father, the Hero*—are subtler, but the characterization of the Frenchman still falls into the "clown" category.)

Spaniards or (in the United States) Hispanic Americans of various national origins are also often subject to caricature and stereotyping which undoubtedly has a basis in ethnic prejudice. As documented by a number of historians, Hispanophobia, which can be traced back to the sixteenth century in England and northern Europe, crossed the Atlantic to North America with northern European and English settlers. Protestant Anglo-Americans inherited a view of Spaniards as the "other"—variously characterized as cruel, treacherous, fanatical, indolent, decadent, authoritarian, amorous, corrupt, and cowardly. These attitudes prevailed throughout the eighteenth and nineteenth centuries, especially in the southwest, southeast, and California, despite a countercurrent of appreciation of things Spanish (especially Spanish architecture) promoted by prominent American novelists, poets, historians, and business tycoons. Exacerbated by a dramatically increasing Latino population (Hispanic Americans will shortly comprise the largest ethnic population in the United States), Hispanophobia endures today, and even the views of historians regarding North America's Spanish legacy are decidedly ambiguous.[2]

Similarly, the Cold War fueled an American view of Russians which was hardly complimentary. An image of Russians, especially Russian political leaders, as godless, vulgar, and vodka-loving buffoons may have mitigated fears of Communist take-over and nuclear holocaust. In any case, a view of French, Spanish (or Hispanic), and Russian people as different, inferior, and "other" seems to be sufficiently pervasive within modern Anglo-American culture that one would expect to find those attitudes brought to bear in the portrayal of these national types in productions of *Love's Labour's Lost*. The result would be portrayals that either reinforce longstanding ethnic and national prejudices or attempt to subvert them by working against a stereotype. In fact, such does not seem to be the case, at least as far as one can infer from the relatively few reviews, promptbooks, and memoirs that describe with sufficient concreteness the approaches that have been taken to characterizing the various Frenchmen, the Spaniard (Don Armado), and the Muscovites.

The prevailing image of Don Armado, for example, is most often identified as "Don Quixote-like." Among the more notable portrayals in this vein is Paul Scofield's Don Armado in the 1946 Royal Shakespeare Company production directed by Peter Brook. Scofield wore a costume and makeup that made him look as if he had stepped out of a Velásquez painting, and gave Don Armado a fantastical dignity, a melancholy sadness that, as Miriam Gilbert writes, resonated "with echoes of Don Quixote."[3] His realistic costume and demeanor differentiated him from the other comic characters, who were treated more as caricatures. Scofield essentially reprised that interpretation in the production directed by Michael Langham in 1961 at Stratford, Ontario. According to Howard Taubman, Scofield minced, fluttered, sighed, and groaned with "an expression of lofty pain as if the demands of chivalry tax his meager brain," but he also allowed the character's humanity and kindness to shine through. Taubman considered it a "comic masterpiece . . . . compounded on the most calculated artifice full of laughing nuances and yet oddly touching."[4] In many respects, Scofield played against the type, humanizing and enriching Armado rather than presenting a parody of the impoverished Spanish grandee as had often before been the case.[5] Indeed, Scofield may have set the direction for many other essentially Don Quixote-like interpretations.

In 1964, the Stratford production was revived for a tour to the Chichester Festival, with William Hutt replacing Scofield and following Scofield's interpretive lead. A decade later, Hutt reprised the interpretation, now polished to a fine degree, in Michael Bawtree's Stratford Festival production set in the Victorian period. The costume was different, but Hutt's Armado was viewed by Berners W. Jackson as "a rickety, grave, enervated fantastic; a meticulous speaker of nonsense." In 1978, Michael Hordern followed suit with an Armado played as "a dotty Quixote" or the White Knight from *Through the Looking Glass*. His costumes suggested both Quixote and mendicant friar, wearing first a metal breast plate, later a grey burlap robe.[6]

Other productions, while continuing to invoke Don Quixote, have taken a different tack towards Armado. Michael Kahn, for example, admitted that he saw Armado as "a melancholy Quixote-like Spaniard," but for his 1968 American Shakespeare Theatre production, transposed to a contemporary India, Armado became "the last of the Edwardians attended by an Indian boy," a holdover from the last days of the Raj. Armado (Josef Sommer) employed a wealth of comic business and sometimes anachronistic interpolations—for example at one point he sang "Tiptoe through the tulips," parodying the eccentric popular 1960s performer Tiny Tim—to satirize not a Spanish but a British Colonial stereotype. Unlike Scofield's melancholy, humanized

Spaniard, Sommer's Armado was a "silly lover" willing "to try anything which might—or so he imagined—make him look like a lover," including at one point breaking into an unconscious parody of a flamenco dance.[7]

A 1992 Georgia Shakespeare Festival production set on a 1950s California campus presented Armado—without resorting to a Spanish accent or ethnic makeup—as a blend of Salvador Dalí and Zorro. In a 1988 Great Lakes Theatre Festival production set in the 1930s, directed by Gerald Freedman, Don Armado was described by one reviewer as "a melancholy Spaniard, . . . an extravagant poseur" who entered "in a somber whirlwind of cape, black hair and anguished eyes like El Greco" and spoke "with a bit of a lisp," presumably a parodic imitation of Castilian.[8] J.H. Bledsoe, artistic director of Virginia Shakespeare Festival, when queried about interpretations of Don Armado, responded that "Shakespeare's Spaniards lend themselves to concepts that emphasize immorality and the exotic."[9]

The Muscovites have almost invariably been played for comedy, but whether or not for the purposes of parodying or satirizing Russians is not easily discernible. Frequently the Muscovites are portrayed as heavily bearded, flamboyantly costumed Cossacks or Boyars, who speak gibberish Russian in Chaliapin-style basso voices. A 1967 production at the Great Lakes Shakespeare Festival in Cleveland, directed by Philip Minor, set in a an elegant contemporary resort hotel, presented the Muscovites costumed as Russian cosmonauts. Since this was at the height of the Soviet-American "space race," the gag undoubtedly had contemporary satiric relevance. (Considering that Soviet cosmonaut Vladimir M. Komarov was killed during the reentry of his Soyuz I early in 1967, the gag may very well have been in poor taste.) In 1972, although the United States had "won" the "race" by landing first on the moon in 1969, British director Toby Robertson's contemporized Prospect Theatre production also presented the Muscovites as Soviet cosmonauts. (Three cosmonauts were killed in 1971 while reentering the earth's atmosphere in their Soyuz II capsule.) Closer to our own time, the 1992 Georgia Shakespeare Festival production portrayed the Muscovites as a 1950s Russian doo-wop *a capella* quartet. The backs of their identical tuxedo jackets bore the name of the group, the "Muscovites," sewn on in sequins.

Evidence for satiric or parodic portrayals of the various Frenchmen (and women) is even scarcer than for comparable portrayals of Don Armado or the Muscovites. But after all, in the context of the dramatic structure, the French characters are the "norm" against which the eccentric and lowlife comic characters are contrasted. As such, they may not lend themselves as easily to interpretations that are clearly designed to satirize Frenchmen. A number of productions of the late 1960s and early 1970s were set in a modern period using settings and costumes designed to parody an entire class or life style rather than a national type. Kahn's 1968 production, for example, presented the French courtiers as versions of the Beatles who escape the modern world (as some of the Beatles did) to go to India/Navarre to study with a version of the Maharishi Mahesh Yogi.[10] A 1977 Alabama Shakespeare Festival production was set in a Noël Coward-world of the south of France in the 1930s, a sophisticated milieu in which the French courtiers could feel at home. The 1992 Georgia Shakespeare Festival production portrayed the bachelors as affluent, preppie Ivy League students of the 1950s, while the Princess of France and her ladies were costumed and made up like young Jackie Kennedys. Artistic director Richard Garner commented that the milieu was selected to reflect an "American sensibility of a class system" that would be accessible to or recognized by the audience. A number of productions have used *fin-de-siècle* England as a period setting for *Love's Labour's Lost,* in which the French courtiers serve to parody upper-class Edwardian behavior. These various examples suggest that social class serves as a more laughable "other" than nationality.[11]

In sum, the amusing touches that have been applied to give these foreign characters some distinctive features either avoid any quality that might smack of national stereotype or caricature, or they transmute the characters' "otherness" into qualities that may be regarded with wry, perhaps even condescending, affection. Ultimately, this pattern of avoidance may in itself be revelatory. It suggests that there is no longer any "other" to serve as the butt of the humor, because the audience itself is the "other"; that is, a body made up of many "others." If the effete Frenchman, the bombastic Spaniard, and the vodka-pickled Russian have gone the way of the Polish joke, can we still find someone or something to laugh at in *Love's Labour's Lost*? Obviously, we don't have to think hard for the answer to that. We can get back to the purer comedic values that underpin our love for so much of Shakespeare: the revelation of universal human foibles that have changed not at all since Elizabethan times. This play shows us pretentiousness, impetuosity, self-centeredness, show-offishness, denial, arrogance, hypocrisy, cruelty. To paraphrase Pogo, we have seen the other, and it is us.

NOTES

1. Taylor, p. 411.
2. Weber, pp. 335–360.
3. Gilbert, p. 48.
4. Taubman, 23 June 1961, 19.
5. For example, Ernest Milton's interpretation in a 1932 Old Vic production

459

directed by Tyrone Guthrie.

6. Gilbert, p. 106.
7. Ibid., p. 85.
8. Review by Marianne Evett included in this book. Original page number was 8-B.
9. Questionnaire sent to members of the Shakespeare Theatre Association of America, December 1993.
10. Gilbert, pp. 78–79.
11. Leiter, pp. 335–339.

Works Consulted

Gilbert, Miriam. *Love's Labour's Lost: Shakespeare in Performance*. New York: Manchester University Press, 1993.

Hulbert, Dan. "Elizabethan love enchants in '50s get-up," *Atlanta Journal Constitution* (16 June 1992), D1, D5.

Jackson, Berners W. "Shakespeare at Stratford, Ontario, 1974." *Shakespeare Quarterly* 25 (Autumn 1974), 395–400.

Lee, Elizabeth. "Festival gives Bard 20th-century twist," *Gwinnett* [Georgia] *Daily News* (9 June 1992), 3.

Leiter, Samuel L., ed. *Shakespeare Around the Globe: A Guide to Notable Postwar Revivals*. Westport, CT: Greenwood Press, 1986. "Love's Labour's Lost," ed. by Felicia Hardison Londré, pp. 335–354.

Taubman, Howard. "The Theatre: A Sparkling 'Love's Labour's Lost,'" *New York Times* (23 June 1961), 19.

_____. "Challenging Trio," *New York Times* (2 July 1961), II, 1.

Taylor, Gary. *Reinventing Shakespeare*. New York: Oxford University Press, 1989.

Weber, David J. *The Spanish Frontier in North America*. New Haven: Yale University Press, 1992.

On Playing Berowne*

Theodore Swetz

You played Berowne with American Players Theatre in a beautiful outdoor hilltop amphitheatre near Spring Green, Wisconsin. It would have been one of five or six shows done in rotating repertory during the summer. Tell me about that experience.

I think we rehearsed *Love's Labour's Lost* in late July or early August. It was the last play put into the repertory that summer. We had been having temperatures of around a hundred degrees every afternoon, and we didn't have any rehearsal space. We rehearsed on stage, out in the sun. It was funny, because Berowne makes a lot of references to sun and light. "But be first advised, in conflict you get the sun of them." Well, Randall Duk Kim's artistic philosophy was that we never cut one word. And Berowne's got the longest speech in Shakespeare—

Longer than Prospero's monologue in The Tempest *?*

Yes, by twenty lines. It's about 75 lines [IV.3.285–360], and there's a redundancy to it, which a lot of people see as two different drafts ending up in the final text. But if you go to the acting of it, the storytelling of it, it's very easy to see how it makes sense and why he goes back over the same ground with different images. Because he's selling an idea. Well, it's a good seven minutes in performance, and you sort of load up for that speech. You're going through the play and you know the "big trick" is coming—the triple. You've got to hit the triple. You're gearing yourself up to it with every circumstance, and, of course, I wasn't usually cast in a leading man role, so I was even more self-conscious about the whole experience.

One afternoon, we were playing a matinee and I finished the long speech. I had completed "the triple"—rather well, I thought. And at that moment, from the stage, I could see dark clouds moving in. At that point, Chuck Bright, our managing director, came out on stage, stopped the show, and said, "Ladies and gentlemen, the weather bureau tells us that in a few minutes we're going to have strong rains hit us, but it's only going to last ten or fifteen minutes, so I think we should stop now and let it happen, then we'll resume." It happened exactly as the weather bureau said it would. It rained like hell for about ten minutes, fifteen minutes, then stopped. So after they cleaned up everything and the audience got back in, it was about half an hour. I was waiting in the wings when the stage manager got the word from Chuck Bright. She said we would start from the beginning of Berowne's speech! "No, no, wait!," I pleaded. "Can I talk to somebody?" Because not only do you peak for that speech—it takes the whole performance to get there—but also I'd have to go out and do it somewhat differently to show that I'm worth my salt as an actor. I mean, I'd already given them one experience; do I go out and serve up exactly the same experience again? It's got to be alive. At APT [American Players Theatre], we used to do tai chi together as a company early in the morning, and we would do the form three times. The whole form might last about ten minutes, so by the time you got to the third repetition of it, doubt and hesitation would set in. You'd be thinking, "Did I do that posture already?" And that's the feeling I dreaded in having to do Berowne's speech again. I've never forgiven Chuck Bright for that. We still joke about it.

So you did have to go through with it?

Oh, yes, we started with my speech. What was really wonderful though is how my situation fit within the play's circumstances: Berowne is at center stage creating a solution, and the other three are there to take it in and judge whether it's going to work. He must impress them. As we took the stage there was a little glimmer in the eyes of my fellow actors. They were standing there looking at me as if to say, "Go ahead, Ted, show us what you can do." And as I courageously carved through the piece, I saw in their eyes: "Very nice!" In the end, it was quite wonderful for me, because what happened was a real application of Morris Carnovsky's technique with regard to the self. It usually happens by accident—or fate—but when those discoveries happen, they teach you everything about an idea you've been trying to grab hold of, such as the self in the role. What happened the second time through that speech was that I put more of myself in it. You know, these are wonderfully mischievous lines. And so, with my having to go out and do them again, it's no longer a storytelling event. That's been done. Now the event is changed. What kind of event is it now? And it all comes down to the actor and technique. The only thing I could call on was the need for Ted to show up more. That creative self that Morris talked about had to be present. My Berowne was much better after that experience.

In what way?

Because I then allowed my *self*—Ted, the power of Ted—to be on stage more, mingling with the character. Morris once told how he discovered this when he was doing a play with the Group Theatre. He said to himself, "I'm going to go out this time, and I'm going to be very aware that I'm in this play with Stella" [Adler]. I think it was in *Awake and Sing* that this happened. He said, "I'm going to be aware that it's Stella doing her work as a storyteller, and that I'm Morris out there with Stella, and together we create the truth of these characters. They are individual energies." And so he went on with that in mind. And after the scene, when they were both off stage, Stella said, "What were you doing out there? It was very interesting." He said, "I just made sure that *I* was present in the creation, that my sensibilities as Morris were there, right on the edge. And without me, you couldn't be doing anything." It was for them on stage just the way we are now: you wouldn't be sitting there having this coffee and conversation without me. It seems a silly thing to say, but sometimes you've got to state the obvious to see the complexity of it. We're totally reliant on each other in order to have a conversation. How many times have you gotten stuck with somebody that you didn't want to . . . give yourself to? Those are the tough conversations, aren't they? So it's a very curious thing I seem to have stumbled on—with Morris's guidance. That moment with Berowne crystallized something—the idea of the self in the role.

It seems to parallel the modern idea of, say, "superimposing" the actor on the character as opposed to the old notion of transforming the actor through makeup to become the character.

Yes, but this idea of the self is basic and universal and is even more important with transforming makeup. When Morris directed *Ivanov* at APT and I played Lebedev, a sixty-year-old man, I created a makeup that actually fooled Morris when I came out for the costume parade. Now there's a wonderful old tradition—the costume parade. We never have them any more, but Morris and Phoebe started out in the 1920s in the theatre, so they wanted one. Well, when I came out as Lebedev, Morris asked, "Who's that?!", because the makeup had truly transformed me. He loved the makeup, but he said: "Make sure Ted shows up. Lebedev needs Ted's sensibilities." So it gets incredibly complex. We would be rehearsing *Ivanov*, thinking we were doing pretty well, when from the seats we'd hear Morris's booming voice: "Talk, talk, talk." We'd think, "Gee, maybe we'd better explore this idea of talking and the use of the self." We learned so much sincerity in character. That's why it was so nice to see Phoebe's work last night [Phoebe Brand in the movie *Vanya on 42nd Street*], to be reminded once more.

Was Berowne the only "leading man" role you've played?

Pretty much. From the very beginning I've always been cast in character roles.

Did you go at it with the idea that now you were a jeune premier *or matinee idol type?*

In a way. I mean, when I look at the one photograph I have of myself as Berowne, I realize that I looked the part. And it was easy for me to bring a "leading man" romantic energy to it. The thing is, I'm a very romantic person. (You notice how this "self" thing keeps coming back?) And if a leading man can be someone who carries a story, I like doing that. There were a lot of similarities between Berowne and me—but I didn't recognize them so much then. I was still quite young in my craft. So I struggled with it—really struggled with it—until I put on the makeup. I react very strongly to visuals. I put on my toupee. Of course, everybody ribbed me about the toupee. I would take it off and put it on a styrofoam head, and it looked like a full wig. They'd say, "Ted, if you need to call it a toupee, go right ahead." And I made a very sculpted beard, very clipped, the kind of beard that has to be trimmed to perfection every day. It took me an hour: I drew it with a pencil, and then I took spirit gum and used very small clippings of crepe hair to give it texture. And as I built it, I started to think differently, because I was becoming handsome in a way I had never thought I could be. Just in my mirror. And it changed my thinking. It totally changed *my* thinking! And I do love poetry, romance, and eating. I adore women—Ted does that. So I had a lot of similarities with Berowne. I just had to get over my theatrical . . . angst, if you will. But you know what helped me a great deal is something Stella Adler said to me once in a class: "Everything is character." I had pigeonholed Berowne in my own definition: "leading man," "romantic lead." But actually *everything* is character. When you think about "what makes us" outside the theatre, what makes our "character" is our appetites. What we pursue tells people about our personality. Again, that's what I loved about Stella and Morris's work: they kept

Theodore Swetz played Berowne in the 1983 American Players Theatre production in Spring Green, Wisconsin. Photo courtesy of Theodore Swetz.

helping me see me. Not that I'm ever enough. I mean, the character can't simply be Ted. But the equation is based on mingling imaginatively with the whole life of the play. And that means the self plus the imagination. You must dig out the reality of Berowne's world, but then you must add your experience.

465

And you have to spend all your artistic life learning how to balance that equation. And that's why you need technique, obviously. Because half of the equation is never enough.

I remember that Jon Smoots—now *he* is a leading man!—do you remember seeing Jon Smoots?

Is he tall?

Yes. He's everything you could imagine. Jon, I think, expected to play Berowne. So when the casting came out with little, balding, pudgy Ted to play Berowne, Jonathan—in a wonderful moment of egotism (and we all have our egos, thank God)—said "Gee, I wonder what they were thinking . . . when they cast you as Berowne." I turned and replied: "Well, they were probably thinking they'd get the best actor to do it." Jon played the King of Navarre and we had a wonderful time together.

You know, this play was my first encounter with extensive wit as the fuel of the play. We would get together and talk about the nature of wit, a vital part of the play's circumstance. When you work in a company like that, you take the time to ask, "What *is* the nature of wit?" Because you're all searching. So now I've transferred that—those conversations exploring the world of the play—to teaching. To ask "what is the nature of wit" is working on circumstances. How can you not ask the question? A lot actors assume they know all they need to know about a play's circumstances, or they're simply not curious enough. So they lose that equation that Morris talked about: are you mingling with the world of the play? When you're just relying on your self, then it's out of balance.

We were also just learning how to become a company when we did *Love's Labour's Lost*. A company gives you the power to go on that kind of search, to ask the creative questions that have to be asked. And all these people were on the search with me! We pulled our talent out of each other. I miss that kind of collaboration.

Who directed Love's Labour's Lost *at APT?*

Fred Ollerman directed it the first summer, and Randy—Randall Duk Kim—directed it the following summer.

Did you use the Quarto or Folio?

We used the Folio, under the guidance of Anne Occhiogrosso.

I know APT did all the plays uncut, so you kept all those obscure puns—

Every one of them.

How did they go over with audiences?

First we had to understand them. We took several rehearsal days, sitting down and looking up every word in the text, so we could paraphrase everything we said. We would read over a scene and add up the circumstances, and we found that, after paraphrasing it, we could follow the path of the text in a clear way. We would make so many discoveries using the Folio. Annie was our main guide in interpreting the Folio's punctuation. It led us to action and a deeper understanding of the moment. So it was never just witty chat. It all comes out of need put into action. Puns are not just played on a joking level; rather the character uses the tool of a pun to get something. So we aimed it all that way. And audiences adored *Love's Labour's Lost*. When we started work on it, we had asked, "Is anybody going to go along with this?" But, you know, when you look at *The Comedy of Errors*, it has difficult language too. I mean, talk about obscure jokes! But if you put it into action, the story takes over.

There is so much to celebrate about playing Berowne. He has a vocabulary I can only dream about having. He has a line something like "light seeking light doth light of light beguile." How many ways is he using the word "light" there? You can't help but be humbled by it. The challenge becomes how to elevate myself up to the story. And if the story warms you, you gravitate to it, and you want to live there for a while. You can't help but become more eloquent in your own life after spending time with that play.

The soliloquies were wonderful to play. Morris had a tremendous definition of soliloquy. In a soliloquy, he said, your deepest desire collides with the circumstances of the story. So taking on a soliloquy, knowing that you have to address the audience, then you have to put something on that audience in a creative way. For example, as you and I talk now, we're not having this conversation out of context. You know who I am, I know who you are, there's a wealth of facts we have about each other as we talk here. Well, if we do that in life, you must do that on the stage. So, as Berowne, what I used to do was talk to all the single men in the audience, all the single men who have trouble with women. And at the beginning when I would speak to them, of course, I would have the upper hand, because I would present myself as "I'm successful, you're not." But then he falls in love. Now when he talks to them, it's harder. They become vital to him. He needs them now; he needs the comfort of his fellow victims.

But audiences adored it, just adored it. Because the only thing it's about is pursuit of love. Of course, that love will be defined differently by everyone. I think that men love to be in love, and women know what it is to love. It's funny how once you start doing a lot of Shakespeare—if you have that privilege—how much every play of his becomes clearer to you. The women vow and they keep their vows, but the men vow in the moment; if the men need to vow again somewhere else, they'll vow again. We see that in *Love's Labour's Lost*. And it makes you learn a hell of a lot about yourself, so that the next time you promise something, you really think about it. I never gave Berowne a chance in hell that he would go work in a hospital for a year. I thought he'd go for a little while, but then his pleasure-seeking nature would take over again. . . .

Oh! Really?

That's what I thought then. I don't know if I would now. I just didn't think he could do it.

For me, it's a fairytale ending; the romance will triumph.

Look at us! That's just what I was talking about! I've been married nineteen years, so I must believe in that. But with Berowne's mentality, I didn't think he could do it. And you do! It's wonderful!

And John Ezell sees it more the way you do. He thinks Berowne will get killed in a war before the year is up.

That's very funny! The structure of the play allows us these different views. Something will do him in. Here you have tremendously intelligent people, and who does them in—the dullards. They come in and wreak havoc on the wit-mongers. I love that.

To me, the most intriguing character is Don Armado.

Oh, yes, he's a wonderful character. And I think it's a tough role to play. He has to be a comic—of the braggart soldier tradition—and he's a greathearted but ineffectual lover. What makes this play vital is that it talks to the lover. So that if you have loved, you will laugh and you will sigh with this play. When we worked on the play, we went back to source materials on all the great stock characters of the *commedia dell'arte*. But I found something else helpful on an old recording I picked up of Charles Laughton doing one of his solo reading performances. He read a piece by Plato called the *Phaedrus*. It explains lovesickness, explains the pangs of love. It says that when we're born into this world we come from the gods, and the gods are the most beautiful things you can imagine, and these celestial creatures have wings. You're born into this world and as an infant you remember the beauty of the gods, but as you get older you lose that memory. However, when you fall in love, you remember—you have a pang of memory of the beauty of the gods, and your soul starts to sprout wings. And this is how Plato describes being in love. And the only way you can ease your pain, the ache of your sprouting wings, is when you behold the beloved. So if you're creative, you take that information and pass it through your talent and do something with, use it when you talk to the audience, and so on. The audience may not have read Plato, but they have all been in love; they have all sprouted wings. And through the actor they recognize it.

Note

*Theodore Swetz teaches acting in the professional theatre training program at the University of Missouri-Kansas City. He was an original member of American Players Theatre and acted with the company for ten years, playing Berowne in the 1983 season and in the 1984 revival. He was interviewed by Felicia Londré on 1 December 1994.

ENVOI*

Melia Bensussen

My first thoughts on staging a production of *Love's Labour's Lost* had to do with earning the ending of the play. In reading and rereading the play, I was struck by Marcade's entrance, by the sudden mention of death, by the apparently instant maturation of the leading characters. How intriguing for Shakespearean comedy: instead of ending in the traditional marriage scene (as in *Much Ado About Nothing*, or *Twelfth Night*, or *As You Like It*, or *A Midsummer Night's Dream* . . .), in *Love's Labour's Lost* we hear vows to wait a year, to suffer for a year, and only *then* to wed.

The promise made by the King and his lords became my point of departure. Would the young men we meet at the beginning, full of adolescently idealistic promises to not sleep, not eat, to form a little "academe," would these same young men be capable of fulfilling such a vow? Apparently they are, and Berowne's language at the end says to us "yes," they have learned, they have changed. The more closely I looked at the text the more I decided that the lords were not alone, but that the ladies also changed greatly in the course of the play. The production began to become about the maturing of the two courts, and ultimately, about the shifting, changing, and growing of the entire world of the play.

This "maturing" of the courtiers became evident in the progression of visual elements and physical movements throughout the production. First, it was visible in their clothing; their costumes changed and traveled through time. Lynda Myers, the costume designer, created initial images for both courts of portrait-like elegance, using images from the mid-1750s: the men in knickers and slippers with fancy buckles, the women in big skirts and wigs and constantly-moving fans. The period clothing helped to point up the artificiality of the world of the self-indulgent and immature lords and ladies. They seemed silly, frilly, and utterly detached from the "locals" around them (Costard, Jaquenetta, Holofernes, etc.). As the play progressed, the courtiers slowly discovered real love and real loss, a process paralleled in the shedding of layers to achieve a simpler, almost "Napoleonic" style (circa 1810). It was a transformation from obvious "dressing up," from wooden, artificial posing and prancing, to a more natural, more apparently "adult" style which allowed the performers to move and breathe more freely. The final scene was played with the ladies in elegant, pastel-colored shifts and the men in trousers and boots. The transition, covering as it did a span of sixty years, was not done in a pointed fashion. We went out of our way to disguise the historical forward movement, and carefully timed the evolution in dress to fit the naturally shifting mood and climate on stage.

The setting of the production was also transformed, affecting not only the two courts but all of the characters moving within it. Here I began with an image of the seasons changing. Within the play itself, time is limited to a few days (although in typical Shakespearean fashion, time is rather elastic within the text), but I chose to see all four seasons come and go, to have the production begin in Spring and end in Winter. The seasons themselves developed in a progression not dissimilar from that of the clothing, beginning as very full, very painterly, very artificial. Spring was too pink, too flowery, too rich and well-composed for nature. Little by little, with each coming season, the set (with its large tree at the center) became more and more stripped down, more and more "real," more and more "natural."

As my work with our set designer, John Ezell, progressed, the play became more about nature intruding, taking over, insinuating herself into this otherwise artificial and "high court" world. It was as if there was an *absence* of nature at the beginning, and through the journey of the play the world became more and more real, ending with an image of vivid (and comforting) Winter. Comforting Winter. Odd I know, to have Winter be the comforting season, but Marcade's entrance was at the end, and with his entrance came the reminder of mortality that defines human experience. And that mortality, that moment that transformed the Princess into a queen, also transformed the brash young men into earnest suitors. The moment when nature was at her cruelest, she was also at her most honest and real. Nature, with whom the young men were dueling at the opening of the play, ceased to be an enemy: both courts stopped fighting to keep their own natures trapped within themselves.

This to me was not a production about a specific historical period, but rather about our growing up, our beginning to understand nature's cycles and the movement within our own lives. When looked at in this light, the play is full of cues, hints, and secrets about this progression in everyone's life on stage. From the mention of Katharine's dead sister, to the cruel ridiculing of the Worthies by the lords, to Armado's admission of being a penitent moments before Marcade's entrance, to the discussion in Act IV about how and when to injure or hunt a deer, there was no shortage of autumnal coloring, or darkening spots on the horizon.

Although I was consciously looking for the cruelty, for the darkness in the play (emphasizing, for example, how hard the ladies are on the men during and after their disastrous Muscovite appearance), in no way did this diminish the lively and ever-present humor of the evening. I relied heavily on *commedia dell'arte* models for Don Armado, Moth, Holofernes, Sir Nathaniel, Costard, and Jaquenetta. Those antecedents helped to inform costume choices and, in some cases, character mannerisms. There is the obvious difficulty of a lot of the language in these scenes being topical and no longer comprehensible, and I did resort to some cutting in the Armado/Moth scenes and well as in the Holofernes/Nathaniel/Dull sequences. But in general I was pleasantly surprised by how funny these scenes can be without an audience's understanding every word. Physical comedy helped to a certain extent, but we also discovered how much of the humor is conveyed by the characters themselves, and it becomes their own idiosyncratic behavior that provokes our laughter and enjoyment. We reveled in the style, in the verse, in the rhymes.

Costard was for me the most "natural" of the characters, the most in tune with his own nature, and therefore the most sexual. Our production gently implied that Costard had actually impregnated Jaquenetta and made Berowne aware of this, and Berowne urged Costard to place responsibility for the pregnancy on Armado. It was Berowne's last cruel joke, which near the end of the play gave him one more misdeed to overcome to win Rosaline's love. It also gave Armado a certain nobility when he agreed to marry Jaquenetta, thereby anticipating all the lords in their own wedding vows.

Music was also a key element, which helped shift the focus in the moments discussed above as well as underscoring the transformation from courtly/artificial to natural and the changes from light to dark in tone. I mostly cut Moth's attempts at songs; thus, the production's only song was at the end. But there was music under many of the scenes and in the transitions, helping to convey a sense of time passing and seasons changing, to emphasize the "dance" of the two courts' encounter and the absurdity of the Muscovites' performance.

At the end, a very pregnant Jaquenetta (more liberties taken here with the passing of time) sang the final song accompanied by Holofernes (aided by Dull) manning the Cuckoo puppet while Nathaniel manned the Owl. In the snowy Winter twilight, the most "natural" characters, all the Worthies, still wearing some of their costume pieces, watched as the courts ceremoniously parted. Black was introduced to the scene with Marcade's entrance at the uppermost portion of the stage, appearing as if over a hill, and then the courtiers donned black shawls and overcoats. Thus, as the light faded, so too did color drain from the stage.

In the opening lines we hear of men striving for immortality, and in the end they learn to accept their own mortality as a gift of their humanity. And in this acceptance of the cycle of life, they are able to mature and move on. The last image, framed by our worthy Worthies, was of couples parting, wiser, sadder, and in hope of rejuvenation: snow gently falling on them, blessing them, Jaquenetta's song rising above them, promising them rebirth in the Spring.

NOTE

*Melia Bensussen directed *Love's Labour's Lost* for the professional theatre training program at the University of Missouri-Kansas City, 21–24 April 1994. She wrote this memoir especially for this volume.

Contributors of New Material to This Volume

Melia Bensussen worked closely with Joseph Papp as an associate artist at the New York Shakespeare Festival. She has directed at dozens of New York and regional theatres, including Oregon Shakespeare Festival, North Carolina Shakespeare Festival, Heart of America Shakespeare Festival, Cleveland Playhouse, and Playwrights Horizons. She has received fellowships from the Princess Grace Foundation, the Drama League of New York, and Theatre Communications Group.

John Ezell is Hall Family Foundation Professor of Theatre at the University of Missouri-Kansas City and resident designer for Missouri Repertory Theatre. His award-winning set designs have graced stages from Broadway to Hong Kong. His numerous credits include Shakespeare Theatre at the Folger, the Old Globe, Great Lakes Theater Festival, and the Royal Danish Ballet. He is a consultant for the Beinecke Library at Yale University.

Gerald Freedman is artistic director of Great Lakes Theater Festival and dean of the North Carolina School of the Arts. He has also been artistic director of the New York Shakespeare Festival (1968–71), co-artistic director of The Acting Company (1974–77), and artistic director of the American Shakespeare Theatre (1978–79). He has directed operas, television specials, and Broadway musicals, including the 1967 premiere of *Hair*.

Péter Huszti, one of Hungary's leading stage and screen actors, is also Rector of the Academy of Drama and Film in Budapest. His many Shakespearean roles include Hamlet, King Lear, and Iago. His autobiography, *Királyok az Alagútban* (Budapest: Szépirodalmi Könyvkiadó, 1986), includes over fifty production photographs.

Toru Iwasaki translated Koshi Nakanori's article from the Japanese. Professor Iwasaki teaches Shakespeare and other English literature at the University of Tokyo.

Felicia Hardison Londré, Curators' Professor of Theatre at the University of Missouri-Kansas City and dramaturg for Missouri Repertory Theatre, is also honorary co-founder of the Heart of America Shakespeare Festival and was the founding secretary of the Shakespeare Theatre Association of America. She has held two Missouri Humanities Council grants for summer seminars on Shakespeare. Her books include *Tennessee Williams* (1979), *Tom Stoppard* (1981), *Federico García Lorca* (1984), and *The History of World Theater: From the English Restoration to the Present* (1991). In 1993 she was a visiting foreign professor at Hosei University in Tokyo, and in 1995 she held the women's chair in humanistic studies at Marquette University. She has given her slide lecture on the Shakespeare authorship question in Hungary, China, Japan, and at various American universities.

Mari Pappas, translator from the French of Jacques Copeau's article, earned her M.A. in theatre at the University of Missouri-Kansas City. Her thesis was on Jacques Copeau. She is currently in the Ph.D. program at the University of Pittsburgh.

Theodore Swetz teaches acting in the professional training program at the University of Missouri-Kansas City. He studied acting under Stella Adler and Morris Carnovsky and was an original member of the American Players Theatre, where he served as assistant artistic director.

Daniel J. Watermeier, professor of theatre at the University of Toledo, has published widely on Shakespearean production history. He was co-editor of *Shakespeare Companies and Festivals: An International Guide* (1995) and associate editor of *Shakespeare Around the Globe: Notable Postwar Revivals* (1986). He has also published two books on the great nineteenth-century actor Edwin Booth, is the recipient of a Guggenheim Fellowship, and was a visiting professor at the University of Southern California.